Cases and Materials in Intellectual Property Law

Cases and Materials in Intellectual Property Law

Second Edition

David I Bainbridge

Reader in Law
Aston Business School
Aston University

FINANCIAL TIMES
PITMAN PUBLISHING

FINANCIAL TIMES
MANAGEMENT

LONDON · SAN FRANCISCO
KUALA LUMPUR · JOHANNESBURG

Financial Times Management delivers the knowledge,
skills and understanding that enable students,
managers and organisations to achieve their ambitions,
whatever their needs, wherever they are.

London Office:
128 Long Acre, London WC2E 9AN
Tel: +44 (0)171 447 2000
Fax: +44 (0)171 240 5771
Website: www.ftmanagement.com

An imprint of Pearson Education Limited

First published in Great Britain in 1995
Second edition published in 1999

© David I Bainbridge 1999

The right of David I Bainbridge to be identified as Author of
this Work has been asserted by him in accordance with the
Copyright, Designs, and Patents Act 1988.

ISBN 0 273 63556 5

British Library Cataloguing in Publication Data
A CIP catalogue record for this book can be obtained from the British Library.

10 9 8 7 6 5 4 3 2 1

Printed and bound in Great Britain by Bell & Bain Ltd, Glasgow

The Publishers' policy is to use paper manufactured from sustainable forests.

Contents

Preface   ix
Acknowledgements   x
Table of cases   xi
Table of legislation   xxiii

Chapter 1   Basic Principles   *1*
    Introduction   *1*
    Justification   *7*
    Contract and Intellectual Property   *10*
    Controls over Abuse of Intellectual Property Rights   *13*
    New forms of works   *26*
    International Cooperation   *28*

Chapter 2   Copyright Law   *37*
    Introduction   *37*
    Expression   *37*
    Subsistence   *41*
    Subsistence - artistic works   *49*
    De Minimis   *55*
    Authorship   *59*
    Ownership of copyright   *61*
    Implied licence   *72*
    Moral rights   *74*
    Infringement of copyright   *76*
    Fair dealing   *100*
    International standards   *103*

Chapter 3   The Law of Breach of Confidence   *117*
    Introduction   *117*
    Basic requirements   *117*
    Springboard doctrine   *124*

Third parties   *126*

Employees   *132*

Trade secrets   *139*

Public interest   *141*

Privacy   *144*

Relief   *154*

Chapter 4   Patent Law   *160*

Introduction   *160*

Development of the patent system   *163*

Justification for the patent system   *171*

Basic requirements for a patent   *173*

    Novelty   *173*

    Anticipation by disclosure   *187*

    Priority   *194*

    Inventive Step   *201*

    Industrial application   *212*

    Excepted matter   *213*

Ownership and employees   *224*

Infringement and claims   *229*

Defences   *235*

Remedies   *238*

Groundless threats actions   *252*

Conventions   *258*

Chapter 5   Design Law   *270*

Introduction   *270*

Requirements for registered designs   *274*

Spare parts   *286*

Infringement   *295*

The design right   *297*

Chapter 6   Trade Marks   *312*

Introduction   *312*

Registrability   *314*

Geographical names   *336*

Invented words   *339*

Containers and packaging   *340*

Disclaimers   *343*

Infringement of a registered trade mark   *346*

Comparative advertising   *358*

Groundless threats of infringement actions   *363*

Rectification and removal of trade marks   *368*

Character merchandising   *371*

International Standards   *376*

Chapter 7   Passing Off   *381*

Introduction   *381*

The development of passing off   *382*

Misrepresentation   *400*

Damage to goodwill   *404*

Common field of activity   *417*

A law of unfair competition?   *422*

Chapter 8   EC Law and Intellectual Property   *425*

Introduction   *425*

The EC Treaty   *426*

Non-discrimination   *428*

Free movement of goods   *432*

Restrictive trade agreements   *448*

Abuse of a dominant position   *456*

Index   477

Preface

The study of intellectual property law is both interesting and challenging. It is a large subject and has a considerable amount of case law associated with it and there has been much written about the subject. One of the problems for the busy student of intellectual property is locating and gaining access to relevant material as a significant number of libraries do not subscribe to all the law reports and journals that a student might want to look at. Many of the law reports on intellectual property cases are quite lengthy, compounding the difficulty for the student.

The purpose of this book is to bring together important and useful materials in such a way as to be helpful to the student of intellectual property law. The content of the book consists largely of extracts from reported cases together with interesting and thought-provoking articles and extracts from books. Also included are extracts from the texts of some of the important international conventions affecting intellectual property law and which are of particular interest in the United Kingdom. The book does not contain substantial extracts from statutory materials as students of intellectual property are likely to have access to an appropriate book of legislation such as Butterworths Intellectual Property Handbook or Blackstone's Statutes on Intellectual Property Law. Rather, the author considered it better to concentrate on materials which *describe* and *critique* intellectual property law rather than simply *state* the law.

There have been some significant additions to the second edition. In particular, there is a new chapter on EC law as it affects intellectual property. Extracts from some important recent patent, design and trade mark cases have also been included.

The book is laid out in eight chapters covering the main areas of intellectual property. The author has added brief descriptive material and commentary on the extracts included.

It has taken a significant amount of work to put this second edition together and many people have been helpful and supportive. In particular, Lorraine Keenan deserves a special mention for her contribution in the preparation of this book, checking and inserting scanned in text and producing the camera ready copy for the book.

Where reference is made to the Treaty of Rome, the Article numbers are those at the time of writing. It should be noted that, during 1999, the Treaty will be renumbered, for example, Articles 85 and 86 becoming Articles 81 and 82 respectively.

David I Bainbridge
December 1998

Acknowledgements

A number of persons, bodies and organisations have kindly given their permission to the inclusion of materials included in this book. The author and publisher express their thanks to them all. They include:

A Booy
The British Library Science Reference and Information Service
Butterworths
Professor W R Cornish
European Patent Office
The Honourable Justice Hammond
Her Majesty's Stationery Office
The Incorporated Council of Law Reporting for England & Wales
Manchester University Press
The Modern Law Review
Dr. P Oliver
Brad Sherman
Sweet & Maxwell
World Intellectual Property Organisation
World Trade Organisation

Table of Cases

A

A.G. für Autogene Aluminium Schweissung v London Aluminium Co. Ltd (No. 2) (1923) 40 RPC 107   *239*

Ahmed Saeed [1989] ECR 803   *458*

Allied Maples Group Ltd. v Simmons & Simmons [1995] 1 WLR 1602   *250*

Amber Size and Chemical Co. Ltd. v Mengel [1913] 2 Ch 239   *136*

American Cynamid v Ethicon [1975] AC 395   *153*

American Braided Wire Co. v Thompson (1889) 6 RPC 518   *210*

Amp Inc. v Utilux Pty. Ltd. [1972] RPC 103   *18, 275, 279, 282, 290*

Anderson, D P, & Co. Ltd. v Lieber Code Co. [1917] 2 KB 469   *56*

Argyll, Duchess of, v Duke of Argyll [1967] Ch 302   *121, 145*

Aristoc Ltd. v Rysta Ltd. (1945) 62 RPC 65   *348*

Asahi Kasei Kogyo KK's Application [1991] RPC 485   *195*

Assidoman Multipack Ltd. v The Mead Corp. [1995] FSR 225   *233*

Attorney-General v Guardian Newspapers (No.2) [1990] 1 AC 7109   *155*

Attorney-General v Jonathan Cape Ltd. [1976] 1 QB 752   *148*

Australia Asset Management Corp. v York Montague Ltd. [1996] 3 WLR 87   *244*

Australian Coastal Shipping Co. v Green [1971] 1 QB 456   *246*

Availablity to the Public Decision G01/92 [1993] EPOR 241   *190*

B

Bailey v Taylor (1825) 1 Russ & M 73   *40*

Bailey, A, & Co. Ltd. v Clark, Son & Morland Ltd. (1938) 55 RPC 253   *338*

Barclays Bank plc v RBS Advanta [1996] RPC 307   *359*

Barings plc v Coopers & Lybrand, *The Times*, 6 December 1996   *249*

Barran v Lomas (1880) 28 WR 973   *283*

Batt, J., and Co.'s Trade Marks (1898) 15 RPC 262   *373*

Bauman v Fussell [1978] RPC 485   *78*

BAYER/Diastereomers Decision T12/81 [1979-85] EPOR Vol B 308   *190*

Beck v Montana Constructions Pty. Ltd. [1964-5] NSWR 229   *73*

Beecham Group Ltd. v Bristol Laboratories Ltd. [1978] RPC 153   *232*

Belasco v Commission [1989] ECR 2117   *474*

Beloff v Pressdram Ltd. [1973] 1 All ER 241   *61*

Berlei (UK) Ltd. v Bali Brassiere Co. Inc. [1969] 2 All ER 812   *369*

Bernstein v Skyviews and General Ltd. [1978] QB 479   *153*

Billhöfer Maschinenfabrik GmbH v Dixon & Co. Ltd. [1990] FSR 105   *94*

Biogen Inc. v Medeva plc [1997] RPC 1   *194*

Birmingham, Dudley and District Banking Co. v Ross (1888) 38 Ch D 295   *21*

Blair v Osborne & Tomkins [1971] 2 WLR 503   *72*

Blofield v Payne (1833) 2 LJ KB 68   *386*

Bollinger, J v Costa Brava Wine Co. Ltd. [1960] Ch 262   *388, 390*
Bollinger, J. v Costa Brava Wine Co. Ltd. (No.2) [1961] 1 WLR 277   *390, 412*
BOSTITCH Trade Mark [1963] RPC 183   *374*
Boulton and Watt v Bull (1793) Court of Common Pleas   *168*
Bowden Wire Ltd. v Bowden Brake Co. Ltd. (1914) 31 RPC 385   *373*
Boyd v The Tootal Broadhust Lee Co. (1894) 11 RPC 175   *239*
Brain, Patrick John v Ingledew Brown Bennison and Garrett (No.3) [1997] FSR 511
   252
Bristol-Myers Co. (Johnson's) Application [1975] RPC 127   *185, 187, 192*
Bristol-Myers Squibb & Others [1997] FSR 102   *443*
British Insulated Wire Co. v Dublin United Tramway Co. (1899) 17 RPC 14   *245*
British Legion v British Legion Club (Street) Ltd (1931) 48 RPC 555   *397*
British Leyland Motor Corp. Ltd. v Armstrong Patents Co. Ltd. [1986] 2 WLR 400
   15, 89, 98, 270, 403
British Northrop Ltd. v Texteam Blackburn Ltd. [1974] RPC 57   *56*
British Oxygen Co. Ltd. v Liquid Air Ltd. [1925] Ch 383   *102*
British Steel PLC's Patent [1992] RPC 117   227
British Sugar PLC v James Robertson & Sons Ltd. [1996] RPC 281   *319, 366*
British Thomson-Houston Co. v Corona Lamp Works Ltd. (1922) 39 RPC 49   *207*
British United Shoe Machinery Co. v A Fussell & Sons Ltd. (1910) 27 RPC 205   *251*
British United Shoe Machinery Co. Ltd. v Simon Collier Ltd. (1908) 26 RPC 21   *199*
British Westinghouse v Braulik (1910) 27 RPC 209   *204*
Broome v Cassell & Co. Ltd. [1972] AC 1027   *241*
Brown v John Hastie & Co. (1904) 21 RPC 445   *251*
Browne v Flower [1911] 1 Ch 219   *21*
BRT v SABAM [1974] ECR 51   *462*
BTH Co. Ltd. v Metropolitan Vickers Electrical Co. Ltd. (1928) 45 RPC 1   *181*
Buck's Invention (1651) 1 WPC 35   163
Buckingham v Francis [1986] 2 All ER 738   *248*
Burberry's v J. C. Cording & Co. Ltd. (1909) 26 RPC 693   *56, 57*
Burgess v Burgess [1853] 22 LJ Ch 675   *385*

C

C. & H. Engineering v F Klucznik & Sons Ltd. [1992] FSR 421   298
Cable & Wireless plc v British Telecommunications plc [1998] FSR 383   *363*
Cadbury Ltd. v Ulmer GmbH [1988] FSR 385   *401*
Canadian Shredded Wheat Co. Ltd. (The) v Kellogg Co. of Canada Ltd. (1938) 55 RPC 125
   320
Canadian Shredded Wheat Co. Ltd. (The) v Kellogg Co. of Great Britain Ltd.(1940) 57 RPC
   137   *320*
Canon Kabushiki Daisha v Green Cartridge Company (Hong Kong) Ltd. [1997] FSR 817
   25
Carflow Products (UK) Ltd. v Linwood Securities (Birmingham) Ltd. [1996] FSR 424   *129*
Carl Zeiss Stiftung v Herbert Smith & Co. (No.2) [1969] 2 Ch 276   *127*
Carpenter v Smith (1841) 1 WPC 530   *186*
Catnic Components Ltd. v Hill & Smith Ltd. [1982] RPC 183   230

Catnic Components Ltd. v Hill & Smith Ltd. [1983] FSR 512   *246*
Cavity Trays Ltd. v RMC Panel Products Ltd. [1996] RPC 361   *257*
Centrafarm BV v Sterling Drug Inc [1974] 2 CMLR 480   *432*
Centrafarm BV v Sterling Drug Inc [1974] ECR 1147   *441*
Chabot v Davies (1936) 3 All ER 221   *19*
Chiron Corp. v Organon Teknika Ltd. (No.3) [1994] FSR 202   *197, 212, 236*
Christian Franceries Case T 16/83 [1988] EPOR 65   *214*
CIVC v Wineworths [1991] 2 NZLR 432   *412*
Clement Talbot Ltd. v Wilson (1909) 26 RPC 467   *245*
CNL-Sucal v Hag [1990] 3 CMLR 571   *354, 445*
Clothworkers of Ipswich (1615) Godbolt 252   *354*
CNL-Sucal v Hag [1990] 3 CMLR 571   *445*
Coca-Cola Co's Applications [1986] 2 All ER 274   *341, 403*
Coca-Cola Co. of Canada Ltd. v Pepsi-Cola Co. of Canada Ltd. (1942) 59 RPC 127
   346, 357
Coco v A.N. Clark (Engineers) Ltd. [1969] RPC 41   *120, 127, 131, 139, 148*
Collins v Imtrat Handellgesellschaft mbH [1994] FSR 166   *428*
Commercial Plastics Ltd. v Vincent [1964] 3 WLR 820   *134*
Commercial Solvents v Commission [1974] 1 ECR 223   *468, 473*
Commission v BASF [1994] ECR 1-2555   *474*
Computer Associates v Altai (1992) 982 F.2d 693   *95*
Cordova, de v Vick Chemical Co. (1951) 68 RPC 103   *357*
Corelli v Gray (1913) 30 TLR 116   *38*
Corruplast Ltd. v George Harrison (Agencies) Ltd. [1978] RPC 761   *246*
Cowan [1989] ECR 195   *431*
Cozens v Brutus [1973] AC 854   *50*
CPC/Flavour Concentrates Decision T303/86 [1989] 2 EPOR 95   *191*
Cramp, G. A., & Sons Ltd. v Frank Smythson Ltd. [1944] AC 329   *44, 48*
Cranleigh Precision Engineering Ltd. v Bryant [1965] 1 WLR 1293   *121*
Crescent Tool Co. v Kilborn & Bishop Co. (1917) 247 F.290   *398*
Croft v Day (1843) 7 Beav 88   *384*
Crosfield, Joseph & Sons Ltd.; In re H. N. Brock & Co. Ltd. [1910] 1 Ch 130   *317*
Cummins v Bond [1927] 1 Ch 167   *59*
Cutler v Wandsworth Stadium Ltd. [1949] AC 398   *390*

D

D v National Society for the Prevention of Cruelty to Children [1976] 2 All ER 993   *143*
Darcy v Allin (1602) 1 WPC 1   *160*
Dart Industries Inc. v Decor Corp. Pty. Ltd. [1994] FSR 567   *244*
Davis v Comitti (1885) 52 LT 539; 54 LJ Ch 419   *17, 58*
Davis v The Sussex Rubber Co. Ltd. (1927) 44 RPC 412   *314*
Day v Brownrigg (1878) 10 Ch D 294   *57*
Deutsche Grammophon (1971) ECR 487   *430*
Deutsche Renault AG v Audi AG [1995] 1 CMLR 461   *355*
Donaldson v Beckett (1774) 2 Bro PC 129   *7*
Dorling v Honnor Marine [1965] 1 Ch 1   *19, 270*

Dunlop Pneumatic Tyre Co. Ltd. v Neal [1899] 1 Ch 807   *22, 23*
Dunlop Pneumatic Tyre Co. Ltd. v Holborn Tyre Co. Ltd. (1901) 18 RPC 222   *22*
Dunlop Pneumatic Tyre Co. Ltd. v David Moseley & Sons Ltd. [1904] 1 Ch 612   *23*

E

Eastman Photographic Materials Co. Ltd. v Comptroller-General of Patents, Designs, and Trade Marks [1898] AC 571   *339*
Edelsten v Edelsten (1863) 1 De GJ & S 185   *386*
Edge, William, & Sons Ltd. v William Nicholls & Sons Ltd. [1911] AC 693   *401*
Electrix Ltd. v Electrolux Ltd. [1960] AC 722   *316*
ELVIS PRESLEY Trade Marks [1997] RPC 543   *324*
Elliott, R. J., & Co. Ltd. v Hodgson (1902) 19 RPC 518   *401*
EMI Electrola [1989] ECR 79   *429*
Erven Warnink B. V. v Townend & Sons (Hull) Ltd. [1979] AC 731   *152, 388, 404*
European, The, v The Economist Newspapers [1996] FSR 431   *395, 399*
Ewing v Buttercup Margarine Co. Ltd. (1917) 34 RPC 232   *397*
Exxon Corp. v Exxon Insurance Consultants International Ltd. [1981] 3 All ER 241   *55, 76*
Exxon/Fuel Oils Decision T409/91 [1994] OJ EPO 653   *197, 201*

F

Faccenda Chicken Ltd. v Fowler [1985] 1 All ER 724   *140*
Faccenda Chicken Ltd. v Fowler [1986] 1 All ER 617   *134*
Fanfold Ltd's Application (1928) 45 RPC 325   *332*
Feist Publications Inc. v Rural Telephone Service Co. Inc. (1991) S Ct 1282   *44*
Financial, The, Times Ltd. v Evening Standard Co. Ltd. [1991] FSR 7   *405*
Fischer, George, (Great Britain) Ltd. v Multi-Construction Ltd. [1995] 1 BCLC 260   *248*
Fisons Plc v Norton Healthcare Ltd. [1994] FSR 745   *348*
Flour Oxidising Co. Ltd. v Carr & Co. Ltd. (1908) 25 RPC 428   *181*
Football League Ltd. v Littlewoods Pools Ltd. [1959] 2 All ER 546   *48*
Ford Motor Co. Ltd.'s Design Applications [1994] RPC 545   *288*
Ford Motor Co. Ltd.'s Design Applications [1995] RPC 167   *292*
Ford-Werke AG's Application [1955] 72 RPC 191   *343*
Franchi v Franchi [1967] RPC 149   *128*
Fraser v Evans [1969] 1 All ER 8   *143, 146, 149*
Fraser v Thames Television Ltd. [1984] 1 QB 44   *126*
Fujitsu Ltd.'s Application [1997] RPC 608   *216*

G

Gadd and Mason v Manchester Corporation (1892) 9 RPC 516   *205*
Gale's Application [1991] RPC 305   *214, 223*

Galloway v Bleaden (1839) 1 WPC 521   *185*
Gardex Ltd. v Sorata Ltd. [1986] RPC 623   *278*
Garrett's Application [1916] 1 Ch 436   *318*
Gartside v Outram (1856) 26 LJ Ch 113   *145*
Gaskell & Chambers Ltd. v Measure Master Ltd. [1993] RPC 76   *295*
Genentech Inc.'s Patent [1989] RPC 147   *196, 201, 214*
Genentech I/Polypeptide expression Decision T292/85 [1989] OJ EPO 275   *196, 198, 201*
General Tire & Rubber Co. v The Firestone Tyre and Rubber Co. Ltd. [1972] RPC 457
   *181, **202**, 209, 211*
General Tire and Rubber Co. v Firestone Tyre and Rubber Co. Ltd. [1976] RPC 197
   ***238**, 247*
Generics and Harris Pharmaceuticals [1992] 1 ECR 5335   *440*
Gerber Garment Technology Inc. v Lectra Systems Ltd. [1997] RPC 443   *242, 256*
Gillette Safety Razor Co. Ltd. v Anglo-American Trading Co. Ltd. (1913) 30 RPC 465
   129, 185
Gorris v Scott (1874) LR 9 Ex 125   *245*
Green v Broadcasting Corporation of New Zealand [1989] RPC 700   *26*
Greer v Kettle [1938] AC 156   *92*
Guccio Gucci v Paolo Gucci [1991] FSR 89   *399*
GVL v EC Commission [1983] ECR 483   *430*

H

Hack's Application (1940) 58 RPC 91   *370*
Haig, John, & Co. Ltd. v Forth Blending Co. Ltd. [1954] SC 35   *401*
Hallen v Brabantia [1991] RPC 195   *209*
Hanfstaengl v Empire Palace [1894] 3 Ch 109   *77*
Harmer v Jumbil (Nigeria) Tin Areas Ltd. [1921] 1 Ch 200   *22*
Harris' Patent [1985] RPC 19   *224*
Harrods Ltd. v Harrodian School Ltd. [1996] RPC 697   *396, **413*
Hauptzollamt Munchen-Mitte v Technische Universitat Munchen [1991] ECR 1-5469   *473*
Hawkes and Son (London) Ltd. v Paramount Film Service Ltd. [1934] 1 Ch 593   *77,*
   101
Heineken Brouwerijen [1984] ECR 3435   *428*
Henderson v Radio Corpn. Pty. Ltd. [1969] RPC 218   *418*
Hensher, George, Ltd. v Restawile Upholstery (Lancs) Ltd. [1976] AC 64   *20, 49*
Herbert Morris Ltd. v Saxelby [1916] 1 AC 688   *135, 139*
Hickton's Patent Syndicate v Patents and Machine Improvements Company Ltd. (1909)
   26 RPC 339   *176*
Hill v William Hill (Park Lane) [1949] AC 530   *350*
Hilti v Commission [1994] ECR 1-667   *469*
Hivac Ltd. v Park Royal Scientific Instruments Ltd. [1946] Ch 169   *139*
Hodgkinson & Corby Ltd. v Wards Mobility Services Ltd. [1994] 1 WLR 1564   *398*
Hoechst v Commission [1989] ECR 2859   *471*
Höfner and Elser v Macrotron [1991] ECR 1-1979   *470*
Hollinrake v Truswell [1894] 3 Ch 420   *57*
Holly Hobbie Trade Mark [1984] FSR 199   *372*

Holt's Trade Mark (1896) 13 RPC 118   *327*
Hoover Plc v George Hulme (Stockport) Ltd. [1982] FSR 565   *20*
Howel v Richards (1809) 11 East 633   *12*
Hubbard v Vosper [1972] 2 QB 84   *100*

I

IBM T 38/86 [1990] EPOR 606   *215*
**Ibcos Computers Ltd. v Barclays Mercantile Highland Finance Ltd. [1994] FSR 275
    *86***
Imperial Group Ltd. v Philip Morris & Co. Ltd. [1982] FSR 72   *345*
Improver Corporation v Remington Products, Landgericht (Regional Court) Dusseldorf, 30
    December 1988   *234*
Improver Corporation v Remington Products [1990] FSR 181   *234*
Initial Services Ltd. v Putterill [1967] 3 All ER 145   *143, 145, 146, 149*
Interlego AG v Tyco Industries Inc. [1989] AC 217   *53, 282*
Iron-Ox Remedy Co. v Co-operative Wholesale Society (1907) 24 RPC 425   *386*
Irving's Yeastvite Ltd. v Horsenail (1934) 51 RPC 110   *358*

J

James's Trade Mark, James v Soulby (1886) 33 Ch D 392   *342*
Jarrold v Houlston (1857) 3 K & J 708   *96*
Jellinek's Application (1946) 63 RPC 59   *370*
Jennings v Stephens [1936] Ch 469   *85*
Jones v Lavington [1903] 1 KB 253   *13*

K

Karo Step Trade Mark [1977] RPC 273   *56*
Katz v United States (1967) 389 US 347   *145*
Kaye v Robertson [1991] FSR 62   *151*
Kenrick v Lawrence (1890) 25 QBD 99   *89*
Kestos Ltd. v Kempat Ltd. (1936) 53 RPC 151   *276, 280*
Keurkoop v Nancy Kean Gifts [1982] ECR 2853   *464, 472*
King, The, v Arkwright [1785] 1 WPC 64   *164, 173*
King Features Inc. v O. and M. Kleeman Ltd. [1941] AC 417   *18*
King Instruments Corp. v Perego (1995) 65 F 3rd 941, 72 F 3rd 855   *247*

L

L.B. (Plastics) Ltd. v Swish Products Ltd. [1979] RPC 551   *20, 53, 81, 89, 94*
Ladbroke (Football) Ltd. v William Hill (Football) Ltd. [1964] 1 All ER 465   *46, 84*

Lancashire Fires Ltd v S A Lyons & Co. Ltd [1996] FSR 629   *139*
Lansing Linde Ltd. v Kerr [1991] 1 WLR 251   *140*
Leather Cloth Company Ltd. v The American Leather Cloth Company Ltd. (1863) 4 De GJ & S 137   *384*
Lego System Aktieselskab v Lego M. Lemelstrich Ltd. [1983] FSR 155   *417*
Leng, Sir W.C., & Co. Ltd. v Andrews [1909] 1 Ch 763   *135*
Leslie v Young & Sons [1894] AC 335   *48*
Liardet's Patent (1773) 1 WPC 52   *165*
Lister & Co.'s Application [1965] FSR 178   *206*
Littlewoods Organisation Ltd. v Harris [1978] 1 All ER 1026   *137*
Liverpool Electric Cable Co. Ltd.'s Application (1929) 46 RPC 99   *337*
London Armoury Co. Ltd. v Ever Ready Co. (Great Britain) Ltd. [1941] 1 KB 742   *390*
Longbottom v Shaw (1891) 8 RPC 333   *203*
Losh v Hague (1838) 1 WPC 202   *186*
Luchtenberg T 84/83 [1979-85] EPOR 796   *182*
Lux Traffic Controls Ltd. v Pike Signals Ltd. [1993] RPC 107   *180, 208, 213*
Lyngstad & Others v Anabas Products Ltd. [1977] FSR 62   *419*

M

Macaura v Northern Assurance Co. [1925] AC 619   *256*
Mackenzie's Application [1967] RPC 628   *343*
Macmillan & Co. Ltd. v K. & J. Cooper (1924) 40 TLR 186   *44, 45, 48*
MADAME Trade Mark [1966] RPC 541   *322*
Malone v Commissioner of Police of the Metropolis (No.2) [1979] 2 All ER 620   *144*
Market Investigations Ltd. v Minister of Social Security [1969] 2 QB 173   *62, 66*
Marsden v Saville Street Co. (1878) LR 3 Ex D 203   *354*
Mason v Burningham [1949] 2 All ER 134   *13*
Matania v National Provincial Bank Ltd. [1936] 2 All ER 633   *22*
May & Baker Ltd. v Boots Pure Drug Co. Ltd. (1950) 67 RPC 23   *197*
McCulloch v L A. May Ltd. (1947) 65 RPC 58   *418*
McDowell's case (1927) 43 RPC 393   *369*
Merchant-Adventurers Ltd. v M. Grew & Co. Ltd. [1972] Ch. 242   *19*
Merck & Co Inc. v Primecrown Ltd. [1997] FSR 237   *438, 439*
Merck v Stephar [1981] ECR 2063   *439*
Merit Trade Marks [1989] RPC 687   *343*
Merrell Dow Pharmaceuticals Inc. v H. N. Norton & Co. Ltd. [1996] RPC 76   *187, 201*
Merrill Lynch's Application [1989] RPC 561   *215, 220*
Meters Ltd. v Metropolitan Gas Meters Ltd. (1911) 28 RPC 157   *241, 245*
Michelin [1983] ECR 3461   *462, 470*
Microbeads AC v Vinhurst Road Markings Ltd. [1976] 1 All ER 529   *11*
Miles v Clarke [1953] 1 WLR 537   *91*
Millar v Taylor (1769) 4 Burr 2303   *6*
Millington v Fox 3 M & Cr 338   *383*
Minnesota Mining & Manufacturing Co. v Bondina Ltd. [1973] RPC 491   *210*
Ministère Public v Deserbais [1988] ECR 4907   *472*
Mirage Studios v Counter-Feat Clothing Co. Ltd. [1991] FSR 145   *329*

MOBIL/Friction reducing additive Decision G02/88 [1990] EPOR 73   *188, 192*
Molins and Molins Machine Co. Ltd. v Industrial Machinery Co. Ltd. (1938) 55 RPC 31
    179
Mölnlycke AB v Procter & Gamble Ltd. [1992] FSR 549   *197*
Mölnlycke AB v Procter & Gamble Ltd. (No.5) [1994] RPC 49   *208*
Monforts v Marsden (1895) 12 RPC 266   *13*
Moody v Tree (1892) 9 RPC 233   *18*
Moore v News of the World Ltd. [1972] 1 QB 441   *75*
Moorgate Tobacco Company Ltd. v Phillip Morris Ltd. (No.2) (1984) 156 CLR 414   *422*
Morison v Moat (1851) 9 Hare 241   *117, 119*
Morris', Philip, Application [1980] RPC 527   *343*
Mothercare U.K. Ltd. v Penguin Books Ltd. [1988] RPC 113   *404*
Musik-Vertrieb Membran and K-tel International v GEMA [1981] ECR 147   *429, 443*

N

National Provincial Bank Ltd. v Ainsworth [1965] AC 1175   *147*
Nederlandsche Banden-Industrie Michelin v The Commission of the European Communities
    [1983] ECR 3461   *467*
Niblett Ltd. v Confectioners' Materials Co. Ltd. [1921] 3 KB 387   *13*
Nichols v Universal Pictures (1930) 45 F (2d) 119   *90*
Noah v Shuba [1991] FSR 14   69, 74
Nold v Commission [1974] ECR 491   *471*
North Cheshire and Manchester Brewery Co. v The Manchester Brewery Co. [1899] AC 83
    404
Northern Office Micro Computers (Pty.) Ltd. v Rosenstein [1982] FSR 124   *134*

O

O'Cedar Ltd. v Slough Trading Co. Ltd. [1927] 2 KB 123   *22*
Ocular Sciences Ltd. v Aspect Vision Care Ltd. [1997] RPC 289   *126, **139, 154, 300***
O'Reilly v Morse (1854) 56 US (15 How) 62   *199*
Origins Natural Resources Inc. v Origin Clothing Ltd. [1995] FSR 280   *356*

P

Parker, Philip v Stephen Tidball [1997] FSR 680   *300*
Parker-Knoll Limited v Knoll International Limited [1962] RPC 243   *406*
Parks-Cramer Co. v G. W. Thornton & Sons Ltd. [1966] RPC 407   205
Paterson Zochonis Ltd. v Merfarken Packaging Ltd. [1983] FSR 273   *246*
Penn v Jack (1867) LR 5 Eq 81   *239, 245*
Pepper v Hart [1993] AC 534   *289, 290, 307*
Perry vTruefitt (1842) 6 Beav 66   *383, 384*
Petterson T1002/92 [1996] EPOR 1   *222*

Pharmon v Hoechst [1985] ECR 2281 *442*
Pianotist Co's Application (1906) 23 RPC 774 *335*
Pillsbury-Washburn Flour Mills Co. v Eagle (1898) 86 Fed R 608 *391*
PLG Research Ltd. v Ardon International Ltd. [1993] FSR 197 *188, 233*
Pneumatic Tyre Co. Ltd. v Puncture Proof Pneumatic Tyre Co. Ltd. (1899) 16 RPC 209 *238*
Polaroid Corp. v Eastman Kodak Co. [1977] RPC 379 *245*
Politechnika Ipari Szovetkezef v Dallas Print Transfers Ltd. [1982] FSR 529 *329*
Prince Albert v Strange (1849) 1 Mac & G 25 *117, 120, 145, 150, 156*
Prince plc v Prince Sports Group Inc. [1998] FSR 21 *368*
Printers and Finishers Ltd. v Holloway [1965] RPC 239 *132, 136, 145*
Proctor v Bayley (1889) 42 Ch D 390 *144*

R

Radio Telefis Eireann & Independent Television Publications Ltd. v The Commission of the European Communities [1995] FSR 530 *466*
Ravenhead Brick Co. Ltd. v Ruabon Brick & Terra Cotta Co. Ltd. (1937) 54 RPC 341 *397*
Reckitt & Colman Products Ltd. v Borden Inc. [1990] 1 All ER 873 *400*
Reddaway v Banham & Co. [1896] AC 199 *385, 387, 402*
Reid & Sigrist Ltd. v Moss and Mechanism Ltd. (1932) 49 RPC 461 *133, 136*
Reymes-Cole v Elite Hosiery Co. Ltd. [1965] RPC 102 *254*
Richardson, John, Computers v Flanders [1993] FSR 497 *90*
Ripley, Edward, & Son's Application (1898) 15 RPC 151 *317*
Rite-Hite Corp. v Kelley Co. Inc. [1996] FSR 469 *247*
Robb v Green [1895] 2 QB 315 *136*
Rodi and Weinenberger A.G. v Harry Showell Ltd. [1969] RPC 367 *230, 231*
Rose Plastics GmbH v William Beckett & Co. (Plastics) Ltd. (unreported), 2 July 1987 *54*

S

Sabel BV v Puma AG [1998] RPC 199 *358*
Saltman Engineering Co. Ltd. v Campbell Engineering Co. Ltd. (1948) 65 RPC 203; [1963] 3 All ER 403 *118, 121, 127, 131*
Samuel Parkes & Co. Ltd. v Cocker Bros. Ltd. (1929) RPC 241 *204*
Savage v Harris & Sons (1896) 13 RPC 364 *210*
Saville Perfumery Ltd. v June Perfect Ltd. (1941) 58 RPC 147 *348*
Scott v Stanford LR 3 Eq. 718 *78*
Seager v Copydex Ltd. [1967] 1 WLR 923 *121*
Sellars v Adelaide Petroleum NL (1994) 179 CLR 332 *251*
Selz, Charles, Ltd.'s Application (1954) 71 RPC 158 *225*
Series 5 Software Ltd v Philip Clarke [1996] FSR 273 *362*
Siddell v Vickers & Sons Ltd. (1890) 15 App Cas 496 *210*
Sifam Electrical Instrument Co. Ltd. v Sangamo Weston Ltd. [1973] RPC 899 *286, 293*

Sim v Heinz [1959] 1 WLR 313   *152*
Sirdar Rubber Co. Ltd. v Wallington, Weston & Co. (1905) 22 RPC 257   *22*
Sirdar Rubber Co. Ltd. v Wallington, Weston & Co. (1907) 24 RPC 539   *22*
Slazenger & Sons v Feltham & Co. (1889) 6 RPC 531   *396*
Smith Hayden & Co's Application (1946) 63 RPC 97   *335*
Smith Kline and French Laboratories Ltd.'s Trade Mark Application [1976] RPC 511   *325*
Smith Kline and French Laboratories Ltd. v Sterling-Winthrop Group Ltd. [1975] 2 All ER
   578   *342*
Smith Kline and French Laboratories Ltd. v Sterling-Winthrop Group Ltd. [1976] RPC 511
   336
Sodastream Ltd. v Thorn Cascade Co. Ltd. [1982] RPC 459   *396*
Solanite Signs Ltd. v Wood (1933) 50 RPC 315   *255*
Solar Thomson Engineering Co. Ltd. v Barton [1977] RPC 537   *23, 24*
Southern Pacific v Jensen (1917) 244 US 205   *147*
Spalding, A. G., & Bros. v A W Gamage Ltd. (1915) 84 LJ Ch 449   *385, 389*
Spectravest Inc. v Aperknit Ltd. [1988] FSR 161   *78*
Stead v Williams (1843) 2 WPC 126   *186*
Stenor Ltd. v Whitesides (Clitheroe) Ltd. (1948) 65 RPC 1   *277*
Stevenson Jordan and Harrison Ltd. v Macdonald and Evans [1952] 1 TLR 110   *62, 71,*
   156
Stroughill v Buck (1850) 14 QB 781   *92*
Summers, John, & Sons Ltd. v The Cold Metal Process Co. (1948) 65 RPC 75   *253*
Sykes v Sykes (1824) 3 B & C 541   *312*

T

Taittinger SA v Allbev Ltd. [1993] FSR 641   *394, 410, 414*
Talbot v General Television Corporation Pty. Ltd. [1981] RPC 1   *127*
Tamworth Herald Co. Ltd. v Thomson Free Newspapers Ltd. [1991] FSR 337   *407*
TARZAN Trade Mark [1970] RPC 450   *326*
Tate v Fulbrook [1908] 1 KB 821   *27*
Tavener Rutledge Ltd. v Trexapalm Ltd. [1977] RPC 275   *57*
Taylor's Patent (1896) 13 RPC 482   *186*
Terrapin v Terranova [1976] ECR 1039   *446*
Terrapin Ltd. v Builders' Supply Company (Hayes) Ltd. [1967] RPC 375   *121, 125,*
   155
Tetra Pak Rausing SA v EC Commission [1991] 4 CMLR 334   *457*
Thomas Marshall (Exports) Ltd. v Guinle [1979] Ch 227   *127, 135*
Tolley v J. S. Fry and Sons Ltd. [1931] AC 333   *153*
Total Information Processing Systems v Daman [1992] FSR 171   *88*
Transfermatic Trade mark [1966] RPC 568   *369*
Trebor Bassett Ltd. v The Football Association [1997] FSR 211   *364*
Turner, Ernest, Electrical Instruments Ltd. v Performing Right Society Ltd. [1943] 1
   Ch 167   *85*

U

Ungar v Sugg (1892) 9 RPC 113   *255*
Union Carbide Corp. v Naturin Ltd. [1987] FSR 538   *99, 156*
United Biscuits (UK) Ltd. v Asda Stores Ltd. [1997] RPC 513   *394*
United Biscuits UK Ltd. v Burton Biscuits Ltd. [1992] FSR 14   *396*
United Brands v Commission [1978] ECR 207   *469*
United Horse Shoe and Nail Co., The v Stewart & Co. (1888) 5 RPC 260   *239, 246*
United Telephone Co. v Walker (1886) 4 RPC 63   *245*
University of London Press Ltd. v University Tutorial Press Ltd. [1916] 2 Ch 601   *42, 56, 101*

V

Valeo Vision S.A. v Flexible Lamps Ltd. [1995] RPC 205   *281*
Van Der Lely N.V. v Bamfords Ltd. [1963] RPC 61   *230*
Van Zuylen Frères v Hag [1974] ECR 731   *445*
Vicom Systems Inc's Patent Application [1987] 2 EPOR 74   *216, 218, 221*
Vine Products Ltd. v Mackenzie & Co. Ltd. [1969] RPC 1   *388, 393, 412*
Vodafone Group plc v Orange Personal Communications Services Ltd. [1997] FSR 34   *363*
Vokes Ltd. v Heather (1945) 62 RPC 135   *135*
Volvo AB v Erik Veng (UK) Ltd. [1989] 4 CMLR 122   *463, 467*

W

W & G du Cros Ltd. (1913) 30 RPC 660   *325, 336, 337*
Wagamama Ltd. v City Centre Restaurants Ltd. [1995] FSR 713   *349, 397, 417*
Walker, John, & Sons Ltd. v Henry Ost & Co. Ltd. [1970] 1 WLR 917   *388*
Walter v Steinkopff [1892] 3 Ch 489   *101*
Wang Laboratories Application [1991] RPC 463   *222*
Ward v Kirkland [1967] Ch 194   *22*
Warner Brothers and Metronome Video v Christiansen [1988] ECR 2605   *442*
Watson Laidlow & Co. Ltd. v Pott, Cassels & Williamson (1914) 31 RPC 104   *247*
Weatherby & Sons v International Horse Agency and Exchange Ltd. [1910] 2 Ch 297   *77*
Weingarten Bros. v Bayer & Co. (1905) 92 LT 511   *401*
Wessex Dairies Ltd. v Smith [1935] 2 KB 80   *136*
Wheatley's Application [1985] RPC 91   *182*
Wilhelm, Walt [1969] ECR 1   *430, 462*
Williams Coulson & Sons v James Coulson and Co. (1887) 3 TLR 46   *153*
Windsor RDC v Otterway & Try Ltd. [1954] 3 All ER 721   *251*
Windsurfing International Inc. v Tabur Marine (GB) Ltd. [1985] RPC 59   *183, 208, 211*
Wineworths Ltd. v CIVC [1992] 2 NZLR 327   *412*
Winthrop [1974] ECR 1183   *443*
Wombles Ltd. v Wombles Skips Ltd. [1977] RPC 99   *57, 421*

Woodward v Hutchins [1977] 2 All ER 751 *141*
Worsley, E, & Co. Ltd. v Cooper [1939] 1 All ER 290 *137*
Worthington Pumping Engine Co. v Moore (1903) 20 RPC 41 *224*

X

X, In re [1984] 1 WLR 1422 *153*

Y

York Trade Mark [1982] FSR 111 *336*
Yorkshire Copper Works Ltd.'s Application (1954) 71 RPC 150 *328, 338*
Young v Rosenthal and Co. (1884) 1 RPC 29 *174*

Table of Legislation

Administration of Justice Act 1969
s 12   *292*
  12(1)   *338*

Australian Trade Practices Act 1974
s 52   *422, 424*

Broadcasting Act 1990
s 176   *475*

Canadian Unfair Competition Act 1932
s 23(5)(b)   *347*

Chancery Amendment Act 1858   *144*

The Consumer Credit Act 1974   *360*

The Consumer Credit (Advertisements)
Regulations 1989   *360*

Contracts of Employment Act 1963   *63, 64*

Copyright Act 1842   *17, 42, 55, 58*

Copyright Act 1911
s 1   *38*
  1(1)   *42, 45, 56*
  1(2)   *18, 38*
s 22   *19*
  22(1)   *18*
s 35   *50*
  35(1)   *45*

Copyright Act 1956   *19, 54*
s 1(1)   *61*
  1(5)(a)   *61*
s 2   *56*
  2(1)   *61*
  2(5)   *61*
s 3   *271*
  3(1)   *49, 53*
  3(1)(a)   *50*
  3(1)(b)   *50*
  3(1)(c)   *49*
  3(2)   *49*
s 4(1)   *61*
  4(4)   *61, 69, 70*
  4(5)   *69, 70*
s 6(2)   *100*
s 9(8)   *19, 20, 84, 270, 273*
s 10   *20, 272, 274, 287*
  10(3)   *271*
s 20(2)   *70*
s 36(1)   *66*
  36(3)   *66*
s 43   *74, 76*
  43(2)   *74*
  43(2)(a)   *75*
  43(8)   *75*
  43(10)   *75*
s 48(1)   *83, 271, 273*
s 49(1)   *83, 271*
  49(2)   *61*
  49(3)(a)   *61*

Copyright, Designs and Patents Act 1988
s 1(1)   *41*
  1(1)(a)   *298*
s 16   *298*
s 30   *76*
s 50A   *14*
s 92   *13*
s 171(3)   *25*
s 213   *290, 298*
  213(1)   *298*
  213(3)(b)(i)   *302, 303, 306*
  213(4)   *298, 306*
s 214   *298*
s 226   *298*
  226(1)   *302*
  226(2)   *302*
  226(3)   *302*
s 237   *286*
s 265   *285*
  265(4)   *298*
s 266   *281*

Schedule 1
para 19   *286*

Copyright (Industrial) Designs Rules 1957
   272

Design Copyright Act 1968   *274, 288*

Food and Drugs Act 1955   *393*

Forgery and Counterfeiting Act 1981   *424*

Industrial Relations Act 1971   *63, 64*

Matrimonial Homes Act 1967   *147*

Patent Law Amendment Act 1852   *170*

Patents Act 1949
s 13(4)   *11*
s 22   *11*
s 32(1)(e)   *181, 194*
s 60   *238*

Patents Act 1977
s 1   *212, 217*
   1(1)   *173, 217*
   1(1)(a)   *222*
   1(2)   *173, 213, 214, 216, 269*
   1(2)(c)   *214, 217, 221*
   1(3)   *173*
s 2(1)   *180*
   2(2)   *180, 187, 190, 209*
   2(3)   *209*
s 3   *209*
s 4(1)   *212*
   4(2)   *213*
s 5   *194*
   5(1)   *195*
   5(2)   *195*
   5(2)(a)   *195*
s 14   *195*
   14(3)   *195*
   14(5)   *196*
   14(5)(c)   *195, 197*
s 39(1)(b)   *225*
s 40   *227, 229*
   40(1)   *227, 229*

s 44   *14, 213, 236*
   44(1)(b)   *236, 237*
   44(3)   *236, 237*
s 60   *243, 256*
   60(1)   *243*
   60(1)(a)   *257*
   60(2)   *187, 243*
   60(3)   *243*
s 61   *238*
   61(1)   *243, 244*
   61(6)   *243*
s 64   *188, 190, 194*
s 67   *237*
s 70   *252, 255*
   70(1)   *252, 253*
   70(2)   *252*
   70(3)   *253, 255*
   70(4)   *252, 253, 255, 256*
s 72   *180, 195, 209*
   72(1)   *196*
   72(1)(c)   *196*
s 74   *209*
s 77(1)   *216*
   77(4)   *216*
s 110   *313*
s 125(1)   *233*
s 130   *236*
   130(7)   *217*

Patents and Designs Act 1907   *18*

Patents, Designs and Trademarks Act 1883
s 58   *17*

Post Office Act 1969
s 9   *148*
s 28   *148*

Registered Designs Act 1949
s 1   *274, 281, 283, 286*
   1(1)   *272, 285, 286, 302*
   1(1)(b)(i)   *281*
   1(1)(b)(ii)   *281, 282, 288, 289, 290, 291*
   1(2)   *272, 281, 287*
   1(3)   *272, 275*
   1(4)   *281*
s 7   *273, 282*
   7(1)   *273, 280, 295*

s 44   *276, 286*
  44(1)   *286, 293*

Sale of Goods Act 1893
s 12   *13*
  12(1)   *12*
  12(2)   *12*

Statute of Anne 1709   *5, 37*

Statute of Monopolies 1623   *4, 163, 182*
s 1(5)   *17*

The Statute of Uses 1535   *120*

Theft Acts 1968 and 1978   *424*

Trade Descriptions Act 1968   *393, 424*

Trade Marks Acts 1883
s 68   *327*

Trade Marks Act 1888   *317*

Trade Marks Act 1905   *317*
s 9   *315*
s 11   *369*
s 19   *369*

Trade Marks Act 1919   *315*

Trade Marks Act 1938
s 2   *369*
s 4   *348*
  4(1)(b)   *358, 405*
s 9   *314, 325, 328, 331, 338*
  9(1)   *331*
  9(1)(a)   *332*
  9(1)(b)   *332*
  9(1)(c)   *58*
  9(1)(d)   *332*
  9(1)(e)   *328, 332*
  9(2)   *325*
  9(3)   *325*
  9(3)(b)   *333*
s 10   *314, 323, 331, 338*
  10(1)   *331*
  10(2)   *331*

  10(2)(a)   *337*
s 11   *325, 331, 334, 368*
s 12   *331, 334, 348, 370*
  12(1)   *334, 369*
s 14   *331, 333*
s 17(2)   *325*
s 28   *374*
  28(6)   *371, 372, 374*
s 31   *349*
s 68(1)   *341*

Trade Marks Act 1994
s 1(1)   *314, 319, 323, 364*
s 1(1) - (4)
s 3   *319, 371*
  3(1)   *323*
  3(1)(a)   *319,320*
  3(1)(b)   *319, 320, 323*
  3(1)(c)   *319, 320, 323, 336*
  3(1)(d)   *319, 320, 323*
s 9   *364*
s 10   *350, 356, 364*
s 10(1)   *365*
  10(2)   *346, 350, 355, 365*
  10(4)   *366*
  10(4)(a)   *367*
  10(4)(b)   *367*
  10(6)   *359*
  11(2)   *339, 365*
  11(2)(b)   *360, 366*
s 21   *363*
s 46   *324*
s 47   *371*
s 47(1)   *319, 320, 324*
s 64(1)   *371*
s 72   *320*
s 105   *320*

Schedule 3
para 4(2)   *365*
para 18(2)   *320*

Trade Marks (Amendment) Act 1937
s 6   *369*
s 8   *374*

Trade Marks Registration Act 1875   *314, 383*

EC Legislation

EC Treaty (The Treaty of Rome 1957)
[Note: the Articles will be renumbered during 1999]
Art 6 (formerly Art 7)   *428*
Art 6(1) (formerly Art 7(1))   *428*
Art 30   *426, 435, 442, 445*
Art 36   *426, 435, 442, 445*
Art 85   *426, 437, 457, 463*
Art 85(1)   *14, 448*
Art 85(2)   *448*
Art 85(3)   *15, 449, 457*
Art 86   *427, 456, 457, 463, 466*
Art 177   *445, 463*
Art 222   *429*

Commission Regulation (EC) No.240/96 on the application of Article 85(3) of the Treaty to certain categories of technology transfer agreements [1996] OJ L31/2   *449*

Directive on the approximation of the laws of the Member States relating to trade marks, OJ [1989] L40/1   *351*
Art 5(1)   *352*

EC Regulation No.1768/92 Supplementary protection certificate for medicinal products [1992] OJ L182/1   *440*

EC Regulation Limiting of Use of Names for Wines of Specified Regions No.823/87 *410*

International Conventions

Agreement on the Trade Related Aspects of Intellectual Property Rights   *34, 114, 158, 266, 309, 376*

Berne Convention for the Protection of Literary and Artistic Works   *103*

European Convention for the Protection of Human Rights and Fundamental Freedoms 1950
Art 8   *144*

European Patent Convention   *258*
Art 50(2)(c)   *215*
Art 50(3)   *215*
Art 52   *217*
Art 52(1)   *217*
Art 52(2)   *214, 217, 269*
Art 52(2)(c)   *215, 218*
Art 52(3)   *214, 217*
Art 54   *187, 192*
Art 54(1)   *190*
Art 54(2)   *188, 190, 193*
Art 69   *233*
Art 84   *197*

Paris Convention for the Protection of Industrial Property 1883   *29*

Chapter 1

Basic Principles

Introduction

This chapter contains a selection of materials which give some feel for the nature of intellectual property rights. Not only does intellectual property law have to provide a framework of protection for inventive and creative works and business goodwill, it also has to take due account of the interests of society as a whole, users and distributors of articles or works subject to intellectual property rights, competitors and others. It has to strike a balance. This is done in two ways: restricting the scope of the rights by limiting their duration and by constructing mechanisms to prevent or control abuse of the rights. Thus, the scope of copyright is constrained by reference to the acts which the owner has the exclusive right to perform or authorise others to perform. A patent cannot endure for more than 20 years and using intellectual property rights to restrict supply so as to drive up prices may be defeated by the grant of a compulsory licence. In terms of all intellectual property rights there are a number of defences and exceptions to infringement.

An important feature of intellectual property is that it is a form of property, albeit intangible. It is separate to and has an existence distinct from the physical articles or goods which 'contain' the rights. Indeed, in some instances, the rights are capable of existence and enforcement with no tangible form whatsoever. Another feature is that the various rights often are not isolated. There is some overlap; two or more rights might subsist in the same thing. For example, a document might be subject to copyright and to an obligation of confidence. An article of manufacture might be subject to patents, design rights and trade marks. A pictorial trade mark might also be subject to copyright. The *British Leyland* case, extracts of which are reproduced in this chapter, shows how the rights may overlap, how they can have similarities and how the law attempts to prevent a potential abuse of the rights or restricts their exploitation in appropriate circumstances.

Intellectual property law has shown itself to be capable of development and growth to take account of changing technology and new forms of invention and human creativity. However, it does not always succeed and is sometimes found wanting as the 'Opportunity Knocks' case shows. Finally, it must be noted that intellectual property rights are important on a global scale and international co-operation is highly desirable. The Paris Convention of 1883 shows early recognition of this aspect of intellectual property and sets out some of the fundamental principles of international recognition and reciprocity. Extracts of the 'Opportunity Knocks' case, the Paris Convention and the general provisions of the Trade Related Aspects of Intellectual Property Rights Agreement (TRIPS) administered by the World Trade Organisation are reproduced in this chapter. First, an extract from an article by Professor Grant Hammond helps to set the scene and to give an excellent discussion and critique of intellectual property law from an historical viewpoint.

Hammond, G., 'The Legal Protection of Ideas - Part 1' [1992] 8 CLSR 111

'The thrust of intellectual property law is today usually expressed in economic terms: the perceived need to enable creators and producers of knowledge-based commodities to capture the full or at least fuller, benefits of those commodities. In broad terms there are two models which address this objective in contemporary legal systems. The first, the protective model, creates a series of discrete protective laws which give proprietary protection on closely defined terms. The second, the state support model, gives creators direct support or rewards, in one form or another, but allows relatively free appropriation by producers. Both models endeavour to encourage creation and dissemination of intellectual creations. The protective model allows greater rewards and more sophisticated interests to be created.

Common law jurisdictions have historically adopted the protective model. Several problems are apparent with it. First, not everybody accepts an overtly economic rationale; cultural and political objectives are inadequately accommodated. Second, there is a long standing controversy as to whether the model actually achieves its stated economic goals. Third, at least in the eyes of the Third World, it is seen as a significant weapon of repression against members of that unfortunate community. Fourth, the model is increasingly being asked to accommodate more than it was designed for, and probably far more than it can ever satisfactorily accommodate. More and more people are trying to accommodate more and more things under the protective umbrella of intellectual property law to achieve private economic gain ... In short, ideas are part of the seamless web of humanity. Breaking pieces out of that web, unless for an overwhelming justification, robs us of part of ourselves. Absent such a justification, we allow ourselves to be taken on the barb of commercial exploitation of ideas. This problem is particularly acute in an age which is increasingly codifying the self and encouraging individuals to turn every aspect of their being into a reducible, divisible, saleable commodity. If merely to think of the idea of a play about the burning of Atlanta or how to present oneself as the latest pop fad (let alone $e = mc^2$) is to be appropriable, the great chain of humanity is broken. At such a point, our humanity is truly transfixed. It is with that ultimate concern in mind that I approach this subject-matter.

The Basic Paradigm

It is as well to begin with the fundamental principle. Perhaps the best known statement of it is found in a 1918 judgment of Justice Brandeis: "The general rule of law is that the noblest of human productions - knowledge, truths ascertained, conceptions and ideas - become, after voluntary communication to others, free as the air to common use." The proposition as thus enunciated is complex. It has philosophical, economic, cultural, and political dimensions. All of these dimensions find practical expression in a legal birdcage mechanism.

Consider the case of Einstein. He is dubious about Newton's views on physics. He thinks - has the idea if you like - that the better truth is e = mc². He has not yet told the world or anybody so, although he has written out his formula with a few explanatory notes. From the standpoint of the individual, the birdcage operates as a protection. Einstein cannot be forced to disclose his idea. The birdcage affirms his right to his innermost thoughts and ideas. In general, Einstein is under no duty to disclose. However, he may be in a position where he has voluntarily assumed a duty to disclose. He may be employed as a paid researcher, and he may have undertaken to commit his ideas to paper for his employers. And if he is on a university faculty, he will be bound by the scientific ethic which requires, even in the absence of a contract, a member of the academy to disseminate his ideas and research. The birdcage thus gives the individual the freedom to think and the right to assess the maturity of an idea before it is released.

From the standpoint of society, the position is more complex again. Einstein cannot be required to disclose his idea unless he has undertaken to do so in response to some ethical requirement or assumed obligation. But society offers no economic incentive to disclose. It may perhaps confer personal glory, or at least public acknowledgement, for whatever that means to Einstein. Society does not, however, confer an economic reward because it fears that Einstein may somehow get a monopoly on e = mc² and whatever it might be applied to. Instead, the idea becomes part of the general heritage of humankind, and any person can make use of it in theoretical or applied modes. Indeed, more accurately stated, what Einstein has come up with is a scientific discovery. It would be anomalous to deprive the public of something it had always enjoyed, but had not thereto recognized: however, society could, and does, reward the application of that discovery. Hence, rewarding Franklin for recognizing the electrical nature of lightning goes too far; rewarding someone for creating a lightning rod does not.

The result of the birdcage mechanism for legal theory is as follows. Einstein can exercise a self-help remedy by not divulging what is in his mind. He can protect his idea in his private papers and if he tells somebody about it in confidence, though probably on conscience rather than proprietary ground. But once the cage door is voluntarily opened, he has no proprietary rights in the idea. Public dedication has taken place. The dedicated idea is not appropriable by him nor by anybody else, although it ought to be attributed to him. Neither, it appears, can he rely on some kind of non-proprietary relational theory to follow his work. Just as Einstein has no proprietary rights of paternity, he has no following rights. As an idea is applied and acquires further value, no compensation of an economic character is afforded him. He can, however, get a patent if he can think of a practical application of his idea. The text of his explanation, but not the underlying theorem, will then attract copyright.

In the overall result, the birdcage model avoids the zero sum trap. Both Einstein and society get some advantages and some disadvantages. A complex bargain is struck between a given individual and the rest of society. I have however probably said enough to indicate the very real intellectual and practical difficulties in this area of the law. What is an idea? What is the expression of it? Should we grant protection to intellectual creations, and if so, for how long and on what terms? And how do we turn our answers to those questions into workable legal formulas? The answers we give are a window both into our vision of society and the workings of the legal mind.

The Evolution of the Basic Paradigm

It is useful to ask: how did this construct come into being? Something like this is rarely, if ever, created in a vacuum in the law. Holmes thought that the life of law lies in experience. Events, not ideas, drive legal development. Others place a greater emphasis on the primacy of ideas. The better answer may be that the life of the law lies in the way events and ideas interact to produce particular constructs. In any event, Justice Brandeis's general proposition cannot be understood apart from the historical context and the ideas about legal ideas which swirled around those events.

The foundations of our present day intellectual property law came about in the transition from the seventeenth to the eighteenth century. The transition was one from a state in which an all-powerful monarchy granted economic favours for its own purposes to one which recognized more directly the rights of individuals. At the same time, the recognition came slowly and painfully that it would be necessary in the new order to balance private right and public need. Patents, the exclusive right to the fruits of a new manner of manufacture, came into being after judges struck down the huge privilege of Crown granted and enforced monopolies in trade. The judicial victory was endorsed by Parliament in the famous *Statute of Monopolies*. And copyright, the right to replicate a work, eventually came to be vested in authors, not publishers. The system of rights turned itself end for end and then struggled into a precarious balance between public and private rights. The story of these developments is one of the most fascinating chapters in legal history, and its jurisprudential significance is routinely missed. I can here only sketch these developments.

We need to go back to England in the seventeenth and eighteenth centuries. The printing press had been invented, and it was a time of flourishing literary endeavour. It was the age of Johnson, Pope, Sheridan, and Swift. But there was a heated debate, what Samuel Johnson called "the great question concerning Literary Property." The problem was that the Crown had for many years strictly controlled printing. Only books registered with the Stationers Company could be printed, and only then within the guild. This amounted both to a form of censorship and a restrictive trade practice. It also deprived authors of whatever natural law rights they might have in their works.

Of course, it could not last. As early as Milton in 1644, authors began to assert that they must have some kinds of rights in their works. They were becoming less dependent on patrons. And happily, creators displayed then the same contempt for legalism they have always displayed. The law was routinely disobeyed. Things like the probate inventories in England show that roughly one third of the books in England were not in fact enrolled and a flourishing black market and underground traffic existed in copyright. Lawyers actually conveyed what we would today describe as copyright interests regardless of the formal state of the law.

The licensing system eventually ended in 1694, thereby opening the way for two important new streams of legal development, the law of libel and the modern law of copyright. The Stationers petitioned Parliament upon the loss of the advantages of a restrictive trade practice. No longer having rights as publishers, they came up with the notion that authors should be protected and have copyright. This was not public spiritedness on their part. If copyright was a property right, it could then be assigned to the publishers, thereby giving them indirectly what they no longer had directly. Faced with pleading publishers and indignant authors, Parliament capitulated. In 1709 the famous *Statute of Anne* was enacted.

This set the stage for some very difficult litigation. The statute did not expressly abrogate pre-existing common law rights, as contemporary Commonwealth copyright statutes now do. Hence, these critical questions were raised: what, if any, common law rights did authors have in published or unpublished works prior to the *Statute of Anne*? And if there was a common law copyright, was it perpetual? And perhaps most importantly of all, what legal effect did the passing of the *Statute of Anne* have on any pre-existing rights? The matter could not be resolved until after the twenty-eight year copyright period on a work had expired and somebody had allegedly pirated it. In the meantime, three things happened.

First, there was an ongoing debate amongst lawyers and intellectuals over the nature of copyright. On the one hand, the licensing system had implied that, however imperfectly, authors had *something*. And to them, it seemed that natural justice, in Milton's terms, required that protection of some kind be given. On the other hand, the notion that an author could withhold work at that person's caprice did not seem right; still less did the idea that Shakespeare should have a perpetual copyright in his works.

Second, some went to the Chancellors and obtained injunctions restraining the publication of unpublished manuscripts which had been surreptitiously purloined. These cases do not rest on the fully reasoned form of judgment we know today. Reports are brief and, in theoretical terms, can be explained either as the exercise of the Chancellors' conscience or the protection of a property interest, the only kind of interest protected by injunction.

Third, a theoretician was now at work. William Blackstone, later Professor of Law at Oxford, was working towards the first systematic treatise on the laws of England. He had to confirm both the general nature of property and this difficult form of intangible property. He espoused a natural law theory of literary property, adopting the Lockean perspective that a man is entitled to the fruits of his labours. Therefore, an author should have the profits to be made from the commercial exploitation of his own creations. From the standpoint of authority, there were no decisions explicitly recognizing authors' rights in their creations. But the old licensing acts and the equity decisions I have mentioned seemed to Blackstone to be based on the assumption that such common law rights existed. The *Statute of Anne*, as he read it, only gave additional remedies. Hence, when the statutory time limit had expired, the common law right would continue.

Blackstone appears to be the first to suggest the idea of public dedication as a watershed. Where did he get this idea? A doctrine of dedication with respect to land had developed earlier in the century and Blackstone seems to have extended it by analogy.

But he complicated matters by classifying copyright in his taxonomy of property rights acquired "by occupancy", along with easements of light, air, and water. In doing so, he created a logical difficulty which he had overlooked. Rights of that kind were subject to a doctrine of abandonment by non-user. It would follow that an author had rights only so long as the work was kept in print. If this was so, the common law right could not be "perpetual" as he argued. Blackstone had the support and encouragement of William Murray, later to become Lord Mansfield, Lord

Chief Justice of the Court of King's Bench. Murray moved in literary circles and he was well aware that conveyancers had been treating copyrights as property rights in wills and attending to the sale of them before 1700. As a barrister, he advised on some of these matters. Murray thought that on this point practice spoke louder than words, and he was sure that the common law right existed in practice. And from a *moral* perspective, he thought there ought to be such a right. Hence, the decision in *Millar* v *Taylor* (1769) 4 Burr 2303 would have come as no surprise to Murray's contemporaries. In *Millar* v *Taylor*, one of the few split decisions ever handed down by Lord Mansfield's court, it was held (3-1) that (1) the plaintiff owned the common law copyright in the work; (2) this right was not lost by publication; and (3) that the *Statute of Anne* did not abrogate that right. *Millar* v *Taylor* is a gold-mine of jurisprudential argument, as fine minds came to grips with the problem at the level of first principle.

Mr Justice Yates delivered a powerful dissenting judgment. He insisted that there was no common law right in published works. His Honour saw things this way. I have an idea. Whilst I keep it to myself it is mine. But now I communicate the idea to you. It is now our idea. I cannot stop your mind from working on the idea or using it. Because I communicated it to you, I had no intention that it should be solely mine. The idea becomes the common property of me and you and, putatively, of all mankind. Nobody had or was suggesting that the English language could be owned. Since neither the ideas (when published) nor the words (published or unpublished) belong to me as an author, there was nothing I as an author could properly lay claim to in a published work under this statute. Thus, whether Parliament realised it or not, what I did was to create a right where none had existed in the *Statute of Anne*. And that right could be no longer than the statute prescribed. Moreover, property was not absolute in the sense being contended for by Mr Blackstone, who appeared as counsel. "All property has its proper limits," asserted the learned Judge. In the case of inventions (what we now call patents), it had already been determined that the inventor of the air pump had a property in the machine, but not in the air, which was common to all. But notice the explanation for the grant. His Honour reasoned that "invention is the discovery of a vacant property, and the inventor then bestows cultivation upon it."

Thus did Mr Justice Yates square himself with Locke's labour theory of property! And since he claimed property is 'founded upon occupancy,' this also reinforced his argument that nobody could own the idea.

The majority judges would have none of this. The *only* sense in which my ideas, having been communicated to you, can be said to be ours relates to the interrelated workings of your mind and mine. If I communicate my ideas to the public in a book, I have externalized those *ideas*. Any economic value then belongs to me. I may have given my ideas to the public, but I have not authorized anyone to make and market copies of my work.

But what is it that the author could actually protect? One possibility was only the identical work. The majority judges thought the net would have to be wider than that. Mr Justice Willes said, "[Whilst] bona fide variations, translations, and abridgements are different [from copies]; and, in respect of the property, may be considered as new works ... colourable and fraudulent variations will not do." But, of course, the seed of the problem was thus sown. Once one admits (as all the judges did) that ideas as such are not appropriable and (as the majority did) that the author owned more than the exclusive right to make and market identical copies of his work, the issue of ideas is never able to be set to one side. And Lord Mansfield could also see a related problem which has become of great contemporary relevance. In his *An Essay Concerning Human Understanding*, John Locke had suggested that "the Mind often exercises an active Power in the making ... [of] several combinations. For it being once furnished with simple Ideas, it can put them together in several Compositions, and so make variety of complex Ideas, without examining whether they exist so together in Nature. And hence I think these ideas are called notions." It was presumably this which Lord Mansfield had in mind when he said in *Millar* v *Taylor* that copyright "is a property in notion." In the result, authors now had both the Statute of Anne and perpetual common law copyright. But the triumph was to be short-lived. The House of Lords several years later, in *Donaldson* v *Beckett* (1774) 2 Bro PC 129, overruled *Millar* v *Taylor* by a margin of one vote. Lord Mansfield did not vote out of reasons of delicacy. There is great debate about that case and which of the eleven judges actually voted for what propositions. The various law reports are, at best, confusing and even contradictory. The casting vote was that of Lord Camden, a bitter political foe of Lord Mansfield. But subsequent judges have seen the decision as holding that the *Statute of Anne* pre-empted the common law right in published works.

The paradigm was thus set. Practically every intellectual property law case of any importance which has been decided since that time rehearses arguments which were traversed in this although it is rarely cited nowadays. Moreover, this legal paradigm mirrored changes in political philosophy and human behaviour. As Leo Braudy has pointed out, the Lockean tradition argued that you are your own property, and therefore only you can sell yourself. It was on this premise that assertive human beings began to consider their minds and their careers as theirs to shape and sell. A road potentially leading to legal realization of the "commodity self" had begun.'

COMMENT

Hammond provides an interesting historical explanation of the evolution of intellectual property rights but does this justify the present day nature of these rights? Why do we need the complexity of legislation and precedent that we now have in this field? Should there simply be a common law right to own and control the fruit of one's mind? If so, why are intellectual property rights not perpetual?

Imagine that you are the ruler of a State with an emerging industrial and commercial economy which you want to encourage and stimulate. At the present time there are no intellectual property laws in your State. What model of intellectual property rights would you propose and what steps would you take to (a) protect the inventive and creative work of your citizens, and (b) encourage foreign investment in the building of factories and commercial activity in your State?

Justification

Intellectual property law is often justified on the basis that it stimulates investment of time and money in the creation of new works. Many authors of works of copyright rely on the income they derive from the publication of their works for their livelihoods. However, the protection granted by law must strike a balance and it should not be too generous in its scope and duration. In the following extract from a debate in the House of Commons in 1841, Macaulay argues emotively against an extension of the term of copyright beyond the author's death.

Macaulay, T.B., *Hansard*, H C Deb. vol. 56 (5 February 1841) c.345

'For the existing law gives an author copyright during his natural life: nor do I propose to invade that privilege, which I should, on the contrary, be prepared to defend strenuously against any assailant. The point in issue is, how long after an author's death the State shall recognize a copyright in his representatives and assigns, and it can, I think, hardly be disputed by any rational man that this is a point which the legislature is free to determine in the way which may appear to be most conducive to the general good. We may now, therefore, I think descend from these high regions, where we are in danger of being lost in the clouds, to firm ground and clear light. Let us look at this question like legislators, and after fairly balancing conveniences and inconveniences, pronounce between the existing law of copyright and the law now proposed to us. The question of copyright, Sir, like most questions of civil prudence is neither black nor white, but grey. The system of copyright has great advantages, and great disadvantages, and it is our business to ascertain what these are, and then to make an arrangement under which the advantages may be as far as possible secured, and the disadvantages as far as possible excluded. The charge which I bring against my hon. and learned Friend's bill is this, that it leaves the advantages nearly what they are at present and increases the disadvantages at least four fold. The advantages arising from a system of copyright are obvious. It is desirable that we should have a supply of good books; we cannot have such a supply unless men of letters are liberally remunerated: and the least objectionable way of remunerating them is by means of copyright. You cannot depend for literary instruction and amusement on the leisure of men occupied in the pursuits of active life. Such men may occasionally produce pieces of great merit. But you must not look to them for works which require deep meditation and long research. Such works you can expect only from persons who make literature the business of their lives ...

It is then on men whose profession is literature, and whose private means are not ample, that you must rely for a supply of valuable books. Such men must be remunerated for their literary labour. And there are only two ways in which they can be remunerated. One of those ways is patronage; the other is copyright. There have been times in which men of letters looked, not to the public, but to the Government, or to a few great men, for the reward of their exertions. It was thus in the time of Mæcenas and Pollio at Rome, of the Medici at Florence, of Louis the Fourteenth in France, of Lord Halifax and Lord Oxford in this country. Now, Sir, I well know that there are cases in which it is fit and graceful, nay, in which it is a sacred duty, to reward the merits or to relieve the distresses of men of genius by the exercise of this species of liberality. But these cases are exceptions. I can conceive no system more fatal to the integrity and independence of literary men, than one under which they should be taught to look for their daily bread to the favour of ministers and nobles. I can conceive no system more certain to turn those minds which are formed by nature to be the blessings and ornaments of our species into its scandal and its pest. We have then only one resource left. We must betake ourselves to copyright, be the inconveniences of copyright what they may. Those inconveniences, in truth, are neither few nor small. Copyright is monopoly, and produces all the effects which the general voice of mankind attributes to monopoly. My hon. and learned Friend talks very contemptuously of those who are led away by the theory that monopoly makes things dear. That monopoly makes things dear is certainly a theory, as all the great truths which have been established by the experience of all ages and nations, and which are taken for granted in all reasonings, may be said to be theories. It is a theory in the same sense in which it is a theory that day and night follow each other, that lead is heavier than water, that bread nourishes, that arsenic poisons, that alcohol intoxicates. If, as my hon. and learned Friend seems to hold, the whole world is in the wrong on this point, if the real effect of monopoly is to make articles good and cheap, why does he stop short in his career of change? Why does he limit the operation of so salutary a principle to sixty years? Why does he consent to anything short of a perpetuity? ...

It is good that authors should be remunerated; and the least exceptionable way of remunerating them is by a monopoly. Yet monopoly is an evil. For the sake of the good we must submit to the evil; but the evil ought not to last a day longer than is necessary for the purpose of securing the good. Now, I will not affirm, that the existing law is perfect, that it exactly hits the point at which the monopoly ought to cease, but this I confidently say, that it is very much nearer that point than the law proposed by my hon. and learned Friend. For consider this; the evil effects of the monopoly are proportioned to the length of its duration. But the good effects for the sake of which we bear with its evil effects are by no means proportioned to the length of its duration. A monopoly of sixty years produces twice as much evil as a monopoly of thirty years, and thrice as much evil as a monopoly of twenty years. But it is by no means the fact that a posthumous monopoly of sixty years, gives to an author thrice as much pleasure, and thrice as strong a motive as a posthumous monopoly of twenty years. On the contrary, the difference is so small as to be hardly perceptible. We all know how faintly we are affected by the prospect of very distant advantages, even when they are advantages which we may reasonably hope that we shall ourselves enjoy. But an advantage that is to be enjoyed more than half a century after we are dead, by somebody, we know not whom, perhaps by somebody unborn, by somebody utterly unconnected with us, is really no motive to action ...

I will take an example. Dr. Johnson died fifty-six years ago. If the law were what my hon. and learned Friend wishes to make it, somebody would now have the monopoly of Dr. Johnson's works. Who that somebody would be, it is impossible to say, but we may venture to guess. I guess, then, that it would have been some bookseller, who was the assign of another bookseller, who was the grandson of a third bookseller, who had bought the copyright from Black Frank, the Doctor's servant, in 1785 or 1786. Now, would the knowledge, that this copyright would exist in 1841, have been a source of gratification to Johnson? Would it have stimulated his exertions? Would it have once drawn him out of his bed before noon? Would it have once cheered him under a fit of the spleen? Would it have induced him to give us one more allegory, one more life of a poet, one more imitation of Juvenal? I firmly believe not. I firmly believe that a hundred years ago, when he was writing our debates for the Gentleman's Magazine, he would very much rather have had twopence to buy a plate of shin of beef at a cook's shop underground. Considered as a reward to him, the difference between a twenty years' term, and a sixty years' term of posthumous copyright, would have been nothing or next to nothing. But is the difference nothing to us? I can buy Rasselas for sixpence; I might have had to give five shillings for it. I can buy the Dictionary, the entire genuine Dictionary for two guineas, perhaps for less; I might have had to give five or six guineas for it. Do I grudge this to a man like Dr. Johnson? Not at all. Show me that the prospect of this boon roused him to any vigorous effect, or sustained his spirits under depressing circumstances, and I am quite willing to pay the price of such an object, heavy as that price is. But what I do complain of is that my circumstances are to be worse, and Johnson's none the better, that I am to give five pounds for what to him was not worth a farthing. The principle of copyright is this. It is a tax on readers for the purpose of giving a bounty to writers. The tax is an exceedingly bad one; it is a tax on one of the most innocent and most salutary of human pleasures; and never let us forget that a tax on innocent pleasures is a premium on vicious pleasures. I admit, however, the necessity of giving a bounty to genius and learning. In order to give such a bounty, I willingly submit even to this severe and burdensome tax. Nay, I am ready to increase the tax if it can be shown that by so doing I should proportionably increase the bounty. My complaint is, that my hon. and learned Friend doubles, triples, quadruples, the tax and makes scarcely any perceptible addition to the bounty ...

My hon. and learned Friend does not propose that copyright shall descend to the eldest son, or shall be bound up by irrevocable entail. It is to be merely personal property. It is therefore highly improbable that it will descend during sixty years or half that term from parent to child. The chance is that more people than one will have an interest in it. They will in all probability sell it and divide the proceeds. The price which a bookseller will give for it will bear no proportion to the sum which he will afterwards draw from the public, if his speculation proves successful. He will give little, if any thing, more for a term of sixty years than for a term of thirty or five-and-twenty. The present value of a distant advantage is always small.'

COMMENT

The above extract reflects the harsh reality at the time, that authors often 'sold' their copyright for little consideration to powerful publishing companies. Nowadays, it is more likely that an author will receive royalties which will remain payable after his death to his estate, assuming the work is still being exploited. Do you agree with the sentiments of Macaulay? Do you think copyright ought to be perpetual? Bear in mind that the work would never have existed without the effort of the author.

Contract and Intellectual Property

Licensing is an extremely common method of exploiting intellectual property. The owner may not wish to exploit the work himself and may prefer to grant a licence, exclusive or non-exclusive, to another. In some cases, the licensor may work the right in some countries but grant permission to work the right to others in respect of other countries. For example, the proprietor of a patent valid in Europe and the United States might make the patented product himself in the United Kingdom for sale in the United Kingdom and the remainder of

Europe whilst granting an exclusive licence to an American manufacturer in respect of working the patent in the United States of America in return for a royalty of, say, £10.00 per product manufactured or a percentage of the net price.

Licences contain terms dealing with, *inter alia*, the manner of exploitation of the right, the payment of royalties and will often include territorial limitations. Other terms may deal with the grant-back of rights arising in respect to improvements designed or invented by the licensee, in addition to terms stating the quality and quantity of products to be made. The essence of the agreement will be the intellectual property right or rights concerned and the licensee will require that the licensor offers some form of guarantee as to the licensor's title to the rights involved.

It is usual for agreements for the licensing or other exploitation of intellectual property rights to contain an indemnity in case there is some unforeseen fetter on the rights concerned. For example, the acts envisaged by the parties might infringe a third party right. Other areas of law may also impinge showing the importance and impact of contract law to the exploitation of intellectual property as the following case demonstrates.

Microbeads AC v *Vinhurst Road Markings Ltd.* [1976] 1 All ER 529, Court of Appeal

The defendant obtained some road marking machines from the plaintiff under a contract of sale. Unknown to both parties, another company had already applied for a patent for such machines but the patent specification had not, at the time of the sale of the machines, been published. A patent is not published until some time after the priority date (the date of first filing). Under the Patents Act 1977 this period is 18 months. The proprietor of the patent claimed that the machines bought by the defendant infringed the patent.

Lord Denning MR (at 531): 'The dates are important. I will start with the owners of the patent. They are an English company, Prismo Universal Ltd. ("Prismo"), who carry on business near Crawley in Sussex. They hold a patent for an apparatus for applying markings on roads. It is done by the machine which carries a spray gun and a quantity of thermoplastic material. This gun sprays the material on to the roads so as to make a white and yellow line.

For some time the invention was kept secret. The application for a patent was filed on 28th December 1966. The complete specification was filed on 28th December 1967. The Patent Office made their various examinations. Eventually, on 11th November 1970, the complete specification was published. It was on that date that it became open to the world to learn about it. It was only after that date that the patentee had any right or privileges in respect of it: see ss13(4) and 22 of the Patents Act 1949. On 12th January 1972 letters patent were granted to Prismo in respect of the invention. It was only then the patentee was entitled to institute proceedings for infringement: see s13(4) of the 1949 Act.

Now, before that invention was made public, Vinhurst bought some road marking machines and accessories from the Swiss company. These machines were sold and delivered to Vinhurst between January and April 1970, that is some months before the Prismo specification was published in November 1970. The price of the machines and accessories was nearly £15,000, of which Vinhurst paid £5,000, leaving the £10,000 balance to be paid. The buyers, Vinhurst, did not know anything about the patent. They had no idea that the machines might be infringing machines. They took them in good faith and used them. But they found the machines very unsatisfactory. They were dissatisfied. They did not pay the balance of the price.

On 30th November 1970 the sellers, the Swiss company, sued Vinhurst for the balance of £10,000 owing for the machines. At first Vinhurst put in a defence saying that the machines were not reasonably fit for the purpose of marking roads.

But then in 1972 Prismo came down on Vinhurst and said these machines (supplied by the Swiss company) infringed their patent. Thereupon Vinhurst amended their defence so as to set up the infringement as a defence and counterclaim. The point was set down as a preliminary issue. The judge found that the sellers, the Swiss company, were not guilty of a breach of contract in this respect. The buyers appeal to this court.

The preliminary issue was directed on these assumptions: (1) that the letters patent were valid; (2) that the machines sold by the Swiss company to Vinhurst were such as to fall within the scope of the claims in the specification; (3) that the property in each of the machines was to pass prior to November 1970. On those assumptions the point of law was whether there was any breach of contract on the part of the Swiss company under s12(1) or s12(2) of the Sale of Goods Act 1893 having regard to the dates of filing and publication of the specification and of the grant of the patent ...

Now I turn to s12(2). It says that there is an "implied warranty that the buyer shall have and enjoy quiet possession of the goods". Taking those words in their ordinary meaning, they seem to cover this case. The words "shall have and enjoy" apply not only to the time of the sale but also to the future; "shall enjoy" means in the future. If a patentee comes two or three years later and gets an injunction to restrain the use of the goods, there would seem to be a breach of the warranty. But it is said that there are limitations on the ordinary meaning such limitations being derived from the civil law or from conveyancing cases.

One such limitation is said to follow from the words of Lord Ellenborough CJ in *Howel* v *Richards* (1809) 11 East 633 when he said (at 642) :

> "The covenant for title is an assurance to the purchaser, that the grantor has the very estate in quantity and quality which he purports to convey, viz. in this case an indefeasible estate in fee simple. The covenant for quiet enjoyment is an assurance against the consequences of a defective title, and of any disturbances thereupon."

Counsel for the Swiss company said that Lord Ellenborough CJ there meant a defective title existing at the time of the sale. The covenant, he said, did not apply to a defective title which only appeared some time after the sale. The defect here appeared after the sale; it entered in November 1970 when the complete specification was published.

The other limitation, derived from the conveyancing cases, was that the covenant for quiet enjoyment protected the purchaser or tenant only from the acts or operations of the vendor or lessor and those claiming under him, but not against the acts or operations of those claiming by title paramount: see *Jones* v *Lavington* [1903] 1 KB 253. Counsel for the Swiss Company submitted that that conveyancing rule applied to s12(2) also. Here the claim by the patentee was by title paramount.

There is one case which supports this contention. It is a decision of Lord Russell of Killowen CJ in 1895 when he was on the Northern Circuit. It is *Monforts* v *Marsden* (1895) 12 RPC 266. But that case was disapproved by this court in *Niblett Ltd.* v *Confectioners' Materials Co. Ltd.* [1921] 3 KB 387 and must be taken to be overruled. Afterwards in *Mason* v *Burningham* [1949] 2 All ER 134 Lord Greene MR made it clear that the conveyancing cases should not be applied to s12 of the Sale of Goods Act 1893. He said:

> "It is to be observed that in the language used in the Sale of Goods Act, 1893 s12(2), there is no exception for any disturbance by title paramount. The words are as I have quoted them, 'that the buyer shall have and enjoy quiet possession of the goods.' I invited counsel for the defendant to refer us to any authority that would justify the insertion into that statutory phrase of an exception in the case of disturbance by title paramount, but he was unable to do so, and in the absence of any authority, I can only express my opinion that the statute means what it says and is not to have any such gloss put on it".

I would follow the guidance of Lord Greene MR. Even if the disturbance is by title paramount - such as by the patentee coming in and claiming an injunction to restrain the use of the machine - there is a breach of the implied warranty under s12(2) ...

It seems to me that when the buyer has bought goods quite innocently and later on he is disturbed in his possession because the goods are found to be infringing a patent, then he can recover damages for breach of warranty against the seller. It may be the seller is innocent himself, but when one or other must suffer, the loss should fall on the seller; because, after all, he sold the goods and if it turns out that they infringe a patent, he should bear the loss. In the present case Prismo sue for infringement now and stop the buyer using the machines. That is a clear disturbance of possession. The buyer is not able to enjoy the quiet possession which the seller impliedly warranted that he shall have. There is a breach of s12(2) of the 1893 Act.

I would therefore allow the appeal and I will answer the preliminary question accordingly.'

Controls over Abuse of Intellectual Property Rights

As already noted, intellectual property is often worked under a licence agreement. Apart from normal contractual principles, intellectual property law lays down specific rules. For example, an exclusive licence of a copyright must be in writing, signed by or on behalf of the owner of the copyright (section 92 of the Copyright, Designs and Patents Act 1988). The law also places constraints upon intellectual property licences, many of which can be explained on the basis that they prevent the abuse of right by its owner. An example from copyright law is that any term in a licence agreement that attempts to prohibit or restrict the making of a back-up copy of a computer program necessary for its lawful use is void and unenforceable at law; section 50A of the Copyright, Designs and Patents Act 1988. In patent law there is the section 44 defence available where particular types of terms go beyond those normally related to the direct supply of a patented product or the working of the patented invention.

Patents Act 1977, section 44 - avoidance of certain restrictive conditions

44. - (1) Subject to the provisions of this section, any condition or term of a contract for the supply of a patented product or of a licence to work a patented invention, or of a contract relating to any such supply or licence, shall be void in so far it purports -

    (a) in the case of a contract for supply, to require the person supplied to acquire from the supplier, or his nominee, or prohibit him from acquiring except from the supplier or his nominee, anything other than the patented product;

    (b) in the case of a licence to work a patented invention, to require the licensee to acquire from the licensor or his nominee, or prohibit him from acquiring from any specified person, or from acquiring except from the licensor or his nominee, anything other than the product which is the patented invention or (if it is a process) other than any product obtained directly by means of the process or to which the process has been applied;

    (c) in either case, to prohibit the person supplied or licensee from using articles (whether patented products or not) which are not supplied by, or any patented process which does not belong to, the supplier or licensor, or his nominee, or to restrict the right of the person supplied or licensee to use any such articles or process. ...

(3) In proceedings against any person for infringement of a patent it shall be a defence to prove that at the time of the infringement there was in force a contract relating to the patent made by or with the consent of the plaintiff or pursuer or a licence under the patent granted by him or with his consent and containing in either case a condition or term void by virtue of this section.

Competition law also impinges upon intellectual property law. European Community competition law has particularly strong teeth in this respect in relation to patent law.

Article 85(1) of the Treaty of Rome 1957 (the EC Treaty) controls and prohibits certain restrictive trading practices and is particularly relevant in relation to patent licences. However, bearing in mind that a patent is an item of property and, in one sense, the grant of a licence gives something that the licensee otherwise would not have, there is provision for exemption from the application of Article 85(1) in some cases. The need for some exemption from the rigours of Article 85(1) can also be justified on the grounds that certain types of restriction are justified in terms of protecting the owner's interests providing they are not generally restrictive of competition. Article 85(3) provides for block exemption and individual exemption is a possibility in other cases such as where two companies decide to pool their patent rights as part of a joint venture.

An example of a block exemption under Article 85(3) is the 'Technology Transfer Regulation' (Regulation 240/96 of 31 January 1996, OJ L 31, 9.2.1996, p.2) which regulates the licensing of patents and 'know-how'. This regulation provides that certain terms are acceptable, such as limited territorial restrictions, whether or not in the presence of other terms, such as an obligation on a licensee not to grant sub-licences. Other terms counteract the benefit of the exemption, for example, an obligation on a licensee to grant back to the licensor any rights in improvements to the licensed technology. Where there are terms not covered by the exemption but which are restrictive of competition, there is a procedure for notifying the European Commission such that, if the Commission does not oppose within four months, the agreement is deemed to be exempt. European Competition law applies where trade between Member States is affected (though this may apply in surprising cases). There is also domestic competition law to be aware of when drafting agreements involving, *inter alia*, intellectual property rights.

Even though competition law can affect a licence agreement, the common law has shown that it too has teeth when it comes to preventing the potential for abuse of intellectual property rights as the following case demonstrates emphatically. The extract is well worth reading for its description of the rationale of copyright, designs and patents and the nature of those rights.

British Leyland Motor Corp. Ltd. v **Armstrong Patents Co. Ltd.** [1986] 2 WLR 400, House of Lords

The plaintiff manufactured motor vehicles and made spare parts for those vehicles. It also granted licences to other companies allowing them to make spare parts for its vehicles. The defendant wanted to make replacement exhaust systems for the plaintiff's Morris Marina car but refused to take a licence. The defendant obtained a Morris Marina car, removed the exhaust system and, by measuring it, determined its dimensions and shape so that the defendant could make exhaust systems to that pattern. The plaintiff sued for an alleged infringement of the copyright subsisting in the drawings it had prepared for making the exhaust systems.

Lord Templeman (at 419): 'Armstrong's defence to the charge that they breach BL's copyright in the engineering drawing when Armstrong make a replacement exhaust pipe is two-fold. First, Armstrong say that copyright does not extend to the direct reproduction of a functional article such as an exhaust pipe which is not protected by patent law and is not a registered design. Secondly, and alternatively, Armstrong say that BL cannot rely on their copyright to prevent the repair of a car supplied by BL and requiring the inevitable replacement of a component part.

As to the first argument Armstrong point out that the Patents Act 1977 confers a right on the inventor of a novel product by the grant of a patent which prevents anyone making the product without the licence of the inventor for a period of 20 years. The Registered Designs Act 1949 confers a right on a designer of a novel design by the grant of design copyright which prevents anyone making any article in respect of which the design is registered without the licence of the designer for a period of 15 years. The Copyright Act 1956 confers a right on the author of an original artistic work by the grant of copyright which prevents anyone reproducing the work without the licence of the author during his life and 50 years thereafter. There is no general provision that all skill and labour shall be protected, rewarded and encouraged by the grant of a total or partial monopoly which prevents anyone making or reproducing an article which is the product of skill and labour. The invention and design of an article may involve vast expense, thought and money but if the product is not patentable, does not incorporate a registered design and is not an artistic work then there is no restriction on the making or reproduction of the product. BL's exhaust pipes are not entitled to protection because they are not patentable, not registrable and they are not artistic works ...

An article embodying an invention which is not patented does not enjoy the 20 years restriction on use of the invention afforded by patent law. An article embodying a design which is not registrable does not attract the 15 years restriction on reproduction afforded by design copyright. An article which is not an artistic work does not attract the life plus 50 years restriction on reproduction afforded by copyright law to artistic works. But if BL are right, an article which is not patented, not registered and is not an artistic work acquires the life plus 50 years restriction on reproduction afforded by copyright to an artistic work ...

BL deny that they are claiming a monopoly in the reproduction of BL's exhaust pipe. Anyone is free to copy BL's exhaust pipe because BL are prepared to licence the reproduction of BL's exhaust pipe on payment of a royalty described as modest. The driver of a Marina will suffer no inconvenience because he will be able to obtain a replacement exhaust pipe as required either from BL or from BL's licensees. But a monopoly remains a monopoly even if it be benevolently administered and an established monopoly will not necessarily be administered with benevolence. In practice BL are claiming a monopoly and a similar monopoly can be claimed by other manufacturers for their models. The same monopoly could be invoked by the manufacture of any article which requires replacement parts from time to time.

In the course of the present appeal some argument was understandably devoted to a justification of the monopoly claimed by BL. It was urged that BL are entitled to charge a royalty for licensing the production of component parts so as to spread the burden of the expenditure by BL on the research and development of the Marina; that a royalty charged by BL on replacement parts enables BL to reduce the price of their cars; that unless BL have a monopoly there will be no obligation on BL or on any other manufacturer of replacement parts to ensure that such parts are available for motorists throughout the lives of their vehicles; that without BL's monopoly there will be cheap imports from the Far East and the safety standards and quality of replacement parts cannot be safeguarded. The advantage to BL of being able to supply spare parts for Ford and other vehicles in the absence of monopoly was not explored.

Armstrong sought to counteract these arguments by extolling the virtues of competition and by asserting that the interests of the public are not to be safeguarded by monopolists.

For my part, I agree with the submissions made on behalf of Armstrong that Parliament did not intend the protection afforded by copyright to a drawing should be capable of exploitation so as to prevent the reproduction of a functional object depicted in a drawing. But there is a good deal of legislative and judicial history to be considered.

Section 1(5) of the Statute of Monopolies 1623 (21 Ja.I,c.3) contains an emphatic declaration that all monopolies:

"for the sole buying, selling, making, working or using of anything within this realm ... (are altogether contrary to the laws of this realm, and so are and shall be utterly void and of none effect ..."

To this declaration there was, however, a proviso in section VI whereby the declaration against monopolies:

"shall not extend to any letters patents and grants of privilege for the term of 14 years or under, hereafter to be made of the sole working or making of any manner of new manufacturers within this realm, to the true and first inventor and inventors of such manufacturers ... so as also they be not contrary to the law, nor mischievous to the state, by raising prices of commodities at home, or hurt of trade, or generally inconvenient: ..."

In the 18th century various Acts were passed which forbade the copying of books and engravings without the consent of the author and which gave a measure of protection to novel designs.

By the Copyright Act 1842 (5 & 6 Vict. c.45) copyright was defined as meaning "the sole and exclusive liberty of printing or otherwise multiplying copies" of any book including every volume, pamphlet, sheet of music, map, chart or plan separately published. By the Act copyright in every book was conferred for the natural life of the author and seven years after his death with a minimum period of 42 years from publication.

In *Davis* v *Comitti* (1885) 52 L.T. 539 the manufacturer of a barometer claimed to restrain the sale of a rival barometer on the grounds that the rival barometer infringed his copyright under the Copyright Act 1842 in the printed face of the barometer which was registered as a book or chart. Chitty J rejected the claim on the grounds that the barometer face was not a book in itself, and was only a necessary part of the barometer ...

By the Patents, Designs and Trademarks Act 1883 (46 & 47 Vict. c.57) the proprietor of a registered design was, by section 58, given the exclusive right to control the use of an original:

"design applicable to any article of manufacture, or to any substance artificial or natural, or partly artificial and partly natural, whether the design is applicable for the pattern, or for the shape or configuration, or for the ornament thereof": section 60.

In *Moody* v *Tree* (1892) 9 RPC 233 there was registered a picture of a basket claimed as a design for "the pattern of the basket, consisting in the osiers being worked in singly and all the butt ends being outside." Pollock B and Vaughan Williams J held that the design should not have been registered because the claim was in reality a process or mode of manufacture and not a design which must be something appealing to the eye and to the eye separate from the object for which it was applied. Pollock B said in relation to a design, at p.235: "you must use your eye and say, looking at the figure or the design, whether it is new or it is not, and beyond that you cannot go." Vaughan Williams J said, at p.236:

> "a mere mode of manufacture is not a design at all. It is not something which is capable of existence as a pattern, or as a shape or configuration, or as a piece of ornamentation to be applied to an article or class of articles ... "

The Patents and Designs Act 1907 consolidated the enactments relating to patents for inventions and the registration of designs. The period of patent protection was fixed at 16 years. The period of protection for registered designs was then and thereafter limited to 15 years.

Until after the turn of the century copyright in the drawing of an exhaust pipe would not have been infringed by a reproduction of the exhaust pipe. BL's exhaust pipe would not have been registrable as a design before the turn of the century and never became registrable thereafter as a design for it lacks novelty and is a mere mechanical device dictated by the function which the exhaust pipe must perform. BL's exhaust pipe corresponds to the electrical termination which in *Amp Inc.* v *Utilux Pty. Ltd.* [1972] RPC 103 this House held not to be registrable because the features of the design were dictated solely by function.

The Copyright Act 1911 introduced changes into the law of copyright. By section 1(2) copyright was conferred on every original literary, dramatic, musical and artistic work. Copyright was defined by section 1(2) as "the sole right to produce or reproduce the work or any substantial part thereof in any material form whatsoever ...". The period of copyright was retained at the life of the author plus 50 years. By section 35 an artistic work was defined as including: "works of painting, drawing, sculpture and artistic craftsmanship, and architectural works of art and engravings and photographs." Overlap between copyright and design copyright was sought to be avoided by section 22 which directed that:

> "(1) This Act shall not apply to designs capable of being registered under the Patents and Designs Act 1907, except designs which, though capable of being so registered, are not used or intended to be used as models or patterns to be multiplied by an industrial process."

In *King Features Inc.* v *O. and M. Kleeman Ltd.* [1941] AC 417 ("the Popeye case") this House held that the copyright in a Popeye cartoon was infringed by the defendant who, without the licence of the author of the cartoon reproduced a Popeye brooch and doll which had been licensed by the author, Viscount Maugham said, at p.427:

> "an industrial object, whether in two or three dimensions, may well be an infringement of the artistic copyright in the preliminary drawings or prints made by the author or in the design registered under ... the Act of 1907. It is not, in my

opinion, open to doubt that the main object of section 22 was to prevent such a result, and to leave the author of a design capable of registration, if he intended to use it industrially, with no more than the rights which the Act of 1907 gave him."

This House held that section 22 of the Copyright Act 1911 did not operate to bring to an end the copyright in the Popeye cartoon because Popeye was not intended to be used industrially when the cartoon was first drawn. However, in the Popeye case the infringing three-dimensional brooch and doll appropriated the skill and labour of the author of the original cartoon character. Different considerations arise, when, as in the case of an exhaust pipe, the three-dimensional reproduction owes everything to the inventor and designer of the exhaust pipe and nothing to the original skill and labour of the draughtsman. In the Popeye case a copier who made a Popeye brooch by copying a Popeye brooch must have known that there was either in existence a prototype Popeye brooch which was or might be an artistic work or a Popeye drawing or cartoon which was an artistic work. The copier knew that he was infringing copyright either directly or indirectly. In the present case, a copier who makes an exhaust pipe by copying an exhaust pipe knows that he is not directly copying an artistic work. If there is only a prototype exhaust pipe or a literary explanation and written dimensions of the exhaust pipe there is not even any indirect copying. A copier only knows of the existence of an antecedent drawing because BL have been careful to obtain copyright in such a drawing and reveal the existence of the drawing. So although the decision in the Popeye case showed that section 22 was not fully effective to separate copyright and copyright design, the decision did not extend the ambit of copyright to indirect reproduction of a drawing of a purely functional object.

Registered designs are now protected under the Registered Designs Act 1949. Copyright law was further amended by the Copyright Act 1956. The precursor to that Act was a report (Report of the Copyright Committee (1952) (Cmd. 8662)) known as the Gregory Report established by the government to consider copyright law. Amongst the problems considered by the Gregory Committee were the possible repercussions and extensions of the Popeye case and *Chabot* v *Davies* (1936) 3 All ER 221 where the copyright in an architect's elevation representing a shop front was held to be infringed by the erection of the shop since this was regarded as a reproduction of the elevation "in a material form" ...

In *Dorling* v *Honnor Marine Ltd.* [1965] Ch.1 and in all cases since 1956 the courts assumed rather than decided that indirect reproduction of drawings of functional articles were affected by the decision in the Popeye case.

In *Merchant-Adventurers Ltd.* v *M Grew & Co. Ltd.* [1972] Ch. 242 Graham J held that copyright in engineering drawings of electric light fittings was infringed by the defendant who copied the plaintiff's electric light fittings. As to section 9(8) Graham J, at p.251, referred to the "extraordinary provision in the Copyright Act 1956" and contained in section 9(8) and concluded, at p.255:

"There is an infringement of drawings by three-dimensional reproduction of those drawings if they are sufficiently clear for a man of reasonable and average intelligence to be able to understand them and from an inspection of them to be able to visualise in his mind what a three-dimensional object if made from them would look like."

He held that the man of reasonable and average intelligence was able to visualise the appearance of the electric light fittings from the engineering drawings.

In *George Hensher Ltd.* v *Restawile Upholstery (Lancs.) Ltd.* [1976] AC 64, a suite of chairs and a settee were held not to be a "work of artistic craftsmanship" and therefore not entitled to copyright protection. The suite was manufactured from a prototype or mock-up and not from drawings. If the suite had instead been manufactured from a drawing it could have been argued that copyright in the drawing had been infringed ...

The decision of this House in *L.B. (Plastics) Ltd.* v *Swish Products Ltd.* [1979] RPC 551 shows clearly that as the law now stands the first argument put forward by Armstrong namely that copyright does not apply to prevent the indirect copying of drawings of functional articles cannot be sustained. That argument was raised, though in an oblique form, in *L.B. (Plastics) Ltd.* v *Swish Products Ltd.* [1979] RPC 551 and was disposed of by Lord Hailsham of St. Marylebone, at p.631:

> "The argument was that although it be conceded that the appellants' draughtsman's drawings were copyright artistic works within section 3, the information acquired by preliminary work going into the drawing was not, and that what was copyright was simply the particular sketch by the particular draughtsman, which was not reproduced in the three-dimensional product. It would follow of course that a three-dimensional moulding of the present sort could not easily infringe the copyright in a drawing of this sort at all and that a two-dimensional drawing would not do so if drawn as a different sketch. The advantage claimed for counsel's argument is that it reduces the danger of the consequences of the overlap between the law relating to registered design and patent and that relating to copyright which has long given trouble to lawyers and legislators. But we must take copyright law as we find it."

Section 10 of the Copyright Act 1956 was amended by the Designs Copyright Act 1968 enacted on the initiative of a private member of the House of Commons prompted by a group of Birmingham jewellers. The amendment recognised the overlapping of copyright law and design copyright by limiting the copyright in a drawing of a design which is applied industrially to the period of 15 years applicable to design copyright. In the present proceedings the Court of Appeal, Oliver LJ overruling Whitford J in *Hoover Plc* v *George Hulme (Stockport) Ltd.* [1982] FSR 565 held [1984] FSR 591, 624 that designs which could not be registered under the Registered Designs Act 1949 are not affected by section 10 of the Copyright Act 1956 as amended and enjoy copyright protection for the full term of the life of the author plus 50 years.

Thus section 9(8) of the Copyright Act 1956 was defective to achieve the intended purpose of preventing the extension of the scope of copyright "into fields far beyond its main or original intent and properly to be covered by other forms of protection if at all" by making it impossible "to protect under the Copyright Act more in the constructional or functional field than is protectable under the Registered Design Act": Gregory Report, paragraph 258. In the result the owner of copyright in a simple drawing of a simple object who proves that the object has been copied is awarded an injunction and damages; but the owner of copyright in a complicated drawing of a sophisticated object who also proves that the object has been copied will be dismissed with costs if the hypothetical non-expert would not recognise the copying when he saw it. I reluctantly echo the comment of my noble and learned friend Lord

Hailsham of St. Marylebone in *L.B.(Plastics) Ltd.* v *Swish Products Ltd.* RPC 551, 631 that "we must take copyright law as we find it."

I turn, therefore, to the alternative submission on behalf of Armstrong. It is said that BL by choosing to manufacture a car by reference to engineering drawings and by marketing the car as a means of transport which can only be kept in running order by repairs which involve indirect reproduction of those engineering drawings cannot assert their copyright so as to prevent repairs being carried out. Put shortly, a vendor cannot deprive a purchaser of the right to repair.

This submission unlike the first submission, has not been the subject of legislation, is not contrary to settled practice but on the contrary is supported by favourable indications in analogous authorities.

We were not referred to any legislation which affects the submission based on the right to repair. As to the practice, the claim to extend copyright to prevent the replacement of exhaust systems by way of repair has been pioneered by BL. Mass production of vehicles and other machinery began about the turn of the century and was extensively practised by Ford shortly after the First World War. A demand for spare parts came into existence not later than the day when the first model T Ford broke down on the highway and since that day there has been established a network of manufacturers of spare parts offering facilities to motorists for the replacement of exhaust pipes and systems and windscreens and other components. BL themselves, formerly copied and supplied replacement component parts for cars of rival manufacturers but now only make parts for the cars of other manufacturers if BL consider they can do so without copying. I am not clear how BL avoid copying or whether their activities have been challenged ...

It is not surprising that some component manufacturers complied with BL's demands for a licensing agreement. T.I. and Armstrong have chosen to resist and the cost of these present proceedings must I apprehend exceed £1 million. Ford have asserted copyright in their replacement parts and have adopted a policy of not granting any licences to manufacture or sell, thus asserting a monopoly which has been stigmatised by the Monopolies and Mergers Commission as an anti-competitive practice which tends to keep prices up. No doubt if BL are successful in these proceedings, every manufacturer, whether of motor vehicles or other articles, will be careful to make and preserve production or engineering drawings and will either require all component replacement parts to be purchased from the original manufacturer or from licensees who pay royalties to the original manufacturer.

As between landlord and tenant and as between the vendor and purchaser of land, the law has long recognised that "a grantor having given a thing with one hand is not to take away the means of enjoying it with the other:" per Bowen LJ in *Birmingham, Dudley and District Banking Co.* v *Ross* (1888) 38 Ch.D. 295, 313.

In *Browne* v *Flower* [1911] 1 Ch. 219, 225, Parker J said:

> "the implications usually explained by the maxim that no one can derogate from his own grant do not stop short with easements. Under certain circumstances there will be implied on the part of the grantor or lessor obligations which restrict the user of the land retained by him further than can be explained by the implication of any easement known to the law. Thus, if the grant or demise be made for a particular purpose, the grantor or lessor comes under an obligation not to use the land retained by him in such a way as to render the land granted

or demised unfit or materially less fit for the particular purpose for which the grant or demise was made."

These principles were followed in *Harmer* v *Jumbil (Nigeria) Tin Areas Ltd.* [1921] 1 Ch. 200; *O'Cedar Ltd.* v *Slough Trading Co. Ltd.* [1927] 2 KB 123; *Matania* v *National Provincial Bank Ltd.* [1936] 2 All ER 633 and *Ward* v *Kirkland* [1967] Ch. 194.

I see no reason why the principle that a grantor will not be allowed to derogate from his grant by using property retained by him in such a way as to render property granted by him unfit or materially unfit for the purpose for which the grant was made should not apply to the sale of a car. In relation to land, the principle has been said to apply

"beyond cases in which the purpose of the grant is frustrated to cases in which that purpose can still be achieved albeit at a greater expense or with less convenience": per Branson J in *O'Cedar Ltd.* v *Slough Trading Co. Ltd.* [1927] 2 KB 123, 127.

The principle applied to a motor car manufactured in accordance with engineering drawings and sold with components which are bound to fail during the life of the car prohibits the copyright owner of the drawings from exercising his copyright powers in such a way as to prevent the car from functioning unless the owner of the car buys replacement parts from the copyright owner or his licensee.

BL own the car and the copyright in a drawing of an exhaust pipe fitted to the car. BL sell the car and retain the copyright. The exercise by BL of their copyright in the drawing will render the car unfit for the purpose for which the car is held. BL cannot exercise their copyright so as to prevent the car being repaired by replacement of the exhaust pipe.

A purchaser of a patented article may carry out repairs to it without being held liable for infringement. On the other hand he cannot manufacture a new article which infringes the patent and claim that he has not infringed merely because in the manufacture he has used parts derived from a patented article sold by the patentee: see *Dunlop Pneumatic Tyre Co. Ltd.* v *Neal* [1899] 1 Ch. 807 and *Dunlop Pneumatic Tyre Co. Ltd.* v *Holborn Tyre Co. Ltd.* (1901) 18 RPC 222. In *Sirdar Rubber Co. Ltd.* v *Wallington, Weston & Co.* (1905) 22 RPC 257 there was a compound patent of a metal wheel rim of a particular shape to receive a rubber tyre. Swinfen-Eady J said at p.266:

"Unless the purchaser is able to have new rubbers placed in the rim, he cannot obtain the use of the patented article for the fair period of its life. This is not a repair amounting to reconstruction, and a new article, but a fair repair; the old metal rim, the distinguishing feature of the invention, being retained, not colourably, but because essential and practically as good as new, and a fresh rubber put to replace the old one worn out."

On appeal to this House (1907) 24 RPC 539 Lord Halsbury said, at p.543:

"The principle is quite clear although its application is sometimes difficult; you may prolong the life of a licensed article but you must not make a new one under the cover of repair."

In *Dunlop Pneumatic Tyre Co. Ltd.* v *David Moseley & Sons Ltd.* [1904] 1 Ch. 612 the Court of Appeal held that the manufacture and sale of a tyre to be used to infringe a combination patent for a tyre and rim for cycle and other vehicle wheels was not itself an infringement of the patent. Having so found Cozens-Hardy LJ said, at p.621:

" ... I think, speaking for myself, that there may be a third class of cases in which the supply by the defendants might be perfectly lawful - I mean for the purpose of repair. The word 'repair' is no doubt a difficult one to construe, but I do not think that *Dunlop Pneumatic Tyre Co. Ltd.* v *Neal* [1899] 1 Ch. 807 justifies the construction which was put upon it by the appellants' counsel. I certainly doubt - I will not say any more than that - whether the holder of a licensed tyre may not replace a worn-out cover without being guilty of an infringement of the patent. It is not necessary to decide that point now, and I only desire to keep that point open for future consideration."

In *Solar Thomson Engineering Co. Ltd.* v *Barton* [1977] RPC 537 the plaintiffs sold a conveyer system which included patented pulley wheels having elastomeric rings in peripheral grooves. The plaintiffs' articles, including the rings were made in accordance with their production drawings in which they claimed copyright. A purchaser of the conveyer system from the plaintiffs instructed repairers to make and fit new steel rings and the plaintiffs then sued the repairers for infringement of patent and infringement of copyright. The Court of Appeal held that there was an implied licence under the patent to repair the pulleys by replacing worn rings and implied licence under the plaintiffs' copyright in their drawings to the extent necessary to enable such repairs to be carried out. Buckley LJ said at p.560:

"If I am right in the view I have expressed about the existence here of an implied licence under the patent to repair pulleys by replacing worn rubber rings, it must, I think, follow that purchasers of Polyrim pulleys are also impliedly licensed to infringe the plaintiff's copyright in their drawings to the extent necessary to enable such repairs to be carried out. To hold otherwise would be to allow the copyright to stultify the implied licence under the patent."

In the course of the present proceedings Oliver LJ said in the Court of Appeal [1984] FSR 591, 611:

"It is, in fact, unnecessary to decide the point, but I can see that there are strong arguments for saying that where a manufacturer sells to a purchaser an expensive piece of machinery containing parts which are inherently likely to wear out during the working lifetime of the machine, he impliedly licences the purchaser to procure, by copying if it is more advantageous to him, those subsidiary parts, even in a case where the manufacturer is itself willing to supply the parts at whatever it regards as an appropriate price. If such a licence can be implied, there can be no reason for inhibiting the purchaser, when he orders one replacement, from having two or more made against future breakdown during the anticipated life of the machine. But even allowing that such manufacture might be within the implied licence, I find myself quite unable to see how that could constitute some sort of blanket licence from the vehicle manufacturer to any member of the public to copy and manufacture, for sale in the market generally and without specific order, equipment to be made available for purchasers or users of the vehicle manufacturer's products."

For my part, I base the right to repair on the principle of non-derogation from grant rather than implied licence and I see no difficulty in concluding that suppliers such as Armstrong may make exhaust pipes to be supplied to those cars of BL which require to be repaired by the replacement of exhaust pipes. Every owner of a car has the right to repair it. That right would be useless if suppliers of spare parts were not entitled to anticipate the need for repair. The right cannot, in my view, be withheld by the manufacturer of the car by contract with the first purchaser and cannot be withheld from any subsequent owner. It was suggested on behalf of BL that any such right would only be effective against the manufacturer of the car and not against a sub-contractor who manufactured parts for the car and was allowed by BL to retain copyright in the engineering drawings. In my view, the same principle applies to a sub-contractor because he knows that he is manufacturing a part of a car to be sold to a purchaser who will need to keep the car in repair. It was also suggested on behalf of BL that if a patentee of a component part, such as a carburettor can prevent the installation of a replacement carburettor which infringes his patent, it follows that a copyright owner can prevent the installation of a replacement exhaust pipe which indirectly reproduces and infringes the drawing of an exhaust pipe.

There are substantial differences between patent law and copyright law in relation to repairs. First, a patent for an invention is only infringed, for present purposes, where the invention is a product, by a person who "makes" or "uses" the product without the consent of the proprietor of the patent. Where therefore a patented product is sold for use with the consent of the proprietor, repair of the patented product will not constitute an infringement: repair amounting to reconstruction will constitute the manufacture of a new and infringing product. A reproduction of an artistic work or a substantial part of an artistic work will constitute an infringement of copyright. In *Solar Thomson Engineering Co. Ltd.* v *Barton* [1977] RPC 537 the plaintiffs' patent was not infringed by repair but in carrying out that repair the defendants were held to have reproduced a substantial part of the plaintiffs' production drawings and to have infringed copyright in the drawings. Nevertheless, the plaintiffs were not allowed to enforce their copyright otherwise as Buckley LJ said, at p.561:

"If it were, any purchaser of a patented article might find himself deprived of his ostensible right to repair that article by the existence of a copyright of which he would probably be ignorant when he made the purchase."

In the second place, a patent is granted by statute in respect of a product. The copyright in a drawing of a functional article is infringed by a reproduction of that article. Nevertheless, copyright is granted by statute in respect of the drawing and not in respect of the article. There is, in my view, no inconsistency between, on the one hand, allowing patent rights to be exercised to prevent the reproduction of an article covered by the patent and, on the other hand, not allowing copyright to be exercised in derogation of grant to prevent the reproduction of an article which is not covered by the copyright. In the third place, BL market and sell a car as a form of transport which requires an exhaust pipe in order to function. BL are not selling exhaust pipes. The car sold by BL can only be kept in repair by the replacement of the exhaust pipe which is not the subject of a patent. In these circumstances, in my opinion, BL are not entitled to assert the copyright in their drawing of an exhaust pipe in order to defeat the right of the purchaser to repair his car. The exploitation of copyright law for purposes which were not intended has gone far enough. I see no reason to confer on a manufacturer the right in effect to dictate the terms on which an article sold by him is to be kept in repair and working order. Both the Court of Appeal and Foster J might have been prepared to come to the same conclusion but balked at extending the rights of an owner of a car to keep it in repair to a manufacturer who makes parts solely for repair. I see no difficulty in such an extension, otherwise the right to repair would be useless.

For these reasons I would allow the appeal, discharge the injunctions granted by the Court of Appeal and dismiss BL's action with costs.'

COMMENT

Does copyright grant monopolies? If not, could the defendant have made replacement exhaust pipes without infringing copyright? Is a 'right to repair' available in respect of all intellectual property rights? Although this decision has been overtaken by the Copyright, Designs and Patents Act 1988 which contains provisions suppressing copyright in drawings as a means of protecting designs, it appears that the British Leyland case lives on as far as non-derogation from grant is concerned, see section 171(3) of the Act. Do you think that the principle is appropriate to intellectual property? Should a line of cases in real property be used as authority in a case involving personal property?

More recently, the Judicial Committee of the Privy Council were met with a case from Hong Kong in which it was argued that the 'right to repair' principle extended to toner cartridges used in printers and photocopiers (*Canon Kabushiki Kaisha* v *Green Cartridge Company (Hong Kong) Ltd.* [1997] FSR 817).

The Judicial Committee distinguished *British Leyland* on the basis that, with printers and copiers, the cost of replacement cartridges was a major expense, costing more than the initial cost of the printer or copier and would be taken into account by a person deciding which make of printer or copier to purchase. This was unlike the case of a motor car where the cost of a replacement exhaust was relatively small in comparison with the cost of a car. The judgment, given by Lord Hoffman, contained some veiled criticism of *British Leyland*, suggesting that the principle should not be extended and expressing disquiet about judicial decision-making on the grounds of public policy overruling a clear, statutory right.

Patent law has long since contained specific statutory provision to guard against abuse. A good example is the compulsory licence provisions. Parliament has chosen not to make similar provision in copyright law (though there are some provisions for licences as of right in exceptional circumstances). Why should this be so?

New forms of works

The changing nature of society and the development of new forms of works and expression have constantly challenged the ability of intellectual property law to keep pace. The following case shows the consequences of this and has led to many calls for the introduction of a new right to protect television show 'formats'.

Green v Broadcasting Corporation of New Zealand [1989] RPC 700, Privy Council

The appellant, Hughie Green, devised a television show called 'Opportunity Knocks'. It was a talent show and allowed new or hitherto 'undiscovered' performers an opportunity to perform before a large television audience. A number of these performers became very famous and the show provided their 'big break'. Hughie Green also compèred the show. Later, the respondent television company broadcast a similar show in New Zealand based on the same overall format.

Lord Bridge of Harwich at (701): 'The appellant commenced proceedings in the High Court of New Zealand claiming damages for passing off and infringement of copyright. His action was dismissed by Ongley J on 23 December 1983. The judgment was affirmed by the Court of Appeal (Somers, Casey and Gallen JJ) on 22 September 1988. The appellant now appeals to Her Majesty in Council by leave of the Court of Appeal. The only issue arising in the appeal relates to the claim of copyright. The Court of Appeal decided against the appellant by a majority, Gallen J dissenting.

The copyright alleged to have been infringed was claimed to subsist in the "scripts and dramatic format" of "Opportunity Knocks" as broadcast in England. The appellant's primary difficulty arises from the circumstances that no script was ever produced in evidence. Ongley J concluded that:

> "There was really no evidence that any part of the show was reduced to a written text which could properly be called a script ... "

He added later:

> "No writing has been produced in evidence in this action in which, in my view, copyright could subsist."

The Court of Appeal differed from the trial judge to the extent that they accepted that the evidence established the existence of scripts. But the evidence as to the nature of the scripts and what their text contained was exiguous in the extreme. It is to be found in two short passages from the evidence given by the appellant himself. He said in the course of examination-in-chief:

> "In the year 1956, I wrote the scripts of Opportunity Knocks shows, such as they were, because we would have what we would call the introductions, our stock

phrases like 'For So-and-So, Opportunity Knocks', phrases such as 'This is your show, folks, and I do mean you.' The other part of the writing dealt with interviews with the people and one could not really call it writing because you were really only finding out what the artists wanted to talk about."

He said in cross-examination:

"The script of Opportunity Knocks has continuously been the same for the catch phrases, the interviews each week with the artists has differed, the script for the past 17 years and long before 1975 contained particularly the end of the show beginning with the words 'make your mind up time' using the clapometer and bringing back the five people."

On the basis of this evidence Somers J concluded that:

" ... the scripts as they are inferred to be from the description given in evidence did not themselves do more than express a general idea or concept for a talent quest and hence were not the subject of copyright."

In the absence of precise evidence as to what the scripts contained, their Lordships are quite unable to dissent from this view.

The alternative formulation of the appellant's claim relies upon the "dramatic format" of "Opportunity Knocks", by which their Lordships understand is meant those characteristic features of the show which were repeated in each performance. These features were, in addition to the title, the use of the catch phrases "for [name of competitor] opportunity knocks," "this is your show folks, and I do mean you," and "make up your mind time," the use of a device called a "clapometer" to measure audience reaction to competitors' performances and the use of sponsors to introduce competitors. It was this formulation which found favour with Gallen J.

It is stretching the original use of the word "format" a long way to use it metaphorically to describe the features of a television series such as a talent, quiz or game show which is presented in a particular way, with repeated but unconnected use of set phrases and with the aid of particular accessories. Alternative terms suggested in the course of argument were "structure" or "package". This difficulty in finding an appropriate term to describe the nature of the "work" in which the copyright subsists reflects the difficulty of the concept that a number of allegedly distinctive features of a television series can be isolated from the changing material presented in each separate performance (the acts of the performers in the talent show, the questions and answers in the quiz show etc.) and identified as an "original dramatic work". No case was cited to their Lordships in which copyright of the kind claimed has been established.

The protection which copyright gives creates a monopoly and "there must be certainty in the subject matter of such monopoly in order to avoid injustice to the rest of the world": *Tate* v *Fulbrook* [1908] 1 K.B. 821, per Farwell J at page 832. The subject matter of the copyright claimed for the "dramatic format" of "Opportunity Knocks" is conspicuously lacking in certainty. Moreover, it seems to their Lordships that a dramatic work must have sufficient unity to be capable of performance and that the features claimed as constituting the "format" of a television show, being unrelated to each other except as accessories to be used in the presentation of some other dramatic or musical performance, lack that essential characteristic.

For these reasons their Lordships will humbly advise Her Majesty that the appeal should be dismissed. The appellant must pay the respondent's costs of the appeal to the Board.'

COMMENT

Lord Bridge described copyright as creating a monopoly. Is he right? Why was the format for the show held not to be a dramatic work? Hughie Green had spent considerable time and expended some degree of skill and invention in devising the format of the show and yet was denied protection. Would a general tort of unfair competition have helped him in this instance? Is the result of this case that television companies can copy the format of United Kingdom game shows without payment whilst United Kingdom television companies have to pay to import game show formats from countries such as the United States, France and Germany?

Is there any way that Hughie Green could have protected his format under current United Kingdom laws?

International Cooperation

International trade has been a feature of society for many hundreds of years and it was not long before counterfeit goods were made in one country to be exported to other countries. Trade marks were fraudulently applied to counterfeit goods in Roman times if not before. With the development of the independent state, one response was to introduce intellectual property laws which could be used to seize infringing articles. However, these laws were inevitably limited to the territory of the state. Thus, a company making articles to a new design could do little to prevent the copying of the design in other countries provided those copies did not enter the territory in which the company was established.

With the advent of the industrialised society which quickly spread across Europe and beyond, it became important to remedy the territorial limitation imposed on intellectual property laws. No longer was it satisfactory to rely on exploiting new inventions and designs in one country. The drive was towards exporting and something had to be done to give some protection in other countries. The Berne Copyright Convention which was first open for signing in 1886 remedied some of the defects in respect of copyright law, extracts from which are contained in the following chapter. For patents, designs and trade marks, the Paris Convention laid the groundwork for international cooperation and protection by permitting the acquisition of rights in territories other than that of the applicant. The rights, however, remained territorial.

More recently, the TRIPs agreement established a further layer of intellectual property integration, harmonisation and cooperation. Extracts from the Paris

Convention are followed by the general provisions and basic principles of the TRIPs agreement.

Paris Convention for the Protection of Industrial Property 1883

(note: the sub-titles in square brackets do not appear in the original text)

Article 1

[Establishment of the Union; Scope of Industrial Property]

(1) The countries to which this Convention applies constitute a Union for the protection of industrial property.

(2) The protection of industrial property has as its object patents, utility models, industrial designs, trademarks, service marks, trade names, indications of source or appellations of origin, and the repression of unfair competition.

(3) Industrial property shall be understood in the broadest sense and shall apply not only to industry and commerce proper, but likewise to agricultural and extractive industries and to all manufactured or natural products, for example, wines, grain, tobacco leaf, fruit, cattle, minerals, mineral waters, beer, flowers, and flour.

(4) Patents shall include the various kinds of industrial patents recognized by the laws of the countries of the Union, such as patents of importation, patents of improvement, patents and certificates of addition, etc.

Article 2

[National Treatment for Nationals of Countries of the Union]

(1) Nationals of any country of the Union shall, as regards the protection of industrial property, enjoy in all the other countries of the Union the advantages that their respective laws now grant, or may hereafter grant, to nationals; all without prejudice to the rights specially provided for by this Convention. Consequently, they shall have the same protection as the latter, and the same legal remedy against any infringement of their rights, provided that the conditions and formalities imposed upon nationals are complied with.

(2) However, no requirement as to domicile or establishment in the country where protection is claimed may be imposed upon nationals of countries of the Union for the enjoyment of any industrial property rights.

(3) The provision of the laws of each of the countries of the Union relating to judicial and administrative procedure and to jurisdiction, and to the designation of an address for service or the appointment of an agent, which may be required by the laws on industrial property are expressly reserved.

Article 3

[Same Treatment for Certain Categories of Persons as for Nationals of Countries of the Union]

Nationals of countries outside the Union who are domiciled or who have real and effective industrial or commercial establishments in the territory of one of the countries of the Union shall be treated in the same manner as nationals of the countries of the Union.

Article 4
[Patents, Utility Models, Industrial Designs, Marks, Right of Priority]

A. - (1) Any person who has duly filed an application for a patent, or for the registration of a utility model, or of an industrial design, or of a trademark, in one of the countries of the Union, or his successor in title, shall enjoy, for the purpose of filing in the other countries, a right of priority during the periods hereinafter fixed.

(2) Any filing that is equivalent to a regular national filing under the domestic legislation of any country of the Union or under bilateral or multilateral treaties concluded between countries of the Union shall be recognized as giving raise to the right of priority.

(3) By a regular national filing is meant any filing that is adequate to establish the date on which the application was filed in the country concerned, whatever may be the subsequent fate of the application.

B. - Consequently, any subsequent filing in any of the other countries of the Union before the expiration of the periods referred to above shall not be invalidated by reason of any acts accomplished in the interval, in particular, another filing, the publication or exploitation of the invention, the putting on sale of copies of the design, or the use of the mark, and such acts cannot give rise to any third-party right or any right of personal possession. Rights acquired by third parties before the date of the first application that serves as the basis for the right of priority are reserved in accordance with the domestic legislation of each country of the Union.

C. - (1) The periods of priority referred to above shall be twelve months for patents and utility models, and six months for industrial designs and trademarks.

(2) These periods shall start from the date of filing of the first application; the day of filing shall not be included in the period ... (paras D to I omitted).

Article 5
[A. - Patents: Importation of Articles: Failure to Work or Insufficient Working: Compulsory Licenses. - B. Industrial Designs: Failure to Work: Importation of Articles. - C ... D. Patents, Utility Models, Marks, Industrial Designs: Marking]

A. - (1) Importation by the patentee into the country where the patent has been granted of articles manufactured in any of the countries of the Union shall not entail forfeiture of the patent.

(2) Each country of the Union shall have the right to take legislative measures providing for the grant of compulsory licenses to prevent the abuses which might result from the exercise of the exclusive rights conferred by the patent, for example, failure to work.

(3) Forfeiture of the patent shall not be provided for except in cases where the grant of compulsory licenses would not have been sufficient to prevent the said abuses. No proceedings for the forfeiture or revocation of a patent may be instituted before the expiration of two years from the grant of the first compulsory license.

(4) A compulsory license may not be applied for on the ground of failure to work or insufficient working before the expiration of a period of four years from the date of filing of the patent application or three years from the date of the grant of the patent, whichever period expires last; it shall be refused if the patentee justifies his inaction by legitimate reasons. Such a compulsory license shall be non-exclusive and shall not be transferable, even in the form of the grant of a sub-license, except with that part of the enterprise or goodwill which exploits such license.

(5) The foregoing provisions shall be applicable, *mutatis mutandis*, to utility models.

B. - The protection of industrial designs shall not, under any circumstance, be subject to any forfeiture, either by reason of failure to work or by reason of the importation of articles corresponding to those which are protected ... (para C omitted).

D. - No indication or mention of the patent, of the utility model, of the registration of the trademark, or of the deposit of the industrial design, shall be required upon the goods as a condition of recognition of the right to protection.

Article 5bis
[All Industrial Property Rights: Period of Grace for the Payment of Fees for the Maintenance of Rights: Patents: Restoration]

(1) A period of grace of not less than six months shall be allowed for the payment of the fees prescribed for the maintenance of industrial property rights, subject, if the domestic legislation so provides, to the payment of a surcharge.

(2) The countries of the Union shall have the right to provide for the restoration of patents which have lapsed by reason of non-payment of fees ... (Articles 5ter and 5quater omitted).

Article 5quinquies
[Industrial Designs]

Industrial designs shall be protected in all the countries of the Union.

Article 6
[Marks: Conditions of Registration; Independence of Protection of Same Mark in Different Countries]

(1) The conditions for the filing and registration of trademarks shall be determined in each country of the Union by its domestic legislation.

(2) However, an application for the registration of a mark filed by a national of a country of the Union in any country of the Union may not be refused, nor may a registration be invalidated, on the ground that filing, registration, or renewal, has not been effected in the country of origin.

(3) A mark duly registered in a country of the Union shall be regarded as independent of marks registered in the other countries of the Union, including the country of origin.

Article 6bis
[Marks: Well-Known Marks]

(1) The countries of the Union undertake, *ex officio* if their legislation so permits, or at the request of an interested party, to refuse or to cancel the registration, and to prohibit the use, of a trademark which constitutes a reproduction, an imitation, or a translation, liable to create confusion, of a mark considered by the competent authority of the country of registration or use to be well known in that country as being already the mark of a person entitled to the benefits of this Convention and used for identical or similar goods. These provisions shall also apply when the

essential part of the mark constitutes a reproduction of any such well-known mark or an imitation liable to create confusion therewith.

(2) A period of at least five years from the date of registration shall be allowed for requesting the cancellation of such a mark. The countries of the Union may provide for a period within which the prohibition of use must be requested.

(3) No time limit shall be fixed for requesting the cancellation or the prohibition of the use of marks registered or used in bad faith ... (Articles 6ter to 6 quinquies omitted).

Article 6sexies
[Marks: Service Marks]

The countries of the Union undertake to protect service marks. They shall not be required to provide for the registration of such marks ... (Articles 6septies to 7 bis omitted).

Article 8
[Trade Names]

A trade name shall be protected in all the countries of the Union without the obligation of filing or registration, whether or not it forms part of a trademark ... (Articles 9 to 10 omitted).

Article 10bis
[Unfair Competition]

(1) The countries of the Union are bound to assure to nationals of such countries effective protection against unfair competition.

(2) Any act of competition contrary to honest practices in industrial or commercial matters constitutes an act of unfair competition.

(3) The following in particular shall be prohibited:
1. all acts of such a nature as to create confusion by any means whatever with the establishment, the goods, or the industrial or commercial activities, of a competitor;
2. false allegations in the course of trade of such a nature as to discredit the establishment, the goods, or the industrial or commercial activities, of a competitor;
3. indications or allegations the use of which in the course of trade is liable to mislead the public as to the nature, the manufacturing process, the characteristics, the suitability for their purpose, or the quantity of the goods ... (Article 10ter omitted).

Article 11
[Inventions, Utility Models, Industrial Designs, Marks: Temporary Protection at Certain International Exhibitions]

(1) The countries of the Union shall, in conformity with their domestic legislation, grant temporary protection to patentable inventions, utility models, industrial designs, and trademarks, in respect of goods exhibited at official or officially recognized international exhibitions held in the territory of any of them.

(2) Such temporary protection shall not extend the periods provided by Article 4. If, later, the right of priority is invoked, the authorities of any country may provide that the period shall start from the date of introduction of the goods into the exhibition.

(3) Each country may require, as proof of the identity of the article exhibited and of the date of its introduction, such documentary evidence as it considers necessary.

Article 12
[Special National Industrial Property Services]

(1) Each country of the Union undertakes to establish a special industrial property service and a central office for the communication to the public of patents, utility models, industrial designs, and trademarks.

(2) This service shall publish an official periodical journal. It shall publish regularly:

(a) The names of the proprietors of patents granted, with a brief designation of the inventions patented;

(b) The reproductions of registered trademarks.

(Remainder of Convention omitted.)

COMMENT

Some of the basic principles of industrial property law can be seen in the Paris Convention, such as the system of priority dates and compulsory licensing. There are currently over 130 member states and this is a reflection of the success of the Convention. The Uruguay round of the General Agreement on Tariffs and Trade (GATT) concluded on 15 December 1993 with a series of agreements including one on Trade-Related Aspects of Intellectual Property Rights (TRIPs). This lays down minimum standards in respect of adequacy of rights, compliance with general GATT principles and effectiveness of enforcement. Article 2 of the TRIPs agreement requires compliance with Articles 1 to 12 and 19 of the Paris Convention and other provisions in other conventions. However, TRIPs goes further in some respects and it lays down minimum terms of protection, for example, 20 years for patents and 10 years for industrial designs. TRIPs also deals with anti-competitive practices and is now administered by the World Trade Organization. There are special transitional provisions for 'developing' and 'least developed countries' giving them longer to comply (1 January 1999 for the former, 1 January 2005 for the latter). It should be noted that the TRIPs agreement does not have direct effect in the United Kingdom and any changes required will be made through EC legislation; *Lenzing AG's European Patent (UK)* [1997] RPC 245.

Agreement on Trade-Related Aspects of Intellectual Property Rights

Part 1. General Provisions and Basic Principles

Article 1
Nature and scope of obligations

(1)   Members shall give effect to the provisions of this Agreement. Members may, but shall not be obliged to, implement in their law more extensive protection than is required by this Agreement, provided that such protection does not contravene the provisions of this Agreement. Members shall be free to determine the appropriate method of implementing the provisions of this Agreement within their own legal system and practice.

(2)   For the purposes of this Agreement, the term 'intellectual property' refers to all categories of intellectual property, that are the subject of Sections 1 through 7 of Part II.

(3)   Members shall accord the treatment provided for in this Agreement to the nationals of other Members.[1] In respect of the relevant intellectual property right, the nationals of other Members shall be understood as those natural or legal persons that would meet the criteria for eligibility for protection provided for in the Paris Convention (1967), the Berne Convention (1971), the Rome Convention and the Treaty on Intellectual Property in Respect of Integrated Circuits, were all Members of the WTO members of those conventions.[2] Any Member availing itself of the possibilities provided in paragraph 3 of Article 5 or paragraph 2 of Article 6 of the Rome Convention shall make a notification as foreseen in those provisions to the Council for Trade-Related Aspects of Intellectual Property Rights (the 'Council for TRIPs').

Article 2
Intellectual property conventions

(1)   In respect of Parts II, III and IV of this Agreement, Members shall comply with Articles 1 through 12, and Article 19, of the Paris Convention (1967).

(2)   Nothing in Parts I to IV of this Agreement shall derogate from existing obligations that Members may have to each other under the Paris Convention, the Berne Convention, the Rome Convention and the Treaty on Intellectual Property in Respect of Integrated Circuits.

Article 3
National treatment

(1)   Each Member shall accord to the nationals of other Members treatment no less favourable than that it accords to its own nationals with regard to the protection[3] of intellectual property, subject to the exceptions already provided in, respectively, the Paris Convention (1967), the Berne Convention (1971), the Rome Convention or the Treaty on Intellectual Property in Respect of Integrated Circuits. In respect of performers, producers of phonograms and broadcasting organizations, this obligation only applies in respect of the rights provided under this Agreement. Any

Member availing itself of the possibilities provided in Article 6 of the Berne Convention (1971) or paragraph 1(b) of Article 16 of the Rome Convention shall make a notification as foreseen in those provisions to the Council for TRIPS.

(2) Members may avail themselves of the exceptions permitted under paragraph 1 in relation to judicial and administrative procedures, including the designation of an address for service or the appointment of an agent within the jurisdiction of a Member, only where such exceptions are necessary to secure compliance with laws and regulations which are not inconsistent with the provisions of this Agreement and where such practices are not applied in a manner which would constitute a disguised restriction on trade.

Article 4
Most-favoured-nation treatment

With regard to the protection of intellectual property, any advantage, favour, privilege or immunity granted by a Member to the nationals of any other country shall be accorded immediately and unconditionally to the nationals of all other Members. Exempted from this obligation are any advantage, favour, privilege or immunity accorded by a Member:

(a) deriving from international agreements on judicial assistance or law enforcement of a general nature and not particularly confined to the protection of intellectual property;

(b) granted in accordance with the provisions of the Berne Convention (1971) or the Rome Convention authorizing that the treatment accorded be a function not of national treatment but of the treatment accorded in another country;

(c) in respect of the rights of performers, producers of phonograms and broadcasting organizations not provided under this Agreement;

(d) deriving from international agreements related to the protection of intellectual property which entered into force prior to the entry into force of the WTO Agreement, provided that such agreements are notified to the Council for TRIPs and do not constitute an arbitrary or unjustifiable discrimination against nationals of other Members.

Article 5
Multilateral agreements on acquisition or maintenance of protection

The obligations under Articles 3 and 4 do not apply to procedures provided in multilateral agreements concluded under the auspices of WIPO relating to the acquisition or maintenance of intellectual property rights.

Article 6
Exhaustion

For the purposes of dispute settlement under this Agreement, subject to the provisions of Articles 3 and 4 nothing in this Agreement shall be used to address the issue of the exhaustion of intellectual property rights.

Article 7
Objectives

The protection and enforcement of intellectual property rights should contribute to the promotion of technological innovation and to the transfer and dissemination of technology, to the mutual advantage of producers and users of technological knowledge and in a manner conducive to social and economic welfare, and to a balance of rights and obligations.

Article 8
Principles

(1) Members may, in formulating or amending their laws and regulations, adopt measures necessary to protect public health and nutrition, and to promote the public interest in sectors of vital importance to their socio-economic and technological development, provided that such measures are consistent with the provisions of this Agreement.

(2) Appropriate measures, provided that they are consistent with the provisions of this Agreement, may be needed to prevent the abuse of intellectual property rights by right holders or the resort to practices which unreasonably restrain trade or adversely affect the international transfer of technology.

NOTES

[1] When 'nationals' are referred to in this Agreement, they shall be deemed, in the case of a separate customs territory Member of the WTO, to mean persons, natural or legal, who are domiciled or who have a real and effective industrial or commercial establishment in that customs territory.

[2] In this Agreement, 'Paris Convention' refers to the Paris Convention for the Projection of Industrial Property; 'Paris Convention (1967)' refers to the Stockholm Act of this Convention of 14 July 1967. 'Berne Convention' refers to the Berne Convention for the Protection of Literary and Artistic Works; 'Berne Convention (1971)' refers to the Paris Act of this Convention of 24 July 1971. 'Rome Convention' refers to the International Convention for the Protection of Performers, Producers of Phonograms and Broadcasting Organizations, adopted at Rome on 26 October 1961. 'Treaty on Intellectual Property in Respect of Integrated Circuits' (IPIC Treaty) refers to the Treaty on Intellectual Property in Respect of Integrated Circuits, adopted at Washington on 26 May 1989. 'WTO Agreement' refers to the Agreement Establishing the WTO.

[3] For the purposes of Articles 3 and 4, 'protection' shall include matters affecting the availability, acquisition, scope, maintenance and enforcement of intellectual property rights as well as those matters affecting the use of intellectual property rights specifically addressed in this Agreement.

COMMENT

Note the provisions on national treatment and most favoured nation treatment. They are designed to prevent nationals from one country being granted more favourable treatment than nationals from other nations. These provisions are, however, subject to a number of exceptions. Also of interest is that the agreement does not address the issue of exhaustion of rights which is deeply ingrained in EC law.

Chapter 2

Copyright Law

Introduction

Copyright law has had a chequered history, being concerned at one time with the control of publishing as much as providing legal protection against unauthorised copying. Originally, works had to be registered at the Stationers' Company prior to publication. Copyright law, however, remained unsatisfactory. Eventually, it became apparent that a stronger and more certain copyright law was desirable and this was effected through the Statute of Anne, the Preamble to which indicates both the problem of a weak law and the benefits to be obtained from an effective copyright law. The importance of copyright as a means of disseminating ideas and information was also recognised.

Statute of Anne 1709, 8 Anne c.19

Preamble: 'An Act for the Encouragement of Learning, by vesting the Copies of printed Books in the Authors or Purchasers of such Copies, during the Times therein mentioned ... Whereas Printers, Booksellers and other Persons have of late frequently taken the Liberty of printing, reprinting and publishing, or causing to be printed, reprinted and published, Books and other Writings, without the Consent of the Authors or Proprietors of such Books and Writings, to their very great Detriment, and too often, to the Ruin of them and their Families.'

COMMENT

Following this Act, which was concerned with literary works, copyright law developed and grew in a very practical manner, taking many disparate types of work under its wing. The basic mechanism of spreading knowledge through the grant of a property right in the work remains as true today as ever. Can you think of any other justifications for copyright law? What would happen if copyright were to be abolished?

Expression

It is often said that copyright does not protect ideas, it only protects the expression of ideas. Thus, the basic idea of a romantic novel is not protected by copyright but the words expressing the story are. However, it soon became clear that such a distinction, in spite of its easy application, was unsatisfactory. Instead of copying the literal words of a story, the detailed plot, scenes, incidents, characters and sequence of events might be taken and the 'new' story would have very few literal similarities. Copyright law had to contemplate protecting the non-literal elements of a work, something lying between the basic idea and the printed words making up the story, otherwise it would be too easy to defeat copyright law by changing the actual words used whilst remaining faithful to the detailed plot or structure of the story.

Corelli v *Gray* (1913) 30 TLR 116, Court of Appeal

The defendant composed a sketch called 'The People's King' which was performed at a number of variety theatres. The plaintiff had written a novel called 'Temporal Power' and claimed that the defendant's work was taken from hers and infringed her copyright. The judge at first instance agreed and granted an injunction. He considered that the aggregate of similarities including similarities in the plot of the two works drew him inevitably to the conclusion that there had been copying. The defendant appealed.

'Cozens-Hardy MR in his judgment said that there had been a great change made in the law by the Act of 1911. Under the old law a person who desired to dramatize a novel could do so with impunity, except so far as it could be shown that he had to a material extent taken the actual words of the copyrighted work. Subject to that limitation he had a free hand, and could use any combination of incidents with impunity. Section 1 of the Copyright Act, 1911, provided for the copyrighting of literary works, and subsection 2 provided that "For the purposes of this Act, 'copyright' means the sole right to produce or reproduce the work or any substantial part thereof in any material form whatsoever, to perform ... the work or any substantial part thereof in public; ... and shall include the sole right ... (c) in the case of a novel or other non-dramatic work ... to convert it into a dramatic work ..."

That was an entirely new right, or such an enlarged right that it deserved to be termed a new right. His Lordship then stated the facts of the present case and said the learned Judge had heard the evidence of the defendant and of three or four other witnesses whom he called to support his story, and the learned Judge, in language which was not less clear and explicit because it was expressed in moderate terms, indicated that he could not trust the defendant as regards his story of the origin of the sketch. That was not, of course, the conclusion of the case, but it coloured the whole of it and rendered it impossible to avoid looking with suspicion at what had taken place. The plaintiff's case was that on the facts it was impossible not to believe that the defendant had written the sketch with her book before his eyes or in his memory. The learned Judge, in a clear and exhaustive judgment had dealt with six incidents which were to be found in the sketch and also in "Temporal Power", and said that not only were they to be found in both works, but that there were most remarkable similarities or identities of language between the two documents. After going through these matters in detail the learned Judge had said that there was nothing very striking or original in either the novel or the sketch. He added:

> "But the combination of these ordinary materials may nevertheless be original, and when such a combination has arrived at a certain degree of complexity it becomes practically impossible that it should have been arrived at independently by a second individual ... In my judgment the similarities and coincidences in this case are such as, when taken in combination, to be entirely inexplicable as the result of mere chance coincidence."

His Lordship said he accepted that passage as an unanswerable statement of the position in the present case, and he thought that they must approach this case on the footing that the defendant Gray had the book "Temporal Power" either under his eyes or in his memory when he wrote his sketch. No doubt it was still open to this defendant to say that he had not infringed the copyright, because he had only taken from the book something which was not the subject of copyright; but when it appeared that not merely one, two, or three stock incidents had been used, but a combination of stock incidents, every one of which had been taken from the plaintiff's book, it would be narrowing the law beyond what was reasonable to say that the plaintiff was not entitled to be protected.

If it was found that a series of incidents in combination had been taken from the plaintiff's book his Lordship thought she might obtain an injunction, even though not one sentence used in the sketch was similar to one used in the book. The result of the new Act was to give protection not merely to the form of the words in a novel but to the situations contained in it. His Lordship said he did not, however, accept the view that all the situations taken were stock situations. He thought that some of them were very original indeed, but it was not necessary to go into that. The mere fact that in a sketch of six scenes there were five scenes which were also in the plaintiff's book and were not found in any other book was quite enough to justify a decision that the case came within section 1 of the Act.

The appeal must be dismissed.

The Lords Justices delivered judgment to the same effect.'

COMMENT

What was the 'new right' referred to by the Master of the Rolls? The distinction between protected expression and unprotected idea is not at all easy to determine but is of fundamental importance. It has become considerably more difficult to apply in the case of computer programs where protection has been extended, both in the United Kingdom and the United States of America, to non-literal elements of programs such as their structure, menu systems, interfaces, screen displays and such like. If the basic idea of a computer program is its primary function (for example, to record and calculate accounts and produce appropriate reports) and its literal expression is its literal, line by line, program code, where should the threshold of protection be drawn on a continuum between that basic idea and the literal expression? Bear in mind that the recording of numbers and the production of accounts reports is of a mundane nature and lies in the public domain.

It could be argued that copyright should not, and indeed does not, protect facts; something that could be calculated independently to arrive at the same figures. However, independent creation is essential for there to be no infringement and simply copying such facts could still infringe copyright.

Bailey v *Taylor* (1825) 1 Russ & M 73, Court of Chancery

'In 1824, the Plaintiff filed his bill for an injunction to restrain the Defendant from publishing the second and third editions of a work, in which he had copied thirteen tables of calculation as to the value of leases and annuities, which had been published by the Plaintiff in three works, one printed in 1802, another in 1808, and the third in 1810: and the bill also prayed an account. ...

The first edition of the Defendant's work was published in 1811; and the Plaintiff admitted that he had licensed that edition, on condition that the Defendant acknowledged in his preface that he had copied some of his tables from the Plaintiff's works. The Defendant published a second edition in 1820, and a third edition in 1823.

In December 1824, soon after the filing of the bill, the Plaintiff moved before the Master of the Rolls, who was then Vice-Chancellor, for an injunction to restrain the publication of the Defendant's work. The motion was refused, upon the ground that the tables, complained of as pirated, formed a very inconsiderable part of the Plaintiff's work, and could be calculated by any competent person in a few hours; and also on the ground of the length of time which had elapsed since the publication of the second edition of the Defendant's book.

Notwithstanding the refusal of the injunction, the Plaintiff proceeded with his cause, and brought it on to a hearing.

The Defendant proved that the successive editions of his book had been regularly and openly advertised and sold; and an actuary, who was examined on his behalf, stated that, in his judgment, £7, 19s. would be a fair and reasonable charge for re-calculating and furnishing in manuscript the tables which had been borrowed from the Plaintiff's work ...

When the cause came on again, the counsel for the Plaintiff contended that, as there had been a piracy of a part of the Plaintiff's work, he was entitled to protection for the future, and that the amount of the past injury ought to be ascertained, either by a reference to the Master, or by directing an issue. The Defendant had made profit by publishing that which was in truth the property of the Plaintiff, and to an account of these profits the Plaintiff was entitled; for, without an account, there would be no means of assessing accurately his damages at law.

On the other hand, it was insisted, on behalf of the Defendant, that the grounds on which the Court had refused the motion for the injunction were equally valid against awarding an injunction by the decree. These grounds were, the length of time during which the Plaintiff had acquiesced in the alleged piracy; the very small proportion, which the tables said to be pirated bore to the whole mass of the Plaintiff's and Defendant's respective books; and the facility with which the Defendant might acquire a title to the tables which were the subject of complaint. If the Plaintiff had sustained any injury, he might seek compensation by an action at law; if he thought that an account of the proceeds of the sale of the Defendant's work would be necessary or useful in that action, he might file a bill for a discovery; but where he failed in establishing his right to equitable protection by means of an injunction, why should the jurisdiction, in a matter which related merely to the invasion of a legal right, be transferred from a court of law to a court of equity? ...

The Master of the Rolls (Sir John Leach) at 75: "This Court has no jurisdiction to give to a Plaintiff a remedy for an alleged piracy, unless he can make out that he is entitled to the equitable interposition of this Court by injunction; and in such case, the Court will also give him an account, that his remedy here may be complete. If this Court do not interfere by injunction, then his remedy, as in the case of any other injury to his property, must be at law.

I agree that, although the Plaintiff failed, upon the answer of the Defendant, to obtain an injunction, he is at liberty to claim it at the hearing. The question then is, whether the Court ought to grant an injunction as the case now appears? Considering the very inconsiderable part of the Defendant's work which is complained of, and that this may be calculated in a few hours, so as to give the Defendant an unquestionable right to its republication; and considering the difficulty which would be imposed upon the Master if an account were directed, of ascertaining what part of the Defendant's profit ought to be attributed to the Plaintiff's tables; and considering also the distance of time at which the injunction is now sought, being nine years after the publication of the Defendant's second edition, I am bound to refuse the injunction, and to leave the Plaintiff to seek his remedy at law; and the injunction being refused, there can be no account. The bill must, therefore, be dismissed, and with costs."'

COMMENT

This case was heard in the Court of Chancery, thus, equitable remedies only were available. It is interesting to see the use of the word 'piracy' used this early to describe copyright infringement. What exactly does the Master of the Rolls suggest? Does he suggest that more than a few hours are required to produce a work of copyright? It was clear that the Defendant had copied the Plaintiff's tables, so why was no relief forthcoming? Was it because copyright did not subsist in the tables or was it due to other factors? The Defendant had saved himself a fee of £7.19s. for the production of the tables. Why was the Plaintiff not awarded this figure in damages if nothing else?

Subsistence

Section 1(1) of the Copyright, Designs and Patents Act 1988 states that copyright is a property right that subsists, in accordance with Part 1 of the Act (which deals with copyright), in original literary, dramatic, musical or artistic works; sound recordings, films, broadcasts or cable programmes, and the typographical arrangement of published editions. Additionally, qualification requirements must be satisfied as they will if, for example, the author is a British Citizen or the work is first published in the United Kingdom. The first category of works, the 'original works' have been subject to considerable judicial consideration in terms of subsistence of copyright. Of particular importance is the meaning of 'original' and it is clear that a work does not have to be original in the sense that it is unique or that it must satisfy some test of novelty as the following case demonstrates.

University of London Press Ltd. v University Tutorial Press Ltd. [1916] 2 Ch 601, Chancery Division

Examiners for the University of London wrote examination papers in mathematics and the plaintiff company became equitably entitled to the copyright. The defendant, after the relevant examination published a book which contained, *inter alia,* the examination papers together with criticisms and answers to the questions in some of the papers. The plaintiff sued for infringement of copyright. One of the issues was whether copyright subsisted in the examination papers.

Peterson J (at 608): 'The first question that is raised is, Are these examination papers the subject of copyright? Sect. 1, sub-s.1, of the Copyright Act of 1911 provides for copyright in "every original literary dramatic musical and artistic work," subject to certain conditions which for this purpose are immaterial, and the question is, therefore, whether these examination papers are, within the meaning of this Act, original literary works. Although a literary work is not defined in the Act, s.35 states what the phrase includes; the definition is not a completely comprehensive one, but the section is intended to show what, amongst other things, is included in the description "Literary work," and the words are "Literary work" including maps, charts, plans, tables and compilations. It may be difficult to define "literary work" as used in this Act, but it seems to be plain that it is not confined to "literary work" in the sense in which that phrase is applied, for instance, to Meredith's novels and the writings of Robert Louis Stevenson. In speaking of such writings as literary works, one thinks of the quality, the style, and the literary finish which they exhibit. Under the Act of 1842, which protected "books", many things which had no pretensions to literary style acquired copyright; for example, a list of registered bills of sale, a list of foxhounds and hunting days, and trade catalogues; and I see no ground for coming to the conclusion that the present Act was intended to curtail the rights of authors. In my view the words "literary work" cover work which is expressed in print or writing, irrespective of the question whether the quality or style is high. The word "literary" seems to be used in a sense somewhat similar to the use of the word "literature" in political or electioneering literature and refers to written or printed matter. Papers set by examiners are, in my opinion, "literary work" within the meaning of the present Act.

Assuming that they are "literary work", the question then is whether they are original. The word "original" does not in this connection mean that the work must be the expression of original or inventive thought. Copyright Acts are not concerned with the originality of ideas, but with the expression of thought, and, in the case of "literary work", with the expression of thought in print or writing. The originality which is required relates to the expression of the thought. But the Act does not require that the expression must be in an original or novel form, but that the work must not be copied from another work - that it should originate from the author. In the present case it was not suggested that any of the papers were copied. Professor Lodge and Mr Jackson proved that they had thought out the questions which they set, and that they made notes or memoranda for future questions and drew on those notes for the purposes of the questions which they set. The papers which they prepared originated from themselves, and were, within the meaning of the Act, original. It was said, however, that they drew upon the stock of knowledge common to mathematicians, and that the time spent in producing the questions was small. These cannot be tests for determining whether copyright exists. If an author, for purposes of copyright, must not draw on the stock of knowledge which is common to himself and others who are students of the same branch of learning, only those historians who discovered fresh historical facts could acquire copyright for their works. If time expended is to be the test, the rapidity of an author like Lord Byron in producing a short poem might be an impediment in the way of acquiring copyright, and, the completer his mastery of his subject, the smaller would be the prospect of the author's success in maintaining his claim to copyright. Some of the questions, it was urged, are questions in book work, that is to say, questions set for the purpose of seeing whether the student has read and understood the books prescribed by the syllabus. But the questions set are not copied from the book; they are questions prepared by the examiner for the purpose of testing the student's acquaintance with the book, and in any case it was admitted that the papers involved selection, judgment, and experience. This objection has not, in my opinion, any substance; if it had, it would only apply to some of the questions in the elementary papers, and would have little, if any, bearing on the paper on advanced mathematics. Then it was said that the questions in the elementary papers were of common type; but this only means that somewhat similar questions have been asked by other examiners. I suppose that most elementary books on mathematics may be said to be of a common type, but that fact would not give impunity to a predatory infringer. The book and the papers alike originate from the author and are not copied by him from another book or other papers. The objections with which I have dealt do not appear to me to have any substance, and, after all, there remains the rough practical test that what is worth copying is *prima facie* worth protecting. In my judgment, then, the papers set by Professor Lodge and Mr Jackson are "original literary work" and proper subject for copyright under the Act of 1911.'

COMMENT

Note that the definition of literary works is different now. Under the 1911 Act, maps, charts and plans were also deemed to be literary works whereas they now fall to be considered as artistic works, in particular, graphic works. Peterson J's judgment typifies the pragmatic view of copyright law as a way of protecting useful work rather than looking for literary or artistic merit or style. He also stresses that originality is easily attained, being no more than that the work originated from the author. In what way could you justify the low standard apparently required for copyright subsistence? As will be seen later, copyright law does not protect every work, so is Peterson J's practical test of what is worth copying is worth protecting of no value whatsoever?

Copyright law rewards the skill and judgment expended in the creation of a work and, in practice, there is nothing to prevent a work which is copied from everyday materials from attracting copyright.

Macmillan & Co. Ltd. v Cooper (1924) 40 TLR 186, Judicial Committee of the Privy Council

The appellant published a book 'Plutarch's Life of Alexander, Sir Thomas North's Translation' which contained passages from Sir Thomas North's translation which were knitted together by the insertion of additional words. At the end was a glossary and notes written for the appellant. North's translation was, itself, out of copyright. The respondent's book contained the 20,000 words of the plaintiff's book plus another 7,000 words in marginal notes, an introduction and summary. In an action for copyright infringement, the question of subsistence of copyright in the appellant's book had to be determined.

Lord Atkinson (delivering the judgment of the court) (at 187): 'The learned Judges in the appellate jurisdiction apparently came to the conclusion that a publication the text of which consisted merely of a reprint of passages selected from the work of an author could never be entitled to copyright. Their Lordships are unable to concur in that view. For instance, it may very well be that in selecting and combining for the use of schools or universities passages of scientific works in which the lines of reasoning are so closely knit and proceed with such unbroken continuity that each later proposition depends in a great degree for its proof or possible appreciation upon what has been laid down or established much earlier in the book, labour, accurate scientific knowledge, sound judgment touching the purpose for which the selection is made, and literary skill would all be needed to effect the object in view. In such a case copyright might well be acquired for the print of the selected passages.'

COMMENT

Copyright law protects the work expended in selecting and arranging materials contained in a compilation. However, in the United States of America, the Supreme Court has ruled that such a work will not be protected by copyright if it is the result of effort only and requires no skill or judgement *(Feist Publications Inc. v Rural Telephone Service Co. Inc.* (1991) 111 S.Ct 1282). In other words, a work that results from the sweat of the brow only is not protected. Is this fair? The position in the United Kingdom is not necessarily different.

G A Cramp & Sons Ltd. v Frank Smythson Ltd. [1944] AC 329, House of Lords

The respondents claimed that the appellants had infringed the copyright in their 'Liteblue' diary. Apart from the usual diary pages, the diary contained information commonly found in diaries such as a calendar, postal information, tables of weights and measures, a percentage table, etc. A former employee of the respondent who had taken up employment with the appellant copied seven of these tables and inserted them in the appellant's diary. The respondents brought an action for infringement of copyright.

Viscount Simon LC (at 333): 'My Lords, both these parties were publishers of pocket diaries. A number of disputes between them have been settled in the litigation which has already taken place, and the question that remains is whether the appellants, in inserting certain tables in their "Surrey Lightweight Diary, 1942", have infringed any copyright that the respondents had in a collection of tables included in their pocket diary known as "Liteblue Diary, 1933". It is not disputed that seven of these tables had been copied from the respondents' diary by one Eckford, who entered the appellants' service (after previously serving the respondents) as diary manager and salesman in 1937, though it is right to add that his employers knew nothing of this copying. If, therefore, the respondents owned any copyright in the compilation of material which was copied by Eckford from their diary, infringement of this copyright by the appellants in their "Surrey Lightweight Diary, 1942" is not, and cannot be, disputed. The question, however, is whether, having regard to its nature and subject-matter, the compilation to be found in the respondents' "Liteblue Diary", which has thus been copied and made use of by the appellants, should be regarded as matter for copyright ...

The principles of law to be applied to this issue are not in any doubt. By s.1, sub-s.1, of the Copyright Act, 1911, copyright subsists under the conditions mentioned in the section "in every original literary ... work" and this expression includes "compilations": s.35, sub-s.1. Nobody disputes that the existence of sufficient "originality" is a question of fact and degree. Lord Atkinson's observation in delivering the judgment of the Judicial Committee in *Macmillan & Co. Ltd.* v *K & J Cooper* (1924) 40 TLR 186 lays down the law on the subject in terms which are universally accepted. He said: "What is the precise amount of the knowledge, labour, judgment or literary skill or taste which the author of any book or other compilation must bestow upon its composition in order to acquire copyright in it within the meaning of the Copyright Act of 1911 cannot be defined in precise terms. In every case it must depend largely on the special facts of that case, and must in each case be very much a question of degree." Applying this rule to the evidence in the present case, and after hearing full arguments at the Bar of the House, I have reached the conclusion that the respondents' copyright is not established and that the appellants have, therefore, not infringed.

The respondents base their claim to copyright on the selection of these tables to form a combination of information, and the declaration made by the Court of Appeal is "that the collection of tables comprised in the plaintiffs' Liteblue Diary for 1933" (other than the calendar), "is a copyright work", and that the infringement by the plaintiffs consists in printing and publishing in "the Surrey Lightweight Diary, 1942" this collection of tables. At the same time, if I understood Mr Shelley aright, he reserved the right to contend, if necessary, on another occasion that there was copyright in an individual table. Granted that the appellants copied the respondents' tables (and this is not only admitted but is indicated by the almost precise similarity of language), there seems to be nothing that can properly be described as an "original literary work" in grouping together this information. A summarized statement of the most important of the postal charges, inland, imperial and foreign, is part of the ordinary contents of any pocket diary. There would, indeed, as it seems to me, be considerable difficulty in successfully contending that ordinary tables which can be got from, or checked by, the postal guide or the Nautical Almanac are a subject of copyright as being original literary work. One of the essential qualities of such tables is that they should be accurate, so that there is no question of variation in what is stated. The sun does in fact rise, and the moon set, at times which have been calculated, and the utmost that a table can do on such a subject is to state the result accurately. There is so far no room for taste or judgment. There remains, I agree, the element of choice as to what information should be given, and the respondents contend that the test of originality is satisfied by the choice of the tables inserted, but the bundle of information furnished in the respondents' diary is commonplace information which is ordinarily useful and is, at any rate to a large extent, commonly found prefixed to diaries, and, looking through the respondents' collection of tables, I have difficulty in seeing how such tables, in the combination in which they appear in the respondents' 1933 diary, can reasonably claim to be "original work." There was no evidence that any of these tables was composed specially for the respondents' diary. There was no feature of them which could be pointed out as novel or specially meritorious or ingenious from the point of view of the judgment or skill of the compiler. It was not suggested that there was any element of originality or skill in the order in which the tables were arranged. My own conclusion is that the selection did not constitute an original literary work.'

COMMENT

Of course, tables are works of copyright, being literary works and, in the above case, the plaintiff was not claiming copyright in the individual tables but, rather, in the work involved in selecting and arranging the tables. Viscount Simon LC suggests that tables containing factual information where no discretion is allowed as to the precise facts cannot be copyright material. Do you agree with this sentiment? What about the work involved in deriving factual information, such as by means of conducting complex scientific experiments? Certainly, where the creator of the work is presented with choices as to what to include and how to arrange the materials chosen, it is probable that copyright will subsist in the work. The issue of the subsistence of copyright in original literary works was considered again in the House of Lords in the following case.

Ladbroke (Football) Ltd. v William Hill (Football) Ltd. [1964] 1 All ER 465, House of Lords

The respondents were bookmakers who had used fixed odds football coupons for a number of years. The coupons had a number of lists of matches which had various wagers associated with them. Obviously, the particular matches varied from week to week. The appellants were also bookmakers and decided to start using fixed odds football coupons and they copied 15 of the respondents' 16 lists, using similar headings and wagers but having different odds attached to the wagers. The matches in the appellants' lists were different to those in the respondent's lists. The appellants argued that, apart from the selection of matches and choice of odds, there was no copyright in the respondent's coupon. At first instance, it was held that the coupons were not original literary works but this was reversed in the Court of Appeal which granted an injunction restraining the appellants from infringing copyright. The appellants appealed to the House of Lords.

Lord Evershed (at 471): 'No doubt the document (that is, the coupon) is *ex facie* a compilation in the sense that it is made up by putting together in writing (that is, in print) a number of individual items or components. Nonetheless, the coupon is peculiar in this respect: it is the actual instrument of trade used by those concerned in the business of bookmaking. It is the thing sent out by the trader to his actual or potential customers and it is then returned by the customers with their selections of the wagers offered, that is, their choices of the numerous alternative forecasts which they are invited to make written thereon by them. In this respect the coupon might be comparable to a list or catalogue used by a trader who had in fact no premises available for visiting by customers - the catalogue containing a list of the items offered by the trader for sale with appropriate spaces in which the customer could indicate which of the items he wanted and would then return the list or catalogue with his name and address written thereon and (perhaps) a statement of the total sum involved. In this case what corresponds to the articles offered for sale by the trader are the wagers offered by the bookmaker. As my noble friend, Lord Reid, has pointed out, the coupon is concerned with the Association Football matches played during the football season. On every Saturday during the season there are some fifty-four matches played by the professional teams of the English divisions and the Scottish League. It is obvious that the different forecasts which such a list of matches could comprehend is in number very large indeed since not only may the punter be invited to forecast which of two teams in any match (that is the home team or the away team) will win or whether the result will be a draw, but he may be also invited to forecast what the position in any match will be at half time, and also how many goals each team in any match may score both at half time and at the end of the match. It is also abundantly clear on the evidence produced in the case that the appropriate odds which the bookmaker may safely or profitably offer in respect of any forecast or group of forecasts is something which only great skill, industry and experience will discover: and further, that the selection and description of the wagers which will attract custom is no less a matter of skill, judgment and experience. It was further made clear that, since potential customers will inevitably tend to be attracted by the same or similar wagers, certain of them have become very commonly adopted by those concerned in the trade - for example the so-called "Nothing barred list"; so that anyone entering this type of business would almost inevitably have to include such a list and other similar wagers commonly found presented by other bookmakers, and would be no more poaching on the preserves of a competitor by so doing than would a newcomer, for example, in the tobacconist trade by offering (and stating that he offered) certain well-known brands of cigarettes which every tobacconist would be expected by the public to offer for sale. To what has been said one other important consideration must be added, namely, that the list of matches played in each week has at all relevant dates been determined by the Football League, who own the copyright in such list.

So it is said on the part of the appellants that the coupon as a document could have no originality, since it is essentially composed merely of a selection of well-known and well-tried wagers, and is composed each week merely by applying these well-known and well-tried wagers to all, or a limited number, of the League's list of matches. It was also said on the appellants' part that the selection involved in making up the coupons was no more that putting in print what were called "ideas" involving, therefore, nothing in the way of original literary work in any sense: and your lordships' attention was directed to the well-known proposition that there is no copyright in ideas. My lords, I have reached a conclusion adverse to these contentions. When one takes one of these coupons in one's hand and looks at it, the right conclusion is, to my mind, that it falls sensibly and properly within the definition of an original literary compilation. True it is that no question of literary taste or quality is involved that would give to the coupon the award of literature as normally understood; but, having regard to the introduction of a compilation into the definition, that clearly cannot be a decisive factor, since otherwise such things as lists or catalogues could never have been held to have been properly subject to copyright. The result, in my opinion, is that the respondents' coupon is in truth a compilation in writing which is distinctive and original. True it is that a great amount of work is devoted to calculating the odds; but this is not a case in which, in my opinion, the resulting document, that is the coupon, has involved no further skill, labour or judgment - any more than was the list of matches themselves treated as involving no distinctive or original work, by Upjohn, J in the case of *Football League Ltd.* v *Littlewoods Pools Ltd.* [1959] 2 All ER 546. There can, in my judgment, be no doubt on the evidence in the present case that when all the hard work has been done in deciding on the wagers to be offered there still remains the further distinct task, requiring considerable skill, labour and judgment (though of a different kind) of devising the way in which the chosen wagers are expressed and presented to the eye of the customer. As I have earlier stated, the case on its facts which might be thought nearest to the present is that already mentioned of *Cramp & Sons Ltd.* v *Frank Smythson Ltd.* [1944] AC 329; for there the document in which copyright was sought was itself the thing, that is the diary, which was handed out by the trader to the customer. In that case, however, as appeared from the statement of facts, there was no evidence whatever bearing on the work which had been incident to the preparation of the plaintiff's diary and particularly to the tables contained in it. On the other hand, it was clearly proved that the various tables which were inserted in the plaintiff's diary were tables commonly so inserted in other diaries ...

[In *Cramp* v *Smythson*] Lord Macmillan said (at 338): "The inclusion or exclusion of one or more of the tables constituting the ordinary stock material of the diary-compiler seems to me to involve the very minimum of labour and judgment."

The distinction may be fine between those cases in which a list or table is regarded as properly entitled to copyright and those cases in which a list or table is not so regarded. This indeed, readily appears from the case of *Leslie* v *Young & Sons* [1894] AC 335 where the compilation from the official railway timetables of a local timetable relating to a particular town was not regarded as constituting an original work entitled to copyright though the compilation of certain circular tours in reference to the same town was regarded as so entitled. It must further be taken as well established, as stated by Lord Atkinson in delivering the judgment of the Judicial Committee in *Macmillan & Co.* v *Cooper* (1924) 40 TLR 186, that the precise amount of knowledge, labour, judgment or skill which must be bestowed on a compilation in order that it should acquire copyright within the meaning of the Act cannot be defined in precise terms but must in every case depend largely on the special facts of that case and be very much a matter of degree.

On the facts of this case, and in the light of the authorities to which I have alluded, I conclude that there was present here the requisite degree of skill, judgment and labour not only in selecting out of the vast possible total of wagers those which should be offered but also in the way in which the result of the selection was presented to the customer, including particularly the arrangement of the document and of its component headings and the way in which such headings were described and were coloured and also in the way in which, in the appropriate notes underneath the headings, the punter was informed of the possibilities open to him under each heading.'

COMMENT

This case is easily distinguished from *Cramp* v *Smythson* because of the far greater thought and work involved in creating the work. One way to look at the diary case is to say that it is an example of the *de minimis* rule, that is, that small or trivial works will not be afforded protection; see the *Exxon* case later. If there were only a few possible wagers that were realistic, would this affect copyright subsistence? What if the independent creation of other fixed odds football coupons would have resulted in very similar coupons - would this fact affect the copyright position?

Subsistence - Artistic Works

Artistic works are, by section 4(1) of the Copyright, Designs and Patents Act 1988, graphic works (for example, drawings, paintings, maps, charts, etc.), photographs, sculptures or collages, all of which are protected by copyright irrespective of artistic quality. Other artistic works are works of architecture and works of artistic craftsmanship and, for these, the phrase 'irrespective of artistic quality' does not apply. Therefore, the basic test of originality is not sufficient and some unspecified quality would seem to be required. The case below shows how the House of Lords attempted to define and apply that test.

George Hensher Ltd. v *Restawile Upholstery (Lancs) Ltd.* [1976] AC 64, House of Lords

The appellants made a prototype for a new design of furniture which was described as 'boat-shaped' because of its appearance. After the appellants offered for sale furniture made to the new design, the respondents brought out a suite of furniture made to a similar design. The appellants sued for infringement of the copyright in their furniture claiming that the prototypes were artistic works, being works of artistic craftsmanship. At first instance, Graham J found that the prototype was a work of artistic craftsmanship but the respondents' appeal to the Court of Appeal was allowed. The appellants appealed to the House of Lords.

Lord Reid (at 77): 'The appellants did not register any design under the Registered Designs Act 1949. They maintain that the respondents have infringed their copyright. Section 3(2) of the Copyright Act 1956, provides that copyright shall subsist in every original artistic work, and section 3(1) provides:

"In this Act 'artistic work' means a work of any of the following descriptions, that is to say, - (a) the following, irrespective of artistic quality, namely paintings, sculptures, drawings, engravings and photographs; (b) works of architecture, being either building or models for buildings; (c) works of artistic craftsmanship, not falling within either of the preceding paragraphs."

The appellants maintain that the prototype of their furniture was a "work of artistic craftsmanship" within the meaning of section 3(1)(c). The respondents admit that the prototype was a work of craftsmanship but deny that it was of "artistic craftsmanship."

It is common ground that we must consider the prototype and not the furniture put on the market by the appellants. Apparently this is because the articles put on the market were not works of craftsmanship. But if there was copyright in the prototype then the furniture put on the market by the appellants was copied from it, and the respondents' products were copied from the furniture which the appellants put on the market. The respondents do not deny that this would be infringement of that copyright.

The respondents have not taken the point that such a prototype however artistic could not be a "work of artistic craftsmanship," and the point was not argued. But I feel bound to say that I have great doubt about this matter. A work of craftsmanship suggests to me a durable useful handmade object and a work of artistic craftsmanship suggests something, whether of practical utility or not, which its owner values because of its artistic character. It appears to me to be difficult to bring within the terms or the intention of the statute an object which, however artistic it might appear to be, is only intended to be used as a step in a commercial operation and has no value in itself. I express no concluded opinion on this matter, on which the decision of this case can be of no authority.

This case must I think be decided on the assumption that a real chair similar to those put on the market had been made by craftsmanship.

Section 3(1) is difficult to understand unless one takes account of its origin. The Copyright Act 1911 covered artistic works. Section 35 contains a definition. "'Artistic work' includes works of painting, drawing, sculpture and artistic craftsmanship, and architectural works of art and engravings and photographs." "Architectural work of art" is defined as meaning any building or structure having an artistic character or design. This brought in artistic craftsmanship and buildings for the first time. It would seem that paintings, drawings, sculpture, engravings and photographs were protected whether they had any artistic character or not, but works of craftsmanship had to be of "artistic" craftsmanship and buildings must have an "artistic" character or design. There is no further explanation of what is meant by "artistic".

The Act of 1956 in section 3(1)(a) makes explicit that the works to which it refers need have no artistic quality. Section 3(1)(b) removes the need for any artistic character or design in buildings. But section 3(1)(c) preserves the limitation that there must be "artistic" craftsmanship.

The word "artistic" is not an easy word to construe or apply not only because it may have different shades of meaning but also because different people have different views about what is artistic. One may have a word which substantially everyone understands in much the same way. Recently we had to consider such a word - "insulting": *Cozens* v *Brutus* [1973] AC 854. Then the matter can and, indeed, must be left to the judge or jury for further explanation will confuse rather than clarify.

But here two questions must be determined. What precisely is the meaning of "artistic" in this context and who is to judge of its application to the article in question? There is a trend of authority with which I agree that a court ought not to be called on to make an aesthetic judgment. Judges have to be experts in the use of the English language but they are not experts in art or aesthetics. In such a matter my opinion is of no more value than that of anyone else. But I can and must say what in my view is the meaning of the word "artistic".

I think we must avoid philosophic or metaphysical argument about the nature of beauty, not only because there does not seem to be any consensus about this but also because those who are ignorant of philosophy are entitled to have opinions about what is artistic. I think that by common usage it is proper for a person to say that in his opinion a thing has an artistic character if he gets pleasure or satisfaction or it may be uplift from contemplating it. No doubt it is necessary to beware of those who get pleasure from looking at something which has cost them a great deal of money. But if unsophisticated people get pleasure from seeing something which they admire I do not see why we must say that it is not artistic because those who profess to be art experts think differently. After all there are great differences of opinion among those who can properly be called experts.

It is I think of importance that the maker or designer of a thing should have intended that it should have an artistic appeal but I would not regard that as either necessary or conclusive. If any substantial section of the public genuinely admires and values a thing for its appearance and gets pleasure or satisfaction, whether emotional or intellectual, from looking at it, I would accept that it is artistic although many others may think it meaningless or common or vulgar.

I think that it may be misleading to equate artistic craftsmanship with a work of art. "Work of art" is generally associated more with the fine arts than with craftsmanship and may be setting too high a standard. During the last century there was a movement to bring art to the people. I doubt whether the craftsmen who set out with that intention would have regarded all their products as works of art, but they were certainly works of artistic craftsmanship whether or not they were useful as well as having an artistic appeal.

I am quite unable to agree with the view of the Court of Appeal ... that "there must at least be expected in an object or work that its utilitarian or functional appeal should not be the primary inducement to its acquisition or retention." The whole conception of artistic craftsmanship appears to me to be to produce things which are both useful and artistic in the belief that being artistic does not make them any less useful. A person who only wants, or has only room for, one of a particular kind of household object may be willing to pay more to get one which he regards as artistic; if a work of craftsmanship it is nonetheless of artistic craftsmanship because his primary purpose is to get something useful.

But on the other hand I cannot accept the appellants' submission or the view of Graham J. Many people - probably too many - buy things on eye appeal or because they are of a new or original design. But they would not claim that therefore they thought that their purchase had artistic merit. They might say that they were not interested in art, or that they would like to have bought an artistic object but that there was none to be had, at least at a price they could pay. It is notorious that manufacturers go to great expense in providing packaging which will catch the eye of customers. But the customer does not regard the packaging as artistic - he throws it away.

In the present case I find no evidence at all that anyone regarded the appellants' furniture as artistic. The appellants' object was to produce something which would sell. It was, as one witness said, "a winner" and they succeeded in their object. No doubt many customers bought the furniture because they thought it looked nice as well as being comfortable. But looking nice appears to me to fall considerably short of having artistic appeal. I can find no evidence that anyone felt or thought that the furniture was artistic in the sense which I have tried to explain. I am therefore of opinion that this appeal should be dismissed ...'

Lord Morris of Borth-y-Gest (at 81): 'In deciding whether a work is one of artistic craftsmanship I consider that the work must be viewed and judged in a detached and objective way. The aim and purpose of its author may provide a pointer but the thing produced must itself be assessed without giving decisive weight to the author's scheme of things. Artistry may owe something to an inspiration not possessed by the most deft craftsman. But an effort to produce what is artistic may, if forced or conscious, for that very reason fail. Nor should undue emphasis be given to the priorities in the mind of a possible acquirer. A positive need to purchase an object or thing in order to put it to practical use may be the primary reason for its acquisition but this may be reinforced by a full appreciation of its artistic merits if they are possessed.

So I would say that the object under consideration must be judged as a thing in itself. Does it have the character or virtue of being artistic? In deciding as to this some persons may take something from their ideas as to what constitutes beauty or as to what satisfies their notions of taste or as to what yields pleasure or as to what makes an aesthetic appeal. If, however, there is a resort to these or other words which may themselves have their own satellites of meanings there must follow a return to the word "artistic" which is apt without exposition to contain and convey its own meaning.

As to the second question, I consider that as in all situations where a decision is required upon a question of fact the court must pay heed to the evidence that is adduced. Though it is a matter of individual opinion whether a work is or is not artistic there are many people who have special capabilities and qualifications for forming an opinion and whose testimony will command respect. In practice a court will not have difficulty in weighing their evidence and in deciding whether it clearly points to some conclusion. In cases where the court is able to see the work which is in question that will not warrant a decision on the basis of a spot opinion formed by the court itself but it will be a valuable aid to an appreciation of the evidence.

In the present case the evidence fell short of establishing that the knock-up qualified to be characterised as a work of artistic craftsmanship. That a buyer for a retailing company approved of a design and shape and considered that the product would be a "winner" only established that it would be likely to attract purchasers. Purchasers might be induced to buy for a variety of reasons which would not include the attraction of possessing a work of artistic craftsmanship. That buyer, who was a witness, expressed herself very clearly. Being asked about one suite which was a variant of the Bronx she said that young people would purchase it because in their case it had an "eye appeal" and because the wide arms of the suite were an added attraction: it was a "wonderful suite" though it was "horrible" and though it was "vulgar" and though it was "brash". One witness (Mr. Carter) had great knowledge and experience in regard to the designs of and the designing of furniture but his evidence did not support a claim that there was artistic character. He was asked about the design of the Bronx suite. In particular he was asked whether 'aesthetically speaking' he considered the design to be good. His revealing reply was, "Personally I do not, no. I think it is mediocre in my opinion, although I can see it has great appeal. I think it is slightly vulgar but it is obviously quite a good commercial design." Though he considered that there was a "distinctive shape" his nearest approach towards asserting an artistic character was when he said that there was a design concept in visual terms which provided artistic originality or lent artistic merit by possessing a strong individual character. The high water mark of his testimony is set out in the passage recited in the judgment of the Court of Appeal. It was not high enough, in my view, to establish that the prototype (or prototypes) qualified to be described as a work of artistic craftsmanship within the meaning of section 3(1) of the Act.

I would dismiss the appeal.'

COMMENT

What features or characteristics should a work of artistic craftsmanship possess? Does the *Hensher* case do anything to make it easier to test for artistic craftsmanship? In view of the practical approach of protecting that which others wish to copy without permission, this case illustrates the difficulty in allowing judges discretion as to what is artistic. However, the design of the furniture could have been protected against unauthorised copying for relatively little expense. How?

Simply updating or re-drawing an artistic work with minor additions only will not cause a new copyright to arise.

Interlego AG v *Tyco Industries Inc* [1989] AC 217, Privy Council

The plaintiff made the famous children's building bricks made from plastic and called LEGO. These were protected by patents and registered designs but these rights had expired. The defendant started manufacturing similar toy bricks and the plaintiff sued, claiming it had a copyright in a re-drawing of an older drawing in which the copyright had expired.

Lord Oliver (at 256): 'Engineering drawings are no doubt "artistic works" within the broad meaning of that expression in the Copyright Act 1956 but it has to be remembered that they are essentially no more than manufacturing instructions for a three-dimensional artefact. Their claim to artistic copyright rests solely upon the fact that they are drawings and not upon the technical significance of the instructions by which they can be interpreted which are frequently represented only by conventional symbols or figures. In the nature of things the original drawings come to be reproduced, probably many times, and updated from time to time as minor modifications are made in design or methods of manufacture. To accord an independent artistic copyright to every such reproduction would be to enable the period of artistic copyright in what is, essentially the same work to be extended indefinitely. Thus the primary question on Tyco's appeal can be expressed in this way: can Lego, having enjoyed a monopoly for the full permitted period of patent and design protection in reliance upon drawings in which no copyright any longer subsists, continue their monopoly for yet a further, more extensive period by re-drawing the same designs with a number of minor alterations and claiming a fresh copyright in the re-drawn designs? ...

Take the simplest case of artistic copyright, a painting or a photograph. It takes great skill, judgment and labour to produce a good copy by painting or to produce an enlarged photograph from a positive print, but no one would reasonably contend that the copy painting or enlargement was an "original" artistic work in which the copier is entitled to claim copyright. Skill, labour or judgment merely in the process of copying cannot confer originality. In this connection some reliance was placed on a passage from the judgment of Whitford J in *L B (Plastics) Ltd.* [1979] RPC 551, 568-569, where he expressed the opinion that a drawing of a three-dimensional prototype, not itself produced from the drawing and not being a work of artistic craftsmanship, would qualify as an original work. That may well be right, for there is no more reason for denying originality to the depiction of a three-dimensional prototype than there is for denying originality to the depiction in two-dimensional form of any other physical object. It by no means follows, however, that that which is an exact and literal reproduction in two-dimensional form of an existing two-dimensional work becomes an original work simply because the process of copying it involves the application of skill and labour. There must in addition be some element of material alteration or embellishment which suffices to make the totality of the work an original work. Of course, even a relatively small alteration or addition quantitatively may, if material, suffice to convert that which is substantially copied from an earlier work into an original work. Whether it does so or not is a question of degree having regard to the quality rather than the quantity of the addition. But copying, *per se,* however much skill or labour may be devoted to the process, cannot make an original work. A well executed tracing is the result of much labour and skill but remains what it is, a tracing. Moreover it must be borne in mind that the Copyright Act 1956 confers protection on an original work for a generous period. The prolongation of the period of statutory protection by periodic reproduction of the original work with minor alterations is an operation which requires to be scrutinised with some caution to ensure that that for which protection is claimed really is an original artistic work. ...

The essence of an artistic work (to adopt the words of Whitford J in a judgment delivered in *Rose Plastics GmbH* v *William Beckett & Co. (Plastics) Ltd.* (unreported), 2 July 1987, of which their Lordships have seen only an approved transcript,) is that which is "visually significant"; and Mr Jacob asks, forensically, what is there in the 1976 drawings which is visually significant and which was not contained in and directly copied from the 1968 drawings? With deference to the Court of Appeal and accepting both the importance of and the skill involved in producing the design information transmitted to the mould makers by the revised figures substituted on the drawing, their Lordships can see no alternation of any visual significance such as to entitle the drawing, as a drawing, to be described as original. ...

There may have been and no doubt was a great deal of labour and skill involved in the evolution of the right dimensions and tolerances, the concept of the best clutch power, and the actual process of copying from the original drawing and inserting onto the copy the figures and symbols resulting from the technical calculations, but the artistic work remained the original artistic work without any substantial visual alteration. In their Lordships' view, Lego's claim for infringement of copyright in their post-1972 drawings fails as regards such of those drawings as were copied either from drawings made prior to 1973 or from other drawings in respect of which no infringement has claimed. It is not sufficient to confer originality upon them that labour and skill were employed in the process of copying them or in the addition to them of fresh written manufacturing instructions.'

COMMENT

If copying requiring skill and judgment does not give rise to a new copyright why does a natural life painter who makes faithful representations of flowers, birds, etc. obtain a copyright in his work?

De Minimis

Very small and trivial works generally will be denied copyright protection. To protect short phrases, titles and the like could make it difficult for writers and traders. The *Exxon* case below shows a determined and inventive argument intended to overcome the *de minimis* rule.

Exxon Corporation v Exxon Insurance Consultants International Ltd. [1981] 3 All ER 241, Court of Appeal

The plaintiff, a large oil company, decided to devise a new corporate name. After some considerable research it decided to use the word 'Exxon' and registered it as a trade mark. The defendant decided to use the word 'Exxon' in its name and the plaintiff sued on the grounds of passing off and infringement of the copyright in the name. At first instance, Graham J found that the claim in passing off succeeded and granted an injunction and awarded damages. However, he held that the word 'Exxon' was not protected by copyright. The plaintiff appealed to the Court of Appeal with respect to that part of the judgment relating to copyright.

Stephenson LJ (at 245): 'The question, therefore, is whether this word Exxon is an original literary work. It was invented, as the statement of claim alleges, after research and testing to find a suitable word, apparently over a period of more than a year. It is therefore difficult, if not impossible, to say that it is not original. It was invented and devised by and originated with the first plaintiff. Is it an original *literary work* ? Counsel for the plaintiffs has submitted that it is. He says that the 1842 Act, by its preamble, was concerned to protect literary works of lasting benefit to the world, but such literary works were confined by the Act, as is clear from all its sections, to printed books; there is no such limitation in copyright in literary works since 1911 in this country. What is now protected as an original literary work is anything which can be, and has been written down for the first time, any combination of letters thought out and written down, any tangible product of intellectual endeavour. Counsel referred us to Webster's dictionary, in which "work" is defined in one place as "something produced or accomplished by effort, exertion, or exercise of skill ... something produced by the exercise of creative talent or expenditure of creative effort". He says that this word satisfies those conditions. It does not matter how much work went into it, subject, perhaps, to the principle *de minimis lex non curat*; it does not matter how poor the quality of the work is, if it was the result, or the product of creative effort, the exercise of some skill and effort, it is a work, and if it is a work which is written down and consists of letters it is a literary work. If you take the phrase "original literary work" to pieces, this word Exxon is original for the reason that I have given, it is literary and it is a work. Why, then, is it not an original literary work? But he concedes, although he submits that it is helpful to split the phrase up into its three component words, that it is the expression as a whole in the context of the Act which has to be construed. "Literary" is given a broader meaning in the 1956 Act than it was given in the 1842 Act, and that broader meaning must colour and extend the meaning of "work". Some skill and care having been exerted in inventing this word by selecting these 4 letters out of the alphabet of 26, the word qualifies as an original literary work. Admittedly there is no authority for treating such a word as the subject of copyright, but counsel submits that in its plain and natural meaning this one word, meaningless though it is unless applied to a company or to goods, is an original literary work.

The only help from the authorities which I have found is the judgment of Peterson J in *University of London Press Ltd.* v *University Tutorial Press Ltd.* [1916] 2 Ch 601 which Graham J cited. In that case, Peterson J had to consider whether examination papers were the subject of copyright under s.1(1) of the Copyright Act 1911, which provided, exactly in the way provided by s.2 of the 1956 Act, for copyright in "every original literary dramatic musical and artistic work". Peterson J pointed out (at 608) that the 1842 Act protected books, and many things which had no pretensions to literary style acquired copyright ...

I think counsel was also entitled to rely on the "code" case of *D P Anderson & Co. Ltd.* v *Lieber Code Co.* [1917] 2 KB 469. In that case Mr Worrall had selected from an enormous number of words 100,000 five-letter words to form a suitable code for cabling purposes and Bailhache J was pressed with the argument that, these words being meaningless, except so far as they were fixed with the arbitrary meaning which the devisor of the code gave them in the so-called "Empire cipher code", they could not be literary, or a literary work. The learned judge rejected that argument and said (at 471):

> "The words - I call them so for want of a better name - are for use for telegraphic purposes, and to each of them a meaning can be attached by the person sending the message and also by the addressee, provided, of course, he is informed of the meaning attached to it by the sender,"

and he came to the conclusion that copyright did exist and that the defendants had infringed it, although it was a copyright in those very numerous and meaningless code words, meaningless only in the sense which I have described.

Counsel also referred us to observations of two learned judges, first of all observations made by Megarry J, in *British Northrop Ltd.* v *Texteam Blackburn Ltd.* [1974] RPC 57 at 68 in which he said:

> "I do not think that the mere fact that a drawing is of an elementary and commonplace article makes it too simple to be the subject of copyright."

He also referred us to an observation of Whitford J in *Karo Step Trade Mark* [1977] RPC 255 at 273:

> "No doubt a drawing may be so simple that it cannot be said to be 'a work' - for example, a straight line or a circle - for the word 'work' itself carries with it the idea of the exercise of some degree of skill and labour; but I am unable to accept the submission of counsel for [the appellant] that the artistic part of this device is of so simple a nature that no copyright can reside in it."

With those observations I do not, of course, quarrel, but I do not find them of much assistance in deciding whether this word Exxon qualifies as an original literary work, when I give those words in their context as ordinary a meaning as I can ...

The authorities to which counsel as *amicus curiae* next referred us are dicta, first of all of Parker J in *Burberry's* v *J C Cording & Co. Ltd.* (1909) 26 RPC 693 at 701, in which the learned judge said: "Apart from the law as to trade marks, no-one can claim monopoly rights in the use of a word or name"; and to dicta of Walton J in two more recent cases, the first being the "Wombles" case, *Wombles Ltd.* v *Wombles Skips Ltd.* [1977] RPC 99 at 101-102 where the learned judge said:

> "It seems to me that the only conceivable ground for suggesting any business connection between the plaintiff and the defendant is that the characters, albeit mythical, are characters who clean up premises, but I do not think that anybody seeing a 'Womble' skip, albeit in the road, albeit on one of the defendant's lorries, would think that there really was any connection between that and any business carried on by the plaintiff. The plaintiff's business is simply to license copyright reproductions. It may be a defect in the law that, having invented the characters known as the 'Wombles', the authoress has not a complete monopoly of the use of that invented word, which she could then assign to the plaintiffs, but such is the law and that being so it seems to me I must in fact dismiss this motion."

Very shortly after considering that matter, Walton J had to pass from considering the word "Wombles" to considering the work "Kojak", and in *Tavener Rutledge Ltd.* v *Trexapalm Ltd.* [1977] RPC 275 at 278 he said:

> " ... it may very well be that in the United States of America there are rights in invented names or invented fictional characters which are not recognised in this country because, so far as the law of England is concerned, we do not recognise any copyright or other species of property in any names or words, whether invented or not. I think that for that I need only quote two cases, *Day* v *Brownrigg* ((1878) 10 Ch D 294), and the well-known case of *Burberry's* v *J C Cording & Co. Ltd.*"

Those are dicta, and, as counsel for the plaintiff pointed out, in the first of those cases they were dicta in connection with the 1842 Act, and the second two cases were passing-off cases, where copyright was not directly in point. Nevertheless, it seems to have been assumed, both by Parker J in 1940 and by Walton J in 1975, that there could be no copyright in a name or a word, including an invented name or word.

As I read the judgment of Graham J, he was not prepared to accept those dicta as a full and complete statement of the law, and I find it unnecessary to decide whether what those learned judges said can be accepted without qualification. It is, however, certain that this is the first time, as far as the researches of counsel go, that any court has been asked to hold that there could be copyright in a single invented word or name. It was for that reason, as I understand it, that in this case Graham J sought the assistance of the Attorney General and invited counsel as *amicus curiae* to befriend the court. He felt that this claim raised a matter which might affect the public interest adversely in other cases and, as he said, it might be far-reaching in its consequences if granted.

I find rather more assistance in the last case to which counsel as *amicus curiae* referred us; in particular, the observations of Davey LJ in *Hollinrake* v *Truswell* [1894] 3 Ch 420 at 427-428. That case was concerned with copyright in a cardboard pattern sleeve with scales and figures and descriptive words on it. In his judgment Davey LJ said:

"The preamble of the Act [that was referring to the 1842 Act, of course] recites that it is expedient 'to afford greater encouragement to the production of literary works of lasting benefit to the world': and although I agree that the clear enactment of a statute cannot be controlled by the preamble, yet I think that the preamble may be usefully referred to for the purpose of ascertaining the class of works it was intended to protect. Now, a literary work is intended to afford either information and instruction, or pleasure, in the form of literary enjoyment. The sleeve chart before us gives no information or instruction. It does not add to the stock of human knowledge or give, and is not designed to give, any instruction by way of description or otherwise; and it certainly is not calculated to afford literary enjoyment or pleasure. It is a representation of the shape of a lady's arm, or more probably of a sleeve designed for a lady's arm, with certain scales for measurement upon it. It is intended, not for the purpose of giving information or pleasure, but for practical use in the art of dressmaking. It is, in fact, a mechanical contrivance, appliance or tool, for the better enabling a dressmaker to make her measurements for the purpose of cutting out of the sleeve of a lady's dress, and is intended to be used for that purpose. In my opinion it is no more entitled to copyright as a literary work than the scale attached to the barometer in *Davis* v *Comitti* ((1885) 54 LJ Ch 419)."

He agreed with Lindley LJ, I think, that the plaintiffs in that case were attempting to use the 1842 Act for a purpose to which it was not properly applicable.

Counsel for the plaintiffs says that those observations of Davey LJ as to what is a literary work must be considered in the light of the preamble to the 1842 Act, to which Davey LJ expressly referred. The words of Davey LJ do, however, appeal to me as stating the ordinary meaning of the words "literary work". I would have thought, unaided or unhampered by authority, that, unless there is something in the context of the 1956 Act which forbids it, a literary work would be something which was intended to afford either information and instruction or pleasure in the form of literary enjoyment, whatever those last six words may add to the word "pleasure". Counsel has not convinced me that this word Exxon was intended to do, or does do, either of those things; nor has he convinced me that it is not of the essence of a literary work that it should do one of those things. Nor has he convinced me that there is anything in the 1956 Act, or in what Peterson J said about the words in the earlier Act, or in any authority, or in principle, which compels me to give a different construction from Davey LJ's to the words "literary work". As I have already said, I agree with the way in which Graham J put the matter; I am not sure whether this can be said to be a "work" at all; I am clearly of the opinion that it cannot be said to be a literary work. I therefore agree with Graham J, and I would dismiss this appeal.

I should add a reference to the final submissions of counsel as *amicus curiae* that if we were to accede to this claim we should be endangering freedom of speech, and we should be ignoring the protection already given by the Trade Marks Act 1938.

I attach little weight to the first submission, because in my view counsel for the plaintiffs is right in saying that the plaintiffs have clearly impliedly licensed the world to use this word properly.

As to his second submission, it is noticeable that s.9(1)(c) of the Trade Marks Act 1938 does give protection to an invented word, or invented words; nevertheless I agree with Graham J that no great weight should be attached to the fact that adequate protection, or apparently adequate protection, is already provided to the plaintiffs under the Trade Marks Act 1938."

COMMENT

Why should the plaintiff not be content to rely on his trade mark registration or passing off to prevent the use of the name *Exxon* by others? Do you think that the *Exxon* case, particularly in relation to its approval of *Hollinrake* v *Truswell*, still represents good law, bearing in mind that computer programs are now protected by copyright as literary works? Do you think that Graham J, the judge at first instance, was correct in holding that the defendant's use of the name *Exxon* was passing off?

Authorship

The author of a work of copyright is, by section 9, the person who creates the work and by section 11, subject to exceptions, the author will be the first owner of the copyright. One might expect the author to be a living individual. The following entertaining and unusual case unsuccessfully challenged the basic rules.

Cummins v *Bond* [1927] 1 Ch 167, Chancery Division

The plaintiff was a medium and took part in séances. In a series of sittings with two others present, including the defendant, the plaintiff claimed to have made contact with a certain 'Cleophas' who had been alive around 2,000 years ago. The plaintiff had produced a written script whilst supposedly under the influence of Cleophas. It was in archaic language and was purported to concern the Apostles. The defendant was allowed to take the script away and he claimed to have added notes. He then attempted to publish the work and the plaintiff sought to prevent this on the basis that she was the owner of the copyright in the script by virtue of her authorship of it.

Eve J (at 172): 'The issue in this action is reduced to the simple question who, if any one, is the owner of the copyright in this work. *Prima facie* it is the author, and so far as this world is concerned there can be no doubt who is the author here, for it has been abundantly proved that the plaintiff is the writer of every word to be found in this bundle of original script. But the plaintiff and her witness and the defendant are all of opinion - and I do not doubt that the opinion is an honest one - that the true originator of all that is to be found in these documents is some being no longer inhabiting this world, and who has been out of it for a length of time sufficient to justify the hope that he has no reasons for wishing to return to it.

According to the case put forward by those entertaining the opinion I have referred to the individual in question is particularly desirous of assisting in further discoveries relating to the ancient Abbey of Glastonbury, and he chooses the Brompton Road as the locality in which, and the plaintiff as the medium through whom, his views as to further works to be undertaken on the site of the Abbey shall be communicated to the persons engaged in the work of excavation. He is sufficiently considerate not to do so in language so antiquated as not to be understood by the excavators and others engaged in the interesting operations, but in order not to appear of too modern an epoch he selects a medium capable of translating his messages into language appropriate to a period some sixteen or seventeen centuries after his death. I am not impugning the honesty of persons who believe, and of the parties to this action who say that they believe, that this long departed being is the true source from which the contents of these documents emanate: but I think I have stated enough with regard to the antiquity of the source and the language in which the communications are written to indicate that they could not have reached us in this form without the active co-operation of some agent competent to translate them from the language in which they were communicated to her into something more intelligible to persons of the present day. The plaintiff claims to be this agent and to possess, and the defendant admits that she does possess, some qualification enabling her, when in a more or less unconscious condition, to reproduce in language understandable by those who have the time and inclination to read it, information supplied to her from the source referred to in language with which the plaintiff has no acquaintance when fully awake.

From this it would almost seem as though the individual who has been dead and buried for some 1900 odd years and the plaintiff ought to be regarded as the joint authors and owners of the copyright, but inasmuch as I do not feel myself competent to make any declaration in his favour, and recognizing as I do that I have no jurisdiction extending to the sphere in which he moves, I think I ought to confine myself when inquiring who is the author to individuals who were alive when the work first came into existence and to conditions which the legislature in 1911 may reasonably be presumed to have contemplated. So doing it would seem to be clear that the authorship rests with this lady, to whose gift of extremely rapid writing coupled with a peculiar ability to reproduce in archaic English matter communicated to her in some unknown tongue we owe the production of these documents. But the defendant disputes the plaintiff's right to be considered the sole author, alleging that he was an element and a necessary element in the production, and claiming, if the authorship is to be confined to persons resident in this world, that he is entitled to the rights incident to authorship jointly with the plaintiff.

In the course of the trial, after reading the correspondence, ... In my opinion the plaintiff has made out her case, and the copyright rests with her.

Upon the same footing it has been further contended on behalf of the defendant that an agreement was come to between him and the plaintiff under which he is beneficially interested in the copyright, or alternatively that the conduct of the plaintiff has been such as to estop her from denying that he has such an interest. In order to determine these questions the evidence and correspondence require some examination ... It is quite clear that no agreement was ever concluded, and I am quite unable to hold that the plaintiff ever abandoned the position she took up in the latter part of the year 1925 or ever so conducted herself as to preclude her from insisting on the claims put forward in this action. Accordingly I hold she is entitled to the declaration for which she asks, that is to say, a declaration that she is the owner of the copyright in this work - it must be identified in some way - delivery up of such parts of the original manuscript as have not already been handed to her, and the defendant must pay the costs of the action.'

COMMENT

Was the plaintiff the joint author (with Cleophas) or the sole author? What if a person creates rules for an expert system to produce financial advice and, after that person's death, another person uses the expert system, supplying necessary answers to questions asked by the system, to produce a financial report? Who is/are the author(s) of the report? Or is it a computer-generated work, being one created in circumstances such that there is no human author? Does copyright law permit non-human authors?

Ownership of Copyright

The basic rule is that the author of a work of copyright will be its first owner. There are some exceptions, a major one being where the author is an employee who has created the work in the course of his employment. Ownership may be transferred by way of an assignment which must be in writing and signed by or on behalf of the then owner of the copyright. The following case examines the question of whether a person is an employee and the capacity of the person signing on behalf of the assignor.

Beloff v Pressdram Ltd. [1973] 1 All ER 241, Chancery Division

The plaintiff was an employee of *The Observer* newspaper although she did not have a written contract of employment. There were some factors that suggested that she may have been an employee for copyright purposes. A third party wrote an article for *Private Eye* containing an attack upon a member of the government (Mr Maudling). The plaintiff wrote a memorandum to the editor of *The Observer* about a conversation she had had with another member of the government who had said that, should anything happen to the Prime Minister, he was sure that Mr Maudling would take over as Prime Minister. The plaintiff then wrote an article attacking the article in *Private Eye*. The author of the *Private Eye* article wrote a reply which contained the full text of the plaintiff's memorandum. In order to enable her to sue for infringement of copyright, the editor of *The Observer* purported to assign the copyright in the memorandum to the plaintiff who then sued the publisher of *Private Eye*.

Ungoed-Thomas J (at 246): '(1) *Was the copyright originally vested in the Observer Ltd. or the plaintiff?* I will deal first with the law. The copyright subsisted in the memorandum as an unpublished literary work and both the plaintiff and The Observer Ltd. were qualified to own the copyright in it: see Copyright Act 1956, ss.1(1), (5)(a), 2(1), (5), 49(2), (3)(a).
    The original ownership of the copyright in this case is governed by s.4(1) and (4). These subsections read;

    "(1) Subject to the provisions of this section, the author of a work shall be entitled to any copyright subsisting in the work by virtue of this Part of this Act."

"(4) Where ... a work is made in the course of the author's employment by another person under a contract of service or apprenticeship, that other person shall be entitled to any copyright subsisting in the work by virtue of this Part of this Act."

So if this case falls within sub-s.(4) the original copyright was in The Observer Ltd. otherwise it was in the plaintiff.

The memorandum was clearly made in the course of the plaintiff's employment by The Observer Ltd: nor was this disputed. The only question is whether the plaintiff's employment was under a contract of service. If yes, the copyright originally vested in The Observer Ltd.; if not, it vested in the plaintiff.

The distinction, familiar to lawyers, is between contract of service and contract for services. ...

In *Market Investigations Ltd.* v *Minister of Social Security* [1969] 2 QB 173 it was held that a part-time interviewer engaged by a market research company was under a contract of service. Cooke J observed (at 184):

"The observations of Lord Wright, of Denning LJ, and of the judges of the Supreme Court in the USA suggest that the fundamental test to be applied is this: 'Is the person who has engaged himself to perform these services performing them as a person in business on his own account?'. If the answer to that question is 'yes', then the contract is a contract for services. If the answer is 'no' then the contract is a contract of service. No exhaustive list has been compiled and perhaps no exhaustive list can be compiled of considerations which are relevant in determining that question, nor can strict rules be laid down as to the relative weight which the various considerations should carry in particular cases. The most that can be said is that control will no doubt always have to be considered, although it can no longer be regarded as the sole determining factor; and that factors, which may be of importance, are such matters as whether the man performing the services provides his own equipment, whether he hires his own helpers, what degree of financial risk he takes, what degree of responsibility for investment and management he has, and whether and how far he has an opportunity of profiting from sound management in the performance of his task."

Cooke J continued (at 188):

"The opportunity to deploy individual skill and personality is frequently present in what is undoubtedly a contract of service. I have already said that the right to work for others is not inconsistent with the existence of a contract of service. Mrs Irving did not provide her own tools or risk her own capital, nor did her opportunity of profit depend in any significant degree on the way she managed her work."

It thus appears, and rightly in my respectful view, that, the greater the skill required for an employee's work, the less significant is control in determining whether the employee is under a contract of service. Control is just one of many factors whose influence varies according to circumstances. In such highly skilled work as that of the plaintiff it seems of no substantial significance. The test which emerges from the authorities seems to me, as Denning LJ said (in *Stevenson Jordan and Harrison Ltd.*

v *Macdonald and Evans* [1952] 1 TLR at 111) whether on the one hand the employee is employed as part of the business and his work is an integral part of the business, or whether his work is not integrated into the business but is only accessory to it, or, as Cooke J expressed it (in *Market Investigations Ltd.* v *Minister of Social Security* [1969] 2 QB at 184), the work is done by him in business on his own account.

The only documents produced relating to the nature of the plaintiff's employment were two letters of 1947 and 1948 and two statements by The Observer Ltd. directed to the plaintiff under the Contracts of Employment Act 1963 and the Industrial Relations Act 1971.

The first letter, dated 19th September 1947, was from the editor of the Observer to the plaintiff confirming her appointment as Paris correspondent with a yearly salary and expenses. It reads:

"We are very pleased to hear that you are willing to become Paris correspondent for The Observer and The Observer Foreign News Service. You have done excellent work for us on the Paris Conference, and I am happy to confirm your appointment, as from November 2nd, 1947, and for an initial period of six months, at the rate of £750 a year, plus expenses incurred on our behalf. We hope it will be possible, as you indicate, to keep the expenses within reasonable limits. In addition to full week-end coverage for The Observer, and the occasional provision of Profile, obituary and Notebook material as the needs arise, we shall require a minimum of one article a week, by mail or telephone, for Servob. (Hitherto we have stipulated two Servob articles weekly from our correspondents, but in practice one is usually sufficient. We should, however, like to be able to call on you for additional Servob articles in special circumstances, which would include occasions like the Paris Conference.) Your name will be used on all Servob contributions; for The Observer our customary rule is that correspondents' names are used on major pieces (leader-page articles, Notebooks, important and exclusive news stories), but not necessarily on all items of straight-forward reporting; and we shall prefer to apply this rather flexible rule to you, too. I understand you will be in London next month; we shall be happy to see you then to discuss any further aspects of your appointment."

The second letter is dated 15th October 1948 and made a different appointment on different terms. It appointed the plaintiff to the staff of the Observer, first in London and then in Washington for some years, on a full-time basis at a yearly salary of £1,200 in London and a salary with living allowance elsewhere. As far as it is material it reads:

"This is to inform you officially that we would like you to come back to London at the end of November and to join our staff on a whole-time basis. We would want you to leave for Washington at the end of December and to remain there for at least one year and more probably for several years. I suggested to you that we should ensure your future by giving you a contract for five years. I am quite confident that you can be an asset to this paper for much longer than that, but would like to ask you if a three year promise of employment would satisfy you. The reason for asking this is simply that five years is much longer than we promise any of the other members of the staff and might therefore cause some indignation amongst them. The promise of employment would be subject to your being willing to write whenever the paper might need you most and not necessarily in Washington all the time. The financial terms of our offer are a combined salary-cum-living-allowance while in Washington of £2,000 per annum; when elsewhere your salary would be at £1,200 with an additional living allowance if outside Britain. We will, of course, have to talk over details of office accommodation, travel expenses, etcetera with you before you go to Washington."

The two statutory statements came after the plaintiff's appointment as political and lobby correspondent of the Observer. The first is addressed to the plaintiff under the Contracts of Employment Act 1963, and states that the Act requires The Observer Ltd. to state certain of the main terms and conditions on which it employs "you Nora Leah Beloff as at August 1, 1964". It states the commencement of employment as 1947, the rate of remuneration as £3,000 per year, the normal hours of work "subject to day to day circumstances", as 10.00am to 6.00pm Tuesday to Friday, "and as required by the Head of your Department on Saturday". "Your employment is subject to six months' notice on either side" and "Your paid holiday entitlement is four weeks per calendar year" with bank holidays, with the provision that, "All holiday dates are to be settled by agreement with the Head of your Department/the Manager": and that sickness payments are considered individually.

The second statement is described as a supplementary statement and is headed by reference to the 1963 Act as amended by the Industrial Relations Act 1971. It is addressed to the plaintiff and includes a statement that she is entitled to receive, and required to give notice of termination of employment under her contract, or national agreements entered into by her trade union or in accordance with the above Acts.

The plaintiff said that she assumed that she was in the Observer as a result of the 1947 letter, but that she did not remember signing it. She was in Washington for the Observer from 1949 to 1950 as contemplated by the 1948 letter, and I have no doubt that those letters stated the terms under which she immediately thereafter entered on her work for The Observer.

She said, however, that she must have received the statutory statements but that she did not think that she read them. It is of course clear that her work was not regulated by any specified hours; that she worked late hours, and had more than four weeks' holiday. It was submitted for the plaintiff that the statements were documents issued by The Observer Ltd. and she was not bound by them. But she recognised that she must have received them, although she might not have read them; and it does at any rate seem that even after the coming into force of the Industrial Relations Act 1971 her employers did not contemplate her as being outside the Act. But I do not rely on these statements in deciding whether or not the plaintiff was under a contract of service.

The editor of the Observer said in evidence in answer to a question whether he could direct the plaintiff to New York or elsewhere, that it was for him to allocate jobs; and since 1948, before her appointment as political and lobby correspondent, she was directed not only to Washington and to Moscow, but to cover Common Market negotiations, and since that appointment she has also done some foreign assignments for The Observer.

Like many journalists, such as Mr Howard, editor of the New Statesman, who gave evidence, she has broadcast and appeared on television. And she has written on occasions for certain other papers such as the Atlantic Monthly and Punch, and she has had leaves from The Observer to write books. But these incidents do not appear to have affected the permanent basis of her salaried employment with The Observer, and appear to have been, in the case of leaves for writing books at any rate, with the consent of The Observer. Indeed, leave itself tends to indicate a permanent full-time job on the staff.

In 1964 the plaintiff was appointed political and lobby correspondent of The Observer, and she has since done that job interspersed with the foreign assignments for The Observer as I have mentioned. As the accredited lobby correspondent for The Observer she holds a very important and regular position in The Observer organisation, and, so far as I know, she is the only person in The Observer organisation who holds such a position. It means that she has on behalf of The Observer the advantages essential to a great national newspaper, of special access to the House of Commons, of arrangements available to the group of lobby correspondents, including various forms of help and briefings which are important, not only for writing informed articles but also for obtaining news items earlier than would otherwise be available for The Observer. This means, of course, that it is essential for The Observer that she keeps in constant touch with Parliament at all hours when any such advantages are likely to be gained by doing so. Her work as lobby correspondent, as she explained, is not just the production of an article but also the reporting of political news. This work includes news and other coverage of Parliamentary occurrences for The Observer, including in particular briefings, news and other advantages which, as I have indicated, the lobby correspondent is appointed by his paper to obtain and supply. The job of political and lobby correspondent for The Observer is essential for and woven into its political coverage. Such a paper as The Observer without its accredited lobby correspondent is hardly conceivable.

The plaintiff writes for The Observer a weekly article headed "Politics - Nora Beloff": it is usually on one theme. She also writes profiles, and on the major speeches of politicians, and she even writes leaders. The editor described her as "a very active member of the general editorial staff" and said that she shared in the editorial responsibility of the newspaper. She is a regular attendant at weekly and *ad hoc* editorial meetings presided over by the editor and whose wide scope is indicated by the functions of those who attend - deputy and assistant editors, chief reporters, the business editor, the leader writer, the news editor, and others as advisable from time to time. The plaintiff said its purpose was to plan the paper for the next issue to look ahead and to have a general discussion and exchange ideas. She said that her article for the following issue was very often discussed. The editor said that she tells him what she is going to write and that discussion only arises if it overlaps with something else. The editor has certainly some strong-minded persons attending these meetings and, as might be expected from his experience and wisdom, he said that "my government is as a rule consensual". The plaintiff said that she was free to decline to write on a suggested topic. Of course, she could not be forced to do so, nor can I imagine Mr Astor attempting to force her. The editorial meetings are for discussion, without power of decision; that rests solely with the editor, and not the less so, although as a rule consensually exercised by him.

I come to other recognised indications of contract of service, in addition to her substantial regular salary for her full-time job and her holidays. Apart from an electric typewriter, which the plaintiff has at home, the plaintiff does not provide any equipment of her own which she uses for her work. All The Observer's resources are available to her to carry out her job. She has an office in The Observer building, and a secretary who is provided by The Observer. She does not use her own capital for the job, nor is her remuneration affected by the financial success or otherwise of The Observer. In addition to PAYE deductions, deduction for the pension scheme to which she belongs is also made by The Observer from her salary. All these indications are in favour of her contract being a contract of service. .

The submission relied on for a contrary conclusion was, as I have indicated, that such contracts were limited to contracts to do lowly tasks under supervision. But this became clearly unsustainable, and at a later stage it was submitted that the overriding consideration was whether the plaintiff produced an article every week or worked full-time for the Observer or, as it was put, whether she was a contributor and not a reporter. But this submission clearly fails on the facts which I have stated - her job was full-time and was far from being limited to a weekly article and in fact included reporting Parliamentary events. Nor (in accordance with, e.g. *Market Investigations Ltd.* v *Minister of Social Security* [1969] 2 QB at 176) does a full-time contract of service exclude some television and broadcasting appearances and the writing of such articles as she wrote for Punch and Atlantic Monthly.

I have increasingly in the course of this case, as the relevant facts came to be deployed, inclined to the conclusion which I now firmly hold that the plaintiff's job is "an integral part of the business" of The Observer and its organisation and that the plaintiff's contract with The Observer Ltd. is a contract of service. My conclusion, therefore, is that the copyright in the memorandum originally vested in The Observer Ltd. and not in the plaintiff.

(2) *Was the purported assignment made without authority?*
The purported assignment is in these terms:

"I DAVID ASTOR, for and on behalf of The Observer Limited of 160 Queen Victoria Street in Greater London, Editor of The Observer, Hereby assign the copyright of The Observer Limited in a Memorandum dated 17th February 1971 entitled 'Maudling' written by Miss Nora Beloff in so far as The Observer Limited may be entitled thereto to Miss Nora Beloff of 25 Walsingham Street, St John's Wood Park, NW 8, together with any accrued rights of action therein. Dated this 26th day of March 1971. Signed by the said DAVID ASTOR for and on behalf of The Observer Limited [and then Mr Astor's signature]."

Assignment of copyright is, so far as is relevant for present purposes, governed by s.36(1) and (3) of the 1956 Act. They read, so far as is material:

"(1) Subject to the provisions of this section, copyright shall be transmissible by assignment ... as personal or moveable property.
(3) No assignment of copyright ... shall have effect unless it is in writing signed by or on behalf of the assignor."

It is, of course, common ground that an assignment cannot be assigned on behalf of an assignor without his authority. Hence this issue.

The articles of association of The Observer Ltd. provide as follows so far as they might conceivably be thought to have any bearing on this question: by art 89 that the directors may entrust to and confer on a managing director any of the powers exercisable by them; by art 90, in the usual way, that the business of the company shall be managed by the directors; by art 94 which deals with the "Editor of The Observer newspaper" and with "General Manager", and which provides:

> "Every appointment of an Editor or General Manager shall be upon such terms and conditions as the Trustees shall prescribe, and if there shall be any vacancy in either of those offices the Directors shall appoint such persons to fill the vacancy as shall be nominated in writing by the Trustees";

by art 108 that the directors may delegate any of their powers to committees consisting of a member or members of their body; by art 112 that directors shall cause proper minutes to be made of proceedings of all meetings of directors and committees and all business transacted thereat; by art 113 that a resolution in writing signed by all the directors shall be as effective as a resolution passed at a meeting of directors.

The crucial evidence on this aspect of the case is that of the editor. He said in his evidence-in-chief that he executed the assignment and was authorised by The Observer Ltd. to do so and that it was within the scope of his authority to execute "such documents" on behalf of The Observer. But the transcript of his cross-examination on this evidence reads:

> "*Q* I can, I think, ask you this. Do you often effect assignments of copyrights?
> *A* No, I do not.
> "*Q* Have you ever assigned a copyright before? *A* I suppose I probably have because people's articles are reproduced in book form and I suppose I would have assigned copyright in those cases.
> "*Q* What do you do if that happens - do they write and ask you for permission? *A* Yes.
> "*Q* And then you write back and say 'Yes, you may'? *A* In effect, yes.
> "*Q* So you give them a licence to publish? *A* Yes, presumably.
> "*Q* I repeat my question: Have you ever signed any such document as this before, which I gather you will take from me *prima facie* constitutes an assignment of copyright? *A* I do not think I have.
> "*Q* When you told Mr Mervyn Davies that you were authorised by The Observer to execute this document, what did you mean? *A* How do you mean?
> "*Q* They are your words, and I am asking you to say what you meant when you gave an affirmative answer. *A* I consulted my colleagues, my directorial colleagues and managerial colleagues, as to whether there was any reason why this should not be done. I assumed in fact as editor I had the right to do it, but in case it required any support from the management I asked my colleagues on the management and they agreed that I have this right.
> "*Q* Was there any meeting of the Board of The Observer? *A* No, not with this.
> "*Q* Do you as editor have any directive from the Board rather as if a General is sent to the Middle East and he is told, 'Your mandate is to re-take Tobruk', or something like that - are you given such a document? *A* No."

It seemed to me clear beyond doubt that when the editor gave his evidence, and it so seems to me now, that the answers in cross-examination were by way of amplifying with the result of limiting and correcting the impression which might be obtained from reading his evidence-in-chief. His answers in cross-examination disclose that he had no specific or general authority from the board of directors to execute an assignment of copyright. Any colleagues whom he consulted clearly did not constitute a board or even all the directors signing a resolution within art 113, and clearly they did not even purport to make any decision at all. Nothing in writing or even oral was referred to as conferring the necessary authority on him. But, of course, it is proved that Mr Astor is editor of The Observer and thus this issue came to turn on whether or not his appointment as editor carried automatically with it authority to assign copyright. It is, of course, for the plaintiff to establish such authority, and so I come to the evidence of the scope of the editor's authority to assign copyright.

In 24 years as editor of The Observer he had never assigned copyright. What he had done or purported to do was by correspondence to agree to the reproduction in a particular book of a particular Observer article, i.e. to give a limited licence, limited to production in a particular book, a particular work already published in the paper of which he was editor. But such licence is, of course, very different from assignment, the out and out parting with all rights in a work for all time, the transfer of the property of The Observer Ltd. And in this case the work whose copyright was assigned was not an article or any other work which had appeared in his newspaper; it had not been published at all. It was purported to be assigned not even for publication but to further an action contemplated by the assignee, an action which would inevitably involve The Observer without The Observer being a party to it. These considerations tell against the editor automatically having by virtue of his appointment authority to assign copyright and, a fortiori, against authority to assign such copyright as is the subject of this action.

It is clear from the first part of the transcript of evidence which I have quoted that Mr Astor did not often even write permitting the reproduction of an Observer article; he was in some confusion about licences and assignments; and even contemplated such licences as "assignments". It was in this state of confusion that he "assumed in fact as editor I had the right to do it", that is execute the assignment. But it appears that he was in sufficient doubt about it to consult colleagues, "my directorial and managerial colleagues", "my colleagues in the management", from which I gather he meant managers and executive directors at hand, possibly in The Observer office. But whatever their number or function, they were not, as I have said, conferring authority or making any decision. They were, at its highest, expressing or concurring with a view. We do not know precisely the circumstances, the questions or the answers, and not one of them has appeared in court to express or substantiate his view with reference to the authority of an editor to assign copyright in general, or in such a work as the memorandum in particular, and to be cross-examined, as Mr Astor was, on his evidence-in-chief. Nor has anyone else been called, as might be expected, to establish that it is in general by custom or practice or otherwise within the ambit of an editor's authority to assign copyright, much less the copyright of such a work as this memorandum.

So my conclusion on the evidence as a whole is that it has not been established that Mr Astor had authority to execute this assignment on behalf of The Observer Ltd.'

COMMENT

When is an employee not an employee? Why did the editor wish to assign the copyright in the memorandum to the plaintiff? Does it seem strange that it was held that the editor of a newspaper does not, on the facts of this particular case, have authority to assign copyright? What is the difference between an assignment and a licence?

The employer will normally be the first owner of the copyright in works created by his employees in the course of their employment. However, this is subject to agreement to the contrary and such agreement may be implied, particularly on the basis of past practice.

Noah v *Shuba* [1991] FSR 14, Chancery Division

The plaintiff, a consultant epidemiologist, was employed by Public Health Laboratory Service (PHLS). The first defendant was the managing director of the second defendant, a company selling products used by beauty therapists. The plaintiff wrote 'A Guide to Hygienic Skin Piercing' which he wrote during evenings and weekends whilst employed by PHLS. It was published by PHLS in 1982 and the plaintiff sent a copy to the first defendant. There was a copyright notice on the copy. The first defendant made some use of the guide but eventually wrote a report for publication in a magazine. The report included extracts of the plaintiff's guide including a reference to a particular cold sterilisation solution. The plaintiff had previously refused to recommend use of the solution but the report gave the impression that the plaintiff endorsed the views of the first defendant that there was no risk of infection following use of the solution. This was done by way of slight alterations to the extracts from the plaintiff's guide. The plaintiff sued for copyright infringement, false attribution and defamation. One preliminary issue was whether the plaintiff was the owner of the copyright in the guide.

Mummery J (at 24): 'The first issue which I have to decide is whether Dr Noah is the owner of the copyright in the *Guide*. It is common ground that:

(1)   Copyright subsists in the *Guide*.
(2)   Dr Noah is the sole author of the *Guide*.
(3)   Dr Noah was employed at the relevant time under a contract of service with PHLS.
(4)   Substantial parts of the *Guide* have been reproduced in the form of two extracts quoted in the article published in the *Health & Beauty Salon* magazine in October 1986.

The contention that Dr Noah is not the owner of the copyright in the *Guide* is based on section 4(4) of the Copyright Act 1956 which provides that where:

" ... a work is made in the course of the author's employment by another person under a contract of service ... that other person shall be entitled to any copyright subsisting in the work ... "

This provision has effect subject, however, in any particular case "... to any agreement excluding the operation thereof in that case": section 4(5).

Before going to the evidence on the terms of Dr Noah's contract of service and of the circumstances in which he wrote the *Guide*, it is important to note that the effect of section 20(2) of the Copyright Act 1956 is to presume that, as Dr Noah's name appeared as author of the *Guide* on the copies of it as published, he is presumed, unless the contrary is proved, not only to be the author of the work but also to have made it in circumstances *not* falling within section 4(4). The burden of proof is, therefore, on Mr Shuba to establish that the *Guide* was made by Dr Noah in the course of his employment by PHLS.

I should also mention that it has been accepted on behalf of Dr Noah that, as a matter of construction, the contrary "agreement" referred to in section 4(5) must have been made *before* the relevant work came into existence. Any agreement made *after* the work came into existence could only take effect, if at all, as an assignment or licence of copyright which had already, by operation of section 4(4), automatically vested in PHLS as employer. The evidence shows that after Dr Noah had almost completed the manuscript for the *Guide* he had discussions with the administrator of PHLS, Mr Adrian Collins, about the copyright position. As a result of those discussions and of enquiries made by Mr Collins from the British Library, the *Guide* was published bearing the copyright notice stating that Dr Noah was the owner of the copyright. Nothing was agreed, however, in those discussions which could be relied upon by Dr Noah as a legal or equitable assignment to him of any copyright in the *Guide* that may have vested in PHLS. The present matter therefore turns on whether section 4(4) and (5) applies to the present case.

The primary submission made on behalf of Dr Noah is that the copyright in the *Guide* did not vest in the PHLS as his employer because he had not made it 'in the course of his employment' with PHLS. His evidence, which I accept, is that he wrote the *Guide* at home in the evenings and at weekends and not at the instigation of or on the direction of PHLS.

On behalf of Mr Shuba many points have been taken on the evidence as indicating that Dr Noah wrote the *Guide* in the course of his employment. It has been pointed out that under the terms of his conditions of service, which do not expressly deal with the matter of copyright, he was expected to report on research work by means of contributions to appropriate scientific journals and before recognized learned societies. Regulation 11 of the Staff Regulations provided that before doing so he should inform the Director of the Service and follow the normal practice of consulting colleagues who have been associated with him in collaborative investigations. It was, however, also provided in regulation 11 that the writing of scientific books or monographs, if undertaken, was "not expected to be done in working hours." It is also clear from regulation 3(b) and (c) that the writing of books and articles was in general to be regarded as something done "in addition to official duties," though staff were entitled to undertake such work at the laboratory or elsewhere and to receive fees, provided that the work would not interfere with their official duties.

Mr Price, on behalf of Mr Shuba, pointed out that the PHLS functions included the provision to persons perceived as needing it information relevant to the control of infectious diseases; that the *Guide* fell within those functions and had been printed and published by PHLS at public expense; that Dr Noah's duties included the making of investigations and provision of information on subjects which were covered by the *Guide*; that the *Guide* had been designed to enable health authorities and other bodies to set and observe high and uniform standards in the implementation of the 1928 Act; that it could not be said that Dr Noah had undertaken the writing of the book in any private capacity and that the preparation of the *Guide* could not be properly described as a "private" venture by Dr Noah, since it was clear from the cover and the title page that it was a PHLS guide. The previous 1979 *Tattooing Guide* had been signed by Dr Noah in his official capacity as a consultant at the Communicable Diseases Surveillance Centre. The evidence showed that Dr Noah had used PHLS notepaper in order to send out letters to those from whom he solicited comments and views before settling on the final version of the *Guide*. The typescript of the *Guide* had been produced by his secretary at the Centre using PHLS time and equipment. In brief, it was submitted that the *Guide* was a PHLS venture involving the collaboration of staff at PHLS premises, including Dr Noah's colleague, Mr Peter Hoffman, who wrote one of the appendices in the *Guide*. Mr Price submitted that, if the court accepted Dr Noah's contention, this would result in the surprising consequence that Dr Noah, as owner of the copyright, would be in a position to invoke that copyright in order to prevent PHLS from reprinting and disseminating the *Guide* without his permission. This was surprising, it was argued, in view of the public functions of PHLS and the public interest in the whole question of hygiene and infectious disease. I have not been persuaded by these points that Mr Shuba has discharged the burden of proving that Dr Noah made the *Guide* in the course of his employment. In my judgment, Dr Noah's position is very similar to that of the accountant in *Stevenson Jordan and Harrison Ltd.* v *McDonald & Evans* [1952] 1 TLR 101 in relation to copyright in lectures delivered by the accountant author who was employed under a contract of service. It was held that the provisions of the Copyright Act 1911 equivalent to section 4(4) did not apply. At page 111 Denning LJ pointed out that it had to be remembered that a man employed under a contract of service may sometimes perform services outside the contract. He gave the instance of a doctor on the staff of a hospital or the master on the staff of a school employed under a contract of service giving lectures or lessons orally to students. He expressed the view that if, for his own convenience, he put the lectures into writing then his written work was not done under the contract of service. It might be a useful accessory to his contracted work, but it was not part of it and the copyright vested in him and not in his employers. Morris LJ also pointed out that, even though the employer in that case paid the expenses of the lecturer incurred in the delivery of a lecture and was prepared to type the lectures as written by any lecturer and even though it would not have been improper for that lecturer to have prepared his lecture in the company's time and used material obtained from its library, it had not been shown that the accountant could have been ordered to write or deliver the lectures or that it was part of his duty to write or deliver them. In those circumstances the lectures were not written in the course of his employment.

Although that conclusion is sufficient to dispose of the issue on ownership of copyright, I should add that, even if I had found that the *Guide* had been written by Dr Noah in the course of his employment, I would have found on the evidence before me that there was an implied term of his contract of service excluding the operation of the statutory rule in section 4(4) vesting the copyright in the work so made in the employer PHLS. Evidence was given by Dr Noah and also by Dr Christine Miller, who was a consultant epidemiologist at PHLS from 1967 to 1987 and the author of numerous publications on vaccination, that it had for long been the practice at PHLS for employees there to retain the copyright in work written by them, usually in the form of articles, in the course of their employment there. If, for example, the articles were published in learned journals, it was the author of the article and not the PHLS who, at the insistence of most learned journals, assigned the copyright to the publishers of the journal in question. At no relevant time has the copyright in those articles been claimed by PHLS. It has acquiesced in a practice under which that copyright was retained and then assigned by the employee authors. The position of the PHLS in relation to this case is consistent with that practice. It has accepted that the copyright in the *Guide* is vested in Dr Noah. In my judgment, this long-standing practice is sufficient material from which I can and do imply that it was a term of Dr Noah's appointment as consultant that he should be entitled to retain the copyright in works written by him in the course of his employment.'

COMMENT

A narrow interpretation of 'in the course of employment' was taken in line with precedent. The operation of an implied term negating the normal rule reinforced the view that Dr Noah owned the copyright in question. Copyright can vest in an employee on the basis of a prior oral or implied term - is this sufficient as regards works previously created, that is, retrospectively? Who owns the copyright in a book written by a university lecturer which is based on his lectures given at the university to the students?

Implied Licence

Where there is a defect in a purported assignment of copyright or, from the facts, it would appear that the intention of the parties was to transfer ownership of copyright, the courts will often use the concept of beneficial ownership of copyright. In other circumstances the court may be prepared to imply a licence to allow a person, possibly a third party, to perform some act restricted by copyright.

Blair v *Osborne & Tomkins* [1971] 2 WLR 503, Court of Appeal

An architect was commissioned to prepare plans for a pair of houses so that the client could obtain planning permission. The architect, the plaintiff in the case, retained ownership of the copyright in the plans. After obtaining planning permission, the client sold the building site to a third party who was given copies of the architect's plans. The third party engaged their own surveyors who modified the plans and, putting their own name on the plans, submitted them for building regulations approval. Eventually, the houses were built in accordance with the plans. The architect sued for infringement of copyright but the county court awarded him nominal damages only. He appealed to the Court of Appeal.

Lord Denning MR (at 506): 'It is quite plain that Mr Blair was entitled to the copyright in his drawings. He drew them himself, and that makes him *prima facie* the owner of the copyright in them. Furthermore, it is one of the RIBA conditions: "Copyright in all drawings and in the work executed from them will remain the property of the architect." As owner of the copyright, Mr Blair was certainly entitled to stop people in general from copying his drawings, or building a house from them; but that is subject to this qualification: he could not complain of anything for which he had given licence or permission. The question in this case is whether he had given a licence.

The RIBA conditions do not give any guidance on this question of licence. But they do contain a condition [Condition of Engagement I] which is of some relevance:

"An engagement entered into between the architect and the client may be terminated at any time by either party upon reasonable notice being given."

Suppose now that after the architect has made the plans, a contract is made by the owner with a builder whereby the builder is to build the house in accordance with the plans: and then the architect says he will go on no longer as architect for the work, and gives one month's notice. Can the architect refuse to let the owner and the builder use the plans and make the house from them? Surely not. At that stage, at any rate, when the owner has placed a contract for the work, the architect must be taken to have impliedly licensed the work to be done in accordance with the plans. Now take it back to an earlier stage, when the architect has drawn plans and obtained planning permission on the faith of them, and been paid for them. Can the architect then withdraw from the work and refuse to let the owner use the plans? Surely not. That shows that, at that stage also, the architect must be taken to have impliedly licensed the building to proceed in accordance with the plans.

Those illustrations show, to my mind, that when the owner of a building plot employs an architect to prepare plans for a house on that site, the architect impliedly promises that, in return for his fee, he will give a licence to the owner to use the plans for the building on that site. The copyright remains in the architect, so that he can stop anyone else copying his plans, or making a house from them; but he cannot stop the owner, who employed him, from doing work on that very site in accordance with the plans. If the owner employs a builder or another architect, the implied licence extends so as to enable them to make copies of the plans and to use them for that very building on that site: but for no other purpose. If the owner should sell the site, the implied licence extends so as to avail the purchaser also.

There is no authority in this country on this subject. But I am glad to find that there is a case in the Supreme Court of New South Wales. It is *Beck* v *Montana Constructions Pty. Ltd.* [1964-5] NSWR 229. I find the reasoning of Jacobs J very convincing. He said, at p.235:

" ... the payment for sketch plans includes a permission or consent to use those sketch plans for the purpose for which they were brought into existence, namely, for the purpose of building a building in substantial accordance with them and for the purpose of preparing any necessary drawings as part of the task of building the building."

I entirely agree.

Applying this principle, it seems to me that the payment of £70 to Mr Blair covered the use of the drawings, not only by Mr Underwood and Mr Norris themselves, but also by the people to whom they sold the plot, and by the surveyors and workmen of the purchasers, so that they might make copies of them and otherwise use them in the accustomed way for building a house on this site. I think that the claim for infringement of copyright fails.

But there is one small point I should mention. When Osborne & Tomkins put in their detail plan to the local council, they put their own name on it as though it were

all their own work; whereas, it was not all their own work. Part of it was Mr Blair's original drawings. It is conceded that the implied licence did not enable them to put forward part of his work as their own. To that extent, therefore, it was not licensed. But no damage flowed from that misdescription. The local authority said that the name on the document did not influence them. For that technical infringement the judge awarded nominal damages of 40s. Subject to that small nominal award, the judge dismissed the claim and gave no further damages. I think that was quite right.
  The appeal should be dismissed.'

COMMENT
The architect had a contract with the original owner of the land but not with the purchaser. The doctrine of privity of contract would not enable the purchaser to require the architect to deliver the plans to him had they not yet been delivered. Yet the law of copyright allows the purchaser to use the plans. Is this equivalent to saying that the benefit of the original agreement was assignable to a third party? Simply changing the architect's name on the plans was not, at the time, an act restricted by copyright (now it would be an infringement of the architect's moral right to be identified as the author of the plans) so how could Lord Denning find that Osborne and Tomkins had infringed the copyright subsisting in the plans? Would this be a suitable case for additional damages?

Moral Rights

The Copyright, Designs and Patents Act 1988 provides for a range of moral rights including a right to be identified as the author of a work (or director of a film) and right to object to a derogatory treatment of a work (or film). One pre-existing right is a right not to have a work falsely attributed. The following case, brought under the 1956 Act, is important as showing that the meaning of a 'work' in this context can be surprising, bearing in mind the *de minimis* rule.

Noah v Shuba [1991] FSR 14, Chancery Division

The facts are stated in the extract of this case reproduced earlier in this chapter.

Mummery J (at 31): 'The offence of false attribution of authorship in section 43 of the Copyright Act 1956 is in terms which impose a restriction in relation to, *inter alia*, literary works. References in the section to a work "shall be construed in reference to such a work." It is provided in subsection (2) that:

"A person (in this subsection referred to as 'the offender') contravenes those restrictions as respects another person if, without the licence of that other person, he does any of the following acts in the United Kingdom, that is to say, he-

(a) inserts or affixes that other person's name in or on a work of which that person is not the author or in or on a reproduction of such a work, in such a way as to imply that the other person is the author of the work."

The offence is actionable as a breach of statutory duty: section 43(8). As regards remedies it is provided in subsection (10) that

"nothing in this section shall derogate from any right of action or other remedy (whether civil or criminal) in proceedings instituted otherwise than by virtue of this section;

Provided that this subsection shall not be construed as requiring any damages recovered by virtue of this section to be disregarded in assessing damages in any proceedings instituted otherwise than by virtue of this section and arising out the same transaction."

Thus, for example, in *Moore* v *News of the World Limited* [1972] 1 QB 441, the claim for the statutory offence under section 43 was linked to a claim for libel. A separate award of damages could be given for the statutory offence if the other cause of action did not cover the injury caused by the false attribution of authorship. In that case the Court of Appeal upheld the jury's award to the plaintiff of £4,300 for libel and £100 for false attribution of authorship. Lord Denning MR observed at page 450C that in most cases of false attribution of authorship there will also be a cause of action for libel or passing off and the damages for those causes of action would cover false attribution as well, so that there would be little extra awarded for false attribution.

There were certain points of agreement between the parties in relation to the section 43 claim:

(1) The effect of the misplaced quotation marks was to imply that Dr Noah was the author of the last seventeen words.

(2) No licence or consent had been granted by Dr Noah consenting to the attribution of those words to him.

(3) If an offence had been committed, that did not derogate in any way from Dr Noah's claim for defamation arising out of the same transaction.

(4) As regards any damages to be awarded it was, however, appropriate to take into account in assessing the damages for false attribution of authorship any amount that might be awarded to Dr Noah for defamation as a result of people wrongly thinking that he had written the words in question.

The point of dispute between the parties is whether Dr Noah's name was inserted or affixed on something that can properly be described as a "work" or a reproduction of a "work" within the meaning of section 43(2)(a). The question is, therefore, what is to be identified as the relevant "work"? It was contended on behalf of Dr Noah that the relevant work is the whole of the passage in quotation marks which was attributed to him, including both the words of which he was the author *and* the words of which he was not the author, that it was implied that he was the author of the whole of that passage and that was a false implication since he was not the author of the last seventeen words. Alternatively, it was submitted that, if only the last seventeen words are relevant to identification of the work, then they on their own constituted a work of which Dr Noah was not the author and the use of his name and the position of the quotation marks in relation to it implied falsely that he was the author.

On the other hand, it was submitted on behalf of Mr Shuba that for the purposes of section 43 the relevant "work" would consist only of those words which the person complaining had not written. The bulk of the passage within quotation marks was in fact written by Dr Noah so that he could not complain about that. His only complaint could be about the last two sentences consisting of seventeen words and they were too short and insubstantial a matter to constitute a literary 'work' within the meaning of section 43.

In my judgment, the main submission made on behalf of Dr Noah is the correct one. Dr Noah's name was inserted on or affixed to the whole of the quoted passage so as to imply that he was the author of the whole of that passage. He was not the author of the whole of that passage. That passage has been falsely attributed to him. If Mr Shuba's argument were right, no offence would be committed under section 43 if a passage was quoted verbatim from an author's work with several key statements of the passage altered to the contrary sense simply by the insertion of the word "not." The result would be that the passage reproduced was still substantially what the author had written, but would convey to the reader the opposite meaning to what the author had written. The effect would be a violation of the author's interests protected by section 43. They are not only economic interests but also an author's interests in his reputation and in the integrity of his work.

It is not necessary for me to decide the alternative argument. I have, however, heard argument from both sides and I can say that I would have rejected Dr Noah's submission that the last two sentences on their own constituted a "work" within the meaning of section 43. Those two sentences on their own do not afford sufficient information, instruction or literary enjoyment to qualify as a work: see *Exxon Corporation* v *Exxon Insurance Consultants International Limited* [1982] Ch. 119.'

COMMENT

This case shows that great care must be taken to make sure that quoted passages are verbatim. The omission of a single 'not' or the replacement of an 'or' with an 'and' can entirely change the meaning of a sentence and result in actions for false attribution and for defamation. Bear in mind that section 30 of the 1988 Act requires a sufficient acknowledgement to be made in terms of fair dealing for criticism or review (or for reporting current events). Might it be safer to omit an acknowledgement and risk a straightforward infringement action where substantiality will be in issue rather than rely on accuracy of copying? If a work is shortened, perhaps by omitting certain passages, or taken 'out of context' could this amount to false attribution?

Infringement of Copyright

Copyright is infringed by the performance (or authorisation of the performance) of one of the acts within the owner's exclusive rights in respect of a substantial part of the work without the licence of the copyright owner. What is substantial is a question of quality as well as, or instead of, quantity.

Hawkes and Son (London) Ltd. v Paramount Film Service Ltd. [1934] 1 Ch 593, Court of Appeal

A film with accompanying sound-track was made of the opening of a new school at which a band was present. When the film was shown in cinemas, part of the tune 'Colonel Bogey' could be heard. The plaintiff which owned the copyright in the musical composition sued the company which made the film and the distribution company for infringement of copyright.

Lord Hanworth MR (at 602): 'I turn therefore simply to look at the statute, and I bear in mind two or three points which have been rightly called to our attention. It is quite plain from what Lindley LJ said in *Hanfstaengl* v *Empire Palace* [1894] 3 Ch 109 at 128, that we have to consider the statute upon broad lines; to bear in mind the necessity for the protection of authors whether of musical or of literary compositions. The Acts have to be construed with reference to that purpose, and they are not to be made the instruments of oppression and extortion. On the other hand, as the learned Lord Justice says, "the intention of an infringer is immaterial," and as Slesser LJ has pointed out, Parker J said in *Weatherby & Sons* v *International Horse Agency and Exchange Ltd.,* [1910] 2 Ch 297 at 305, that the right of the owner of a copyright is not determined or measured by the amount of actual damage to him by reason of the infringement; copyright is a right of property, and he is entitled to come to the Court for the protection of that property, even though he does not show or prove actual damage. Lindley LJ says this, [1894] 3 Ch 109 at 129, "Guided by the foregoing considerations ... I ask myself whether these sketches are such copies of the plaintiff's pictures, or such reproductions of the designs thereof, as are struck at by the statute which confers copyright in such pictures." That was his test ... But it is said, first, that there is no substantial part of this musical work taken, and that the cases show that we must look into the question of the degree and what was the nature of the reproduction. In one case to which Lindley LJ refers, he points out that in that case a worsted work copy of an engraving was held not to be an infringement of the copyright therein. On the other hand, photographs of pictures have been held to infringe the copyright, although there is a vast difference between a photographic reproduction and the picture itself. Therefore, when one deals with the word "substantial", it is quite right to consider whether or not the amount of the musical march that is taken is so slender that it would be impossible to recognize it.

In order that we might give the defendants every chance, we decided to go and see this film reproduced, and we have done so this morning, and it appeared plain to us that there is an amount taken which would be recognized by any person ... Having considered and heard this film, I am quite satisfied that the quantum that is taken is substantial, and although it might be difficult, and although it may be uncertain whether it will be ever used again, we must not neglect the evidence that a substantial part of the musical copyright could be reproduced apart from the actual picture film.'

Slesser LJ (at 606): 'Mr Archer is perfectly right when he points out that the authorities indicate that other matters beyond mere quantity may and have to be looked at; indeed it is a criticism, I think, if I may respectfully make it, of the judgment in this case, that the only ground on which the learned judge held that no substantial part had been reproduced was that the whole work would take not more than four minutes to play, and the part recorded on the news reel took 20 seconds. I agree with my Lord that this reproduction is clearly a substantial part of "Colonel Bogey", looked at from any point of view, whether it be quantity, quality, or occasion. Any one hearing it would know that it was the march called "Colonel Bogey", and though it may be that it was not very prolonged in its reproduction, it is clearly, in my view, a substantial, a vital, and an essential part which is there reproduced. That being so, it is clear to my mind that a fair use has not been made of it; that is to say, there has been appropriated and published in a form which will or may materially injure the copyright, that in which the plaintiffs have a proprietary right. As is pointed out by Sir W. Page Wood VC in *Scott* v *Stanford* LR 3 Eq. 718 at 723: "If, in effect, the great bulk of the plaintiff's publication - a large and vital portion of his work and labour - has been appropriated and published in a form which will materially injure his copyright, mere honest intention on the part of the appropriator will not suffice, as the Court can only look at the result, and not at the intention in the man's mind at the time of doing the act complained of, and he must be presumed to intend all that the publication of his work effects." So far, therefore, it is clear that a substantial part has been appropriated; or to use the language before the Act of 1911 I should have held in accordance with the authorities that there had not been a fair use made of the matter.'

COMMENT

It is unsatisfactory to talk in terms of either quality or quantity when deciding whether a substantial part has been taken. Can you frame the test of substantiability in better terms? The following case shows that even significant changes to a work will not necessarily defeat an infringement action.

Spectravest Inc. v *Aperknit Ltd*. [1988] FSR 161, Chancery Division

The plaintiff owned the copyright in designs of cats sitting in a pair of boots known as 'Puss-N-Boots'. These designs could be printed onto clothing. The defendant printed a design which was similar, but with dogs and boots, onto garments. The plaintiff obtained an order restraining the defendant from infringing copyright but, after taking legal advice, the defendant resumed sales of its garments having the 'dogs-in-boots' design. The legal advice was to the effect that the defendant's design did not infringe the plaintiff's copyright. The plaintiff moved to commit the defendant for contempt of court. The issue of infringement of copyright was central to the case.

Millet J (at 170): 'In *Bauman* v *Fussell* [1978] RPC 485, the Court of Appeal pointed out that a man may reproduce a substantial part of another work even though the whole which he produces is not a reproduction of the original in its essential features. Accordingly, where the reproduction of a substantial part of the plaintiffs' work is alleged, a sensible approach is first to identify the part of the plaintiffs' work which is alleged to have been reproduced and to decide whether it constitutes a substantial part of the plaintiffs' work. The test is qualitative and not, or not merely, quantitative. If it does not, that is an end of the case. If it does, the next question is whether that part has been reproduced by the defendant. Reproduction does not mean exact replication. A man may use another's work as an inspiration to make a new work of his own, treating the same theme in his own manner; but he is not entitled to steal its essential features and substance and retain them with minor and inconsequential alterations. The question is whether there is such a degree of similarity between the salient features of the two works that the one can be said to be a reproduction of the other. In considering whether a substantial part of the plaintiffs' work has been reproduced by the defendant, attention must primarily be directed to the part which is said to have been reproduced, and not to those parts which have not.

In *Bauman* v *Fussell* itself an artist was alleged to have copied a photograph of two cocks fighting. All three members of the court agreed upon the test to be applied, but disagreed whether the same passage in the judgment below applied it correctly. This can only have been because the majority in the Court of Appeal considered that the finding, which was implicit in the judgment of the county court judge, that the attitudes of the two fighting cocks was not a substantial part of the plaintiff's work, was one to which he was entitled to come, while the dissenting Lord Justice thought that it was not.

It is, however, important not to adopt an analysis which is over-elaborate, for the two questions I have described are merely different aspects of the same question: whether the defendants' work is or includes a reproduction of a substantial part of the plaintiffs' work. There may be only a fine distinction between asking whether what has been reproduced is a substantial part of the plaintiffs' work, and asking whether what is a substantial part of the plaintiffs' work has been reproduced. The question is one of degree, and turns on the impression made on the mind by a comparison of the two works.

I will now describe these more fully. Both are what are called all-over designs, consisting of a number of individual variations on the same theme, some or all of which are repeated at intervals all over the garment, back, front and sleeves. In each case all but one of the individual designs depicts a young animal, in the one case a kitten, in the other a puppy nestling in or clambering out of a boot; in each case the remaining design depicts a pair of young animals in a pair of similar boots.

The plaintiffs have five different individual designs; the defendants have eight (of which two are almost but not quite identical). The plaintiffs' arrangement has six individual designs on each main panel, only one of which is repeated, with the double boot in the centre and not repeated. The defendants' arrangement has eleven individual designs, more closely packed, on each main panel, three of which are repeated; the double boot is reversed, is not in the centre, and is repeated. In my judgment, the arrangement of the defendants' design is not sufficiently similar to that of the plaintiffs to say that the arrangement of the plaintiffs' design has been reproduced by the defendants.

I now turn to the individual designs, for each of the six different designs of the plaintiffs is entitled to its own separate protection. In my judgment, the defendants' dogs are not reproductions or colourable imitations of the plaintiffs' cats. They are quite distinctive. They appear in different attitudes, and in different positions relative to the boots. All the cats are shown full-face; many (and by far the most artistically successful) of the dogs are shown in profile.

The boots, however, are quite a different matter. There are several differences; the plaintiffs' boots have no toecaps or heel counter areas and no decoration on the upper part of the leg, and have a barely visible heel and instep, together with a double or two-coloured sole. The defendants' boots have prominent toecaps and heel counter areas in a different colour, and a star on the upper part of the leg on most, though not all, designs but appear to have no heel or instep and have only a single sole.

These differences are not insignificant; but the boots themselves, that is to say, the basic shape and outline of the boots, the angles and perspectives in which they are seen, and even the detailed arrangement of the tongues and laces, are identical. Even without direct evidence to that effect, the conclusion that one had been copied from the other would be inescapable.

The colouring of the individual designs is virtually identical, the only differences being due to the inferior quality of the defendants' work. In both cases, whatever the colour of the garment, the animals themselves and the soles and laces of the boots (and in the defendants' case the stars on the boots) are white and printed in a rubberised solution which gives them a raised or embossed effect and a different feel to the touch from the rest of the fabric. In both cases, the boot itself is grey, while the inside of the boot and the tongue (and, in the defendants' case, the toecap and heel counter area) are in the same colour as the garment or, where the garment is white, in pink. The only differences are that in the plaintiffs' case, where the garment is not white, the inside of the boot and tongue are in a deeper shade than the garment, probably because the colour has been printed twice, while in the defendants' case they are in the same shade, probably because it has not been thought necessary to print again over the existing background; and that in the case of the defendants' pink garments, unlike the plaintiffs', the colour of the background has affected the colour of the boot, turning it into a greyish-puce.

The first question is whether the boots form a substantial part of the plaintiffs' work. I have no doubt that they do, both qualitatively and quantitively. The next question is whether the boots in the defendants' work reproduce the essential features of those in the plaintiffs' work. The question is one of impression, but again I have no doubt that they do. Despite the evidence that has been given, and to which I shall refer later, I do not think that it is a borderline case, on which different minds might reasonably reach different conclusions. I think it is a clear case. The resemblances are striking and of the essence. It needed the defendants to point out the differences rather than the plaintiffs to point out the similarities. The impression made on my mind, that the one is a reproduction of the essential features of the other, is very strong. In my judgment, Mr Hilton did not merely borrow the theme of animals in footwear but, when he came to design the footwear, he took the essential features of the plaintiffs' work.

That is enough to dispose of this question but, even if the cats or dogs are taken in conjunction with the boots, the result is the same. The dogs are obviously different from the cats, are shown in different attitudes and their positions relative to the boots are different. But the colour scheme is retained, and not only are the essential features of the boots reproduced, they are made to serve the same purpose. The concept is the same. While this would not be a breach of copyright if it stood alone, it hardly lessens the impression of copying produced by the boots themselves. On the contrary, the overall impression of reproduction or colourable imitation is reinforced.

I find, therefore, that the defendants' "Dog-N-Boots" design reproduces a substantial part of the plaintiffs' "Puss-N-Boots" design, and infringes the copyright in that design which the plaintiffs claim to own, contrary to the terms of the orders and undertakings.'

COMMENT

Millet J said it was important not to be over-elaborate in the analysis of infringement. Did he follow that advice? Was the infringement in respect of the boots, the cats and dogs or the boots together with cats and dogs? Is it possible that copyright can subsist in a colour combination?

The following case shows how strong copyright could be in protecting a design through drawings depicting the design.

L B Plastics Ltd. v *Swish Products Ltd.* [1979] RPC 551, House of Lords

The appellants made a plastic 'knock-down' drawer system, known as the Sheerglide, which could be assembled and fitted into furniture carcasses. Its main market was furniture manufacturers, one of which, Grovewood Products Ltd., showed the Sheerglide drawers to the respondent, an associated company. Grovewood suggested that the respondent make a 'knock-down' drawer system for its furniture but asked that it be interchangeable with the Sheerglide system. The respondent's system was known as the Swish design.

The appellant sued for the infringement of the copyright subsisting in its drawings showing the Sheerglide design. The respondent denied copying, although it accepted that it had access to the appellant's drawers, arguing that it had reproduced nothing more than the idea underlying the design.

Lord Hailsham (at 626): 'Before the decision to commission the market survey had been taken, at the end of March 1975, the head of the design and development team had written:

> "I have spoken to"- the respondents' patent agent - "regarding the possibility of using the *L.B. principle*," (sic, emphasis mine) "in part *or in whole*", (emphasis mine) "for a corner bracket and front fixing bracket ... I also raised once again ... the possibility of *minor changes to the design"* (sic, emphasis again mine) "which could possibly get around any patents and registered designs which they or others may have on this type of fixing principle".

To my mind this language illustrates as well as anything could both the intention to copy, the alertness to the danger of patent infringement, and the blindness to the possibility of copyright infringement which seems to have animated the respondents from March 1975 onwards.

But this is not all. After the receipt of the market survey report the same author wrote directly to the patent agent as follows:

> "As I stressed on my visit to you this matter is extremely urgent and any guidance you can offer in order to help decide whether we should risk changing to the new proposed design would be very much appreciated. Considerable time and money can be saved if we can adopt a similar principle (sic) to the L.B. (Plastics) design". (sic) ...

The matter does not quite stop there. As I have said, Grovewood had supplied the sister company with actual tracings of the appellants' drawings and, if they had not already got them, examples of the appellants' range of products. Coupled with the similarity of design, the availability of these objects, and the short time taken to achieve complete success, the inference seems almost irresistible that there was actual copying, and in fact in one apparently trivial respect the Court of Appeal was driven to accept that there was. In the screwholes in the facia pieces were two small countersinks or recesses which, as the appellants' evidence showed, they had themselves developed as the result of experience in order to accommodate the debris or sawdust produced by sinking the customers' connecting screws through the suppliers' facia pieces into the customers' front piece. This countersink is reproduced in the "Swish" drawer, and with regard to it the Court of Appeal said this:

> "This reverse countersink has, we think, clearly been taken by the defendants from the plaintiffs' design. To this extent we think the defendants should be held to have copied the plaintiffs' design".

The Court of Appeal, however, went on to hold (quite rightly in my opinion) that this in itself was trivial detail, and certainly not by itself "a substantial part" of the appellants' work. But this seems to me to miss its entire significance. If the respondents' design, as to the role of copying in which such an abundance of *prima facie* evidence exists, reproduces the appellants' design down to an apparently trivial detail like this, does this not shed a flood of light on the real source of the more substantial resemblances? Is it not quite incredible that the substantial resemblances had an independent origin when a small detail like this was directly copied? To my mind the question has only to be asked to be answered. Certainly the respondents' counsel, directly challenged, was unable to offer the smallest innocent explanation of this point of identity and only asked your Lordships to attach no importance to such an apparently small matter. I find myself unable to do so.

Before I leave the documents I must draw attention to one other comparatively trivial matter which seems to me equally to reinforce the argument. The appellants were able to point to a document disclosed by the respondents in which they had actually superimposed a tracing of the appellants' drawing on one of their own, obviously for the purpose of comparison. Their own explanation was that this was just to correct to the minutest degree the intricate dimensions necessary to make their own drawer truly interchangeable with the appellants', the general information for which they had obtained by other means. I find myself unable so to regard it. Appellants' counsel was able to establish, at least to my satisfaction, that the dimensions so minutely copied were precisely the critical dimensions necessary to reproduce the appellants' design in a form acceptable to Grovewood. Substantiality for the purposes of the Copyright Act is to be judged by quality rather than quantity, and the critical dimensions can hardly be judged to be less than substantial just because they are measured only in millimetres ...

I cannot therefore but conclude that, by the time the case was complete, so far from the appellants being bound, as the Court of Appeal thought, to "discharge a burden of proof" that the respondents had copied, the boot was heavily on the other foot. The respondents had a most formidable case to meet on the oral evidence and documents, and had sought to answer it with an alternative explanation by oral evidence which the judge had felt constrained to reject.

How then had the Court of Appeal fallen into this error? First, as I have said, they seem to have been influenced by their mistaken belief that the judgment of the trial judge rested solely on inference based on the inspection of similarities and dissimilarities. But generally they seem to have been led into error by two independent but closely related chains of reasoning of their own. The first is the belief that, subject to the second chain, all the respondents were shown to have "adopted" was the appellants' "concept" or "idea", and that this was not copyright. Of course, it is trite law that there is no copyright in ideas, and it may be that if all the respondents were shown to have copied from the appellants was the idea of some sort of external latching of the moulded corner pieces and clips to the extrusions this would have been a sound enough conclusion. But, of course, as the late Professor Joad used to observe, it all depends on what you mean by "ideas". What the respondents in fact copied from the appellants was no mere general idea. It was, to quote the respondents' own language to "follow the pattern" or principle "in part or in whole" with "minor changes" to the design, with the same choice of principal members interfitting in the same way to the same critical dimensions, and even incorporating such a trivial element as the reverse countersink, and then to countercheck their work by superimposing their own drawings on the appellants' to make sure that they had made no mistake.

It is here, however, that the second chain of reasoning adopted by the Court of Appeal assumes its importance. Some of the points of identity found between the drawings and the alleged infringements were due, it is said, not to the adoption of the "concept" or "idea", but the insistent demand by the customer for "interchangeability" with the appellants' dimensions so that, like the appellants' product, the respondents' drawer fitted into the customer's carcass. But this theory breaks down for at least two distinct reasons. First, and perhaps more important, it ignores the fact, which I have already pointed out, that the appellants were able to establish from the evidence that the customer's carcass was in fact a mirror image of the drawers made from the appellants' drawings and not vice versa. It was not argued in this case that the respondents had inadvertently copied the appellants' drawers by designing drawers directly from the dimensions of the carcass. That might indeed set up a chain of causation in an appropriate case. But it is not what is alleged here. They did not copy the carcass, or the dimensions of the carcass. Why should they? They had been supplied with the drawers and the drawings to which the drawers were made, and they copied these. Thus the requirement of interchangeability was not as the Court of Appeal assumed so much a badge of respectability as an incitement to copy. Secondly, the appellants showed quite clearly that the "design" or "pattern" which the respondents had copied in "whole or in part" was no more limited to the few critical measurements necessary to fit the carcass than it was limited to the "idea" of external latching. There was a wide option of choice available to them to achieve interchangeability, in the number of spigots, and other details. They chose to copy the appellants' design not merely in small details but in its overall shape and the relation of its parts, and therefore apart from these proceedings, would have saved themselves "considerable time and money" ...

However, I must make one or two observations about the decision of the Court of Appeal on the point. Read with sections 48(1) and 49(1) of the Act the [section 9(8)] defence only arises if there is a reproduction of a part of the copyright work sufficiently substantial to be otherwise an infringement of copyright. When a court finds that in fact there is no such reproduction, as the Court of Appeal did here, I rather doubt the possibility, and certainly the prudence, of attempting the intellectual exercise of trying to decide whether, if there were such a substantial reproduction a non-expert observer, notional or actual, could or could not have seen it. Were it to be attempted, I believe a court would be wise to specify with sufficient clarity what are the points of resemblance about which they assumed themselves to be wrong and which are assumed to be reproductions of a substantial part of the copyright work, and which the non-expert is supposed to be able (or unable) to recognise in the three-dimensional form of the alleged infringement. This the Court of Appeal did not attempt, and, in failing to do so fell into what appears to me to be a logical, and therefore a legal, error, for they seem to me to have reproduced in their endeavours to decide the point under section 9(8) the same exercise as regards substantiality, concept, interchangeability and originality as they had attempted under the primary issue of copying, and I believe this to have been wrong. Certainly I would regard it as a wrong approach in deciding a question under section 9(8) to enumerate dissimilarities which are really there and which a non-expert would have recognised as dissimilarities, or points of identity which are not really there which a non-expert would have mistakenly thought he saw as points of identity. There are passages in the Court of Appeal judgment which seem to me to do just this. The defence under section 9(8) is concerned with points of resemblance or identity which are really there, but which the non-expert would have failed to recognise as points of resemblance or identity in the three-dimensional form with the result that it would not have appeared to him that there had been the reproduction of any substantial part of the original artistic work. Be that as it may, I consider that the defence under section 9(8) must fail.

It remains to me to consider the almost metaphysical point raised by junior counsel for the respondents in an admirably concise following argument. This he based on what I fear is in this case an insubstantial foundation, namely a paragraph of Lord Pearce's speech on page 293 of the report of *Ladbroke (Football) Ltd.* v *William Hill (Football) Ltd.* [1964] 1 WLR 273. The argument was that although it be conceded that the appellants' draughtsman's drawings were copyright artistic works within section 3, the information acquired by preliminary work going into the drawing was not, and that what was copyright was simply the particular sketch by the particular draughtsman, which was not reproduced in the three-dimensional product. It would follow of course that a three-dimensional moulding of the present sort could not easily infringe the copyright in a drawing of this sort at all and that a two-dimensional drawing would not do so if drawn as a different sketch. The advantage claimed for counsel's argument is that it reduces the danger of the consequences of the overlap between the law relating to registered design and patent and that relating to copyright which has long given trouble to lawyers and legislators. But we must take copyright law as we find it. I do not believe the *Ladbroke* passage in its context has any bearing on this case, which, unlike *Ladbroke,* is not a compilation case. I believe the drawing was a team effort by the whole of the appellants' drafting and design body and all the information embodied in the drawing can, if a substantial part of the drawing be reproduced in a three-dimensional form, be considered for the purpose of deciding whether the three-dimensional form is an infringement, subject of course to section 9(8), and though I admired the elegance and subtlety of the presentation, I feel bound to reject junior counsel's argument.'

COMMENT

Would the defendant's actions infringe copyright under the 1988 Act and, if so, how? Note the importance of copying an apparently trivial feature in proving copying more significant features. The section 9(8) defence in the Copyright Act 1956, the 'lay recognition test', was not re-enacted in the 1988 Act.

Several tests could be used to determine what is a substantial part of a work. It could be based on recognition or competition. That is, is it possible to recognise the first work from the extract taken or does the second work compete unfairly with the first as a result of the copying? In practice, the qualitative test is difficult to predict in its application and copyright infringement where only a part of the first work has been taken must tend towards a subjective analysis. Would it be simpler and more just if the question was whether the defendant had simply made use of the plaintiff's work in creating his own? That deliberate copying, no matter how tiny a proportion, should infringe unless permitted by the exceptions to infringement such as fair dealing?

One of the acts restricted by copyright is performing, playing or showing a work in public. The meaning of 'public' is obviously central to determine infringement. The right of persons to be on premises by virtue of a contract or an implied licence only does not prevent a performance on those premises from being a public performance.

Ernest Turner Electrical Instruments Ltd. v *Performing Right Society Ltd.* [1943] 1 Ch 167, Court of Appeal

The owner of a factory played music to the employees. The music had been broadcast by the BBC and some gramophone records had also been played in the factory. Although no strangers were allowed to enter the factory, the Performing Right Society, which had obtained an assignment of the public performance rights in the music, sued on the basis that the playing of the music in question was a public performance and, thus, infringed copyright.

Lord Greene MR (at 171): 'We have been referred to a number of authorities, but I propose to base my judgment on the latest authority in this court where the previous cases were considered and reviewed. That authority is *Jennings* v *Stephens* [1936] Ch 469, and I refer to two short sentences in the judgments of Lord Wright MR and Romer LJ. Lord Wright said (at 479):

"The true criterion seems to be the character of the audience",

and Romer LJ said (at 482):

"The question whether an entertainment is given in public or in private depends, in my opinion, solely upon the character of the audience."

That, of course, does not mean that any element is to be excluded from consideration which throws light on the matter. In the present case the nature of the audience puts the matter beyond doubt. In each case the audience constituted a substantial part of the working population of the district. ...

It was said that it was not legitimate to consider what the effect would be of a decision in favour of the employers in the present cases, having regard to the fact that there are thousands of factories in the country, employing, no doubt, hundreds of thousands, indeed millions, of workpeople. If performances can be given without infringement of copyright in these two cases, they can be given in every case. To discover the real nature of the audience and the effect on the monopoly of treating these performances as private performances, it seems to me to be relevant to consider what the result would be if performances of this kind were given in all the other factories in the country. The result would be that the employers of millions of workpeople would be giving to those workpeople without payment the fruit of the brains, skill, imagination, and taste of various authors and composers, or the property of their successors in title, without any remuneration to him or them, and would be getting the advantage of that work, taste and skill, in obtaining increased or improved output. The effect would be largely to destroy the value of the statutory monopoly by depriving the owners of copyright of the exclusive right to sell their goods to the public. I think it is legitimate to take those matters into consideration, not to turn a rightful act into a wrongful act in these two cases, but to see what in each case is the nature of the audience that is having the benefit of the music. Looking at the matter in that way confirms me in my view that the audience, in the case of each factory, must be regarded as a section of the public. The legitimacy of taking these matters into consideration is clearly recognized by Lord Wright in his judgment in *Jennings* v *Stephens* [1936] Ch. 469 at 480, when he says in reference to the case before him:

"If that were not a performance in public, and might be repeated indefinitely all over the country, the performing right would not be of much value".

There Lord Wright was regarding the question from much the same angle as I am. He is taking into account the extent to which the value of the statutory monopoly would be whittled down as a material factor in dealing with these questions. In my opinion, the learned judge came to the only possible conclusion in these cases and the appeals must be dismissed, with costs.'

COMMENT

A very wide view of what constitutes a public performance was taken. Would playing music in a hotel foyer, a hairdressers or a record shop constitute a public performance? What about showing a film to students in a student hall of residence? Do you think that the reasoning is sound? Preference for one interpretation because of the consequences of the other is not good law. After all, the general public were excluded from entry to the premises.

Ibcos Computers Ltd. v *Barclays Mercantile Highland Finance Ltd.* [1994] FSR 275, Chancery Division

The second defendant, Mr Poole, had written accounting software which he licensed to Mr Clayton's agricultural dealership in 1979. The software looked promising and Mr Poole and Mr Clayton developed the software and used a company PK Ltd. to market the software, known as ADS, in 1982. At the time Mr Poole owned 40% of the shares, was the sole employee and managing director of PK Ltd., Mr Clayton and his family owned the remaining 60% of the shares in PK Ltd.

The software was successful and PK Ltd. engaged additional employees to further develop the software.

In 1986 Mr Poole left PK Ltd. and an agreement was prepared which included a term to the effect that Mr Poole recognised that PK Ltd. owned the software and included a restrictive covenant, of two years duration, whereby Mr Poole undertook not to sell competing software and not to work for a company selling competing software.

On leaving PK Ltd., Mr Poole wrote software, called Unicorn, to perform the same function as ADS. This was marketed by the first defendant. He also wrote file transfer programs to convert files used with ADS to a suitable format for use with Unicorn.

In 1991, the first defendant stopped marketing Unicorn and Mr Poole formed a Company, UDS Ltd., to do so. Ibcos Computers Ltd., the successor in title to PK Ltd. sued alleging that Unicorn was developed from ADS and this infringed the copyright in ADS, breach of confidence and that Mr Poole was in breach of the restrictive covenant. Jacob J found that Mr Poole was not in breach of the restrictive covenant.

Jacob J (at 289): 'Logically therefore the claim in copyright calls to be tested in the following order:
  (1)   What are the work or works in which the plaintiff claims copyright?
  (2)   Is each such work "original"?
  (3)   Was there copying from that work?
  (4)   If there was copying, has a substantial part of that work been reproduced?

I have set forth the tests which are taken directly from the statute because not only is this what the law requires but because by doing this one can avoid aphorisms such as "there is no copyright in an idea" or "*prima facie* what is worth copying is worth protecting." The courts have used these in the past but they can only serve as a guide. There are dangers in departing from the Act too far. For instance the latter aphorism, taken literally, would mean that all a plaintiff ever had to do was to prove copying. Originality, appropriate subject matter for copyright and a taking of a substantial part would all be proved in one go. One would not need the Act if the aphorism represented the law. It proves too much.

I therefore propose to follow that order, so far as I can, on what are clearly very messy and partly inchoate facts.

The copyright works
The ADS "program" is in fact a complicated composite of interrelated programs, routines and sub-routines. Mr Turner gives the following figures: 335 program files, 171 record layout files and 46 screen layout files. Mr Howe submitted that not only each individual program has copyright (and perhaps several since each of these will have been modified and updated) but also the package as whole has a copyright - as a kind of compilation. The submission was that the program of all programs is an original program. This must be right. The Act specifically confers copyright on a compilation subject to its being original. The amount of skill, labour and judgment which went into the ADS package as a whole is very substantial, well above the threshold of originality accepted in other fields of copyright.

Accordingly in my judgment the copyright works include not only the individual programs but the whole package. Moreover in every case where a program was revised or modified enough for a fresh copyright to be created, that copyright is also a relevant work.

Originality

In connection with the whole package being a copyright compilation I should mention *Total Information Processing Systems* v *Daman* [1992] FSR 171. It was not a full trial, the matter concerned unusually being dealt with as a preliminary issue in an interlocutory motion, with the result that there was no testing by cross-examination of the evidence. The preliminary point was:

> "whether there was an arguable case that the copying of the Field and Record specifications in a program called a Contract Costing Program is an infringement of copyright."

His Honour Judge Paul Baker made a number of observations which, taken out of context could be misleading. He said (at 179):

> "The mere linking of several programs is not in my judgment itself an original literary or artistic work in the way that the collective presentation of literary works by diverse authors is. Nor could the compilation be regarded as a computer program separate from and in addition to the individual programs."

Whilst that may be right on the facts of that case it cannot be correct as a general statement. Indeed no counsel before me accepted it as accurate. There is no reason why a compilation of computer programs should not itself acquire a separate copyright. Someone might, for instance, produce a selection of games on a disk. If there was enough originality in that selection it would surely be afforded copyright. The games might be wholly separated or they might have linking elements, e.g. common joystick control programs. In my view it is all a question of degree, just as it is in the case of any other compilation.

He went on to say:

> "To accord it copyright protection (that is to say the compilation) would lead to great inconvenience. It would mean that the copyright owners of one of the components could not interface with another similar program to that of the other components without the licence of the compiler."

No counsel supported this and I cannot agree. Of course the owner of the copyright in an individual program could interface his program with that of another. What he could not do is to put his program into an *original* compilation of another without that other's licence. The same is true of any other copyright works, be they poems, songs or whatever. All that the copyright owner of an original compilation of programs gets is a right to stop another compilation which is substantially the same as, and copied from, his.

Floating around on the question of originality was another notion. It was sometimes suggested in a general sort of way that because a particular program had a function, and especially if that function could only be achieved in one or a limited number of ways, there could be no copyright in it. The extreme form of this idea is expressed by Judge Baker in the *Total* case. He said:

"Secondly, stemming from the principle that copyright does not exist in ideas but in the expression of them is the line of authorities commencing with *Kenrick v Lawrence* (1890) 25 QBD 99 that if there is only one way of expressing an idea that way is not the subject of copyright."

That statement is in error in two ways. First, *Kenrick* (the case about a drawing of a hand showing voters which way to vote on a voting slip) did not decide that if there is only one way of expressing an idea no copyright can subsist in it. What was held was that there was no copyright infringement in taking the idea of using a picture of a hand showing how to vote. Accordingly a different picture embodying the same idea was not a taking of a substantial part of the copyright work. In that sense only the principle that there is no copyright in an idea applied.

Secondly there is, I think, danger in the proposition that, "If there is only one way of expressing an idea that way is not the subject of copyright." As Lord Hailsham observed in *LB Plastics* v *Swish* [1979] RPC 551:

"But of course as the late Professor Joad used to observe it all depends on what you mean by "ideas." What the respondents in fact copied from the appellants was no mere general idea."

It is of course true that copyright cannot protect any sort of general principle, such as the principle of drawing a hand to show how to vote, but it can protect a detailed literary or artistic expression. Thus in the case of an exhaust pipe it was said that the copyright was protecting the engineering principles which went into its design. Nevertheless there was copyright in the drawing and the copying of the drawing (via the medium of an exhaust pipe made from it) amounted to an infringement. This was so even though there was also a copying of the engineering principles that went into the original design. Thus Oliver LJ said in *British Leyland* v *Armstrong* [1986] RPC 279 at 296:

"What the plaintiffs seek to protect is not the idea of an exhaust system, but their monopoly in the drawings of this particular exhaust system, the salient feature of which is the flow-line into which months of research have gone, and for the embodiment of which the drawings, taken together, form a complete set of working instructions.

The question in every case is no doubt, whether a given three-dimensional object 'reproduces' the substance of the two-dimensional drawing or drawings, but I can see nothing in the Act which justifies a distinction being drawn, so far as the ambit of 'reproduction' is concerned, between drawings which are purely functional, and drawings which have some aesthetic appeal. I can find no context at all for giving the word some different and more extended or restricted meaning according to the intention of the author, or the emotional response of the beholder."

To my mind that passage is inconsistent with Judge Baker's statement, which was not supported by any counsel before me. The true position is that where an "idea" is sufficiently general, then even if an original work embodies it, the mere taking of that idea will not infringe. But if the "idea" is detailed, then there may be infringement. It is a question of degree. The same applies whether the work is functional or not, and whether visual or literary. In the latter field the taking of a plot (i.e. the "idea") of a novel or play can certainly infringe - if that plot is a substantial part of the copyright work. As Judge Learned Hand said (speaking of the distinction between "idea" and "expression") (*Nichols* v *Universal Pictures* (1930) 45 F (2d.) 119): "Nobody has ever been able to fix that boundary and nobody ever can."

It should be noted that the aphorism "there is no copyright in an idea" is likely to lead to confusion of thought. Sometimes it is applied to the question of subsistence of copyright (is there a "work" and if there is, is it "original"?). Sometimes it is applied to the different question of infringement (has a substantial part been taken?). That is not to say that the expression has no use: for instance if all a defendant has done is to copy a general idea then it does not matter whether there is copyright in the plaintiff's work, or whether the plaintiff owns that copyright.

[Jacob J then discussed US copyright law and its exclusion from protection of function resulting from differences in the US Copyright Code and the UK Statute]

That is not to say that American case law on copyright is never of assistance. But I do not think it assists me in relation to subsistence of copyright. Ferris J in *John Richardson Computers* v *Flanders* [1993] FSR 497 found the American approach of some assistance at the later stage of considering whether a substantial part of a program had been taken. To this I will return.

The consequence of regarding ADS as a whole as a copyright work is that it is right to consider what Mr Turner called the program structure as a whole and the design features as a whole as part of the work, in addition to the literal bits of code and the program structure within an individual program.

The individual programs within ADS are also each the subject of copyright for their creation was plainly the result of work, skill and judgment. But to say as much might not end matters so far certain of the programs are concerned. In relation to those first created after Mr Poole became managing director of PK in 1982 there is no problem. They must, as is conceded, belong fully to PK. But there are programs within ADS which were written before then. Some extend back to Mr Poole's Mark 3. Some were written for Mr Clayton during the period 1979-82. Moreover most of these were modified to a greater or lesser amount once the company started. In the latter connection I had some evidence from Mr Wright who joined PK in June 1984. He produced a schedule of programs which had been modified. This included modifications before he joined, which was, of course, hearsay. Mr Lambert at one time seemed to be going to take a point on this, and overnight Mr Wright had to produce an additional version of his schedule indicating the matter of which he had direct knowledge. That was a waste of time because Mr Lowe (who, it will be recalled, was willing to give both sides witness statements) joined the company much earlier and proved (by his witness statement) the schedule directly. In the end I heard no submissions on the schedule.

It makes sense to consider the contractual position as regards pre-1982 programs first. Determination of this will set the dividing line between programs which wholly belonged to PK (including any fresh copyrights arising out of modification) and programs whose copyright belongs to Mr Poole. I propose to consider the question as a matter of contract as between the parties. The formal requirements of the Act as regards title (particularly the requirement that certain assignments be in writing) have nothing to do with the *inter partes* position. Indeed it was not submitted that they had.

Who owns the copyrights?

As I have said, the defendants accept that any software writing that Mr Poole did whilst he was employed by PK belongs to them. The dispute relates to the software with which the company started. There are three possible candidates for what PK owned after Mr Poole left:

(i) the copyright in the software which Mr Poole wrote when he was managing director of the company and only that software;

(ii) the copyright in item (i) plus the copyright in the software as modified especially for Mr Clayton in the period 1979-82, *i.e.* the software with which the company started;

(iii) the copyright in the entire software including the unmodified software Mark 3 originally sold by way of licence to Mr Clayton in 1979.

Logically one must consider first the position before the agreement and secondly the effect of the agreement, particularly clause 6.

So what was the position when the company started operation? Prior to then Mr Poole and Mr Clayton were in an informal partnership. There was (and to my mind this is important) no version of the Mark 3 program as it existed back in 1979. All there was was a large disk (we are back in the days before convenient floppies) about the size of a cake which could he loaded into and out of Mr Clayton's computer. Any alterations of the 1979 program involved overwriting it so that one could not as a practical matter distinguish between the 1979 work and the modified and added-to form.

Who owned the copyright in the modified form? In my view it was the partnership. Mr Lambert submitted otherwise on the authority of *Miles* v *Clarke* [1953] 1 WLR 537. In that case there had been an informal partnership of photographers. The partnership had used premises, furniture and equipment originally belonging to one partner. When the partnership broke up it was contended that the lease and plant had been contributed to the partnership "pot". Harman J held otherwise, saying (at 540):

> "In my judgment no more agreement between the parties should be inferred than is absolutely necessary to give business efficacy to that which has happened and that is the only safe way to proceed."

The difficulty in Mr Lambert's way is twofold: first the program as it then stood was the very foundation of the venture. Moreover even though he had not contributed to it by way of programming, Mr Clayton contributed to it in other ways - by considerable discussion as to what the program should do and by some payment. Mr Lambert suggested that he was doing that solely for his own benefit. I do not so hold on the evidence. He was for some time with Mr Poole intending that the developments should result in a vendible product. No doubt he also got a benefit in his own business but the parties' intention at the time was a two-fold benefit. I think it was indeed "absolutely necessary" that the company should own the copyright in the program as it was in 1982. If the position were otherwise once the program was established commercially Mr Poole could have left the company and sold the same product on his own account. Or if there was a third party pirate, it would not be the company's right to sue for infringement and claim damages. Neither of these would make any commercial sense.

More difficult is the position as regards the copyright in the 1979 Mark 3 program. The problem is that the parties never considered this at all. Indeed they probably did not know there was a separate copyright or copyrights in that. To my mind the answer to this question is to be found in how Mr Poole had treated the physical embodiment of that program. He had not sought to retain this program separately. He may have happened to have some listings from then (a matter which on the evidence remained murky both in relation to the position in late 1981 and early 1982 but also later when Mr Poole was writing Unicorn). If the intention had been to keep the 1979 programs separate in copyright terms then the same would have been done physically. So in the end I hold that the copyright in the 1979 programs also came to the company. There is some slight corroboration for this in that when the company tried to sell ADS for a different field of use altogether (laboratory equipment) it felt entirely free to do so and Mr Poole did not suggest that his original copyrights were being used in a way which had not been contemplated when the venture was set up.

Even if the foregoing be wrong, I have no doubt that clause 6 of the 1986 agreement settled the position as between the parties. That is what it was intended to do. "D B Poole recognises that all PK software [is] the sole property of PK" means all copyrights in that software are PK's.

Mr Lambert suggested that the clause merely recognises the legal position that the material written whilst an employee belongs to the employer. He put forward a fanciful submission to the effect that at the date there was some uncertainty in law as to works written by a managing director and the clause was dealing with that. But it is manifest that neither of these parties had ever even heard of any such uncertainty. They cannot have been trying to deal with something they knew nothing about.

Mr Lambert also placed some reliance on the word "recognise" which he said was not a word of conveyance. I do not think that clause 6 has that limited effect. I think the clause was intended to ensure that all the rights in the PK software were indeed PK's. This makes sense. Both parties knew that Mr Poole was leaving to write a different program for Highland. The 1979 software had become inextricably mixed in with PK's and was in any event very old - to the point that if ever Mr Poole was to write new accounting software he would not need or want to refer to the old material.

This meaning does not have the effect that Mr Poole could not write new accounting software or that he could not make use of his undoubted skills and general memory of sub-routines and the like. That he can do (contrary to what he appeared to think in the witness box). All it means is that he (like anyone else) may not copy the PK software exactly or substantially.

There is a further reason for this construction. For if Mr Poole retained some copyrights embodied within ADS (particularly the 1979 copyrights) then, as I have said above, it would be necessary to imply a licence to use those copyright works. The court will not, unless there is no other reasonable construction, construe a clause in such a way that it then has to go on to imply a term to make sense of the contract as a whole.

Mr Howe reinforced his argument on construction by reference to the so-called doctrine of "estoppel by recital". He referred me to *Greer* v *Kettle* [1938] AC 156 in which Lord Maugham (with whom Lords Atkin and Roche agreed) approved what Patteson J said in *Stroughill* v *Buck* (1850) 14 QB 781, namely:

"When a recital is intended to be a statement which all the parties to the deed have mutually agreed to admit as true it is an estoppel upon all. But when it is intended to be the statement of one party only, the estoppel is confined to that party, and the intention is to be gathered from construing the instrument."

Mr Howe said that this case is even stronger than a mere recital. It is in fact a contractual statement of the position as between the parties in the operative part of the contract itself. I agree. Mr Poole cannot now contend that PK software is not that of the company.

Accordingly I hold that the whole of the PK ADS program and the individual copyrights within it belong to PK.

The programs contributed by Mr White
But what about the two programs originally written by Mr White? Clearly the legal ownership of these remains in Mr White and he clearly gave an irrevocable licence to PK to use them and if necessary to modify them. What happened to them is that they were indeed modified by Mr Poole when they were received. On the evidence it is likely that the modifications were more than trivial: Mr White said so in general terms, though it is not possible to know precisely what the modifications were. The programs had to be integrated into the package as a whole. So it is likely that the programs, as they are in ADS, have two copyrights: the copyright in the original White program and the copyright in the Poole edition of those programs. The latter belong to PK.

Copyright in source code
It was the plaintiffs' case that the defendants had infringed copyright in their source code. This inherently raises the question of whether there is copyright in source code. The defendants did not dispute this, rightly so in my view. I mention the point only because of another passage in the judgment in *Total:*

"Considerable steps are frequently taken to preserve confidentiality of the source code. This suggests a doubt that taken by itself it is the subject of copyright."

I do not understand this observation. Again no counsel supported it. Because people keep confidential material which would be of considerable use to pirates is no reason for saying that copyright does not protect it. If you do not want your property stolen it is better to hide it away than give thieves easy access to it. Historically the very foundations of copyright in part lie in the law of confidence. I unhesitatingly say that source code can be the subject of copyright. Whether it is or not depends upon the normal requirement of originality.

Was there copying?
For infringement there must be copying. Whether there was or not is a question of fact. To prove copying the plaintiff can normally do no more than point to bits of his work and the defendant's work which are the same and prove an opportunity of access to his work. If the resemblance is sufficiently great then the court will draw an inference of copying. It may then be possible for the defendant to rebut the inference - to explain the similarities in some other way. For instance he may be able to show both parties derived the similar bits from some third party or material in the public domain. Or he may be able to show that the similarity arises out of a

functional necessity - that anyone doing this particular job would be likely to come up with similar bits. So much is common ground between the parties. The concept of sufficient similarities shifting the onus onto the defendant to prove non-copying is well recognised in copyright law. Thus Lord Wilberforce in *LB Plastics* v *Swish* (at 621) asked whether the inference of copying:

> "could be displaced by evidence from the respondents showing how in fact they had arrived at their design and that they had not done so by copying?"

Actually I think the proposition is not so much one of law as of plain rational thought.

It should be noted that at this stage (namely "Was there copying?") both the important and the unimportant bits of the works being compared count. Indeed it is often identity of trivial matter which traps a copyist. As Hoffmann J observed in *Billhöfer Maschinenfabrik GmbH* v *Dixon & Co. Ltd.* [1990] FSR 105 at 123:

> "It is the resemblances in *inessentials,* the small, redundant, even mistaken elements of the copyright work which carry the greatest weight. This is because they are least likely to have been the result of independent design."

What then is the position here? Is there an inference of copying? I have no doubt that there is. It is overwhelming. There are bits of ADS in Unicorn which cannot really be explained in any other way. It would be burdensome in this judgment to set out all the similarities which raise the inference. They were all well identified in Mr Turner's report for the plaintiffs before the trial began. I find it surprising that the defendant's experts did not seem to have addressed or faced up to these resemblances. Only at moments in the witness box did Mr Kenny (the better of the defendants' experts) seem to recognise that there were real difficulties in the way of a case of independent design.

I must set out some of the key items.

[Jacob J then considered common features including common spelling mistakes, redundant code, etc.]

In any copyright infringement case it is elementary as a first stage to compare the two works with a critical eye for inexplicably similar detail. Spelling mistakes and idiosyncrasies are often the sign of copying. They are, in my judgment, here.

My conclusion that there was disk-to-disk copying has serious consequences so far as Mr Poole's evidence is concerned. It is seldom easy for a judge to assess merely by demeanour whether a witness is telling the truth, though Mr Poole was certainly uncomfortable at times. That is why documents and inherent probabilities can be of such assistance. Here I rest my opinion in relation to Mr Poole's evidence on the objective facts of inexplicable (save for copying) similarities between the programs.

"Substantial part": general considerations
There is a danger in jumping from a conclusion that there was copying to a conclusion that a substantial part of a work has been taken. It is all too easy to say that a defendant who has lied about copying must have taken a lot. Of course it is likely in most cases that this is so. But the court must always go on to look at the further question of whether a substantial part was copied. In relation to conventional

kinds of work this it can do reasonably readily. Even in the case of technical drawings it is possible to examine the parties' drawings to see whether a substantial part of the plaintiff's work is to be found in the defendant's. A good example of the right way to go about the problem is the *Billhöfer* case. Even though there was copying (betrayed by the inessential details) there was no taking of sufficient visual features of the copyright drawing. In a computer program case, however, the court cannot so readily assess the question of substantial part unaided by expert evidence. I believe I should therefore be largely guided by such evidence. Before turning to this I should mention some other considerations.

The problem may be bedevilled by the "no copyright in an idea" argument - along the lines of the United States Code, section 102(b). As I have indicated that has no relevance in United Kingdom law once one goes beyond a mere general idea. As I have said, Ferris J in *John Richardson* obtained some assistance from the American cases. An important United States case is *Computer Associates* v *Altai* (1992) 982 F.2d 693 (2nd Cir.). Ferris J said (at 526):

"In the test propounded in *Computer Associates* the discovery of a program's abstraction is the first step. The second step is to filter these abstractions in order to discover a 'core of protectable material'. In the process of filtration there are to be excluded from consideration (a) elements dictated by efficiency; (b) elements dictated by external factors and (c) elements taken from the public domain."

Later he said:

"There is nothing in any English case which conflicts with the general approach adopted in the *Computer Associates* case. I think that in preference to seeking the 'core of protectable expression' in the plaintiff's program an English court will first decide whether the plaintiff's program as a whole is entitled to copyright and then decide whether any similarity attributable to copying which is to be found in the defendant's program amounts to the copying of a substantial part of the plaintiff's program. This was the approach which was held to be correct in the *William Hill* case."

I would interpolate that it is the approach called for by our statute. Going on:

"But at the stage at which the substantiality of any copying falls to be assessed in an English case the question which has to be answered, in relation to the originality of the plaintiff's program and the separation of an idea from its expression, is essentially the same question as the United States court was addressing in *Computer Associates*. In my judgment it would be right to adopt a similar approach in England."

For myself I do not find the route of going via United States case law particularly helpful. As I have said, United Kingdom copyright cannot prevent the copying of a mere general idea but can protect the copying of a detailed "idea". It is a question of degree where a good guide is the notion of overborrowing of the skill, labour and judgment which went into the copyright work. Going via the complication of the concept of a "core of protectable expression" merely complicates the matter so far as our law is concerned. It is likely to lead to overcitation of United States authority based on a statute different from ours. In the end the matter must be left to the value judgment of the court. Having expressed this reservation however, I thoroughly agree with what Ferris J went on to say: "Consideration is not restricted to the text of the code..." That must be right: most literary copyright works involve both literal matter (the exact words of a novel or computer program) and varying levels of abstraction (plot, more or less detailed of a novel, general structure of a computer program).

I therefore think it right to have regard in this case not only to what Mr Turner called "literal similarities" but also to what he called "program structure" and "design features".

Some of the similarities relate to the data divisions of the programs. In *Total* (at 180) Judge Baker said (speaking of the data division):

"The part copied can be likened to a table of contents. It would be very unusual that that part of a book could be described as a substantial part of it. The specification in high level language of fields and records in the data division tells one little or nothing about the costing program and so, in my judgment, cannot be regarded as a substantial part of it within the meaning of section 16(3)."

I do not agree that it would be "very unusual" that a table of contents would be a substantial part of a book. It is all a question of degree. Very often the working out of a reasonably detailed arrangement of topics, sub-topics and sub-sub-topics is the key to a successful work of non-fiction. I see no reason why the taking of that could not amount to an infringement. Likewise there may well be a considerable degree of skill involved in setting up the data division of a program. In practice this is done with the operating division in mind and its construction may well involve enough skill, labour and, I add, judgment, for it to be considered a substantial part of the program as a whole.

Before turning to Mr Turner's views I have to add one further matter. I have concluded that there was disk-to-disk copying. This happened in relation to a substantial range of ADS programs. This shifts the onus to the defendants to prove non-copying of matter which is similar in ADS and Unicorn. And I have real difficulties in relation to those parts of Mr Poole's evidence which are not corroborated. Is similar matter due to the fact that it was the same programmer and therefore a consequence of mere style or is it due to copying and modification? I have come to the conclusion that I should not accept the mere style explanation from Mr Poole. Why else would he have told untruths about the disk-to-disk copying? My difficulties are the same as those of Vice-Chancellor Sir William Page Wood over a hundred years ago when faced with a defendant who denied copying but who manifestly had copied. He said (in *Jarrold* v *Houlston* (1857) 3 K & J 708 at 717):

"That Mr Philp has made use of the Plaintiffs' book to a certain extent I find to be clear. The extent to which he has done so is another subject of consideration with regard to the injunction. But ... I have come, with great regret, to the conclusion that the statement in his affidavit denying that he has taken any idea or language from the work of Dr Brewer is wholly inconsistent with any conclusion I can arrive at, after looking at the numerous passages to which I have been referred. I extremely regret that he did not take the frank and candid course of stating how he had used the book. Had he done so, the case might very possibly now wear a different aspect."

It is of course possible for two programs to be similar as a result of mere style. Such was the case of a minor program within Unicorn written not by Mr Poole but by one Joy Masters who had learned programming with Mr Poole at Supaflo many years earlier. In the case of Mr Poole's programs however the question is not whether the similarities could have arisen by reason of style and programming habits, but did they? Mr Poole was capable of producing something like Unicorn independently (though probably not in the time-frame within which it was done). He is manifestly good at programming. His skill in producing both ADS and Unicorn shows this. Unicorn is undoubtedly to the user a much friendlier program than ADS was at the time (it has now been much enhanced I understand). It has got convenient cursor movements, colour, error correction and so on, all absent from ADS as I was shown. Users doubtless think of the programs as very different because they present differently. Indeed Mr Dance, a customer, told me that was so in his case. But I think Mr Poole was taking short-cuts by starting with ADS and making considerable additions and modifications. Unicorn is a major enhancement of ADS, not a wholly independent creation. Given his failure to be "frank and candid" I think the proper inference is that the similarities identified by Mr Turner and not explained by independent evidence are due to copying. That is the guide by which I think it right to judge the question of whether a substantial part was taken. I turn to Mr Turner's similarities.

[Jacob J then considered the similarities identified by Mr Turner, the plaintiff's expert witness. Jacob J found that the suite of programs and some of the individual programs had been infringed.]

File transfer programs
Finally as regards specific programs it was alleged that the file transfer programs of Unicorn also infringe. These are a kind of program not present in ADS. Their function is to take data stored on a different overall program and render it suitable for Unicorn. This is obviously necessary commercially if a dealer is to be persuaded to change programs. Otherwise all his data would have to be re-keyed. There are three file transfer programs, each designed to take data on an IBCOS program (*i.e.* an ADS program). Thus the comment to the program PRTRIS is "Transfer IBCOS Parts System as a Whole (all versions)".
Mr Turner said of all three file transfer programs:

"It is my opinion that these UNICORN file transfer programs could only have been written at an economic cost with access to the equivalent ADS record file layouts."

Mr Kenny did not challenge this in a further report. Mr Poole said he recreated the record layouts of ADS fields from memory, even though there are a substantial number of ADS variable names used. I do not accept that evidence. Nor do I think it matters. If one deliberately copies a substantial part of another's work by memory, one still infringes.
    A defence advanced was along the lines of licence. It was said that a user of the ADS system had an implied right to change to another system and therefore to do

that which was necessary to do that. He could exercise his right by the services of a third party, who accordingly must also have the right to make such use of ADS as was necessary to create file transfer programs. The argument was by analogy with the right to repair a motor car held to exist in *British Leyland*. I doubt that the analogy is good but did not hear substantial argument on the point, for it would not apply to taking a source code and using that direct. The "right to repair" would not apply to someone who got unauthorised access to drawings and copied them in two dimensions directly for the purpose of making spare parts.

Mr Howe conceded that if a customer were to take the ADS Manual and use that or allow someone else to use that to obtain the file records that would not infringe. But that is not what happened here.

In my judgment therefore the creation of the file transfer programs took the ADS file record layouts which themselves form a substantial part of ADS. The file transfer programs infringe.

Unicorn 2

This is a further revision of Unicorn issued in 1993. Many of the literal similarities which were present in Unicorn have disappeared. There has been a considerable cleaning up of comments. Mr Turner in an uncrossexamined further report concluded:

> "In this brief examination into whether the literal similarities between the ADS and Unicorn software packages identified in [his earlier report] also exist in [Unicorn 2] no clear pattern has emerged. At one extreme many similarities no longer exist and original work has obviously been done to create an alternative solution. At the other, some similarities still exist intact, and no attempt has been made to create an alternative, original solution. Between the two extremes I have found a complete spectrum of cases including many instances of minimal cosmetic changes."

Plainly Unicorn 2 was made starting from Unicorn.

Mr Turner has considered whether the literal similarities in his 49 examples are present still in Unicorn 2 and has concluded that many are not. I do not have much detail on the evidence and in the circumstances I find myself in considerable difficulty in deciding one way or the other whether what remains in Unicorn is or is not a substantial part of an ADS copyright work. I do not propose to find infringement of matter I have been unable to consider in detail. However where Mr Turner has given unchallenged evidence that there has been virtually no change, or that changes were merely cosmetic, I accept that evidence. On that basis I hold that the following programs of Unicorn 2 infringe: TAX, MESS, NOMCBS, DATST, PRINT, PAMUPP, ASSAPM, PAYDIN, CUSCSH, PAYNAL, NAREC.

The overall structure remains virtually unchanged. Mr Turner says so. The copyright in ADS as a whole is likewise infringed.

Breach of confidence

I have concluded that Mr Poole had access to and made use of the source code of ADS when writing Unicorn. Quite apart from questions of copyright infringement, this was a breach of confidence. I have already observed that source code is normally kept confidential by software houses. Normally of course customers do not themselves ever get any source code. It seems that some may have done in the early days of the distribution of ADS but it also seems likely that this was done under conditions of confidence. Mr Poole was indeed responsible for arranging for the preparation of the PK standard terms and conditions which were in operation by at least 1983. Those require the customer to treat the programs as trade secrets. In the end I do not think it was disputed that the source code of ADS was confidential. It follows that the plaintiffs succeed so far as breach of confidence is concerned against Mr Poole and his company.

Highland may stand in different case. Their position is that they had no knowledge of any breach of confidence whilst they were selling Unicorn. If that were wholly right then there could be no liability for breach of confidence as against them. However by late 1989 they had the source codes of both programs and were able to make the comparison themselves. They also had Mr Turner's first report. As I have said that points out enough literal similarities to indicate copying. Some of the spelling mistakes for example are pointed out there. It follows in my judgment that Highland should be taken to have had sufficient knowledge that Unicorn was written using the ADS source code from - and the date is a bit arbitrary - the beginning of 1990 at the latest. The plaintiffs say that from the date when Highland had sufficient notice that Unicorn was made in breach of confidence Highland are themselves liable for breach of confidence. Hence the third action. The argument is that there is liability even though Unicorn itself does not embody any confidential information. The argument was raised late in the day by Mr Howe who relied upon the "skins for skinless sausages" case, *Union Carbide Corp.* v *Naturin Ltd.* [1987] FSR 538. As the Court of Appeal indicated in that case, the issue of law is important and difficult. I do not think it right, Mr Howe having only raised the point in reply, to deal with it here.

The point does not matter in this case because there is admitted liability for infringement of copyright if Mr Poole is liable for that - as I hold that he is. Since Highland are no longer interested in this kind of program, the question of an injunction against them in respect of breach of confidence (or in respect of copyright) is essentially academic.'

COMMENT

Do you think Jacob J is correct in his attack upon the use of aphorisms such as 'copyright does not protect ideas'? An important feature of this case is that copying can be proved, in the absence of a plausible explanation by the defendant, by proof of taking something trivial or by copying mistakes. Does it make good sense for copyright owners to include deliberate mistakes in their works?

Note that a software product can have a great many separate copyrights. The product as a whole may be protected as a compilation in addition to each and every item, such as the programs, data files, dictionaries, etc. Furthermore, modifying software may give rise to fresh copyrights. Under what circumstances do you think this will be so?

This case and the *John Richardson Computers* case referred to have gone a long way in clarifying the scope of copyright protection for computer programs. However, *Ibcos* was a case involving literal copying whilst *John Richardson Computers* involved non-literal copying. Hence, Ferris J's interest in United States authorities. Although Jacob J made some veiled criticism of using United States precedent in the manner in which Ferris J did, that criticism is somewhat unfair. Ferris J did not proceed via the 'core of protectable expression' as implied by Jacob J but, primarily, used *Computer Associates* to support the view that copyright is not limited to the literal program code. Do you think the criticisms of the *Total Information* case are justified? If so, why?

Fair Dealing

It is not an infringement of copyright to perform a restricted act for the purposes of fair dealing, for example, for research or private study, for criticism or review or for reporting current events, subject to a sufficient acknowledgement in some cases. The scope of fair dealing is difficult to predict but the following case shows how it may be decided in terms of fair dealing for criticism or review.

Hubbard v *Vosper* [1972] 2 QB 84, Court of Appeal

The defendant wrote a book which was very critical of the cult of Scientology. He had been a member of the cult for a number of years but had left it after becoming disillusioned and being declared 'in a condition of enemy' by the cult. The defendant's book entitled *The Mind Benders* contained extracts from books and other documents concerning Scientology written by the plaintiff, the leader of the cult.

The plaintiff sued for infringement of copyright and breach of confidence. The defendant claimed fair dealing in respect of the copyright action and public interest in relation to the confidence action.

Lord Denning MR (at 92): 'Whatever one may think of Mr Hubbard's books, letters and bulletins, they are the subject of literary copyright. His name appears as author on every book, letter and bulletin. So he is presumed to be the owner of the copyright in them.

In writing *The Mind Benders* Mr Vosper has made free use of Mr Hubbard's books, letters and bulletins. He has taken very little from some, but from others he has taken very substantial parts. For instance, he has taken quite big extracts from the *Introduction to Scientology Ethics*, and put them into his book. He has also taken substantial parts of the letters and bulletins. The parts taken are so substantial that Mr Vosper will be guilty of infringement of copyright unless he can make good his defence. And his defence is that his use of them is fair dealing within section 6(2) of the Copyright Act 1956. This says that:

> "No fair dealing with a literary, dramatic or musical work shall constitute an infringement of the copyright in the work if it is for purposes of criticism or review, whether of that work or of another work, and is accompanied by a sufficient acknowledgement."

The last words of the section are satisfied. At the end of his book Mr Vosper said: "Quotations are used from the following books by L Ron Hubbard" - setting them out.

The question is, therefore, whether Mr Vosper's treatment of Mr Hubbard's books was a "fair dealing" with them "for the purposes of criticism or review." There is very little in our law books to help on this. Some cases can be used to illustrate what is not "fair dealing". It is not fair dealing for a rival in the trade to take copyright material and use it for his own benefit. Such as when "The Times" published a letter on America by Rudyard Kipling. The *St. James' Gazette* took out half-a-dozen passages and published them as extracts. This was held to be an infringement: see *Walter* v *Steinkopff* [1892] 3 Ch 489. So also when the University of London published examination papers. The Tutorial Press took several of the papers and published them in their own publication for the use of students. It was held to be an infringement: see *University of London Press Ltd.* v *University Tutorial Press Ltd.* [1916] 2 Ch 601. Likewise when a band played 20 bars of "Colonel Bogey" - to entertain hearers - it was not fair dealing: see *Hawkes & Son (London) Ltd.* v *Paramount Film Service Ltd.* [1934] Ch 593.

In this case Mr Vosper has taken considerable extracts from Mr Hubbard's works and has commented freely upon them. I will give some illustrations. On p.28 of Mr Vosper's book, he gives a quotation from Mr Hubbard's *Axioms and Logics*. I will emphasise the words taken:

"Scientology Axiom One is the assumption upon which the rest of the subject stands. *'Life is basically a static.'* and this is further defined - *'a Life Static has no mass, no motion, no wave-length, no location in space or in time. It has the ability to postulate and to perceive.'*

Hubbard has redefined in modern, scientific-sounding terms the ancient Hindu Vedanta concept of a soul or spirit that whilst appearing to inhabit the physical universe is of a distinctly separate order."

Another illustration is on p.141 of Mr Vosper's book:

" ... Hubbard in his book Introduction to Scientology Ethics, 1968 states: *'A Suppressive Person or Group becomes "Fair Game".* By Fair Game is meant, without right for self, possessions or position, and no Scientologist may be brought before a Committee of Evidence or punished for any action taken against a Suppressive Person or Group during the period that person or group is "fair game".'

"Would a Scientologist who takes it into his head to murder a declared Suppressive Person be regarded by Scientologists as fully within his rights? That murder has not occurred as far as is known, is not to the credit of L Ron Hubbard's Ethics but more to the credit of police and courts of the old-fashioned, repressive type."

Those illustrations enable me to state the conflicting arguments. Mr Pain for Mr Hubbard says that what Mr Vosper has done is to take important parts of Mr Hubbard's book and explain them and amplify them. That, he says, is not fair dealing. Mr Caplan for Mr Vosper says that Mr Vosper has, indeed, taken important parts of Mr Hubbard's book, but he has done it so as to expose them to the public, and to criticise them and to condemn them. That, he says, is fair dealing.

It is impossible to define what is "fair dealing". It must be a question of degree. You must consider first the number and extent of the quotations and extracts. Are they altogether too many and too long to be fair? Then you must consider the use made of them. If they are used as a basis for comment, criticism or review, that may be fair dealing. If they are used to convey the same information as the author, for a rival purpose, that may be unfair. Next, you must consider the proportions. To take long extracts and attach short comments may be unfair. But, short extracts and long comments may be fair. Other considerations may come to mind also. But, after all is said and done, it must be a matter of impression. As with fair comment in the law of libel, so with fair dealing in the law of copyright. The tribunal of fact must decide. In the present case, there is material on which the tribunal of fact could find this to be fair dealing.

Mr Pain took, however, another point. He said that the defence of "fair dealing" only avails a defendant when he is criticising or reviewing the plaintiff's literary work. It does not avail a defendant, said Mr Pain, when he is criticising or reviewing the doctrine or philosophy underlying the plaintiff's work. In support of this proposition, Mr Pain relied on the words of Romer J in *British Oxygen Co. Ltd.* v *Liquid Air Ltd.* [1925] Ch 383, 393:

> "I am inclined to agree with Mr Upjohn that, in this proviso [as to 'fair dealing'], the word 'criticism' means a criticism of the work as such."

But, when you refer back to Mr Upjohn's arguments, you will see that all he means is that the criticism must be a criticism of the plaintiff's work, and not of the plaintiff's conduct.

I do not think that this proviso is confined as narrowly as Mr Pain submits. A literary work consists, not only of the literary style, but also of the thoughts underlying it, as expressed in the words. Under the defence of "fair dealing" both can be criticised. Mr Vosper is entitled to criticise not only the literary style but also the doctrine or philosophy of Mr Hubbard as expounded in the books.

Mr Pain took yet another point. This was on the bulletins and letters. These, he said, were not published to the world at large, but only to a limited number of people and, in particular, to those who took classes in Scientology. He said that, whilst it might be "fair dealing" to criticise the books, it was not "fair dealing" to take extracts from these bulletins and letters and criticise them. He quoted again the words of Romer J in *British Oxygen Co. Ltd.* v *Liquid Air Ltd.* [1925] Ch 383, 393:

> " ... it would be manifestly unfair that an unpublished literary work should, without the consent of the author, be the subject of public criticism, review or newspaper summary. Any such dealing with an unpublished literary work would not, therefore, in my opinion, be a 'fair dealing' with the work".

I am afraid I cannot go all the way with those words of Romer J. Although a literary work may not be published to the world at large, it may, however, be circulated to such a wide circle that it is "fair dealing" to criticise it publicly in a newspaper or elsewhere. This happens sometimes when a company sends a circular to the whole body of shareholders. It may be of such general interest that it is quite legitimate for a newspaper to make quotations from it, and to criticise them - or review them - without thereby being guilty of infringing copying. The newspaper must, of course, be careful not to fall foul of the law of libel. So also here, these bulletins and letters may have been so widely circulated that it was perfectly "fair dealing" for Mr Vosper to take extracts from them and criticise them in his book.

It seems to me, therefore, that Mr Vosper may have a good defence of "fair dealing" to raise at the trial.'

COMMENT

Note the reference to the presumption of ownership of copyright resulting from the name of the author on the books and other materials. Is Lord Denning right to suggest that fair dealing goes to the ideas and thoughts expressed in a literary work in addition to the literary style? If the ideas were criticised without copying any extracts would there be any need to rely on fair dealing?

There is also a public interest defence under common law for copyright infringement actions and in respect of breach of confidence. The public interest defence was used to excuse the breach of confidence. Would it have been more appropriate to use the public interest as a defence to copyright infringement also?

International Standards

Standards of copyright protection internationally were promoted through the Berne Copyright Convention which brought about a degree of harmonisation between the copyright laws of its member countries and which provides for reciprocal protection between those countries. However it must be said that Berne is very much a 'broad brush' approach and whilst basic principles of copyright law in member countries are the same, there remain many differences in detail, compounded by the inclusion of a number of derogations in the Convention. At the moment, there are well over 100 countries in the Berne Convention.

Following the extracts from the Berne Convention are the copyright provisions of the TRIPs agreement.

Berne Convention for the Protection of Literary and Artistic Works

of September 9, 1886, completed at PARIS on May 4, 1896, revised at BERLIN on November 13, 1908, completed at BERNE on March 20, 1914, revised at ROME on June 2, 1928, at BRUSSELS on June 26, 1948, at STOCKHOLM on July 14, 1967, and at PARIS on July 24, 1971, and amended on September 28, 1979

The countries of the Union, being equally animated by the desire to protect, in as effective and uniform a manner as possible, the rights of authors in their literary and artistic works ...

Note: each Article has been given a title to facilitate identification. There are no titles in the signed (English) text.

Article 1
[Establishment of a Union]

The countries to which this Convention applies constitute a Union for the protection of the rights of authors in their literary and artistic works.

Article 2
[Protected Works: 1. 'Literary and artistic works'; 2. Possible requirement of fixation; 3. Derivative works; 4. Official texts; 5. Collections; 6. Obligation to protect; beneficiaries of protection; 7. Works of applied art and industrial designs; 8. News]

(1)   The expression 'literary and artistic works' shall include every production in the literary, scientific and artistic domain, whatever may be the mode or form of its expression, such as books, pamphlets and other writings; lectures, addresses, sermons and other works of the same nature; dramatic or dramatico-musical works; choreographic works and entertainments in dumb show; musical compositions with or without words; cinematographic works to which are assimilated works expressed by a process analogous to cinematography; works of drawing, painting, architecture, sculpture, engraving and lithography; photographic works to which are assimilated works expressed by a process analogous to photography; works of applied art; illustrations, maps, plans, sketches and three-dimensional works relative to geography, topography, architecture or science.

(2)   It shall, however, be a matter for legislation in the countries of the Union to prescribe that works in general or any specified categories of works shall not be protected unless they have been fixed in some material form.

(3)   Translations, adaptations, arrangements of music and other alterations of a literary or artistic work shall be protected as original works without prejudice to the copyright in the original work.

(4)   It shall be a matter for legislation in the countries of the Union to determine the protection to be granted to official texts of a legislative, administrative and legal nature, and to official translations of such texts.

(5)   Collections of literary or artistic works such as encyclopaedias and anthologies which, by reason of the selection and arrangement of their contents, constitute intellectual creations shall be protected as such, without prejudice to the copyright in each of the works forming part of such collections.

(6)   The works mentioned in this Article shall enjoy protection in all countries of the Union. This protection shall operate for the benefit of the author and his successors in title.

(7)   Subject to the provisions of Article 7(4) of this Convention, it shall be a matter for legislation in the countries of the Union to determine the extent of the application of their laws to works of applied art and industrial designs and models, as well as the conditions under which such works, designs and models shall be protected. Works protected in the country of origin solely as designs and models shall be entitled in another country of the Union only to such special protection as is granted in that country to designs and models; however, if no such special protection is granted in that country, such works shall be protected as artistic works.

(8)   The protection of this Convention shall not apply to news of the day or to miscellaneous facts having the character of mere items of press information.

Article 2bis

[Possible Limitation of Protection of Certain Works: 1. Certain speeches; 2. Certain uses of lectures and addresses; 3. Right to make collections of such works]

(1) It shall be a matter for legislation in the countries of the Union to exclude, wholly or in part, from the protection provided by the preceding Article political speeches and speeches delivered in the course of legal proceedings.

(2) It shall also be a matter for legislation in the countries of the Union to determine the conditions under which lectures, addresses and other works of the same nature which are delivered in public may be reproduced by the press, broadcast, communicated to the public by wire and made the subject of public communication as envisaged in Article 11bis(1) of this Convention, when such use is justified by the informatory purpose.

(3) Nevertheless, the author shall enjoy the exclusive right of making a collection of his works mentioned in the preceding paragraphs.

Article 3

[Criteria of Eligibility for Protection: 1. Nationality of author; place of publication of work; 2. Residence of author; 3. 'Published' works; 4. 'Simultaneously published' works]

(1) The protection of this Convention shall apply to:
  (a) authors who are nationals of one of the countries of the Union, for their works, whether published or not;
  (b) authors who are not nationals of one of the countries of the Union, for their works first published in one of those countries, or simultaneously in a country outside the Union and in a country of the Union.

(2) Authors who are not nationals of one of the countries of the Union but who have their habitual residence in one of them shall, for the purposes of this Convention, be assimilated to nationals of that country.

(3) The expression 'published works' means works published with the consent of their authors, whatever may be the means of manufacture of the copies, provided that the availability of such copies has been such as to satisfy the reasonable requirements of the public, having regard to the nature of the work. The performance of a dramatic, dramatico-musical, cinematographic or musical work, the public recitation of a literary work, the communication by wire or the broadcasting of literary or artistic works, the exhibition of a work of art and the construction of a work of architecture shall not constitute publication.

(4) A work shall be considered as having been published simultaneously in several countries if it has been published in two or more countries within thirty days of its first publication.

Article 4

[Criteria of Eligibility for Protection of Cinematographic Works, Works of Architecture and Certain Artistic Works]

The protection of this Convention shall apply, even if the conditions of Article 3 are not fulfilled, to:

(a) authors of cinematographic works the maker of which has his headquarters or habitual residence in one of the countries of the Union.

(b) authors of works of architecture erected in a country of the Union or of other artistic works incorporated in a building or other structure located in a country of the Union.

Article 5
[Rights Guaranteed: 1. and 2. Outside the country of origin; 3. In the country of origin; 4. 'Country of origin']

(1) Authors shall enjoy, in respect of works for which they are protected under this Convention, in countries of the Union other than the country of origin, the rights which their respective laws do now or may hereafter grant to their nationals, as well as the rights specially granted by this Convention.

(2) The enjoyment and the exercise of these rights shall not be subject to any formality; such enjoyment and such exercise shall be independent of the existence of protection in the country of origin of the work. Consequently, apart from the provisions of this Convention, the extent of protection, as well as the means of redress afforded to the author to protect his rights, shall be governed exclusively by the laws of the country where protection is claimed.

(3) Protection in the country of origin is governed by domestic law. However, when the author is not a national of the country of origin of the work for which he is protected under this Convention, he shall enjoy in that country the same rights as national authors.

(4) The country of origin shall be considered to be:
    (a) in the case of works first published in a country of the Union, that country; in the case of works published simultaneously in several countries of the Union which grant different terms of protection, the country whose legislation grants the shortest term of protection;
    (b) in the case of works published simultaneously in a country outside the Union and in a country of the Union, the latter country;
    (c) in the case of unpublished works or of works first published in a country outside the Union, without simultaneous publication in a country of the Union, the country of the Union of which the author is a national, provided that:
        (i) when these are cinematographic works the maker of which has his headquarters or his habitual residence in a country of the Union, the country of origin shall be that country, and
        (ii) when these are works of architecture erected in a country of the Union or other artistic works incorporated in a building or other structure located in a country of the Union, the country of origin shall be that country.

Article 6
[Possible Restriction of Protection In Respect of Certain Works of Nationals of Certain Countries Outside the Union: 1. In the country of the first publication and in other countries; 2. No retroactivity; 3. Notice]

(1) Where any country outside the Union fails to protect in an adequate manner the works of authors who are nationals of one of the countries of the Union, the latter country may restrict the protection given to the works of authors who are, at the date of the first publication thereof, nationals of the other country and are not

habitually resident in one of the countries of the Union. If the country of first publication avails itself of this right, the other countries of the Union shall not be required to grant to works thus subjected to special treatment a wider protection than that granted to them in the country of first publication.

(2) No restrictions introduced by virtue of the preceding paragraph shall affect the rights which an author may have acquired in respect of a work published in a country of the Union before such restrictions were put into force.

(3) The countries of the Union which restrict the grant of copyright in accordance with this Article shall give notice thereof to the Director General of the World Intellectual Property Organization (hereinafter designated as 'the Director General') by a written declaration specifying the countries in regard to which protection is restricted, and the restrictions to which rights of authors who are nationals of those countries are subjected. The Director General shall immediately communicate this declaration to all the countries of the Union.

Article 6bis

[Moral Rights: 1. To claim authorship; to object to certain modifications and other derogatory actions; 2. After the author's death; 3. Means of redress]

(1) Independently of the author's economic rights and even after the transfer of the said rights, the author shall have the right to claim authorship of the work and to object to any distortion, mutilation or other modification of, or other derogatory action in relation to, the said work, which would be prejudicial to his honour or reputation.

(2) The rights granted to the author in accordance with the preceding paragraph shall, after his death, be maintained at least until the expiry of the economic rights, and shall be exercisable by the persons or institutions authorised by the legislation of the country where protection is claimed. However, those countries whose legislation, at the moment of their ratification of or accession to this Act, does not provide for the protection after the death of the author of all the rights set out in the preceding paragraph may provide that some of these rights may, after his death, cease to be maintained.

(3) The means of redress for safeguarding the rights granted by this article shall be governed by the legislation of the country where protection is claimed.

Article 7

[Term of Protection: 1. Generally; 2. For cinematographic works; 3. For anonymous and pseudonymous works; 4. For photographic works and works of applied art; 5. Starting date of computation; 6. Longer terms; 7. Shorter terms; 8. Applicable law: 'comparison' of terms]

(1) The terms of protection granted by this Convention shall be the life of the author and fifty years after his death.

(2) However, in the case of cinematographic works, the countries of the Union may provide that the terms of protection shall expire fifty years after the work has been made available to the public with the consent of the author, or, failing such an event within fifty years from the making of such a work, fifty years after the making.

(3) In the case of anonymous or pseudonymous works, the terms of protection granted by this Convention shall expire fifty years after the work has been lawfully made available to the public. However, when the pseudonym adopted by the author leaves no doubt as to his identity, the term of protection shall be that provided in paragraph (1). If the author of an anonymous or pseudonymous work discloses his

identity during the above-mentioned period, the term of protection applicable shall be that provided in paragraph (1). The countries of the Union shall not be required to protect anonymous or pseudonymous works in respect of which it is reasonable to presume that their author has been dead for fifty years.

(4) It shall be a matter for legislation in the countries of the Union to determine the term of protection of photographic works and that of works of applied art in so far as they are protected as artistic works; however, this term shall last at least until the end of a period of twenty-five years from the making of such a work.

(5) The term of protection subsequent to the death of the author and the terms provided by paragraphs (2), (3) and (4) shall run from the date of death or of the event referred to in those paragraphs, but such terms shall always be deemed to begin on the first of January of the year following the death or such event.

(6) The countries of the Union may grant a term of protection in excess of those provided by the preceding paragraphs.

(7) Those countries of the Union bound by the Rome Act of this Convention which grant, in their national legislation in force at the time of signature of the present Act, shorter terms of protection than those provided for in the preceding paragraphs shall have the right to maintain such terms when ratifying or acceding to the present Act.

(8) In any case, the term shall be governed by the legislation of the country where protection is claimed; however, unless the legislation of that country otherwise provides, the term shall not exceed the term fixed in the country of origin of the work.

Article 7[bis]
[Term of Protection for Works of Joint Authorship]

The provisions of the preceding Article shall also apply in the case of a work of joint authorship, provided that the terms measured from the death of the author shall be calculated from the death of the last surviving author.

Article 8
[Right of Translation]

Authors of literary and artistic works protected by this Convention shall enjoy the exclusive right of making and of authorizing the translation of their works throughout the term of protection of their rights in the original works.

Article 9
[Right of Reproduction: 1. Generally; 2. Possible exceptions; 3. Sound and visual recordings]

(1) Authors of literary and artistic works protected by this Convention shall have the exclusive right of authorizing the reproduction of these works, in any manner or form.

(2) It shall be a matter for legislation in the countries of the Union to permit the reproduction of such works in certain special cases, provided that such reproduction does not conflict with a normal exploitation of the work and does not unreasonably prejudice the legitimate interests of the author.

(3) Any sound or visual recording shall be considered as a reproduction for the purposes of this Convention.

Article 10
[Certain Free Uses of Works: 1. Quotations; 2. Illustrations for teaching; 3. Indication of source and author]

(1) It shall be permissible to make quotations from a work which has already been lawfully made available to the public, provided that their making is compatible with fair practice, and their extent does not exceed that justified by the purpose, including quotations from newspaper articles and periodicals in the form of press summaries.

(2) It shall be a matter for legislation in the countries of the Union, and for special agreements existing or to be concluded between them, to permit the utilization, to the extent justified by the purpose, of literary or artistic works by way of illustration in publications, broadcasts or sound or visual recordings for teaching, provided such utilization is compatible with fair practice.

(3) Where use is made of works in accordance with the preceding paragraphs of this Article, mention shall be made of the source, and of the name of the author if it appears thereon.

Article 10bis
[Further Possible Free Uses of Works: 1. Of certain articles and broadcast works; 2. Of works seen or heard in connection with current events]

(1) It shall be a matter for legislation in the countries of the Union to permit the reproduction by the press, the broadcasting or the communication to the public by wire of articles published in newspapers or periodicals on current economic, political or religious topics, and of broadcast works of the same character, in cases in which the reproduction, broadcasting or such communication thereof is not expressly reserved. Nevertheless, the source must always be clearly indicated; the legal consequences of a breach of this obligation shall be determined by the legislation of the country where protection is claimed.

(2) It shall also be a matter for legislation in the countries of the Union to determine the conditions under which, for the purpose of reporting current events by means of photography, cinematography, broadcasting or communication to the public by wire, literary or artistic works seen or heard in the course of the even may, to the extent justified by the informatory purpose, be reproduced and made available to the public.

Article 11
[Certain Rights in Dramatic and Musical Works: 1. Right of public performance and of communication to the public of a performance; 2. In respect of translations]

(1) Authors of dramatic, dramatico-musical and musical works shall enjoy the exclusive right of authorizing:
- (i)   the public performance of their works, including such public performance by any means or process;
- (ii) any communication to the public of the performance of their works.

(2) Authors of dramatic or dramatico-musical works shall enjoy, during the full term of their rights in the original works, the same rights with respect to translations thereof.

Article 11bis

[Broadcasting and Related Rights: 1. Broadcasting and other wireless communications, public communication of broadcast by wire or rebroadcast, public communication of broadcast by loudspeaker or analogous instruments; 2. Compulsory licenses; 3. Recording; ephermeral recordings]

(1) Authors of literary and artistic works shall enjoy the exclusive right of authorizing:

    (i) the broadcasting of their works or the communication thereof to the public by any other means of wireless diffusion of signs, sounds or images;

    (ii) any communication to the public by wire or by rebroadcasting of the broadcast of the work, when this communication is made by an organization other than the original one;

    (iii) the public communication by loudspeaker or any other analogous instrument transmitting, by signs, sounds or images, the broadcast of the work.

(2) It shall be a matter for legislation in the countries of the Union to determine the conditions under which the rights mentioned in the preceding paragraph may be exercised, but these conditions shall apply only in the countries where they have been prescribed. They shall not in any circumstances be prejudicial to the moral rights of the author, nor to his right to obtain equitable remuneration which, in the absence of agreement, shall be fixed by competent authority.

(3) In the absence of any contrary stipulation, permission granted in accordance with paragraph (1) of this Article shall not imply permission to record, by means of instruments recording sounds or images, the work broadcast. It shall, however, be a matter for legislation in the countries of the Union to determine the regulations for ephemeral recordings made by a broadcasting organization by means of its own facilities and used for its own broadcasts. The preservation of these recordings in official archives may, on the ground of their exceptional documentary character, be authorized by such legislation.

Article 11ter

[Certain Rights in Literary Works: 1. Right of public recitation and of communication to the public of a recitation; 2. In respect of translations]

(1) Authors of literary works shall enjoy the exclusive right of authorizing:

    (i) the public recitation of their works, including such public recitation by any means or process;

    (ii) any communication to the public of the recitation of their works.

(2) Authors of literary works shall enjoy, during the full term of their rights in the original works, the same rights with respect to translations thereof.

Article 12

[Right of Adaptation, Arrangement and Other Alteration]

Authors of literary or artistic works shall enjoy the exclusive right of authorizing adaptations, arrangements and other alterations of their works.

Article 13
[Possible Limitation of the Right of Recording of Musical Works and Any Words Pertaining Thereto: 1. Compulsory licenses; 2. Transitory measures; 3. Seizure on importation of copies made without the author's permission]

(1) Each country of the Union may impose for itself reservations and conditions on the exclusive right granted to the author of a musical work and to the author of any words, the recording of which together with the musical work has already been authorized by the latter, to authorize the sound recording of that musical work, together with such words, if any; but all such reservations and conditions shall apply only in the countries which have imposed them and shall not, in any circumstances, be prejudicial to the rights of these authors to obtain equitable remuneration which, in the absence of agreement, shall be fixed by competent authority.

(2) Recordings of musical works made in a country of the Union in accordance with Article 13(3) of the Conventions signed at Rome on June 2, 1928, and at Brussels on June 26, 1948, may be reproduced in that country without the permission of the author of the musical work until a date two years after that country becomes bound by this Act.

(3) Recordings made in accordance with paragraphs (1) and (2) of this Article and imported without permission from the parties concerned into a country where they are treated as infringing recordings shall be liable to seizure.

Article 14
[Cinematographic and Related Rights: 1. Cinematographic adaptation and reproduction; distribution; public performance and public communication by wire of works thus adapted or reproduced; 2. Adaptation of cinematographic productions: 3. No compulsory licenses]

(1) Authors of literary or artistic works shall have the exclusive right of authorizing:
  (i)   the cinematrographic adaptation and reproduction of these works, and the distribution of the works thus adapted or reproduced.
  (ii) the public performance and communication to the public by wire of the works thus adapted or reproduced.

(2) The adaptation into any other artistic form of a cinematographic production derived from literary or artistic works shall, without prejudice to the authorization of the author of the cinematographic production, remain subject to the authorization of the authors of the original works.

(3) The provisions of Article 13(1) shall not apply.

Article 14bis
[Special Provisions Concerning Cinematographic Works: 1. Assimilation to 'original' works; 2. Ownership; limitation of certain rights of certain contributors; 3. Certain other contributors]

(1) Without prejudice to the copyright in any work which may have been adapted or reproduced, a cinematographic work shall be protected as an original work. The owner of copyright in a cinematographic work shall enjoy the same rights as the author of an original work, including the rights referred to in the preceding Article.
  (2) (a) Ownership of copyright in a cinematographic work shall be a matter for legislation in the country where protection is claimed.
      (b) However, in the countries of the Union which, by legislation, include among the owners of copyright in a cinematographic work authors

who have brought contributions to the making of the work, such authors, if they have undertaken to bring such contributions, may not, in the absence of any contrary or special stipulation, object to the reproduction, distribution, public performance, communication to the public by wire, broadcasting or any other communication to the public, or to the subtitling or dubbing of texts, of the work.

(c) The question whether or not the form of the undertaking referred to above should, for the application of the preceding subparagraph (b), be in a written agreement or a written act of the same effect shall be a matter for the legislation of the country where the maker of the cinematographic work has his headquarters or habitual residence. However, it shall be a matter for the legislation of the country of the Union where protection is claimed to provide that the said undertaking shall be in a written agreement or a written act of the same effect. The countries whose legislation so provides shall notify the Director General by means of a written declaration, which will be immediately communicated by him to all the other countries of the Union.

(d) By 'contrary or special stipulation' is meant any restrictive condition which is relevant to the aforesaid undertaking.

(3) Unless the national legislation provides to the contrary, the provisions of paragraph (2)(b) above shall not be applicable to authors of scenarios, dialogues and musical works created for the making of the cinematographic work, or to the principal director thereof. However, those countries of the Union whose legislation does not contain rules providing for the application of the said paragraph (2)(b) to such director shall notify the Director General by means of a written declaration, which will be immediately communicated by him to all the other countries of the Union.

Article 14ter

['Droit de suite' in Works of Art and Manuscripts: 1. Right to an interest in resales; 2. Applicable law; 3. Procedure]

(1) The author, or after his death the persons or institutions authorized by national legislation, shall, with respect to original works of art and original manuscripts of writers and composers, enjoy the inalienable right to an interest in any sale of the work subsequent to the first transfer by the author of the work.

(2) The protection provided by the preceding paragraph may be claimed in a country of the Union only if legislation in the country to which the author belongs so permits, and to the extent permitted by the country where this protection is claimed.

(3) The procedure for collection and the amounts shall be matters for determination by national legislation.

Article 15

[Rights to Enforce Protected Rights: 1. Where author's name is indicated or where pseudonym leaves no doubt as to author's identity; 2. In the case of cinematographic works; 3. In the case of anonymous and pseudonymous works; 4. In the case of certain unpublished works of unknown authorship]

(1)   In order that the author of a literary or artistic work protected by this Convention shall, in the absence of proof to the contrary, be regarded as such, and

consequently be entitled to institute infringement proceedings in the countries of the Union, it shall be sufficient for his name to appear on the work in the usual manner. This paragraph shall be applicable even if this name is a pseudonym, where the pseudonym adopted by the author leaves no doubt as to his identity.

(2)   The person or body corporate whose name appears on a cinematographic work in the usual manner shall, in the absence of proof to the contrary, be presumed to be the maker of the said work.

(3)   In the case of anonymous and pseudonymous works, other than those referred to in paragraph (1) above, the publisher whose name appears on the work shall, in the absence of proof to the contrary, be deemed to represent the author, and in this capacity he shall be entitled to protect and enforce the author's rights. The provisions of this paragraph shall cease to apply when the author reveals his identity and establishes his claim to authorship of the work.

(4) (a)   In the case of unpublished works where the identity of the author is unknown, but where there is every ground to presume that he is a national of a country of the Union, it shall be a matter for legislation in that country to designate the competent authority which shall represent the author and shall be entitled to protect and enforce his rights in the countries of the Union.

(b)   Countries of the Union which make such designation under the terms of this provision shall notify the Director General by means of a written declaration giving full information concerning the authority thus designated. The Director General shall at once communicate this declaration to all other countries of the Union.

Article 16
[Infringing Copies: 1. Seizure; 2. Seizure on importation; 3. Applicable law]

(1)   Infringing copies of a work shall be liable to seizure in any country of the Union where the work enjoys legal protection.

(2)   The provisions of the preceding paragraph shall also apply to reproductions coming from a country where the work is not protected, or has ceased to be protected.

(3)   The seizure shall take place in accordance with the legislation of each country.

Article 17
[Possibility of Control of Circulation, Presentation and Exhibition of Works]

The provisions of this Convention cannot in any way affect the right of the Government of each country of the Union to permit, to control, or to prohibit, by legislation or regulation, the circulation, presentation, or exhibition of any work or production in regard to which the competent authority may find it necessary to exercise that right.

Article 18

[Works Existing on Convention's Entry Into Force: 1. Protectable where protection not yet expired in country of origin; 2. Non-protectable where protection already expired in country where it is claimed; 3. Application of these principles; 4. Special cases]

(1)   This Convention shall apply to all works which, at the moment of its coming into force, have not yet fallen into the public domain in the country of origin through the expiry of the term of protection.

(2)   If, however, through the expiry of the term of protection which was previously granted, a work has fallen into the public domain of the country where protection is claimed, that work shall not be protected anew.

(3)   The application of this principle shall be subject to any provisions contained in special conventions to that effect existing or to be concluded between countries of the Union. In the absence of such provisions, the respective countries shall determine, each in so far as it is concerned, the conditions of application of this principle.

(4)   The preceding provisions shall also apply in the case of new accessions to the Union and to cases in which protection is extended by the application of Article 7 or by the abandonment of reservations.

Article 19

[Protection Greater than Resulting from Convention]

The provisions of this Convention shall not preclude the making of a claim to the benefit of any greater protection which may be granted by legislation in a country of the Union.

Article 20

[Special Agreements Among Countries of the Union]

The Governments of the countries of the Union reserve the right to enter into special agreements among themselves, in so far as such agreements grant to authors more extensive rights than those granted by the Convention, or contain other provisions not contrary to this Convention. The provisions of existing agreements which satisfy these conditions shall remain applicable.

Agreement on Trade-Related Aspects of Intellectual Property Rights

Part II. Standards concerning the availability, scope and use of Intellectual Property rights
Section 1. Copyright and related rights

Article 9
Relation to the Berne Convention

1.   Members shall comply with Articles 1 through 21 of the Berne Convention (1971) and the Appendix thereto.   However, Members shall not have rights or

obligations under this Agreement in respect of the rights conferred under Article 6bis of that Convention or of the rights derived therefrom.

2.   Copyright protection shall extend to expressions and not to ideas, procedures, methods of operation or mathematical concepts as such.

Article 10
Computer programs and compilations of data

1.   Computer programs, whether in source or object code, shall be protected as literary works under the Berne Convention (1971).

2.   Compilations of data or other material, whether in machine readable or other form, which by reason of the selection or arrangement of their contents constitute intellectual creations shall be protected as such.   Such protection, which shall not extend to the data or material itself, shall be without prejudice to any copyright subsisting in the data or material itself.

Article 11
Rental rights

In respect of at least computer programs and cinematographic works, a Member shall provide authors and their successors in title the right to authorize or to prohibit the commercial rental to the public of originals or copies of their copyright works. A Member shall be excepted from this obligation in respect of cinematographic works unless such rental has led to widespread copying of such works which is materially impairing the exclusive right of reproduction conferred in that Member on authors and their successors in title. In respect of computer programs, this obligation does not apply to rentals where the program itself is not the essential object of the rental.

Article 12
Term of protection

Whenever the term of protection of a work, other than a photographic work or a work of applied art, is calculated on a basis other than the life of a natural person, such term shall be no less than 50 years from the end of the calendar year of authorized publication, or, failing such authorized publication within 50 years from the making of the work, 50 years from the end of the calendar year of making.

Article 13
Limitations and exceptions

Members shall confine limitations or exceptions to exclusive rights to certain special cases which do not conflict with a normal exploitation of the work and do not unreasonably prejudice the legitimate interests of the right holder.

Article 14
Protection of performers, producers of phonograms (sound recordings) and broadcasting organizations

1.   In respect of a fixation of their performance on a phonogram, performers shall have the possibility of preventing the following acts when undertaken without their

authorization: the fixation of their unfixed performance and the reproduction of such fixation. Performers shall also have the possibility of preventing the following acts when undertaken without their authorization: the broadcasting by wireless means and the communication to the public of their live performance.

2. Producers of phonograms shall enjoy the right to authorize or prohibit the direct or indirect reproduction of their phonograms.

3. Broadcasting organizations shall have the right to prohibit the following acts when undertaken without their authorization: the fixation, the reproduction of fixations, and the rebroadcasting by wireless means of broadcasts, as well as the communication to the public of television broadcasts of the same. Where Members do not grant such rights to broadcasting organizations, they shall provide owners of copyright in the subject matter of broadcasts with the possibility of preventing the above acts, subject to the provisions of the Berne Convention (1971).

4. The provisions of Article 11 in respect of computer programs shall apply *mutatis mutandis* to producers of phonograms and any other right holders in phonograms as determined in a Member's law. If on 15 April 1994 a Member has in force a system of equitable remuneration of right holders in respect of the rental of phonograms, it may maintain such system provided that the commercial rental of phonograms is not giving rise to the material impairment of the exclusive rights of reproduction of right holders.

5. The term of the protection available under this Agreement to performers and producers of phonograms shall last at least until the end of a period of 50 years computed from the end of the calendar year in which the fixation was made or the performance took place. The term of protection granted pursuant to paragraph 3 shall last for at least 20 years from the end of the calendar year in which the broadcast took place.

6. Any Member may, in relation to the rights conferred under paragraphs 1, 2 and 3, provide for conditions, limitations, exceptions and reservations to the extent permitted by the Rome Convention. However, the provisions of Article 18 of the Berne Convention (1971) shall also apply, *mutatis mutandis,* to the rights of performers and producers of phonograms in phonograms.

Chapter 3

The Law of Breach of Confidence

Introduction

The law of confidence provides a useful weapon in the fight against the unauthorised disclosure, use or misappropriation of a person's ideas and information. It is particularly important in the early days of the development of a creative work or invention before there is sufficient of a tangible nature to be protected by other intellectual property rights such as a patent or copyright.

The scope of the subject-matter of confidential information is very wide, ranging from secret industrial processes to names and addresses of business customers. It also covers personal secrets and government intelligence. An obligation of confidence will be imposed in a large number of situations, sometimes expressly, but the beauty of this area of law is that it is implied into many relationships, contractual or otherwise. For example, an obligation of confidence will be implied in the doctor-patient or advisor-client relationship. In this way, the law of confidence can be seen as giving rise to a fiduciary duty; a duty of good faith not to disclose or misuse confidential information without the permission of the person who has disclosed it willingly on the implicit understanding that it will go no further or be used for other purposes.

The primary remedy is the *quia timet* injunction to prevent an anticipated unauthorised disclosure or use of the information by the person to whom it was imparted in confidence. This is the main strength and rationale of this area of law. Lying in equity, confidence requires fast action by the plaintiff for effective control but nowhere is the need for speed so important, as the public domain is the graveyard of confidences.

Basic Requirements

Although the equitable doctrine of breach of confidence is quite old, its development to its modern form is only quite recent. There were a flurry of cases in Victorian times, such as *Prince Albert* v *Strange* (1849) 1 Mac & G 25 and *Morison* v *Moat* (1851) 9 Hare 241, but the greatest recognition of the usefulness of an action in breach of confidence has come in the last 50 years or so. Even so, Lord Greene MR, in a case decided in 1948, considered the nature of confidence to be well settled.

Saltman Engineering Co. Ltd. v *Campbell Engineering Co. Ltd.* [1963] 3 All ER 403, Court of Appeal.

The plaintiff owned the copyright in engineering drawings of tools for making leather punches. The drawings were given to Monarch Engineering which passed them on to the defendant, as sub-contractor, for the purpose of manufacturing the tools and making some 5,000 leather punches at 3s 6d each. The defendant was acting as agent or subcontractor to the plaintiff. Following delivery of the punches, the defendant retained the drawings and the tools made in accordance with them. It was alleged that there was an implied undertaking of confidence such that the defendant could not use the drawings or the tools otherwise than to fulfil its obligations under the sub-contract.

Lord Greene MR (at 414): 'The main part of the claim is based on breach of confidence, in respect of which a right may be infringed without the necessity of there being any contractual relationship. I will explain what I mean. If two parties make a contract, under which one of them obtains for the purpose of the contract or in connexion with it some confidential matter, then, even though the contract is silent on the matter of confidence, the law will imply an obligation to treat that confidential matter in a confidential way, as one of the implied terms of the contract: but the obligation to respect confidence is not limited to cases where the parties are in contractual relationship. The learned judge, having declined to find any contract between Monarch and the defendants, went on, if I understand his judgment correctly, to hold that for that reason there could be no relationship of confidence between any of the plaintiffs and the defendants. In my opinion, the learned judge erred in law in coming to that conclusion. He did not deal with the really substantial point in the case, namely, whether or not the defendants had committed a breach of confidence which infringed the rights of Saltmans, who owned the confidential matter. Into that question he did not go and the consequence is, from our point of view, that we have not the advantage of any findings of his on matters of fact which are relevant to the issue of breach of confidence as between Saltmans and the defendants ...

The other point is that, even if Mr Ransom did not make a contract with the defendants, it does not alter the fact that the confidential drawings handed to the defendants for the purpose of executing the order placed with them were the property of Saltmans, and the defendants knew that at a comparatively early date in this history. They knew that they were drawings belonging to Saltmans. Saltmans had not in fact paid for them, but that did not alter the fact that they were Saltman's drawings. The defendants knew that those drawings had been placed in their possession for a limited purpose, namely, the purpose only of making certain tools in accordance with them, the tools being tools required for the purpose of manufacturing leather punches.

Without going further into the matter it seems to me that the existence of a confidential obligation in relation to these drawings, as between Saltmans and the defendants, is abundantly proved; in fact it is not disputed. I need not go into the law, which I think is correctly stated in a formula which leading counsel for the defendants himself accepted. I will read it:

"If a defendant is proved to have used confidential information, directly or indirectly obtained from a plaintiff, without the consent, express or implied of the plaintiff, he will be guilty of an infringement of the plaintiff's rights."

There are several cases which deal with that (*Morison* v *Moat* (1851), 9 Hare 241, is one of the better known of them) and I need not examine them further. The principle is established and is not disputed: and it is perfectly clear that an obligation, based on confidence, existed and bound the conscience of the defendants down to November 22, 1945 ... I think that I shall not be stating the principle wrongly, if I say this with regard to the use of confidential information. The information, to be confidential, must, I apprehend, apart from contract, have the necessary quality of confidence about it, namely, it must not be something which is public property and public knowledge. On the other hand, it is perfectly possible to have a confidential document, be it a formula, a plan, a sketch, or something of that kind, which is the result of work done by the maker on materials which may be available for the use of anybody; but what makes it confidential is the fact that the maker of the document has used his brain and thus produced a result which can only be produced by somebody who goes through the same process.

What the defendants did in this case was to dispense in certain material respects with the necessity of going through the process which had been gone through in compiling these drawings, and thereby to save themselves a great deal of labour and calculation and careful draughtsmanship. No doubt, if they had taken a finished article, namely the leather punch, which they might have bought in a shop, and given it to an expert draughtsman, that draughtsman could have produced the necessary drawings for the manufacture of machine tools required for making that particular finished article. In at any rate a very material respect they saved themselves that trouble by obtaining the necessary information either from the original drawings or from the tools made in accordance with them. That, in my opinion, was a breach of confidence. In the view that I take this case is a simple one: there has been a breach of confidence, the duty of confidence owed in the circumstances of this case by the defendants to Saltmans. It is not necessary to go into the question whether there was an implied obligation of confidence as between the two contracting parties, Monarch and the defendants. I need say nothing about that, because quite obviously in the circumstances, if Monarch obtained any relief based on that, they could hold it only for the benefit of Saltmans, who are the owners of the confidential matter ... In my opinion the plaintiffs are entitled to the appropriate relief in respect of the infringement of their right.'

COMMENT

There were also issues under copyright and contract but these were not relevant to the appeal. Lord Greene MR confirmed that there is no need for a contract for an action in confidence, something which had been accepted for over 100 years. However, an interesting aspect of his judgment is that the law of confidence can apply even if the information is not unique and could be derived by someone else. In this way, what is protected is the work required to obtain or create the information.

Does re-creating confidential information by a process of reverse engineering constitute a breach of confidence? How could the defendant later make punches to compete with those made under the sub-contract without being in breach of confidence? Does the law of confidence conflict with competition law?

Megarry J further considered the nature of an action in breach of confidence in *Coco* v *A. N. Clark (Engineers) Ltd.* [1969] RPC 41 which involved information concerning an engine designed for a moped.

Coco v A. N. Clark (Engineers) Ltd. [1969] RPC 41, Chancery Division

The plaintiff designed a new moped with a new design of two-stroke engine and had a prototype made. Following an initial discussion between the plaintiff and the defendant company, which was interested in making mopeds to the design, the plaintiff delivered the prototype and there were a number of meetings and further negotiations. The plaintiff also supplied further information and drawings. However, eventually, because of an alleged defect in the transmission envisaged by the plaintiff for his moped (by means of roller friction on the rear tyre of the moped) the defendant announced that it did not want to use the plaintiff's design and that it had decided to make mopeds to its own design. The plaintiff believed that this was a ruse to obtain his engine design without having to pay for it. He claimed that the alleged transmission problem was a mere excuse. No agreement had been executed between the plaintiff and defendant. The plaintiff sued for breach of confidence after he suspected that the defendant was about to market a moped that had an engine with a similar piston and carburettor to his.

Megarry J (at 46): 'Mr Mowbray bases himself on the defendant company's misuse of information given to the company under circumstances of confidence. The essence of his case is breach of confidence. He expressly disclaims any contention that he could enjoin mere copying such as might have occurred if the Coco [engine] had been manufactured and put on the market by the plaintiff, and the defendant company had then bought one of them, dismantled it and slavishly copied it. Mr Mowbray says that what happened here was that the plaintiff supplied confidential information to the defendant company for one particular purpose, namely, a joint venture in producing the Coco, and that for the defendant company to use this information for its own purposes without the plaintiff's consent is a breach of confidence ... The equitable jurisdiction in cases of breach of confidence is ancient: confidence is the cousin of trust. The Statute of Uses, 1535, is framed in terms of "use, confidence or trust": and a couplet, attributed to Sir Thomas More, Lord Chancellor avers that

> "Three things are to be helpt in Conscience:
> Fraud, Accident and things of Confidence."

(See 1 Rolle's Abridgement 374). In the middle of the last century, the great case of *Prince Albert* v *Strange* (1849) 1 Mac. & G. 25 reasserted the doctrine. In the case before me, it is common ground that there is no question of any breach of contract, for no contract ever came into existence. Accordingly, what I have to consider is the pure equitable doctrine of confidence, unaffected by contract. Furthermore, I am here in the realms of commerce, and there is no question of any marital relationship such as arose in *Duchess of Argyll* v *Duke of Argyll* [1967] Ch 302. Thus limited, what are the essentials of the doctrine?

Of the various authorities cited to me, I have found *Saltman Engineering Co. Ltd. v Campbell Engineering Co. Ltd.* (1948) 65 RPC 203; *Terrapin Ltd.* v *Builders' Supply Co. (Hayes) Ltd.* [1960] RPC 128 and *Seager* v *Copydex Ltd.* [1967] 1 WLR 923; [1967] RPC 349 of the most assistance. All are decisions of the Court of Appeal. I think it is quite plain from the *Saltman* case that the obligation of confidence may exist where, as in this case, there is no contractual relationship between the parties. In cases of contract, the primary question is no doubt that of construing the contract and any terms implied in it. Where there is no contract, however, the question must be one of what it is that suffices to bring the obligation into being; and there is the further question of what amounts to a breach of that obligation.

In my judgment, three elements are normally required if, apart from contract a case of breach of confidence is to succeed. First, the information itself, in the words of Lord Greene, MR in the *Saltman* case, must "have the necessary quality of confidence about it." Secondly, that information must have been imparted in circumstances importing an obligation of confidence. Thirdly, there must be an unauthorised use of that information to the detriment of the party communicating it. I must briefly examine each of these requirements in turn.

First the information must be of a confidential nature. As Lord Greene said in the *Saltman* case, "something which is public property and public knowledge" cannot *per se* provide any foundation for proceedings for breach of confidence. However confidential the circumstances of communication, there can be no breach of confidence in revealing to others something which is already common knowledge. But this must not be taken too far. Something that has been constructed solely from materials in the public domain may possess the necessary quality of confidentiality: for something new and confidential may have been brought into being by the application of the skill and ingenuity of the human brain. Novelty depends on the thing itself, and not upon the quality of its constituent parts. Indeed, often the more striking the novelty, the more commonplace its components. Mr Mowbray demurs to the concept that some degree of originality is requisite. But whether it is described as originality or novelty or ingenuity or otherwise, I think there must be some product of the human brain which suffices to confer a confidential nature upon the information: and, expressed in those terms, I think that Mr Mowbray accepts the concept.

The difficulty comes, as Lord Denning, MR pointed out in the *Seager* case, when the information used is partly public and partly private: for then the recipient must somehow segregate the two and although free to use the former, must take no advantage of the communication of the latter. To this subject I must in due course return. I must also return to a further point, namely, that where confidential information is communicated in circumstances of confidence the obligation thus created endures, perhaps in a modified form, even after all the information has been published or is ascertainable by the public; for the recipient must not use the communication as a spring-board. I should add that, as shown by *Cranleigh Precision Engineering Ltd.* v *Bryant* [1965] 1 WLR 1293; [1966] RPC 81, the mere simplicity of an idea does not prevent it being confidential. Indeed, the simpler an idea, the more likely it is to need protection.

The second requirement is that the information must have been communicated in circumstances importing an obligation of confidence. However secret and confidential the information, there can be no binding obligation of confidence if that information is blurted out in public or is communicated in other circumstances which negative any duty of holding it confidential. From the authorities cited to me, I have not been able to derive any very precise idea of what test is to be applied in determining whether the circumstances import an obligation of confidence. In the *Argyll* case, Ungoed-Thomas, J concluded his discussion of the circumstances in which the publication of marital communications should be restrained as being confidential by saying, "If this was a well-developed jurisdiction doubtless there would be guides and tests to aid in exercising it." In the absence of such guides or tests he then in effect concluded that part of the communications there in question would on any reasonable test emerge as confidential. It may be that that hard-worked creature, the reasonable man, may be pressed into service once more; for I do not see why he should not labour in equity as well as at law. It seems to me that if the circumstances are such that any reasonable man standing in the shoes of the recipient of the information would have realised that upon reasonable grounds the information was being given to him in confidence, then this should suffice to impose upon him the equitable obligation of confidence. In particular, where information of commercial or industrial value is given on a business-like basis and with some avowed common object in mind, such as a joint venture or the manufacture of articles by one party for the other, I would regard the recipient as carrying a heavy burden if he seeks to repel a contention that he was bound by an obligation of confidence: see the *Saltman* case. On that footing, for reasons that will appear, I do not think I need explore this head further. I merely add that I doubt whether equity would intervene unless the circumstances are of sufficient gravity; equity ought not to be invoked merely to protect trivial tittle-tattle, however confidential.

Thirdly, there must be an unauthorised use of the information to the detriment of the person communicating it. Some of the statements of principle in the cases omit any mention of detriment; others include it. At first sight, it seems that detriment ought to be present if equity is to be induced to intervene; but I can conceive of cases where a plaintiff might have substantial motives for seeking the aid of equity and yet suffer nothing which could fairly be called detriment to him as when the confidential information shows him in a favourable light but gravely injures some relation or friend of his whom he wishes to protect. The point does not arise for decision in this case, for detriment to the plaintiff plainly exists. I need therefore say no more than that although for the purposes of this case I have stated the propositions in the stricter form, I wish to keep open the possibility of the true proposition being that in the wider form ... I should mention one point on the substantive law that caused me some difficulty during the argument. This is what may be called the "spring board" doctrine. In the *Seager case*, Lord Denning quoted a sentence from the judgment of Roxburgh, J in the *Terrapin* case, which was quoted and adopted as correct by Roskill, J in the *Cranleigh* case. It runs as follows:

"As I understand it, the essence of this branch of the law, whatever the origin of it may be, is that a person who has obtained information in confidence is not allowed to use it as a spring-board for activities detrimental to the person who made the confidential communication, and spring-board it remains even when all the features have been published or can be ascertained by actual inspection by any member of the public."

Salmon, LJ in the *Seager* case also states: "The law does not allow the use of such information even as a spring-board for activities detrimental to the plaintiff."

Quite apart from authority, I would recognise the principle enshrined in those words as being salutary. Nevertheless, I am not entirely clear how it is to be put into practical effect in every case. Suppose a case where there is a confidential communication of information which is partly public and partly private; suppose that the recipient of the information adds in confidence ideas of his own, improving the initial scheme; and suppose that the parties then part, with no agreement concluded between them. How is a conscientious recipient of the ideas to comply with the requirements that equity lays upon him? For in the words of Lord Denning in the *Seager* case, he:

> "must take special care to use only the material which is in the public domain. He should go to the public source and get it: or, at any rate, not be in a better position than if he had gone to the public source. He should not get a start over others by using the information which he received in confidence."

Suppose that the only confidential information communicated is that some important component should be made of aluminium instead of steel and with significant variations in its design and dimensions. The recipient knows that this change will transform a failure into a success. He knows that, if he had persevered himself, he might have come upon the solution in a week or in a year. Yet he is under a duty not to use the confidential information as a spring-board or as giving him a start.

What puzzles me is how, as a law-abiding citizen, he is to perform that duty. He could, I suppose, commission someone else to make the discovery anew, carefully abstaining from saying anything to him about aluminium or the design and dimensions which will achieve success; but this seems to me to be artificial in the extreme. Yet until this step is taken and the discovery made anew, he cannot make use of his own added ideas for the further improvement of the design which he had already communicated in confidence to the original communicator, ideas which would perhaps make a success into a triumph. He cannot build his super-structure as long as he is forbidden to use the foundations. Nor is the original communicator in a much better case. He is free to use his own original idea, which converted failure into success; but he cannot take advantage of the original recipient's further ideas, of which he knows, until such time as he or someone commissioned by him would, unaided by any confidence, have discovered them.

For those who are not law-abiding and conscientious citizens there is, I suppose, a simple answer: ignore the duty, use the information, and then pay damages. This may be the course which Lord Denning envisaged in the *Seager* case: for after stating that the recipient should not get a start over others by using the confidential information, he continued "At any rate, he should not get a start without paying for it. It may not be a case for injunction or even for an account, but only for damages, depending on the worth of the confidential information to him in saving him time and trouble." I also recognise that a conscientious and law-abiding citizen, having received confidential information in confidence, may accept that when negotiations break down the only honourable course is to withdraw altogether from the field in question until his informant or someone else has put the information into the public domain and he can no longer be said to have any start. Communication thus imposes on him a unique disability. He alone of all men must for an uncertain time abjure this field of endeavour, however great his interest. I find this scarcely more reasonable than the artificiality and uncertainty of postponing the use of the information until others would have discovered it.

The relevance of the point, I think is this. If the duty is a duty not to use the information without consent, then it may be the proper subject of an injunction restraining its use, even if there is an offer to pay a reasonable sum for that use. If, on the other hand, the duty is merely a duty not to use the information without paying a reasonable sum for it, then no such injunction should be granted. Despite the assistance of counsel, I feel far from assured that I have got to the bottom of this matter. But I do feel considerable hesitation in expressing a doctrine of equity in terms that include a duty which law-abiding citizens cannot reasonably be expected to perform. In other words, the essence of the duty seems more likely to be that of not using without paying, rather than of not using at all. It may be that in fields other than industry and commerce (and I have in mind the *Argyll* case) the duty may exist in the more stringent form; but in the circumstances present in this case I think that the less stringent form is the more reasonable. No doubt this matter may be canvassed and resolved at the trial: but on motion, in a case where both the probabilities and the evidence support the view that the fruits of any confidential communication were to sound in monetary compensation to the communicator, I should be slow to hold that it was right to enjoin the defendant company from making any use of the information.'

COMMENT

In the event, Megarry J refused to grant an interlocutory injunction but ordered that 5s 0d. per engine made by the defendant be paid into a special joint bank account on trusts. Megarry J's three elements for a successful action provide an excellent formula for analysing breach of confidence cases. Although this was an interlocutory hearing only it marks the coming of age of the action.

The *Coco* case demonstrates the difficulty in deciding who is free to use what information when negotiations between an inventor and potential manufacturer break down. Allowance must be made for the possibility that the person to whom the information has been disclosed has developed the original idea and done other work in respect of it. Is injunctive relief inappropriate in such circumstances and, if so, would damages or an account of profits be a sufficient remedy? Megarry J was unable to formulate an effective test for identifying situations where an obligation of confidence would arise. Can you suggest a test with more predictive value than calling upon the services of the reasonable man yet again?

Springboard Doctrine

In the *Coco* case, Megarry J found the springboard doctrine to be somewhat unsatisfactory. The doctrine itself was most succinctly set out by Roxburgh J in the *Terrapin* case below. That case went to appeal and is reported in [1960] RPC 130 but, as the judgment in the Chancery Division was used in a number of subsequent cases, it was decided to publish a report of that hearing later.

Terrapin Ltd. v *Builders' Supply Company (Hayes) Ltd.* [1967] RPC 375, Chancery Division

The defendant made prefabricated portable buildings to the plaintiff's design as part of a joint venture. The plaintiff communicated information concerning manufacturing details, technical information and know-how to the defendant for this purpose. After the joint venture came to an end, the defendant offered for sale prefabricated buildings incorporating many of the features of the plaintiff's design. The defendant argued that sale of the buildings by the plaintiff together with the publication of brochures had disclosed all the relevant design features to the public.

Roxburgh J (at 391): '... Mr Aldous in his able and patient argument said that the obligation to treat the foregoing information as confidential was discharged when the plaintiffs published all the general features of the Mark 24 building unit, and later the Mark 36 building unit, in one publication (which Mr Aldous quite properly emphasised was important in his submission), either in the brochures or by putting the goods on the market, and thereby enabling every member of the public, by an elementary process of dismantling (which is easier, of course, in the case of a building which is designed to be easily dismantled than it is in the case of any other conceivable type of building) to obtain such information. Says Mr Aldous:

> "Either the brochures or that activity resulted in the publication of all the general features: indeed, it would enable anybody to see exactly how the building unit was constructed."

The brochures would not enable anybody to see exactly how the unit was constructed. They would give the general idea, but not the details. The dismantling would, of course, enable any competent carpenter to see exactly how the building was constructed. "And," says Mr Aldous, "that publication discharges the confidential obligation."

Frankly he admitted that there is no suggestion of such a doctrine in any reported case. I go further and say that it is inconsistent with the principles stated by Lord Greene in *Saltman's* case.

As I understand it, the essence of this branch of the law, whatever the origin of it may be, is that a person who has obtained information in confidence is not allowed to use it as a spring-board for activities detrimental to the person who made the confidential communication, and spring-board it remains even when all the features have been published or can be ascertained by actual inspection by any member of the public. The brochures are certainly not equivalent to the publication of the plans, specifications, other technical information and know-how. The dismantling of a unit might enable a person to proceed without plans or specifications, or other technical information, but not, I think, without some of the know-how, and certainly not without taking the trouble to dismantle. I think it is broadly true to say that a member of the public to whom the confidential information had not been imparted would still have to prepare plans and specifications. He would probably have to construct a prototype, and he would certainly have to conduct tests. Therefore, the possessor of the confidential information still has a long start over any member of the public. The design may be as important as the features. It is, in my view, inherent in the principle upon which the *Saltman* case rests that the possessor of such information must be placed under a special disability in the field of competition in order to ensure that he does not get an unfair start: or, in other words, to preclude the tactics which the first defendants and the third defendants and the managing director of both of those companies employed in this case.

COMMENT

How does one calculate the temporary incapacitation necessary to cancel out the advantage that the defendant has over any member of the public who is free to access the relevant information by dismantling an article and/or reading detailed trade literature? Is it true that, in an industrial context, all that is protected by the law of confidence is the first manufacturer's lead time; that is, the time taken for competitors to derive the information for themselves, independently? Are competitors free to dismantle products put onto the market by the first manufacturer in order to obtain technical information?

In *Ocular Sciences Ltd.* v *Aspect Vision Care Ltd.* [1997] RPC 289, Laddie J (at 396) cast some doubt on the springboard doctrine, saying that he did not think Roxburgh J had meant that information which has become public knowledge could be the subject-matter of an injunction. Rather, it was a case of preventing a defendant from using confidential information to get an illegitimate head start. Is this proposition consistent with Roxburgh J's judgment? Where the information has become public, it would be more appropriate for a court to grant financial relief instead.

Third Parties

It might be thought that a third party to whom confidential information is subsequently disclosed would be free to make use of that information providing he did not know it was confidential. The position of third parties is touched on in the following case which also looks at confidence in ideas.

Fraser v Thames Television Ltd. [1984] 1 QB 44, Queen's Bench Division

The plaintiffs, three actresses and their manager, told one of the defendants, a scriptwriter, of their idea for a television series about a three-girl rock group. The scriptwriter disclosed the idea to a producer and to Thames TV, the other defendants. There was agreement that a series would be made to be called the 'Rock Follies'. However, one of the plaintiffs was unable to take part because of another commitment and Thames TV decided to go ahead and they offered the parts of the members of the rock group to other actresses contrary to the agreement between the plaintiffs and Thames TV. The plaintiffs claimed that all the defendants were in breach of confidence and, further, that Thames TV were in breach of contract.

Hirst J (at 65): 'In my judgment there is no reason in principle why an oral idea should not qualify for protection under the law of confidence, provided it meets the other criteria I discuss below. Neither the originality nor the quality of an idea is in any way affected by the form in which it is expressed. No doubt both the communication and the content of an oral idea may be more difficult to prove than in the case of a written idea, but difficulties of proof should not affect the principle any more than in any other branches of the law where similar problems arise (e.g. contract and defamation).

I do not accept Mr Harman's argument that this will cause unfairness to third parties, since it is clear that, in order to be fixed with an obligation of confidence, a third party must know that the information was confidential; knowledge of a mere assertion that a breach of confidence has been committed is not sufficient: see *Carl Zeiss Stiftung* v *Herbert Smith & Co. (No.2)* [1969] 2 Ch. 276.

Nor do I accept Mr Harman's argument that an idea which is capable of development in more than one format is not entitled to protection. In my judgment the precise format is a matter for the writer to decide, and the fact that it is developable in more than one format in no way diminishes its intrinsic value.

I accept that to be capable of protection the idea must be sufficiently developed, so that it would be seen to be a concept which has at least some attractiveness for a television programme and which is capable of being realised as an actuality: see *per* Harris J in *Talbot* v *General Television Corporation Pty. Ltd.* [1981] RPC 1, 9, lines 20-22. But I do not think this requirement necessitates in every case a full synopsis. In some cases the nature of the idea may require extensive development of this kind in order to meet the criteria. But in others the criteria may be met by a short unelaborated statement of an idea. In *Talbot's* case itself I do not think the detailed submission, quoted at p.5, added very much of substance to the idea which is set out in one sentence starting at line 10 on p.5.

Unquestionably, of course, the idea must have some significant element of originality not already in the realm of public knowledge. The originality may consist in a significant twist or slant to a well known concept (*Talbot's* case). This is, I think, by analogy, consistent with the statements in *Saltman Engineering Co. Ltd.* v *Campbell Engineering Co. Ltd.* 65 RPC 203 and *Coco* v *A. N. Clark (Engineers) Ltd.* [1969] RPC 41, that novelty in the industrial field can be derived from the application of human ingenuity to well known concepts.

To the best of my recollection, every witness in the theatre or television business on both sides agreed that if he or she received an idea from another, it would be wrong to make use of it without the consent of the communicator. They of course were expressing their views in the context of a moral usage in their profession rather than of a strict legal obligation. However, the authorities, and in particular *Saltman's* case (*per* Somervel LJ) and *Thomas Marshall (Exports) Ltd.* v *Guinle* [1979] Ch 227, strongly support Mr Strauss's argument that the existence of such a usage is a factor of considerable force in deciding whether a legal obligation exists. I think the law as laid down in the authorities I have cited clearly establishes that the obligation which the witnesses saw as moral is in fact also legal in character.

This of course does not mean that every stray mention of an idea by one person to another is protected. To succeed in his claim the plaintiff must establish not only that the occasion of communication was confidential, but also that the content of the idea was clearly identifiable, original, of potential commercial attractiveness and capable of being realised in actuality. With these limitations, I consider there is no basis for Mr Harman's fears that authors' freedom to develop ideas will be unduly stultified.

Applying these principles to the facts of the present case, Miss Leventon's communication of the idea to the scriptwriter, in particular at the meeting on January

22, 1974, was clearly in confidence; indeed it was in the nature of a professional occasion, since she was sounding out the scriptwriter's willingness to write a series based on the idea, Mr Rosenthal having declined (cf. *Coco's* case). I reject Mr Harman's attempt to distinguish *Coco's* case on the grounds that there was no joint enterprise between Miss Leventon and the scriptwriter, because each had their separate role as actress and author respectively. I think that on January 22, 1974, they were jointly concerned commercially in the possible use of the idea.

That the idea could be seen as a concept which had commercial attractiveness for a television programme and was something which was capable of being realised as an actuality is clearly proved by Mr Rosenthal's evidence. Its originality is also clearly proved by Mr Rosenthal, supported by the evidence of other witnesses. This originality, as Mr Rosenthal indicated, lies in the slant or twist the plaintiffs' idea gave to well-known concepts. It is difficult to think of anybody in a better position to prove this aspect than a television writer of Mr Rosenthal's stature. Quite apart from all this evidence, the scriptwriter's own success in turning the idea into a much-acclaimed television series is eloquent testimony of its commercial attractiveness, its ability to be realised in actuality and its originality.

Consequently, I hold that the scriptwriter owed an obligation of confidence in relation to the plaintiffs' idea.

The producer knew from the scriptwriter that the idea was the plaintiffs' and had been imparted to the scriptwriter in confidence. He is therefore fixed with an obligation of confidence.

Thames, through Miss Lambert, knew, either from the scriptwriter or the producer or both, that the idea was the plaintiffs' and had been imparted to the scriptwriter in confidence, and so Thames also are fixed with an obligation of confidence. I reject Mr Harman's argument that any obligation of confidence resting upon Thames was "washed out" once the contract of October 4, 1974, was entered into. I see no reason in principle why this result should ensue; nor was there any such provision in the contract. Furthermore, in this particular case, if Thames had declined to exercise their option, as they were perfectly free to do, they would then (on Mr Harman's argument) have been free of any obligation of confidence in relation to the idea. Such a result would be absurd.

I also reject Mr Harman's argument that, whatever its original status, the plaintiffs' idea lost its confidentiality once they disclosed it to others (for example, Mr Degas). Since such disclosure to others was plainly also in confidence, confidentiality remained intact: see *Franchi* v *Franchi* [1967] RPC 149.

Mr Harman accepts that, in relation to the claim in confidence, all four plaintiffs stand or fall together, so that there is no distinction to be drawn between Mr Fraser and the other three plaintiffs.

Mr Strauss accepts that, on the plaintiffs' own case, the communication of the idea by the scriptwriter and producer to Thames in the spring or summer of 1974 was legitimate, since it was done with the plaintiffs' consent. His claim for breach of confidence is therefore confined to the user of the idea after the breakdown.

I hold that the scriptwriter was in breach of confidence in using the idea in his writing of the two Rock Follies series after May 1975.

I hold that the producer was in breach of confidence in using the plaintiffs' idea in his production of the two Rock Follies series after May 1975. I reject Mr Harman's argument that the producer can escape liability, because his activity as producer was under Thames' aegis, and added nothing to the harm caused to the plaintiffs by Thames' breach of confidence. In my judgment the producer's liability falls to be judged by reference to his conduct on its own separate merits, irrespective of Thames.

I hold that Thames were in breach of confidence in using the idea in the making and screening of the two Rock Follies series, all of which took place after May 1975.'

COMMENT

It was also held that Thames TV were in breach of contract on the basis of an implied negative covenant not to use other actresses if the plaintiffs agreed to perform in the series (Thames TV had refused to make arrangements to work around one of the plaintiff's commitments).

What is the position where a third party is given information without knowledge that it is confidential but later finds out about its confidential nature? Should knowledge of the confidential nature of information be judged on a subjective basis only?

Carflow Products (UK) Ltd v *Linwood Securities (Birmingham) Ltd.* [1996] FSR 424, Patents Court

In an action for infringement of a registered design applied to a steering wheel lock, the defendants claimed that the registration was invalid for lack of novelty. The first defendant claimed to have designed and made a prototype steering wheel lock which was shown to a buyer from the second defendant, Argos. No express obligation of confidence was imposed on the Argos buyer. This disclosure was prior to the registration of a similar design by the plaintiff. If it was not in confidence, express or implied, that would mean either that the plaintiff's design registration was invalid, or the defendant's design fell outside the plaintiff's registration and, thus, did not infringe. This is the *'Gillette'* defence, after the case in which it was first used, *Gillette Safety Razor Co. Ltd.* v *Anglo-American Trading Co. Ltd.* (1913) 30 RPC 465.

Jacob J (at 428): 'There are two possible approaches in law: what did the parties themselves think they were doing by way of imposing or accepting obligations and what would a reasonable man think they were doing? The difference between the two approaches is that the former takes into account the subjective unspoken views of the parties. One would not do so in relation to the making of a contract, but in relation to the equitable obligation of confidence it seems right to do so - equity looks at the conscience of the individual. So I prefer the subjective view. As it happens, overall I do not think in this case it matters whether one approaches the problem from the subjective or objective points of view.

I begin with the unchallenged evidence of Mr Bond. Subjectively he did not think he was imposing any duty of confidence on Argos or Mr Spencer Jones. His evidence may be summarised as follows:

(1) he knew about imposing obligations of confidence expressly and had done so with a number of suppliers by a written document;
(2) he did not think he was imposing an obligation of confidence on Argos;

(3) he knew that buyers at Argos were apt to leave samples around their rooms in such a way that others could see them and was prepared to leave a sample;

(4) he in fact left a sample of another product which had not yet been made available to others with Mr Spencer Jones;

(5) he would not have liked it if Mr Spencer Jones had shown the sample to a rival manufacturer with a view to that manufacturer producing the item cheaper.

This last point is neutral. I imagine no-one would like that, whether the product shown was confidential or not. It is also somewhat artificial. In practice Mr Bond would have had design right over the sample and it could not be copied. Curiously neither party to the meeting seems to have been conscious of possible intellectual property rights in the design, even though Argos do later make inquiries about these if a product is actually ordered.

Next I turn to the subjective view of Mr Spencer Jones. He was not asked directly whether or not he regarded the disclosure to him as confidential. He was asked about his personal ethics. He made it clear that his personal ethics and conscience would be against showing a prototype given to him by one manufacturer to another manufacturer. But on the other hand he would not sign any agreement not to do so if he had been asked. He said that Argos would not undertake in writing not to show something they were offered to a third party. Indeed that had happened on previous occasions. And he said, even though he personally thought it would be unethical: "I could discuss the details of any products with anybody I liked and it is a right that any buyer has."

He took the same view about prices: "Ethically" he would not tell anyone else the prices agreed with a particular manufacturer, but he felt free to do so. Overall he took the view that people coming to sell to Argos would know that they are "quite a hard-nosed company". He plainly did not think people would refuse to show new products to Argos unless Argos accepted confidentiality. The amount of business at stake would make it worth the risk all the same. Overall I conclude on Mr Spencer Jones' evidence that he did not think there was any enforceable obligation imposed on his using what he learned from a prospective seller of a proposed new design. Nor did he think that such a seller would be intending to impose such an obligation (rightly so in this case).

I think there is confirmation for this view provided by the fact that Argos buyers do not take special precautions to keep prototypes left with them secret, and from what Mr Spencer Jones actually did with a sample of another product of Mr Bond's which he did keep. Mr Spencer Jones took it and used it in his car where it would be visible to the public. He plainly would not have done that if he thought the device was supposed to be a secret with which he was entrusted. It is true that the product was in final manufactured form, but it was not suggested that it had in fact been disclosed to anyone else at the time of the meeting.

On a subjective basis, therefore, neither party to the meeting thought there was an obligation of confidence - an enforceable obligation - being imposed or accepted.

On an objective basis what is the position? What would a bystander say about the meeting, assuming he heard and saw all that went on but could not see into the minds of the parties? He would know that the product was a prototype. He would know, I think it fair to assume, that our law provides a variety of ways in which the design of a product may be protected (unregistered design right, registered design, or even patent for an invention). He would know that the would-be seller is promoting his wares or potential wares. I cannot think that on an objective basis the reasonable man would think an obligation of confidence was being imposed merely because a prototype of what was being offered for sale was shown. Furthermore I think it would lead to much difficulty if the position were otherwise. People are habitually showing things they have designed or invented to would-be manufacturers. If the latter are put under an obligation of confidence merely by seeing a prototype - which they would as reasonable men know could be the subject of independent protection, then they would be far less willing to look at things. The reasonable man will not look at the transaction myopically, blinding himself to the panoply of potential intellectual property rights the law provides.

Now it is true that in *Coco v A. N. Clark (Engineers) Ltd* [1969] RPC 41 Megarry J said at page 48:

"It seems to me that if the circumstances are such that any reasonable man standing in the shoes of the recipient of the information would have realised that upon reasonable grounds the information was being given to him in confidence, then this should suffice to impose upon him the equitable obligation of confidence. In particular, where information of commercial or industrial value is given on a business-like basis and with some avowed common object in mind, such as a joint venture or the manufacture of articles by one party for the other, I would regard the recipient as carrying a heavy burden if he seeks to repel a contention that he was bound by an obligation of confidence."

And it is often the case that the courts will spell out an obligation of confidence where information is given for one purpose. One can readily, without more, hold that it may not be used for another. But all depends on the circumstances. And where the law provides a variety of methods, optional (in the case of rights which must be registered) or automatic (in the case of copyright and design right) I do not think the reasonable recipient must assume that he is placing himself under an obligation of confidence in respect of matter which could be protected independently. Things would be very different if more than such matter were disclosed - for example the detailed plans of the *Coco* case or of *Saltman Engineering Co. Ltd* v *Campbell Engineering Co. Ltd* (1948) 65 RPC 203.

Accordingly on an objective basis the mere showing of the prototype in this case does not impose an obligation of confidence.

What then of Mr Spencer Jones' ethics? Should the law impose an enforceable obligation of confidence notwithstanding that either on a subjective view or an objective view there is none. I cannot think they do. His views cannot be relevant at all to the objective view: they were unspoken. As to the subjective view, one has to consider all that he said, which I have summarised above. Mr Spencer Jones did not subjectively think he was receiving information in confidence. Nor were there reasons why he should have thought that he was receiving information in confidence. And he did not come under a duty of confidence.'

COMMENT

The *Gillette* defence succeeded and the plaintiff's action was dismissed. The design was left on the register, the court leaving the matter of validity undecided.

This case shows that it is dangerous to rely on the courts implying an obligation of confidence when prototypes are being shown to potential buyers or customers. The same must apply in the context of showing articles made to new designs or embodying new inventions to others, such as potential manufacturers or 'product champions'. The basic question is whether the conscience of the person to whom the article has been shown is fixed by equity. It is far safer, where there is any doubt whatsoever, to impose an express obligation of confidence, or better still, file an application for a patent or registered design if appropriate.

Employees

Many cases involving issues of confidence result from allegations that previous employees have misused confidential information given to them by their former employers. A major problem for the courts is to reconcile the need to protect the previous employer's confidential information with the desirability of permitting past employees to make use of their skill and experience for the benefit of new employers. A very strict approach in favour of the employer would make it difficult for employees to obtain alternative employment but full liberalisation would defeat the effectiveness of the law of confidence in this area. It should be noted that a present employee owes a very strong duty of fidelity to his employer and most problems involve ex-employees.

Printers and Finishers Ltd. v Holloway [1965] RPC 239, Chancery Division

The plaintiff had a flock printing plant. (Flock printing is a method of printing on fabric by applying fibre in a pattern to the fabric, using an adhesive to produce an embossed effect.) The defendant was a manager at the plaintiff's factory and, whilst still employed there, he contacted a rival company, which was setting up a flock printing plant, and disclosed details of his employer's plant to the rival company. The defendant assisted in other ways and the plaintiff sought damages for breach of confidence in addition to a perpetual injunction. The plaintiff had commenced flock printing under a know-how agreement with an American company. At the time flock printing was unknown in the United Kingdom and Europe and the plaintiff operated strict conditions of secrecy at the factory and no strangers were permitted to enter the factory without leave of the director. The defendant had shown employees of the rival company round the plaintiff's secret factory. He had also visited the rival factory on two occasions, staying overnight and receiving £25.00.

Cross J (at 255): 'The second part of the injunction sought against Holloway is directed to the use or disclosure by him of information in his head, and the question whether or not it should be granted involves a consideration of the principles on which the court should act in cases of this kind. The wording of the proposed injunction is based on the description of each step in their process given by the plaintiffs in general terms in their particulars dated 5th November 1959, and in detail in the evidence of their managing director Mr Elliot given "in camera" at the trial, with the omission of a few matters in regard to which the evidence at the trial showed clearly that Mr Elliot was wrong in thinking that what the plaintiffs did was peculiar to them. The mere fact that the confidential information is not embodied in a document but is carried away by the employee in his head is not, of course, of itself a reason against the granting of an injunction to prevent its use or disclosure by him. If the information in question can fairly be regarded as a separate part of the employee's stock of knowledge which a man of ordinary honesty and intelligence would recognise to be the property of his old employer, and not his own to do as he likes with, then the court, if it thinks that there is a danger of the information being used or disclosed by the ex-employee to the detriment of the old employer, will do what it can to prevent that result by granting an injunction. Thus an ex-employee will be restrained from using or disclosing a chemical formula or a list of customers which he has committed to memory. Again in *Reid & Sigrist Ltd.* v *Moss and Mechanism Ltd.* (1932) 49 RPC 461 the defendant was restrained from disclosing any methods of construction or features of design of turn indicators for use in aeroplanes evolved by the plaintiffs and made known to the defendant or evolved by him whilst in their employment. The salient point there was that in the course of the development of the instrument by the plaintiffs the defendant took part in confidential discussions with an outside expert called in to advise the plaintiffs as to the best method of dealing with certain problems which had arisen. It appears, indeed, that after the discussions and while he was still in the plaintiff's employ, the defendant made and later took away with him drawings embracing the various matters discussed. But even if he had not done so and relied simply on his memory of the confidential discussions I think that an injunction would still have been granted.

What is asked for here, however, goes far beyond any relief granted in any case which was cited to me. The plaintiffs are saying, in effect:

"True it is that other flock printers use plant and machinery similar to ours and that as we did not trouble to exact any covenant from him not to do so Holloway was entitled to go and work for a trade competitor who uses such plant and machinery. Nevertheless we are entitled to prevent him from using for the benefit of his new employers his recollection of any features of our plant, machinery or process which are in fact peculiar to us."

If this is right, then it seems to me, an ex-employee is placed in an impossible position. One naturally approaches the problem in this case with some bias in favour of the plaintiffs, because Holloway has shown himself unworthy of their trust; but to test their argument fairly one must take the case of an employee who has been guilty of no breach of contract. Suppose such a man to be told by his new employers that at this or that stage in the process they encounter this or that difficulty. He may say to himself: "Well, I remember that on the corresponding piece of machinery in the other factory such-and-such a part was set at a different angle or shaped in a different way": or again, "When that happened we used to do this and it seemed to work", "this" being perhaps something which he had been taught when he first went to the other factory, or possibly an expedient which he had found out for himself by trial and error during his previous employment.

Recalling matters of this sort is, to my mind, quite unlike memorising a formula or list of customers or what was said (obviously in confidence) at a particular meeting. The employee might well not realise that the feature or expedient in question was in fact peculiar to his late employer's process and factory: but even if he did, such knowledge is not readily separable from his general knowledge of the flock printing process and his acquired skill in manipulating a flock printing plant, and I do not think that any man of average intelligence and honesty would think that there was anything improper in his putting his memory of particular features of his late employer's plant at the disposal of his new employer. The law will defeat its own object if it seeks to enforce in this field standards which would be rejected by the ordinary man. After all, this involves no hardship on the employer. Although the law will not enforce a covenant directed against competition by an ex-employee it will enforce a covenant reasonably necessary to protect trade secrets (see the recent case of *Commercial Plastics Ltd.* v *Vincent* [1964] 3 WLR 820, in which the plaintiff only failed because the covenant was too widely drawn as regards area). If Mr Elliot is right in thinking that there are features in his process which can fairly be regarded as trade secrets and which his employers will inevitably carry away with them in their heads, then the proper way for the plaintiffs to protect themselves would be by exacting covenants from their employees restricting their field of activity after they have left their employment, not by asking the court to extend the general equitable doctrine to prevent breaking confidence beyond all reasonable bounds.'

COMMENT

Cross J took a robust view in favour of ex-employees though having no particular sympathy with the employee in the present case. This approach was also taken in South Africa where, in *Northern Office Micro Computers (Pty.) Ltd.* v *Rosenstein* [1982] FSR 124, Marais J said that an employee, upon termination of his employment, would not have to 'wipe the slate of his mind clean'. Cross J made a distinction between memorising a formula or list of customers and other information which an employee should be free to place at the disposal of other employers. How can such a distinction be made in practice and is there any effective way of preventing the subsequent use of the latter type of information for an indefinite period? In the absence of a covenant in restraint of trade are trade secrets really not protected?

In the following case, the ex-employee's obligation of confidence in respect of his previous employer's information was developed further.

Faccenda Chicken Ltd. v *Fowler* [1986] 1 All ER 617, Court of Appeal

The plaintiff sold fresh chickens from refrigerated vans to butchers, supermarkets and restaurants. The defendant was the plaintiff's sales manager, who had thought up the idea, and he left the plaintiff's employment to set up a rival business in the same geographical area. The plaintiff brought an action alleging improper use of sales information concerning customers of the plaintiff and their orders and regarding delivery routes. There was no covenant in restraint of trade.

Neill LJ (at 624): 'Counsel for Faccenda Chicken Ltd. made a number of criticisms of the judge's formulation of the law. We can summarise the most important of these criticisms as follows: (a) that the judge erred in law in holding that there were two classes or categories of confidential information which an employer might acquire in the course of his service: there was only one such class or category. Confidential information remained confidential even after the employee had left the employer's service: (b) that the law of confidence relating to employees was merely a branch of the general law of confidence, and, although the obligations of an employee were based on an implied term of the contract of service, this was immaterial because the scope of the implied term was coextensive with the obligations imposed by equity on a person to whom confidential information was entrusted in circumstances where no contract existed between the parties: (c) that the judge erred in law in holding that confidential information in his second class could be protected by a restrictive covenant. It was plain, it was submitted, that a restrictive covenant would not be enforced unless the protection sought was reasonably necessary to protect a trade secret or to prevent some personal influence over customers being abused in order to entice them away: see *Herbert Morris Ltd.* v *Saxelby* [1916] 1 AC 688 at 709, [1916-17] All ER Rep 305 at 317 per Lord Parker: (d) that, although some of the information, for example the names and addresses of customers, could not by itself be treated as confidential, the sales information did constitute confidential information when looked at as a whole: (e) that in any event information about the prices charged to individual customers was confidential information: (f) that a clear distinction could be drawn between the skill and general knowledge of a trade or business which an employee might acquire in the course of his employment and which he was entitled to use in subsequent employment, and the special knowledge of a former employer's business which the employee could not use thereafter. In support of this proposition and of the special importance of prices, we were referred to the judgment of Farwell LJ in *Sir W C Leng & Co. Ltd.* v *Andrews* [1909] 1 Ch 763 at 774, where in a formulation of principle (which was subsequently approved by Lord Atkinson in *Herbert Morris Ltd.* v *Saxelby* [1916] 1 AC 688 at 705, [1916-17] All ER Rep 305 at 311) he said:

"To acquire the knowledge of the reasonable mode of general organization and management of a business of this kind, and to make use of such knowledge, cannot be regarded as a breach of confidence in revealing anything acquired by reason of a person having been in any particular service, although the person may have learnt it in the course of being taught his trade; but it would be a breach of confidence to reveal trade secrets, such as prices, &c., or any secret process or things of a nature which the man was not entitled to reveal."

Reference was also made to the judgment of Megarry VC in *Thomas Marshall (Exports) Ltd.* v *Guinle* [1978] 3 All ER 193 at 209, [1979] Ch 227 at 248 where he said: "Costs and prices which are not generally known may well constitute trade secrets or confidential information."

In the course of his submissions, in support of the appeal counsel for Faccenda Chicken Ltd. took us on an instructive and valuable tour of many of the cases dealing with the law of confidence in the context of the relationship between employer and employee and also referred us to some of the cases on restrictive covenants.

It is not necessary, however, for us for the purpose of this judgment to travel this ground again. It is sufficient to set out what we understand to be the relevant principles of law. Having considered the cases to which we were referred, we would venture to state these principles as follows.

(1) Where the parties are, or have been, linked by a contract of employment, the obligations of the employee are to be determined by the contract between him and his employer: cf *Vokes Ltd.* v *Heather* (1945) 62 RPC 135 at 141.

(2) In the absence of any express term, the obligations of the employee in respect of the use and disclosure of information are the subject of implied terms.

(3) While the employee remains in the employment of the employer the obligations are included in the implied term which imposes a duty of good faith or fidelity on the employee. For the purpose of the present appeal it is not necessary to consider the precise limits of this implied term, but it may be noted: (a) that the extent of the duty of good faith will vary according to the nature of the contract (see *Vokes Ltd.* v *Heather*): (b) that the duty of good faith will be broken if an employee makes or copies a list of the customers of the employer for use after his employment ends or deliberately memorises such a list, even though, except in special circumstances, there is no general restriction on an ex-employee canvassing or doing business with customers of his former employer (see *Robb* v *Green* [1895] 2 QB 315, [1895-9] All ER Rep 1053 and *Wessex Dairies Ltd.* v *Smith* [1935] 2 KB 80, [1935] All ER Rep 75).

(4) The implied term which imposes an obligation on the employee as to his conduct after the determination of the employment is more restricted in its scope than that which imposes a general duty of good faith. It is clear that the obligation not to use or disclose information may cover secret processes of manufacture such as chemical formulae (see *Amber Size and Chemical Co. Ltd.* v *Mengel* [1913] 2 Ch 239), or designs or special methods of construction (see *Reid Sigrist Ltd.* v *Moss Mechanism Ltd.* (1932) 49 RPC 461), and other information which is of a sufficiently high degree of confidentiality as to amount to a trade secret.

The obligation does not extend, however, to cover all information which is given to or acquired by the employee while in his employment, and in particular may not cover information which is only "confidential" in the sense that an unauthorised disclosure of such information to a third party while the employment subsisted would be a clear breach of the duty of good faith.

This distinction is clearly set out in the judgment of Cross J in *Printers and Finishers Ltd.* v *Holloway* [1964] 3 All ER 731, [1965] 1 WLR 1, where he had to consider whether an ex-employee should be restrained by injunction from making use of his recollection of the contents of certain written printing instructions which had been made available to him when he was working in his former employer's flock printing factory. In his judgment, delivered on 29 April 1964 (not reported on this point in the Weekly Law Reports), Cross J said [1964] 3 All ER 731 at 738n):

"In this connexion one must bear in mind that not all information which is given to a servant in confidence and which it would be a breach of his duty for him to disclose to another person during his employment is a trade secret which he can be prevented from using for his own advantage after the employment is over, even though he has entered into no express covenant with regard to the matter in hand. For example, the printing instructions were handed to [the first defendant] to be used by him during his employment exclusively for the plaintiffs' benefit. It would have been a breach of duty on his part to divulge any of the contents to a stranger while he was employed, but many of these instructions are not really 'trade secrets' at all. [The first defendant] was not, indeed, entitled to take a copy of the instructions away with him; but insofar as the instructions cannot be called 'trade secrets' and he carried them in his head, he is entitled to use them for his own benefit or the benefit of any future employer."

The same distinction is to be found in *E Worsley & Co. Ltd.* v *Cooper* [1939] 1 All ER 290, where it was held that the defendant was entitled, after he had ceased to be employed, to make use of his knowledge of the course of the paper supplied to his previous employer. In our view it is quite plain that this knowledge was nevertheless "confidential" in the sense that it would have been a breach of the duty of good faith for the employee, while the employment subsisted, to have used it for his own purposes or to have disclosed it to a competitor of his employer.

(5) In order to determine whether any particular item of information falls within the implied term so as to prevent its use or disclosure by an employee after his employment has ceased, it is necessary to consider all the circumstances of the case. We are satisfied that the following matters are among those to which attention must be paid. (a) The nature of the employment. Thus employment in a capacity where "confidential" material is habitually handled may impose a high obligation of confidentiality because the employee can be expected to realise its sensitive nature to a greater extent than if he were employed in a capacity where such material reaches him only occasionally or incidentally. (b) The nature of the information itself. In our judgment the information will only be protected if it can properly be classed as a trade secret or as material which, while not protected if it can properly be classed as a trade secret or as material which, while not properly to be described as a trade secret, is in all the circumstances of such a highly confidential nature as to require the same protection as a trade secret *eo nomine*. The restrictive covenant cases demonstrate that a covenant will not be upheld on the basis of the status of the information which might be disclosed by the former employee if he is not restrained unless it can be regarded as a trade secret or the equivalent of a trade secret; see for example *Herbert Morris Ltd.* v *Saxelby* [1916] 1 AC 688 at 710, [1916-17] All ER Rep 305 at 317 per Lord Parker and *Littlewoods Organisation Ltd.* v *Harris* [1978] 1 All ER 1026 at 1037, [1977] 1 WLR 1472 at 1484 per Megaw LJ.

We must therefore express our respectful disagreement with the passage in Goulding J's judgment where he suggested that an employer can protect the use of information in his second category, even though it does not include either a trade secret or its equivalent by means of a restrictive covenant (see [1985] 1 All ER 724 at 731). As Lord Parker made clear in *Herbert Morris Ltd.* v *Saxelby* [1916] 1 AC 688 at 709, [1916-17] All ER Rep 305 at 317, in a passage to which counsel for Faccenda Chicken Ltd. drew our attention, a restrictive covenant will not be enforced unless the protection sought is reasonably necessary to protect a trade secret or to prevent some personal influence over customers being abused in order to entice them away.

In our view the circumstances in which a restrictive covenant would be appropriate and could be successfully invoked emerge very clearly from the words used by Cross J in *Printers and Finishers Ltd.* v *Holloway* [1964] 3 All ER 731 at 736, [1965] 1 WLR 1 at 6 (in a passage quoted later in his judgment by Goulding J (see [1985] 1 All ER 724 at 732-733)):

"If [the managing director] is right in thinking that there are features in his process which can fairly be regarded as trade secrets and which his employees will inevitably carry away with them in their heads, then the proper way for the plaintiffs to protect themselves would be by exacting covenants from their employees restricting their field of activity after they have left their employment, not by asking the court to extend the general equitable doctrine to prevent breaking confidence beyond all reasonable bounds."

It is clearly impossible to provide a list of matters which will qualify as trade secrets or their equivalent. Secret processes of manufacture provide obvious examples, but innumerable other pieces of information are *capable* of being trade secrets, though the secrecy of some information may be only short-lived. In addition, the fact that the circulation of certain information is restricted to a limited number of individuals may throw light on the status of the information and its degree of confidentiality. (c) Whether the employer impressed on the employee the confidentiality of the information. Thus, though an employer cannot prevent the use or disclosure merely by telling the employee that certain information is confidential, the attitude of the employer towards the information provides evidence which may assist in determining whether or not the information can properly be regarded as a trade secret. It is to be observed that in *E Worsley & Co. Ltd.* v *Cooper* [1939] 1 All ER 290 at 307 Morton J attached significance to the fact that no warning had been given to the defendant that "the source from which the paper came was to be treated as confidential". (d) Whether the relevant information can be easily isolated from other information which the employee is free to use or disclose. In *Printers and Finishers Ltd.* v *Holloway* [1964] 3 All ER 731 at 736, [1965] 1 WLR 1 at 6 Cross J considered the protection which might be afforded to information which had been memorised by an ex-employee. He put on one side the memorising of a formula or a list of customers or what had been said (obviously in confidence) at a particular meeting, and continued:

> "The employee might well not realise that the feature or expedient in question was in fact peculiar to his late employer's process and factory; but even if he did such knowledge is not readily separable from his general knowledge of the flock printing process and his acquired skill in manipulating a flock printing plant, and I do not think that any man of average intelligence and honesty would think that there was anything improper in his putting his memory of particular feature of his late employer's plant at the disposal of his new employer."

For our part we would not regard the separability of the information in question as being conclusive, but the fact that the alleged "confidential" information is part of a package and that the remainder of the package is not confidential is likely to throw light on whether the information in question is really a trade secret.'

COMMENT

What is the difference between a trade secret and confidential information? Neill LJ suggests that an employee has a duty of good faith to his present employee which would be broken if the employee copies or memorises a list of customers for use after his employment ends. He then goes on to say that information which does not contain a trade secret or its equivalent cannot be protected by a covenant in restraint of trade. Can those propositions be reconciled? Is a list of customers a trade secret? Bear in mind that what Neill LJ says in respect of restrictive covenants is *obiter*.

Ocular Sciences Ltd. v Aspect Vision Care Ltd. [1997] RPC 289, Patents Court

The facts of this case are very complex and occupy some 43 pages of the law report. Fortunately, they are not particularly important as regards the legal issues discussed in the extracts from the judgment of Laddie J reproduced in this book. In very basic terms, the case involved allegations of breach of confidence and infringements of copyright, design right and a patent in relation to the design and manufacture of soft contact lens.

Laddie J (at 370): 'I have some difficulty with *Faccenda* category (1). *Faccenda* says that the employee is free to disclose even to his master's competitor all information which is trivial or which is easily accessible from public sources. I do not think that necessarily is true. Indeed, *Hivac Ltd.* v *Park Royal Scientific Instruments Ltd.* [1946] Ch. 169 indicates that a restraint on an employee, while employed, from assisting a competitor has nothing to do with whether that assistance involves disclosure of confidential information. Once again, what an employee can or cannot make available to a competitor during the period of his employment has little to do with the law of confidence.

In the end, it seems to me that the law as expounded in *Faccenda* and reviewed by the Court of Appeal in *Lancashire Fires* comes down to this. An employer, like anyone else, is entitled (all other usual defences aside) to restrain unauthorised disclosure or use of information which, in the *Coco v Clark* sense, is confidential. On the other hand, for public policy reasons, an employee is entitled to use and put at the disposal of new employers all his acquired skill and knowledge. That is so, no matter where he acquired that skill and knowledge and whether it is secret or was so at the time he acquired it. Where the employer's right to restrain misuse of his confidential information collides with the public policy, it is the latter which prevails. The critical question is how to distinguish information which can be treated as an employee's acquired skill and knowledge from that which is not. As the Court of Appeal pointed out in *Lancashire Fires,* that may be a difficult borderline to detect and where it lies will depend on the particular facts of the case.

COMMENT

A useful clarification of the nature of an employee's duty whilst still in employment, and a robust position as regards the protection of trade secrets *vis-à-vis* public policy. Does this leave trade secrets vulnerable in the context of an increasingly mobile labour market?

Trade Secrets

The ability to distinguish between 'genuine' trade secrets and other information that an ex-employee is free to use, in the absence of a covenant in restraint of trade, is of fundamental import. This has troubled judges for some time. In *Herbert Morris Ltd.* v *Saxelby* [1916] 1 AC 688 Lord Parker spoke of trade secrets in terms of their detailed character. He said (at 712): '[charts, sheets and drawings] of special machines, the costs index, and other documents, all of which may be considered confidential ... far too detailed for the defendant to carry away the contents thereof in his head. All that he could carry away was the general method and character of the scheme and organisation practised by the plaintiff company. Such scheme and method can hardly be regarded as a trade secret.'

The question of what constitutes a trade secret arose more recently in the following case.

Lansing Linde Ltd. v *Kerr* [1991] 1 WLR 251, Court of Appeal

The defendant was a manager of the plaintiff company which manufactured fork lift trucks. Soon after termination of his employment he commenced work as managing director of a competitor. The plaintiff sought an interlocutory injunction to restrain the defendant from working for the other company or divulging trade secrets or other confidential information or enticing away the plaintiff's customers. The defendant was under a covenant in restraint of trade of 12 months duration. The judge refused to grant the injunction requested because the covenant was probably too wide (being a world-wide restriction) and that, in any case, the covenant would have expired before a full trial could be arranged. The appeal to the Court of Appeal was dismissed and it was held that a wider view of the balance of convenience ought to be taken in such cases and the employer would have to show not only a serious issue to be tried but also that it was more likely than not that the employer would succeed at the trial. There was some discussion of the nature of a trade secret.

Staughton LJ (at 249): 'In *Faccenda Chicken Ltd.* v *Fowler* [1985] 1 All ER 724 ... Goulding J at first instance had defined three classes of information: (i) information which, because of its trivial character or its easy accessibility from public sources of information, cannot be regarded by reasonable persons or by the law as confidential at all; (ii) information which the servant must treat as confidential ... but which once learned reasonably remains in the servant's head and becomes part of his skill and knowledge; (iii) specific trade secrets so confidential that, even though the servant may have left the service, they cannot lawfully be used for anyone's benefit but the master's ...

It appears to me that the problem is one of definition: what are trade secrets, and how do they differ (if at all) from confidential information? Mr Poulton suggested that a trade secret is information which, if disclosed to a competitor, would be liable to cause real (or significant) harm to the owner of the secret. I would add first, that it must be information used in a trade or business, and secondly, that the owner must limit the dissemination of it or at least not encourage or permit widespread publication ... It can thus include not only secret formulae for the manufacture of products but also, in an appropriate case, the names of customers and the goods which they buy. But some may say that not all such information is a trade secret in ordinary parlance. If that view be adopted, the class of information which can justify a restriction is wider, and extends to some confidential information which would not ordinarily be called a trade secret.'

COMMENT

Staughton LJ implicitly approves of Goulding J's exposition of classes of information even though, in *Faccenda Chicken*, Neill LJ submitted that Goulding J's second category of information could not be protected. In practice, confidential information, not being a trade secret, is not particularly well protected following termination of employment. In the absence of a covenant in restraint of trade, how would you advise a person about to take up new employment or set up business in his own right as regards the use he can or cannot make of information concerning his former employer's customers, suppliers, delivery routes, and methods of fixing prices, marketing and the like?

Public Interest

The major defence to a breach of confidence action is that of public interest. Whilst there is a general public interest in maintaining confidential relationships (such as between doctor and patient) there is also a public interest in the truth. However, what is interesting to the public (and is, for example, of the type commonly published in certain newspapers) is not necessarily in the public interest. The case below concerns material that is interesting to the public and yet also falls within the public interest defence. It also shows that an injunction will not normally be granted if there is a possibility of a defamation action and the defendant is likely to plead justification.

Woodward v *Hutchins* [1977] 2 All ER 751, Court of Appeal

A number of pop singers conducted their business through a management company which employed Mr Hutchins, one of the defendants, as a public relations officer. He was responsible for making sure that the singers received favourable publicity and were shown to the public in the best light. Mr Hutchins signed a letter promising not to disclose information concerning the group to outsiders. This letter was later torn up in the presence of the managing director of the management company after, according to Mr Hutchins, he had agreed that it should be rescinded. When Mr Hutchins left the employment of the management company he wrote articles for the Daily Mirror newspaper containing lurid details of the behaviour of the pop singers who applied for an injunction to prevent publication of the remaining articles following publication of the first article.

Lord Denning MR (at 753): 'The first article came out last Saturday, 16th April. It was headed: "Why Mrs. Tom Jones threw her jewellery from a car-window and Tom got high in a Jumbo jet". It goes on to give a description of a very unsavoury incident in a jumbo jet. Mr Tom Jones is said to have become inebriated and to have behaved outrageously on the aircraft. Then on Monday, 18th April 1977, the Daily Mirror came out with the headline: "Tom Jones and Marji" [that is the name of a woman called Marjorie Wallace] "The truth! Starts today: the most explosive show-business story of the decade. The Family by Chris Hutchins, the man on the inside. I lived it. I'm telling it." The article gives a long description of what is called "The Marji Wallace Affair. Enter a Sexy Lady", with a photograph of them kissing one another. Now this morning, 19th April 1977, there is an article on the first page: "Tom Jones's Superstud. More Startling Secrets of The Family by Chris Hutchins", together with an account of many more discreditable incidents in which members of the group were concerned.

These articles have produced a swift reaction. Today Tom Jones and others of the group have issued a writ seeking an injunction to restrain the further publication of the series. This afternoon, after a hearing for two hours from 2.15pm to 4.20pm, Slynn J has granted an injunction. The newspaper appeals to this court, and we have heard it from 4.30 to 6.30pm. The reason for the urgency is because the newspaper wishes to publish the next article tomorrow morning. The case requires consideration of three possible causes of action: libel, breach of contract and breach of confidential information.

So far as libel is concerned, the Daily Mirror and Mr Hutchins intimate that they are going to plead justification. They are going to say that the words in the article are true in substance and in fact. In these circumstances it is clear that no injunction would be granted to restrain the publication. These courts rarely, if ever, grant an injunction when a defendant says he is going to justify. The reason is because the interest of the public in knowing the truth outweighs the interest of a plaintiff in maintaining his reputation.

So far as the cause of action for breach of contract is concerned, it is based on the letter in 1972 which I have read. Even if that letter still stood, I doubt whether the promise in it would be enforced. A serious question would arise as to whether it was reasonable to impose such a fetter on freedom of speech. But I need not pursue the point. On the evidence as it stands at the moment, as to the tearing up of the letter, it is a permissible view that the promise was rescinded. So no injunction should be granted on that ground.

The remaining cause of action is for breach of confidential information. It is on this ground that the judge granted an injunction in these words:

> "An injunction restraining the Defendants and each of them from disclosing, divulging or making use of, or from writing, printing, publishing or circulating any confidential information acquired during the course of employment with the Plaintiffs or any of them relating to the private lives, personal affairs or private conduct of the Plaintiffs or any of them."

No doubt in some employments there is an obligation of confidence. In a proper case the court will be prepared to restrain a servant from disclosing confidential information which he has received in the course of his employment. But this case is quite out of the ordinary. There is no doubt whatever that this pop group sought publicity. They wanted to have themselves presented to the public in a favourable light so that audiences would come to hear them and support them. Mr Hutchins was engaged so as to produce, or help to produce, this favourable image, not only of their public lives but of their private lives also. If a group of this kind seek publicity which is to their advantage, it seems to me that they cannot complain if a servant or employee of theirs afterwards discloses the truth about them. If the image which they fostered was not a true image, it is in the public interest that it should be corrected. In these cases of confidential information it is a question of balancing the public interest in maintaining the confidence against the public interest in knowing the truth. That appears from *Initial Services Ltd.* v *Putterill* [1967] 3 All ER 145, [1968] 1 QB 396, *Fraser* v *Evans* [1969] 1 All ER 8, [1969] 1 QB 349 and *D* v *National Society for the Prevention of Cruelty to Children* [1976] 2 All ER 993 at 999, [1976] 3 WLR 124 at 132. In this case the balance comes down in favour of the truth being told, even if it should involve some breach of confidential information. As there should be "truth in advertising", so there should be truth in publicity. The public should not be misled. So it seems to me that the breach of confidential information is not a ground for granting an injunction.

There is a further point. The injunction is so vaguely worded that it would be most difficult for anyone, Mr Hutchins, or the newspaper or any court afterwards, to know what was prohibited and what was not. It speaks of "confidential information". But what is confidential? As Bridge LJ pointed out in the course of the argument, Mr Hutchins, as a press agent, might attend a dance which many others attended. Any incident which took place at the dance would be known to all present. The information would be in the public domain. There could be no objection to the incidents being made known generally. It would not be confidential information. So in this case the incident on this jumbo jet was in the public domain. It was known to all the passengers on the flight. Likewise with several other incidents in the series. The injunction is framed in such wide terms that it would be impossible for the newspaper or Mr Hutchins to know where the line should be drawn.

There is a parallel to be drawn with libel cases. Just as in libel, the courts do not grant an interlocutory injunction to restrain publication of the truth or of fair comment. So also with confidential information. If there is a legitimate ground for supposing that it is in the public interest for it to be disclosed, the courts should not restrain it by an interlocutory injunction, but should leave the complainant to his remedy in damages. Suppose that this case were tried out and the plaintiffs failed in their claim for libel on the ground that all that was said was true. It would seem unlikely that there would be much damages awarded for breach of confidentiality. I cannot help feeling that the plaintiffs' real complaint here is that the words are defamatory; and as they cannot get an interlocutory injunction on that ground, nor should they on confidential information.

Finally, there is the balance of convenience. At this late hour, when the paper is just about to go to press, the balance of convenience requires that there should be no injunction. Any remedy for Mr Tom Jones and his associates should be in damages and damages only.

I would allow the appeal, and discharge the injunction ...'

Bridge LJ (at 755): 'I agree with both judgments and, at this hour, I add but a very few words of my own. It seems to me that those who seek and welcome publicity of every kind bearing on their private lives so long as it shows them in a favourable light are in no position to complain of an invasion of their privacy by publicity which shows them in an unfavourable light.'

COMMENT

The public relations officer was paid, presumably, a large sum of money for his articles. Why was his motive for writing the articles not taken into account? What, precisely, was the public interest in this case? Would an application for a more narrowly drawn injunction, restricted to things that happened out of the public view, have been more likely to be granted?

Privacy

It is often claimed that there is no general right to privacy under English law. In some circumstances, data protection law may control or prohibit the use or disclosure of personal information. In other cases, the law of breach of confidence may provide some protection. The ability of the law of confidence to provide a remedy appears severely limited where the information has been obtained surreptitiously, for example, by industrial espionage. The increasing use of technology to store and transmit confidential information exposes the weakness of the law of confidence in this respect. The growth of networking and the threat of computer hacking are particularly relevant.

Malone v *Commissioner of Police of the Metropolis (No.2)* [1979] 2 All ER 620, Chancery Division

The plaintiff was an antique dealer and was being tried in the Crown Court for a number of offences of handling stolen property. Some of the evidence concerned telephone conversations between the plaintiff and others which had been intercepted on behalf of the police authorised by a warrant issued by the Home Secretary. The plaintiff sued the police claiming a declaration that the 'phone tap was illegal and was a breach of his rights of property, privacy and confidentiality'. He also claimed that the tapping of his telephone line was contrary to Article 8 of the European Convention for the Protection of Human Rights and Fundamental Freedoms 1950.

Megarry VC (at 633): 'I now turn to the third ground on which counsel for the plaintiff supports his first proposition, the right of confidentiality. This is an equitable right which is still in course of development, and is usually protected by the grant of an injunction to prevent disclosure of the confidence. Under Lord Cairns's Act, the Chancery Amendment Act 1858, damages may be granted in substitution for an injunction; yet if there is no case for the grant of an injunction, as when the disclosure has already been made, the unsatisfactory result seems to be that no damages can be awarded under this head: see *Proctor* v *Bayley* (1889) 42 Ch D 390. In such a case, where there is no breach of contract or other orthodox foundation for damages at common law, it seems doubtful whether there is any right to damages, as distinct from an account of profits. It may be, however, that a new tort is emerging (see Goff and Jones on Restitution 2nd Edn (1978), pp 518-519 and Gareth Jones, Restitution of benefits obtained in breach of another's confidence (1970) 86 LQR 463 at 491), though this has been doubted: see Street on Torts, 6th Edn (1976), p 377. Certainly the subject raises many questions that are so far unresolved, some of which are discussed in the Younger report, Cmnd 5012, pp 296-299, para 32.

The application of the doctrine of confidentiality to the tapping of private telephone lines is that in using a telephone a person is likely to do it in the belief that it is probable (though by no means certain) that his words will be heard only by the person he is speaking to. I do not think that it can be put higher than that. As the Younger report points out, those who use the telephone are-

"aware that there are several well understood possibilities of being overheard. A realistic person would not therefore rely on the telephone system to protect the confidence of what he says because, by using the telephone, he would have discarded a large measure of security for his private speech."

Extension lines, private switchboards and so-called "crossed lines", for example, all offer possibilities of being overheard. The report then pointed out that what would not be taken into account would be an unauthorised tap by induction coil or infinity transmitter. The report, which was dealing only with incursions into privacy by individuals and companies, and not the public sector, said nothing about tapping authorised by the Home Secretary. However, the substantial publicity attending the Birkett report, and the general interest in films, television and affairs of notoriety in other countries, must mean that few telephone users can be ignorant of the real possibility that telephones are subject to the risk (which most people will probably regard as being very small in their own cases) of being tapped by some governmental body with access to the telephone system.

It is against that background that I must consider counsel's submissions for the plaintiff. He contended that the categories of confidentiality were not closed, and that they should be extended. The leading case in this branch of the law is *Prince Albert v Strange* (1849) 1 Mac & G 25, 41 ER 1171; *affg* 2 De G & Sm 652, 64 ER 293, as applied in *Margaret, Duchess of Argyll v Duke of Argyll* [1965] 1 All ER 611, [1967] Ch 302; and without citing the former, counsel for the plaintiff read me passages from the latter. If A makes a confidential communication to B, then A may not only restrain B from divulging or using the confidence, but also may restrain C from divulging or using it if C has acquired it from B, even if he acquired it without notice of any impropriety: see the authorities cited in Snell's Equity, 27th Edn (1973), p.651, one of which, *Printers & Finishers Ltd. v Holloway* [1965] 1 WLR 1 at 7, was put before me. In such cases it seems plain that, however innocent the acquisition of the knowledge, what will be restrained is the use or disclosure of it after notice of the impropriety. In the case of a telephone conversation, said counsel for the plaintiff, any conversation that was "reasonably intended to be private" (in the words of Harlan J in *Katz v United States* (1967) 389 US 347 at 362) should be treated as a confidential communication. Even if the using of the telephone must be taken as implying some sort of consent to some risk of being overheard, that could not be taken to be any kind of consent to any publication to any third party.

Counsel for the plaintiff agreed that there were limits to the doctrine of confidentiality. He accepted the dictum of Page Wood VC in *Gartside v Outram* (1856) 26 LJ Ch 113 at 114 that "There is no confidence as to the disclosure of iniquity". This view was applied in *Initial Services v Putterill* [1967] 3 All ER 145 at 148, [1968] 1 QB 396 at 405, where Lord Denning MR held that it extended "to any misconduct of such a nature that it ought in the public interest to be disclosed to others", and was not confined to cases of crime or fraud. Counsel for the plaintiff agreed that if through what are often called "crossed lines" a person overhears what is plainly a confidential conversation, and this discloses plans to commit a crime, that person should inform the police, and he could not be said to have committed any breach of the obligation of confidentiality. But that, he contended, was very different from tapping a telephone in the hope of obtaining information about some crime, whether already committed or being planned.

In *Fraser* v *Evans* [1969] 1 All ER 8 at 11, [1969] 1 QB 349 at 362, Lord Denning MR stated that he did not look on the dictum of Page Wood VC (1956) 26 LJ Ch 113 at 114 as expressing a principle, and said:

> "It is merely an instance of just cause or excuse for breaking confidence. There are some things which may be required to be disclosed in the public interest, in which event no confidence can be prayed in aid to keep them secret."

In a judgment a mere four sentences long, Davies LJ agreed with Lord Denning MR on one ground of his decision, but expressly refrained from saying anything about two other points, of which the exegesis of iniquity was one. The judgment of the third member of the court, Widgery LJ, consisted of a single sentence. He said: "I entirely agree", and went on to state that he would not take time "in an endeavour to repeat the reasons given by my lord". This might be read as being a complete agreement with what Davies LJ had said, or with what the other two members of the court were agreed on (which comes to the same thing), or it might be read as an agreement with all that Lord Denning MR had said, including that part of it on which Davies LJ had refrained from expressing any view.

I do not think that I need explore the problem, which often arises, of the significance and effect of the simple words "I agree" when uttered in the Court of Appeal. Russell LJ did this in his presidential address to the Holdsworth Club in 1969, and I could add little. I readily accept and adopt what Lord Denning MR said, whether or not it expresses a majority view. I also accept the other formulation by Lord Denning MR that I have mentioned, that in *Initial Services Ltd.* v *Putterill* [1967] 3 All ER 145 at 148, [1968] 1 QB 396 at 405, based on whether disclosure is in the public interest. Lord Denning MR extended this to all crimes, frauds and misdeeds, whether actually committed or in contemplation, but limited it to cases where the disclosure was to someone who had a proper interest to receive the information, as where the disclosure is to the police in relation to a crime. As in the case before me this is the only kind of disclosure in question, I need say no more on this limitation. Winn LJ expressly concurred in Lord Denning MR's judgment, and I do not think Salmon LJ disagreed. As between the two formulations, I think I would prefer *Fraser* v *Evans* [1965] 1 WLR 1 at 7, since that is not confined to misconduct or misdeeds. There may be cases where there is no misconduct or misdeed but yet there is a just cause or excuse for breaking confidence. The confidential information may relate to some apprehension of an impending chemical or other disaster, arising without misconduct, of which the authorities are not aware, but which ought in the public interest to be disclosed to them. However, I need not pursue this, since in the circumstances of the present case the two formulations produce no significant difference ...

Third, there is the right of privacy. Here the contention is that, although at present no general right of privacy has been recognised by English law, there is a particular right of privacy, namely, the right to hold a telephone conversation in the privacy of one's home without molestation. This, it was said, ought to be recognised and declared to be part of English law, despite the absence of any English authority to this effect. As I have indicated I am not unduly troubled by the absence of English authority: there has to be a first time for everything, and, if the principles of English law, and not least analogies from the existing rules, together with the requirements of justice and common sense, pointed firmly to such a right existing, then I think the court should not be deterred from recognising the right.

On the other hand, it is no function of the courts to legislate in a new field. The extension of the existing laws and principles is one thing, the creation of an altogether new right is another. At times judges must, and do, legislate; but, as Holmes J once said, they do so only interstitially, and with molecular rather than molar motions: see *Southern Pacific* v *Jensen* (1917) 244 US 205 at 221, in a dissenting judgment. Anything beyond that must be left for legislation. No new right in the law, fully-fledged with all the appropriate safeguards, can spring from the head of a judge deciding a particular case; only Parliament can create such a right. The most obvious recent example of this is the so-called deserted wife's equity to occupy the matrimonial home. There was much uncertainty as to the ambit and operation of this right, and whether it arose from desertion alone, or whether there was also a betrayed wife's equity, a battered wife's equity, and so on, or, for that matter, a deserted husband's equity. After some 15 years of controversy and litigation, with its accompanying burden of costs, in *National Provincial Bank Ltd.* v *Ainsworth* [1965] 2 All ER 472, [1965] AC 1175 it was held that the equity had never existed. Parliament then enacted the Matrimonial Homes Act 1967, laying down a complete code which the courts could not possibly have laid down by way of judicial decision. The fact that the code has its difficulties does not affect the matter: the point is that the 1967 Act dealt with a wide variety of circumstances, and provided a number of safeguards, in a way that no court could properly have done. Where there is some major gap in the law, no doubt a judge would be capable of framing what he considered to be a proper code to fill it: and sometimes he may be tempted. But he has to remember that his function is judicial, not legislative, and that he ought not to use his office so as to legislate in the guise of exercising his judicial powers.

One of the factors that must be relevant in such a case is the degree of particularity in the right that is claimed. The wider and more indefinite the right claimed, the greater the undesirability of holding that such a right exists. Wide and indefinite rights, while conferring an advantage on those who have them, may well gravely impair the position of those who are subject to the rights. To create a right for one person, you have to impose a corresponding duty on another. In the present case, the alleged right to hold a telephone conversation in the privacy of one's own home without molestation is wide and indefinite in its scope, and in any case does not seem to be very apt for covering the plaintiff's grievance. He was not "molested' in holding his telephone conversations: he held them without "molestation", but without their retaining the privacy that he desired. If a men telephones from his own home, but an open window makes it possible for a near neighbour to overhear what is said, and the neighbour, remaining throughout on his own property, listens to the conversation, is he to be a tortfeasor? Is a person who overhears a telephone conversation by reason of a so-called "crossed line" to be liable in damages? What of an operator of a private switchboard who listens in? Why is the right that is claimed confined to a man's own home, so that it would not apply to private telephone conversations from offices, call boxes or the houses of others? If they were to be included, what of the greater opportunities for deliberate overhearing that they offer? In any case, why is the telephone to be subject to this special right of privacy when there is no general right?

That is not all. Suppose that there is what for brevity I may call a right to telephonic privacy, sounding in tort. What exceptions to it, if any, would there be? Would it be a breach of the right if anyone listened to a telephone conversation in which some act of criminal violence or dishonesty was being planned? Should a listener be restrained by injunction from disclosing to the authorities a conversation that would lead to the release of someone who has been kidnapped? There are many, many questions that can, and should, be asked. ...

Fourth, there is the right of confidentiality. Let me at the outset dispose of one point. If telephone services were provided under a contract between the telephone subscriber and the Post Office, then it might be contended that there was some implied term in that contract that telephone conversations should remain confidential and be free from tapping. To meet such a possible contention, the Solicitor-General took me through a series of statutes and cases on the point, ending with certain sections of the Post Office Act 1969. The combined effect of ss.9 and 28 is that the Post Office is under a duty to provide certain services, including telephone services (though this duty is not enforceable by proceedings in court), and that the Post Office has power to make a scheme of charges and other terms and conditions for those services, the charges being recoverable "as if" they were simple contract debts. Under s.28, the Post Office Telecommunications Scheme 1976 was duly made, bearing the name Scheme T1/1976: this was published as a supplement to the London Gazette of 25th May 1976. By para 6 of the scheme, neither the scheme, nor anything done under it, nor any request for any service for which the scheme fixes or determines any charges, terms or conditions, is to "constitute or lead to the formation of a contract between the Post Office and any other person". At the end of the Solicitor-General's submissions on the point counsel for the plaintiff conceded that there was no contract as such between the plaintiff and the Post Office; and that, I think, is the end of any contention based on implied terms.

The right of confidentiality accordingly falls to be considered apart from any contractual right. In such a case, it has been said that three elements are normally required if a case of breach of confidence is to succeed:

"First, the information itself, in the words of Lord Greene MR in the *Saltman* case (1948) [1963] 3 All ER 413n at 415 must 'have the necessary quality of confidence about it'. Secondly, that information must have been imparted in circumstances importing an obligation of confidence. Thirdly, there must be an unauthorised use of that information to the detriment of the party communicating it."

See *Coco v A N Clark (Engineers) Ltd.* [1969] RPC 41 at 47 cited by Lord Widgery CJ in *Attorney-General v Jonathan Cape Ltd.* [1975] 3 All ER 484 at 494, [1976] 1 QB 752 at 769. Of the second requirement, it was said in the *Coco* case [1969] RPC 41 at 47 that "However secret and confidential the information, there can be no binding obligation of confidence if that information is blurted out in public or is communicated in other circumstances which negative any duty of holding it confidential". What was in issue in the *Coco* case [1969] RPC 41 was a communication by an inventor or designer to a manufacturer, and the alleged misuse of that information by the manufacturer. In the present case, the alleged misuse is not by the person to whom the information was intended to be communicated, but by someone to whom the plaintiff had no intention of communicating anything: and that, of course, introduces a somewhat different element, that of the unknown overhearer.

It seems to me that a person who utters confidential information must accept the risk of any unknown overhearing that is inherent in the circumstances of communication. Those who exchange confidences on a bus or a train run the risk of a nearby passenger with acute hearing or a more distant passenger who is adept at lip-reading. Those who speak over garden walls run the risk of the unseen neighbour in a tool-shed nearby. Office cleaners who discuss secrets in the office when they think everyone else has gone run the risk of speaking within earshot of an unseen member of the staff who is working late. Those who give confidential information over an office intercommunication system run the risk of some third party being connected to the conversation. I do not see why someone who has overheard some secret in such a way should be exposed to legal proceedings if he uses or divulges what he has heard. No doubt an honourable man would give some warning when he realises that what he is hearing is not intended for his ears: but I have to concern myself with the law, and not with moral standards. There are, of course, many moral precepts which are not legally enforceable.

When this is applied to telephone conversations, it appears to me that the speaker is taking such risks of being overheard as are inherent in the system. As I have mentioned, the Younger report referred to users of the telephone being aware that there were several well-understood possibilities of being overheard, and stated that a realistic person would not rely on the telephone system to protect the confidence of what he says. That comment seems unanswerable. In addition, so much publicity in recent years has been given to instances (real or fictional) of the deliberate tapping of telephones that it is difficult to envisage telephone users who are genuinely unaware of this possibility. No doubt a person who uses a telephone to give confidential information to another may do so in such a way as to impose an obligation of confidence on that other: but I do not see how it could be said that any such obligation is imposed on those who overhear the conversation, whether by means of tapping or otherwise.

Even if any duty of confidentiality were, contrary to my judgment, to be held to bind those who overhear a telephone conversation, there remains the question of the limits to that duty. I have already discussed and accepted the formulation of Lord Denning MR's in *Fraser* v *Evans* [1969] 1 All ER 8 at 11, [1969] 1 QB 349 at 362, namely, that of "just cause or excuse for breaking confidence", as well as his formulation in *Initial Services Ltd.* v *Putterill* [1967] 3 All ER 145 at 148, [1968] 1 QB 396 at 405, based on whether the disclosure is in the public interest. I shall not repeat these alternative formulations; I treat the former as including the latter. If what is overheard, though confidential, is itself an iniquity, it is plain that it is subject to no duty of confidence. But if there is merely a suspicion of iniquity, does that justify a deliberate overhearing by means of a tap? Even if from time to time the tap provides information about iniquity, does that justify a process of recording entire conversations, and listening to those recordings, when much of the conversations may be highly confidential and untainted by any iniquity? Further, if there is a reasonable suspicion of iniquity, can that suspicion justify tapping in order to find out whether the suspicion is well-founded, if in fact the conversations are wholly innocent?

I think that one has to approach these matters with some measure of balance and common sense. The rights and liberties of a telephone subscriber are indeed important; but so also are the desires of the great bulk of the population not to be the victims of assault, theft or other crimes. The detection and prosecution of criminals, and the discovery of projected crimes, are important weapons in protecting the public. In the nature of things it will be virtually impossible to know beforehand whether any particular telephone conversation will be criminal in nature. The question is not whether there is a certainty that the conversation tapped will be iniquitous, but whether there is just cause or excuse for the tapping and for the use made of the material obtained by the tapping.

If certain requirements are satisfied, then I think that there will plainly be just cause or excuse for what is done by or on behalf of the police. Those requirements are, first, that there should be grounds for suspecting that the tapping of the particular telephone will be of material assistance in detecting or preventing crime, or discovering the criminals, or otherwise assisting in the discharge of the functions of the police in relation to crime. Second, no use should be made of any material obtained except for these purposes. Third, any knowledge of information which is not relevant to those purposes should be confined to the minimum number of persons reasonably required to carry out the process of tapping. If those requirements are satisfied, then it seems to me that there will be just cause or excuse for carrying out the tapping, and using information obtained for those limited purposes. I am not, of course, saying that nothing else can constitute a just cause or excuse: what I am saying is that, if these requirements are satisfied, then in my judgment there will be a just cause or excuse. I am not, for instance, saying anything about matters of national security: I speak only of what is before me in the present case, concerning tapping for police purposes in relation to crime.'

COMMENT

In *Prince Albert* v *Strange* (1849) 1 Mac & G 25, the information (prints taken from etchings made by Prince Albert and Queen Victoria) was surreptitiously obtained yet an injunction was granted. This case was not fully considered in *Malone*. In 1980, the Law Commission produced a draft Bill to codify the law of confidence which contained specific provision dealing with eavesdropping and industrial espionage.

Under the law of confidence as it now stands, is a computer hacker under a duty of confidence in respect of information of a confidential nature that he has gained unauthorised access to?

The position of innocent acquirers of confidential information has been uncertain. Can such a person be under an obligation of confidence if he discovers its true nature a) before he has made use of it or disclosed it to others, or (b) after such use or disclosure? Is Megarry VC correct in considering that damages are not available in a breach of confidence action commenced subsequent to an unauthorised disclosure to the public; that is, where an injunction would no longer be appropriate?

The law of confidence is insufficiently wide to give a general right to privacy nor does it seem to be capable of development to that extent. Other areas of English law may be of some assistance, but even here, their application may be very limited as the following article shows.

Markesinis, B.S. 'Our Patchy Law of Privacy - Time to do Something about it' , (1990) 53 *MLR* 802

'The Facts

In *Gordon Kaye (by Peter Froggatt his next friend)* v *Andrew Robertson and Sport Newspapers Ltd.* [now reported in [1991] FSR 62] the Court of Appeal unanimously condemned an offensive intrusion into the actor Mr Gordon Kaye's privacy and made what are, so far, the strongest appeals to Parliament to reform our patchy law on the important issue of privacy. Mr Kaye's sufferings started with the storms of last winter. He was then severely injured by a detached piece from an advertisement hoarding. It smashed through the windscreen of his car and severely injured his head. For three days after this incident which occurred on 25 January, he was on a life-support machine; another seven days followed in intensive care. His condition remained critical throughout this period. Visits were severely restricted, not least in order to limit the risk of infection. As is usual, complete calm and peace was ordered to facilitate recovery; and so as to ensure that those medical decisions were observed, a special notice was pinned on the door of his room to this effect.

The two defendants were the editor and owning company of the *Sunday Sport*. This is a weekly publication which the Judge at first instance described as having "a lurid and sensational style". Lord Justice Glidwell who, along with his brother judges inspected some recent copies of this publication, thought it had a strong bias to pornography. The issue of 4 March, which eventually published the Kaye story, leaves little doubt of this since over a photo of Mr Kaye lying asleep (or, probably, unconscious) in bed is printed a photo of a scantily-clad woman with the title "red-hot Donna had four men in the snow".

Disregarding the notice on the door the defendants' agents entered Mr Kaye's hospital room where they photographed him with a flash light and took an interview of sorts. At the trial the editor admitted - proudly one suspects - that his staff had achieved "a great old-fashioned scoop". He also accepted that other publications might well be willing to "pay large sums of money for the privilege" of talking to and photographing Mr Kaye. Though the defendants claimed Mr Kaye had consented to all this, the available medical evidence suggested that he was, at best, only in very limited control of his faculties. Indeed, a quarter of an hour after the alleged "voluntary" interview had taken place Mr Kaye had no recollection of the event. Though in the subsequent publication the defendants claimed to have been motivated by a desire to inform Mr Kaye's fans of the state of his health, the facts described above (and given more fully in the judgment) point in another direction. For the average reader this lurid and sensational journalism must have had much baser motives.

Mr Justice Porter issued a series of orders, in effect banning the publication of the story (in its original form). The defendants appealed and Glidwell, *(sic)* Bingham and Legatt LJJ essentially upheld the plaintiff's claim but, as a result of their careful review of our patchy law, had to issue a more restricted order. Basically, this allowed the defendants to publish some photos and their story provided they made it clear that neither had been obtained with Mr Kaye's consent. The reasoning of the learned justices as well as the reduced protection which, to their obvious regret, they were able to give to Mr Kaye, reveal (a) the legal contortions that have to be made in order to protect deserving victims and (b) the need to establish some wider principle of privacy. Indirectly, the case and judgments also show how inadequate are the

Press's current attempts to demonstrate that they can police themselves on this matter.

The Judgments

The leading judgment was delivered by Lord Justice Glidwell; but the other two Justices delivered concurring opinions which present particular interest not least because of their comparative content. In these judgments four causes of action were considered. In inverse order of likely success they were: passing off, trespass to the person, libel, and malicious falsehood.

Passing off was dealt with briefly. It was rejected since the case was not considered to be covered by the House of Lords decision in *Warnink* v *Townend & Sons* [1979] AC 731. The plaintiff's claim seemed to have foundered mainly on the grounds that he was "not in the position of a *trader* (italics supplied) in relation to his interest in his story about his accident". True; but an extension of the tort could have been made, indeed was almost made, in the case of *Sim* v *Heinz* [1959] 1 WLR 313 where Heinz, the food manufacturers, apparently used the actor Ron Moody to simulate the voice of another well-known actor, Alistair Sim, in advertising their products. Mr Sim's attempt to obtain an interlocutory injunction on the grounds of defamation failed, though the alternative argument that an actor has an interest in his voice similar to the one that a trader has in his wares, held out some appeal both to McNair J who heard the application at first instance, and to Hodson LJ who decided the case on appeal. *Sim* v *Heinz* which was not, apparently, cited to or by the court in either *Warnink* or *Kaye*, shows that an extension of this very "commercial" tort could be attempted in order to avoid the "grave defect in the law [of allowing one] party, for the purpose of commercial gain, to make use of the voice of another party without his consent". And if that could be done for the voice of an actor, why not for his image, especially when the appropriation of the likeness is used to enrich another person?

The attempt to use trespass to protect Mr Kaye did not fare much better. Two reasons were given, the first more convincing than the second. The first was that no case could be found to support the view that the taking of the flashlight photograph amounted to battery; and the second that there was no causal evidence to show that, as a result of their act, Mr Kaye had suffered stress and a set-back in his recovery. In Lord Justice Glidwell's words there was "no evidence that the taking of the photographs did in fact cause him [Mr Kaye] any damage". The second point is, it is submitted, not very telling since battery is a tort actionable *per se* and will succeed without proof of any damage. But the first point presented a greater obstacle given that, apparently, "there can be no battery unless there is *contact* with the plaintiff", *Street on Torts* (London: Butterworths, 8th ed 1988) at 23. Now, flashlight contact might be treated as sufficiently close to physical contact to justify, as Glidwell LJ was willing to entertain, an extension of the tort of battery. (The same might just be arguable in German law as well but it would, probably, fail.) It must be noted, however, that in novel situations the current tendency is to resort to the tort of negligence rather than expand the older tort of battery and even to by-pass the latter tort by having resort to criminal law. Why not then try negligence? This ever-growing tort, unlike battery, requires proof of the existence of a duty of care - something which would have caused no problem in the instant case; but it also requires proof of damage which, as stated, was not forthcoming. It may thus be that the two elements of the two torts were inadvertently telescoped into one. Clearly, the learned Judge regarded this part of his judgment as secondary to the main thrust of his arguments which came in the remaining two causes of action: libel and malicious falsehood.

Libel was, according to Glidwell and Bingham LJJ, strongly arguable. *Tolley* v *J S Fry and Sons Ltd.* [1931] AC 333 was the authority that persuaded the judge who heard the application at first instance; and it also appealed to the appeal court judges. If it was not used in the end it was because of the rule in *Williams Coulson & Sons* v *James Coulson and Co.* (1887) 3 TLR 46 which held that interim injunctions are to be used sparingly in libel actions - a rule confirmed in *Herbage* v *Times Newspapers Limited and Others* (unreported), despite the decision of the House of Lords in *American Cyanamid* v *Ethicon* [1975] AC 395. So, though the judges felt that the publication was libellous, they also felt that a jury might well not take the same view and, in the circumstances, a general injunction should not be and was not granted.

But was the publication libellous on the authority of *Tolley* v *Fry?* Tolley succeeded because an innuendo was discovered. It was in 1931 - but would it still be now? - defamatory for an amateur golfer to give the impression that he had "prostituted his amateur status for gain". But the ratio of the case would not have covered a professional golfer even though he, too, needs (perhaps even more strongly than the amateur) to prevent the unauthorised use of his image. So where is the innuendo here? Given the nature of the publication in question, one could argue that any respectable member of society who appears to be associated with the *Sunday Sport* is, automatically, defamed. But the learned Judge, hinting, perhaps, at this suggestion was right in suggesting that such "a conclusion is [not] inevitable". And if a jury were to decide that there was no defamation, that would be the end of Mr Kaye's interest to be left in peace in his hospital bed. Yet, as Lord Justice Bingham said, "If ever a person has a right to be let alone by strangers with no public interest to pursue, it must surely be when he lies in hospital recovering from brain surgery and in no more than partial command of his faculties". And yet this right, *de lege lata*, depends on the quaint facts of *Tolley* v *Fry*; and the result, judging from the Court of Appeal judgment in *Tolley* [1930] 1 KB 467 was not that obvious even in those halcyon days of the 1930s when sportsmen played for their sport and not for money.

In the end Mr Kaye succeeded by the skin of his teeth because the judges were able to rely on the tort of malicious falsehood. This is not an easy tort, as any reading of a text book will reveal; nor is it frequently used. But, at least, it avoided the injunction problems of *Coulson* v *Coulson* since in malicious falsehood the test of that case applies only to the requirement that the plaintiff must show that the words are false; and the (original) statement by the *Sunday Sport* that the photos and interview were taken with Mr Kaye's consent were, clearly, false.

So Mr Kaye won; but he won only limited protection in that the publication of the photos and story could only go ahead if the paper made it clear that they were taken without his consent. Moreover he won, but only just, because judges anxious to do justice were willing "to be persuaded" that something, somehow, should be done. In this, they were following other distinguished courts which had tried to put old torts on the procrustean bed in order to protect privacy (*Bernstein* v *Skyviews and General Ltd.* [1978] QB 479) or resort to old procedures (wardship) (*re X* [1984] 1 WLR 1422) in order to rectify the patchy way in which English law has faced a new problem: our increased ability to collect, collate and disseminate information about other persons under the pretence of *public* interest but, often, for no better reason than *private* gain.'

COMMENT

Professor Markesinis suggests that statutory intervention is required to reform the law and to provide for an effective right to privacy. See also Bedingfield, D., 'Privacy or Publicity? The Enduring Confusion Surrounding the American Tort of Invasion of Privacy', (1992) 55 *MLR* 111 and Markesinis, B.S., 'The Calcutt Report Must not be Forgotten', (1992) 55 *MLR* 118. How does one provide an effective law of privacy without unduly interfering with the principle of free speech?

Relief

Ocular Sciences Ltd. v *Aspect Vision Care Ltd.* [1997] RPC 289, Patents Court

For a note about the facts of this case, see the extract from this case earlier in this chapter.

Laddie J (at 395): '(1) Injunctive relief.
It is common to classify injunctions as either prohibitory or mandatory. However the expression "prohibitory injunction" is a broad one. It covers a wide variety of orders made by the courts which share the common feature that the court restrains the addressee from doing one or more acts. The terms of a prohibitory injunction will be tailored to meet the particular facts of the case before the court. In the case of actions for breach of confidence it is possible to split the prohibitory injunction which the plaintiff will normally invite the court to make into two distinct parts. First there is the order which restrains the wrongdoer from continuing to use, or benefit from the use of, the confidential information. Secondly there is the order preventing the wrongdoer from making the information public. The first is primarily directed to prevent the wrongdoer from benefiting from his wrongful acts or continuing to inflict damage on the plaintiff while the second is directed more to preserving the confidential nature of the information, that is to say preserving the subject matter of the suit. There is no reason why a court should feel constrained to choose simply between granting both or neither. The factors which may justify granting or refusing one type of prohibitory injunction may not be identical to those relevant to the grant or refusal of the other. Particularly in relation to this type of relief, the court has a duty to frame the relief ordered to secure a just and equitable result ...

(a) Injunctions against continued use
Before considering whether in this case it would be appropriate to restrain the defendants from using their current technology or running their business, it is right to consider precisely what the injunction is going to stop and how that relates to the plaintiffs' rights which have been breached. In particular what is the effect of an injunction, as sought here, which prohibits a defendant from "making any use of" the confidential information? Where the defendant continues to possess the confidential information and his products incorporate or disclose it or their manufacture continues to use it, an injunction against use will automatically restrain continued operation of the process and sale of products. But what would be the effect of an injunction in those terms where the defendant's products or process do not themselves continue to incorporate or disclose confidential information although they were brought into

existence or were perfected or owe their commercial success to the fact that confidential information was used in the past? Such products or processes can be referred to conveniently as "derivative" or "derived". If exploitation by the defendant of such derived products and processes is considered to be continued use of the information employed in their creation or development, an injunction against use would have the effect of prohibiting further exploitation of the derived matter. If that is so, the court should consider whether injunctive relief which goes that far is intended and appropriate.

There are at least two types of case in which derivative works may be in issue. The first is where, at the date of judgment, the information is no longer confidential but it was at the time the products were made or when the production equipment or process was designed or constructed. In that case even if the products incorporate or disclose, or the process uses, the information, it is not *confidential* information. This touches upon a part of the so-called "springboard" principle based on the well known passage in Roxburgh J's judgment in *Terrapin Ltd.* v *Builders' Supply Co. (Hayes) Ltd.* [1967} RPC 375 ...

This could be understood as meaning that, after the information has become public knowledge, it can still be the subject of an injunction. I do not think that that is what Roxburgh J meant. All that he indicated was that where confidential information has been used by a defendant to get an illegitimate head start, that head start is still illegitimate even if, at a subsequent date, the information becomes public. It does not address what relief should be granted ...

This is not a simple issue but I must admit that I am attracted by Lord Goff's analysis [in *Attorney-General* v *Guardian Newspapers (No.2)* [1990] 1 AC 109]. It seems to me that, at least in the area of breach of confidence, injunctions are granted not against the continued flow of a wrongful benefit arising out of or caused by breach of the plaintiff's rights but to prevent continuation of the breach. If a continuing activity of the defendant does not constitute a breach of confidence then it ought not to be injuncted even if it produces an unfair benefit to the defendant. Lord Griffiths agreed that that would be a conclusive answer to a claim against a third party recipient of the information. Like Lord Goff, I can not see why it should not be a conclusive answer to a claim against the confidant. The way the court reduces or eliminates the unfair benefit is by imposing financial penalties or, possibly, by the creation of a constructive trust. The latter is a form of relief sought by the plaintiffs in this action and I will consider it in due course.

The second type of case is where the defendant's derivative products, process or business have been made from or with the assistance of information which is still confidential but where they do not themselves directly disclose or incorporate the information. If the derivative products or process are regarded merely as illicit benefits flowing from misuse of confidential information, then, for the reasons set out above, I do not think that is a basis which would justify the court in granting an injunction. On the other hand it may be possible to argue that the continued use or exploitation of the derived product is to be regarded as a continued use or exploitation of the confidential information which was utilised for their creation. This is of relevance here. Even if I grant an injunction to restrain continued use of the MPS program, the defendant's business will have been assisted by its use in the past and it could be said that continuation of the business represents a continued exploitation of or benefit from it. In addition, Mr Anthony Galley may have looked at the plaintiffs' Lens Design Program when creating his spreadsheet for the purpose of reassuring himself or confirming the steps he had already taken. The plaintiffs argue that if the defendants continue to use their spreadsheet they are continuing to take the benefit of the still secret Lens Design Program. They want the court to grant injunctions to restrain breach of confidence which would prevent continued operation of the AVCL business and use of the defendants' lens design spreadsheet.

The way the plaintiffs put their case is as follows. They say that the court has power to grant an injunction even where the information is not embodied in the product of the use. They submit that the principle stated in *Prince Albert* v *Strange* (1849) 1 Mac. & G. 25 namely:

"the court will interfere by injunction to prevent a party availing himself in any manner of a title arising out of a violation of right or breach of contract or confidence"

applies here. They say that this should apply regardless of whether the ultimate product of the violation discloses the confidential information. They say that, as a matter of equity, the court should also seek to prevent the defendants benefiting from their unlawful acts. The plaintiffs also rely on *Union Carbide Corp.* v *Naturin Ltd.* [1987] FSR 538. In that case the plaintiff's confidential method of making sausage skins had been stolen and taken abroad where it was used to set up a factory. Sausage skins from the offending factory were imported into England. The skins said nothing about how they were made. The plaintiff brought proceedings for breach of confidence here against the importer. The defendant importer applied to strike out on the ground that the statement of claim disclosed no reasonable cause of action. In the Court of Appeal the application was unsuccessful. Slade LJ said at page 547:

"The argument on this issue has been interesting and has raised important questions of law. However, I do not think it appropriate for this court to attempt a definitive answer to them on this striking out application. Suffice it to say that, subject to the important question of notice, to which I will shortly turn, I am of the opinion that the 'cardinal principle' referred to by Lloyd-Jacob J is wide enough to afford the plaintiffs an arguable claim against Naturin on the basis that, by marketing the casings received from Viscofan, they are availing themselves of a title derived from a breach of confidence and are thus to be treated as making use of the confidential information itself. Possibly there may be other conceptually sounder legal routes by which the same result could be reached. However, I am not yet persuaded that a plaintiff whose confidential know-how has been stolen and used by the thief to manufacture a product would necessarily be left without rights or remedies, at least against a third party who was in possession of the product and at all material times had full knowledge of all the circumstances in which the product had come into existence. I am not yet convinced that the arm of the law or of equity would necessarily be too short to reach the third party in such a case."

In coming to the conclusion that the plaintiff's case was at least arguable, the Court of Appeal relied on the passage in *Prince Albert* v *Strange* cited above and also on a similar passage in the judgment of Lloyd-Jacob J in *Stevenson Jordan Harrison Ltd.* v *MacDonald & Evans* (1951) 68 RPC 190.

Since *Union Carbide* was a strike out application, the Court of Appeal did not have to decide whether or not the plaintiffs' claim was maintainable, only whether it was arguably so. I do not read it as supporting the argument that the very broad statement quoted from *Prince Albert* is adequate of itself to define those cases in which the courts will grant injunctions. Slade LJ's suggestion that there might be other conceptually sounder legal routes to support the plaintiffs' case suggests that he also harboured misgivings about simply adopting the statement in *Prince Albert* as unqualified.

A broad principle that courts of equity should grant injunctions to prevent wrongdoers from "getting away with it" has a tabloid appeal. However, it seems to me that the statement in *Prince Albert* must be treated with the same care as Lord Goff treated the somewhat similar broad statement "a man shall not be allowed to profit from his own wrong". I cannot believe that the use of any title which has arisen in some way, whether direct or indirect, substantial or insubstantial, proximate or remote from a breach of a right or contract will always be stopped by the court. The broad field covered by that statement of principle must contain areas into which it would be quite inappropriate for the arm of equity to reach.

It seems to me that whether or not the use of a derived product, say, should be treated as a use of the information employed in its creation must be determined on the particular facts of the case ...

If I had considered this to be a borderline case as far as the grant of this type of injunctive relief is concerned, their deliberate attempts to mislead the court would have led me to decline to make an order in the plaintiffs' favour.

However I do not think this is a borderline case. Having taken into account the various matters referred to above, I am not prepared to make an order restraining the defendants from using the confidential information on which the plaintiffs have succeeded. The plaintiffs' relief must sound in money, assuming, of course, that they can prove any loss to them or benefit to the defendants.

(b) Injunctions against disclosure

Although I am not prepared to grant injunctions against continued use of those items of confidential information on which the plaintiffs' claims have succeeded, different considerations apply to the claims for injunctions to restrain publication of the information. In the special circumstances of this case, one of the major factors which has led me to refuse to prevent continued use of that information by the defendants is that an injunction to that effect would cause enormous damage to the defendants when no or very little relevant injury is being suffered by the plaintiffs. Nevertheless the information, so long as confidential, has some value even if it is of minor technical significance and narrow scope. To a company which wishes to enter this industry, it may be useful to have a set of drawings of the machinery necessary for making lenses together with the confidence that those drawings are of a working production line. There has been no suggestion that the defendants have disclosed the details of their machinery to anyone save their employees and suppliers and two licensees. The latter are under express obligations of confidence in relation to the total package of material they have obtained or will obtain under their licences. It has not been suggested that confidentiality in any of the plaintiffs' information has been compromised by the defendants' activities or that a restraint imposed on the defendants preventing them from making public the details of that information would cause the defendants any significant inconvenience. The defendants did not appear to be concerned to resist an injunction to that effect, even though it has not been asserted that the defendants have threatened to make the information public.

Refusal of an injunction restraining publication would have the effect of destroying the subject matter of the litigation. Notwithstanding the unpalatable way in which the plaintiffs have conducted this litigation, in my view it would not be right for the court to go so far as to decline to preserve the existence of their asset when, as here, such preservation will cause no harm or significant inconvenience to the defendants. In the absence of any notable objection from the defendants I am prepared to grant an injunction against the defendants restraining them from publishing the information which I have held to be confidential. That injunction will need to be drafted in a way which makes it clear that it will not have the effect of preventing the defendants from making such disclosure as is necessary for the proper operation of their manufacturing operation.'

COMMENT

A useful description of injunctive relief and its applicability. Laddie J also casts some doubt on the 'Springboard Doctrine', as it has been understood by some, following *Terrapin*. Laddie J granted an injunction restraining publication of the relevant information by the defendant but he refused to grant an injunction against continued use. However, the plaintiff may be entitled to damages in respect of such use.

Laddie J identified two cases where derivative works, being works which are based on confidential information but which do not themselves incorporate or disclose confidential information. The first is where the information is no longer confidential, the second being where it still is confidential.

What is the significance of this distribution in terms of whether or not an injunction should be granted?

Agreement on Trade-Related Aspects of Intellectual Property Rights

Section 7. Protection of undisclosed information

Article 39

1. In the course of ensuring effective protection against unfair competition as provided in Article 10[bis] of the Paris Convention (1967), Members shall protect undisclosed information in accordance with paragraph 2 and data submitted to governments or governmental agencies in accordance with paragraph 3.

2. Natural and legal persons shall have the possibility of preventing information lawfully within their control from being disclosed to, acquired by, or used by others without their consent in a manner contrary to honest commercial practices[1] so long as such information:

(a) is secret in the sense that it is not, as a body or in the precise configuration and assembly of its components, generally known among or readily accessible to persons within the circles that normally deal with the kind of information in question;

(b) has commercial value because it is secret; and

(c) has been subject to reasonable steps under the circumstances, by the person lawfully in control of the information, to keep it secret.

3. Members, when requiring, as a condition of approving the marketing of pharmaceutical or of agricultural chemical products which utilize new chemical entities, the submission of undisclosed test or other data, the origination of which involves a considerable effort, shall protect such data against unfair commercial use. In addition, Members shall protect such data against disclosure, except where necessary to protect the public, or unless steps are taken to ensure that the data are protected, against unfair commercial use.

Note:

1. For the purpose of this provision, 'a manner contrary to honest commercial practices' shall mean at least practices such as breach of contract, breach of confidence and inducement to breach, and includes the acquisition of undisclosed information by third parties who knew, or were grossly negligent in failing to know, that such practices were involved in the acquisition.

Chapter 4

Patent Law

Introduction

Patents are the strongest form of intellectual property, giving rise to a monopoly in the working of an invention either in relation to a product or a process. Originally, patents were granted by the Crown for a wide variety of trades and business ventures, many of which owed little to invention. Thus, a monopoly was granted to Flemish weavers to encourage them to practise their trade in England. Monopolies were also granted in respect of trade in commodities such as salt. Nevertheless, some patents were granted for inventions such as a new method of making stained glass as used in Canterbury Cathedral.

A monopoly is capable of abuse, for example, if the owner limits supply of a patented product and charges extortionately for it. A monopoly should only be granted in circumstances that give rise to appropriate benefits in the wider public interest such as the stimulation of investment and the progress of science. This was recognised early as the following case, known as the case of monopolies, shows.

Darcy v Allin (1602) 1 WPC 1

'This was an action for the infringement of letters patent for the sole making and selling of cards, and the declaration stated, that the queen, perceiving that divers subjects of able bodies, which might go to plough, did employ themselves in the art of making of cards, she did, by her letters patent, (13 Jun. 30 El.) grant to Ralph Bowes, that he, by himself, his factors, and assigns, as well denizens as strangers, might buy and provide beyond the seas playing cards, and cause them to be brought into England, or into her dominions, by whatsoever means, and utter, sell, or distribute the same, in gross or by retail; and that he should have the whole trade of making and selling of cards in England, &c., and that none should have the making and selling of cards within her dominions but he, for 12 years, straitly restraining all her subjects, other than the said Ralph Bowes, his factors and assigns, from the making and selling thereof: that by other letters patent, of 11 Aug. 40 El., reciting those above recited, the same exclusive privilege was granted to the plaintiff for 21 years, to begin after the expiration of the former term of 12 years; and that plaintiff was possessed of that interest; and that the former term expired 13 Jun. 42 El.; and that plaintiff after the expiration of the said term, to wit, on the, &c., caused 4,000 gross of cards to be made in London at his charges, amounting to &c., for the necessary use of the subjects.

That the defendant, knowing the premises, 15 May, 44 El. caused 80 gross of cards to be made, he being a subject, and no assignee or factor to the plaintiff; and 16 May, 44 El., did sell half a gross of playing cards to, &c., for &c., which were not made in England, or brought into England, by the plaintiff or his factor, without license of the queen, or consent of the plaintiff he being a subject, whereby the plaintiff was defrauded of the benefit which he was to enjoy by his charter, to his damage of £200 ...

To this plea the plaintiff demurred, and the case was argued before Popham, C.J., and the court, upon the two following questions, on the two distinct grants in the letters patent; first whether the said grant to the plaintiff, of the sole making of cards within the realm, was good, or not; secondly, whether the license or dispensation, to have the sole importation of foreign cards, granted to the plaintiff, was available, or not, in law.

As to the first question, it was resolved, that the said grant to the plaintiff, of the sole making of cards within the realm, was utterly void; and that for two reasons. First, that it is a monopoly, and against the common law. Secondly, that it is against divers acts of parliament. Against the common law for four reasons. As to the first ground, 1. All trades, as well mechanical as others, which prevent idleness (the bane of the commonwealth), and exercise men and youth in labour, for the maintenance of themselves and their families, and for the increase of their substance, to serve the Queen when occasion shall require, are profitable for the commonwealth; and therefore the grant to the plaintiff, to have the sole making of them, is against the common law, and the benefit and liberty of the subject, as was adjudged in this court in *Davenant* v *Hurdis*; where the case was, that the company of Merchant Tailors in London, having power by charter to make ordinances for the better rule and government of the company, so that they are consonant to law and reason, made an ordinance, 'that every brother of the same society who should put any cloth to be dressed by any cloth-worker, not being a brother of the same society, should put one-half of his cloths to some brother of the same society, who exercised the art of a cloth-worker, upon pain of forfeiting ten shillings, &c.; and to distrain for it, &c.,' and it was adjudged that that ordinance, although it had the countenance of a charter, was against the common law, because it was against the liberty of the subject. For every subject, by the law, has freedom and liberty to put his cloth to be dressed by what cloth-worker he pleases, and cannot be restrained to certain persons, for that in fact would be a monopoly, and therefore such ordinance by colour of a charter, or any grant by charter to such effect, would be void. As to the second ground, the sole trade of any mechanical artifice, or any other monopoly, is not only a damage and prejudice to those who exercise the same trade, but also to all other subjects, for the end of all these monopolies is for the private gain of the patentees ...

As to the third ground. The queen was deceived in her grant; for the queen, as by the preamble appears, intended it to be for the weal public, and it will be employed for the private gain of the patentee, and for the prejudice of the weal public. Moreover, the queen meant that the abuse should be taken away, which shall never be by this patent, but rather the abuse will be increased, for the private benefit of the patentee; and therefore, as it is said in the Earl of Kent's case, this grant is void *jure regio*. As to the fourth ground. This grant is *primae impressionis*, for no such was ever seen to pass by letters patent under the great seal before these days, and therefore it is a dangerous innovation, as well without any precedent or example as authority of law or reason ...

As to the second question, it was resolved, that the dispensation, or license, to have the sole importation and merchandizing of cards, without any limitation or stint, notwithstanding the act of 3 E. 4, is utterly against law. For it is true that, forasmuch as an act of parliament which generally prohibits a thing, upon a penalty which is popular, or only given to the king, may be inconvenient to divers particular persons, in respect of person, place, time, &c., for this reason, the law has given power to the king to dispense with particular persons; but when the wisdom of the parliament has made an act to restrain, *pro bono publico*, the importation of many foreign manufacturers, to the intent that the subjects of the realm might apply themselves to the making of the said manufacturers, &c., and thereby maintain themselves and their family with the labour of their hands; now for a private gain to grant the sole importation of them to one or divers, without any limitation, notwithstanding the said act, is a monopoly against the common law, and against the end and scope of the act itself; for this is not to maintain and increase the labours of the poor card makers within the realm, at whose petition the act was made, but merely to take away and destroy their trade and labours, and that without any reason of necessity or inconvenience, in respect of person, place, or time; and the more so, because it was granted in reversion for years, as hath been said; but only the benefit of a private man, his executors and administrators, for his particular commodity, and in prejudice of the commonwealth. And Edward the 3d, by his letters patent, granted to one John Pechey the sole importation of sweet wine into London; and at a parliament held 50 E.3, this grant was adjudged void. Also, admitting that such grant or dispensation was good, yet the plaintiff cannot maintain an action on the case against those who import any foreign cards, but the remedy which the act of 3 E. 4. in such case gives ought to be pursued. And judgment was given and entered, *quod querens nihil caperet per billam.'*

COMMENT

In this case, the patent offended against common law and statute and, in highlighting the dangers of monopolies too easily granted, paved the way for the Statute of Monopolies. Is the denial of a monopoly in *Darcy* v *Allin* based truly on the principle that it would unduly inhibit other tradesmen from practising their trade? If this is so, how do you reconcile this with the fact that the grant of a monopoly may stimulate invention and innovation which, in turn, lead to greater employment?

The reasoning in *Darcy* v *Allin* indicates one source of danger resulting from monopolies. Guilds were being established and, by using their monopoly, they could prevent competition by non-members. This could operate against the public good by allowing the members of such guilds to fix prices and charge fees to non-members if they were allowed to manufacture the relevant goods. This form of privilege permitting undue manipulation of the market was unsatisfactory and had to be contained in some way. One solution was to restrict monopolies to new inventions, thereby providing an incentive for these alone. If the right balance was struck this surely would be in everyone's interest.

Statute of Monopolies, 1623 21 Jac. I c.3

'Provided also, and be it declared and enacted, That any Declaration before-mentioned shall not extend to any Letters Patents and Grants of Privilege for the Term of fourteen Years or under, hereafter to be made, of the sole Working or Making of any manner of new Manufactures within this Realm, to the true and first Inventor and Inventors of such Manufactures, which others at the Time of Making such Letters Patents and Grants shall not use, so as also they be not contrary to the Law, nor mischievous to the State, by raising Prices of Commodities at home, or Hurt of Trade, or generally inconvenient: The said fourteen Years to be accounted from the Date of the first Letters Patents, or Grant of such Privilege hereafter to be made, but that the same shall be of such Force as they should be, if this Act had never been made, and of none other.'

COMMENT

Thus monopolies were limited and the origins of the patent system were set down. However, monopolies that have nothing to do with inventions still exist. Can you think of any? Can any person represent another in court? Until recently, only a chartered patent agent could act as an agent in respect of a patent application. Although professional monopolies are gradually being eroded (perhaps law is the last bastion) some still exist. Can they be justified?

Development of the Patent System

The patent system slowly evolved after the Statute of Monopolies and, over the next 200 years or so, some of the basic principles were identified and refined. For example, the need for the applicant to make a full disclosure of his invention and submit a detailed specification. The meaning of the basic statement of what constituted a patentable invention was fleshed out.

Patents were, at one time, granted by private Acts, as the one below shows. It states the duration of 14 years and the fact that the use of existing methods of melting ores, etc. may continue, confirming that the patent is limited to its novel features only.

Buck's Invention (1651) 1 WPC 35

'Whereas Jeremy Buck, of Minchinhampton, in the county of Gloucester, Esq., by a new invention, doth undertake to melt or cause to be melted down iron, lead, tin, copper, brass, and other metals, with stone coal, pit coal, or sea coal, without charking thereof: Be it therefore enacted by this present parliament and by the authority thereof, that the said Jeremy Buck, his executors, administrators and assigns, and such as he, or they, or any of them, by writing under his, their, or any of their hands and seals, shall from time to time appoint (and none other), shall and may use, exercise and enjoy the art, skill and mystery of melting down iron ore and cinders into raw iron, and of other ore and metal, with stone coal, pit coal, or sea coal, without charking thereof, and the sole and only benefit of his new invention aforesaid, for and during the term of fourteen years from the first day of March, in the year of our Lord God, 1650; and that no person or persons, bodies politic or corporate, whatsoever, shall make use of the said new invention within the commonwealth of England, or any the dominions thereof, during the said time of fourteen years.

Provided always, and it is hereby declared and enacted, that all and every person and persons may use such ways and works for melting down any iron ore, cinder, or other metals, as they now use or have heretofore lawfully used to do, or any other way or works hereafter by them newly to be invented, so as they make not use of the said new invention of him the said Jeremy Buck.

And it is further enacted, by the authority aforesaid, that every person offending against this act for every day wherein such offence shall be committed, shall forfeit and lose to the said Jeremy Buck, his executors, administrators and assigns, respectively, the sum of 10*l*. in the name of a pain or penalty to be recovered by the said Jeremy Buck, his executors, administrators and assigns, by action of debt to be grounded upon this act, in any court of record within this commonwealth, where any action of debt now doth or shall hereafter be tryable, together with damages for non-payment thereof, and costs of suit; in which action of debt, or for the staying whereof, no essoyn, wager of law, protection or injunction, or any other means of delay, shall or may be granted, admitted, or allowed.

Provided also, that the said Jeremy Buck, and his assigns, after seven years of the term hereby granted, do and shall take apprentices, and teach them the knowledge and mystery of the said new invention.'

COMMENT

Note the provision for taking apprentices after seven years. An apprenticeship was for seven years, thus, at the time of expiry of the patent, there would be skilled tradesmen able to work the patent freely. This patent was granted before the need for the invention to be fully disclosed, hence the need to train apprentices as a way of putting the invention into the public domain after expiry of the patent. Indeed, later, failure to fully disclose how to work a particular invention could render a patent invalid as Arkwright discovered in the case below.

The King v Arkwright [1785] 1 WPC 64

Buller J (at 65): 'Gentlemen of the jury, this is a *scire facias*, brought to repeal a patent granted to the defendant for the sole use of instruments or machines which he represented to his majesty that he had invented, and which would be of great utility to the public in preparing silk, cotton, flax and wool for spinning; and that these machines are constructed on easy and simple principles, very different from any that had ever yet been contrived: that he was the first and sole inventor thereof, and that the same had never been practised by any other person whatsoever. It was upon this representation made by the defendant, that he obtained the patent now in question. The questions for your decision are three: First, whether this invention is new? Secondly, if it be new, whether it was invented by the defendant? And, thirdly, whether the invention is sufficiently described by the specification?

It seems to me the last is the question of the greatest importance; because, if you should be of opinion upon that question that the specification is not certain enough, it may have the effect of inducing people who apply for patents in future times to be more explicit in their specifications, and, consequently, the public will derive a great benefit from it: and, therefore, I will state to you the evidence upon that point first, and will endeavour to state it separately from all the evidence which is applicable to the other points of the cause. Upon this point it is clearly settled at law, that a man to entitle himself to the benefit of a patent for a monopoly, must disclose his secret and specify his invention in such a way that others may be taught by it to do the thing for which the patent is granted, for the end and meaning of the specification is, to teach the public, after the term for which the patent is granted, what the art is, and it must put the public in possession of the secret in as ample and beneficial a way as the patentee himself uses it. This I take to be clear law, as far as it respects the specification; for the patent is the reward, which, under the act of parliament, is held out for a discovery; and, therefore, unless the discovery be true and fair, the patent is void. If the specification, in any part of it, be materially false or defective, the patent is against law, and cannot be supported.

It has been truly said by the counsel, that if the specification be such that mechanical men of common understanding can comprehend it, to make a machine by it, it is sufficient; but then it must be such that the mechanics may be able to make the machine by following the directions of the specification, without any new inventions or additions of their own. The question is, whether, upon the evidence, this specification comes within what I have stated to you to be necessary by law, in order to support it ...'

COMMENT

What is the rationale behind full disclosure of the patent? Is this the valuable consideration that the patentee brings in return for the grant of the monopoly? Sometimes, patents were granted for longer periods in the public interest. The one below was granted for 18 years but the Act limited the payment to be made to the patentee.

Liardet's Patent (1773) 1 WPC 52

'An Act for vesting in John Liardet, his, &c., the sole use and property of a certain composition or cement of his invention throughout his Majesty's kingdom of Great Britain for a limited time.

After reciting the grant of the letters patent, and further reciting, "unless the term granted by the said letters patent be prolonged, and the property of the said John Liardet in the said invention better secured, not only within that part of Great Britain called England, the dominion of Wales, the town of Berwick upon Tweed, and in his Majesty's colonies and plantations abroad, but also within that part of Great Britain called Scotland, it will neither be possible for the said John Liardet to receive an adequate recompense for his labour, expense and time, nor for the public at large to reap the various advantages in point of utility and economy, as well as ornament in building, which would arise from this invention were its use universally diffused, and its price lowered, upon which the demand, and consequently the profits of the proprietor, must depend: And whereas the cement from its nature grows too hard for use if not used soon after it is made, and therefore must be made where used, or near it, from which circumstance the use thereof has hitherto been confined to the metropolis and a few miles about it, as training workmen and erecting works is difficult and expensive: And whereas, if the term is not enlarged, the same narrow plan must be continued, a general plan of erecting works and training men all over the kingdom, which is necessary if the use of the cement is to be universal, cannot upon so short a prospect be undertaken, the circle cannot be enlarged, and the price must continue such as may indemnify the proprietor for his expense, out of the profits arising from a very small consumption only during his present term; to the end therefore that the said John Liardet may be enabled and encouraged to prosecute and complete his said invention, so that the public may reap all the advantages to be derived therefrom in their fullest extent," it is enacted, that the said letters patent should be vested in the said Liardet, his, &c., for 18 years from the passing of the act.

S.2. And whereas the said John Liardet has hitherto furnished the said cement at the rate of sixpence per foot square on the surfaces of all plain buildings, and twopence per foot running measure for arrises; to the end therefore that the public may be assured of the advantage of this invention at the same price, be it further enacted, by the authority aforesaid, that it shall not be lawful for the said John Liardet, his, &c., during the continuance of this act, to ask, demand, or take any greater price than sixpence by the foot square, and twopence per foot as aforesaid for arrises, so covering any plain work with the aforesaid cement or composition.

3. Proviso, that the act shall not hinder the making any composition or cement not the invention or application of the said Liardet, or which has been publicly used or exercised before the date of the letters patent; but that all such not the invention of the said Liardet, or not particularly ascertained and described in the specification thereinafter mentioned, should remain to the public or inventor as if the said act had not been made.

4. That every objection which might have been made to the said cement, not being a new invention within the true intent and meaning of an act of the 21st of James the First, may be made in bar to any action brought by virtue or in consequence of this act.

5. Proviso against transfer to more than five persons.

6. Proviso that Liardet shall enrol a specification within four months after the passing of the act.'

COMMENT

Why was the above patent granted for a longer term? If that rationale is accepted why was there any need to control the payment made to the proprietor of the patent by others exploiting the invention? Is this an early form of compulsory licence? Note the requirement for a specification to be filed.

The following extract is taken from Dr. Davenport's excellent descriptions of the trials and tribulations suffered by James Watt in respect of the patent system.

A. N. Davenport, *James Watt and the Patent System* (London: The British Library, 1989)

'The term "patent" is an abbreviation of "letters patent", the name of a document containing a command from the Sovereign and authenticated by the presence at the foot of a wax impression of the Great Seal of the Realm. The seal was attached by a silken cord in such a way that it did not have to be broken before the document could be read - hence the Latin name "litterae patentes", meaning "open letters", which gave rise to "letters patent".

At least from the beginning of the 13th century letters patent were issued for a host of administrative purposes from the Chancery, the office of the Lord Chancellor who was the King's secretary and custodian of the Great Seal. A patent was a document of such power that an elaborate procedure was evolved to ensure that no document was sealed with the Great Seal which was not fully approved by the sovereign and, incidentally, to provide fees for many of those involved in the procedure.

When monopolies came to be granted for inventions, the grants were made by letters patent and so until its reform by the 1852 Act, the English patent system was encumbered by an application procedure which was slow, elaborate and expensive. This procedure, requiring the Sovereign's signature at two stages, has been summarised by Gomme and, more recently, by the present author.

The first English patent for a manufacture was that granted in 1449 by King Henry VI to John of Utynam for a method of making coloured glass for the Royal Chapel windows. It was to be more than one hundred years later, in 1552, that the second was granted by King Edward VI, and this also was for glass making. After 1552, patents for manufacturing processes became more frequent so that by 1617, the date at which the series of patent specifications printed by the Patent Office commences, about one hundred such grants had been made.

A patent of invention was, and still is, considered to provide a monopoly which is beneficial because it encourages innovation and hence industry and trade. Other commercial monopolies are liable to prove objectionable through providing a well-nigh irresistible temptation to profiteer. As a means of raising revenue, Queen Elizabeth I granted some monopolies in everyday necessities such as salt, vinegar and starch. These caused so much unrest that in 1601 she issued a proclamation revoking the more obnoxious patents and giving her subjects the right to take any complaints about monopolies to the courts of common law. Some monopoly abuses continued, despite three further proclamations by King James I, so that in 1624 the famous "Statute of Monopolies" was enacted which declared all monopolies to be illegal but which excluded certain monopolies from the general prohibition. ...

Watt's patent litigation

All the litigation in which Watt became involved was under his first patent of 1769, the term of which had been extended until 1800 by the 1775 Act. Watt had taken Dr.

Small's advice and filed a specification describing just the principles of his method of lessening the consumption of steam in fire engines. Those most relevant to the litigation are quoted below in full:

> "FIRST, that vessel in which the powers of steam are to be employed to work the engine, which is called the Cylinder in common fire engines, and which I call the Steam Vessel, must, during the whole time the engine is at work, be kept as hot as the steam that enters it; first by inclosing it in a case of wood, or any other materials that transmit heat slowly; secondly, by surrounding it with steam or other heated bodies; and, thirdly, by suffering neither water nor any other substance colder than the steam to enter or touch it during that time.
>
> SECONDLY, in Engines that are to be worked wholly or partially by condensation of steam, the steam is to be condensed in vessels distinct from the steam vessels or cylinders, although occasionally communicating with them; these vessels I call Condensers; and, whilst the engines are working, these condensers ought at least to be kept as cold as the air in the neighbourhood of the engines, by application of water, or other cold bodies.
>
> THIRDLY, whatever air, or other elastic vapour, is not condensed by the cold of the condenser, and may impede the working of the engine, is to be drawn out of the steam vessels or condensers by means of pumps, wrought by these engines themselves, or otherwise.
>
> FOURTHLY, I intend in many cases to employ the expansive force of steam to press on the pistons, or whatever may be used instead of them, in the same manner as the pressure of the atmosphere is now employed in common fire engines: in cases where cold water cannot be had in plenty, the engines may be wrought by this force of steam only, by discharging the steam into the open air after it has done its office.
>
> FIFTHLY, where motions round an axis are required, I make the steam vessels in form of hollow rings ... [there follows a description of weights and valves which with appropriate steam inlets and outlets enable the desired motions to be achieved. Watt worked intermittently on this idea of a 'steam wheel' over many years].
>
> SIXTHLY, I intend, in some cases, to apply a degree of cold not capable of reducing the steam to water, but of contracting it considerably, so that the engines shall be worked by the alternate expansion and contraction of steam.
>
> LASTLY, instead of using water to render the piston, or other parts of the engines, air and steam-tight. I employ oils, wax, resinous bodies, fat of animals, quicksilver, and other metals, in their fluid state."

Clearly these Principles cover almost any conceivable steam engine, other than a Newcomen, and so Newcomen engines continued to be made. ...

Boulton and Watt v Bull

a) Court of Common Pleas. June 1793 ...
The main point at issue throughout the Boulton and Watt patent litigation was whether or not Watt's specification was sufficient. ... Despite all the attacks made, the jury found in favour of Boulton and Watt. But the judge said:

"I confess I have myself very great doubt whether this specification is sufficient ... I think the Jury would have no great difficulty in collecting from the whole of this evidence that a good mechanic would be able to constitute an engine from this specification which would produce the effect of lessening the consumption of steam and fuel in fire engines ... the only question is whether the particular Instrument must not be organized and described as organized".

The jury's verdict was therefore made subject to the opinion of the Court on the validity of the Specification.
b) Meanwhile, the Court of Chancery granted an injunction restraining Bull from further infringement. ...
   Court of King's Bench, Michaelmas Term 1798 and 25 January 1799 Hornblower and Maberley contended "that the invention for which letters patent were granted is not an invention of any formed or organized machine, instrument, or manufacture, but of mere principles only, for which no such letters patent could, by law, be granted". The case was argued in 1798 and again the following year, and the four judges then gave their verdicts.
   Lord Kenyon, Chief Justice: "I confess I am not one of those who greatly favour patents; for though in many instances, and particularly in this, the public are benefited by them, yet, on striking the balance upon this subject, I think that great oppression is practised on inferior mechanics by those who are more opulent. The principal objection made to this patent by the plaintiffs in error is, that it is a patent for a philosophical principle only, neither organized or capable of being organized; and if the objection were well founded in fact, it would be decisive; but I do not think it is so. No technical words are necessary to explain the subject of a patent; as Lord Hardwicke said, upon another occasion, 'there is no magic in words'. The questions here are, whether, by looking at the patent, explained as it is by the specification, it does not appear to be a patent for a manufacture, and whether the specification is not sufficient to enable a mechanic to make the thing described? The jury have not, indeed, answered those questions in the affirmative in terms; but they have impliedly done so by finding a general verdict for the plaintiffs below. By comparing the patent and the manufacture together, it evidently appears that the patentee claims a monopoly for an engine or machine, composed of material parts, which are to produce the effect described, and that the mode of producing this is so described as to enable mechanics to produce it. Having said thus much, it appears that the subject, as far as we have to treat it, is exhausted ... But having now heard everything that can be said on the subject, I have no doubt in saying that this is a patent for a manufacture, which I understand to be something made by the hands of man." ...

Mr Justice Grose: ... "But I do not consider it as a patent for the whole engine, but only for the addition to, or improvement of the old engine, and so the Act of Parliament considers it. The inventor 'took out his patent not for the engine, but for his method for lessening the consumption of steam and fuel in fire-engines'. The method is disclosed in the specification, and there is no pretence to say that he claims, or could claim, the sole making of the old engine. But a doubt is entertained whether there can be a patent for an addition to an old manufacture: this doubt rests altogether upon *Bircot's case,* 3 Inst. 184 ... If indeed a patent could not be granted for an addition, it would be depriving the public of one of the best benefits of the

Statute of James. Lord Coke's opinion therefore seems to have been formed without due consideration, and modern experience shows that it is not well founded".'

COMMENT

It is interesting to see the patent system described by Lord Kenyon as a 'great oppression ... practised on inferior mechanics by those who are more opulent'. Grose J confirms that patents for additions are possible; that is, a patent for an improvement to an existing product or process. This is an important feature of the patent system. Why? Although the patent system had seen significant development and refinement, the process of obtaining the grant of a patent had become cumbersome and expensive. No less a person than Charles Dickens had written about this and, eventually, the whole system was reformed by the Patent Law Amendment Act 1852 which laid down the foundations of the modern patent system. In the following short extract from Dickens' Poor Man's Tale of a Patent, the bureaucracy of obtaining a patent is described.

Dickens, C., *A Poor Man's Tale of a Patent* (1850), reprinted in Phillips, J., *Charles Dickens and the 'Poor Man's Tale of a Patent'* (Oxford: ESC Publishing, 1984)

'... Now, teaching had not come up but very limited when I was young. So much the worse for me you'll say. I say the same. William Butcher is twenty year younger than me. He knows a hundred year or more. If William Butcher had wanted to Patent an invention, he might have been sharper than myself when hustled backwards and forwards among all those offices, though I doubt if so patient. Note. William being sometimes cranky, and consider porters, messengers, and clerks.

Thereby I say nothing of my being tired of my life, while I was Patenting my invention. But I put this: Is it reasonable to make a man feel as if, in inventing an ingenious improvement meant to do good, he had done something wrong? How else can a man feel, when he is met by such difficulties at every turn? All inventors taking out a Patent MUST feel so. And look at the expense. How hard on me, and how hard on the country if there's any merit in me (and my invention is took up now, I am thankful to say, and doing well), to put me to all that expense before I can move a finger! Make the addition yourself, and it'll come to ninety-six pound, seven, and eightpence. No more, and no less.

What can I say against William Butcher, about places? Look at the Home Secretary, the Attorney-General, the Patent Office, the Engrossing Clerk, the Lord Chancellor's Purse-bearer, the Clerk of the Hanaper, the Deputy Clerk of the Hanaper, the Deputy Sealer, and the Deputy Chaff-wax. No man in England could get a Patent for an Indian-rubber band, or an iron-hoop, without feeing all of them. Some of them, over and over again. I went through thirty-five stages. I began with the Queen upon the Throne. I ended with the Deputy Chaff-wax. Note. I should like to see the Deputy Chaff-wax. Is it a man, or what is it?

What I had to tell, I have told. I have wrote it down. I hope it's plain. Not so much in the handwriting (though nothing to boast of there), as in the sense of it. I will now conclude with Thomas Joy. Thomas said to me, when we parted, "John, if the laws of this country were as honest as they ought to be, you would have come to London

- registered an exact description and drawing of your invention - paid half-a-crown or so for doing of it - and therein and thereby have got your Patent."

My opinion is the same as Thomas Joy. Further. In William Butcher's delivering "that the whole gang of Hanapers and Chaff-waxes must be done away with, and that England has been chaffed and waxed sufficient". I agree.'

COMMENT

William Butcher is a friend of the narrator, a smith from Birmingham who decided to take out a patent. Thomas Joy is an acquaintance who helps. Why should a simple deposit of a description and drawing together with payment of a small fee not be sufficient to obtain a patent?

Justification for the Patent System

A number of theories have been postulated justifying the patent system. It is not a foregone conclusion that the grant of patents is in the wider interests of society and some countries even experimented with abolition of patents, notably Switzerland and the Netherlands. Dutton, in the following extract from his book which looks at patents during the industrial revolution, a time surely when the justification for patents was most keenly felt, looks at four particular arguments in favour of a strong patent system.

Dutton, H.I., *The Patent System and Inventive Activity during the Industrial Revolution* (Manchester: Manchester University Press, 1984) at p.17ff

'During the industrial revolution the patent system was justified by four arguments: the natural-law thesis, the reward-by-monopoly thesis, the monopoly-profit thesis, and the exchange-for-secrets thesis. The "natural rights" thesis was the least important and was practically abandoned by the late 1820s, but the remaining three were widely advanced before and during the patent controversy of the mid-Victorian period ... During the industrial revolution the theories supporting the patent system went largely unchallenged. Most endorsed the economic philosophy expressed in the 1624 Statute of Monopolies, which, as one writer noted, provided the "first germ of the Patent Law, springing forth from the destruction of despotic privilege, like the young tree from the ruined feudal castle" ...

The natural-law thesis assumes that individuals have a natural right of property in their own ideas. On this argument, using the ideas of others without some form of compensation amounted to theft, and since property was personal and exclusive, the State was morally obliged to enforce exclusivity. This reasoning was enshrined in the French patent law of 1791 and openly advocated by J R McCulloch during the patent reform campaign of the 1820s: "If anything can be called a man's exclusive property, it is surely that which owes its birth entirely to combinations formed in his own mind, and which, but for his ingenuity, would not have existed" ...

The reward-by-monopoly thesis, in contrast, was widely used to justify patents. It was based on the notion that inventors should be rewarded according to the usefulness of their invention. Since this reward cannot be guaranteed by ordinary market forces, the State should intervene to provide a temporary monopoly. Adam Smith, more than most other political economists, was careful to appreciate that the happy miracle of economic harmony was not simply created out of chaos by the invisible hand. The law and lawmaker were crucially important in ensuring competition and the most efficient allocation of resources. For Smith the institutional framework, which included legal and non-legal elements, was logically prior to the market ...

Bentham also justified patents principally because they provided the inventor with a reward for his efforts. He came to this conclusion by distinguishing between two categories of labour. Firstly, there is the physical kind of labour which merely produces goods. When imitated, this kind of labour requires an equal amount of labour to produce an equivalent output: the inputs per unit of output are the same. The second kind of labour is qualitatively different and is defined by the skill or mental power used in the production of goods. The imitation of this kind of labour leads to relatively lower input costs because, while knowledge is expensive to produce, it is inexpensive to reproduce: "of skill ... it is the property to be capable of being indefinitely imbibed and diffused and that without any exertion of mental labour comparable to that, at the expense of which it was acquired". This is the free-rider problem elliptically expressed. "A man will not be at the expense and trouble of bringing to maturity [an] invention unless he has a prospect of an adequate satisfaction, that is to say, at least of such a satisfaction as to his eyes appears an adequate one, for such troubles and expense." Bentham never doubted that patents, compared with any other system of encouraging and protecting invention, were "proportionately and essentially just" ...

The monopoly-profit-incentive thesis was probably the most quoted argument in support of patents. Private reward, it is clear, can also act as an incentive to invent, but the reward argument is concerned with some just profit which the inventor in some sense deserves to make within the monopoly period. The incentive argument is concerned with the duration and exclusiveness of the monopoly itself and is linked with the notion that economic growth is inherently desirable. It assumes that the supply of invention (which was also assumed to be a major cause of growth) would be less than it would otherwise be if patents were not used to protect the inventor. Here inventive activity was associated with progress as well as private profit, and this probably explains why the argument was so popular during the early nineteenth century.

There is ample evidence of the belief in the causal link between patents, invention and industrial development. In 1791 Sir William Pultney could write to Lord Kenyon that "I think [patents] have been one of the great causes of the important discoveries which in this country have so much improved our manufactures and trade". Another writer held that patents encouraged "some of the most valuable inventions which the various and astonishing powers of mechanics have produced. If new inventions," he concluded, "are not protected, England's sun is set ... [and] ... the mechanical genius of this country will sleep" ...

The final justification for patents was the exchange-for-secrets thesis, or the disclosure agreement. It was based on the eighteenth century idea of contract, where society and the inventor made a bargain, one offering temporary protection, the other knowledge of new techniques. Unlike the incentive argument, disclosure was not related to the supply of inventive output. It was merely concerned with the dissemination of information of existing technology which would otherwise remain secret. It did, however, assume - as did the incentive argument - that invention and progress were causally linked.

This rationale had its origins in the Elizabethan period, although then disclosure was of a quite different form. Inventors were compelled to use the patent to introduce the trade, and to teach the mystery of the art to native tradesmen. In the early eighteenth century the form and condition of disclosure changed. Patentees now had to describe the nature and manner of their inventions in a specification. In 1734 the law officers made it a condition of the contract by a provision in the patent itself, and in the 1778 Liardet and Johnson case Lord Mansfield gave this form of contract a secure legal basis. This was confirmed by Buller, J, in *King v Arkwright* (1785) and in *Williams v Williams,* Lord Eldon held that patentees were "purchasers from the public": patents were exchanged for secrets.'

COMMENT
Which of the four arguments bears most credibility today? What would happen if the patent system were to be abolished and the exploitation of new inventions left to the vagaries of market forces? Patents may be renewed for up to 20 years. Is this period of protection too long, too short or just about right?

Basic Requirements for a Patent

By section 1(1) of the Patents Act 1977 a patent may be granted only for an invention that is new, involves an inventive step, is capable of industrial application and is not excluded by section 1(2) and 1(3). Novelty, inventive step and industrial application are further defined in sections 2 to 4. Novelty can be said to be the primary feature. It is determined by reference to the 'state of art'.

Novelty

A patent gives the proprietor a monopoly in respect of working the invention. Subject to a number of defences and legal controls, the monopoly is very strong. It is essential, therefore, that a patent will only be granted for an invention that is new. Novelty may be compromised in a number of ways. For example, someone may have patented the invention some time before or the invention may have been used previously in such a way that it was disclosed to the public. When a patent application is processed a search is made through earlier patents to see if they disclose the invention subject to the present application.

Novelty (and inventive step) is frequently put at issue by a defendant to an action for an alleged infringement action. If the defendant can show that the patent is invalid because it was not novel when it was applied for, he has a total defence and can continue the act complained of.

Young v Rosenthal and Co. (1884) 1 RPC 29, Queen's Bench Division

The plaintiff's patent claimed an improvement in the design of corsets or stays which involved arranging the seams joining the individual parts diagonally. The plaintiff alleged that the defendant had infringed the patent but the defendant argued that the invention was not novel due to an earlier, now expired, patent.

Grove J (at 31): 'Originally the Crown granted monopolies, and could grant monopolies for almost anything it liked. The Crown granted monopolies on salt, sugar, or anything else, excluding other persons from that monopoly; but in the reign of James II, a statute was passed, which remains law to this day, declaring that monopolies should be abolished; or rather it declared that they were contrary to the laws of the realm, except Letters Patent granted to the true and first inventor of any manner of new manufacture which others could not have used, that is to say, a person should be allowed to have a monopoly to preclude other persons from using for 14 years (which was the term originally given, but it is not material how long at present because this is within 14 years) any manner of new manufacture, except the true and first inventor. Therefore, the invention must be new. It must not have been used before, and it must be an invention of a manufacture. An invention of an idea or mathematical principle alone, mathematical *formulae* or anything of that sort, could not be the subject of a patent. For instance, supposing a person discovered that three angles of a triangle are equal to two right angles, that is an abstract discovery, and would not be the subject of a patent. It must be a manufacture, and it must be a manufacture which must be new in this realm. Shortly afterwards, it was found necessary for the protection of the public that the Patentee should enrol a specification, and in that he was required to describe the nature of his invention, in order that the rest of the public might know what his invention really is, so that they may not unintentionally infringe it, and so that they may know what they are prohibited from using without his leave or license. He must also describe the means of performing his invention, in order that when his patent expires people may know how to make it. Letters Patent are in fact granted to a person so to speak upon the condition that he enrols a specification in which he states truly the nature of his invention and the means of performing it. Here the Patentees took out Letters Patent in the year 1879, and they have filed a specification, and they are bound in that specification to fulfil the two requisites I have mentioned; they must state the nature of their invention clearly, so that any person reading their specification may understand what the nature of their invention is, and they must state the means of performing it, so that the public, when the patent has expired, may be enabled to use it. Otherwise a Patentee might do this: first of all, with regard to the first point, he might say nothing about the nature of his invention, and he might simply describe the thing he makes, e.g. "This stay is my patent," and then the public might say, "In this stay there is a good deal that is old as well as something that may be new; the cloth is old, the whalebone is old, the direction of the whalebone or the direction of the cloth is old, and the gores are old," and therefore the public would not know unless he specified it what the Patentee claimed to be his invention, and the public would not know whether they were infringing or not when they made other sets of stays. They might know that he did not claim the gores for instance, but when they made a gore they might be infringing his patent. Therefore, he is bound to state in what the nature of his invention consists. If he does that properly, the public reading his specification will know what they ought not to do in making stays, and know the sort of stays they ought not to make and use. Then he is also bound so to describe it in his specification as that any workman acquainted with the subject, or any stay-maker, being a practical workman, would know how to make it; and the reason of that is this, that if he did not do so, when the patent expired he might have some trade mystery which people would not be able actually to use in accordance with his invention (although they had a right to use it after his invention had expired), because they would not know how to make it. That would not apply to a thing of this sort, but to some things it might apply. Therefore he is bound to do these two things, namely, to tell the public what is the nature of his invention, and to tell them how the invention is to be made in practice. Take, for instance, a chemical invention. A man might make a chemical discovery, and he might claim a patent for it, and call it by his own name, "Thomas's this" or "Thomas's that"; and when the patent came to an end, the public might not know the least in the world how to make it, and he would still continue by that means to have a monopoly which he had no right to continue, and which was granted to him for 14 years only, unless it was prolonged, and then, when the 14 years were at an end, the public might not know how his chemical invention is made. It might be a particular sort of varnish. He might make the varnish and sell it for 14 years, and not tell the public how it was made, and then he might get not only 14 years but twice or three times 14 years' monopoly by keeping secret his manufacture. Therefore, in the interest of the public, the law says the Patentee must fairly and properly describe the nature of his invention in what is now publicly called his claim, and also the means or mode by which it can be performed.

With regard to the specification in the present case, it appears to me that no difficulty has occurred as to the description of the means by which it is performed. On reading this specification no point has been made about it, nor do I see any fair and reasonable point. The description in the specification is such that any man who understands the claim can understand how the stay is made and make it. Whether the Patentees have sufficiently discriminated between what is new and what is old is a question upon which I will not trouble you now, but I will hear that matter argued hereafter. It would have been better if it had been argued before, because then I might have been assisted by the argument of counsel in putting a right construction upon it, and that would have been very convenient to me: but I must run the risk and give you my view of what the specification substantially means. Now, with regard to infringement and novelty, they are two quite distinct issues. A man may infringe a patent although the patent is not new, because to infringe a patent is to imitate it - to use not necessarily the whole but any material part of the invention. It may turn out that a man infringes a patent, and that the jury would be right in finding that he had infringed the patent, but then it might be said "The patent is not new," and, therefore, although you have technically infringed it, that is, although you have made stays or parts of stays in the same manner as the patent, yet, if what you have made, or if, indeed any portion of the material part of the patent which is claimed is not new, then the patent is invalid, because the Patentee has got a patent for a thing which he did not invent, or if he did invent it he was not the true and first inventor. He invented it, but the public had used it before. It is not because a Patentee does not know what was in existence before that he can claim a monopoly, otherwise, as a learned judge once said, a Patentee would get a patent for exclusive ignorance instead of exclusive knowledge. You may patent a thing which is known. For instance, if I were to take out a patent for stays, without having seen what I have seen during these last two days, I very likely should think I was inventing something very new in inventing something which the stay-makers in London knew perfectly well. I could not get a patent for that, although I really invented it and found it out. Suppose a man knew only the common description of stays, and said, "It would be very much better to make stays with the stitches or seams diagonal or horizontal, as the case may be." He might invent that honestly and truly; but that is not enough, for if people had been using such things before, a Patentee cannot go back and adopt them. Therefore, it must not only have been new in his invention, he must not only, so to speak, have "found it out," but he must have found something out which was not in use before, because if it was in public use before, even by one person, his patent is bad. Mere private use in the closet, mere experimental working in a laboratory, without publishing the invention, but keeping it a secret with a view possibly of a patent being taken out, would not invalidate it. But, if it is once publicly used or sold in a shop, or publicly used in a carriage, or on the person, or in any such way, then the public have a right to it, and the patent is bad. Then another thing is required for a patent, namely, that the invention must be something useful to the public, and in measuring that, you must have regard to what was previously known. It is not useful to the public to invent a thing which has been invented before. A patented invention must have some utility beyond that which, with regard to a particular thing, has been known before. If it has any utility beyond that the patent is good. If it has not any such utility, that is, if it is not a bit better than anything that went before, then the patent is bad.'

COMMENT

Novelty is to be judged objectively and, if the invention has been in public use before the patent was applied for, it will be invalid. Under the 1977 Act, the test of prior publication is whether the invention has been made available to the public in the United Kingdom or elsewhere. Note again the requirement for full disclosure. Did the plaintiff make full disclosure in this case? Was it relevant?

Hickton's Patent Syndicate v Patents and Machine Improvements Company Ltd. (1909) 26 RPC 339, Court of Appeal

The patent in suit related for an invention involving traversing the carriages and bobbins in a lace machine in order to equalise the consumption of thread on the numerous bobbins. The defendant, who had infringed the patent, argued that the invention was not new as this method, called 'shogging', was already known. The patent was held to be invalid at first instance and the plaintiff appealed on the basis that, although the technique was old, its use in order to equalise the consumption of thread from the bobbins was new.

Cozens-Hardy MR (at 346): 'This is an appeal from a decision of Mr Justice Swinfen-Eady, and with the greatest possible respect to that learned judge, I think he has arrived at a wrong conclusion. It seems to me to be a reasonably plain case. The point is this: it is said that the machines, lever machines, or lace machines, are perfectly old and well-known; but it was also well known that their use involved the loss of a very considerable percentage of thread, because some of the bobbins had to do much more work than the others. The evil thus ascertained was attempted to be remedied by the operator putting his hand in and changing a few of the most exhausted bobbins and putting them in the place where some less exhausted bobbins were to be found. This operation was costly in time, and it was really not highly efficient, because it did not get that equality and evenness which is so desirable and essential in manufacturing things of this kind. The Patentee had got the idea that the equalisation of the use of the thread might be obtained by "shogging" the comb-bar, and thus securing that each bobbin does first an easy task, and then a hard task, with the result that if you "shog" through the complete width of the strip of lace you produce a practical equality in the working of all the bobbins and thus greatly minimise, in fact almost destroy, the loss of thread which existed before. Was that a new idea, was it a meritorious idea, was it a useful invention? I think it was upon the evidence plainly a new idea. Certain it is that, although need for some invention to obviate this waste had been before the eyes of all persons engaged in the trade, it had never been discovered before. It was new in that sense, and it was none the less new because the operation of "shogging" was as old as the hills. It was a new application of "shogging," an application never applied to a machine of this class, nor for any analogous purpose. It is true that "shogging" being old, "shogging" was applied in other lace machines, but it either was so annulled as not to produce the equalisation which was aimed at here, or if by accident it did produce the equalisation, it was not a use so analogous to that which is found here as to render the thing so obvious as to compel us to state that there is no subject-matter in the Patent. Utility is not denied and infringement is not denied, and I think the conclusion to which we are bound to come is, that there was subject-matter in this Patent which entitled the Plaintiffs to the relief which they sought by their action.

The learned Judge in his judgment states a proposition, which, with the greatest possible respect, seems to me to be a great deal too wide. "An idea may be new and original and very meritorious, but unless there is some invention necessary for putting the idea into practice it is not patentable." That, I venture to say, is not in accordance with the principles which have hitherto been applied in Patent cases, and I do not think it ought to be recognised as the law. When once the idea of applying some well-known thing for a special and new purpose is stated, it may be very obvious how to give effect to that idea, and yet none the less is that a good subject-matter for a Patent.

For these reasons I think the appeal succeeds and in consequence the relief asked for ought to be granted.'

Fletcher Moulton LJ (at 347): 'I am of the same opinion. The only point here is subject-matter. It is clear that none of the anticipations are anticipations of this new machine if they are examined. There is not one which could make the article which is produced; that is to say, lace in which there is exactly that movement of the thread which in that way, without disfiguring the laces, absolutely equalises the expenditure of the thread.

After the judgment of the Master of the Rolls I do not intend to enter into the facts of the case, but I do wish to deal with the dictum of the learned Judge in the Court below, which really gives the ground for his decision. The Defendants contend that although the idea of traversing by "shogging" in order to equalise is new, yet it is not proper subject-matter for a Patent as no invention whatever was necessary to carry it out. The learned Judge says:

"An idea may be new and original and very meritorious, but unless there is some invention necessary for putting the idea into practice it is not patentable".

With the greatest respect for the learned Judge, that, in my opinion is quite contrary to the principles of patent law, and would deprive of their reward a very large number of meritorious inventions that have been made. I may say that this dictum is to the best of my knowledge supported by no case, and no case has been quoted to us which would justify it. But let me give an example. Probably the most celebrated Patent in the history of our law is that of *Boulton and Watt,* which had the unique distinction of being renewed for the whole fourteen years. The particular invention there was the condensation of the steam, not in the cylinder itself, but in a separate vessel. That conception occurred to Watt and it was for that that his Patent was granted, and out of that grew the steam engine. Now can it be suggested that it required any invention whatever to carry out the idea when once you have got it? It could be done in a thousand ways and by any competent engineer, but the invention was in the idea, and when he had once got that idea, the carrying out of it was perfectly easy. To say that the conception may be meritorious and may involve invention and may be new and original, and simply because when you have once got the idea it is easy to carry it out, that that deprives it of the title of being a new invention according to our patent law, is, I think, an extremely dangerous principle and justified neither by reason, nor authority.

I have taken the case of *Boulton and Watt* with the condenser, but I can give another. Take the case of the safety valve for boilers. The man who first discovered the idea of a properly weighted valve in the boiler solely for the purpose of relief, if the pressure rose too high, would have been making a most valuable and meritorious invention. So soon as he conceived the idea of guarding against the danger of explosion the carrying out of the idea required no invention at all. In my opinion, invention may lie in the idea, and it may lie in the way in which it is carried out, and it may lie in the combination of the two; but if there is invention in the idea plus the way of carrying it out, then it is good subject-matter for Letters Patent. As a matter of fact in the present case I have not the slightest doubt that there is a good subject-matter.'

COMMENT

A new use for an old invention may be patentable for there may be inventive skill in determining the new use. However, it is arguable that this case is wrongly decided. Had the invention been made available to the public? Were the judges confusing novelty with inventive step? Can you discover any novelty sufficient for the grant of a patent? Compare this case with the *Molins* case below.

Molins and Molins Machine Co. Ltd. v **Industrial Machinery Co. Ltd.** (1938) 55
RPC 31, Court of Appeal

The plaintiff was the proprietor of a patent for a method of making cigarettes which,
by applying movement to the trough of the machine, improved the consistency of the
distribution of the tobacco in cigarettes. The plaintiff sued the defendant for an
alleged infringement of the patent and the defendant counterclaimed, arguing that
the patent was anticipated by an earlier machine with a similar movement though
moving at a slower speed (the *Bonsack* invention).

Lord Greene MR (at 37): 'In the early days of cigarette making machines, the speed
attained was slow, being at the rate of some 250 cigarettes a minute. This was the
highest speed at which, according to the evidence, machines constructed in
accordance with the invention of one *Bonsack,* hereinafter referred to, could
operate. Progressive improvements enabled a much higher speed to be obtained.
Automatic feeding of the tobacco into the hopper, improvements in the design of the
rollers enabling the tobacco to be made uniform at a quicker rate, lengthening of the
picker roller and improvements in its design, were some of the improvements which
led to this result. But as the speed of the machines was increased a defect came to
be observed, a defect which, although it may have been, and no doubt was, present
so to speak, in embryo all along, nevertheless became of practical importance when
the speed of the machines was substantially increased. This defect consisted of an
irregularity in the filling of the cigarettes. Some cigarettes would contain rather more
tobacco than they should have contained, others less, and even where the presence
of the defect in an individual cigarette might escape attention, the fact that it existed
was established when it was found that a given quantity of tobacco was producing
fewer or more cigarettes than it ought to have produced. The reason for this was
that owing to the lack of uniformity in the rod of tobacco some portions of it
contained too much and some too little tobacco.

Apart from the specification of *Bonsack,* to which I shall refer, there is no
suggestion in the evidence than anyone before the present Patentee had discovered
the cause of this defect or suggested a remedy for it ...

But here an argument is put forward which I have some difficulty in following. It
appears to be of this nature. *Bonsack's* Specification does not explain for what
purpose in the construction of his machine the trough is to be inclined. Various
hypotheses as to *Bonsack's* reasons were put forward by the expert witnesses, but I
do not find it necessary or profitable to engage in speculations of this kind. It is said,
as I follow the argument, that *Bonsack* cannot be an anticipation because it does not
appear and ought not to be assumed that, in giving directions for the inclination of
his trough, he was envisaging the same problem as that with which the present
inventor was concerned; and that if the problems were not the same, the validity of
the present claim is not affected by the fact that this particular element is to be found
inserted for no apparent purpose in *Bonsack's* machine ...   *Bonsack's* instruction is
to make a machine of a particular kind. No question of adjustment arises. The
inclination which he gives to his trough is a physical fact necessarily present in each
machine made in accordance with his specification, and is as much a part of the true
nature of that machine as any other element in it.'

COMMENT

The specification was held invalid because it had been anticipated by the earlier *Bonsack* patent which described similar apparatus running at a slower speed. Inclining the trough cured the problem with higher speed machines but the *Bonsack* patent also had an inclined trough though the problem of uneven tobacco distribution did not occur with slow speed machines. However, the court allowed an amendment to the specification which restricted it to faster machines. Can this case and *Hickton's* case be reconciled? (*Hickton* was not mentioned in *Molins*.)

Lux Traffic Controls Ltd. v Pike Signals Ltd. [1993] RPC 107, Patents Court

The plaintiff claimed that the defendant had infringed its two patents for traffic control systems. The first related to the minimum green period (minimum time for which traffic lights will remain green after detecting a vehicle) and the second to the inter-green period (the safety period between changes of lights). The defendant argued that the patents were invalid on the grounds of obviousness and that there was not an invention. For the first patent, the defendant also alleged that it lacked novelty because of prior publication and field trials in public. The first patent was held to be invalid for lack of novelty. (The second patent was held to be valid and infringed.)

Aldous J (at 128): 'Novelty: Section 72 of the 1977 Act sets out the grounds upon which a patent may be revoked. The first ground is, that the invention is not a patentable invention. A patentable invention is defined in section 1 as inter alia, being an invention which is new. Section 2(1) states that an invention should be taken to be new if it does not form part of the state of the art. The state of the art is defined in sub-section (2) as:

> "The state of the art in the case of an invention shall be taken to comprise all matter (whether a product, a process, information about either, or anything else) which has at any time before the priority date of that invention been made available to the public (whether in the United Kingdom or elsewhere) by written or oral description, by use or in any other way."

The defendants alleged that claim 1 was not new because the invention was made available to the public in a paper entitled *Vehicle Control by Portable Traffic Lights* by Mr K Holford; the oral disclosure by Mr Lux at a meeting of the Association of Road Traffic Sign Makers held on 28 September 1982; disclosure by Lux to the Department of Transport in a letter dated 22 June 15 1982, and by the use by Lux of a prototype traffic controller in Somerset between 20 September 1982 and February 1983.

There is no dispute that the Holford paper was published before the priority date and that Mr Lux attended the ARTSM meeting on 28 September 1982. Further the publication of the 22 June, 1982, letter and use of a prototype before the priority date were admitted. Thus the only question for decision is whether those prior disclosures and the prior use made the invention available to the public. The standard of proof required is that set out in the judgment of the Court of Appeal in

General Tyre and Rubber Co. v *Firestone Tyre and Rubber Co. Ltd.* [1972] RPC 457 at 485, line 37:

"When the prior inventor's publication and the patentees claim have respectively been construed by the court in the light of all properly admissible evidence as to technical matters, the meaning of words and expressions used in the art and so forth, the question whether the patentees claim is new for the purposes of s.32(1)(e) falls to be decided as a question of fact. If the prior inventor's publication contains a clear description of, or clear instructions to do or make, something that would infringe the patentees claim if carried out after the grant of the patentees patent, the patentees claim will have been shown to lack the necessary novelty, that is to say, will have been anticipated. The prior inventor, however, and the patentee may have approached the same device from different starting points and may for this reason, or it may be for other reasons, have so described their devices that it cannot be immediately discerned from a reading of the language which they have respectively used that they have discovered in truth the same device; but if carrying out the directions contained in the prior inventor's publication will inevitably result in something being made or done which, if the patentees patent was valid, would constitute an infringement of the patentees claim, this circumstance demonstrates the patentees claim has in fact been anticipated.

If, on the other hand, the prior publication contains a direction which is capable of being carried out in a manner which would infringe the patentees claim, but would be at least as likely to be carried out in a way which would not do so, the patentees claim will not have been anticipated, although it may fail on the ground of obviousness. To anticipate the patentees claim, the prior publication must contain clear and unmistakable directions to do what the patentee claims to have invented (*Flour Oxidising Co. Ltd.* v *Carr & Co. Ltd.* (1908) 25 RPC 428, 457, line 34, approved in *B.T.H. Co. Ltd.* v *Metropolitan Vickers Electrical Co. Ltd. (1928)* 45 RPC 1 at 24, line 1). A signpost, however clear, upon the road to the patentees invention will not suffice. The prior inventor must be clearly shown to have planted his flag at the precise destination before the patentees ..."

The invention was conceived by the middle of 1982 and on 16 January 1982, Lux demonstrated it in confidence to Mr Hodgetts and Mr Burdass of the Department of Transport. Subsequently Lux sought approval to convert ten controllers for use in trials in Somerset. Permission was given and Lux modified two controllers so that they incorporated the features of the invention. In mid-September 1982, those prototype controllers were delivered to Mr Brewer who was in charge of Lux's Bridgwater depot. In broad terms, he was told how they worked and was informed of the importance of keeping information about them secret. He remembered that one of the controllers was used intermittently over about five months on commercial jobs. He also remembered four of the sites where it was used, but could not recall the others. He himself set the controls and remembered that on the early jobs the cabinet housing of the control box was locked, but he could not remember whether it was locked thereafter. It was left at sites for two or three days at a time, but never over the weekend.

The defendants submitted that I should infer that on-site the cabinet housing of the prototype controller would not always have been locked, because contractors would require to have access to the controls so as to be able to use it in manual. I cannot make that inference. There is no reason why Mr Brewer should not have continued his practice of locking the cabinet.

There is no evidence as to what happened when the prototype was used nor that anybody, other than Mr Brewer, realised that it provided a minimum green extension. But the parties accept that on some, perhaps a few, occasions the minimum green extension facility would have been operated. The parties also accept that with the cabinet locked an interested skilled man would only be able to observe the colour of the lights and whether a detector recorded a demand.

It is settled law that to invalidate a patent a disclosure has to be what has been called an enabling disclosure. That is to say the disclosure has to be such as to enable the public to make or obtain the invention. Further it is settled law that there is no need to prove that anybody actually saw the disclosure provided the relevant disclosure was in public. Thus an anticipating description in a book will invalidate a patent if the book is on a shelf of a library open to the public, whether or not anybody read the book and whether or not it was situated in a dark and dusty corner of the library. If the book is available to the public, then the public have the right to make and use the information in the book without hindrance from a monopoly granted by the State.

Prior to the 1977 Act, patents were invalidated by prior use of an invention which included use in secret and use which did not involve disclosure of the details of the invention to the public (see *Wheatley's Application* [1985] RPC 91). Thus agreement to sell a product before applying for a patent invalidated a subsequent patent covering that product because the inventor was using the invention to reap benefits and thereby prolonging his statutory monopoly. That was one of the vices the Statute of Monopolies 1623 was intended to prevent. The 1977 Act changed the law. Patents are now only invalidated if prior to application, the invention formed part of the state of the art which comprises all matter which has been made available to the public anywhere in the world by *inter alia* use or in any other way.

The defendants' primary submission was that the invention had been made available to the public in that the prototype controller had been used in public. They submitted that whether the green extension facility was used or observed by anybody was not material. It was sufficient if a contractor operating a site could test the equipment, and upon such a test the claimed invention would be made available to it. The plaintiffs submitted that the correct approach was to decide what the interested skilled man would have seen and thereafter decide whether the events observed gave a clear disclosure of the claimed invention. They also submitted that if the defendants' submissions as to law were correct, then on the facts the skilled man would not have had the invention disclosed to him.

There is no English authority which decides the issue between the parties, but some guidance can be obtained from decisions of the European Patent Office.

In *Luchtenberg* T84/83 1979-85 EPOR 796, the Technical Board of Appeal had to consider an opposition to the grant of a patent for an invention for a car mirror. A mirror embodying the invention had been prior used in a private car. They held that the circumstances were such that the features of the mirror could have been seen by members of the public without the fetter of confidence. That was sufficient to invalidate a patent and therefore was sufficient to prevent the patent being granted. ... In the present case, a light system with a prototype controller was on a number of occasions made available to contractors over five months. Those contractors were free in law and equity to examine it. When doing so, they could observe the lights, test the detectors and observe when a detection had been made. They could not, upon my conclusion as to fact, have seen the control panel which had a light showing that a demand had been recorded.

If a skilled man had taken the time to test the way the lights worked, using the prototype controller, he would have seen that the system used standard lights and standard detectors. The detectors had at their back a light which was normally lit, but which went out when a demand was registered. He would also have appreciated that the system worked in a standard manner, except that in circumstances equivalent to those encountered when a vehicle stalled or red runners took place, the green period was longer. He would see that the vehicle had been detected as the light behind the detector would have gone out. He would also see that the vehicle detected had not moved off. In essence he would have understood that an extended green period was provided. He must, I believe, conclude that the extended green period was a consequence of the controller recording the demand from the vehicle and not receiving a signal of any vehicle movement thereafter.

I conclude that such an examination would be sufficient to disclose the invention of claim 1. Once the prototype controller was made available to the contractors, then all the details of the invention were also made available to them. I conclude that claim 1 lacked novelty.'

COMMENT

Why was not an implied duty of confidence imposed on the contractor's workmen? How could the plaintiff have carried out field trials without jeopardising the novelty of the patent application? What physical and legal measures should have been taken? This case demonstrates the care that a prospective applicant for a patent must exercise to keep the invention secret until the filing date of the application. A patent application is normally published 18 months after filing (or an earlier priority date, if applicable). Are there any good reasons why the applicant should not disclose details of the invention except in confidence after filing but before publication? In the following case, a patent was anticipated by prior use by a 12 year old boy!

Windsurfing International Inc. v Tabur Marine (Great Britain) Ltd. [1985] RPC 59, Court of Appeal

As is often the case, an infringement action results in a counterclaim that the patent should be revoked on the basis of, typically though not limited to, anticipation or obviousness. This case is yet another example. The patent in suit was for a sailboard and the defendant argued that it had been anticipated by a 12 year old boy who had built such a device and used it in public near Hayling Island on weekends and also that it was obvious in the light of such prior use and due to a printed publication containing a description of a sailboard that differed from the patented sailboard in some respects only. The patent was held to be invalid in the Patents Court.

Oliver LJ (at 75): '... we ought to deal with the other two points raised by the defendants, one of which formed the primary ground for the learned judge's decision. These relate to the evidence of Mr Chilvers, whose evidence was that, in 1958 when he was 12 years old, he had made a sailboard which he has used for sailing in an inlet at Hayling Island on summer weekends during two consecutive seasons. There is no doubt that that user was in public in the sense that it was open and visible to anyone in the vicinity of the caravan site at Hayling Island where the family stayed, and it was relied upon by the defendants to support objections based both on anticipation and obviousness ... [referring to the judgment of Whitford J in the Patents Court] Now, it is clear from that description that the Chilvers sailboard constituted, beyond argument, an anticipation of the patent in suit save for one point, namely the arcuate booms employed in the Schweitzer patent, for it embodies every other feature of the alleged invention. The defendants pray it in aid as an anticipation but they also sought to rely upon it as something which was "used in the United Kingdom" within sub-paragraph (f) and thus as the foundation for an argument that, quite apart from Darby, the alleged invention was obvious. In the light of the view which he took that the Chilvers sailboard was an anticipation and that the Schweitzer patent was obvious having regard to Darby, the learned judge found it unnecessary to determine this point, merely contenting himself with observing that interesting questions might arise as to the extent to which a use of this kind, ten years before the date of the patent, ought in any event to be allowed to form a satisfactory basis for an attack on the ground of obviousness. Assuming, for the moment, that the learned judge was wrong in concluding that Chilvers was an anticipation of the Schweitzer patent, the limited and fairly distant use of the Chilvers board appears indeed to constitute the only ground upon which the attack on the ground of obviousness could be resisted. The arcuate booms form the only feature of the Schweitzer patent which differs in any material respect from the Chilvers board, and although their substitution may not have been immediately apparent to a 12 year old boy - all other considerations apart they would be more difficult to manufacture - anybody with a reasonable degree of sailing knowledge, looking at the Chilvers board, must at once have seen that the perfectly well known device of a wishbone boom would be an obvious substitute for the primitive split boom actually employed.

The real question is how far Peter Chilvers' relatively isolated user of his device - albeit carried out publicly - can be relied on in support of a case of obviousness as opposed to anticipation. Mr Pumfrey submits that it cannot be relied upon at all - it was, he suggests, a "freak" use which no man skilled in the art would have considered for one moment as seriously meriting his attention, let alone any development. It is, he submits, contrary to common-sense that a patent which has resulted in a considerable commercial success over the past ten years should be invalidated as the result of the use, years ago and on a comparatively obscure holiday beach, of a primitive plaything put together by an adventurous youth.

We do not see why such a notion should be repulsive to common-sense. If Peter Chilvers had adopted, as part of his device, the conventional wishbone boom in place of the more primitive straight split boom which he in fact used, it would, we should have thought, have been quite unarguable that this would not have been an anticipation under sub-paragraph (e), for the notion behind anticipation is, as we understand it, that it would be wrong to enable the patentee to prevent a man from doing what he has lawfully done before the patent was granted. No doubt, the philosophy behind sub-paragraph (f) is different to this extent, that a patent is granted only for an invention and that which is obvious is not inventive, but it also must, we think, take into account the same concept as anticipation, namely that it would be wrong to prevent a man from doing something which is merely an obvious extension of what he has been doing or of what was known in the art before the priority date of the patent granted. This emerges perhaps most clearly from the following passages from the speech of Lord Moulton in *Gillette Safety Razor Co. Ltd. v Anglo-American Trading Co. Ltd.* (1913) 30 RPC 465 at 480:

"But he" - a prior inventor - "has shown the world how to make a safety razor by clamping a blade in the way which I have described ... The knowledge so communicated applies to blades of any section. After the public has been shown how thus to clamp a blade, one cannot make a novel invention by saying that, instead of clamping a thick blade, one will clamp a thin one ... If the claims of such a patent were so wide as to include it, the patent would be bad, because it would include something which differed by no patentable difference from that which was already in possession of the public. Such a patent would be bad for want of novelty ... from the point of view of the public it is important that this method of viewing their rights should not be overlooked. In practical life it is often the only safeguard to the manufacturer. It is impossible for an ordinary member of the public to keep watch on all the numerous patents which are taken out and to ascertain the validity and scope of their claims. But he is entitled to feel secure if he knows that that which he is doing differs from that which has been done of old only in non-patentable variations, such as the substitution of mechanical equivalents or changes of material shape or size."

Mr Chilvers, of course, and indeed, any of the persons who witnessed or copied his aquatic feats, are members of the public and one asks then on what principle should such persons, who clearly cannot be prevented from doing exactly that which they did before, be prevented from doing that which is no more than an obvious variant of what they did before?

It is, of course, perfectly true that the user proved was relatively short, extending over two summer seasons, that it can, of its nature, have had only a limited audience, and that there is no evidence that it excited anything more than mild amusement in those who witnessed it. But it was certainly not secret and it was not accidental. Mr Chilvers knew perfectly well what he was doing and he was doing it to achieve exactly the same result as the patent in suit (see the speech of Lord Reid in *Bristol-Myers Co. (Johnson's) Application* [1975] RPC 127 at 141 lines 1-15). Nor can it matter that the user was of relatively short duration. In his speech in *Bristol-Myers* (at pages 144-5), Lord Morris recognised that it was possible to conceive of circumstances in which prior user was so trivial as to be capable of being disregarded, but said that he could find no warrant either in reason or in authority for the contention that what amounts to a user is not to be so regarded if it is "merely temporary"; and Lord Diplock (at page 159) observed that:

"it is, at any rate by now, clear law that prior use which defeats a patent, need not be habitual - one single instance is enough ..."

Nor can it be said that Mr Chilvers was merely carrying out an uncompleted experiment (as postulated in the summing-up in *Galloway* v *Bleaden* (1839) 1 WPC 521 at 525). No doubt the craft was initially experimental in the sense that it had not been done before, but Mr Chilvers in fact worked it and used it for two seasons for the recreational purpose for which it was constructed. It cannot legitimately be objected that his user was simply recreational and non-commercial. The purpose, indeed, of the patentee's embodiment is recreational and the commercial success of the product has been achieved by popularising the recreation; and it is clearly established that non-commercial user for the private purpose of the user is sufficient to found an objection based on prior user, so long as the user is overt, in the sense of being exposed to public view: *Stead* v *Williams* (1843) 2 WPC 126, *Carpenter* v *Smith* (1841) 1 WPC 530, *Taylor's Patent* (1896) 13 RPC 482. The user, Lord Diplock observed in *Bristol-Myers* (at page 159) need not be for the purposes of trade "if it is use from which the user derives a practical benefit". Finally, it is no objection that the user excited no interest and created no public demand (*Losh* v *Hague* (1838) 1 WPC 202 at 205). In our judgment, Mr Chilvers' user is clearly user to which regard must be had under sub-paragraph (e) and we can see no context for giving the words 'having regard to what was used' any different meaning for the purposes of sub-paragraph (f). "A man cannot be said to be the inventor of that which has been exposed to public view and which he might have had access to if he had thought fit" (*Carpenter* v *Smith*) (1841) 1 WPC 530 at 536 *per* Lord Abinger C.B.).

If that be right, then one asks "upon what ground could it be said that the substitution of a wishbone boom was not obvious?" Only, we think, upon the ground that the hypothetical skilled man in 1958 would have been so uninterested in this child's plaything that he would not have applied his mind to the matter at all for, on the evidence, it is, we think, clear that any skilled adult who applied his mind to Chilvers' device would at once have seen it as obvious that the unconventional and primitive split boom devised by Chilvers ought to be replaced by the conventional wishbone boom which, even though not in everyday use, would then have been familiar to anyone skilled in yachtbuilding.

Judging the patent in suit by this test, we are clearly of the opinion that the learned judge was right in the conclusion to which he came. It is, in our judgment, beyond doubt that a skilled man reading the specification would at once identify what was described as "arcuate booms" as a wishbone boom. Chilvers used what was clearly a primitive form of wishbone boom and, if he had manufactured his article in 1980 instead of 1958, it would, in our judgment, quite clearly have constituted an infringement of the plaintiff's patent.'

COMMENT

What does the word 'arcuate' mean and how did the boy's boom anticipate the plaintiff's boom? A nice test for novelty is to swap the dates and decide whether the article that allegedly anticipates the patent would infringe that patent if the patented invention was first in time. This is the basis of a defence which was used in the *Gillette* case mentioned in the *Windsurfing* case. That is, the defendant's product was not novel at the time of filing of the patent. Therefore, if the defendant's product is within the patent claims, the patent is invalid or alternatively, the defendant's product is not within the patent claims and does not infringe.

Anticipation by disclosure

The following extract concerns anticipation by disclosure. Some doubt is cast on the correctness of certain aspects of decisions on anticipation at the European Patent Office, notwithstanding the desirability of adopting the same approaches in the United Kingdom.

The case hinged on whether a claim to a substance formed in the human liver, as a result of taking the anti-histamine drug terfenadine, was patentable.

Merrell Dow Pharmaceuticals Inc. v H. N. Norton & Co. Ltd. [1996] RPC 76, House of Lords

The appellants had a patent for an anti-histamine drug, terfenadine, which had the advantage of not making the person taking it drowsy. This patent expired in 1992. After taking out this patent, the appellants discovered that taking terfenadine produced an acid metabolite in the human liver. They then applied for a patent in relation to this substance. It had five years to run at the time of the hearing.

The appellants brought an infringement action against the respondents who had started making and selling terfenadine after its patent had expired. The appellants maintained that, by doing so, they were infringing the second patent under section 60(2) of the Patents Act 1977 (supplying the means, relating to an essential element of the invention, for putting the invention into effect). By taking terfenadine, a person must necessarily produce the acid metabolite.

If the second patent was valid it would mean, in effect, that the appellants would be able to extend their monopoly in terfenadine after its patent had expired. First, Lord Hoffmann dealt with anticipation by use, holding that the invention was not anticipated by use.

Lord Hoffmann (at 86): *'The New Law*

Mr Floyd submitted that *Bristol-Myers Co. (Johnson's) Application* was still good law. In section 2(2), the state of the art comprised "all matter," which could be "a product, a process, information about either, or anything else" which had been "made available to the public" in any way, including by "use". Mr Floyd said that "all matter" must include products or processes which conveyed no information about themselves. Otherwise, why make separate mention of "information about either"? The product itself therefore counted as part of the state of the art and could be made available to the public by use. Thus the acid metabolite had been made available to the public by use, even though such use conveyed no information to the public about the nature of the product or how to make it.

I think that this argument, which in any event depends upon a rather refined *inclusio unius* construction of the parenthetical expansion of the words "all matter", dissolves completely when one looks, as one must, at Article 54. This provision makes it clear that to be part of the state of the art, *the invention* must have been made available to the public. An invention is a piece of information. Making matter available to the public within the meaning of section 2(2) therefore requires the communication of information. The use of a product makes the invention part of the state of the art only so far as that use makes available the necessary information.

The 1977 Act therefore introduced a substantial qualification into the old principle that a patent cannot be used to stop someone doing what he has done before. If the previous use was secret or uninformative, then subject to section 64, it can. Likewise, a gap has opened between the tests for infringement and anticipation. Acts done secretly or without knowledge of the relevant facts, which would amount to infringements after the grant of the patent, will not count as anticipations before.

This construction of section 2(2) is supported by a number of authorities both in the courts of this country and the EPO. I shall refer to only two. In *PLG Research Ltd.* v *Ardon International Ltd.* [1993] FSR 197, 225, Aldous J said:

> "Mr Thorley submitted that if a product had been made available to the public, it was not possible thereafter to patent the product whether claimed as a product claim or a product-by-process claim. That submission is too broad. Under the 1977 Act, patents may be granted for an invention covering a product that has been put on the market provided the product does not provide an enabling disclosure of the invention claimed. In most cases, prior sale of the product will make available information as to its contents and its method of manufacture, but it is possible to imagine circumstances where that will not happen. In such cases a subsequent patent may be obtained and the only safeguard given to the public is section 64 of the Act."

And in *MOBIL/Friction reducing additive Decision G02/88* [1990] EPOR 73 the Enlarged Board of Appeal of the EPO said (at page 88):

> "[T]he Enlarged Board would emphasise that under Article 54(2) EPC the question to be decided is what has been 'made available' to the public: the question is not what may have been 'inherent' in what was made available (by a prior written description, or in what has previously been used (prior use), for example). Under the EPC, a hidden or secret use, because it has not been made available to the public, is not a ground of objection to [the] validity of a European patent. In this respect, the provisions of the EPC may differ from the previous national laws of some Contracting States, and even from the current national laws of some non-Contracting States. Thus, the question of 'inherency' does not arise as such under Article 54. Any vested right derived from prior use of an invention is a matter for national law . . ."

Mr Thorley is therefore right in saying that his claim cannot be dismissed simply on the ground that making the acid metabolite is something which has been done before. To that extent, the intuitive response is wrong.

Anticipation by disclosure

I turn therefore to the ground upon which the respondents succeeded before Aldous J and the Court of Appeal, namely that the disclosure in the terfenadine specification had made the invention part of the state of the art. This is different from the argument on anticipation by use because it relies not upon the mere use of the product by members of the public but upon the communication of information. The question is whether the specification conveyed sufficient information to enable the skilled reader to work the invention.

Mr Thorley says that no one can know about something which he does not know exists. It follows that if he does not know that the product exists, he cannot know how to work an invention for making that product in any form. The prior art contained in the terfenadine specification gave no indication that it would have the effect of creating the acid metabolite in the human body. Therefore it did not contain sufficient information to enable the skilled reader to make the substance in that or any other form. It did not make the acid metabolite available to the public.

What does Mr Thorley mean when he says that no one knew that the acid metabolite existed? What Merrell Dow's research revealed was that something was created in the liver which could be given a chemical description. But the same thing may be known under one description and not known under another. For example, the inhabitants of a village may know the elderly gentleman of military bearing as a prize-winning rose grower without knowing that he had won the VC in the war. In answer to the question: "Do you know the holder of the VC in your village?" they would truthfully answer "I did not know that such a person existed".

There is an infinite variety of descriptions under which the same thing may be known. Things may be described according to what they look like, how they are made, what they do and in many other ways. Under what description must it be known in order to justify the statement that one knows that it exists? This depends entirely upon the purpose for which the question is being asked. Let me elaborate upon an example which was mentioned in argument. The Amazonian Indians have known for centuries that cinchona bark can be used to treat malarial and other fevers. They used it in the form of powdered bark. In 1820, French scientists discovered that the active ingredient, an alkaloid called quinine, could be extracted and used more effectively in the form of sulphate of quinine. In 1944, the structure of the alkaloid molecule ($C_{20}H_{24}N_2O_2$) was discovered. This meant that the substance could be synthesised.

Imagine a scientist telling an Amazonian Indian about the discoveries of 1820 and 1944. He says: "We have found that the reason why the bark is good for fevers is that it contains an alkaloid with a rather complicated chemical structure which reacts with the red corpuscles in the bloodstream. It is called quinine." The Indian replies: "That is very interesting. In my tribe, we call it the magic spirit of the bark." Does the Indian know about quinine? My Lords, under the description of a quality of the bark which makes it useful for treating fevers, he obviously does. I do not think it matters that he chooses to label it in animistic rather than chemical terms. He knows that the bark has a quality which makes it good for fever and that is one description of quinine.

On the other hand, in a different context, the Amazonian Indian would not know about quinine. If shown pills of quinine sulphate, he would not associate them with the cinchona bark. He does not know quinine under the description of a substance in the form of pills. And he certainly would not know about the artificially synthesised alkaloid.

I recognise that there is a distinction between cinchona bark and terfenadine. The former is a substance occurring in nature and the latter is an artificial product. This might have been relevant if the medicinal qualities of the bark had been unknown and a person who discovered them had tried to patent the bark or the natural alkaloid. But the distinction is not material to the present question, which is essentially an epistemological one: what does it mean to know something, so that it can be part of the state of the art? The quinine example shows that there are descriptions under which something may in a relevant sense be known without anyone being aware of its chemical composition or even that it has an identifiable molecular structure. This proposition is unaffected by whether the substance is natural or artificial.

So far I have been considering what it means to know about something in ordinary everyday life. Do the same principles apply in the law of patents? Or does patent law have a specialised epistemology of its own? Mr Thorley argues that it does. He says that for a substance to be known so as to be part of the state of the art within the meaning of section 2, it must be known (or be readily capable of being known) by its chemical composition. No other description will do. He says that by 1977 the science of chemistry had advanced so far that the chemical composition of virtually everything was either known or readily ascertainable by analysis. Therefore the legislature assumed that knowledge that something existed could safely be equated with knowledge of its chemical composition. Section 64 would provide a safety net for people like Amazonian Indians who were doing things with substances which did not readily yield to analysis.

My Lords, I think that on this point the Patents Act 1977 is perfectly clear. Section 2(2) does not purport to confine the state of the art about products to knowledge of their chemical composition. It is the *invention* which must be new and which must therefore not be part of the state of the art. It is therefore part of the state of the art if the information which has been disclosed enables the public to know the product under a description sufficient to work the invention.

For most of the purposes of a product claim, knowledge of its chemical composition will be necessary to enable the public to work the invention. It is something they will need to know in order to be able to make it. So in *Availability to the Public Decision GO1/92* [1993] EPOR 241 the President of the EPO referred to the Enlarged Board of Appeal the question of the circumstances in which making a product available to the public would count as making available its chemical composition. The Board answered that the composition or internal structure of a product becomes part of the state of the art if it is possible for a skilled person to discover it and reproduce it without undue burden. Mr Thorley took this case to mean that in no context can a product be part of the state of the art unless its chemical composition is readily discoverable. But that is not what the case says. The Board was asked about the circumstances in which the chemical composition of a product becomes part of the state of the art. It was not asked about the circumstances in which knowing its chemical composition was necessary for the purpose of treating the product as part of the state of the art.

Other decisions of the EPO seem to me to make it clear that, at least for some purposes, products need not be known under their chemical description in order to be part of the state of the art. In *BAYER/Diastereomers Decision T12/81* [1979-85] EPOR Vol B 308, 312, the Technical Board of Appeal said:

"... [T]he concept of novelty must not be given such a narrow interpretation that only what has already been described in the same terms is prejudicial to it. The purpose of Art 54(1) EPC is to prevent the state of the art being patented again. Art 54(2) EPC defines the state of the art as comprising everything made available to the public before the date of filing in any way, including by written description. There are many ways of describing a substance in chemistry and this is usually done by giving its precise scientific designation. But the latter is not always available on the date of filing ... [It] is the practice of a number of patent offices to accept the process parameter, in the form of a product-by-process claim, for closer characterisation of inventions relating to chemical substances.

To the Board's knowledge this is also the practice at the European Patent Office. If inventions relating to chemical substances defined by claims of this kind are patented, it necessarily follows that the resulting patent documents, once they enter the state of the art, will be prejudicial to the novelty of applications claiming the same substance although in a different and perhaps more closely defined form."

In other words, if the recipe which inevitably produces the substance is part of the state of the art, so is the substance as made by that recipe. *CPC/Flavour Concentrates Decision T303/86* [1989] 2 EPOR 95 was a case about actual recipes for cooking. The application was to patent a process for making flavour concentrates from vegetable or animal substances by extraction with fat solvents under pressure in the presence of water. The claim specified certain parameters for the ratio between the vapour pressure of the water in the meat or vegetables and the vapour pressure of the free water. Opposition was based upon two cookbook recipes for pressure-frying chickens and making stews which in non-technical terms disclosed processes having the same effect. The Technical Board of Appeal said (at page 98):

"It is sufficient to destroy the novelty of the claimed process that this process and the known process are identical with respect to starting material and reaction conditions since processes identical in these features must inevitably yield identical products."

Furthermore, it did not matter that the cook did not realise that he was not only frying a chicken, but also making a "flavour concentrate" in the surplus oil. It was enough, as the Board said, that "some flavour of the fried chicken is extracted into the oil during the frying process even if this is not the desired result of that process."

Mr Thorley said that *CPC/Flavour Concentrates* can be explained on the ground that the flavour concentrates as made according to the cooking recipes could have been analysed and chemically identified. Perhaps they could. But this was not the ground for the Board's decision. It proceeded on the basis that for the purpose of being part of the state of the art, a process for making flavour concentrates was sufficiently described by a recipe for cooking food which did not expressly refer to the flavour concentrates but would inevitably have the effect of making them.

In this case, knowledge of the acid metabolite was in my view made available to the public by the terfenadine specification under the description "a part of the chemical reaction in the human body produced by the ingestion of terfenadine and having an anti-histamine effect". Was this description sufficient to make the product part of the state of the art? For many purposes, obviously not. It would not enable anyone to work the invention in the form of isolating or synthesising the acid metabolise. But for the purpose of working the invention by making the acid metabolise in the body by ingesting terfenadine, I think it plainly was. It enabled the public to work the invention by making the acid metabolite in their livers. The fact that they would not have been able to describe the chemical reaction in these terms does [not *(sic)*] mean that they were not working the invention. Whether or not a person is working a product invention is an objective test independent of what he knows or thinks about what he is doing. (The position may be different when the invention is a use for a product; in such a case, a person may only be working the invention when he is using it for the patented purpose: see the discussion of the *MOBIL/Friction reducing additive* case in the next section). The Amazonian Indian who treats himself with powdered bark for fever is using quinine, even if he thinks that the reason why the treatment is effective is that the tree is favoured by the Gods. The teachings of his traditional medicine contain enough information to enable him to do exactly what a scientist in the forest would have done if he wanted to treat a fever but had no supplies of quinine sulphate. The volunteers in the clinical trials who took terfenadine were doing exactly what they would have done if they had attended Merrell Dow's Strasbourg symposium and decided to try making the acid metabolite in their livers by ingesting terfenadine.

It may be helpful at this point to highlight the similarities and the distinctions between the case for anticipation by use, which I have rejected, and the case for anticipation by disclosure, which I have accepted. In both cases no one was aware that the acid metabolite was being made. In the case of anticipation by use, however, the acts relied upon conveyed no information which would have enabled anyone to work the invention, i.e. to make the acid metabolite. The anticipation in this form relies solely upon the fact that the acid metabolite was made, as the anticipation in *Bristol-Myers Co. (Johnson's) Application* relied solely upon the fact that ampicillin trihydrate had been made and sold to the public. It disavows any reliance upon extraneous information, such as the formula for making terfenadine and the instructions to take it for its anti-histamine effect. Anticipation by disclosure, on the other hand, relies upon the communication to the public of information which enables it to do an act having the inevitable consequence of making the acid metabolite. The terfenadine specification teaches that the ingestion of terfenadine will produce a chemical reaction in the body and for the purposes of working the invention in this form, this is a sufficient description of the making of the acid metabolite. Under the description the acid metabolite was part of the state of the art.

The MOBIL/Friction reducing additive case
Mr Thorley claimed support from the decision of the Enlarged Board of Appeal, to which I have already referred, in *MOBIL/Friction reducing additive Decision G02/88* [1990] EPOR 73. Mobil had attempted to patent a substance for use as a friction reducing additive in lubricating oil. This was opposed by Chevron, who were able to show that the substance was already known and in use for inhibiting rust-formation in ferrous metal. There was no dispute that this put an end to the product claim, which would have entitled Mobil to a monopoly of the product for every possible use. But Mobil then applied to amend the application to restrict it to the *use* of the substance for reducing friction, saying that its usefulness for this purpose had not been previously appreciated. The Technical Board of Appeal, hearing an appeal by Mobil from a successful opposition by Chevron, referred three questions to the Enlarged Board of Appeal, of which the third was:

"Is a claim to the use of a compound for a particular non-medical purpose novel for the purpose of Art 54 EPC, having regard to a prior publication which discloses the use of that compound for a different non-medical purpose, so that the only novel feature in the claim is the purpose for which the compound is used?"

(The reference to "non-medical" purpose is because patents for a second use of medical products give rise to certain special problems under the EPC. It can for present purposes be ignored.)

The Enlarged Board accepted Chevron's submission that while using an old substance in a new way to achieve a new purpose might be novel, the use of an old substance in an old way to achieve a new purpose would not. In the latter case, the only difference would lie in the mind of the user: he would be doing the same thing with the same substance but with a different purpose in mind. One might expect this to lead to the conclusion that if the additive was the same and it was being used in the same way (e.g. by pouring it into the engine) then an attempt to patent its use as a friction reducer when it was previously thought only to inhibit rust should fail.

The Enlarged Board went on to say, however, that a claim for the use of an old compound in an old way for a new purpose (B) could be interpreted to include "the function of achieving purpose B (because this is the technical result)." In such case, the fact that the substance achieved that purpose would be an objective "functional technical feature" of the invention, not residing only in the mind of the user. Thus the fact that the substance did reduce friction was a new technical feature which, if novel, could constitute a patentable invention.

I think it is fair to say that, in the United Kingdom at least, this aspect of the Enlarged Board's decision has been criticised on the ground that a patent for an old product used in an old way for a new purpose makes it difficult to apply the traditional United Kingdom doctrine of infringement. Liability for infringement is, as I have said, absolute. It depends upon whether the act in question falls within the claims and pays no attention to the alleged infringer's state of mind. But this doctrine may be difficult to apply to a patent for the use of a known substance in a known way for a new purpose. How does one tell whether the person putting the additive into his engine is legitimately using it to inhibit rust or infringing by using it to reduce friction? In this appeal, however, we are not concerned with this aspect of the case. The part upon which Mr Thorley relies is the decision that the claimed technical feature, i.e. the friction reducing quality, was novel even though it was "inherent" in the substance. The Enlarged Board said, in a passage which I have already quoted:

"... under Article 54(2) EPC the question to be decided is what has been 'made available' to the public: the question is not what may have been 'inherent' in what was made available (by a prior written description, or in what has previously been used (prior use), for example). Under the EPC, a hidden or secret use, because it has not been made available to the public, is not a ground of objection to [the] validity of a European patent."

My Lords, I do not think that this principle is in issue in this appeal. I have accepted it fully in the discussion of anticipation by use, in which the above passage has already been quoted. It was applied by the Technical Board of Appeal to the facts of MOBIL/Friction reducing additive when that case went back to the Technical Board of Appeal after the decision in principle by the Enlarged Board: see [1990] EPOR 514. The Technical Board decided that so far as friction reduction had been an inevitable concomitant of the use of the additive for other purposes, it was a case of uninformative use like Bristol-Myers Co. (Johnson's) Application. Or to put the same thing in another way, a description of the product by its chemical composition or as "something in the lubricating oil which inhibits rust formation" or any other of the descriptions under which it was previously known would not enable anyone to use it for the purpose of reducing friction, even though this would be the inevitable consequence of doing so. It did not therefore prevent the invention in the form sanctioned by the Enlarged Board from being novel.

But the argument in this appeal for anticipation by disclosure involves no "doctrine of inherency". It does not claim that the acid metabolite must be deemed to have been made available by the teachings of the terfenadine patent even though all information about it remained hidden. It claims instead that the acid metabolite was sufficiently disclosed under the description "an antihistamine chemical reaction in the human body which occurs after taking terfenadine". The respondents say that for the purposes of the particular invention in issue, the specification contained sufficient information about the acid metabolite to make it part of the state of the art. For the reasons I have given, I think it did. I would therefore dismiss the appeal.'

COMMENT

Why was the patent anticipated? What is the difference between anticipation by use and anticipation by disclosure and in what respect is the difference important?

Under section 32(1)(e) of the Patents Act 1949, an invention had to be new "...having regard to what was *known or used*, before the priority date of the claim". In his judgment Lord Hoffmann refers to section 64 of the Patents Act 1977. This gives a right to continue to do an act which was done in good faith before the priority date even though that act would infringe the patent were it in force. The same applies in respect of effective and serious preparations to do the act.

Are Lord Hoffmann's comments on the approach of the European Patent Office's Enlarged Board of Appeal a criticism of that approach?

Priority

Under section 5 of the Patents Act 1977, a patent application may claim the priority of an earlier application filed not more than 12 months before, providing the invention in the application in suit is supported by matter disclosed in the earlier application. In the following case, the House of Lords held that the invention in the second application was not supported by matter in the earlier application.

Biogen Inc. v *Medeva plc* [1997] RPC 1, House of Lords

This case was the first before the House of Lords to concern an invention in the field of genetic engineering.

The plaintiff sued for infringement of its patent and the defendant counterclaimed for revocation of the patent on several grounds. The patent in suit claimed the priority of an earlier application, Biogen 1.

Lord Hoffmann (at 46): *'Priority date*

The next question is whether, given that Biogen 1 disclosed what would at the time have been a patentable invention, it "supports" the invention actually claimed in the patent in suit. This question must be answered in the affirmative if Biogen is to be able to rely on the date of Biogen 1 as its priority date in accordance with section 5(2)(a). The relevant provisions are as follows:

"5(1) For the purposes of this Act the priority date of an invention to which an application for a patent relates and also of any matter (whether or not the same as the invention) contained in any such application is, except as provided by the following provisions of this Act, the date of filing the application.

(2) If in or in connection with an application for a patent (the application in suit) a declaration is made, whether by the applicant or any predecessor in title of his, complying with the relevant requirements of rules and specifying one or more earlier relevant applications for the purposes of this section made by the applicant or a predecessor in title of his and each having a date of filing during the period of twelve months immediately preceding the date of filing the application in suit, then -
(a) if an invention to which the application in suit relates is supported by matter disclosed in the earlier relevant application or applications, the priority date of that invention shall instead of being the date of filing the application in suit be the date of filing the relevant application in which that matter was disclosed or, if it was disclosed in more than one relevant application, the earliest of them."

In *Asahi Kasei Kogyo KK's Application* [1991] RPC 485 this House decided that for matter to be capable of supporting an invention within the meaning of section 5(2)(a) it must contain an "enabling disclosure", that is to say, it must disclose the invention in a way which will enable it to be performed by a person skilled in the art. This construction has not been challenged by the appellants before your Lordships' House. It is however important to notice the relationship between the requirement of "support" in section 5(2)(a) and certain other provisions of the Act which share the concept of an enabling disclosure.

The concept of an enabling disclosure is central to the law of patents. For present purposes, it touches the matters in issue at three different points. First, as we have seen, it forms part of the requirement of "support" in section 5(2)(a). Secondly, it is one of the requirements of a valid application in section 14. And thirdly, it is essential to one of the grounds for the revocation of a patent in section 72. I shall start with section 14. Subsection (3) says:

"The specification of an application shall disclose the invention in a manner which is clear enough and complete enough for the invention to be performed by a person skilled in the art."

This is plainly a requirement of an "enabling disclosure". In addition, subsection (5)(c) says that the claim or claims shall be "supported by the description". It was by reference to subsection (3) that Lord Oliver of Aylmerton, who gave the leading speech in *Asahi,* reasoned at page 536 that a description would not "support" the claims for the purpose of subsection (5)(c) unless it contained sufficient material to enable the specification to constitute the enabling disclosure which subsection (3) required: "the Act can hardly have contemplated a complete application for a patent

lacking some of the material necessary to sustain the claims made". By parity of reasoning, he said that "support" must have the same meaning in section 5(2)(a).
The absence of an enabling disclosure is likewise one of the grounds for the revocation of a patent specified in section 72(1). Paragraph (c) says that one such ground is that -

> "the specification of the patent does not disclose the invention clearly enough and completely enough for it to be performed by a person skilled in the art."

This is entirely in accordance with what one would expect. The requirement of an enabling disclosure in a patent application is a matter of substance and not form. Its absence should therefore be a ground not only for refusal of the application but also for revocation of the patent after grant. Similarly, the same concept is involved in the question of whether the patent is entitled to priority from an earlier application. This is not to say that the question in each case is the same. The purposes for which the question is being asked are different. But the underlying concept is the same.

The explanation of section 14(5)(c) in *Asahi* seems to me to provide an answer to a point which puzzled the Court of Appeal in *Genentech Inc.'s Patent* [1989] RPC 147. The court noted that although section 14(5)(c) is a statutory requirement for a valid patent application, non-compliance is not a ground for revocation of a patent which has been granted. Section 72(1) states exhaustively the grounds upon which a patent may be revoked. These grounds do not, as such, include non-compliance with section 14(5). But the substantive effect of section 14(5)(c), namely that the description should, together with the rest of the specification, constitute an enabling disclosure, is given effect by section 72(1)(c). There is accordingly no gap or illogicality in the scheme of the Act.

The need for an enabling disclosure to satisfy the requirements of support under section 5(2)(a), valid application under section 14 and sufficiency under section 72(1)(c) has, I think, been plain and undisputed since the decision in *Asahi*. What has been less clear is what the concept of an enabling disclosure means. Part of the difficulty has been caused by a misinterpretation of what the Technical Board of Appeal of the EPO said in *Genentech I/Polypeptide expression* (T 292/85) [1989] 0J EPO 275. This was a patent for a plasmid suitable for transforming a bacterial host which included an expression control sequence or "regulon" which could enable the expression of foreign DNA as a recoverable polypeptide. The Examining Division was willing to grant a patent only in respect of the plasmids, bacteria and polypeptides known at the date of application. The Technical Board of Appeal allowed the appeal, saying that the Examining Division had taken too narrow a view of the requirement of enabling disclosure:

> "What is also important in the present case is the irrelevancy of the particular choice of a variant within the functional terms 'bacteria', 'regulon' or 'plasmid'. It is not just that *some* result within the range of polypeptides is obtained in each case but it is the *same* polypeptide which is expressed, independent of the choice of these means ... Unless variants of components are also embraced in the claims, which are, now or later on, equally suitable to achieve the same effect in a manner which could not have been envisaged without the invention, the protection provided by the patent would be ineffectual ... The character of the invention this time is one of general methodology which is fully applicable with

any starting material, and is, as it was already stated, also independent from the known, trivial, or inventive character of the end-products."

In other words, the applicants had invented a general principle for enabling plasmids to control the expression of polypeptides in bacteria and there was no reason to believe that it would not work equally well with any plasmid, bacterium or polypeptide. The patent was therefore granted in general terms.

In *Mölnlycke AB* v *Procter & Gamble Ltd.* [1992] FSR 549, however, Morritt J interpreted this decision to mean that it was a general rule of European patent law that an invention was sufficiently disclosed if the skilled man could make a single embodiment. This interpretation was followed by Aldous J in *Chiron Corporation* v *Organon Teknika Ltd.* [1994] FSR 202, although I think I detect in his judgment some surprise that the EPO should have adopted such a mechanistic and impoverished approach to the concept of enabling disclosure. As we shall see, he applied the same rule in the present case.

In fact the Board in *Genentech I/Polypeptide expression* was doing no more than apply a principle of patent law which has long been established in the United Kingdom, namely, that the specification must enable the invention to be performed to the full extent of the monopoly claimed. If the invention discloses a principle capable of general application, the claims may be in correspondingly general terms. The patentee need not show that he has proved its application in every individual instance. On the other hand, if the claims include a number of discrete methods or products, the patentee must enable the invention to be performed in respect of each of them.

Thus if the patentee has hit upon a new product which has a beneficial effect but cannot demonstrate that there is a common principle by which that effect will be shared by other products of the same class, he will be entitled to a patent for that product but not for the class, even though some may subsequently turn out to have the same beneficial effect: see *May & Baker Ltd.* v *Boots Pure Drug Co. Ltd.* (1950) 67 RPC 23, 50. On the other hand, if he has disclosed a beneficial property which is common to the class, he will be entitled to a patent for all products of that class (assuming them to be new) even though he has not himself made more than one or two of them.

Since *Genentech I/Polypeptide expression* the EPO has several times reasserted the well established principles for what amounts to sufficiency of disclosure. In particular, in *Exxon/Fuel Oils* (T 409/91) [1994] OJ EPO 653, paragraph 3.3, the Technical Board of Appeal said of the provision in the European Patent Convention equivalent to section 14(5)(c) of the Act:

"Furthermore, Article 84 EPC also requires that the claims must be supported by the description, in other words, it is the definition of the invention in the claims that needs support. In the Board's judgment, this requirement reflects the general legal principle that the extent of the patent monopoly, as defined by the claims, should correspond to the *technical contribution* to the art in order for it to be supported, or justified."

Support for the claims
I come therefore to the question of whether Biogen 1 contained an enabling disclosure which supported the claims in the patent in suit. The argument before Aldous J seems to have concentrated on the questions of whether it had been

shown that Professor Murray's method was capable of making both HBcAg and HBsAg and whether it would work in eukaryotic as well as bacterial hosts. The judge, following his earlier decision in *Chiron Corporation* v *Organon Teknika Ltd.* [1994] FSR 202, said that it would be enough if the specification enabled one embodiment to be made. As there was no doubt that Professor Murray had made HBcAg in cultures of *E. coli,* that was an end of the matter. In case it was considered that the claims really amounted to two inventions, one for making HBcAg and another for HBsAg, he found that the skilled man would also have been able to make HBsAg. Having heard the evidence of Professor Murray and others, he said:

> "Upon the evidence, I conclude that Biogen did express and demonstrate expression of the surface antigen using the techniques described in the specification." ([1995] RPC 25, 50).

The disclosure was therefore sufficient in respect of both inventions.

In the opposition proceedings in the EPO, the argument proceeded upon similar lines. The only issue on sufficiency seems to have been whether the invention could produce HBsAg as well as HBcAg. The Technical Board, like Aldous J, found as a fact that it could. The question of whether the method could be used in other hosts was not argued, the opponents thinking (probably rightly) that this point was concluded against them by the EPO decision in *Genentech I/Polypeptide expression.* In fact, if Professor Murray's method worked in a prokaryotic host, despite the possibility that such a host might not be able to cope with introns, it was even more likely to work in a eukaryotic host, which was better equipped for dealing with them. For my part, therefore, I would not differ from the findings of either Aldous J or the Technical Board in rejecting both these grounds of opposition.

In the Court of Appeal, Hobhouse LJ began his judgment by saying that he did not believe that the court was differing from Aldous J "on any question of the acceptance of the evidence of witnesses or primary scientific fact". He nevertheless made a thorough re-examination of the evidence on whether the method disclosed in Biogen 1 had enabled the making of HBsAg and came to the conclusion that it had not. He said:

> "The outcome of this evidence is that whatever results the plaintiff obtained in 1978 did not amount to evidence justifying a claim to have produced a recombinant DNA molecule which enabled the expression of HBsAg in *E. coli* (or any other host)." ([1995] RPC 25, 112).

I am bound to say that I regret the decision of the Court of Appeal to revisit the evidence upon which the judge made his finding of fact. For the reasons given earlier in relation to the issue of obviousness, I think that this was a question on which greater respect should have been paid to the judge's findings. The Court of Appeal's reversal of the judge on this issue greatly lengthened the hearing before your Lordships' House, as no doubt it had done in the Court of Appeal. The House was invited to undertake a minute examination of the facts with a view to restoring the findings of the judge. It was even offered inspection of the autoradiographs claimed to show the positive results upon which Professor Murray had based his claim to success - an offer which your Lordships felt able to decline. But I think that your Lordships learned enough of the detailed facts to form the view that the judge's decision was one which was open to him upon the evidence and should not have been disturbed.

But the fact that the skilled man following the teaching of Biogen 1 would have been able to make HBcAg and HBsAg in bacterial cells, or indeed in any cells, does not conclude the matter. I think that in concentrating upon the question of whether Professor Murray's invention could, so to speak, deliver the goods across the full width of the patent or priority document, the courts and the EPO allowed their attention to be diverted from what seems to me in this particular case the critical issue. It is not whether the claimed invention could deliver the goods, but whether the claims cover other ways in which they might be delivered: ways which owe nothing to the teaching of the patent or any principle which it disclosed.

It will be remembered that in *Genentech I/Polypeptide expression* the Technical Board spoke of the need for the patent to give protection against other ways of achieving the same effect "in a manner which could not have been envisaged without the invention". This shows that there is more than one way in which the breadth of a claim may exceed the technical contribution to the art embodied in the invention. The patent may claim results which it does not enable, such as making a wide class of products when it enables only one of those products and discloses no principle which would enable others to be made. Or it may claim every way of achieving a result when it enables only one way and it is possible to envisage other ways of achieving that result which make no use of the invention.

One example of an excessive claim of the latter kind is the famous case of *O'Reilly v Morse* (1854) 56 U.S. (15 How) 62 in the Supreme Court of the United States. Samuel Morse was the first person to discover a practical method of electric telegraphy and took out a patent in which he claimed any use of electricity for "making or printing intelligible characters, signs, or letter, at any distances". The Supreme Court rejected the claim as too broad. Professor Chisum, in his book on Patents (vol 1, § 1.03[2] summarises the decision as follows:

"Before Morse's invention, the scientific community saw the possibility of achieving communication by the 'galvanic' current but did not know any means of achieving that result. Morse discovered one means and attempted to claim all others."

A similar English case is *British United Shoe Machinery Co. Ltd.* v *Simon Collier Ltd.* (1908) 26 RPC 21. The patentee invented a piece of machinery for automatically trimming the soles of boots and shoes by means of a cam. One of the claims was in general terms for automatic means of trimming soles. Parker J said, at pages 49-50:

"[T]he problem was simply how to do automatically what could already be done by the skill of the workman. On the other hand, the principle which the inventor applies for the solution of the problem is the capacity of a cam to vary the relative positions of two parts of a machine while the machine is running. Assuming this principle to be new, it might be possible for the inventor, having shown one method of applying it to the solution of the problem, to protect himself during the life of his patent from any other method of applying it for the same purpose, but I do not think that the novelty of the principle applied would enable him to make a valid claim for all means of solving the problem whether the same or a different principle were applied to its solution."

I return therefore to consider the technical contribution to the art which Professor Murray made in 1978 and disclosed in Biogen 1. As it seems to me, it consisted in showing that despite the uncertainties which then existed over the DNA of the Dane particle - in particular, whether it included the antigen genes and whether it had introns - known recombinant techniques could nevertheless be used to make the antigens in a prokaryotic host cell. As I have said, I accept the judge's findings that the method was shown to be capable of making both antigens and I am willing to accept that it would work in any otherwise suitable host cell. Does this contribution justify a claim to a monopoly of *any* recombinant method of making the antigens? In my view it does not. The claimed invention is too broad. Its excessive breadth is due, not to the inability of the teaching to produce all the promised results, but to the fact that the same results could be produced by different means. Professor Murray had won a brilliant Napoleonic victory in cutting through the uncertainties which existed in his day to achieve the desired result. But his success did not in my view establish any new principle which his successors had to follow if they were to achieve the same results. The inventive step, as I have said, was the idea of trying to express unsequenced eukaryotic DNA in a prokaryotic host. Biogen 1 discloses that the way to do it is to choose the restriction enzymes likely to cleave the Dane particle DNA into the largest fragments. This, if anything, was the original element in what Professor Murray did. But once the DNA had been sequenced, no one would choose restriction enzymes on this basis. They would choose those which digested the sites closest to the relevant gene or the part of the gene which expressed an antigenic fragment of the polypeptide. The metaphor used by one of the witnesses was that before the genome had been sequenced everyone was working in the dark. Professor Murray invented a way of working with the genome in the dark. But he did not switch on the light and once the light was on his method was no longer needed. Nor, once they could use vectors for mammalian cells, would they be concerned with the same problem of introns which had so exercised those skilled in the art in 1978. Of course there might be other problems, but Biogen 1 did not teach how to solve them. The respondents Medeva, who use restriction enzymes based on knowledge of the HBV genome and mammalian host cells, owe nothing to Professor Murray's invention.

It is said that what Professor Murray showed by his invention was that it could be done. HBV antigens could be produced by expressing Dane particle DNA in a host cell. Those who followed, even by different routes, could have greater confidence by reason of his success. I do not think that this is enough to justify a monopoly of the whole field. I suppose it could be said that Samuel Morse had shown that electric telegraphy could be done. The Wright Brothers showed that heavier-than-air flight was possible, but that did not entitle them to a monopoly of heavier-than-air flying machines. It is inevitable in a young science, like electricity in the early nineteenth century or flying at the turn of the last century or recombinant DNA technology in the 1970s, that dramatically new things will be done for the first time. The technical contribution made in such cases deserves to be recognised. But care is needed not to stifle further research and healthy competition by allowing the first person who has found a way of achieving an obviously desirable goal to monopolise every other way of doing so. (See Merges and Nelson, *On the Complex Economics of Patent Scope* (1990) 90 Columbia Law Review 839.)

I would therefore hold that Biogen 1 did not support the invention as claimed in the European Patent and that it is therefore not entitled to the priority date of Biogen 1.

As it is conceded that the invention was obvious when the patent application was filed, it is invalid.

The EPO decision.
I must at this point say something about the decision of the Technical Board of the EPO, which dismissed opposition proceedings and held the patent valid. Decisions of the EPO on questions of law are, as this House said in *Merrell Dow Pharmaceuticals Inc v H N Norton & Co. Ltd.* [1996] RPC 76, 82, of considerable persuasive authority. But the decision of the EPO in this case did not, as it seems to me, proceed on any principle different from those I have endeavoured to apply. The Board held, as I have been willing to assume, that the invention described in Biogen 1 was not obvious at the priority date. On the other hand it held that the disclosure in Biogen 1 was in respect of the same invention as that claimed in the patent and, contrary to my view hereafter expressed, that such disclosure was sufficient to enable the invention to be performed to the full extent of the claims. But in arriving at this conclusion, the Board directed its attention solely to the question of whether the teaching in Biogen 1 would enable the man skilled in the art to achieve expression of HBsAg as well as HBcAg. Nothing was said about whether the claims were too broad because expression could also be achieved without the use of the teaching which it contained, by a method of which it could not be said, in the words of the Technical Board in *Genentech I,* that it was "in a manner which could not have been envisaged without the invention". But the principle upon which I have come to the conclusion that on this ground the patent is invalid is also, as I have said, clearly stated in decisions of the EPO such as *Genentech I* and *Exxon.* I would not therefore regard the outcome of this appeal as suggesting any divergence between the jurisprudence of this court and that of the EPO.'

COMMENT
Being obvious at the time of applying for the patent meant that, in the absence of the priority of Biogen 1, the patent was invalid. It was also invalid for insufficiency.

In *Genentech Inc.'s Patent* [1989] RPC 147, the Court of Appeal highlighted the fact that section 72(1) (the sole grounds for revocation of a patent) does not expressly include failure to comply with section 14(5) (that the claim or claims be clear and concise, fully supported by the description, etc.). How does this case reconcile the two provisions?

The case also contains a lengthy discussion of inventive step. The House of Lords were prepared to assume that Biogen 1 was not obvious without deciding the point. Why?

Inventive Step

An invention involves an inventive step if it is not obvious to persons skilled in the art, having regard to the state of the art. The notional skilled worker is not endowed with inventive faculties or else all inventions might be deemed to be obvious. Sometimes, commercial success is a useful indicator of inventive step.

The General Tire & Rubber Company v The Firestone Tyre and Rubber Company Ltd. [1972] RPC 457, Court of Appeal

The patent related to a method of making oil-extended rubber to be used for making tyre treads. The defendant alleged, *inter alia*, that the patent was obvious to persons skilled in the art of rubber manufacture. Although the invention was a commercial success this was due to other factors and the defendant also pointed out that other manufacturers independently found the same solution soon after the plaintiff.

Sachs LJ (at 497): "'Obvious" is, after all, a much-used word and it does not seem to us that there is any need to go beyond the primary dictionary meaning of "very plain".

When head (f) is invoked it is, of course, as previously indicated, for whoever seeks revocation of a patent to show that the alleged inventive step was obvious to a normally skilled addressee in the art. On the way to that end there are here a number of preliminary questions to be resolved. These include the common general knowledge to be imputed to that addressee; whether what had to be done to achieve the step was truly a matter of inventive experiment or merely a matter of that type of trial and error which forms part of the normal industrial function of such an addressee; what documents he would find in the course of such researches as he would be expected to make; and how he would regard those documents in the light of common general knowledge. Then finally one has to consider whether the step is properly described as a new combination of integers or merely as a collocation of old ones. None of these questions, some of which inevitably overlap, is easy to resolve, and on each it is for the appellants to establish their contentions.

As regards obviousness as a whole the trial judge approached the matter correctly when he said, [1970] FSR at 302 ([1971] RPC at 237):

> "The question of obviousness is seldom easy to decide. It has been said to be a kind of jury question and, in the days when patent actions were tried before a judge and jury, was treated so. The decision is ultimately one for the court which cannot let its function in this respect be usurped by the witnesses, though undoubtedly the evidence of the witnesses may help the court to arrive at its decision. It must be decided objectively and, being a jury question, it is right that all the relevant circumstances of the case should be taken into account. That this is the correct view of the matter is clear both from the old cases and the new."

His observations naturally apply with equal force to each of the questions which need resolution on the way to giving final answer on the issue.

It is as well in relation to the evidence in the instant case at this point to refer to the need for objective as opposed to subjective tests. The question is whether the step was obvious to a normally qualified skilled addressee in 1950 - as opposed to the person who in fact claims to be the inventor or to any particular rival of his. Indeed, it is not infrequent that the inventor is not himself called as a witness in a patent action. That, however, does not rule out evidence as to how the problems were in fact approached at the relevant time by the patentee, by his rivals, or by others. What they did may provide significant signposts leading to the answer to the objective test. In this behalf the literature - both the widely read documents and the internal memoranda of Goodyear and the Office of Rubber Reserve already mentioned - provide valuable evidence: as also do the actual experiments carried out by the plaintiffs in the year proceeding the date of the patent-in-suit - though this material happens originally to have been admitted into evidence on an issue other than obviousness ...

Commercial success is, of course, not of itself conclusive on an issue of obviousness, but it has been treated in case after case as a valuable weight in favour of the patent. Mr Templeman sought to minimise that weight in the instant case by aid of what Lord Herschell said in *Longbottom* v *Shaw* (1891) 8 RPC 333, a case concerning an improvement in the method of forming a row of hooks. The improved article had supplanted the old article in the market, but in relation to that particular commercial success Lord Herschell, at page 336, said:

> "If nothing be shown beyond the fact that the new arrangement results in an improvement, and that this improvement causes a demand for an apparatus made in accordance with the patent, I think it is of very little importance."

He went on to say that the position would be different if it were shown "that men's minds were likely to have been engaged upon a mode of remedying the defects".

That, however, was a case in which the patentee had failed to adduce any evidence of the history of the alleged invention. In particular, there was no evidence of any previous demand for an improvement in the subject matter. In the instant case, however, there is, contrary to the submissions made on behalf of the appellants, ample evidence of such a demand: we have already referred to the interest in the gap and the investigations in the U.S.A. - which in the circumstances are relevant to this aspect of obviousness. It is, however, as well to add that proof of previous demand for a particular improvement is not, of course, a necessary prerequisite to establishing that commercial success is of weight: for instance, resigned acceptance of an existing state of affairs may exist and be relevant - especially when there is in effect a tied body of consumers, as for tyres, who must anyway take the only available products. Indeed, we find it difficult to think that there are competitive commercial concerns who are not continually interested in and seeking advances in the economic production of whatever article they may be selling: the phrase of Mr Baker as to a manufacturer's interest in "the dollar value" (overall performance and cost) of tyres illustrates this factor.

In our judgment the very widespread adoption of the plaintiffs' process both for its economies in the use of raw polymer and for its improvements in the properties of the finished article is of value on the issue of obviousness.

It being apparent from what has already been said that there is a considerable weight of material in the balance of the scales against the plea of obviousness, we now turn to consider what are submitted to be the main factors to be put into them on the opposite side.

As regards commercial success it was contended that the vastly increased use of synthetic rubber for tyres after June, 1951, was due not to the adoption of oil-extended rubber but to other factors such as the advent of cold rubber, the adoption of an improved carbon black known as HAF, and the exigencies of the Korean war - which created both a demand for rubber and a shortage of natural rubber. We naturally assume that each of those factors - and notably the Korean war, which affected the U.S.A. as from June, 1950 - would increase the demand both for synthetic rubber for tyre treads and for pressure for improvements in processing it. On the other hand, this does not in our judgment affect the true point made on behalf of the plaintiffs, that whatever may have been the effects of the other factors, nonetheless the widespread adoption of the oil-extended rubber process was due to its own intrinsic merits and would have occurred whether or not the other factors had operated - though the extent of its use might have been initially less had there been no Korean war. Upon the evidence it is correct to say that the combined saving in cost of production coupled with the increased treadwear and other beneficial properties were such as would have catered for a long-felt want and would have been of great value whether or not there had been such a war ...

That leaves the final question as to whether a skilled addressee who is assumed to have read and remembered amongst all other available material the three specifications Semperit (a), Semperit (c) and Wilmington, would by reason of these have come to regard the plaintiffs' solution of the problem as obvious, despite the fact that his common general knowledge would have biased him against exploring the chances of oil-extended rubber providing a solution. In this behalf we agree with the approach adopted by the trial judge when he correctly said ([1970] FSR at page 312): ([1971] RPC at 246).

"It seems to me to be very dangerous and in law not permissible to assess obviousness in the light of carefully selected pieces of prior knowledge only".

Whether or not in that particular passage he had in mind the three specifications as being the "carefully selected pieces", it is in our judgment right to apply to them the process of reasoning adopted by the trial judge. Bearing in mind what has, when discussing anticipation, already been said as regards each of these three specifications, we have come to the conclusion that, assuming Mr Templeman's submissions as to their position in this case to be correct, they would not affected a skilled addressee's mind in the way that he submits.

Having regard to our assessment of the evidence on the issue of obviousness we do not find it necessary to examine in detail the authorities cited to us on this subject. It is sufficient to refer to two passages in judgment that have been much cited and are of high authority.

The first is that in the judgment of Fletcher Moulton, LJ in *British Westinghouse v Braulik* (1910) 27 RPC 209. Though it was quoted in the first instance judgment, [1970] FSR at page 313-C, ([1971] RPC at 246, lines 39 to 45) it provides such an apt warning against an ex post facto analysis of an invention of the type which the appellants sought to apply in the important case that it merits citation.

"I confess that I view with suspicion arguments to the effect that a new combination, bringing with it new and important consequences in the shape of practical machines, is not an invention, because, when it has once been established it is easy to show how it might be arrived at by starting from something known, and taking a series of apparently easy steps. This ex post facto analysis of invention is unfair to the inventors and in my opinion it is not countenanced by English patent law."

The second is in the judgment of Tomlin J (as he then was) in *Samuel Parkes & Co. Ltd.* v *Cocker Bros. Ltd.* (1929) RPC 241 at 248:

"Nobody, however, has told me, and I do not suppose anybody ever will tell me, what is the precise characteristic or quality the presence of which distinguishes invention from a workshop improvement ...The truth is that, when once it had been found ... that the problem had waited solution for many years and that the device is in fact novel and superior to what had gone before and has been widely used, and used in preference to alternative devices, it is, I think, practically impossible to say that there is not present that scintilla of invention necessary to support the patent."

In our judgment the evidence in the instant case shows that there is far more than a "scintilla of invention" in the process for which protection is claimed in the patent-in-suit. The appellants have failed by a considerable margin to establish their plea of obviousness. On the contrary, the plaintiffs have positively established that the invention for which protection is claimed in the patent was not obvious.'

COMMENT

In a counterclaim based on lack of inventive step, the burden of proof is on the defendant. The process of bringing together several pieces of prior knowledge is sometimes referred to as 'mosaicing'. It rarely succeeds in showing obviousness. Why not? What factors may assist a judge in resolving the question of obviousness? What is a 'long felt want'?

Parks-Cramer Co. v *G W Thornton & Sons Ltd.* [1966] RPC 407, Court of Appeal

The plaintiff was granted a patent in respect of a method of cleaning between rows of machines in textile mills. It comprised, essentially, an overhead vacuum cleaner which automatically travelled along overhead rails and had attached to it long flexible hoses reaching almost to the floor with nozzles mounted at intervals along the hoses. The defendant, who was sued for infringement argued that every housewife knows that the passage of a vacuum cleaner over a floor removes dust and debris and that, as a consequence, the invention was obvious.

Diplock LJ (at 417): '... "Obviousness" is not a concept which can be clarified by elaborate exegesis, and we do not propose to cite the many cases to which we have been referred in which various judges at various times, both before and after the phrase "is obvious and does not involve any inventive step" was first inserted in the Patents Acts, have expressed the concept of obviousness, or lack of subject-matter as it was previously called, in various ways appropriate to the particular invention whose validity was challenged on this ground.

There is, however, one authority which we must mention for it was upon this rather than upon the short and simple phrase later used in the statute that counsel for the defendants chiefly relied to support his contention that claim 1 was invalid. It was the case of *Gadd and Mason* v *Manchester Corporation* (1892) 9 RPC 516 which contains the much-cited words of Lindley, LJ.

"1. A patent for the mere new use of a known contrivance, without any additional ingenuity in overcoming fresh difficulties, is bad, and cannot be supported. If the new use involves no ingenuity, but is in manner and purpose analogous to the old use, although not quite the same, there is no invention: no manner of new manufacture within the meaning of the Statute of James. 2. On the other hand, a patent for a new use of a known contrivance is good and can be supported if the new use involves practical difficulties which the patentee has been the first to see and overcome by some ingenuity of his own. An improved thing produced by a new and ingenious application of a known contrivance to an old thing, is a manner of new manufacture within the meaning of the statute ... If, practically speaking, there are no difficulties to be overcome in adapting an old contrivance to a new purpose, there can be no ingenuity in overcoming them, there will be no invention, and the first rule will apply. The same rule will, I apprehend, also apply to cases in which the mode of overcoming the so-called difficulties is so obvious to every one of ordinary intelligence and acquaintance with the subject-matter of the patent, as to present no difficulty to any such person. Such cases present no real difficulty to people conversant with the matter in hand, and admit of no sufficient ingenuity to support a patent".

As Lord Parker, LCJ said recently of this same citation in re Lister & Co.'s Patent [1965] FSR 178 "there is a real danger when one has a criterion laid down like that, a criterion adopted over and over again in later cases, of treating the words used as if they were the words of a statute". We agree and would add that it seems to us that there is an additional danger in summarising what Lindley, LJ said by calling it "the doctrine of analogous use," since this involves selecting a single and imprecise adjective to convey the characteristics of a particular kind of obviousness, which it took the expositor of the doctrine 18 lines of print to express. What Lindley, LJ meant by an "analogous use" of a known contrivance is plain from what he said. The new use to which the known contrivance is put must involve no ingenuity, scilicet it must itself be obvious: the manner in which the known contrivance is used and the purpose for which it is used must *both* be similar to the previous manner and purpose of its use though they need not be "quite the same."

As in all other cases of obviousness, the question is one of degree. There may be an inventive step in recognising that a problem exists at all: but given a problem which is known to exist which it is the object of the invention to solve, the question always is: "Is the solution claimed by the patentee one which would have occurred to everyone of ordinary intelligence and acquaintance with the subject-matter of the patent who have his mind to the problem?"

A court, however, experienced in the general field of patents for inventions, cannot have the same acquaintance with the subject-matter of a particular patent as those whose work has been concerned with the particular kind of manufacture in which the disputed invention is intended to be used. Where the evidence discloses that the existence of a problem and the desirability of finding a solution to it has been recognised by those conversant with the matter in hand, the steps which were in fact taken to solve the problem before the priority date of the patent may provide very cogent evidence as to whether the solution adopted by the patentee was obvious or not.

The evidence in the present case shows that the problem of preventing the accumulation of fly upon the floors of cotton mills in the aisles and under the machines themselves, and the desirability of collecting and removing it continuously while it was being produced, was recognised early in the 1950s. It shows too that attempts to solve it were made throughout the period from 1952 to 1958 not only by the plaintiffs but by at least two other inventors and that the plaintiff's efforts to find a solution went to the length of putting on the market machines which afforded some alleviation of the problem but were not a commercial success. These attempts by the plaintiffs and others had one feature in common, that they all involved blowing currents of air across the floor of the mill in one direction to drive the fly towards collecting points. One thing which did not in fact occur to anyone of ordinary intelligence and acquaintance with the problem was that the solution lay not in blowing the fly towards fixed collecting points but in passing a suction nozzle repeatedly over the same relatively narrow track in the aisles while the machines were in production. The solution embodied in the plaintiffs' patent was an immediate commercial success, not only for the plaintiffs themselves, as sellers of the patented apparatus - such commercial success may be due to other causes than the intrinsic usefulness of the apparatus - but also for the users of the apparatus who achieved substantial savings in production costs from its use.

This evidence fortifies the view which we have already expressed that it was *not* obvious that by causing a vacuum cleaner to traverse at frequent intervals, the same relatively narrow path along the aisle between the machines it would collect the fly not only from that part of the floor which was directly in its path but also from the rest of the floor as well: and if this is what the plaintiffs' invention claims it is in our judgment valid.

It has, however, been argued by the defendants that the specification by using the word "repeatedly" does not sufficiently disclose the need for frequent passage of the suction nozzle along the aisles. It would cover, it is suggested, a method in which the nozzle traversed the aisle once very two hours - like the former labourer with the broom. If there is substance in this objection it would seem to go to sufficiency or to utility rather than to obviousness, for if the apparatus traversed the aisles at such lengthy intervals, it would not perform its stated task. But we do not think that there is any substance in it. It is well settled that where general dimensional words of this kind are used in a claim they must be given the meaning which they would convey to an intelligent person conversant with the subject-matter reading the specification as a whole. (See *British Thomson-Houston Co.* v *Corona Lamp Works Ltd.* 39 RPC 49 at 76, 77). At the date of the specification travelling cleaning equipment moving upon rails above the rows of machines was a commonplace, and the pace at which such equipment travelled was well-known. This is the sort of pace which we should expect someone familiar with cotton mills to understand from the expression "repeatedly moving said suction current longitudinally of an aisle." But the matter does not end there. The specification contemplates that the patented apparatus would be used in conjunction with such blowing equipment and where this was done would travel upon the same rails and therefore, of necessity, move at the same pace. Thus the word "repeatedly" tells the well-versed reader all he needs to know to make the process work.

We are, therefore, of opinion that claim 1 is valid; and it is conceded that if this be so the defendants have infringed it.'

COMMENT

Commercial success coupled with a history of attempts by others to find a solution to a long felt want is a useful indicator of non-obviousness though it can never be conclusive. What other factors could account for commercial success? Does lack of commercial success show that an invention is obvious? In many cases, as this, careless drafting of patent claims can assist a defendant to formulate an attack on the patent based on obviousness.

Lux Traffic Controls Ltd. v Pike Signals Ltd. [1993] RPC 107, Patents Court

The facts are briefly outlined earlier in this chapter.

Aldous J (at 135): 'Obviousness: In view of the conclusion I have reached as to the Somerset prior use, it is not necessary for me to come to a conclusion on obviousness. However, I will shortly set out my conclusions upon the assumption that none of the prior art relied on disclosed the idea of a second detection within the minimum green period which is used to deal with consequential traffic flow and, if there is no movement, extends the green period.

The correct approach to obviousness is that advocated by Oliver LJ in *Windsurfing International Inc* v *Tabur Marine (GB) Ltd.* [1985] RPC 59 at 73, line 45:

> "There are, we think, four steps which require to be taken in answering the jury question. The first is to identify the inventive concept embodied in the patent in suit. Thereafter, the court has to assume the mantle of the normally skilled but unimaginative addressee in the art at the priority date and to impute to him what was, at that date, common general knowledge in the art in question. The third step is to identify what, if any, differences exist between the matter cited as being "known or used" and the alleged invention. Finally, the court has to ask itself whether, viewed without any knowledge of the alleged invention, those differences constitute steps which would have been obvious to the skilled man or whether they require any degree of invention."

... It is always easy to postulate the obvious route to an invention once the solution is known. Many judges have realised that and have cautioned against such an *ex post facto* analysis ...'

COMMENT

The *Windsurfing* test for inventive step is used in this case based on patents under the 1977 Act, showing the test to be still relevant. Is there any reason why the *Windsurfing* test should not be used to determine inventive step under the 1977 Act?

Mölnlycke AB v Procter & Gamble Ltd (No.5) [1994] RPC 49, Court of Appeal

This case concerned a patent for refastenable disposable nappies which included an external plastic strip with an embossed surface to allow repeated fastening and unfastening (in order to allow inspection of the state of the nappy) without tearing. In the infringement action, the defendant attacked the validity of the patent on several grounds including obviousness. At trial, the patent was held to be valid and infringed. The Court of Appeal confirmed this finding and, in giving the judgment of the court, the Vice-Chancellor set out the test for obviousness; again adopting the *Windsurfing* test.

Nicholls VC (at 111): 'The patent law of the United Kingdom is now contained in the Patents Act 1977 which is a statutory code and which was passed "to establish a new law of patents", to amend the law, and to give effect to certain international conventions, most importantly the European Patent Convention of 1973 ...

The requirement that the invention involves an inventive step is defined in section 3 [of the 1977 Act]:

> "3. An invention shall be taken to involve an inventive step if it is not obvious to a person skilled in the art, having regard to any matter which forms part of the state of the art by virtue only of section 2(2) above and disregarding section 2(3) above."

Section 2 is the section which deals with novelty and provides that an invention shall be taken to be new if it does not form part of the state of the art. What is meant by "the state of the art" both for the purposes of section 2 and section 3 is defined in section 2(2):

> "(2) The state of the art in the case of an invention shall be taken to comprise all matter (whether a product, a process, information about either, or anything else) which has at any time before the priority date of that invention been made available to the public (whether in the United Kingdom or elsewhere) by written or oral description, by use or in any other way."

Sub-section (3) of section 2 extends the definition in respect of the criterion of novelty, but not in respect of the criterion of obviousness, to matter which had been the subject of an earlier application not published until after the priority date of the patent in question.

Under the statutory code (which is further confirmed in its completeness by sections 74 and 72) the criterion for deciding whether or not the claimed invention involves an inventive step is wholly objective. It is an objective criterion defined in statutory terms, that is to say whether the step was obvious to a person skilled in the art having regard to any matter which forms part of the state of the art as defined in section 2(2). We do not consider that it assists to ask whether the patent discloses something sufficiently inventive to deserve the grant of a monopoly. Nor is it useful to extract from older judgments expressions such as "that scintilla of invention necessary to support a patent". The statute has laid down what the criterion is to be: it is a qualitative not a quantitative test. The warning against coining phrases given by the Court of Appeal in *General Tire & Rubber Co.* v *Firestone Tyre & Rubber Co. Ltd.* [1972] RPC 457 at 497 to 498 is even more apt under the 1977 Act. (See also the rejection of semantic arguments by the Court of Appeal in *Hallen* v *Brabantia* [1991] RPC 195 at 211 to 212.)

The Act requires the court to make a finding of fact as to what was, at the priority date, included in the state of the art and then to find again as a fact whether, having regard to that state of the art, the alleged inventive step would be obvious to a person skilled in the art.

In applying the statutory criterion and making these findings the court will almost invariably require the assistance of expert evidence. The primary evidence will be that of properly qualified expert witnesses who will say whether or not in their opinions the relevant step would have been obvious to a skilled man having regard to the state of the art. All other evidence is secondary to that primary evidence. In the past, evidential criteria may have been useful to help to elucidate the approach of the common law to the question of inventiveness. Now that there is a statutory definition, evidential criteria do not form part of the formulation of the question to be decided.

In the nature of things, the expert witnesses and the court are considering the question of obviousness in the light of hindsight. It is this which may make the court's task difficult. What with hindsight, seems plain and obvious, often was not so seen at the time. It is for this reason that contemporary events can be of evidential assistance when testing the experts' primary evidence. For instance, many people may have been industriously searching for a solution to the problem for some years without hitting upon the allegedly obvious invention. When this type of evidence is adduced, the court can quickly find itself caught up in an investigation of what was or was not obvious to certain identified individuals at certain dates during the history of the development of the product or process involved. This gives rise to complications because the state of knowledge of these individuals, though skilled, may not correspond to the statutory definition of the state of the art. A particular inventor may have been unaware of some aspect of the state of the art as defined in section 2(2), and may therefore have genuinely taken what was actually an inventive step, but nevertheless be unable to claim a patentable invention since the step was, in the terms of the statute, obvious. Further, this type of evidence invites the court to speculate whether particular individuals were of an inventive disposition, because the earlier making of the same invention by another or others does not necessarily mean that at a later date the invention was obvious. Yet again, evidence of the commercial success of the invention can lead into an investigation of the reasons for this success; there may be commercial reasons for this success unrelated to whether the invention was or was not obvious in the past.

Secondary evidence of this type has its place and the importance, or weight, to be attached to it will vary from case to case. However, such evidence must be kept firmly in its place. It must not be permitted, by reason of its volume and complexity, to obscure the fact that it is no more than an aid in assessing the primary evidence.

We had cited to us authorities extending back over a hundred years in which various evidential considerations are discussed in relation to what were the common law or statutory precursors of the present statutory definition. It appears that the word "obvious" was first used in this connection by Lord Herschell in 1889 in *American Braided Wire Co.* v *Thompson* (1889) 6 RPC 518 at 528. As Lord Herschell pointed out in *Siddell* v *Vickers & Sons Ltd.* (1890) 15 App. Cas. 496, and adapting his language to the new statutory definition, obviousness connotes something which would at once occur to a person skilled in the art who was desirous of accomplishing the end, or, in Lopes LJ's much quoted phrase, "it must not be the obvious or natural suggestion of what was previously known": see *Savage* v *Harris & Sons* (1896) 13 RPC 364 at 370.

There are many reported decisions by courts which have had to distinguish between an invention and mere workshop improvement where the evidentiary considerations are discussed and forensic tools developed ... Citing previous decisions on a question of fact is not a useful, nor is it a proper exercise.

On the need to distinguish between inventiveness and novelty, we are rightly referred to what Sir Lionel Heald QC had said in *Minnesota Mining & Manufacturing*

Co. v *Bondina Ltd.* [1973] RPC 491 at 521-3, where he drew attention to the importance of always keeping the distinction in mind and the different criteria involved. At page 34 of the transcript of his judgment in the present case Morrit J said:

> "To ascertain the difference between Mesek and the patent in suit, I must ascertain what Mesek teaches. For this purpose it seems to me that the clear and unmistakable direction test exemplified in *General Tire & Rubber* v *Firestone Tyre & Rubber* [1972] RPC 457 at 486 in relation to novelty is appropriate."

In our judgment this was not correct. The clear and unmistakable directions test is not part of the statutory criterion of obviousness and should not be used in this connection. Indeed the Court of Appeal itself in *General Tire*, at the page cited, makes this clear; the two concepts are different as are the criteria.

The question to be answered under section 3 of the Act is a question of fact. In some cases it may be a very complex question; in others the question may involve no complexity although it may still be difficult to answer with confidence. In the present case the technology is reasonably straightforward and the inventive step claimed involved an idea for the application of that technology in relation to a particular product. It exemplifies a case where, despite the fact that no doubt large sums of money are at stake, the resolution of the question of fact is obscured, not assisted, by an over-elaboration of the evidence or a failure to recognise that the relevant question is the primary question.

Although formulated with reference to the Patents Act 1949, the analysis of Oliver LJ in *Windsurfing International* v *Tabur Marine* [1985] RPC 59 at 73 continues to provide assistance. There are four steps:

(1) What is the inventive step said to be involved in the patent in suit?

(2) What was, at the priority date, the state of the art (as statutorily defined) relevant to that step?

(3) In what respects does the step go beyond, or differ from, that state of the art?

(4) Having regard to such development or difference, would the taking of the step be obvious to the skilled man?

The value of this analysis is not that it alters the critical question; it remains the question posed by the Act. But it is that it enables the fact-finding tribunal to approach the exercise of answering that question in a structured way. This was [what] Morritt J did in the present case.

The burden of proof is upon the person attacking the validity of the patent to show that no inventive step was involved. It is therefore for him to make out the case of obviousness and prove it by appropriate expert evidence. Accordingly in any given case it will be for that person to marshal and prove those aspects of the state of the art which he alleges make the relevant step obvious. The matter will come before the court on the basis of certain allegations which have to be used for the purposes of deciding upon the answer to the second and third questions posed above. In the present case the defendants did just that. Before the trial judge they made wider allegations regarding the relevant state of the art but before us they focused their case upon what was to be learnt from two particular patents which formed part of the prior art, the Japanese Utility Model No. 74910/1982, known as "Unicharm", and the US Patent No. 3,867,9540 known as "Mesek". Mr Thorley QC, to whom we are indebted for his able and clear argument, accepted that the defendants could not succeed on the question of obviousness in this court save by reference to what was to be learnt from those two patents. He did of course also pray in aid other aspects of the supporting evidence and he sought to criticise inferences favourable to the plaintiffs which the judge was prepared to draw from other parts of the evidence.'

COMMENT

Many inventions seem obvious with hindsight. How does a judge avoid the effect of hindsight? Is obviousness a question of fact or a question of law? Nicholls VC usefully distinguishes between novelty and inventive step. Do over-elaborate submissions by counsel blur that distinction?

Industrial Application

The third requirement is that the invention must be capable of industrial application. Usually, this will not be problematic but it could be argued that an invention was not capable of industrial application because the invention simply did not work or there was no conceivable use of it. Industrial application does not extend to methods of treatment of the human or animal body.

Chiron Corporation v *Organon Teknika Ltd. (No.3)* **[1994] FSR 202, Patents Court**

The plaintiff alleged an infringement of its patent for a diagnostic test for Hepatitis C Virus. The defendant set up a number of defences, one of which was that one claim did not have an industrial application.

Aldous J (at 239): 'It is a requirement of section 1 of the Act that patentable inventions should be capable of industrial application. Section 4(1) states:

"4. (1) Subject to subsection (2) below, an invention should be taken to be capable of industrial application if it can be made or used in any kind of industry, including agriculture."

The defendants submitted that claim 11 was not limited to polypeptides whose sequence was related to HCV [Hepatitis C Virus]. They submitted that claim 11 covered polypeptides that had no conceived use. Thus it was submitted that the claim sought to monopolise products which had no industrial application.

It is important to remember that the old law which provided for revocation if the claims were not fairly based on the description or lacked utility was swept away by the 1977 Act. The law is now that set out in the 1977 Act. Section 4(1) states that inventions shall be taken to be capable of industrial application "if it can be made ... in any kind of industry." Although the range of polypeptides falling within the claims, and in particular claim 11, may be large, there is no evidence to suggest that once the sequence is known they could not be made by industry. I therefore reject this submission of the defendants.

Section 4(2) provides:

> "(2) An invention of a method of treatment of the human or animal body by surgery or therapy or of diagnosis practised on the human or animal body shall not be taken to be capable of industrial application."

The defendants submitted that claim 17, being a claim for testing blood for HCV, was a claim to an invention for a method of diagnosis practised on the human or animal body. Therefore it was not capable of being patented.

That submission is also untenable. Although the test of claim 17 can be used for diagnosing HCV, it is not a method practised on the human body.'

COMMENT

One of the defences to infringement action was that a licence granted by the plaintiff offended against section 44 and, accordingly, provided a full defence. Does the exclusion in section 4(2) prohibit the patenting of drugs?

Excepted Matter

The excluded matter in section 1(2) of the Patents Act 1977 has continued to cause problems. To some extent, this is a reflection of the perceived attractiveness of the grant of a patent resulting in attempts to overcome the exclusions.

Lux Traffic Controls Ltd. v Pike Signals Ltd. [1993] RPC 107, Patents Court

The facts are briefly outlined earlier in this chapter.

Aldous J (at 137): 'Not an invention: Section 1(2) of the Patents Act 1977 states:

> "It is hereby declared that the following (among other things) are not inventions for the purposes of this Act, that is to say, anything which consists of:
> (a) a discovery, scientific theory or mathematical method;
> (b) a literary, dramatic, musical or artistic work or any other aesthetic creation whatsoever;
> (c) a scheme, rule or method for performing a mental act, playing a game or doing business, or a program for a computer;
> (d) the presentation of information;

but the foregoing provision shall prevent anything from being treated as an invention for the purposes of this Act only to the extent that a patent or application for a patent relates to that thing as such."

The defendants submitted that the invention of the patent was a scheme for doing business within s.1(2)(c) of the Act and therefore was not patentable. As I understand their submission, they contended that what was claimed was in essence a scheme or method for controlling traffic which was not a patentable invention.

Nicholls LJ in *Gale's Application* [1991] RPC 305 at 323, said:

"I turn now to section 1(2) of the Act. When considering these provisions, it is helpful to have in mind the principle of patent law, well established before the Act, that an idea or discovery as such is not patentable. It is the practical application of an idea or discovery which leads to patentability. It leads to patentability even if, as frequently happens, the practical application of the discovery is inherent in the discovery itself or is obvious once the discovery has been made and stated. On this I need refer only to three authorities."

He went on to cite passages from those authorities and, at p.324, line 26, he continued:

"... The language of section 1(2), and of the corresponding article, Article 52(2) and (3), of the European Patent Convention, is apt as an embodiment of this principle of the United Kingdom patent law. Section 1(2) comprises a non-exhaustive catalogue of matters or things, starting with 'a discovery', which as such are declared not to be inventions. Thus a discovery as such is not patentable as an invention under the Act. But when applied to a product or process which, in the language of the 1977 Act, is capable of industrial application, the matter stands differently. This was so held in *Genetech Inc.'s Patent* [1989] RPC 147. There, this court by a majority decision, held that section 1(2) did not depart from the established principle mentioned above. Purchas LJ, at page 208, and also Dillon LJ, at page 240, decided that the quotation from Whitford J set out above still represented the law. Dillon LJ said:

'In so far as a patent claims as an invention the practical application of a discovery, the patent does not, in my judgment, relate only to the discovery as such, even if the practical application may be obvious once the discovery has been made, even though unachievable in the absence of discovery.'"

As Nicholls LJ pointed out, s.1(2) of the Act comprises a non-exhaustive catalogue of matters or things which are not patentable. Although not specifically mentioned, I believe a method of controlling traffic as such is not patentable, whether or not it can be said to be a scheme for doing business. The field expressly excluded by the section concerns mere ideas not normally thought to be the proper subject for patents which are concerned with manufacturing. That conclusion is consistent with the decision of the Technical Board of Appeal in *Christian Franceries case,* T 16/83 [1988] EPOR 65. They considered Article 52(2) of the EPC and said at p.70:

"From this non-restrictive listing, the Board of Appeal concludes that at the very least abstract terms, principles and methods are excluded from patentability by

Article 50(2)(c) and (3) EPC. The extent of this exclusion from patentability not being specified by the examples listed, the precise meaning of the terms of this listing has become secondary. In consequence, a process for regulating traffic flow consisting of establishing directives for regulating urban traffic whose effect consists of a simple economic advantage constitutes a plan within the scope of economic activities which are excluded according to Article 52(2)(c) and (3) EPC. The case in point in fact concerns a creation or concept which, although it brings economic advantage, does not extend beyond an abstract plan as such".

Mr Jacob for Lux did not submit that a method of controlling traffic as such could be a patentable invention. He submitted that the invention involved traffic control, but also made a contribution to the art in a field not excluded from patentability. That, he submitted, was patentable. (See the decision of the Technical Board in *IBM* T 38/86, [1990] EPOR 606 at 611.)

On behalf of the defendants, it was submitted that the invention was similar to that in the *Christian Franceries* case and that I should come to the same conclusion, namely that the invention related to a method of traffic control as such. It was submitted that the only matter than the invention contributed was a way of processing and applying information.

It is clear both from the decisions of the European Patents Office and judgments of the Court of Appeal that the form of the claim in a patent cannot be decisive as to whether or not the invention relates solely to excluded matter. For instance the invention in the *Christian Franceries* case was claimed both as a process for regulating traffic and as a device. The Board held that the invention was not patentable. Fox LJ came to a similar conclusion in *Merrill Lynch's Application* [1989] RPC 561. He said, at p.569, line 2:

"On the other hand, it seems to me to be clear, for the reasons indicated by Dillon LJ, that it cannot be permissible to patent an item excluded by section 1(2) under the guise of an article which contains that item - that is to say, in the case of a computer program, the patenting of a conventional computer containing that program. Something further is necessary. The nature of that edition [sic] is, I think, to be found in the *Vicom* case where it is stated:

'Decisive is what technical contribution the invention makes to the known art. There must, I think, be some technical advance on the prior art in the form of a new result (e.g. a substantial increase in processing speed as in Vicom).'"

At the heart of many inventions is a discovery which is an excluded matter. What can be patented is the incorporation of that discovery into technology. As Fox LJ stated, something more than excluded matter is required to enable an invention to be patented. That something extra is a technical contribution to the art.

I have found the *Christian Franceries* case helpful when considering the principles to apply, but I do not believe it would be right in this case to come to the same conclusion merely because the patent in suit is concerned with traffic regulation. The discovery behind the application in the *Christian Franceries* case is not the same as that of the patent in suit and it does not follow that the invention of the patent in suit is also excluded. I must decide whether the invention relates to a manner of regulating traffic as such or whether the invention includes something extra, namely a technical contribution.

There can be no doubt that devices that regulate traffic flow can have a technical contribution and are patentable. For example, a claim to a process of regulating traffic using lights with a detector which used sound waves would undoubtedly be patentable. It would be patentable because of the technical contribution provided by a detector which used sound waves.

The minimum green extension patent does include as part of its invention a technical contribution. The inventors realised that a different controller was needed to deal with the problem of stalled cars and red runners. They appreciated that a detector which detected movement could be used to detect no movement. Thus they re-arranged the electrical connections so that the controller provided an extended green period if no detection was made during the minimum green period. The idea of regulating traffic was incorporated into the controller, thereby producing a novel technical machine which operated if no detection was made.

I conclude that the invention claimed is not an excluded matter and is patentable. That conclusion appears to have been the same as that of the Comptroller as he granted the patent.'

COMMENT

Are the exclusions simply examples of things that do not have an industrial application and, if so, is section 1(2) redundant? Can you distinguish discoveries, scientific theories, mathematical methods and computer programs from the other exceptions? Why was the particular invention in this case not caught by section 1(2)?

Fujitsu Limited's Application [1997] RPC 608, Court of Appeal

Aldous LJ (at 611): 'Those provisions have to be construed in the light of the European Convention and with the help of the judgments given by the European Patent Office. As Nicholls LJ said in *Gale's Application* [1991] RPC 305 at 322:

"One of the purposes of the 1977 Act was to give effect to the European Patent Convention. Thus, section 77(1) provides that a European patent (UK), by which is meant a European patent designating the United Kingdom, shall as from a prescribed date be treated for the purposes of parts 1 and 3 of the Act as if it were a patent under the Act granted in pursuance of an application made under the Act. Section 77(4) provides that where a European patent (UK) is revoked in accordance with the European Patent Convention, the patent shall be treated for the purposes of parts 1 and 3 of the Act as having been revoked under the Act.

The Act had a further purpose. The Act did not merely enact the statutory provisions necessary for the provisions of the Convention regarding European patents to take effect in this country. The Act also had a harmonisation objective. On the signature of the Convention for the European Patent for the Common Market, referred to in the Act as the Community Patent Convention, and not to be confused with the European Patent Convention, the governments of the member states of the European Community resolved to adjust their laws relating to patents so as to bring those laws into conformity with the corresponding provisions in the European Patent Convention and other conventions. Accordingly, when construing and applying section 1(1) and (2) of the Act, the court must have regard to the legislative intention with which those subsections were framed, namely, that they were framed so as to have, as nearly as practicable, the same effect in the United Kingdom as the corresponding provisions in Articles 52(1), (2) and (3) of the European Patent Convention have in the territories in which that Convention applies. That is the effect of section 130(7) in the present case.

From this brief reference to the European Patent Convention one point which emerges is that it is of the utmost importance that the interpretation given to section 1 of the Act by the courts in the United Kingdom, and the interpretation given to Article 52 of the European Patent Convention by the European Patent office, should be the same. The intention of Parliament was that there should be uniformity in this regard. What is more, any substantial divergence would be disastrous. It would be absurd if, on an issue of patentability, a patent application should suffer a different fate according to whether it was made in the United Kingdom under the Act or was made in Munich for a European patent (UK) under the Convention. Likewise in respect of opposition proceedings."

... The law
Section 1(2)(c) of the Act has been considered by this court in *Merrill Lynch's Application* [1989] RPC 561 and in *Gale's Application.* In both those cases the court drew attention to the proviso to section 1(2) which states that the "things", referred to in the subsection, should only be excluded "to the extent that a patent or an application for a patent relates to that thing as such."

In *Merrill Lynch* the applicants submitted that the question for the court was to decide whether the subject matter of the claim was a computer program. If it was, it was not patentable. If it was not, then the invention was not excluded from patentability by section 1(2). Thus it was said that a piece of machinery (a computer) which follows the instructions of a computer program was patentable, although the program itself would be excluded from patentability by the section. That was rejected by the Court of Appeal. Fox LJ said at page 569:

> "It seems to me to be clear, ... that it cannot be permissible to patent an item excluded by section 1(2) under the guise of an article which contains that item - that is to say, in the case of a computer program, the patenting of a conventional computer containing that program. Something further is necessary. The nature of that addition is, I think, to be found in the *Vicom* case where it is stated: 'Decisive is what technical contribution the invention makes to the known art.' There must, I think, be some technical advance on the prior art in the form of a new result *(e.g.* a substantial increase in processing speed as in *Vicom). "*

By that statement Fox LJ was making it clear that it was not sufficient to look at the words of the claimed monopoly. The decision as to what was patentable depended upon substance not form. He also went on to point out the importance of considering whether the invention made a technical contribution, despite the fact that neither the statute nor Article 52 of the Convention lays down that the matter, which would result in the invention not relating to the thing as such, must provide a technical contribution. It would therefore seem that as a matter of words, if for instance the patent was not confined to a computer program, then it could not be excluded under subsection (2), as to an extent the patent would not relate to the computer program as such. However it is and always has been a principle of patent law that mere discoveries or ideas are not patentable, but those discoveries and ideas which have a technical aspect or make a technical contribution are. Thus the concept that what is needed to make an excluded thing patentable is a technical contribution is not surprising. That was the basis for the decision of the Board in *Vicom.* It has been accepted by this court and by the EPO and has been applied since 1987. It is a concept at the heart of patent law.

The reasons for the decision of the Technical Board in *Vicom* T208/84, [1987] 2 EPOR 74 have to be read against the background of the invention claimed. It was for a method of digitally processing images and an apparatus for carrying out the method. The invention as claimed involved scanning the elements of a data array to produce a convolved array and then repeating the scanning so that the last convolved data array generated had the enhanced qualities required. That claim was objected to as being a method of performing a mental act as such and as a computer program as such contrary to Articles 52(2) and (3) of the Convention.

The Board allowed the appeal. They drew a distinction between a method of performing a mental act which was not patentable and a technical process. They pointed out that use of a mathematical process did not produce a technical result. They went on:

"In contrast thereto, if a mathematical method is used in a technical process, that process is carried out on a physical entity (which may be a material object but equally an image stored as an electric signal) by some technical means implementing the method and provides as its result a certain change in that entity. The technical means might include a computer comprising suitable hardware or an appropriate programmed general purpose computer.

The Board, therefore, is of the opinion that even if the idea underlying an invention may be considered to reside in a mathematical method a claim directed to a technical process in which the method is used does not seek protection for the mathematical method *as such.*"

The Board then came to consider the objection that the invention was excluded as it related to a computer program as such. They rejected that objection, essentially upon the same reasoning. They said:

"Generally claims which can be considered as being directed to a computer set up to operate in accordance with a specified program (whether by means of hardware or software) for controlling or carrying out a technical process cannot be regarded as relating to a computer program *as such* and thus are not objectionable under Article 52(2)(c) and (3) EPC.
....
Generally speaking, an invention which would be patentable in accordance with conventional patentability criteria should not be excluded from protection by the mere fact that for its implementation modern technical means in the form of a computer program are used. Decisive is what technical contribution the invention as defined in the claim when considered as a whole makes to the known art."

Mr Birss submitted that the decision in *Vicom* showed that patent applications for processing images of real things were not excluded from being patentable. He took us to the claim which had been considered by the Examining Division which limited the invention to a method of filtering a two-dimensional data array and compared that with the claim that was allowed which claimed a method of processing images. He submitted that it was the change from filtering to processing real images that supplied the technical contribution.

The reasoning in *Vicom* as to what was the technical contribution is not easy to ascertain. However, I do not read the decision as concluding that all claims to processing real images are patentable and I can see no reason why, if they are, the same reasoning should not apply to all useful images. As I read the decision, the Board saw a technical contribution, namely the generation of the enhanced picture. As the Principal Examiner pointed out:

> "..., the numbers which are mathematically processed in *Vicom* do not merely determine the intellectual content of the images which are displayed, but are also the technical means which cause the display to operate to a technical level. Thus in *Vicom* manipulating numbers in the manner described affects the technical quality of the image. So in *Vicom,* the invention concerned the technical representation, or technical control of what is displayed and not the information content of what is displayed."

In my view *Vicom* does not support the submission that claims to processing of real images are allowable. The technical contribution was not the fact that an image was being produced. It was the way the enhanced image was produced.

In *Gale* this court had to consider a patent application for a ROM programmed to carry out a method of calculating a square root of a number. Nicholls LJ who gave the leading judgment described the working of a computer and said:

> "In principle, the instructions in a computer program do no more than prescribe a particular manner of operation for which it was constructed. Thus writing a fresh set of instructions for use in a computer in particular circumstances or for particular purposes cannot in itself be regarded as inventive."

He went on to point out that, to be used in a computer, a series of instructions had to be recorded in some physical form perhaps on a disc in a ROM. He said that if the instructions *qua* instructions were not patentable, they were not patentable merely because they were recorded on or in a known piece of apparatus. The disc on ROM was "merely the vehicle used for carrying" the instruction.

> "... the physical differences are not material for patent purposes, because they constitute no more than the use of a compact disc for its intended purpose. Likewise with a disc or ROM which records or reproduces a new set of instructions, if those instructions are recorded on a conventional disc, or are stored in a ROM using conventional methods. To decide otherwise would be to exalt form over substance."

He went on to conclude that the application before him did not contain a technical contribution and therefore was a computer program which was excluded from patentability.

I, like Nicholls LJ, have difficulty in identifying clearly the boundary line between what is and what is not a technical contribution. In *Vicom* it seems that the Board concluded that the enhancement of the images produced amounted to a technical contribution. No such contribution existed in *Gale's* Application which related to a ROM programmed to enable a computer to carry out a mathematical calculation or in *Merrill Lynch* which had claims to a data processing system for making a trading market in securities. Each case has to be decided upon its own facts.

Does the application consist of a program for a computer as such?
The judge held ([1996] RPC 511 at 518):

> "I have already referred to the essence of Fujitsu's development. It is clear that, in form at least, the claims are not to programs as such. It follows that, *prima facie,* they avoid the 'program' exclusion under section 1(2). However as Fox LJ said in *Merrill Lynch* something further is needed. The real issue it seems to me, is whether the application also avoids the other exclusions under section 1(2). If it does not, the application will fail. Whether, in those circumstances, the grounds of failure are stated to be that the invention is only for a program or that it is, for example, a method for performing a mental act is a matter of semantics."

He went on to hold that the application was excluded as it consisted in substance of a scheme or method for performing a mental act.

I am not sure whether the judge came to any conclusion as to whether the application consisted of a computer program as such. Clearly he considered that in form the claims were not excluded from being patented, but seemed to believe that there was no difference in this case between the two grounds of exclusion.

Mr Birss sought to rely upon the form of the claims. He submitted that claim 10, directed as it was to a computer apparatus having a number of features and claim 9 directed to a method of manufacturing a structure could not be said to relate to an invention consisting of a computer program as such.

That submission cannot be right having regard to the judgment of Nicholls LJ in *Gale.* In that case, I held at first instance that the ROM claimed was not excluded as it was an article which had been altered during manufacture so as to perform the function of the method or program defined by the claim. The Court of Appeal decided that that was not correct and that the court should look at the claims as a matter of substance. It was both convenient and right to strip away, as a confusing irrelevance, the fact that the claim was for "hardware".

There is only one invention. The fact that it is claimed as a method, a way of manufacture or an apparatus having appropriate features is irrelevant. Further there is no dispute as to what the invention is. In summary it uses a computer program so that an operator can select an atom, a lattice vector and a crystal face in each of two crystal structures displayed. The computer, upon instruction and using the program, then converts data representing the physical layouts of the two crystal structures into data representing the physical layout of the structure that is obtained by combining the original two structures in such a way that the selected atoms, the selected lattice vectors and the selected faces are superposed. The resulting data are then displayed to give a picture of the resulting combined structure. Clearly the whole operation revolves around the computer program and the question for decision is whether there is a technical contribution so that it cannot be said that the invention consists of a computer program as such.

Mr Birss put forward two grounds for concluding that the application included a technical contribution. First, relying on *Vicom,* he submitted that the technical contribution was provided by the processing of real images or structures. I have already concluded that *Vicom* does not support so rigid a view. Thus this submission must be rejected. Second, he submitted that the application provided a new tool for modelling crystal structure combinations which relieved the chemist of the laborious task of building a model. It provided a solution to the problem of providing a quick and error free way of creating real images of two crystal structures joined together.

Mr Birss is right that a computer set up according to the teaching in the patent application provides a new "tool" for modelling crystal structure combinations which avoids labour and error. But those are just the sort of advantages that are obtained by the use of a computer program. Thus the fact that the patent application provides a new tool does not solve the question of whether the application consists of a program for a computer as such or whether it is a program for a computer with a technical contribution.

I believe that the application is for a computer program as such. I agree in general with the reasons of the Principal Examiner which I have quoted. In *Vicom* the technical contribution was provided by the generation of the enhanced display. In the present case the combined structure is the result of the directions given by the operator and use of the program. The computer is conventional as is the display unit. The two displays of crystal structures are produced by the operator. The operator then provides the appropriate way of superposition and the program does the rest. The resulting display is the combined structure shown pictorially in a form that would in the past have been produced as a model. The only advance is the computer program which enables the combined structure to be portrayed quicker.

I conclude that the application does not relate to a patentable invention as it is excluded by section 1(2)(c) as being a program for a computer as such.

Does the claim consist of a method of performing a mental act as such?
The fact that a patent application consists of a program for a computer does not mean that it does not also consist of a method of performing a mental act. The contrary is not true. In this case the computer program is the result of intellectual input, but whether the claimed invention, which incorporates operator control, consists of a method of performing a mental act as such is doubtful. As there is no need to decide this issue, I conclude that an in-depth analysis is best left to be dealt with on another occasion. However, in the light of the submissions of counsel I will set out my views on the point of construction that was argued.

Mr Birss submitted that the words "a method for performing a mental act" in section 1(2)(c) should be construed as only covering methods which the human mind carries out.

They should not be construed to include the sort of acts which a human mind could [not] do. If so, the Fujitsu application was not excluded as it related to a specific way of modelling crystal structures not carried out by the human mind.

Mr Silverleaf QC who appeared for the Comptroller submitted that the narrow construction sought to be placed upon the words "for performing a mental act" was wrong, contrary to authority and involved reading into the Act words such as: "as done by the mind".

In support of the narrow construction Mr Birss referred to the Board's decision in *Vicom.* He suggested that the invention in that case could have been performed by the human mind, but was held to be patentable because the human mind did not actually work in the way claimed. The distinction drawn by Mr Birss may be correct in fact, but the reasoning is not. The reason why the Board concluded that the invention was patentable was because they concluded there was a technical contribution. The Board did not analyse how the human mind works and therefore that did not play a part in their considerations.

Mr Birss also relied on *Pettersson T1002/92* [1996] EPOR 1. The invention in that case related to a system for handling customers queuing for a number of service points. The Technical Board held at page 8:

> "The wording of claim 1 leaves no doubt that protection is sought for a 'system which is capable to determine the queue sequence of customers', and thus for a three-dimensional object with the aforementioned capacities. Claim 1 explicitly indicates that this system comprises: 'a turn-number allocation unit, a selection unit, terminals, an information unit and computing means'. Hence, the wording employed in the claim defines a technical item with at least five construction components, which item clearly belongs to the category of an apparatus."

The Board concluded that in such a case there was a mix of technical and non-technical elements which meant that the claim was not excluded from patentability. Again there was no analysis of how the human mind works. The invention was held to be patentable because there was a technical contribution with the result that it did not relate to a method of performing a mental act as such.

There are good reasons to reject the narrow construction. First, a decision as to whether an invention is patentable as consisting of a method of performing a mental act as such should be capable of determination without recourse to evidence as to how the human mind actually works. If it were to the contrary, the section would pose an extremely difficult problem. Second, the narrow interpretation appears to introduce a consideration of novelty which is covered in section 1(1)(a). Third, the words used as "a mental act" suggest any mental act whether done before or not.

A similar but not identical submission was made in *Wang Laboratories Inc.'s Application* [1991] RPC 463 as appears from this extract of my judgment at page 472:

> "Before turning to the claims, I must deal with a submission of Mr Burkill, who appeared for the applicant. He submitted that the words 'a scheme, rule or method for performing a mental act' in section 1(2)(c) only excluded schemes, rules or methods which were intended to be performed and were capable of being performed in the human mind. He submitted that the word 'for' introduced a subjective element. Thus, as claim 1 had as its basis steps which were not intended to be carried out by a human, in that the human mind would not go through those steps, the basis of the claim was not excluded matter.
>
> The word 'for' does not, in my view, introduce a subjective element. It means 'for the purposes of'. The fact that the scheme, rule or method is part of a computer program and is therefore converted into steps which are suitable for use by a person operating the computer does not matter. What is excluded from being patented is a scheme, rule or method for performing a mental act, whatever mental steps or process is involved. As I pointed out in *Gale's Application*, it is a question of fact to be decided in each case whether the claimed invention is

more than a claim to an invention for a disqualified matter. Just as a claim to a disc containing a program can be in fact a claim to an invention for a computer program, so can a claim to steps leading to an answer be a claim to an invention for a performing a mental act. The method remains a method for performing a mental act, whether a computer is used or not. Thus a method of solving a problem, such as advising a person whether he has acted tortiously, can be set out on paper, or incorporated into a computer program. The purpose is the same, to enable advice to be given, which appears to me to be a mental act. Further, the result will be the advice which comes from performance of a mental act. The method may well be different when a computer is used, but to my mind it still remains a method for performing a mental act, whether or not the computer program adopts steps that would not ordinarily be used by the human mind."

Mr Birss submitted that the reasoning in my judgment in *Wang* was flawed. He submitted that it was not possible to perform a mental act using a computer and a claim to a method of using a computer could not be a claim to a method of performing a mental act. As a matter of semantics that may be right, but as has been made clear in *Merrill Lynch* and *Gale,* it is necessary to look at the substance of the application when dealing with the question of whether it is patentable. A claim to a computer operating in a particular way is no more patentable than a claim to a computer program. A claim to a method of carrying out a calculation (a method of performing a mental act) is no more patentable when claimed as being done by a computer than when done on a piece of paper. Methods of performing mental acts, which means methods of the type performed mentally, are unpatentable, unless some concept of technical contribution is present.

The task of arriving at the conclusion I have reached, namely that this appeal should be dismissed, has been made easier by the clear and pertinent submissions of counsel.'

Roch LJ (at 621): 'I agree. The creation of diagrammatic images of physical objects on the visual display units of computers which can be turned, revolved and altered at the bidding of the computer operator is not new. In my opinion, what the appellants have done here is no more than to produce, brilliant though it may be, a new computer program. The invention may be new but as it is no more than a computer program it is not patentable.'

COMMENT

Leave to appeal to the House of Lords was refused. Do you think leave to appeal should have been granted? Some aspects of the judgment of Aldous LJ are, arguably, unsatisfactory.

Computer programs, even if they clear the exclusion as computer programs *as such*, may fail on the basis of being a method for performing a mental act. This latter exception, as interpreted in this case and previous cases in England, is potentially very wide ranging.

The wide interpretation taken by Aldous LJ means that the exclusion may apply even if the algorithm used in the computer program is completely different to that used in the human mind. Furthermore, it may still apply even if it would be impossible or unrealistic for a human to attempt the mental act, for example because of the length of time and massive number of processing operations involved. Do you think a better approach would be to limit the exception to methods for performing a mental act which could or are carried out in practice by human beings? If it was, would this cause any practical difficulties for the court in determining whether the exception applied?

What is more important, the substance or the form of a patent application? Is it true that, for patent specifications and claims, the primary focus should be on the form rather than the substance?

The TRIPS Agreement (see the relevant extracts at the end of this chapter) does not expressly exclude computer programs as such from patentability. The Fujitsu invention was granted a patent in Japan.

A cynical view of the *Fujitsu* case is that all the reasoning and that part of the decision (the major part) dealing with the exclusions were totally unnecessary. The case could simply have been dealt with by refusing a patent on the ground that the invention lacked novelty, that it did no more than automate a process that used to be done manually, using physical models instead of computer images. Roch LJ says this but then goes on, in his brief statement, to contradict himself by saying the invention is new!

Ownership and Employees

Many inventions are made by employees and, usually, it will be the employer who will be entitled to be the proprietor of the patent. The employee will be named as inventor, however. The rules for ownership of employee inventions are somewhat different to those applying to copyright works and extend to situations where the employee has a special obligation to further the interests of the employer.

Harris' Patent [1985] RPC 19, Patents Court

Harris invented an improved version of a slide valve (known as a 'Wey valve') for controlling the flow of material such as coal dust through a duct. When he made the invention Harris worked for a company (Reiss Engineering) which made Wey valves under licence to a Swiss Company (Sistag). He was employed as a Sales Manager and, at the time he made the invention, he had been notified of his redundancy. Harris filed his patent application in 1979 and his employer sought a declaration that it was entitled to the patent.

Falconer J (at 38): 'It is in considerations of this sort that, in my view, as I have already indicated, guidance may be offered by the earlier cases decided before the coming into operation of the statutory provisions as to employees' inventions contained in the Patents Act 1977. It will suffice to refer to two of those earlier cases, both of which were cited to me, as they were to the superintending examiner.

In *Worthington Pumping Engine Co.* v *Moore* (1903) 20 RPC 41, always regarded as a leading authority in this field, the defendant was a vice-president of the plaintiff company, an American corporation, and head and responsible manager of, and with sole control of, the English branch of their business and conducting their business outside the United States of America and Canada. His salary was $10,000 per annum, a very large salary by any standards at the turn of the century - I should interpolate that the case was heard in 1903 - and in addition he received a commission on sales. His position and the nature of his obligations were described by Byrne J thus at page 46, line 1:

"I do not think I shall be wrong in saying that the defendant was in effect the alter ego of the plaintiff corporation outside the United States. The correspondence which has been referred to in the case shows that the relationship between the plaintiff corporation in America and the defendant as their agent and manager in England was of the closest and most confidential character. The requirements of customers and the methods of meeting new wants and demands was the subject of frequent communications between them, and I think it is beyond question that it was part of the defendant's duty to communicate and consult with the head office about any modifications and alterations in construction required to suit the demands of customers, and to offer such suggestions as might occur to him as advantageous to the plaintiff corporation in relation to the business he controlled. I think that he would not have been acting in accordance with the good faith implied in his contract had he kept back new ideas or details of construction suggested or carried out in the ordinary course of business between the parties (even though such ideas or details might have been in the hands of a third person properly subject-matter for Patent) with a view to his personal profit at the expense of the plaintiff corporation. It appears to me that the degree of good faith due from the defendant to the plaintiff company was little, if at all, less than that required from a partner towards the firm of which he is a member."

It was held that two patents which he had taken out in his own name but employed in the plaintiff company's business were held by him in trust for the plaintiff company.

In *Charles Selz Ltd.'s Application* (1954) 71 RPC 158 the respondent was the manager of a factory making lampshades. While on a visit, in the course of his duties as such manager, to a trade exhibition, he saw a demonstration of a process for plastic packaging by spraying and appreciated it might be applied to make plastic coatings to frameworks for display articles and signs and also for making lampshades. He applied for a patent and his employers sought, in effect, a declaration that any patent granted would be held in trust for them. Lloyd-Jacob J upheld the decision of the assistant comptroller rejecting the employers' claim, finding that the respondent had not at any time been directed to apply his mind for the purpose of devising an invention or anything in the nature of an invention and had no express duty to consider the possibility of finding some additional scope for the activities of his company and that in the circumstances the invention belonged to the respondent.

In his consideration of the appellants' case under paragraph (b) of section 39(1), the superintending examiner stated his finding as to the status, duties and responsibilities of Mr Harris in these terms:

"... it is contended that by reason of his position as Manager of the Way valve department, a position of trust and responsibility, Mr Harris had a particular and special obligation to further Reiss's interests. Mr Pumfrey submitted that he was better paid than most other employees, being a manager and senior employee of great experience. Details of salary are given in exhibit HFSR.5, but contrary to any impression that may be given thereby he was not the only member of staff to receive 'perks' such as a bonus and use of a company car, as became clear in the later evidence.

Mr Harris did receive a salary only just short of the maximum shown on the list in that exhibit, but in spite of the suggestion that he had a position of special responsibility, it is clear that his powers were extremely limited. For example he was not involved in the hiring or discharging of staff, or even the agreeing of holiday dates. He did not attend board meetings, even as a manager when his department might have been under discussion. Certainly, in my view, his position in Reiss Engineering bears no relation to the position of Moore in *Worthington*, and he was clearly not the alter ego of Reiss."

As to Mr Harris's salary, I would just add that it was £6,900 per annum at the time he received the letter of 4 August 1978 informing him of his redundancy ...

There is one incident in evidence which throws some light on the nature of Mr Harris's duties and responsibilities. In paragraph 4 of the counterstatement an occasion is referred to when Mr Harris attempted to suggest an improvement to a Wey valve, but was instructed not to consider improvements to the valves which he sold, but to limit his endeavours to sales of the valves. Mr Reiss in paragraph 17 of his first declaration stated he had no recollection of any such conversation, but Mr Harris testified to it in paragraph 20 of his first declaration and that it took place in the presence of Mr Nott-Macaire, a former draughtsman, who was, in fact, Mr Harris's assistant. Mr Nott-Macaire in his declaration testifies to the incident and that "Mr Reiss made it clear that he was not interested and wanted Mr Harris simply to get on with the job of selling the valves".

It seems to me that, having regard to his status and the nature of his duties and responsibilities, as they were in fact under that status, the obligation which he had by reason of the nature of his duties and particular responsibilities arising therefrom was no more than to do the best he could to effect sales of the Wey valves which Reiss Engineering sold, valves made by Sistag or strictly to Sistag's drawings, and to ensure to customers after-sales service of valves supplied. Beyond that obligation, in my judgment, he had no special obligation to further the interests of Reiss Engineering's valve business. Accordingly, I hold that Mr Harris's invention is not one falling within paragraph (b) of section 39(1).'

COMMENT

The nature of the employment is an obvious key to the question of entitlement to an employee invention. The seniority of the employee's position might also be relevant. Would any invention made by the managing director of a company that was useful to that company and related to that company's line of business always be deemed to belong to the company? What if the employee was a sales director? What would the position be where an invention was disclosed to the company by an employee, for example, by way of a company suggestions scheme?

British Steel PLC's Patent [1992] RPC 117, Patent Office

Some inventions can bring massive returns and huge profits to a company. Section 40 of the Patents Act 1977 has a provision for compensation to be paid to an employee by his employer if the invention proves to be of outstanding benefit. In this case, the employee designed a new valve for a vessel used in steel-making. It proved to be a significant advance and the employee was awarded an MBE and received an *ex gratia* payment of £10,000 from his employer. He applied for compensation under section 40.

Dr P Ferdinando (at 121): 'It is common ground between the parties that the invention was regarded as a great advance. In British Steel's own publicity, as well as in reports in the press, the rotary valve was variously described as a "key development", "a world beater", "revolutionary", "miracle valve", "vital cost-saving technology", "a winner". Mr Broughton, however, suggested that it was significant that this high degree of praise was lavished chiefly in the early stages of the life of the rotary valve, before its development for full-scale practical application ... It is agreed that the application is made under section 40(1), which reads:

> "Where it appears to the court or the comptroller on an application made by an employee within the prescribed period that the employee has made an invention belonging to the employer for which a patent has been granted, that the patent is (having regard among other things to the size and nature of the employer's undertaking) of outstanding benefit to the employer and that by reason of those facts it is just that the employee should be awarded compensation to be paid by the employer, the court or the comptroller may award him such compensation of an amount determined under section 41 below."

Mr Tritton and Mr Broughton both made submissions to me about the interpretation to be placed on this sub-section, and on particular words and phrases used in it. In this respect I was referred to the sole precedent case, an unreported Patent Office decision dated 8 February 1989 regarding Ellis's application for an award in respect of GEC Avionics Ltd.'s patent No. 2088079 (hereafter "GEC"). I think it appropriate at the outset for me to consider these matters in the context of the present application, since they determine what the applicant's evidence must demonstrate if he is to be successful ...

Secondly, section 40(1) specifies that regard must be had to the "size and nature of the employer's *undertaking*" (my emphasis). The question arises as to what precisely is the "undertaking" to which I must have regard in reaching a decision in this case. In the present case, the only firm evidence which has been supplied has concerned the size and nature of British Steel's operation considered as a whole. I pressed Mr Tritton for clarification of whether this, or a particular sector of it, constituted the "undertaking" in respect of which the application had been made, but I did not find his submissions altogether clear in this regard. Although he noted that the evidence established that the patented valve had been used by British Steel only at its South Teesside works, and suggested that the benefit needed to be judged in that context, he also stated that he regarded the "undertaking" as relating to British Steel in its entirety. There being no clear argument or evidence leading me otherwise, I have no option in this case but to have regard to the size and nature of the undivided totality of the British Steel operation. In coming to this conclusion, though, I do not rule out the possibility that in appropriate circumstances, and when supported by evidence to justify such an interpretation, the proper "undertaking" to be considered might be constituted by a particular sector or site of the employer's total organisation.

Thirdly, sub-section (1) makes clear that the patent must be of "outstanding" benefit if the application is to succeed. Mr Tritton submitted that, taken at face value, this indicated that the patent must stand out from the rest. In *GEC*, the hearing officer noted that the statute did not use words such as "significant" or "substantial", and opined that 'something out of the ordinary was required'. While Mr Tritton was plainly correct in describing "outstanding" as a comparative term, I would regard it as going further than that, implying a superlative. The test I must apply in reaching my decision as to whether an award is warranted must be correspondingly stiff.

The final point of interpretation I need to deal with in relation to section 40(1) concerns the distinction to be drawn between the patent and the patented invention in assessing the benefit enjoyed by the employer. The hearing officer addressed this point in some detail in the *GEC* case, and concluded "that the initial evidential burden of raising a *prima facie* case to show that no benefit is derived from the patent falls on the patentee". In circumstances where the patentee "secures a monetary benefit from goods or services which are the subject of an invention, there is a presumption where that invention is covered by a patent, that at least a part of that benefit derives from the patent". In other words, if the patentee cannot demonstrate *prima facie* that he derived no benefit from the patent, then it is to be assumed that any benefit he derived from the invention is at least partly due to the existence of the patent ...

Thus, the total benefit to British Steel of the patented invention for which I am satisfied that there is evidentiary support amounts to between £100,000 and £500,000 a year. I am required by section 40(1) to decide whether this benefit is outstanding having regard to the size and nature of the employer's undertaking. For the reasons I elaborated earlier, I am obliged in doing so to set the total benefit against the overall British Steel PLC operation, which in 1988/89 had a turnover of some £4900 million and a pre-tax profit of £593 million. The proven benefit therefore represents no more than 0.01% of turnover or 0.08% of profits. In this context, even if the benefits of the patented invention were to be considered due wholly to the patent, it does not appear to me that they can be described as "outstanding".

Although it is not strictly necessary for me to do so, for the sake of completeness I shall briefly consider what the position would be if I had accepted all of Mr Monks' assertions about the benefits British Steel enjoyed from the use of the patented invention. Assuming one major incident avoided a year, the annual benefit comes to £5,428,000. This is only some 0.11% of turnover and 0.92% of profits for British Steel PLC. Even on this basis, I would not feel about to adjudge the benefit as being "outstanding".

A number of Mr Broughton's counters to Mr Monks' claim that particular benefits had arisen from the use of the rotary valve were to the effect that, even had the rotary valve not been developed, some other new development would have emerged to produce comparable advantage. I would observe that I do not regard this as an effective argument in itself, at least in relation to the estimation of benefit *per se*. Section 40 requires me, in deciding whether to order an award, to consider real benefits, not hypothetical ones, and a benefit calculated for a particular invention is not, in my view, diminished by the possibility that a different invention might have produced a similar benefit, though this might have some bearing on whether I considered the benefit to be outstanding.

Several of Mr Tritton's submissions went to the notion that the benefit of the patented invention, and so of the patent, would have been greater to British Steel had its exploitation been more effectively pursued. The principle of such an argument is not one which fits comfortably with section 40(1), which requires that "the patent is (...) of outstanding benefit" to the employer. As I have already indicated, I take this to mean that the benefit needs to be actual, not potential; whether an employer patentee chooses to exploit an invention may depend as much on his commercial strategy as on the intrinsic worth of the invention. In the present instance, British Steel has sought to exploit the invention, but the argument that it could have done so more successfully is not in my view germane for the same reasoning.

Notwithstanding that I regard the basic principle of the argument flawed ...

In summary, while I recognise that the rotary valve is a valuable invention, I am not satisfied that, at least at this stage in the life of the patent, it can be adjudged to be of outstanding benefit to the patentee having regard *inter alia* to the size and nature of its undertaking. In the light of my findings, I make no order for the payment of compensation under section 40(1).

Incidental to the main proceedings, I feel I should comment on an observation made by Mr Broughton to the effect that had I decided that an award should be made, an enquiry similar to that usual in infringement proceedings should follow. It seems to me that section 40 proceedings are not such as would call for an enquiry; they are in this sense more akin to the determination of an appropriate royalty in licence of right proceedings. Had I been minded to make an award, on the basis of the evidence, I should also have decided on that basis what it should be. I believe I should have borne in mind the size of the benefit derived from the patent, and that reasonably expected to be derived, having regard to Mr Monks' salary of about £14,000 and the awards he had already received for his invention, namely the £10,000 *ex gratia* payment from British Steel and the MBE. In view of my finding, however, that is not now necessary.'

COMMENT

What if the employer fails to take full advantage of the patent? The case shows that 'outstanding' means what it says. Do you think many employees receive compensation under Section 40? Of course, employees receive income through their salary or wages. If an employee is engaged to carry out research and development, would he be entitled to compensation if he invented, in the normal course of his employment, an invention of truly outstanding benefit to his employer?

Infringement and Claims

The scope of the monopoly granted by a patent is determined, in legal terms, from the patent claims. It is the claims against which an alleged infringement will be measured and it is, therefore, essential that the manner in which they are interpreted is well-settled. However, patent claims can be very complex and highly technical and patent agents tend to use language to increase the robustness of the claims. For example, rather than say 'two' or 'three' or even 'two or three' a patent agent will tend to say 'a plurality'. Another factor is that patent claims are written, primarily, for technical persons so that they can evaluate the state of the art or determine whether their planned course of action is likely to infringe an existing patent. The *Catnic* case shows that interpretation of patent claims is treated differently to the interpretation of conventional legal documents such as contracts or wills.

Catnic Components Ltd. v *Hill & Smith Ltd.* [1982] RPC 183, House of Lords

The plaintiff was the proprietor of a patent relating to steel lintels of a box-section type of design. The plaintiff sued for infringement and the defendant modified its design including the rear member by 6 to 8 degrees from the vertical. The relevant patent claim described the rear member as 'extending vertically' and the defendant argued that its modified lintel was outside the claim because the rear member was not vertical. The Court of Appeal held that an essential feature of the relevant claim was that the rear member should extend vertically and, as a result, there was no infringement. The plaintiff appealed to the House of Lords which upheld the appeal.

Lord Diplock (at 242): 'Whitford J held that on the proper interpretation of the claim the modified design DH4 did not amount to what he described as an "infringement in terms", but he went on to hold it to be an infringement under the "pith and marrow doctrine".

The majority of the Court of Appeal (Buckley and Waller LLJ) disagreed with the learned judge on the application of the pith and marrow doctrine to the alleged infringement: the third member (Sir David Cairns) would have upheld his judgment. There was no discernible difference of opinion between the three members of the court as to the applicable law, which they derived principally from the speeches in this House in *Van Der Lely N.V.* v *Bamfords Ltd.* [1963] RPC 61 and *Rodi and Weinenberger A.G.* v *Harry Showell Ltd.* [1969] RPC 367. Where they differed was as to the application of the law to the facts of the instant case. Buckley LJ was of the opinion that although it was not in fact essential to the working of the invention that the back plate should be precisely vertical (i.e. at an angle of 90° exactly to the horizontal) the patentee nevertheless by the language used in his specification had made such precision an essential feature of the monopoly he claimed. Waller LJ regarded "vertical," and presumably also the adverb "vertically," as capable only of being used as a word of precision; and for him this was decisive against any claim for infringement by any lintel in which the back plate was not at an angle of 90° exactly to the horizon. Sir David Cairns expressed the view that DH4 was not "a textual infringement" of the patent, but held it to infringe the "pith and marrow" of claim 1.

My Lords, in their closely reasoned written cases in this House and in the oral argument, both parties to this appeal have tended to treat "textual infringement" and infringement of the "pith and marrow" of an invention as if they were separate causes of action, the existence of the former to be determined as a matter of construction only and of the latter upon some broader principle of colourable evasion. There is, in my view, no such dichotomy; there is but a single cause of action and to treat it otherwise, particularly in cases like that which is the subject of the instant appeal, is liable to lead to confusion.

The expression "no textual infringement" has been borrowed from the speeches in this House in the hay-rake case. *Van Der Lely* v *Bamfords,* where it was used by several of their Lordships as a convenient way of saying that the word "hindmost" as descriptive of rake wheels to be dismounted could not as a matter of linguistics mean "foremost": but this did not exhaust the question of construction of the specification that was determinative of whether there had been an infringement of the claim or not. It left open the question whether the patentee had made his reference to the "hindmost" (rather than any other wheels) as those to be dismounted, an essential feature of the monopoly that he claimed. It was on this question that there was a division of opinion in this House and in the Court of Appeal in the hay-rack case.

My Lords, a patent specification is a unilateral statement by the patentee, in words of his own choosing, addressed to those likely to have a practical interest in the subject matter of his invention (i.e. "skilled in the art"), by which he informs them what he claims to be the essential features of the new product or process for which the letters patent grant him a monopoly. It is those novel features only that he claims to be essential that constitute the so-called "pith and marrow" of the claim. A patent specification should be given a purposive construction rather than a purely literal one derived from applying to it the kind of meticulous verbal analysis in which lawyers are too often tempted by their training to indulge. The question in each case is; whether persons with practical knowledge and experience of the kind of work in which the invention was intended to be used, would understand that strict compliance with a particular descriptive word or phrase appearing in a claim was intended by the patentee to be an essential requirement of the invention so that any variant would fall outside the monopoly claimed, even though it could have no material effect upon the way the invention worked.

The question, of course, does not arise where the variant would in fact have a material effect upon the way the invention worked. Nor does it arise unless at the date of publication of the specification it would be obvious to the informed reader that this was so. Where it is not obvious, in the light of then-existing knowledge, the reader is entitled to assume that the patentee thought at the time of the specification that he had good reason for limiting his monopoly so strictly and had intended to do so, even though subsequent work by him or others in the field of the invention might show the limitation to have been unnecessary. It is to be answered in the negative only when it would be apparent to any reader skilled in the art that a particular descriptive word or phrase used in a claim cannot have been intended by a patentee, who was also skilled in the art, to exclude minor variants which, to the knowledge of both him and the readers to whom the patent was addressed, could have no material effect upon the way in which the invention worked.

My Lords, upon analysis of the speeches in this House in *Van Der Lely* v *Bamfords* the division of opinion between Lord Reid and the remainder of their Lordships appears to have been due to his thinking that it would be obvious to the informed reader that dismounting the "foremost" rather than the "hindmost" wheels was an immaterial variant, whereas the majority were not satisfied that this was even the fact, let alone that it was obviously so. In the bracelet case, *Rodi and Weinenberger A.G.* v *Harry Showell Ltd.* (ubi sup.) where this House was more evenly divided, the difference between the majority and the minority appears to have turned upon their respective views as to whether the particular variant alleged to be an infringement, had a material effect upon what were claimed to be the advantages obtained by the patented invention - as to which they differed. In the third of the trilogy of leading cases in this House upon this topic, the ampicillin case, *Beecham Group Ltd.* v *Bristol Laboratories Ltd.* [1977] FSR 215; [1978] RPC 153, the descriptive phrase was "an amino group in the alpha position". In the alleged infringing antibiotic, hetacillin, this amino group had been temporarily converted by a further chemical reaction into a molecular structure that was no longer an amino group, but the reaction was reversible and upon being put to use as an antibiotic, (which necessitated contact with water) it reverted to its original form as an amino group and in that form produced its prophylactic effects. This House unanimously held that this temporary masking of the amino group amounted to an immaterial variant. It would be obvious to anyone skilled in the specialised art of selecting and synthesising polymers for use as antibiotics that the essential feature of the invention was that when put to use for its intended purpose, the product should have an amino group in the alpha position; and that, accordingly, the patentee's reference to this feature of his claim cannot have been intended by him to exclude products in which the amino group in that position was temporarily displaced during a period before the product was put to any prophylactic use.

The essential features of the invention that is the subject of claim 1 of the patent in suit in the instant appeal are much easier to understand than those of any of the three patents to which I have just referred; and this makes the question of its construction simpler. Put in a nutshell the question to be answered is: Would the specification make it obvious to a builder familiar with ordinary building operations that the description of a lintel in the form of a weight-bearing box girder of which the back plate was referred to as "extending vertically" from one of the two horizontal plates to join the other, could *not* have been intended to exclude lintels in which the back plate although not positioned at precisely 90° to both horizontal plates was close enough to 90° to make no material difference to the way the lintel worked when used in building operations? No plausible reason has been advanced why any rational patentee should want to place so narrow a limitation on his invention. On the contrary, to do so would tender his monopoly for practical purposes worthless, since any imitator could avoid it and take all the benefit of the invention by the simple expedient of positioning the back plate a degree or two from the exact vertical.

It may be that when used by a geometer addressing himself to fellow geometers, such expressions descriptive of relative position as "horizontal", "parallel", "vertical" and "vertically" are to be understood as words of precision only; but when used in a description of a manufactured product intended to perform the practical function of a weight-bearing box girder in supporting courses of brickwork over windows and door spaces in buildings, it seems to me that the expression "extending vertically" as descriptive of the position of what in use will be the upright member of a trapezoid-shaped box girder, is perfectly capable of meaning positioned near enough to the exact geometrical vertical to enable it in actual use to perform satisfactorily all the functions that it could perform if it were precisely vertical; and having regard to those considerations to which I have just referred that is the sense in which in my opinion "extending vertically" would be understood by a builder familiar with ordinary building operation. Or, putting the same thing in another way, it would be obvious to him that the patentee did not intend to make exact verticality in the positioning of the back plate an essential feature of the invention claimed.

My Lords, if one analyses line by line the ways in which the various expressions are used in the specification, one can find pointers either way as to whether in particular lines various adjectives and adverbs descriptive of relative position are used as words of precision or not. Some of these are discussed in the judgments of the majority of the Court of Appeal who found the pointers in favour of precision stronger than those to the contrary, of which one example is the description of the two "horizontal" plates as being only "*substantially* parallel". For my part I find the result of such analysis inconclusive and of little weight as compared with the broad considerations to which I have referred and which are a consequence of giving as I think one should, a purposive construction to the specification.

It follows that I have reached the same conclusion as the trial judge and Sir David Cairns, although not by the route of drawing a distinction between "textual infringement" and infringement of the "pith and marrow" of the invention. Accordingly I would allow the appeal.'

COMMENT

What is the 'pith and marrow' of an invention? What does the word 'vertical' mean? Is the purposive approach to interpretation of patent claims fair or even workable? *Catnic* was decided under the 1949 Act. Although frequently used and approved under the 1977 Act, in *PLG Research Ltd.* v *Ardon International Ltd.* [1995] FSR 116, Neill LJ doubted its appropriateness, saying that if it was the same as the Protocol under Article 69 of the European Patent Convention (on the interpretation of claims) it was unnecessary or, if it was different, it should no longer be used. However, subsequent case law has firmly defended the continued ability of the *Catnic* test as being valuable guidance as to the application of the Protocol. See, for example, *Assidoman Multipack Ltd.* v *The Mead Corp.* [1995] FSR 225 and *Kastner* v *Rizler Ltd.* [1995] RPC 585. The approach in *Catnic* mirrors that taken in respect of the European Patent Convention and is discussed in the extract from the article by Sherman below.

Sherman, B., *Patent Claim Interpretation: The Impact of the Protocol on Interpretation* (1991) 54 MLR 499

'Introduction

The European Patent Convention (EPC), signed in Munich in 1973, marked an important turning point in the patent laws of the various contracting states. While the main aim of the EPC was to provide an efficient mechanism for the grant of European patents, in order to achieve this end it was also necessary to ensure that the substantive patent laws of the contracting states were harmonised. Much of the groundwork for the task of harmonisation had, however, already been laid by the 1963 Strasbourg Convention. For our purposes, one of the most important decisions made at the Strasbourg Convention was the agreement that the role of the patent claims was to demarcate the scope of the monopoly. This provision was adopted by the drafters of the EPC and is now to be found in Article 69 of the EPC (Section 125(1) Patents Act 1977). One of the problems facing the drafters of the EPC, however, was the fear that the harmonisation of patent laws would be hindered by the idiosyncratic interpretations of the national courts. In part, it was this fear of divergency of interpretation that led the drafters of the EPC to take the unprecedented step of attaching to Article 69 the Protocol on Interpretation. This is, in effect, an attempt to ensure uniformity of interpretation by stipulating the permissible readings of the patent claims.

The Protocol on Interpretation reads:

> Article 69 should not be interpreted in the sense that the extent of the protection conferred by a European patent is to be understood as that defined by the strict literal meaning of the working used in the claims, the description and drawings being employed only for the purposes of resolving ambiguity found in the claims. Neither should it be interpreted in the sense that the claims serve only as a guideline and that the actual protection conferred may extend to what, from a consideration of the description and drawings by a person skilled in the art, the patentee has contemplated. On the contrary, it is to be interpreted as defining a position between these extremes which combines a fair protection for the patentee with a reasonable degree of certainty for third parties.

It is the aim of this paper to examine the Protocol on Interpretation, its effects upon the interpretation of patent claims and the lessons that the Protocol offers to other areas of intellectual property law. The first section of the paper briefly outlines two recent decisions in EPC countries in which different approaches to the interpretation of the claims were adopted, decisions which suggest that the Protocol has not fulfilled the aim of harmonising interpretation. Given that these differences could be remedied by the introduction of an Appeal Court, or a change in interpretation, these conclusions are hardly startling. What is important, however, are the reasons for the Protocol's ineffectiveness in regulating patent claim interpretation. In the second section of the paper some of these reasons will be examined. The third and final section examines whether, in the light of these findings, it is correct to suggest that the Protocol has failed.

Interpretation and Infringement

Given the relationship between the various member countries of the EPC, it is not surprising that there are many similarities as to the way patent claims are to be read. These similarities range from the basic agreement as to the use of purposive interpretation as the standard form of interpretation, through to a general acceptance of the doctrine of equivalents. Despite this initial agreement, as the Bundesgerichshof said recently, "significant differences [still exist] both with respect to the method of determination of the factual scope of protection of patents and the scope of protection granted". Perhaps the best example of the different approaches to, and the importance of, the interpretation of the patent claims can be seen in the recent decisions in Germany (*Improver Corporation* v *Remington Products, Landgericht* (Regional Court) Dusseldorf, 30 December 1988) and the UK (*Improver Corporation* v *Remington Products,* [1990] FSR 181) concerning the alleged infringement of the Improver Corporation patent. The primary question in these cases was whether the Improver Corporation's patents had been infringed by the manufacture and sale of the Remington Corporation's "Smooth and Silky" shaver in the respective jurisdictions. The patent in suit was a European patent, issued by the

European Patent Office and designated valid for a considerable number of contracting states including the UK and West Germany. The interesting feature of these decisions is that with fixed subject matter - that is, the patent and the infringing article - being interpreted in the light of identical (or very similar) laws, the cases can be read like a controlled experiment in legal interpretation.

While there were a number of important differences at the interlocutory stages of the actions, the most striking difference arose in the trial decisions where, in the UK, Hoffmann J found for the defendant, while in Germany the Landegericht (District Court) of Dusseldorf found in favour of the plaintiff. The primary reason for these conflicting conclusions was that the claims were interpreted differently by the respective courts. That is, despite both courts expressly referring to and utilising the Protocol, two alternative interpretations of the claims were adopted, with the consequence that the ultimate decisions were different. As the reasoning used is not important for the purposes of this paper, suffice it to say that the main difference between the decisions lay with Hoffmann J's reliance upon the language of the claims (and a corresponding willingness to limit them to their primary or literal meaning), whereas the German court interpreted the claims from the standpoint of the person skilled in the art, adopting the "open" style traditional in that country (and indeed, most others on the Continent).

Undoubtedly, if the differences as to the interpretation of patent claims outlined in the *Improver Corporation* decisions continue, they will lead to irreconcilable differences as to the understanding of Article 69 and its Protocol between the British courts on the one hand, and the German (and probably other Continental) courts on the other. A consequence of this will be that patents granted in the same terms by the European Patent Office may well be treated as being of crucially different scope in different EPC states. Since one of the central features of a harmonised legal system is the uniformity of approach and interpretation, the current differences can only serve as a barrier to the aims of the EPC.

The differing interpretations of similar terms of the EPC is not, however, without precedent, and in the absence of an overriding appeal body, not surprising. While the current differences in understanding may, like the divergences surrounding the second medical use exception, be remedied by a change in interpretation, or the introduction of a Patents Appeal court, these decisions remind us that the aim of the Protocol, that is to harmonise patent interpretation, has not, and arguably can never be, achieved in the manner in which it was designed ...'

COMMENT

What would the effect be if a strict literal interpretation was always applied to patent claims? Is a purposive approach simply a concession to bad drafting? What is a variant? How does one decide whether a variant infringes?

Defences

A patent gives the proprietor such a powerful right that it is not surprising that a large number of defences are provided for. Private and non-commercial acts or acts done for experimental purposes do not infringe. Acts done in good faith before the priority date also do not infringe. 'Euro-defences' based on the Treaty of Rome may be available, depending on the circumstances. In many cases, the defendant to an infringement action may put the validity of the patent in issue under section 70, perhaps claiming that it is not a patentable invention within the meaning of section 1 of the Act. One defence in particular has been described as draconian. This is where, at the time of the infringement, there was a contract of licence in force which contained a term or condition void by virtue of section 44. This is a complete defence and an example of its successful use is given below.

Chiron Corp. v Organon Teknika Ltd. (No.3) [1994] FSR 202, Patents Court

The facts are briefly outlined earlier in this chapter.

Aldous J (at 246): 'The defendants allege that they have a defence to the action as a term or terms of licences offend section 44 of the Patents Act 1977. [The judge then recited section 44 (see chapter 1)] ... Chiron and Ortho Diagnostic Systems Inc. entered into a written agreement on 3 October 1986. That agreement was followed by another written agreement dated 17 August 1989. Under Clause 5.1 of that Agreement Chiron granted "to Ortho an exclusive worldwide license, without the right to sub-licence except to principal affiliates ... to the Chiron know-how and any existing Chiron patents ..."

Under the Agreement Ortho obtained an exclusive licence under *inter alia* the patent in suit. Clause 6.1 of the 1989 Agreement applied to supply of antigens and antibodies. It stated:

6.1 *Supply.* Chiron, within the limitations contained in this Article, shall supply Ortho with such quantities of Raw Material manufactured under GMP conditions as Ortho may require for manufacture and sale of Products. Ortho agrees during the term of this Agreement to obtain solely from Chiron all raw materials that Ortho requires ...

The defendants submitted that Clause 6.1 contravened section 44(1)(b); thus it was void and they had a defence pursuant to section 44(3). They submitted that the 1989 Agreement was, *inter alia,* both a patent licence and a contract for the supply of a patented product. Clause 6.1 required Ortho, the licensee, to acquire from Chiron the licensor, and also prohibited Ortho from acquiring from anybody except Chiron Raw Material, e.g. Antigens for HIV, which were not the patented product (HCV products).

The plaintiffs submitted that the 1989 Agreement was an agreement between the two United States companies seeking to co-operate and that section 44 was not directed to preventing such co-operation. They submitted that at the date of the Agreement, 17 August 1989, there was no United Kingdom patent and therefore section 44 did not apply as section 44 was only concerned with the conditions or terms of a contract for the supply of a patented product or a licence to work a patented invention. They submitted that as section 130 defined a patented product as "means any product which is a patented invention, or, in relation to a patented process, a product obtained directly by means of the process or to which the process has been applied" and the word patent was defined as "a patent under this Act," section 44 only applied where the relevant patent was granted before the agreement was concluded.

I cannot accept the plaintiffs' submissions. The 1989 Agreement must be construed as of August of that year. At that date, the patent in suit had been applied for and the Agreement contemplated that Ortho would, upon grant, become exclusive licensees under the patent. The agreement licenses Ortho under the patent and sets out conditions for the supply of certain products.

I conclude that the defendants are right. Clause 6.1 falls within section 44(1)(b).

I suspect that the plaintiffs realised that it was at least possible that Clause 6.1 of the 1989 Agreement fell within section 44(1)(b). After the defendants pleaded that section 44 gave them a defence, Chiron and Ortho entered into a waiver agreement

...

The plaintiffs relying on the terms of the waiver submitted that, in so far as exports were still restricted, that restriction could not be a term or condition of the grant of the United Kingdom patent licence. It was only a term of the collaboration agreement between Chiron and Ortho having no connection with the United Kingdom patent. That submission is, I believe, wrong. The agreement is a collaboration agreement, but it is also a licence to Ortho to work the United Kingdom patent. Tied to that licence is an agreement that Ortho will buy Raw Material from Chiron for use for kit manufacture. Thus if Ortho want to manufacture such material in the United Kingdom and export it to another country for kit manufacture, they must purchase it from Chiron, whether it is patented or not. Such an obligation offends section 44(1)(b) ...

I cannot accept that submission. An exclusive licensee obtains his right to sue under section 67 of the Act. That section states:

Subject to the provisions of this section, the holder of an exclusive licence under a patent shall have the same right as the proprietor of the patent to bring proceedings in respect of any infringement of the patent committed after the date of the licence; and references to the proprietor of the patent in the provisions of this Act relating to infringement shall be construed accordingly.

Thus Ortho Ltd. has the same right to bring proceedings as Chiron and I do not believe that it has any better right than Chiron. Thus if section 44(3) prevents Chiron succeeding in this action, Ortho Ltd. cannot succeed either.'

COMMENT

What would the position have been had the agreement been dated before the first filing of the patent application? Clearly, great care must be taken when drafting patent licences or contracts for the supply of patented products.

Remedies

Remedies for infringement of a patent, set out in section 61 of the Patents Act 1977, are: an injunction, an order for delivery up or destruction, damages, an account of profits and a declaration that the patent is valid and infringed by the defendant. Damages and accounts are, as usual, alternatives.

The determination of the quantum of damages has long been a thorny problem. Using as a basis the 'willing licensor' and 'willing licensee' concept (that is what the defendant would have paid in licence fees had he obtained a licence from the plaintiff) will only work in a limited number of cases. The proprietor may not want to grant licences, preferring to work the patent himself. What would have been a monopoly has been turned into a duopoly by the defendant's act with all the economic consequences that follow. The case below resulted from an argument about the measure of damages to be awarded as a result of the patent infringement action discussed earlier in this chapter and includes a useful discussion of the assessment of damages in patent cases.

General Tire and Rubber v Firestone Tyre and Rubber Co. Ltd. [1976] RPC 197, House of Lords

The facts are briefly outlined earlier in this chapter.

Lord Wilberforce (at 211): 'Examination of these various bases of computation must necessarily be preceded by some statement of legal principle. This I can do fairly briefly since I do not believe that there is much room for dispute. One who infringes the patent of another commits a tort, the foundation of which is made clear by the terms of the grant. This, after conferring the monopoly of profit and advantage upon the patentee, concludes by declaring infringers "answerable to the patentee according to law for his damages thereby occasioned".

As in the case of any other tort (leaving aside cases where exemplary damages can be given) the object of damages is to compensate for loss or injury. The general rule at any rate in relation to "economic" torts is that the measure of damages is to be, so far as possible, that sum of money which will put the injured party in the same position as he would have been in if he had not sustained the wrong (*Livingstone* v *Rawyards Coal Co.* 5 A.C. 25, 39, per Lord Blackburn.)

In the case of infringement of a patent, an alternative remedy at the option of the plaintiff exists by way of an account of profits made by the infringer - see Patents Act, 1949, section 60. The respondents did not elect to claim an account of profits: their claim was only for damages. There are two essential principles in valuing that claim: first, that the plaintiffs have the burden of proving their loss; second, that the defendants being wrongdoers, damages should be liberally assessed but that the object is to compensate the plaintiffs and not punish the defendants (*Pneumatic Tyre Co. Ltd.* v *Puncture Proof Pneumatic Tyre Co. Ltd.* (1899) 16 RPC 209 at page 215).

These elemental principles have been applied in numerous cases of infringements of patents. Naturally their application varies from case to case. Reported authorities, many of which were cited in argument, may be useful as illustrations of judicial reasoning, but are capable of misleading if decisions on a particular set of facts and observations in judgments leading up to such decisions are later relied upon as establishing a rule of law. Nevertheless I think it useful to refer to some of the main groups of reported cases which exemplify the approaches of courts to typical situations.

1. Many patents of inventions belong to manufacturers, who exploit the invention to make articles or products which they sell at a profit. The benefit of the invention in such cases is realised through the sale of the article or product. In these cases if the invention is infringed, the effect of the infringement will be to divert sales from the owner of the patent to the infringer. The measure of damages will then normally be the profit which would have been realised by the owner of the patent if the sales had been made by him (see *The United Horse-shoe and Nail Co. Ltd.* v *John Stewart & Co.* 13 A.C. 401). An example of this is *Boyd* v *The Tootal Broadhust Lee Co.* (1894) 11 RPC 175 where the plaintiff manufacturers proved that a profit of 7/- per spindle would have been made, and settlements of litigation for lesser rates were discarded.
2. Other patents of inventions are exploited through the granting of licences for royalty payments. In these cases, if an infringer uses the invention without a licence, the measure of the damages he must pay will be the sums which he would have paid by way of royalty if instead of acting illegally, he had acted legally. The problem, which is that of the present case - the respondents not being manufacturers in the United Kingdom - is to establish the amount of such royalty. The solution to this problem is essentially and exclusively one of evidence, and as the facts capable of being adduced in evidence are necessarily individual from case to case, the danger is obvious in referring to a particular case and transferring its conclusions to other situations.

Two classic cases under this heading are *Penn* v *Jack* 14 LT 494, LR 5, Eq. 81 and *A.G. für Autogene Aluminium Schweissung* v *London Aluminium Co. Ltd (No. 2)* (1923) 40 RPC 107. In *Penn* v *Jack* the patentee was shown to have approached all users of the invention and to have successfully required the vast majority to pay him a royalty of 2/6d. per horse-power. The defendant was one of the few who refused and it was held that he should pay damages for infringement based on the accepted royalty rate on the basis that he might have expected to have got a licence at the same rate. The *Aluminium* case contains a clear statement by Sargent J.

"... what has to be ascertained is that which the infringer would have had to pay if, instead of infringing the patent, he had come to be licensed under the patent. I do not mean by that that the successful patentee can ascribe any fancy sum which he says he might have charged, but in those cases where he has dealt with his property merely by way of licence, and there have been licences at certain definite rates, there prima facie, apart from any reason to the contrary, the price or royalty which has been arrived at by means of a free bargain between the patentee and the person desiring to use the patented article has been taken as being the price or royalty that presumably would have to be paid by the infringer. In doing that, it seems to me that the court is certainly not treating the infringer unduly harshly; he should at least, in my judgment, have to pay as much as he would in all probability have had to pay had he to deal with the patentee by way of free bargain in the way in which the other persons who took licences did in fact pay."

These are very useful guidelines, but the principle of them must not be misapplied. Before a "going rate" of royalty can be taken as the basis on which an infringer should be held liable, it must be shown that the circumstances in which the going rate was paid are the same or at least comparable with those in which the patentee and the infringer are assumed to strike their bargain. To refer again to *Boyd v Tootal* (ante): when it was argued that because numerous other persons had agreed to pay at the rate of 4/- per spindle the infringer should also pay at that rate (rather than at 7/- per spindle, which represented the normal profit), it was relevant to show that the rate of 4/- was negotiated by way of settlement of litigation in which the validity of the patent was in doubt. This was not the equivalent of that which the court had to assume: for that purpose the patent must be assumed to be valid. This line of argument is very relevant in the present case, for, as I shall show, the appellants adduced a great deal of evidence as to the royalties actually agreed by various licensees, and this was discarded, totally. by the learned judge and the Court of Appeal. They had every right to discard it if the bargains which led to these royalties being agreed were reached in circumstances differing from those which must be assumed when the court is attempting to fix a bargain as between patentee and infringer. The central question in the present case is whether this difference existed.

3. In some cases it is not possible to prove either (as in 1) that there is a normal rate of profit, or (as in 2) that there is a normal, or established, licence royalty. Yet clearly damages must be assessed. In such cases it is for the plaintiff to adduce evidence which will guide the court. This evidence may consist of the practice, as regards royalty, in the relevant trade or in analogous trades: perhaps of expert opinion expressed in publications or in the witness box; possibly of the profitability of the invention; and any other factor on which the judge can decide the measure of loss. Since evidence of this kind is in its nature general and also probably hypothetical, it is unlikely to be of relevance, or if relevant, of weight, in the face of the more concrete and direct type of evidence referred to under (2). But there is no rule of law which prevents the court, even when it has evidence of licensing practice, from taking these more general considerations into account. The ultimate process is one of judicial estimation of the available indications. The true principle, which covers both cases when there have been licences, and those where there have not, remains that stated by Fletcher Moulton, LJ in the *Meters* case: though so often referred to, it always bears recitation.

"There is one case in which I think the manner of assessing damages in the case of sales of infringing articles has almost become a rule of law, and that is where the patentee grants permission to make the infringing article at a fixed price - in other words, where he grants licences at a certain figure. Every one of the infringing articles might then have been rendered a non-infringing article by applying for and getting that permission. The court then takes the number of infringing articles, and multiplies that by the sum that would have had to be paid in order to make the manufacture of that article lawful, and that is the measure of the damage that has been done by the infringement. The existence of such a rule shows that the courts consider that every single one of the infringements was a wrong, and that it is fair where the facts of the case allow the court to get at the damages in that way to allow pecuniary damages in respect of every one of them. I am inclined to think that the court might in some cases, where there did not exist a quoted figure for a licence, estimate the damages in a way closely analogous to this. It is the duty of the defendant to respect the monopoly rights of the plaintiff. The reward to a patentee for his invention is that he shall have the exclusive right to use the invention, and if you want to use it your duty is to obtain his permission. I am inclined to think that it would be right for the court to consider what would have been the price which - although no price was actually quoted - could have reasonably been charged for that permission, and estimate the damage in that way. Indeed, I think that in many cases that would be the safest and best way to arrive at a sound conclusion as to the proper figure. But I am not going to say a word which will tie down future judges and prevent them from exercising their judgment, as best they can in all the circumstances of the case, so as to arrive at that which the plaintiff has lost by reason of the defendant doing certain acts wrongfully instead of either abstaining from doing them, or getting permission to do them rightfully."

(Meters Ltd. v *Metropolitan Gas Meters Ltd.* (1911) 28 RPC 157 at 164-5).

A proper application of this passage, taken in its entirety, requires the judge assessing damages to take into account any licences actually granted and the rates of royalty fixed by them, to estimate their relevance and comparability, to apply them so far as he can to the bargain hypothetically to be made between the patentee and the infringer, and to the extent to which they do not provide a figure on which the damage can be measured, to consider any other evidence, according to its relevance and weight, upon which he can fix a rate of royalty which would have been agreed. If I may anticipate, I have to find that the process carried out by the courts below does not satisfy this requirement ...

I must now consider the reasoning which led the learned judge and the Court of Appeal to reject this basis, for that they totally did. The Court of Appeal generally adopted the learned judge's reasoning but in some respects went further, so that I need not separately discuss the latter. There are two relevant strands in the judgment of the Court of Appeal. First, though citing authorities which, classically, vouch the proposition that the measure of damages is the loss suffered by the plaintiffs through the wrongful act of the defendant, they appear to diverge from this principle in their assessment of the evidence. They recite a contention of the respondents "that the search is not for the amount which they can be shown to have lost in the peculiar circumstances of the case, but what Firestone UK ought fairly to have paid for the use of the invention ... the court (is concerned) to discover ... not what Firestone UK would have paid but what they should have paid". This argument, after discussion, they appear to accept: the appropriate inquiry, they later find, is not to determine what sum the respondents had lost in not negotiating a licence with Firestone UK in (say) 1959, but to put a value on Firestone's use.

Given that the respondents were not claiming an account of profits, the consequence of departing from the conception of loss can only be to discover a *tertium quid* defined, it seems, by reference to what the infringer ought fairly to have paid. But there is no warrant for this in authority or principle; indeed it seems to reflect an inclination towards punitive damages (see *Broome* v *Cassell & Co.Ltd.*

[1972] AC 1027 at page 1089 per Lord Reid). This was disclaimed by counsel in this House.

The second strand can be discerned from two brief extracts:

"In our judgment, a distinction must be drawn between commercial considerations or other matters affecting the value of the subject matter of the supposed negotiations on the one hand and circumstances which have a direct bearing upon the relevant bargaining powers on the other.

When using the royalty method to assess (the value of the use) we must assume that the hypothetical negotiations take place between parties bargaining on equal terms; in other words, there must be eliminated from the circumstances of the supposed market those elements of the circumstances of the actual market which would in any way distort the bargaining powers of the hypothetical negotiators".

My Lords, this passage is, in my opinion, unsupportable in law or in fact. In law it rests upon the hypothesis that what has to be considered, in measuring the loss a patentee sustains through an infringement, is some bargain struck between some abstract licensor and some abstract licensee uncontaminated by the qualities of the actual actors. But this is not so. The "willing licensor" and "willing licensee" to which reference is often made (and I do not object to it so long as we do not import analogies from other fields) is always the actual licensor and the actual licensee who, one assumes, are each willing to negotiate with the other - they bargain as they are, with their strengths and weaknesses, in the market as it exists. It is one thing (and legitimate) to say of a particular bargain that it was not comparable or made in comparable circumstances with the bargain which the court is endeavouring to assume, so as, for example, to reject as comparable a bargain made in settlement of litigation. It is quite another thing to reject matters (other than any doubt as to the validity of the patent itself) of which either side, or both sides, would necessarily and relevantly take account when seeking agreement.'

COMMENT

What is the purpose of damages to be awarded in a case of patent infringement? The plaintiff has the burden of proving the loss suffered and apart from aspects such as lost profit on sales or lost royalties, what other information would be useful? How does the plaintiff determine other effects such as a depression in prices charged for the patented product or products made using a patented process? Are lost parasitic sales allowable? (A parasitic sale is, for example, the sale of non-patented products alongside the sale of patented products.)

Gerber Garment Technology Inc. v Lectra Systems Ltd. [1997] RPC 443, Court of Appeal

The patents which had been infringed related to fabric cutting machines. At the trial, the judge awarded damages for infringement of the patents, damages in respect of non-infringing design machines sold alongside the infringing machines, damages based on the sale of spare parts and servicing the machines. Damages were also awarded for price depression and 'springboard' damages. A substantial part of the damages claimed related to losses to subsidiary companies in which the plaintiff owned all the shares. The defendants appealed.

Staughton LJ (at 451): '*What is the scope of recovery for infringement of a patent?* The rights which a patent confers are demonstrated by section 60 of the Patents Act 1977, which is headed "Meaning of infringement". Subsection (1) deals with what might be called direct infringement; subsections (2) and (3) provide that there is also infringement if a person supplies ...

> any of the means, relating to an essential element of the invention, for putting the invention into effect ...

unless the supply is of a staple commercial product. (I omit provisions which are not relevant for present purposes.)

Mr Hobbs submits that the damages which a patentee can recover from an infringer by way of loss of profits are limited to the profits that would have been earned in activities for which the patent provides a monopoly. In other words, any activities of the infringer that do not in themselves constitute infringements cannot form part of a claim for lost profits. For the purpose of the present case, that submission would disqualify the claim in respect of the CAD systems. They could be sold by the infringers without infringing any right of the patentees; they are not within section 60(2) and (3); at most they are what are called convoyed goods (or "fellow travellers" as I would say), because they are commonly sold together with the patented product. The argument also extends to spare parts, servicing, and the springboard damages which relate to goods sold after the patent has expired.

There is no such limitation to be found in the Patents Act. Section 61(1) deals with remedies, as follows:

> 61. (1) Subject to the following provisions of this Part of this Act, civil proceedings may be brought in the court by the proprietor of a patent in respect of any act alleged to infringe the patent and (without prejudice to any other jurisdiction of the court) in those proceedings a claim may be made -
> (a) for an injunction or interdict restraining the defendant or defender from any apprehended acts of infringement;
> (b) for an order for him to deliver up or destroy any patented product in relation to which the patent is infringed or any article in which that product is inextricably comprised;
> (c) for damages in respect of the infringement;
> (d) for an account of the profits derived by him from the infringement;
> (e) for a declaration or declarator that the patent is valid and has been infringed by him.

There is also subsection (6):

> (6) Subject to the following provisions of this Part of this Act, in determining whether or not to grant any kind of relief claimed under this section and the extent of the relief granted the court or the comptroller shall apply the principles

applied by the court in relation to that kind of relief immediately before the appointed day.

It should be noticed that delivery up or destruction can only be ordered of patented articles, or of any article in which they are inextricably comprised. Naturally enough there could not be an order for delivery up of convoyed items such as the CAD systems. They are not an infringement. It may be that the remedy of an account of profits is also somewhat confined, since it speaks of "profits ... derived from the infringement": see *Encyclopaedia of UK and European Patent Law* para 10-124A and n.(63), *Dart Industries Inc v Decor Corp Pty Ltd.* [1994] FSR 567. As to whether that would include convoyed goods I express no opinion; it seems to me of little or no weight in determining the extent of the words "damages in respect of the infringement" in section 61(1).

Infringement of a patent is a statutory tort; and in the ordinary way one would expect the damages recoverable to be governed by the same rules as with many or most other torts. We were referred to *Halsbury's Laws of England* (4th edn) vol.12 para 1128 and following, to establish the elementary rules (i) that the overriding principle is that the victim should be restored to the position he would have been in if no wrong had been done, and (2) that the victim can recover loss which was (i) foreseeable, (ii) caused by the wrong, and (iii) not excluded from recovery by public or social policy. The requirement of causation is sometimes confused with foreseeability, which is remoteness. The two are different - see *Halsbury* para 1141:

> 1141. Causation in tort. Subject to foreseeability and the principles of public policy it is prima facie necessary and sufficient for a plaintiff to prove that a defendant's wrongdoing was a cause and not necessarily the sole or dominant cause of his injuries, as a matter of physical consequences or common sense, but subsidiary principles associating foreseeability and causation have been evolved in certain categories of concurrent or intervening causes.

It is not enough that the loss would not have occurred but for the tort; the tort must (for present purposes at any rate) be, as a matter of common sense, a cause of the loss.

There is no dispute about foreseeability or causation in the present case. It is conceded that both requirements (if there are two) are satisfied. What is said is that either the general rules in *Halsbury* do not apply to the Patents Act, or else there is now a fourth limitation which must be satisfied.

That fourth limit is to be derived from the speech of Lord Hoffmann in *South Australia Asset Management Corporation* v *York Montague Ltd.* [1996] 3 WLR 87 (aka the *Banque Bruxelles case*) at pages 92-94:

> "Much of the discussion, both in the judgment of the Court of Appeal and in argument at the Bar, has assumed that the case is about the correct measure of damages for the loss which the lender has suffered...

> I think that this was the wrong place to begin. Before one can consider the principle on which one should calculate the damages to which a plaintiff is entitled as compensation for loss, it is necessary to decide for what kind of loss he is entitled to compensation. A correct description of the loss for which the valuer is liable must precede any consideration of the measure of damages. For

this purpose it is better to begin at the beginning and consider the lender's cause of action....

In the present case, there is no dispute that the duty was owed to the lenders. The real question in this case is the kind of loss in respect of which the duty was owed.

How is the scope of the duty determined? In the case of a statutory duty, the question is answered by deducing the purpose of the duty from the language and context of the statute: *Gorris* v *Scott* (1874) LR 9 Ex. 125. In the case of tort, it will similarly depend upon the purpose of the rule imposing the duty.

Rules which make the wrongdoer liable for all the consequences of his wrongful conduct are exceptional and need to be justified by some special policy. Normally the law limits liability to those consequences which are attributable to that which made the act wrongful. In the case of liability in negligence for providing inaccurate information, this would mean liability for the consequences of the information being inaccurate."

My answer would be, at first impression, that the Patents Act is aimed at protecting patentees from commercial loss resulting from the wrongful infringement of their rights. That is only a slight gloss upon the wording of the statute itself. In my judgment, again as a matter of first impression, it does not distinguish between profit on the sale of patented articles and profit on the sale of convoyed goods. So I must look to see whether any such distinction emerges from the case law. I do not pause to consider (and it would probably be wrong for me to express an opinion) whether Lord Hoffmann's requirement is indeed a fourth rule for the recovery of damages, as Mr Hobbs submits, or an aspect of one of the other three, or a test for the ascertainment of duty rather than damages for breach.

Turning now to the patent cases, there are four occurring between 1867 and 1909 which seem to me to be merely decisions of fact, although they all disallow or deprecate loss of profit on the sale of goods other than those covered by the patent: *Penn* v *Jack* (1867) LR 5 Eq.81, *United Telephone Company* v *Walker* (1886) 4 RPC 63, *British Insulated Wire Co.* v *Dublin United Tramway Co.* (1899) 17 RPC 14, *Clement Talbot Ltd.* v *Wilson* (1909) 26 RPC 467. I get no help from them.

That last case was distinguished in *Meters Ltd.* v *Metropolitan Gas Meters Ltd.* (1910) 27 RPC 721, (1911) 28 RPC 157. The defendants sold gas meters which contained a small part that infringed a patent of the plaintiffs. Eve J and the Court of Appeal held that loss of profit on the sale of whole meters was recoverable by the plaintiffs, Eve J saying that the mechanism protected by the patents was "of the very essence of the meter". That decision does not, of course, go nearly as far as the patentees in the present case would wish, in awarding damages for loss of profit on convoyed goods. But it does go further than a limit to the loss of profit on the patented mechanism alone.

Next there is *Polaroid Corporation* v *Eastman Kodak Co.* [1977] RPC 379. That was an appeal against the grant of an interlocutory injunction. It was set aside, apparently on the ground that damages would be a sufficient remedy. The plaintiffs relied on loss which they would suffer, not only to their business in the integral system of instant photography (which was patented), but also to their business in the peel-apart system (which for the most part was not). That, as it seems to me, was not a case of convoyed goods; a photographer would buy one system or the other but not both. Infringing the patents relating to the integral system might, in the event, damage the business in the peel-apart system. But such loss would surely fail the test of causation, or else (as Goff LJ said at page 397) be too remote. In any event both he and Buckley LJ (at page 394) declined to express a concluded view on an interlocutory application.

The same two Lords Justice were part of the court which heard the appeal in *Corruplast Ltd.* v *George Harrison (Agencies) Ltd.* [1978] RPC 761. That was a case of springboard or bridgehead damages - loss that will be felt after the expiry of a patent by reason of infringing conduct during its lifetime. It is one of the heads of damage challenged in this appeal as outside the scope of patent damages. Buckley LJ said (at page 764) that "arguably at least" such damage "could not be recovered under the heading of infringement". He apparently regarded that as a ground for granting an interlocutory injunction. That seems to conflict with the reasoning of Goff LJ in the *Polaroid* case at page 397 ("one is not entitled to an injunction to avoid damages which, if suffered, would be too remote").

The case of *Catnic Components Ltd.* v *Hill & Smith Ltd.* [1983] FSR 512 is directly in point. The claim was for loss of profit on the sale of lintels which were patented; and there was also a claim in respect non-patented lintels which would have been sold along with the patented lintels. Falconer J held that the second claim did not succeed. He found (at page 533) that:

"it is common practice in the building industry for a builder to obtain from one supplier all his requirements for lintels for the erection of a particular building."

However, he ruled (at page 537) that:

"any loss of sales of non-patented lintels did not arise out of the acts of infringement and was not the natural and direct consequence of those acts; in the language of Goff LJ such damage was too remote."

The reference to natural and direct consequence was derived from the speech of Lord Macnaghten in *The United Horse Shoe and Nail Co.* v *Stewart & Co.* (1888) 5 RPC 260 at page 268. That case, besides being an appeal from Scotland, was decided at the time when "direct" was the accepted test for causation or remoteness or both: see Lord Denning MR in *Australian Coastal Shipping Co.* v *Green* [1971] 1 QB 456 at page 481. It is no longer the test for torts in general; I do not see why it should survive in the particular case of infringement of a patent.

The last of the English cases is *Paterson Zochonis Ltd.* v *Merfarken Packaging Ltd.* [1983] FSR 273. Printers infringed the copyright of the plaintiffs by printing cartons and leaflets which could be, and were in fact, used for a competitor's products. It was held that they were not liable for the loss caused by the competitors in passing off their products as those of the plaintiffs. The claim was for loss of sales and damage to reputation.

The argument for the printers was that they were liable for "loss caused by the infringement" (page 280), which "can only be nominal and cannot include any damage flowing from the delivery of the material to" the competitor. Both Oliver LJ (at page 282) and Fox LJ (page 287), as it seems to me, treated the problem as one of causation. Robert Goff LJ (at page 295) took a different route:

"I know however of no principle that, whenever one interest of a plaintiff has been wrongfully damaged, consequential damage to another interest of the plaintiff is necessarily recoverable. In each case it has to be considered whether, as a matter of policy, the latter damages should be recoverable in an action founded upon the wrongful invasion of the plaintiff's first interest. I know of no authority which enables a plaintiff, suing for damages for infringement of his copyright, to recover as part of such damages loss he has suffered because the commission by a third party of the tort of passing off has been facilitated by the defendant's infringement of his copyright; and as a matter of policy it is, in my judgment, undesirable to extend the scope of recoverable damages in an action for infringement of copyright in this way. The law of copyright is a self-contained branch of the law, concerned with the protection of a particular proprietary right. The provisions regulating the protection of that right, including (for example) those which provide for strict liability or liability based on fault are framed with regard to a particular interest, viz. the proprietary right in question. It would be undesirable as a matter of policy to extend the statutory remedies available for the protection of that interest to the recovery of damages in respect of the invasion of a different interest."

Viewing the cases as a whole, I cannot find any rule of law which limits the damages for infringement in a patent case in such a way as to exclude the loss claimed by the patentees in the present case. In *General Tire & Rubber Co.* v *Firestone Tyre & Rubber Co. Ltd.* [1976] RPC 197 at page 214 Lord Wilberforce approved a passage in the judgment of Fletcher Moulton LJ in the *Meters case* which concluded:

"But I am not going to say a word which will tie down future judges and prevent them from exercising their judgment, as best they can in all the circumstances of the case, so as to arrive at that which the plaintiff has lost by reason of the defendant doing certain acts wrongfully instead of either abstaining from doing them, or getting permission to do them rightfully."

Beyond that the assessment of damages for infringement of a patent is in my judgment a question of fact. There is no dispute as to causation or remoteness in the present case; nor can I see any ground of policy for restricting the patentees' right to recover. It does not follow that, if customers were in the habit of purchasing a patented article at the patentee's supermarket, for example, he could claim against an infringer in respect of loss of profits on all the other items which the customers would buy in the supermarket but no longer bought. The limit there would be one of causation, or remoteness, or both. But the present appeal, in so far as it seeks to restrict the scope of recovery, should be dismissed.

It remains to mention first that in *Watson Laidlow & Co. Ltd.* v *Pott, Cassels & Williamson* (1914) 31 RPC 104 at pages 116 and 117 the House of Lords sanctioned damages for "accessories, extensions, repairs etc," and for "machines and frames". Secondly, the recent United States cases of *Rite-Hite Corp.* v *Kelley Co. Inc.* [1996] FSR 469 including the dissenting opinions, and *King Instruments Corporation* v *Perego* (1995) (but decided after *Rite-Hite)* 65 F 3rd 941, 72 F 3rd 855 are certainly interesting; and provide support for each side in the present dispute in some degree. But I do not think that we can rely on them as solving the problem in our courts.

Can the patentees claim by virtue of their shareholding for losses suffered by their subsidiaries?

For the reasons given by Hobhouse LJ I agree that, in law, the parent of a wholly-owned subsidiary can recover damages in respect of the parent's loss by reason of misfortune that has fallen upon the subsidiary, at all events when the subsidiary has no cause of action against the wrongdoer. I am of course assuming that the parent does have a cause of action.

I do, however, differ from Hobhouse LJ on the question whether the patentees have proved in the present case that they have suffered loss, and, how much in terms of money is needed to compensate them. I readily acknowledge that this is a question on which two views are possible. But I prefer the conclusion of Jacob J that as a self-evident starting point, a dollar lost to the subsidiary is a dollar lost to the parent.

There are many ways in which the prosperity of a subsidiary will result in a monetary receipt by the parent. The subsidiary may pay a dividend, or repay capital to the parent, provided in either case that company law permits that course to be taken. Or the parent may sell the subsidiary. There was evidence at the trial that those possibilities existed, although a judge of the Chancery Division would scarcely need to be told that by a witness. There was not any evidence that any of the possibilities was likely to be imminent. In the nature of things it would, I suppose, be rare for such evidence to be available, at any rate as to capital repayment or sale of the subsidiary. Furthermore in terms of amount it can rarely be possible to forecast by how much a loss of profits in the sum of £x will reduce some future dividend, or capital repayment, or sale price of the subsidiary. Companies are often bought and sold not by reference to their net assets, but by reference to profits in a number of recent years, or other considerations such as the effect of an amalgamation or the prospect of acquiring talented employees; see for example *Buckingham* v *Francis* [1986] 2 All ER 738. The market value of shares in a wholly-owned subsidiary is liable to be entirely a matter of speculation, unless and until a purchaser is found.

Counsel for the infringers goes further and observes that, on the evidence in the present case, a dollar lost to the subsidiary would not have reached the parent company in one form or another, because in some instances the subsidiary made a loss for the year in question. I cannot accept that argument. The missing dollar, had it appeared, would have reduced the loss and increased the net assets of the company. If and when a dividend was lawfully paid, or capital repaid or the subsidiary sold, there would be one more dollar in the till to be taken into account.

Things may change, the dollar may be lost by improvident trading in the future, or it may be multiplied by successful trading. For the present all that one can say is that, where a subsidiary is 100 per cent owned,

> "a [one dollar] loss to the subsidiary company ... would result in a [one dollar] loss to the balance sheet or profits of the holding company, unless some other extraneous factor produced a different result."

That, according to Glidewell LJ, was the effect of the expert evidence for the plaintiff in the *Fischer case* [1995] 1 BCLC 260 at page 269. The expert witness for the third party did not disagree. Evidence to the same effect was given by Mr Demco in the present case in his second affidavit. It is quoted in the judgment of Hobhouse LJ which I have had the advantage of reading. It was accepted by the Official Referee and the Court of Appeal in the *Fischer case* and by Jacob J in the present case. I would accept it too.

I do not suppose that this is a case where the evidence of the plaintiffs is deficient through idleness or incompetence. It seems to me that there was no evidence which the patentees could have adduced beyond that of Mr Demco, except that they might have called the expert who gave evidence in the *Fischer case* or some other expert witness to the like effect. The same is very likely to be true of any other parent company which has a cause of action but can only point to loss suffered, in the first instance, by its subsidiary. On occasion it may be possible to point to an impending sale of the subsidiary, and to show how the price will be affected; or the dividend expected from a subsidiary may be shown to be affected. But in at least a majority of cases I would expect no such evidence to be available. If the view of Hobhouse and Hutchison LJJ prevails, then justice will not be done in the majority of cases where the parent has a cause of action and the subsidiary does not but the loss falls in the first instance on the subsidiary. Added to that majority is likely to be the case of *Barings plc v Coopers & Lybrand,* The Times 6 December 1996, when it comes to trial. To avoid injustice I would stay with the simple view that a pound lost to the subsidiary is a pound lost to the parent, unless there are extraneous circumstances.

That conclusion is in truth a presumption of fact. As Hobhouse LJ points out, no appeal on fact was allowed in the *Fischer case;* and Glidewell LJ said (at page 269):

"I view this as a matter of fact."

However, I wonder whether the existence of a presumption of fact is not as much a question of law as a question of fact. Suppose that in a future case it were submitted that, where a subsidiary is 100 per cent owned, a one pound loss to the subsidiary company would result in a one pound loss to the parent company, unless some other extraneous factor produces a different result. Would it be necessary to call an expert witness to prove that? Or would the court say that it can be assumed, both in law and in common sense, until the contrary be proved? I certainly am prepared to assume it, in the light of the unanimity which has greeted the proposition before Jacob J and in the *Fischer case,* and whether or not that aspect of the *Fischer case* is binding upon us.

There are two examples of extraneous circumstances which may be relevant in this case. First, if the subsidiary is insolvent the dollar is, again prima facie, of value to the creditors but of no value to the parent. There is no suggestion that either of the subsidiaries was insolvent in the present case. Secondly, the incidence of taxation may mean that the subsidiary's dollar is worth less (or perhaps more, for all I know) to the parent. That is not a circumstance that has yet been taken into account in the present case. Otherwise, as I say, the present worth of one dollar in the subsidiary is one dollar to the parent. Amid all the changes and chances of this mortal life, the worth of that dollar may change; the subsidiary may make losses and become worthless; or it may make profits and double its worth. Those possibilities can either be left out of account, as extraneous circumstances occurring after the loss; or they can be treated, when proved, as displacing the prima facie presumption. We need not in this case decide which is the right solution.

I would therefore uphold the judge's conclusion on this issue, but for the question of taxation. This was not dealt with in evidence at the trial; but the topic was mentioned in argument. For the patentees it was said that, as the damages would be subject to tax in their hands, there was no need to consider tax that would have been payable had the lost profits in fact been earned. I am by no means sure that that is correct, particularly as one of the subsidiaries is a Belgian company. I would remit this aspect of the case to the judge, with liberty to the parties to call further evidence if desired, for further consideration as to whether the damages should be reduced (but not increased) due to the hypothetical and actual incidence of tax.

Another point argued under this head was that it was wrong to take the marginal cost of production and sale in calculating lost profits. Presumably it was said that some proportion of overheads should have been added to the marginal cost. This is an interesting point, and I am surprised that there is no authority on it, or at any rate none to which we were referred. But the claim is in truth not for lost profits; it is for lost income, from which must be deducted the expenses saved. If it is only the marginal cost which is saved, the remainder of the lost income is recoverable. That is a misfortune which falls upon the wrongdoer.

Damages based on an average of the loss of several chances
As I have already said, the judge awarded damages on the basis that the patentees would have achieved 15 sales if the infringers had not made their 25 wrongful sales. There was extensive evidence of the circumstances of those 25; but the judge did not identify 15 which would in fact have been achieved by the patentees. Nor, in consequence, did he identify the profit lost on each particular machine featuring in his calculation. He simply awarded 60 per cent of the total sum claimed as loss of profit on the 25 machines. One can infer that he must have found the figures for loss of profit for each machine proved.

The judge adopted a similar method of calculation for spare parts, servicing and CAD systems. Mr Hobbs QC for the infringers says that the judge was wrong in law to adopt the method which he did; and he should have made findings relating to the individual machines. His clients, as he put it, were entitled to a speaking award. The judge's calculation of price depression and springboard damages was subject to similar criticism.

In *Allied Maples Group Ltd.* v *Simmons & Simmons* [1995] 1 WLR 1602 the Court of Appeal drew a distinction between (1) questions of historical fact - whether something did or did not happen in the past - and hypothetical questions as to what the plaintiff would have done in other circumstances, on the one hand, and (2) questions as to what a third party would have done, on the other. A plaintiff must prove on the balance of probability that he is entitled to succeed on any question in the first class. In other words he must prove to that standard that historical facts did happen, and that hypothetical conduct on his part would have occurred. If he does achieve that task, there is no discount from his damages because he only just achieved it.

As to the second class of question, Stuart-Smith LJ (with whom Hobhouse LJ agreed) said at page 1611:

"In many cases the plaintiff's loss depends on the hypothetical action of a third party, either in addition to action by the plaintiff, as in this case, or independently of it. In such a case, does the plaintiff have to prove on balance of probability, as Mr Jackson submits, that the third party would have acted so as to confer the benefit or avoid the risk to the plaintiff, or can the plaintiff succeed provided he shows that he had a substantial chance rather than a speculative one, the evaluation of the substantial chance being a question of quantification of damages?

Although there is not a great deal of authority, and none in the Court of Appeal, relating to solicitors failing to give advice which is directly in point I have no doubt that Mr Jackson's submission is wrong and the second alternative is correct."

That seems to me consistent with the decision of the High Court of Australia in *Sellars v Adelaide Petroleum NL* (1994) 179 CLR 332; and also with *British United Shoe Machinery Co. v A Fussell & Sons Ltd.* (1910) 27 RPC 205, and *Brown v John Hastie & Co.* (1904) 21 RPC 445.

In my judgment the issue as to the amount of the patentees' loss in the present case was a question in the second class; it depended on the hypothetical actions of third parties, that is to say the buyers of the infringing machines (or spare parts, servicing and CAD systems). The judge was entitled to conclude that the patentees had lost a chance of making sales to those buyers - no doubt a chance of differing probability in each case. He was entitled to evaluate the chances as a whole, rather than separately, if he chose to do so. The contrary view, that if the judge found 25 chances of a sale, each of 49 per cent probability, he should award nothing is absurd.

As to the suggestion that the infringers were entitled to a speaking award, I can understand their disappointment (or at any rate of their advisers) when their elaborate evidence was not analysed in detail by the judge in his judgment. It must, after all, have made quite a contribution to the duration and expense of an 8-day trial.

Devlin J in *Windsor RDC v Otterway & Try Ltd.* [1954] 3 All ER 721 at page 723 said -

"The court is not at the beck and call of the arbitrator ..."

So too a judge in a civil case, whilst in many respects wise to comply with wishes that are common to both parties, is not obliged to do so. Still less is he obliged to comply with the wishes of one party only, when to do so may unnecessarily impinge on judicial time that is much needed by others.'

COMMENT

Staughton LJ dissented on the 'every dollar lost to a subsidiary was a dollar lost to the parent company' point. Hobhouse and Hutchinson LJJ held that there was no authority for such an approach and that the basic principle, that the plaintiff must prove his own financial loss, must still apply in such a case.

What are springboard damages in the context of a patent? Do the same rules apply to the recoverability of damages for the infringement of a patent as apply in relation to tort generally? This case shows that a plaintiff is not limited to claiming damages based on a royalty and, although difficult to prove and assess, damages can be awarded for other losses.

Groundless Threats Actions

Section 70 provides for an action against groundless threats of infringement proceedings. Although it may be thought that this provision is intended to protect 'secondary infringers' such as retailers the reference in the section to 'a person aggrieved' means that the action is not so limited. For example, a 'primary infringer' may be a person aggrieved if threats directed at a retailer cause the retailer to stop ordering the product in question from the primary infringer. Some acts can, however, be threatened without triggering a groundless threats action. The case below examines these aspects of groundless threats of infringement proceedings.

Patrick John Brain v *Ingledew Brown Bennison and Garrett (No. 3)* [1997] FSR 511, Chancery Division

The plaintiff set up a company to exploit a technology known as 'Wet Oxidation'. The defendant, a firm of solicitors, was instructed by a Danish research institute to write to the plaintiff's company informing it of the institute's pending patent application at the European Patent Office and that appropriate action would be taken to protect the process subject to the application. Another letter was sent to a potential customer of the plaintiff's company. As a result, the plaintiff claimed his company's projects came to nothing and that he had suffered considerable losses. The plaintiff company was struck off the register of companies in 1994. The plaintiff brought a 'threats' action under section 70 of the Patents Act 1977. In an interlocutory hearing ([1995] FSR 552) Jacob J, in refusing to strike out the action declared that:

(a) the letters constituted threats within section 70;
(b) the plaintiff was a 'person aggrieved' within section 70(1);
(c) one particular threat was actionable in spite of section 70(4) which excludes threats of infringement alleged to consist of making or importing a product for disposal or of using a process.

The Court of Appeal held that those declarations should not have been made on a summary application, being dependent upon an assessment of evidence not before the court ([1996] FSR 341). They remain, therefore, live issues.

Later, the plaintiff applied to the court to strike out certain parts of the defence. In that hearing (reported at [1997] FSR 271), Laddie J struck out the defence based on section 70(2), (that is, justification - the defendant proves the act infringes a patent and the patent is not shown by the plaintiff to be invalid in a relevant respect. Aldous LJ in the Court of Appeal had suggested, *obiter,* that the court could look at the published specification and decide, on a balance of probabilities, whether the alleged act would infringe the patent when granted and whether a valid patent would be granted. However, Hobhouse LJ was unconvinced in the absence of further argument (Beldam LJ agreed with both judgments!).

Laddie J held that a defence under section 70(2) could not be sustained absent a granted patent. It would be unsatisfactory to decide the issue on the basis of hypothetical claims in the patent specification; the applicant could well be asked to amend his claims in a way which could not be predicted by the court.

The issues now before Laddie J included whether the plaintiff was a person aggrieved and whether the section 70(4) defence was available. In the event, he found the threats actionable and ordered an inquiry as to damages.

Laddie J (at 516): *'Person Aggrieved*
It is not now in dispute that the letters of which complaint are made in this action threaten proceedings for infringement of patent. What is in dispute is at who those threats are directed and who can sue to restrain them and for compensation for any damage caused by them.

So far as material for the purposes of this action, section 70 of the Act provides: "(1) Where a person ... by circulars, advertisements or otherwise threatens another person with proceedings for any infringement of a patent, a person aggrieved by threats (whether or not he is the person to whom the threats are made) may, subject to subsection (4) below, bring proceedings in the court against the person making the threats, claiming any relief mentioned in subsection (3) below."

Mr Platts-Mills, QC, who appeared on behalf of the plaintiff, argues that his client is a person aggrieved for two reasons. First he says that the threats taken individually or as a whole were made to or were directed at Mr Brain personally. Therefore, basing himself on *John Summers & Sons Ltd.* v *The Cold Metal Process Co.* (1948) 65 RPC 75, he says that Mr Brain is to be treated as a person aggrieved. Secondly he says that he is a person aggrieved by the threats made to Intox Corporation Limited and to its potential partners. As paragraphs 1 to 3 of the statement of claim plead, Mr Brain set up Intox for the purpose of exploiting Wet Oxidation technology, he is and at all material times has been its managing director and controls it and Intox is and at all material times has been his "vehicle" for that exploitation.

Mr Pumfrey, QC, who appeared on behalf of the defendants, does not dispute that if the threats were made against Mr Brain personally he is to be treated as a person aggrieved. However, he argues that in this case none of the threats were so made. He says that the status of Mr Brain must be assessed on the basis that his claim to being a person aggrieved is dependent on the indirect effect on him of threats made to and against others. He says that where the plaintiff is not himself the recipient of the threat, he is not a person aggrieved unless he has suffered loss by reason of the threat. He says that Mr Brain's claim to be a person aggrieved has to be tested against the response he gave to a request for particulars of all matters relied on in support of that claim. That response included the following:

"The Plaintiff had identified a business opportunity from which he expected to benefit financially. The Plaintiff chose to exploit that opportunity through a limited company... Intox Corporation Limited. The Plaintiff had the sole power to choose who should become the directors, secretary and shareholders of Intox Corporation Limited. ... The Plaintiff was at all material times the driving force behind Intox. The Plaintiff at all times had a commercial interest in the success of the venture to be carried on through Intox Corporation Limited. His own financial benefit would have derived from salary and/or director's remuneration from Intox Corporation Limited, and from the value of the shares in that company. The actions of the Defendant were intended to, and did, prevent the venture from succeeding. This had a direct financial effect on the Plaintiff."

Insofar as Mr Brain relies on his position as director of Intox, Mr Pumfrey argued that he must prove that the threats have deprived him of some loss which is capable of quantification. Insofar as Mr Brain claims to be a person aggrieved by virtue of his shareholding in Intox Corporation Limited, Mr Pumfrey says that he must show by evidence that by virtue of that shareholding he would, on the balance of probabilities, have benefited from Wet Oxidation business which would have been conducted by Intox and that those benefits have been reduced or destroyed as a result of the threats made to or in relation to Intox. He says that on this issue, the nature of the shareholdings, the company or companies which would be involved in the business, the size of the shareholding, the manner of trading of Intox and the manner in which the profits of trading would have been remitted to Mr Brain are all relevant.

Mr Pumfrey accepts that if the plaintiff in a threats action has to prove damage or likelihood of damage before be can be treated as a person aggrieved, it may cause some problems in cases such as this where, in accordance with usual Chancery Division practice, the trial is directed to issues of liability, quantum being left to a subsequent inquiry. But these are essentially procedural considerations. They cannot stand in the way of the court considering properly the issue of status.

Mr Pumfrey's argument is based upon the decision of the Court of Appeal in *Reymes-Cole* v *Elite Hosiery Co. Ltd.* [1965] RPC 102. In that case the plaintiff owned a number of patents relating to the manufacture of ladies' stockings. The defendant was another manufacturer. The plaintiff sued the defendant for patent infringement. The defendant counterclaimed in respect of a threatening letter which had been sent, not to it, but to one of its supposed customers, Lucas Brothers. Willmer LJ said:

"... the defendants' right to relief must thus depend upon whether they can show that they were persons aggrieved. It seems to me that the defendants could only be aggrieved if it were shown that Messrs Lucas Brothers' reaction, or likely reaction, to the threat contained in the letter complained of was such as to be damaging to the defendants.

The defendants' own case ... was that the particular type of stocking complained of had not then been in production for some considerable time. The defendants could not be damaged by Messrs Lucas Brothers refusing to buy further supplies of this type of stocking, if it is true that the defendants were no longer producing it. The only other way in which the defendants could be aggrieved would be if the evidence showed that Messrs Lucas Brothers refused altogether to do any further business with the defendants. It seemed to me at one time that this could well be a point of some substance. But it is a point that could be established only by evidence. No witness was called from Messrs Lucas Brothers to speak as to their reaction to the letter complained of, so that in the result the question whether the defendants were likely to suffer any damage was left completely in the air. In the circumstances I do not think that the defendants proved that they were in any sense persons aggrieved. I have accordingly come to the conclusion that the learned judge's decision with regard to this aspect of the case cannot be supported."

Mr Pumfrey also relied on the decision of the Court of Appeal in the interlocutory hearing of this action. Whether, in the absence of any evidence, it was open to

Jacob J to declare, as he did, that Mr Brain was a person aggrieved was one of the issues before the court. Having set out the above passage from *Reymes-Cole,* Aldous LJ, with whom the other members of the Court agreed on this subject, said: "As is apparent from the reasoning of Willmer LJ, the question of whether or not a person is aggrieved by a threat is in the main a question of fact to be established by evidence. If the threat is not made to the person himself, then he must establish by evidence that the threats have or are likely to cause him damage which is not minimal."

Furthermore, relying on *Solanite Signs Ltd* v *Wood* (1933) 50 RPC 315, and *Ungar* v *Sugg* (1892) 9 RPC 113 at 118, lines 25-41, Mr Pumfrey said that it was not sufficient for the plaintiff to point to a general loss of business. The plaintiff must be able to point to specific contracts which have been lost by reason of the threats and not for some other reason. Based on these cases, Mr Pumfrey concluded that it was necessary to have something like a mini inquiry as to damages during the trial. Absent that, the plaintiff could not prove that he had suffered damage and, in consequence, could not show he was a person aggrieved. I am not persuaded that Mr Pumfrey is right.

I think a useful starting point for analysis is the *John Summers* case in which Romer J said:

> "As I have come to the conclusion that *Summers* themselves were threatened different considerations arise. It is true that *Summers* called no evidence to prove the damage which they pleaded, but in my judgment it was not necessary for them to do so. I am clearly of the opinion that any person who is threatened with an action for infringement of patent, as I find that *Summers* were, is a 'person aggrieved' for the purposes of Sec. 36 and need not prove actual damage at the trial in order to found a claim for relief."

As mentioned above, neither party has suggested that this approach is wrong. Yet section 70 provides that a person aggrieved by threats "whether or not he is the person to whom the threats are made" may sue. In other words, whether the plaintiff is threatened directly or not, he must in all cases show he is a person aggrieved. The Act does not create two different standards of grievance depending upon whether the threat is made directly or not. So, if the directly threatened party can be a person aggrieved without the need to prove actual damage at the trial, as Romer J decided, it is difficult to see why an indirectly threatened party should have to prove such actual damage in order to qualify to sue.

Furthermore, there is nothing about the structure of section 70 which lends obvious support to the suggestion that an indirectly threatened party must prove actual damage before he has status to sue. Once it is shown that threats have been made and the party suing is aggrieved by them, and assuming that no special defence under section 70(4) is made out, then he may seek any of the relief set out in section 70(3), namely a declaration that the threats are unjustifiable, an injunction and damages. But this does not mean that damages are a necessary prerequisite to the bringing of the action. If it were, much of the practical value of the section would be destroyed. In most cases section 70 is invoked as soon as threats are issued. The plaintiff applies for interlocutory relief so as to avoid any possibility of the threats causing harm to his commercial interests in the future ... The admitted threats were directed not only at Intox and Jensen but also "any other person or company" which had entered into or might enter into an agreement with

Severn-Trent Water Board. Although Mr Brain had not entered into an agreement with Severn-Trent, and was not actively contemplating doing so, I do not think the reader of the letter would have construed it that precisely. In the end this is a matter of impression. I think a non-lawyer businessman would consider this to be a threat directed at anyone who became involved in assisting Severn-Trent to exploit the Wet Oxidation process.   The last sentence clearly is intended to convey the message that the only legitimate source of help was Risø. I think a reasonable reader asked whether any other person referred to in this letter included Mr Brain, would have replied "probably". It follows that this is a threat directed at Mr Brain personally. The fact that it was addressed to Severn-Trent does not prevent it being directed at him (see Romer J in *Summers* at page 96 line 15 to page 97 line 31).

In addition to this, it seems to me that Mr Brain is a person aggrieved in respect of all the threats made directly and indirectly against Intox. In the light of the approach of the Court of Appeal in *Gerber Garment Technology Inc.* v *Lectra Systems Ltd* (December 18, 1996, unreported [now reported at [1997] RPC 443]), Mr Pumfrey eschewed any attempt to apply the reasoning of *Macaura* v *Northern Assurance Co.* [1925] AC 619 to this case. In other words, he did not argue that because the threats were made to a limited company, shareholders and directors could not have a relevant and recognisable interest. In adopting this approach, I am sure that Mr Pumfrey was correct.

Whether a director, executive or shareholder has a sufficient personal interest in threats made to the company to give him status to sue in respect of threats directed at the company will depend on all the circumstances. Mr Platts-Mills was prepared to accept that a shareholder in, say, ICI would be unlikely to have locus to sue in respect of patent threats made to that company. But he says the facts here are very different. He argues that Mr Brain is a person aggrieved because of what was done to his chosen means of exploiting the wet oxidation process, namely the company that he set up. Intox was his then current proposed route. Intox and Mr Brain were for many purposes to be looked at interchangeably. He says Mr Brain is aggrieved if, as a result of the threat to Intox, his ability to exploit the wet oxidation process through Intox or in any other way is hindered. I accept that submission. In reality the moving force behind the proposed exploitation of the Wet Oxidation process obtained or to be obtained from Mr Jensen was Mr Brain. It is not in dispute that all the running costs of Intox and the losses it incurred were borne by Mr Brain. Whether he used Intox or another custom-created company as a conduit for these activities, his personal involvement was substantial. The success or failure of Intox would be regarded as his success or failure. Mr Brain's commercial interests were or were likely to be adversely affected in a real as opposed to a fanciful or minimal way by the threats made directly or indirectly to Intox. I have come to the conclusion that he was a person aggrieved by those threats.

The Defence under Section 70(4)
In addition to the person aggrieved point, the defendants ran a special defence in relation to Letter No. 2 under section 70(4) of the Act, which provides: "Proceedings may not be brought under this section for a threat to bring proceedings for an infringement alleged to consist of making or importing a product for disposal or of using a process." Mr Pumfrey argued that the letter to Severn-Trent was in respect of the use of a process and therefore could not constitute an actionable threat.

Section 60 of the Act defines the activities which can constitute patent infringement.   Section 70(1) makes it wrongful to threaten patent infringement.

Section 70(4) excludes from the generality of the prohibition in section 70(1) threats in relation to certain types of infringement. It is difficult to detect the legislative philosophy underlying the list of exclusions in section 70(4). In *Cavity Trays Limited v RMC Panel Products Limited* [1996] RPC 361, the Court of Appeal was faced with an argument that a primary infringer who both made an infringing product and then sold it could be threatened with infringement proceedings under the protective umbrella of section 70(4) although the latter subsection only expressly exempted from suit threats in respect of making, not threats in relation to selling. The court rejected this contention. Aldous LJ said:

> "The subsection prevents proceedings being brought for threats which are alleged to consist of certain acts. The word 'consist' confines the types of alleged threats to the specified acts set out in the subsection. The ambit of the words specifying these acts is not open to doubt. There is no ambiguity in the meaning of the subsection which only prevents proceedings being brought for threats of making or importing a product for disposal or using a process. Other threats of proceedings against manufacturers or importers, for example threats of proceedings alleging disposal or use, do not fall within the subsection."

By the same reasoning, although section 70(4) allows a patentee to issue threats in respect of use of a process, it does not permit threats to be made in respect of offering a process or use in the United Kingdom which is a separately identified category of infringement prescribed by section 60(1)(a) of the Act. That was the view arrived at by Jacob J at the interlocutory stage in this action and his conclusion is referred to with tacit approval by Aldous LJ in *Cavity Trays*. If, therefore, Letter No. 2 goes beyond threatening anyone for use of the patented process, it is actionable.

I am prepared to accept that a reasonable reader would understand the letter to be limited, so far as Severn-Trent was concerned, to threatening it with proceedings if it was to use the Wet Oxidation process. That threat would be immune from suit under section 70(4). However, that is not the totality of the threat contained in Letter No. 2. It is also directed to telling Severn-Trent that it would take an "extremely serious view" and "appropriate action" if that process was used as a result of co-operation with Intox, Mr Jensen or any other person or company, I have no doubt that this would be read by a reasonable person as indicating that Risø would bring infringement proceedings against any person supplying the process to Severn-Trent, thereby cutting off its source of technology. That threat is not saved by section 70(4) and is actionable at the suit of a person aggrieved, such as Mr Brain. This view is reinforced when all the correspondence is read as a whole. Letter No. 1 made it clear that Risø objected to Intox offering to help potential customers or partners to erect facilities. In other words it objected to Intox supplying the process to others to use.'

COMMENT

In deciding that Mr Brain was a 'person aggrieved' important factors were that he was the driving force behind Intox and the success or failure of that company had a direct financial effect on him. Under what circumstances would a shareholder be a person aggrieved in relation to threats made to the company of which he is a shareholder?

Does a person aggrieved have to be able to prove damage in order to succeed in a 'threats' action?

The defence to a threats action in section 70(4) is restricted to alleged infringements consisting of making or importing a product for disposal or using a process and does not extend to the other infringing acts. Why is this so? What are the other infringing acts?

Conventions

Patents are usually exploited in a number of countries and it will usually be worth applying for patents in several countries to avoid severe territorial limitation. To assist in obtaining patents in other countries, there is the European Patent Convention and the Patent Co-operation Treaty. Extracts from the former are reproduced below.

European Patent Convention (extracts)

Preamble
The Contracting States,
DESIRING to strengthen cooperation between the States of Europe in respect of the protection of inventions.
DESIRING that such protection may be obtained in those States by a single procedure for the grant of patents and by the establishment of certain standard rules governing patents so granted.
DESIRING, for this purpose, to conclude a Convention which establishes a European Patent Organisation and which constitutes a special agreement within the meaning of Article 19 of the Convention for the Protection of Industrial Property, signed in Paris on 20 March 1883 and last revised on 14 July 1967, and a regional patent treaty within the meaning of Article 45, paragraph 1, of the Patent Cooperation Treaty of 19 June 1970,
HAVE AGREED on the following provisions;

Part I - General and institutional provisions
Chapter I   General Provisions

Article 1   European law for the grant of patents.

A system of law, common to the Contracting States, for the grant of patents for invention is hereby established.

Article 2   European patent

(1) Patents granted by virtue of this Convention shall be called European patents.

(2) The European patent shall, in each of the Contracting States for which it is granted, have the effect of and be subject to the same conditions as a national patent granted by that State, unless otherwise provided in this Convention.

Article 3 Territorial effect

The grant of a European patent may be requested for one or more of the Contracting States.

Article 21 Boards of Appeal

(1) The Boards of Appeal shall be responsible for the examination of appeals from the decisions of the Receiving Section, Examining Divisions, Opposition Divisions and of the Legal Division.

(2) For appeals from a decision of the Receiving Section or the Legal Division, a Board of Appeal shall consist of three legally qualified members.

(3) For appeals from a decision of an Examining Division, a Board of Appeal shall consist of:
   (a) two technically qualified members and one legally qualified member, when the decision concerns the refusal of a European patent application or the grant of a European patent and was taken by an Examining Division consisting of less than four members;
   (b) three technically qualified members and two legally qualified members, when the decision was taken by an Examining Division consisting of four members or when the Board of Appeal considers that the nature of the appeal so requires;
   (c) three legally qualified members in all other cases.

(4) For appeals from a decision of an Opposition Division, a Board of Appeal shall consist of:
   (a) two technically qualified members and one legally qualified member, when the decision was taken by an Opposition Division consisting of three members;
   (b) three technically qualified members and two legally qualified members, when the decision was taken by an Opposition Division consisting of four members or when the Board of Appeal considers that the nature of the appeal so requires.

Article 22 Enlarged Board of Appeal

(1) The Enlarged Board of Appeal shall be responsible for:
   (a) deciding points of law referred to it by Boards of Appeal;
   (b) giving opinions on points of law referred to it by the President of the European Patent Office under the conditions laid down in Article 112.

(2) For giving decisions or opinions, the Enlarged Board of Appeal shall consist of five legally qualified members and two technically qualified members. One of the legally qualified members shall be the Chairman.

Part II - Substantive Patent Law
Chapter I   Patentability

Article 52   Patentable inventions

(1) European patents shall be granted for any inventions which are susceptible of industrial application, which are new and which involve an inventive step.
(2) The following in particular shall not be regarded as inventions within the meaning of paragraph 1:
   (a) discoveries, scientific theories and mathematical methods;
   (b) aesthetic creations;
   (c) schemes, rules and methods for performing mental acts, playing games or doing business and programs for computers;
   (d) presentations of information.
(3) The provisions of paragraph 2 shall exclude patentability of the subject-matter or activities referred to in that provision only to the extent to which a European patent application or European patent relates to such subject-matter or activities as such.
(4) Methods for treatment of the human or animal body by surgery or therapy and diagnostic methods practised on the human or animal body shall not be regarded as inventions which are susceptible of industrial application within the meaning of paragraph 1. This provision shall not apply to products, in particular substances or compositions, for use in any of these methods.

Article 53   Exceptions to patentability

European patents shall not be granted in respect of:
   (a) inventions the publication or exploitation of which would be contrary to 'ordre public' or morality, provided that the exploitation shall not be deemed to be so contrary merely because it is prohibited by law or regulation in some or all of the Contracting States;
   (b) plant or animal varieties or essentially biological processes for the production of plants or animals; this provision does not apply to microbiological processes or the products thereof.

Article 54   Novelty

(1) An invention shall be considered to be new if it does not form part of the state of the art.
(2) The state of the art shall be held to comprise everything made available to the public by means of a written or oral description, by use, or in any other way, before the date of filing of the European patent application.
(3) Additionally, the content of European patent applications as filed, of which the dates of filing are prior to the date referred to in paragraph 2 and which were published under Article 93 on or after that date, shall be considered as comprised in the state of the art.
(4) Paragraph 3 shall be applied only in so far as a Contracting State designated in respect of the later application, was also designated in respect of the earlier application as published.

(5) The provisions of paragraphs 1 to 4 shall not exclude the patentability of any substance or composition, comprised in the state of the art, for use in a method referred to in Article 52, paragraph 4, provided that its use for any method referred to in that paragraph is not comprised in the state of the art.

Article 55   Non-prejudicial disclosures

(1) For the application of Article 54 a disclosure of the invention shall not be taken into consideration if it occurred no earlier than six months preceding the filing of the European patent application and if it was due to, or in consequence of:

(a) an evident abuse in relation to the applicant or his legal predecessor, or

(b) the fact that the applicant or his legal predecessor has displayed the invention at an official, or officially recognised, international exhibition falling within the terms of the Convention on international exhibitions signed at Paris on 22 November 1928 and last revised on 30 November 1972.

(2) In the case of paragraph 1(b), paragraph 1 shall apply only if the applicant states, when filing the European patent application, that the invention has been so displayed and files a supporting certificate within the period and under the conditions laid down in the Implementing Regulations.

Article 56   Invention Step

An invention shall be considered as involving an inventive step if, having regard to the state of the art, it is not obvious to a person skilled in the art. If the state of the art also includes documents within the meaning of Article 54, paragraph 3, these documents are not to be considered in deciding whether there has been an inventive step.

Article 57   Industrial application

An invention shall be considered as susceptible of industrial application if it can be made or used in any kind of industry, including agriculture.

Chapter II   Persons entitled to apply for and obtain European patents - Mention of the inventor

Article 60   Right to a European patent

(1) The right to a European patent shall belong to the inventor or his successor in title. If the inventor is an employee the right to the European patent shall be determined in accordance with the law of the State in which the employee is mainly employed; if the State in which the employee is mainly employed cannot be determined, the law to be applied shall be that of the State in which the employer has his place of business to which the employee is attached.

(2) If two or more persons have made an invention independently of each other, the right to the European patent shall belong to the person whose European patent application has the earliest date of filing; however, this provision shall apply only if this first application has been published under Article 93 and shall only have effect in respect of the Contracting States designated in that application as published.

(3) For the purposes of proceedings before the European Patent Office, the applicant shall be deemed to be entitled to exercise the right to the European patent.

Article 62   Right of the inventor to be mentioned

The inventor shall have the right, vis-à-vis the applicant for or proprietor of a European patent, to be mentioned as such before the European Patent Office.

Chapter III   Effects of the European patent and the European patent application

Article 63   Term of the European patent

(1) The term of the European patent shall be 20 years as from the date of filing of the application.
(2) Nothing in the preceding paragraph shall limit the right of a Contracting State to extend the term of a European patent under the same conditions as those applying to its national patents, in order to take into account a state of war or similar emergency conditions affecting that State.

Article 64   Rights conferred by a European patent

(1) A European patent shall, subject to the provisions of paragraph 2, confer on its proprietor from the date of publication of the mention of its grant, in each Contracting State in respect of which it is granted, the same rights as would be conferred by a national patent granted in that State.
(2) If the subject-matter of the European patent is a process, the protection conferred by the patent shall extend to the products directly obtained by such process.
(3) Any infringement of a European patent shall be dealt with by national law.

Article 66   Equivalence of European filing with national filing

A European patent application which has been accorded a date of filing shall, in the designated Contracting States, be equivalent to a regular national filing, where appropriate with the priority claimed for the European patent application.

Article 69   Extent of protection

(1) The extent of the protection conferred by a European patent or a European patent application shall be determined by the terms of the claims. Nevertheless, the description and drawings shall be used to interpret the claims.
(2) For the period up to grant of the European patent, the extent of the protection conferred by the European patent application shall be determined by the latest filed claims contained in the publication under Article 93. However the European patent as granted or as amended in opposition proceedings shall determine retroactively the protection conferred by the European patent application, in so far as such protection is not thereby extended.

Chapter IV   The European patent application as an object of property

Article 71   Transfer and constitution rights

A European patent application may be transferred or give rise to rights for one or more of the designated Contracting States.

Article 72   Assignment

An assignment of a European patent application shall be made in writing and shall require the signature of the parties to the contract.

Article 73   Contractual licensing

A European patent application may be licensed in whole or in part for the whole or part of the territories of the designated Contracting States.

Article 74   Law applicable

Unless otherwise specified in this Convention, the European patent application as an object of property shall, in each designated Contracting State and with effect for such State, be subject to the law applicable in that State to national patent applications.

Part III - Application for European Patents
Chapter I   Filing and requirements of the European patent application

Article 78   Requirements of the European patent application

(1) A European patent application shall contain:
   (a) a request for the grant of a European patent;
   (b) a description of the invention;
   (c) one or more claims;
   (d) any drawings referred to in the description or the claims;
   (e) an abstract.
(2) A European patent application shall be subject to the payment of the filing fee and the search fee within one month after the filing of the application.
(3) A European patent application must satisfy the conditions laid down in the Implementing Regulations.

Article 79   Designation of Contracting States

(1) The request for the grant of a European patent shall contain the designation of the Contracting State or States in which protection for the invention is desired.
(2) The designation of a Contracting State shall be subject to the payment of the designation fee. The designation fees shall be paid within twelve months after filing the European patent application or, if priority has been claimed, after the date or priority; in the latter case, payment may still be made up to the expiry of the period specified in Article 78, paragraph 2, if that period expires later.

(3) The designation of a Contracting State may be withdrawn at any time up to the grant of the European patent. Withdrawal of the designation of all the Contracting States shall be deemed to be a withdrawal of the European patent application. Designation fees shall not be refunded.

Article 80   Date of filing

The date of filing of a European patent application shall be the date on which documents filed by the applicant contain:

(a) an indication that a European patent is sought;

(b) the designation of at least one Contracting State;

(c) information identifying the applicant;

(d) a description and one or more claims in one of the languages referred to in Article 14, paragraphs 1 and 2, even though the description and the claims do not comply with the other requirements of this Convention.

Article 81   Designation of the inventor

The European patent application shall designate the inventor. If the applicant is not the inventor or is not the sole inventor, the designation shall contain a statement indicating the origin of the right to the European patent.

Article 82   Unity of invention

The European patent application shall relate to one invention only or to a group of inventions so linked as to form a single general inventive concept.

Article 83   Disclosure of the invention

The European patent application must disclose the invention in a manner sufficiently clear and complete for it to be carried out by a person skilled in the art.

Article 84   The claims

The claims shall define the matter for which protection is sought. They shall be clear and concise and be supported by the description.

Article 85   The abstract

The abstract shall merely serve for use as technical information; it may not be taken into account for any other purpose, in particular not for the purpose of interpreting the scope of the protection sought nor for the purpose of applying Article 54, paragraph 3.

Chapter II   Priority

Article 87   Priority right

(1) A person who has duly filed in or for any State party to the Paris Convention for the Protection of Industrial Property, an application for a patent or for the

registration of a utility model or for a utility certificate or for an inventor's certificate, or his successors in title, shall enjoy, for the purpose of filing a European patent application in respect of the same invention, a right of priority during a period of twelve months from the date of filing of the first application.

(2) Every filing that is equivalent to a regular national filing under the national law of the State where it was made or under bilateral or multilateral agreements, including this Convention, shall be recognised as giving rise to a right of priority.

(3) By a regular national filing is meant any filing that is sufficient to establish the date on which the application was filed, whatever may be the outcome of the application.

(4) A subsequent application for the same subject-matter as a previous first application and filed in or in respect of the same State shall be considered as the first application for the purposes of determining priority, provided that, at the date of filing the subsequent application, the previous application has been withdrawn, abandoned or refused, without being open to public inspection and without leaving any rights outstanding, and has not served as a basis for claiming a right of priority. The previous application may not thereafter serve as a basis for claiming a right of priority.

(5) If the first filing has been made in a State which is not a party to the Paris Convention for the Protection of Industrial Property, paragraphs 1 to 4 shall apply only in so far as that State, according to a notification published by the Administrative Council, and by virtue of bilateral or multilateral agreements, grants on the basis of a first filing made at the European Patent Office as well as on the basis of a first filing made in or for any Contracting State and subject to conditions equivalent to those laid down in the Paris Convention, a right of priority having equivalent effect.

Article 89   Effect of priority right

The right of priority shall have the effect that the date of priority shall count as the date of filing of the European patent application for the purposes of Article 54, paragraphs 2 and 3, and Article 60, paragraph 2.

COMMENT

This convention has proved highly successful and business in the European Patent Office has grown significantly. The Patents Act 1977 was enacted in the light of this Convention. Can you identify the equivalent provisions in the United Kingdom Act? Note also the influence of the Paris Convention for the Protection of Industrial Property on the above Convention.

There follow extracts from the 'TRIPS' Agreement relevant to patents. Compare the provisions with the equivalent provisions of the European Patent Convention and the United Kingdom Act.

Trade-related Aspects of Intellectual Property Rights

Section 5 Patents

Article 27
Patentable subject matter

(1) Subject to the provisions of paragraphs 2 and 3, patents shall be available for any inventions, whether products or processes, in all fields of technology, provided that they are new, involve an inventive step and are capable of industrial application.[1] Subject to paragraph 4 of Article 65, paragraph 8 of Article 70 and paragraph 3 of this Article, patents shall be available and patent rights enjoyable without discrimination as to the place of invention, the field of technology and whether products are imported or locally produced.

(2) Members may exclude from patentability inventions, the prevention within their territory of the commercial exploitation of which is necessary to protect *ordre public* or morality, including to protect human, animal or plant life or health or to avoid serious prejudice to the environment, provided that such exclusion is not made merely because the exploitation is prohibited by their law.

(3) Members may also exclude from patentability:
   (a) diagnostic, therapeutic and surgical methods for the treatment of humans or animals;
   (b) plants and animals other than micro-organisms, and essentially biological processes for the production of plants or animals other than non-biological and microbiological processes. However, Members shall provide for the protection of plant varieties either by patents or by an effective *sui generis* system or by any combination thereof. The provisions of this subparagraph shall be reviewed four years after the date of entry into force of the WTO Agreement.

Article 28
Rights conferred

(1) A patent shall confer on its owner the following exclusive rights:
   (a) where the subject matter of a patent is a product, to prevent third parties not having the owner's consent from the acts of making, using, offering for sale, selling, or importing[2] for these purposes that product;
   (b) where the subject matter of a patent is a process, to prevent third parties not having the owner's consent from the act of using the process, and from the acts of: using, offering for sale, selling, or importing for these purposes at least the product obtained directly by that process.

(2) Patent owners shall also have the right to assign, or transfer by succession, the patent and to conclude licensing contracts.

Article 29
Conditions on patent applicants

(1) Members shall require that an applicant for a patent shall disclose the invention in a manner sufficiently clear and complete for the invention to be carried out by

a person skilled in the art and may require the applicant to indicate the best mode for carrying out the invention known to the inventor at the filing date or, where priority is claimed, at the priority date of the application.

(2) Members may require an applicant for a patent to provide information concerning the applicant's corresponding foreign applications and grants.

Article 30
Exceptions to rights conferred

Members may provide limited exceptions to the exclusive rights conferred by a patent, provided that such exceptions do not unreasonably conflict with a normal exploitation of the patent and do not unreasonably prejudice the legitimate interests of the patent owner, taking account of the legitimate interests of third parties.

Article 31
Other use without authorization of the right holder

Where the law of a Member allows for other use[3] of the subject matter of a patent without the authorization of the right holder, including use by the government or third parties authorized by the government, the following provision shall be respected:

(a) authorization of such use shall be considered on its individual merits;

(b) such use may only be permitted if, prior to such use, the proposed user has made efforts to obtain authorization from the right holder on reasonable commercial terms and conditions and that such efforts have not been successful within a reasonable period of time. This requirement may be waived by a Member in the case of a national emergency or other circumstances of extreme urgency or in cases of public non-commercial use. In situations of national emergency or other circumstances of extreme urgency, the right holder shall, nevertheless, be notified as soon as reasonably practicable. In the case of public non-commercial use, where the government or contractor, without making a patent search, knows or has demonstrable grounds to know that a valid patent is or will be used by or for the government, the right holder shall be informed promptly;

(c) the scope and duration of such use shall be limited to the purpose for which it was authorized, and in the case of semi-conductor technology shall only be for public non-commercial use or to remedy a practice determined after judicial or administrative process to be anti-competitive;

(d) such use shall be non-exclusive;

(e) such use shall be non-assignable, except with that part of the enterprise or goodwill which enjoys such use;

(f) any such use shall be authorized predominantly for the supply of the domestic market of the Member authorizing such use;

(g) authorization for such use shall be liable, subject to adequate protection of the legitimate interests of the persons so authorized, to be terminated if and when the circumstances which led to it cease to exist and are unlikely to recur. The competent authority shall have the authority to review, upon motivated request, the continued existence of these circumstances;

(h) the right holder shall be paid adequate remuneration in the circumstances of each case, taking into account the economic value of the authorization;

(i) the legal validity of any decision relating to the authorization of such use shall be subject to judicial review or other independent review by a distinct higher authority in that Member;

(j) any decision relating to the remuneration provided in respect of such use shall be subject to judicial review or other independent review by a distinct higher authority in that Member;

(k) Members are not obliged to apply the conditions set forth in subparagraphs (b) and (f) where such use is permitted to remedy a practice determined after judicial or administrative process to be anti-competitive. The need to correct anti-competitive practices may be taken into account in determining the amount of remuneration in such cases. Competent authorities shall have the authority to refuse termination of authorization if and when the conditions which led to such authorization are likely to recur;

(l) where such use is authorized to permit the exploitation of a patent ('the second patent') which cannot be exploited without infringing another patent ('the first patent'), the following additional conditions shall apply:

　(i) the invention claimed in the second patent shall involve an important technical advance of considerable economic significance in relation to the invention claimed in the first patent;

　(ii) the owner of the first patent shall be entitled to a cross-licence on reasonable terms to use the invention claimed in the second patent; and

　(iii) the use authorized in respect of the first patent shall be non-assignable except with the assignment of the second patent.

Article 32
Revocation/forfeiture

An opportunity for judicial review of any decision to revoke or forfeit a patent shall be available.

Article 33
Term of protection

The term of protection available shall not end before the expiration of a period of twenty years counted from the filing date.[4]

Article 34
Process patents: burden of proof

(1) For the purposes of civil proceedings in respect of the infringement of the rights of the owner referred to in paragraph 1(b) of Article 28, if the subject matter of a patent is a process for obtaining a product, the judicial authorities shall have the authority to order the defendant to prove that the process to obtain an identical product is different from the patented process. Therefore, Members shall provide, in at least one of the following circumstances, that any identical product when produced without the consent of the patent owner shall, in the absence of proof to the contrary, be deemed to have been obtained by the patented process:

(a) if the product obtained by the patented process is new;

(b) if there is a substantial likelihood that the identical product was made by the process and the owner of the patent has been unable through reasonable efforts to determine the process actually used.

(2) Any Member shall be free to provide that the burden of proof indicated in paragraph 1 shall be on the alleged infringer only if the condition referred to in subparagraph (a) is fulfilled or only if the condition referred to in subparagraph (b) is fulfilled.

(3) In the adduction of proof to the contrary, the legitimate interests of defendants in protecting their manufacturing and business secrets shall be taken into account.

Notes:

[1] For the purposes of this Article, the terms 'inventive step' and 'capable of industrial application' may be deemed by a Member to be synonymous with the terms 'non-obvious' and 'useful' respectively.

[2] This right, like all other rights conferred under this Agreement in respect of the use, sale, importation or other distribution of goods, is subject to the provisions of Article 6.

[3] 'Other use' refers to use other than that allowed under Article 30.

[4] It is understood that those Members which do not have a system of original grant may provide that the terms of protection shall be computed from the filing date in the system of original grant.

COMMENT

Note that there is no equivalent to section 1(2) of the Patents Act 1977 (see also Article 52(2) of the European Patent Convention). Does this mean that discoveries, methods for performing mental acts, computer programs, etc. are patentable as such? Would many 'inventions' fail to be patentable under any of the basic requirements apart from novelty?

An alleged infringer of a patented process who produces an identical product to that made by the patented process, without the consent of the proprietor, may be presumed to have made his product by means of that process (Article 34(1)). He would, therefore, have the burden of proving that he did not use the process. Is the United Kingdom Act to the same effect?

Chapter 5

Design Law

Introduction

Until recently design law in the United Kingdom was most unsatisfactory. Designs that had eye-appeal and that were potentially registrable under the Registered Designs Act 1949 could be protected either by registration or through the copyright subsisting in drawings showing the design. In both cases, the maximum term of protection was 15 years. However, a design that had no eye-appeal at all, that is to say, a functional design, was protected through the copyright in any drawings showing the design for the life of the author of the drawing plus fifty years. This was clearly an untenable position and largely accounted for the House of Lords decision in *British Leyland* v *Armstrong Patents*, extracts from which are reproduced in Chapter 1. The only limitation to protection of designs through drawings was that a lay person would recognise that the drawing was of the design, the 'lay recognition' test in section 9(8) of the Copyright Act 1956. This was not a difficult hurdle in most cases.

The Copyright, Designs and Patents Act 1988 attempted to rationalise design law and make it more satisfactory. It retained the Registered Designs Act 1949, with modifications, and introduced a new unregistered design right intended primarily for functional designs. However, there is a large overlap between registered designs and the design right and both may subsist in the same design. Conceptually, a registered design gives a monopoly right not unlike a patent whilst the design right is more like a copyright. The design right is still relatively untested in the courts although there have been some helpful cases, extracts from which are reproduced in the second part of this chapter.

Dorling v *Honnor Marine* below shows the confused state of affairs that existed prior to the amendments to design law made by the Copyright, Designs and Patents Act 1988. Even if a design had not been registered, its registrability was crucial to the question of copyright protection.

Dorling v *Honnor Marine* [1965] 1 Ch 1, Court of Appeal

The plaintiff designed a sailing dinghy and granted a licence to the second defendant allowing him to build boats to the design and to make kits of parts from which the boats could be assembled. The kits were sold with instructions, photographs, plans and drawings. Following unsuccessful negotiations between the plaintiff and second defendant concerning the formation of a boat-building business, the second defendant assigned his licence to the first defendant a company formed by the second defendant. The plaintiff sued for infringement of the copyright subsisting in the plans of the boat by the defendants' reproduction of the plans and photographs by making a three-dimensional representation of them.

Although it was accepted that the boat was registrable under the Registered Designs Act 1949, it had not been registered. At first instance the judge held that the licence was not assignable but that the plaintiff had 'lost' the copyright in the plans by virtue of section 10(3) of the Copyright Act 1956 which suppressed artistic copyright in registrable designs.

Danckwerts LJ (at 17): 'This is an appeal from a judgment of Cross J dated April 10, 1963. The questions to be decided are essentially matters of law ... There is no appeal against the decision in favour of Colonel Honnor and this court is only concerned with the conduct of a company called "Honnor Marine Ltd." which was formed by Colonel Honnor on July 8, 1960, and to which Colonel Honnor purported to assign the licence which he held from the plaintiff. The judge held that the licence was personal to Colonel Honnor and so not assignable to the company. Nonetheless, he held that the action failed against the company and the appeal is against the effect of the judge's decision so far as it affects that company, and this involves consideration of the plaintiff's rights against that company having regard to the Copyright Act, 1956, and the Registered Designs Act, 1949 ...

The company completed two complete dinghies and a certain number of kits and had prepared advertisements of the 14 ft. "Scorpion" sailing dinghy and instructions for building from the kit of parts. These advertisements and instructions contained photographs of the dinghy or parts of it, which had not been taken directly of the plaintiff's plans, but had been taken of the completed boat or of the various parts made from the plans. The result, at any rate in my opinion, was a series of pictures which strongly resembled the drawings in the plaintiff's set of plans.

It is common ground that under the Copyright Act, 1956, the plaintiff had copyright in the plans as an artistic work, unless and except in so far as he had failed to register something which he ought to have registered under the Registered Designs Act, 1949. That is the result of section 3 of the Copyright Act, 1956, under which the copyright in the work would continue to subsist until the end of the period of 50 years from the end of the calendar year in which the author died. It should be observed that there is no requirement of registration under the Copyright Act, 1956.

The importance of copyright consists in the right which the owner of the copyright has to prevent the reproduction of his work by other persons, causing an infringement of his copyright. Section 48(1) of the Act provides that "reproduction," in the case of an artistic work, includes a version produced by converting the work into a three-dimensional form, or if it is in three dimensions, by converting it into a two-dimensional form, and references to reproducing a work are to be construed accordingly. Under section 49(1) it is sufficient if a substantial part of the work is reproduced.

One of the questions to be considered is whether the company by photographing the boat and the parts (which are conversions, it appears, of the plaintiff's artistic work, the plans, into three dimensional form) have committed an infringement of the plaintiff's copyright in his plans.

Section 10 of the Copyright Act contains provisions which appear to be intended to prevent the owner of copyright having at the same time, copyright in the same thing both under the Copyright Act, 1956, and under the provisions of the Registered Designs Act 1949, relating to industrial copyright ... Nothing has been registered by the plaintiff under the Registered Designs Act, 1949, and accordingly it is necessary to refer to that Act to see whether anything could have been registered by the plaintiff under that Act and what effect (if any) that Act has upon the plaintiff's copyright.

The essential object of the Registered Designs Act, 1949, is the protection of designs intended to be reproduced in quantity for industrial purposes. Section 1(1) permits the proprietor to be registered under the Act in respect of any article or set of articles. But "set of articles" seems to have a limited meaning, being concerned with something like a tea-set ...

The previous statutory provisions permitted registration in respect of classes. The present Act only permits registration in respect of an article (apart from a set of articles as above mentioned), and apparently if the design is to be applied to several different articles a separate registration is required in respect of each. By the Copyright (Industrial) Designs Rules, 1957, a design is to be taken to be applied industrially for the purpose of section 10 of the Copyright Act, 1956, if it is applied to more than 50 articles. The design has to be new and original (section 1(2)).

Section 1(3) contains the vital provision in the Act. It is as follows: "In this Act the expression 'design' means features of shape, configuration, pattern or ornament applied to an article by any industrial process or means, being features which in the finished article appeal to and are judged solely by the eye, but does not include a method or principle of construction or features of shape or configuration which are dictated solely by the function which the article to be made in that shape or configuration has to perform."

"Shape or configuration" are the only features in the category which can be material to the present case. It is essential that these are applied to some article and they cannot be considered in the abstract. They are judged solely by the eye. Methods of construction are ruled out, as are also features which are purely functional. The application of this subsection is of the greatest importance in the present case, because if there is nothing in the plaintiff's plans or the articles to be produced from them which is registrable, the Registered Designs Act has no application and the plaintiff's copyright remains unimpaired and unaffected by any of the provisions of the Registered Designs Act and the provisions of section 10 of the Copyright Act, 1956, are irrelevant.

It was common ground that the plans were not registrable under the Registered Designs Act, and that also the parts or kits were not registrable under that Act because they were essentially functional. It was suggested that the one thing which was registrable under the Act was the shape of the completed dinghy and the arguments proceeded on the footing that the shape of the completed boat was a registrable design. I feel the greatest doubt whether that was correct. I should have thought that the shape of the boat was necessarily functional, and was, therefore, not registrable under the Registered Designs Act, 1949. If it is not registrable, of course, the provisions of the Registered Designs Act, 1949, and provisions in section 10 of the Copyright Act, 1956, designed to prevent the proprietor of a design having both artistic copyright and the protection of a registered design, would be irrelevant.

It would be unnecessary to consider some troublesome provisions in the Registered Designs Act, 1949, which, on the assumption that they are relevant, must now be considered. This involves the consideration of "Right given by registration" (section 7).

On the assumptions which have been accepted in argument, the main part of this subsection [section 7(1)] creates no real problem because it can only affect the shape or configuration of the completed boat at the most. But an extremely difficult question is what is the true meaning of the concluding provision, "anything for enabling any such article to be made as aforesaid", and it has been argued strongly that this brings in, under the registrability of the shape of the completed boat, the parts and the kits with which a complete boat might be constructed.

Some argument has turned on the words "any such article as aforesaid", which it has been contended on behalf of the plaintiff means the article previously referred to as an article to be made for sale or for use for any trade or business, and it is suggested that the kits of parts are intended to enable amateurs to construct their own boats and therefore are not intended for sale or for use for the purposes of any trade or business.

There is, in my opinion, great force in this argument. It was submitted on behalf of the defendants that this point was not open to the plaintiff in this court and that there was no evidence that the kits were intended for amateurs. The onus of proving that the kits were for sale or for use for the purposes of any trade or business, however, seems clearly to be on the defendants. Moreover, the words in the defendants' circular "Scorpion - Build her yourself" indicate that the kits were intended for amateurs. But, in any case, I do not think that the provision in question can be intended to bring in, by a side wind, articles which are purely functional, and would not otherwise be within the registration of a design. My conclusion, therefore, is that, so far as copyright under the Copyright Act, 1956, is concerned, the plaintiff is not troubled with difficulties from the Registered Designs Act, 1949, except so far as the shape of the completed boat is concerned, and for my part I do not think that the plaintiff is really affected as regards that part of his artistic work, because I do not think that it is registrable. I shall return, therefore to consideration of the Copyright Act, 1956, with the object of ascertaining whether the plaintiff's rights under that Act have been infringed by the operations of the defendant company.

If the shape of the completed boat ought to have been registered as a design under the Registered Designs Act, 1949, the plaintiff is deprived of his remedies under the Copyright Act, 1956, by virtue of section 10 of that Act. But if the shape of the completed boat could not be registered, the shape of the completed boat is in the same position as the parts of the kits, and maybe protected as well as the plans under the definition of "reproduction" in section 48(1) of the Copyright Act, 1956, because reproduction includes in the case of an artistic work "a version produced by converting the work into a three-dimensional form." The provisions of section 49(1) of the Act, which brings in the copying of a substantial part of the work, should also be borne in mind.

Reliance was placed on behalf of the defendants on the extraordinary provision in section 9(8) of the Act (which was the subject of a cross-appeal). It may be that the section was intended to prevent claims of infringement except in obvious cases. But the subsection presents the court with a very difficult, if not impossible, task. The courts are well used to matters depending on the evidence of experts, whose opinion can thus be readily obtained, even if they are not often in agreement. But how is the impact of the appearance of an object on a non-expert (perhaps "the man on the Clapham bus") to be ascertained? Neither the judge nor this court had the advantage of seeing a kit of parts, though the judge (unlike this court) had the advantage of viewing a completed boat, it appears.

The judge, who said that he knew nothing whatever about boats or plans of boats, appears to have considered that he was, therefore, a qualified non-expert for the purposes of section 9(8). The conclusion to which he came was "that some of the parts - sufficient together to constitute a substantial part of the whole boat - would have appeared to a non-expert, who did not know that they were in fact based on the plans, to be reproductions of the corresponding drawings on the plans, but that he would not have felt any strong conviction that the completed boat was a three-dimensional version of the plans".

I am in a somewhat more difficult position than the judge because I am used to reading plans for the purpose of making models. But, applying my mind to the problems as best I can, I agree with the judge's conclusion as regards the parts. As regards the completed boat, I should have thought that a non-expert would have recognised it as the boat shown in the plans, because Dorling's "Scorpion" is rather a striking and individual design, and the first sheet of the plans contains very clear representations of the completed boat. But I feel that the decision to be made is extremely difficult without seeing the kits of parts of the completed boat, without the assistance of any evidence from non-experts, and without the assistance of a jury. In the result, I agree with the conclusion of the judge that the defendant company gets no help from section 9(8).

The judge, however, thought that the plaintiff was defeated by the operation of section 10 of the Copyright Act, 1956, and section 7 of the Registered Designs Act, 1949. As I have indicated already, I do not agree with these conclusions ...

In my opinion, the plaintiff is entitled to succeed in the Chancery action against the company, and I agree that the appeal should be allowed, and the cross-appeal should be dismissed.'

COMMENT

The Design Copyright Act 1968 modified the Copyright Act 1956 to the effect that dual protection under registered designs law and artistic copyright was a possibility. Failing to register a registrable design would leave the owner of the design with copyright protection for 15 years.

Danckwerts LJ expressed doubts as to whether the shape of the boat as a whole was registrable. Was he right to entertain such doubts? Should carelessness in failing to register a design be rewarded with alternative protection under copyright law? Compare with the situation where an inventor discloses his invention to the public before applying for a patent. Does the inventor have any protection at law in respect of unauthorised copying or use of his invention?

Requirements for Registered Designs

Section 1 of the Registered Designs Act 1949 contains a statement of the basic requirements for registration of a design. For the purposes of the Act, a 'design' means features of shape, configuration, pattern or ornament applied to any article by an industrial process being features which in the finished article appeal to and are judged by the eye. There are a number of exceptions, notably methods or principles of construction or features of shape or configuration which are dictated solely by the function which the article has to perform or which are dependent upon the appearance of another article of which the article is intended by the author to form an integral part.

In the following case, the meaning of the functional exception was considered as well as the eye-appeal requirement. It shows some generosity to the proprietor of a design in both respects, though, in the event, the designs were held to be invalid.

Amp Inc. v *Utilux Pty. Ltd.* [1972] RPC 103, House of Lords

The plaintiff alleged that the defendant had infringed its registered designs in relation to electric terminals which were small metal connectors with two sets of ears to be crimped around an electrical wire. They were originally made for use in washing machines. It was argued that the designs were dictated by their function and this was accepted by the trial judge. The Court of Appeal reversed the judgment at first instance and held that the exclusion in section 1(3) of the Registered Designs Act 1949, to the effect that a registrable design does not include features dictated solely by the function the article had to perform, only applied if an article to perform the function could be made in that shape or no other. The defendant appealed to the House of Lords.

Lord Reid (at 107): 'There had been protection of new or original designs against infringement in a succession of statutes for over a century before 1949. The present definition dates in part from 1919 and in part from 1949. I get little assistance from the way in which it has evolved. It remains obscure in several respects. Before considering its terms I would enquire what is the problem and what is the apparent policy of the legislation.

Those who wish to purchase an article for use are often influenced in their choice not only by practical efficiency but by appearance. Common experience shews that not all are influenced in the same way. Some look for artistic merit. Some are attracted by a design which is strange or bizarre. Many simply choose the article which catches their eye. Whatever the reason may be one article with a particular design may sell better than one without it: then it is profitable to use the design. And much thought, time and expense may have been incurred in finding a design which will increase sales.

Parliament has been concerned to see that the originator of a profitable design is not deprived of his reward by others applying it to their goods. But it has not given protection under the 1949 Act to everything which could be called a design. To be protected the design must come within the definition. Designs which do not come within this definition may or may not be protected by other legislation. We are not concerned with that in this case. The question in this case is whether this terminal has a design which comes within this definition.

The definition includes features of shape, configuration, pattern or ornament. We are not concerned with pattern or ornament. Configuration may have a meaning slightly different from shape: no point is made of that in this case. The first requirement is that the shape is "applied" by an industrial process. "Applied" is an appropriate word for pattern or ornament but is an awkward word with regard to shape. The idea must be that there can be two articles similar in every respect except shape, and that the novel features of shape which is the design has been added to the article by making it in the new shape instead of in some other shape which is not novel.

Then there come the words "being features which in the finished article appeal to and are judged solely by the eye". This must be intended to be a limitation of the foregoing generality. The eye must be the eye of the customer if I am right in holding that the policy of the Act was to preserve to the owner of the design the commercial value resulting from customers preferring the appearance of articles which have the design to that of those which do not have it. So the design must be one which appeals to the eye of some customers. And the words "judged solely by the eye" must be intended to exclude cases where a customer might choose an article of that shape not because of its appearance but because he thought that the shape made it more useful to him.

In the case of finished articles sold to members of the public for use by them I doubt whether this limitation is of much importance. The onus is on the person who attacks the validity of the registration of a design. So he would have to shew on a balance of probability that an article with the design would have no greater appeal by reason of its appearance to any member of the public than an article which did not have this design. Looking to the great variety of popular tastes this would seem an almost impossible burden to discharge.

But the definition of "article" in section 44 of the Act includes any part of an article made and sold separately. So it includes components like these terminals which are sold to manufacturers to be incorporated in the machines which they make. In such a case it might well be possible to prove that no manufacturer who wanted to buy terminals to use as components would be influenced by their appearance: he would only be influenced by their suitability for the use which he proposed to make of them.

In the present case this was not fully explored in evidence and I do not intend to consider whether the appellants might have succeeded on this ground.

I must, however, say something about a more limited meaning of this provision which has obtained considerable support. It has been said that it merely means - being features which have a distinctive appearance. But every feature of shape must have a distinctive appearance; and I cannot imagine any draftsman using the words of this provision if that was all he meant to say, nor can I imagine anyone thinking that worth saying in a definition. I think this despairing refusal to give any real meaning to the provision has arisen from failure to perceive any acceptable alternative ...

Much of the controversy has centred round the word "dictated" which is a metaphorical word out of place in a statutory definition. Unfortunately the draftsman, instead of saying what he meant in his own words, chose to lift words from a judgment where metaphor may be useful and illustrative: it is not the function of a judge to draft definitions. In *Kestos v Kempat* (1936) 53 RPC 139 Luxmoore J said: "A mere mechanical device is a shape in which all the features are dictated solely by the function or functions which the article has to perform". I think that he probably meant that all the features served purely functional purposes and that no feature was there for any other purpose. But we are not concerned with what he meant: we are concerned with what this word "dictated" means in the context of this definition. There it is ambiguous as the draftsman would have seen if he had paused to reflect.

The respondents' argument is that a shape is only dictated by function if it is necessary to use that precise shape and no other in order to perform the function. Admittedly if that is the meaning the scope of this provision would be reduced almost to vanishing point because it is difficult to imagine any actual case where one shape and one shape alone will work. A key was suggested. Its function is to turn a particular lock, and only one shape of key will do that. But that is not quite true. In most cases at least a skeleton key of a different shape will also turn the lock. In the end no actual case was found where only one precise shape would do.

It seems improbable that the framers of this definition could have intended to insert a provision which has virtually no practical effect, so I look to see whether any other meaning produces a more reasonable result.

Again I think that a clue can be found from a consideration of which must have been the object of the provision. If the purpose of the Act was to give protection to a designer where design has added something of value to the prior art then one would expect an exclusion from protection of those cases where nothing has been added because every feature of the shape sought to be protected originated from purely functional considerations.

Stenor Ltd. v *Whitesides (Clitheroe) Ltd.* (1948) 65 RPC 1; [1948] AC 107 was a case decided under the old definition before the words of Luxmoore J had been imported into the definition but his words were taken as "a useful and accurate test" (per Lord Simon at page 121). The question related to the design of a fuse which had to fit as a kind of key into a vulcanising machine. In the Court of Appeal Morton LJ had said that its "shape possesses no features beyond those necessary to enable the article to fulfil its function". That ground of judgment was approved (page 122) by Lord Simon. Lord Porter said (page 128): "Primarily the object of the Act is to protect shape not function, and not to protect functional shape". Lord Uthwatt said (page 139): "Every feature in the design was apt to serve a mechanical object and no feature had any other substantial quality. In the sum of the qualities of the design there was a mechanical device and nothing else". It may be that *Stenor's* case is distinguishable on the facts but in my view the grounds of judgment greatly assist the appellants.

It is fair to say that some other authorities assist the respondents to some extent although admittedly none has to be overruled or even disapproved if this appeal is allowed. Plainly Lloyd-Jacob J did not feel happy with that trend of authority for he said in this case:

"Before entering upon a detailed consideration of the contentions which have been raised in respect of these matters, it is only right to acknowledge a sense of unreality in endeavouring to relate the product of an avowedly functional exercise to the requirements of an Act which offers protection for attempts to provide individuality of appearance. As Mr Collier frankly acknowledged, neither he nor his customer were concerned with any matter of eye-appeal except in the sense of seeing that the terminal would be suitable for the performance of the duty it was required to perform ..."

I do not think that we should allow that unreality to continue. There must be a blend of industrial efficiency with visual appeal. If the shape is not there to appeal to the eye but solely to make the article work then this provision excludes it from the statutory protection.

I would add to avoid misunderstanding that no doubt in the great majority of cases which the Act will protect the designer had visual appeal in mind when composing his design. But it could well be that a designer who only thought of practical efficiency in fact has produced a design which does appeal to the eye. He would not be denied protection because that was not his object when he composed the design.'

COMMENT

A registrable design had to have features which appealed to and were judged solely by the eye. Did the design under consideration have such features? The plaintiff admitted that the designs in question were the result of functional considerations only. How has the "eye-appeal" requirement been changed by the amendments made by the Copyright, Designs and Patents Act 1988? In practice, will these changes have any effect at all?

The eye-appeal requirement has been liberally interpreted in the past as the following case, concerning the design of a shower tray, demonstrates.

Gardex Ltd. v Sorata Ltd. [1976] RPC 623, Chancery Division

The plaintiff had a registered design in respect of a shower tray. In an infringement action there was a challenge on the validity of the registration on the basis that the underside of the shower tray, which included particular features that were registered, lacked eye-appeal because, once fitted, no-one would ever see the underside. Another of the defendant's arguments was that the design features of the underside of the shower tray were only a method or principle of construction.

Falconer J (at 636): 'The features put forward by the plaintiffs as constituting the features of the registered design are the particular shaping of the surround with the sharp corners and straight shape from the bottom portion against the floor, which is flat, up to where it is adjacent the flat under-board portion, giving the appearance of a picture frame surrounding the centre board; the shape of the four feet or supports, the diagonal distribution of those feet or supports; and the disposition of the hole of the waste escape which is placed symmetrically between those two supports nearest the back wall so as to produce a symmetrical effect. Also to be seen in the registered design, if one looks at the illustrations of the underside, is to be seen in the wall adjacent the waste exit a little wedge portion which has been cut out of the sloping wall, which is really, of course, the foam wall in the actual article. It is conceded that that cut out is purely functional in order to accommodate the waste pipe when the vent is in position, and it is not suggested or been sought to say that that is any feature which appeals to the eye and is therefore part of the registered design.

It is accepted by the plaintiffs that primarily the underside depicted in the registered design is functional, but nevertheless they submit that separate considerations played a part in the actual design, and particularly the shaping of the surround (which in the actual article, of course, is a foam surround) so as to produce that picture framing effect upon which they rely, and the particular disposition of the feet or supports and shape of the feet or supports, and the disposition of the waste exit symmetrically centrally between two of those feet or supports. That was the effect of the evidence of Mr Burgess. His evidence was that in designing that under-side, as he did in 1974, there were two considerations. First there was a consideration of function, which he at once said was a strong consideration. Equally he said the aesthetic appeal of the underside was important and he had it in mind because, he said, in the eye of the purchaser or the builder's merchant or the plumber who was going to install it, "the thing must look good".

He was cross-examined at considerable length on this aspect of the case, as well as others, but while he agreed with the functional aspects of the features which are seen in the registered design on the under-side, he maintained his position that the particular configuration and shape that can be seen in the registered design was in part at least due to the aesthetic considerations to which he referred. In that regard one can see that there is no need, for example, for the corners of the surround which support the wall to be sharp, although they are; as a matter of design, they could have been rounded, for example. There is no need for the surround to be the particular shape it is, that is to say a flat portion immediately adjacent the moulded tray walls followed by a straight section going up to adjacent the under-wall; that could be either straight from the edge without a flat portion adjacent the floor, or, of course, it could be a curved shape. Again, there is no need for the feet or supports to be trapezoidal in shape, and even if trapezoidal, there is no need for them to be diagonally disposed; they could be disposed parallel to the side, or across the corner rather like the soap dishes. And there is no need, as Mr Burgess was at pains to explain in cross-examination, for the waste-hole to be in the centre, in fact from a functional point of view his evidence was it would be better in a corner.

... Going back for a moment to the passage that I read from the opinion of Lord Reid in *AMP* v *Utilux* at page 108, line 22, the words I read, I do emphasise:

"And the words 'judged solely by the eye' must be intended to exclude cases where a customer might choose an article of that shape not because of its appearance but because he thought that the shape made it more useful to him."

Here there was no evidence from the defendants to that effect at all, and the onus is upon the defendants in attacking the validity of the design.

The second objection was that the features constituted only a method or principle of construction. Mr Whittle, in his development of this argument, referred to one of the plaintiffs' patents now revoked but originally in this action, No. 1508595, which is to be found in Bundle J at page 62, and he took me through the claims of that patent on which he made some submissions.

Before I go to that, I read a portion from the 5th Edition of *Russell-Clark on Copyright in Industrial Design* to be found on page 27. Under the heading "No method of principle of construction can be a design" this is stated:

"A method or principle of construction of a process or operation by which a shape is produced as opposed to the shape itself. To say that a shape is to be denied registration because it amounts to a mode or principle of construction is meaningless. The real meaning is this, that no design shall be construed so widely as to give to its proprietor a monopoly in a mode or principle of construction. What he gets a monopoly for is one particular individual and specific appearance. If it is possible to get several different appearances which all embody the general features which he claims, then those features are too general and amount to a mode or principle of construction. In other words any construction which is so general as to allow of several different appearances being read within it is too vague and may be invalid."

That passage has appeared in all the editions of the late Mr Russell-Clarke's work and it was in fact specifically cited, approved and applied by Luxmoore J in *Kestos Ltd.* v *Kempat Ltd. and Kemp* (1936) 53 RPC 151 ...

[The foam filling] in section could be straight from the edge of the outer shell to the underboard, or it could be curved, or it could be discontinuous, and there is nothing about the corners, and in particular there is nothing to suggest or specify sharp corners which contribute to the picture frame effect of the registered design. In my judgment, there is nothing in this particular objection and I hold the registered design to be valid.

Coming to infringement, section 7(1) of the Registered Designs Act 1949 defines the right given by registration to the proprietor as

"the exclusive right"

- and the next part does not matter for present purposes -

"to make or import for sale or for use for the purposes of any trade or business or to sell, hire or offer for sale or hire, any article in respect of which the design is registered, being an article to which the registered design or a design not substantially different from the registered design has been applied";

and Mr Russell-Clarke has pointed out in his book (at page 83):

"The question is: has the alleged infringement substantially the same appearance as the registered design?"

The defendants say that their shower base, of which P.4 is the example before the court, has not got the wedge shaped cut out feature, but that, as I have already pointed out, cannot be relied upon, and is not relied upon, as one of the features of the registered design, being purely functional, so that does not enter into the consideration on infringement. As to the rest of the features, the only difference that I can see from the registered design is that in P.4 the feet, although diagonally disposed, are not adjacent the corners in the way they are depicted in the registered design. They are off-set a little from the corners, as can be seen. It seems to me that it is not really possible to argue that the defendants' shower base does not have substantially the same design as that of the registered design and, in my judgment, there is plainly infringement. So on the registered design part of the case I hold the design to be valid and infringed.'

COMMENT

Notice that the burden of proof, when attacking the validity of the design, in an infringement action, is on the defendant. The managing director of the plaintiff company had given evidence to the effect that when he had finished designing the shower tray he was so pleased with the appearance, including that of the underside, that he thought it merited registration as a design. Does this case show that the eye-appeal requirement is almost redundant? Should design registration be available for all new designs, subject to limited exceptions, whether or not they have or are intended to have eye-appeal? Is there any logical reason why designs that are purely functional should be denied the protection of the registered design system?

The following case considers, *inter alia,* novelty in respect of designs for rear light clusters for motor vehicles. Although the registrations were ordered to be revoked, the plaintiff was successful in a claim to copyright infringement in drawings which existed prior to 1 August 1989 and which depicted the designs in question.

Valeo Vision S.A. v *Flexible Lamps Ltd.* [1995] RPC 205, Patents Court

The plaintiffs made rear light clusters for vehicles and were the proprietors of two registered designs in respect of them. They also owned the copyright in drawings of light clusters and confidential information in relation to them. The drawings and information had been disclosed to a third party in confidence who then disclosed them to the defendant who manufactured competing lamp clusters.

The plaintiff sued for infringement of their registered designs and copyright and in respect of breach of confidence. The defendants counterclaimed for revocation of the registered designs and argued that a substantial part of the drawings had not been reproduced by it. Furthermore, the defendant denied being bound by an obligation of confidence.

Aldous J (at 213): 'The defendant alleges that the registered designs were not new and are therefore invalid. That allegation was a ground of revocation before s 1 of the 1949 Act was amended. It follows that if the registered designs were not novel, the registrations will be revoked. The defendant also alleges that the registered designs do not relate to designs as defined, in that they relate to features which are dictated solely by the function which the article has to perform. That also was an allegation which, if established, ensured revocation under the section before amendment and does so after amendment. The defendant goes further and alleges that the features of the registered designs are dependent upon the appearance of another article of which the lamp screens are intended to form an integral part (see s1(b)(ii) as amended). That ground of invalidity was added by the 1988 Act. It follows that if it is established, s266 applies and a licence of right will come available on 1 August 1988 [sic, 1989]. If an appropriate undertaking is offered, then any injunction granted should lapse on that date. Thus the matters to be considered are:

(1) Novelty (sections 1(2) and (4));
(2) Whether the features are solely dictated solely by the function (section 1(1)(b)(i));

(3) Whether the features are dependent upon the appearance of another article (section 1(1)(b)(ii));

(4) Infringement (s 7).

The definition of "design" set out in the 1949 Act has been considered by the courts in a number of cases. The most recent and definitive statement as to its interpretation is contained in the judgment of Lord Oliver in *Interlego A. G.* v *Tyco Industries Inc.* [1989] AC 217. Although Lord Oliver considered s 1 before amendment, I believe that what he said applies to the amended section. At page 241D, he came to consider the definition of design in s 1 and its legislative history. Having concluded that the definition required "eye-appeal", he said at page 242C:

> "There are, apart from authority, three possible constructions of the definition taken as a whole, as was pointed out by Megaw LJ in the Court of Appeal in *Amp Inc.* v *Utilux Pty Ltd.* [1970] RPC 397, 433. It could mean that all that is registrable or is to be considered in connection with an application for registration is that part of the shape or configuration which has eye-appeal, any purely functional feature being excluded from registration. Alternatively, it could mean that any design which includes any feature which is dictated solely by function is to be excluded from registration. Or, finally, it could mean that a design which, ex hypothesi, has eye-appeal will be excluded from registration only if every feature of it is one which is dictated solely by function.
>
> No one has contended for the first of these possibilities and such a construction would, indeed, make very little sense. In approaching the definition it is always to be borne in mind what is to be registered. It is a shape, configuration or pattern to be applied to a particular specified article and it is the shape or configuration of the whole article in respect of which there is to be a commercial monopoly. That necessarily involves taking the design and the article as a whole. Thus, the effective choice must be between excluding the whole shape or configuration from registration because there is a part of it that is purely functional or treating the whole shape or configuration as registrable (assuming that is has eye-appeal) unless the whole of it is dictated solely by functional considerations.
>
> In their Lordship's view the latter construction is the one which makes better sense and it is in fact the construction which is supported by the authorities."

In that passage Lord Oliver made it clear that it was only in the case where all the features of the design were dictated by function would protection not be possible. He went on to analyse the speeches in *Amp Inc.* v *Utilux Pty* and concluded at 245G:

> "Lord Morris, at p113, contemplated that it would not and Viscount Dilhorne, at p118, too appears to have contemplated that any feature which went beyond those dictated solely by function and provided eye-appeal would entitle the shape as a whole to protection. This is, in their Lordship's view, clearly right in principle. The incorporation into the shape as a whole of *some* (perhaps a majority of) features dictated only by functional requirements will not bring the

exclusion into operation so as to deprive it of protection, if there are also some features of the shape which are not attributable solely to function."

It follows that if the design is not excluded from registration because all its features are dictated by function, protection is given to the shape as a whole. That being so, the design which comprises the features appealing to and judged by the eye, can include both features dictated by function and those that are not. If the registered designs depict designs not excluded from registration by the definition in the section, then the court must look at the totality of the design features when deciding whether the registered designs are novel and infringed.

It is established law that when deciding what are the features which in the finished article appeal to and are judged by the eye, commonly referred to as the features of "eye-appeal", the court must adopt the mantle of a prospective purchaser of the relevant article, taking into account what had been on the market before. It is not the mantle of the expert that should be worn as he is trained to discern small differences which may not have eye-appeal. In this case, the screens are purchased by truck manufacturers and designed to be seen by members of the public and I believe it right to look at the designs through the eyes of a truck manufacturer taking into account the attitude of members of the public.

On behalf of the plaintiffs, it was submitted that it was permissible and correct in this case to take into account the colours of the screens as shown in the registered designs. I cannot accept that submission. Section 1 of that Act defines a design as "features of shape, configuration, pattern or ornament". The statement of novelty of both registrations limits them to features of shape and configuration. Colour is not a feature of shape nor is it a feature of configuration. It may form part of pattern or ornament.

The plaintiffs also submitted that despite the statement of novelty stating that the features of the design for which novelty was claimed resided in the shape and configuration, it was right to take into account features of pattern and ornament. To support that submission, I was referred to *Barran v Lomas* (1880) 28 WR 973. In that case there was no statement of novelty and it is therefore not an authority which supports the submission; the submission is completely untenable. The whole purpose of a statement of novelty is to confine the design to certain features. In this case, it is clear that both pattern and ornament are excluded from the ambit of the design by limitation to features of shape and configuration.

For the reasons I have given, the colours of the lens shown in the registered designs cannot be taken into account. That being so, the only difference between the two designs is the number of lines running across the lenses. The plaintiffs submitted that these would be seen by the appropriate addressee as being depending ribs. There is no evidence to support that submission and I reject it. The appropriate addressee would see lines, but would be unable to see any ribs. Those lines could be joins either produced by sequential moulding or by welding.

Anybody with any knowledge of lens design would appreciate that the pattern on the lenses was the effect of pillow case optics. They are a well known method of light dispersion used by lens manufacturers and would be felt on the reverse side of the lens. I do not believe that such optics form part of the shape and configuration of the design. If anything they are pattern or ornament. In any case they are purely functional and were and are normal in lenses.

The plaintiffs also suggested that I should compare their LC6 and LC7 lamps, as embodiments of the registered designs, with the prior art and the defendant's lenses when deciding validity and infringement. Such a course can in certain cases be appropriate. However the Act requires the comparison to be made between the registered designs and the prior art and the alleged infringements. That is the course which I have adopted in this case, as details, not apparent from the registered designs, become apparent when the LC6 and LC7 lamps are looked at.

In view of the conclusion that I have reached as to the relevance of colour and the lines across the lenses, the features of shape and configuration of both registered designs appear to be the same. Any conclusion reached as to the validity and infringement of one of those registered designs will apply to the other.

The registered designs must be looked at as a whole, but it is the features of shape and configuration which have eye-appeal which are relevant. The defendant submitted that there was no feature of the design that had eye-appeal, whereas the plaintiffs submitted to the contrary.

For the purpose of this judgment, it is convenient to consider the design as having features and thereafter go on to decide validity and infringement. The following features are apparent:

(i)   The overall shape is rectangular;
(ii) The top edge and corners are rounded;
(iii) The overall proportions of the height to length to width;
(iv) The four lens fixing screw holes arranged in two sets.

The overall impression of the designs is of a shallow rectangular lens with four screw holes.

Novelty

Under the 1949 Act, before and after amendment, a design to be registrable must be novel. That means that it must not be registered in respect of a design which has been prior published or differs in immaterial features or features which are variants commonly used in the trade.

The defendant alleged that the registered designs had been prior published by the prior sale of eight types of rear lamps. Past sale of seven of them were admitted and they were displayed on "Board 1".

The first lamp displayed on Board 1 was a rear lamp manufactured by Cibié. Its lens is rectangular with rounded edges and corners. Dimensionally it appears similar to the registered designs and the only readily apparent difference is the positioning and number of the screw fixing holes. The second was a Vignal lamp. It is also rectangular *in shape* with rounded corners and edges, but is considerably deeper than the registered design. It has two screw fixing holes. The third was made by Hella. Although this has a generally rectangular lens, its top and bottom edges are curved. It does however have four lens fixing screws arranged in a similar pattern to that depicted in the registered design. The fourth was made by Talmu. It has a rectangular lens with rounded edges and corners. Its proportions are substantially the same as that of the registered designs and the only difference readily apparent is that the four lens fixing screws are in a line. The fifth is another Vignal lens. It is generally rectangular. Its relevance is that it has four lens fixing screw holes arranged in the same way as depicted in the registered designs. The sixth was made by Ulo. It also is generally rectangular and has four lens fixing screw holes arranged as in the registered designs. The seventh was made by the defendant. It is rectangular, but does not have any lens fixing screws.

The nearest lenses on Board 1 to the registered designs are the Cibié, the Talmu and the Vignal (No. 5). As to the Cibié and Talmu, the overall shape and dimensions and the shape of the corners and edges are in essence the same. In so far as they differ from the registered design, the differences are immaterial. As to the position and number of the lens fixing screw holes, these vary from lamp to lamp and the arrangement used in the registered designs are variants commonly used in the trade as appears from the Hella, Vignal and Ulo lenses. I conclude that the designs lack novelty over the Cibié and Talmu lenses and are therefore invalid.

It was also submitted that the registered designs were invalid as all the features were dictated solely by function. The evidence was that the eye-appeal of rear lamps for trucks was not of major importance, but the defendant did not establish that it was irrelevant. Further the defendant did not establish that the overall shape and dimensions of the lenses depicted in the registered designs was dictated solely by function. No doubt the designs were led by the functional requirements of the lamps, but other shapes could have been used and have been used. The basic shape of rear lamps has been rectangular for many years, but that does not mean that the particular shape depicted in the registered designs is dictated solely by function. I am therefore not convinced that the designs depicted in the registered designs would not have been registrable, if they had been novel.

The defendant also submitted that the features of the registered designs were dependent upon the appearance of another article of which the lens was intended by the author of the design to form an integral part. Thus it was said that the registered designs were unregistrable having regard to s 1(1) of the 1949 Act as amended by s 265 of the Copyright, Designs and Patents Act 1988. That submission, the plaintiffs submitted, was untenable because the features of the lens depicted in the registered designs were not dependent upon the appearance of the base as the only feature dependent upon the appearance of the base was the outside perimeter. The plaintiffs also submitted that the defendant's submission could not succeed because the lens was designed before the base, with the result that, if there was any dependency, it was the base that was dependent upon the lens and not vice versa.

I believe that the last submission of the plaintiffs is mistaken. The subsection requires the court to look at "another article", in this case the base, and decide whether the shape and configuration of the article depicted in the design is dependent on the appearance of that other article. It matters not whether the other article was made or designed before the article depicted in the registered design. However the first submission of the plaintiffs is correct. To come within the subsection, all the features of shape and configuration which make up the design features must be dependent upon the appearance of the other article and they are not.

If I had held the registered designs valid, I would have held them to have been infringed. As the registered designs are invalid, they must be revoked.'

COMMENT

The registered designs lacked novelty, being variants commonly used in the trade. For the design right (see later in this chapter) a design is not original if it is commonplace in the design field in question at the time of its creation. Are these two tests the same? If not, should the same test apply to both the registered design and the design right?

On the copyright issue, it was held that the copyright in the drawings had been infringed. However, licences have been available as of right in respect of copyright in drawings representing designs since 1 August 1994. Provided the defendant undertook to take such a licence, there could be no injunction after that date; see section 237 and paragraph 19 of Schedule 1 to the Copyright, Designs and Patents Act 1988. There was no evidence that the defendant had made use of confidential information or knew or ought to have known it was confidential. As the information was now in the public domain, no injunction to restrain further use of it would be granted.

Spare Parts

Spare parts, or replacement parts for compound articles, are denied registration on the basis of two provisions in the Registered Designs Act 1949. First, a design must be applied to an article which is, by section 44(1), 'any article of manufacture and includes any part of an article if that part is *made and sold separately*' (emphasis added). Thus, there must be a trade in those parts as such (rather than the parts being bought simply as replacements for damaged or worn out parts); they must be articles of commerce in their own right.

The second exception that is particularly important in relation to spare parts is the 'must-match' exception, introduced by the Copyright, Designs and Patents Act 1988 which inserted the exception in the Registered Designs Act 1949. Features of shape or configuration which are dependent upon the appearance of another article of which the article is intended by the author of the design to form an integral part are excepted by the 'must-match' exception. These two exceptions are considered judicially in the following two cases, the first being concerned with the meaning of 'article' only.

Sifam Electrical Instrument Co. Ltd. v *Sangamo Weston Ltd.* [1973] RPC 899, Chancery Division

The plaintiff alleged that the defendant had copied the design of the front of his electrical meter. The question arose as to whether the meter front was registrable as a design.

Graham J (at 913): 'I come then to the final question: Was the design of the meter front in sketch No. 10 registrable under the Designs Act, 1949? This depends on the words of sections 1 and 44 of that Act. Section 1(1) reads: "A design may be registered under this Act in respect of any article or set of articles specified in the application". Section 44 defines article as including "any part of an article if that part is made and sold separately".

The meter front here is not now and never has been sold separately nor was it ever intended that it should be. The words of the section are, however, difficult because they cannot be read strictly literally. If an article or part of an article is in fact being sold at the time of the application to register that in itself would invalidate the registration because the design would have been published and would not be "new or original" within subsection (2). What then do the words mean? The defendants say they mean "susceptible of being sold separately", which they say this meter front is. But here again any part of any article is susceptible of being sold separately even if, for example, the part has to be forcibly removed from the whole of the article of which it forms part. A possible dividing line might be drawn between parts which are detachable and parts which are not, but again nowadays it is common to sell parts of larger articles which are intended to be permanently fixed to the larger article of which they are to form part by welding or other permanent fixing. Why should designs not be registrable for such parts which are susceptible of industrial design and of being dealt with as article of commerce? However to give the words such a meaning would have the result that any part of any article could then be registered and thus would defeat the apparent intention of the Act. One might also then ask: When is part of an article not an article in its own right?

I find the matter difficult to decide, but on the whole I think the intention must be to grant registration only for such articles as are intended by the proprietor of the design to be put on the market and sold separately, such as for example a hammer handle, or the bit of a bradawl. This happens also, I understand, to be in accordance with the present practice of the Registrar, that is, the Comptroller General of Patents, Designs and Trade Marks.

By way of contrast reference in this connection may be made to designs Nos.935,397, 941,702 and 946,801 of the defendants in this case. These designs are really to cover their design of new meter fronts, but they have only been allowed to be registered as shown there, that is as forming part of the whole meter illustrated in each case, though novelty is only claimed in respect of the parts coloured blue, that is the new fronts. The whole position is to my mind not at all satisfactory, and ought to be considered with a view to clarification by suitable amending legislation.

In the meantime I have to decide what the phrase means, and consider, as I say, that the only possible interpretation, which does not do undue violence to the intention of the Act or present Office practice, which it is not desirable to upset if it can be avoided, is to give them the meaning "is to be sold separately".

The words used are "if that part is made and sold separately", and the phrase as a whole, to my mind, confirms that both the manufacture and sale of the part in question must be operations which are distinct from the manufacture and sale of the whole article of which the "part" forms a component. It is necessary to imply the words "to be" in order to construe the phrase as not including sale of the part prior to or at the date of the application for registration since this would produce an absurd result contrary to section 1(2), would invalidate the registration, and cannot possibly have been the intention of the legislature.

If this is right the plaintiffs on the facts could not register under the Registered Designs Act, 1949, and their copyright under the Copyright Act, 1956, always was in full force. If I am wrong and the designs should have been registered the defendants had a complete defence under section 10 of the Copyright Act of 1956 in its original form until it was amended and the amending section came into force on the 25th October 1968. Thereafter their defence was no longer available and the plaintiffs can succeed under the Act as amended.'

COMMENT
What is the difference between the phrases 'made and sold separately' and 'made separately and is to be sold separately'? This case again shows the problem with the interaction between copyright and registered design law and the section 10 defence under the Copyright Act 1956 which was removed by the Design Copyright Act 1968. However, the defendant contended that he could still avail himself of the section 10 defence because the plaintiff's artistic copyright had been destroyed as the meter fronts were designed before the 1968 Act came into force. Before that time the defendant could copy the meter fronts. Why?

The following case (and the subsequent appeal to the House of Lords) is of enormous significance to the motor trade where the market in spare parts and the protection of those parts is of some considerable importance.

Ford Motor Co. Ltd.'s Design Applications [1994] RPC 545, Queen's Bench Division

The Ford Motor Company made a large number of applications to the Design Registry to register various parts of their motor vehicles. These were all rejected and the company appealed to the Registered Designs Appeal Tribunal which allowed the appeal in respect of three designs only. The company appealed to the Divisional Court of the Queen's Bench Division for judicial review of the decisions of the Registrar of Designs and the Tribunal.

McCowan LJ (at 551): 'Mr Jeffs [sitting as a deputy judge in the Registered Designs Tribunal] said at [1993] RPC 399 at 419:

"Here the door panels have no reality as articles of commerce apart from their forming part of a complete vehicle, unlike the hammer handle postulated by the judge which could presumably be fitted to any number of different heads. I am therefore of the view that door panels are not registrable".

He continued at F on that page:

"That would be enough to deny registration to any of the articles which I put in the first group, but in case I am wrong about that, I shall now consider section 1(1)(b)(ii) - the 'must match' section.

In the context of this case, 'another article' must refer to the vehicle as a whole. Various possible meanings for the word 'integral' have been urged upon me, but giving the words their normal English meaning, the door panel is the first 'article' and the other 'article', of which the article intended by the author of the design to form an integral part, is the vehicle. The door panel is part of the door and the door forms an essential, integral, part of the vehicle. The word 'integral' was, I am informed, inserted at a late stage in the passage of the bill to avoid difficulties with items which do not stand alone but which nevertheless do not form part of a whole, such as cups and saucers or knife and forks. The word is apt for the purpose of avoiding the difficulties that such items might otherwise pose.

Some parts of a vehicle may be replaceable with parts of a different configuration. For instance, a steering wheel may be replaced deliberately with an alternative wheel of a sportier design while leaving the general appearance of the vehicle unchanged, but that does not apply to a door panel. As a matter of practical commonsense, if a door panel is to be replaced, it must be replaced by one which, for all practical purposes, is the same as the original. This approach would deprive all the body components of the kind listed in the first group for registrability. To overcome this sweeping consequence, the appellants /applicants urge me (as they urged the superintending examiner) to adopt an 'n-1' approach. On such an approach, one could consider the vehicle with the door removed, but in my judgment this approach is not the right one. The designer of the door did not intend it to form an integral part of a vehicle with a door missing. From its first conception, the door was intended to form an integral part of a complete vehicle. Moreover, one has the difficulty that there are doors on both sides. One is generally the mirror image of the other, though there may be minor differences, as when an additional window is inserted low down in the driver's door of a lorry and is omitted from the passenger's door. But even when there are slight modifications such as that, the general shape and configuration of one door is decided by the other. It must match. To overcome the difficulty, it was suggested that I should adopt an n-2 approach, notionally taking off both doors, but it appears to me that this approach is even more artificial than the n-1 approach and I reject it for the same reason. Such components are 'must match' and are unregistrable owing to the provisions of section 1(1)(b)(ii) of the Act.

I come now to the second group of components, such items as wing mirrors, wheels, seats and steering wheel. All of them are visible on the car as sold but substitutions can be made without radically affecting the appearance or identity of the vehicle. It is such standard practice that I can take judicial notice of the fact that alternatives may be offered for items such as these and an owner may choose to substitute proprietary items in order to give his vehicle a sportier appearance, or (where a seat is concerned) for greater comfort, or for a variety of other reasons. Although if any substitution is made the owner may wish it to blend in the general style of vehicle, I am of the view that such items are not 'dependent upon the appearance of another article'".

I am able to leave out the next few sentences and take it up at [1993] RPC 399 at 420.

"While I propose to allow these appeals in respect of components of the second group, it does not of course follow that they will in fact be registered. The applications are frozen in a preliminary stage and the Registrar still has to be satisfied about such requirements as novelty."

The Tribunal went on to consider *Pepper* v *Hart* and Mr Jeffs then said, at [1993] RPC 399 at 421:

"I have been shown long extracts from the Parliamentary debates, as was the superintending examiner. This is a case in which I think it proper to look at those debates as the Act is undoubtedly ambiguous and obscure. Unfortunately many of the ministerial statements to which I was referred were as obscure as the Act but some were undoubtedly helpful."

... having cited from the statements [Mr Jeffs] quoted from the superintending examiner's decision:

"... the cited extracts do seem to provide a clear and consistent indication that the 'must match' exception was intended to exclude vehicle body panels and other parts contributing to the appearance of the vehicle. I have been unable to find any contrary indications which would tend to support the alternative interpretations argued for by Ford and Iveco Fiat."

He said that, in contrast to the superintending examiner, he had the assistance of the applicants on this question of looking at the statements of the pilots of the Bill, but that in any event he concluded that those extracts confirmed the construction that he had put upon the Act without reference to the debates.

He then turned to look at the specific components in the Ford applications and held that all that fell within his first group were unregistrable but that the three components which fell within the second group, namely a wheel and two wheel covers, were inherently registrable and the question of their registrability should be remitted to the Registrar.

Mr Wilson appearing for the applicant has stressed to this court that it is a matter of general importance whether "spare part rights" have been swept away by the amendments to the 1949 Act, or indeed that there never was any such protection. He concedes that neither Act specifically refers to spare parts, but neither, he points out, is there any exclusion of them. Dealing with the first point as to what is an article within the 1949 Act as amended, he submits that the interpretation given in section 44 means no more than "capable of being made and sold separately". If Mr Jeffs' view is right, Mr Wilson asks rhetorically, what was the point of section 1(1)(b)(ii)? It must, he argues, have been put in the Act to deal with spare parts.

On the second point, the proper interpretation of section 1(1)(b)(ii), he first took us to the House of Lords decision in *AMP Inc.* v *Utilux Pty. Ltd.* [1972] RPC, 103, where it was held that the phrase "dictated by" in "dictated solely by the function" means "attributable to, or caused or prompted by". That he characterises as a broad interpretation of section 1(1)(b)(ii). In contrast, he argues, the "must fit" exception in section 213 should be interpreted much more narrowly. If that is to be interpreted narrowly, so too should the "must match" exception. But the "must match" exception is in virtually the same words as section 1(1)(b)(ii). Therefore, his argument runs, the latter should also be interpreted narrowly. By that process he asks the court to arrive at a conclusion that if the applicant can identify a design which does not fall foul of the "must match" exception, that is a design which can be registered since it would not be right to give a broad exclusionary interpretation to the virtually identical provisions of section 1(1)(b)(ii).

He further submits that the notion of "design freedom" is the key to this case. There was no intention on the part of the legislature to exclude parts where there was "design freedom". If, however, he says, the respondent's argument is right, it is never possible to consider "design freedom". He says that both the Registry and the Tribunal were wrong in holding that "another article" in section 1(1)(b)(ii) is the composite article including the part in issue. One should look at n-1 or n-2, that is to say the whole minus the part, or parts, in issue. This must, in his submission, have been intended to be the right approach because otherwise many things intended to be protected would not be.

Turning to the arguments of Mr Silverleaf for the respondent, he says that the question of whether something is an "article" depends on whether it is an article of commerce in its own right. Thus, decorated wheels are registrable because they have a commercial life of their own, whereas nobody buys a wing for a Ford Escort save to replace a wing on a Ford Escort. There is no trade in such a wing for any other purpose. Ford makes no distinction on the production line between wings made to be put on cars before they are sold and those to be put into the spare parts store.

In my judgment, the interpretation given to the word "article" in the 1949 Act as amended is of crucial importance, an interpretation which is not provided for the new unregistered design right in Part III of the 1988 Act. Within the interpretation the key words are 'made and sold separately'. To be that, an article has to have an independent life as an article of commerce and not merely be an adjunct of some larger article of which it forms a part. The selling of a mere replacement part is not separate from the sale of the article as a whole. Consequently, I agree with the Tribunal's decision on the first point.

As to the interpretation of section 1(1)(b)(ii), Mr Silverleaf says quite simply that to consider the other article minus the part in issue is not what the statute requires. I agree with him. In my judgment, Mr Jeffs was right to conclude that "another article" must refer to the vehicle as a whole. As to design freedom, Mr Silverleaf says that the question is whether the manufacturer of the spare part has design freedom. If he has, then he is a candidate for registration. If he has not, then he is not such a candidate. The design freedom in the latter instance is in the original designer of the car. So, with a particular spoiler which figured a fair amount in the argument, the maker of that spare part will have to produce one that looks exactly like the original, or it is unsaleable. He has no design freedom. I accept that argument.

It follows that I have arrived at the same general conclusion as Mr Jeffs. In so doing I have not been influenced by the statements of Government ministers in piloting the 1988 Act through the Houses of Parliament, although we looked at many passages in those statements *de bene esse.* I have not considered it appropriate to have regard to those statements because, in accordance with the words of Lord Browne-Wilkinson in *Pepper* v *Hart,* [1993] AC 534, I do not consider the legislation to be ambiguous or obscure, or that the literal meaning of it leads to an absurdity. In any event, again in accordance with Lord Browne-Wilkinson's words, I do not consider that in this case the ministerial statements clearly disclose the mischief aimed at or the legislative intention. In fact, I have sympathy with Mr Silverleaf's description of them as "long and diffuse and varied". That may be why both sides were able to find comfort in passages in the statements.

I would, therefore, dismiss the appeal save in respect of one application for registration, that being No.2004659, which is for a rear lamp. Mr Jeffs deals with that at page 22 of his judgment, [1993] RPC 399 at 424 line 23. Of this application Mr Silverleaf said that as the suggestion was that the Tribunal may have misunderstood Mr Wilson's argument with regard to that lamp, he would not oppose the remission of this application for consideration by the Registrar of Designs. Accordingly, I would so remit it.'

COMMENT

Leave to appeal to the House of Lords was granted under the 'leapfrog' procedure (section 12 of the Administration of Justice Act 1969). Note the reference to *Pepper* v *Hart* and McCowan LJ's refusal to be influenced by Hansard. Why did he not make use of ministerial statements regarding the changes to design law? Can you distinguish between spare parts that may be registrable and those that are not? Should all spare parts be registrable though for a short duration only of, say, three years? Current European proposals for harmonising design law envisage full protection for certain types of spare parts such as body panels for vehicles, subject only to the anti-competitive controls in the Treaty of Rome.

The House of Lords affirmed the Divisional Court's decision: see below. The basis for the decision in the House of Lords, as in the Divisional Court, was the definition of the article rather than the 'must-match' exception.

Ford Motor Co. Ltd.'s Design Applications **[1995] RPC 167, House of Lords**

For the facts see Divisional Court of Queen's Bench Division above.

Lord Mustill (at 177): 'The outcome of the dispute so far is therefore that some of the items selected as representative have qualified as "articles", and have not been ruled out under section 1(1)(b)(ii); these have been remitted to the Registry for further consideration. There is no appeal in respect of them. As regards the remainder, it has been held by the deputy judge and the Divisional Court that they are not "articles", and all three tribunals have decided that in any event they are excluded from registration by section 1(1)(b)(ii). These are the matters arising from the judgment under appeal, although the Registrar has sought to raise additional questions to which I will return. I will begin with the issue of "article". For convenience I repeat the definition:

"'article' means any article of manufacture and includes any part of an article if that part is made and sold separately;"

The argument in support of the appeal has been put in various ways. Of these the most attractive, and the one which reflects most closely the use of the present tense in the definition ("... if that part is made and sold separately"), is to consider the component as at the time when the relevant operation takes place. In relation to a spare part one asks first whether it is made separately, and finds that it is; for its fabrication is not part of the manufacture of an entire vehicle. Equally, the part is sold separately; for the customer buys it without at the same time buying the rest of the car. The article thus satisfies both tests.

Whilst acknowledging the attractions of this approach, I am unable to adopt it. In the first place it must, I believe, entail that every spare part is an article, with the exception of those acquired at the time of the original purchase, a result which if intended could have been achieved by a much more direct form of words. Furthermore, in some circumstances the proposed reading would be unworkable. Take, for instance, the case of prefabricated components put into stock when made and then drawn upon either to be incorporated into complete units or sold as spare parts. If one attends to the way in which the components are actually employed the position will be that some are made and sold separately, and hence qualify as articles, and others are not; yet the design of each is exactly the same, and the design must be either registrable or not registrable. This anomaly exists because the argument looks at the characteristics of each individual article once produced and put into circulation.

If the Act had been concerned with, say, consumer protection, this would no doubt have been correct. But here the legislation is concerned not with finished articles but with the design sought to be registered, *ex hypothesi* before the articles are made; and the articles themselves are relevant only because they form the media through which the designs intended to be registered under the statute will be put into effect. One must therefore look, not to the history of articles which already exist, but to the characteristics which they will have when the design fulfils its intended purpose. I can therefore see no escape from the conclusion reached by Graham J in the *Sifam* case ([1973] RPC 899) that section 44(1) must be read as meaning "... if that part is to be made and sold separately".

This is however only a first step, for the meaning of "separately" must still be ascertained. With cases at either end of the scale this can without strain be read in its ordinary sense. The design of the meter face in the *Sifam* case was conceived because the meter which the applicants intended to manufacture was useless without a face, and for no other reason. Nobody would sell a meter without a face or buy a face without a meter. The meter and the face were for commercial, if not for purely mechanical, purposes inseparable. At the other extreme one finds what have been called "generic" articles. Taking up the example of the brace and bit, although these are often sold in sets, the components may well be interchangeable with those of different design and manufacture. Whilst the manufacturer of the brace no doubt intends that purchasers of the brace will also be purchasers of the bit, he also hopes that bits will be purchased by those who have bought a brace made by someone else. Thus, although the two components are in many cases associated, when one bears in mind that the Act is concerned with designs, and not with sales, they can properly be regarded as separate. So also with the kind of fancy steering wheel or wheel cover offered by a manufacturer as an option, which may be designed with the intention that some of the sales will be for use with vehicles other than those marketed by the manufacturer himself.

Thus far, I do see no great difficulty. Matters are different in cases where those who brief the designer contemplate that although the component will not be capable of incorporation into complete artifacts outside the manufacturer's own range, nevertheless there will be a substantial ancillary market as replacement goods, over and above the market for the parts when incorporated in the original vehicle. As a rule, these replacement parts will not be purchased at the same time as the original artifact, and in the event they may be bought by someone other that the original purchaser. Thus, even on the assumption that it is right to read the test of section 44(1) as embracing parts which are to be made and sold separately, the design will apply equally to some parts which comply and others which do not: yet there is only one design tendered for registration, and this cannot be both registrable and not registrable at the same time.

My Lords, for these reasons I have been compelled to give up the attempt to read the words of the definition literally, and will instead look behind them for the intention of the legislature. In my opinion the purpose was to distinguish between, on the one hand, an item designed for incorporation, whether as a spare part or as an original component, in a particular article or range of articles made by the manufacturer of the component, and on the other an item designed for general use, albeit perhaps aimed principally at use with manufacturer's own artifacts. Whilst it is often unwise to restate the effect of a statute in different words, since this may lead to the new formula being subjected to the kind of textual analysis which ought to be reserved to the statute itself, an answer will I believe be supplied in many cases by applying the criterion given by McCowan LJ, namely: that to qualify under section 44(1) a spare part has to have an independent life as an article of commerce and not be merely an adjunct of some larger article of which it forms part.

This conclusion is sufficient to dispose of the appeal, which is concerned solely with the deputy judge's first group of components. His decision that items in the second group were in principle registrable was not the subject of any application for judicial review or of any order by the Divisional Court, and accordingly is not before the House. As to the first group of items, because the issue under section 44 did not arise until the hearing before the deputy judge, the case is wholly denuded of any evidence about the intentions of Ford as to the independence or otherwise of the components as articles of commerce. Nevertheless, inspection of the list of components shows that they cannot have been conceived as items of commerce on their own, and indeed I did not understand Ford to have suggested that they were registrable if the interpretation of section 44 which I have preferred is correct.

In the light of this conclusion the question arises whether your Lordships should express an opinion on the second issue, which concerns the identification of "another article" with which the design sought to be registered must, by virtue of section 1(1)(b)(ii), be compared. At first sight there is much to be said for doing so. This is the only issue which has been in contention throughout. All three of the tribunals previously seized of the case have expressed opinions about it, and full argument has been devoted to it in this House. From the point of view of the industry and of those who administer the law of registered designs it will no doubt be regretted if the House leaves the matter in the air.

Nevertheless, for more than one reason I believe that your Lordships should not engage this question ...'

COMMENT

The reasons given by Lord Mustill for not looking further at the 'must-match' exception included the fact that it would not affect the outcome of the appeal and its consideration required two assumptions to be made. He also criticised the manner in which new arguments had been introduced at a late stage. Lord Mustill declined an invitation to 'ramble through the statute, with a pause for your Lordships to express an opinion on every point of interest ...'.

As the House of Lords disposed of the case on the basis of the definition of 'article', does this mean the 'must-match' exception is redundant?

Infringement

A registered design is infringed by any person who does anything which is within the exclusive right of the proprietor. The proprietor has, by section 7(1), the exclusive right to make or import, for sale or hire or use for trade or business purposes or to sell, hire or offer or expose for sale or hire an article to which the registered design or a design not substantially different from it has been applied.

Where the defendant's design is not identical to the registered design belonging to the plaintiff, the question of substantial difference arises. Case law shows that an overall resemblance does not mean that the two designs are not substantially different. The case below shows that registration of a new design that is unlike any previous design does not prevent competitors making use of a similar design concept providing they do not follow the first design too closely.

Gaskell & Chambers Ltd. v Measure Master Ltd. [1993] RPC 76, Patents Court

The plaintiff registered a design for a spirits dispenser to be used in public houses to measure out quantities of whiskey, gin, etc. The dispenser was intended to fit in the neck of an upturned bottle, it had a round plastic lens through which the measured quantity of drink could be seen and was operated by placing a glass under it and pressing the glass laterally against a plastic lever. The defendant's spirit measure also had a round lens and lever. The plaintiff sued for infringement of the registered design.

Aldous J (at 80): 'Mr Thorley, who appeared for the plaintiff, emphasised the differences between the registered design and the prior art devices. Clearly there are differences and my conclusion is the same as Mr. Bowskill, the managing director of a company which distributes bar equipment, namely, the dispenser of the registered design looks completely different to the traditional type. I accept also that it has an appearance which attracts custom and therefore the interested addressee would not concentrate on the small details of the design.

Infringement
The defendant started trading in 1978 and has, since about that time, made dispensers. Prior to the introduction of the DIAMOND range in the late 1980s, its main product was a dispenser having the traditional shape, being a shape similar to the plaintiff's COT range. The defendant's DIAMOND dispensers were designed by Sams Design which is a partnership between Mr. Sams and his wife. Mr Sams gave evidence as to how he came to design the DIAMOND dispensers and what he had before him when he was producing the design. That evidence appears to have been given to refute the allegation that the DIAMOND design was copied from the plaintiff's design.

   Whether or not copying took place is, I believe, irrelevant. The test of infringement is an objective test based on a comparison of the registered design and the alleged infringement. Thus a bad copy or a copy of only a part may not infringe but an independent design may do so.

Neither party submitted to the contrary. However Mr Thorley submitted that the evidence of Mr Hanson, that he formed the view that the similarities between the DIAMOND dispensers and the plaintiff's design were such that he concluded that there had been copying, was relevant. He submitted that if the similarities were such that a reasonable man could infer copying then that was persuasive evidence that the design of the alleged infringement was not substantially different from that of the registered design.

That submission is not correct. Copying can be inferred by one or more similarities but that does not mean that the two designs are not substantially different, which is the test for infringement. I am concerned with the extent of similarity not the derivation of the defendant's design.

The DIAMOND Mark I dispenses one-sixth of a gill of liquid [Aldous J then referred to the photographs of the dispenser]. It has a front lens and an advertising plaque at the top, a lever, internal mechanism, spout and inlet. Its internal mechanism for dispensing the liquid differs from that used by the plaintiff. It has a family likeness to the registered design in that its sight glass is a round lens at the front and it is operated by a depending lever but, such a family likeness does not mean that the two designs are substantially the same or different. Therefore I turn to compare the various features of the registered design and the DIAMOND Mark I.

1. In the registered design the front lens appears concave whereas the lens of the Mark I is flat. That is apparent by a side by side comparison but would not, I believe, be prominent to the eye of the interested addressee after what I have called a now and later approach. However, I do find the absence of the annulus in the DIAMOND Mark 1 as striking. The annulus in the registered design strikes the eye not only because it is emphasised by the black colour of the plastic, but also because of the way it cooperates with the advertising rectangle at the top.

2. The lever. The plaintiff submitted that the two levers were similar in design in that both depended and bent in at the bottom. To my eye they are completely different. Their only similarity is that they are levers positioned to be pushed backwards when a glass is placed under the outlet.

3. The cover plate. The plaintiff accepted that the DIAMOND Mark I did not have sides to its cover plate but submitted that in the Mark I the operating parts were visible and there was a triangular effect produced by the lines of the plastic moulding. I understood what was being referred to but the absence of sides to the cover plate strikes the eye and would, I believe, be remembered by an interested addressee adopting a "now and later" approach.

4. The internal mechanism. In the registered design the internal mechanism is blurred by the sides of the cover plate; but even so the details are very different to those of the Mark I. The Mark I does not have the generally rectangular mechanism.

5. The spout. This cannot be seen properly in the first representation of the registered design but is readily apparent in the front perspective view from below. It is completely different to the spout of the Mark I.

6. The inlet and cork. Although there are differences in detail between the registered design and the Mark I, I do not consider them to be material.

Even though the registered design depicts a design which is a substantial departure from the prior art and the DIAMOND Mark I has a family resemblance to it, I have come to the conclusion that the Mark I does not infringe. The registration is for the shape and configuration of the dispenser as a whole and the Mark I has a substantially different design to that shown in the registration. The absence of side cover plates, the completely different shape of lever and the absence of an annulus make that conclusion inevitable. The differences of the internal mechanism and spout emphasise it.

As to the DIAMOND Mark II, the plaintiff accepted that it did not infringe if the Mark I did not. Thus I hold that the Mark II does not infringe the plaintiff's design. If I am wrong as to the Mark I and it does infringe I suspect I would have concluded that the changes made would not have removed the Mark II from the ambit of the plaintiff's registered design.

As to the DIAMOND 5cl, this is similar to the Mark II but has a prominent conical sight glass. That is a striking feature which would be noted and remembered by the interested addressee. It creates a substantially different appearance. Clearly the 5cl does not infringe as the Mark II does not infringe but, the difference in shape of the sight glass does, in my view, render the 5cl a substantially different design to that depicted in the registered design. Therefore I suspect that I would have concluded that the 5cl would not have infringed even if the Mark II had infringed.

I conclude that the defendant has not infringed the plaintiff's registered design.'

COMMENT

There was evidence given to show that the defendant had not copied the plaintiff's design. Was this evidence relevant to a finding of infringement? Do you think that a totally new design concept should be given wider protection than it apparently has, on the basis of the view of infringement taken in this case? Is there any way in which the proprietor of the design for the dispenser could have obtained better protection?

The Design Right

The Copyright, Designs and Patents Act 1988 introduced a new unregistered design right intended to replace artistic copyright protection through drawings for functional designs. There are some similarities in the basic requirements for a registered design and the design right and the exceptions are similar. However, there is no need for a design in which the design right subsists to have eye-appeal.

In many respects, the design right is similar to copyright and there are no formalities for the right to subsist. Also the design right is subject to qualification and the remedies are as for primary infringement of copyright. The design must be original though, unlike copyright, the test for originality is stated in the statutory provisions as being a question of whether the design was commonplace in the relevant design field at the time of its creation; section 213 of the Copyright, Designs and Patents Act 1988.

The following case, which also concerned copyright issues, looks at originality in the context of the design right in addition to the test for infringement.

C & H Engineering v F Klucznik & Sons Ltd. [1992] FSR 421, Chancery Division

The parties made agricultural equipment. The plaintiff alleged that the defendant had infringed the plaintiff's copyright subsisting in drawings of lamb creep feeders. The defendant counter-claimed that the plaintiff had infringed the defendant's design right subsisting in its design of pig-fender, being a device used in free-range pig farming to retain the piglets in the sty whilst allowing the sow to step over the fender and wander about the field. The defendant fixed a two-inch metal tube along the top edge of the fender to prevent scratching of the sow's teats.

Aldous J (at 426): 'Design right was created in the Copyright, Designs and Patents Act 1988. The intention of Parliament was to amend copyright law so as to phase out full copyright protection for drawings of functional articles and to substitute a new unregistered design right ... [Aldous J then set out the statutory provisions governing the design right and relevant to the dispute - sections 213, 214 and 226 of the Copyright, Designs and Patents Act 1988].

The word "original" in section 213(1) is not defined, but I believe that it should be given the same meaning as the word " original" in section 1(1)(a) of the Act, namely not copied but the independent work of the designer. It should be contrasted with novelty which is the requirement for registration of a registered design: see section 265(4) of the Act.

Section 213(4) says that the design is not original if it is commonplace in the design field in question. The word "commonplace" is not defined, but this subsection appears to introduce a consideration akin to novelty. For the design to be original it must be the work of the creator and that work must result in a design which is not commonplace in the relevant field. The designer is the creator and no design right will subsist until the design has been recorded in a document or in an article. Thus the creator is not necessarily the person who records the design but usually will be.

Section 226 appears to require the owner of a design right to establish that copying has taken place before infringement can be proved; that is similar to copyright. However the test of infringement is different. Under section 16 copyright will be infringed if the work, or a substantial part of the work is copied. Under section 226 there will only be infringement if the design is copied so as to produce articles exactly or substantially to the design. Thus the test for infringement requires the alleged infringing article or articles be compared with the document or article embodying the design. Thereafter the court must decide whether copying took place and, if so, whether the alleged infringing article is made exactly to the design or substantially to that design. Whether or not the alleged infringing article is made substantially to the plaintiff's design must be an objective test to be decided through the eyes of the person to whom the design is directed. Pig fenders are purchased by pig farmers and I have no doubt that they purchase them taking into account price and design. In the present case, the plaintiff's alleged infringing pig fenders do not have exactly the same design as shown in the defendant's design document. Thus it is necessary to compare the plaintiff's pig fenders with the defendant's design drawing and, looking at the differences and similarities through the eyes of a person such as a pig farmer, decide whether the design of the plaintiff's pig fender is substantially the same as the design shown in the drawing.

By 1990 pig fenders were commonplace and had been made in metal and wood. In essence Mr Butler wanted a commonplace pig fender with a metal roll bar on the top. He had seen fenders with a wooden roll bar. He gave Mr Jackson the basic measurements needed and the only part of the pig fender shown in the drawing which was not commonplace was the 2 inch tube on the top. Thus the design is the incorporation of the 2 inch pipe into a commonplace pig fender.

The first matter for decision is: who created the design? The defendant submitted that it was Mr Jackson and the plaintiff submitted it was Mr Butler; nobody submitted that they were joint creators. The creator was the person who thought of using a 2 inch pipe on top of a commonplace form of pig fender. I do not know whether it was Mr Jackson or Mr Butler who thought of that design and created it. As I have said, the evidence is conflicting and any conclusion as to who thought of it would be a matter of guesswork. I therefore conclude that the defendant has not established that it is the owner of the design right in its drawing of a pig fender and thus the action for infringement must fail.

Even if I had come to the conclusion that the defendant owned the design right in its drawing, I would have held that the plaintiff had not infringed as its pig fenders are not made to the same design, nor substantially to that design.

The plaintiff produced its pig fender at the suggestion of Mr Kingston. At a meeting with Mr Kingston, Mr Holliday saw one of the defendant's pig fenders and was given by Mr Kingston the basic dimensions needed for such a device. Those dimensions were incorporated on to a rough sketch which was given to Mr Coleman. Mr Coleman was given a free hand, but was told that the customer insisted on having a round tube on the top. The fenders were made stackable by flaring out the sides.

I have no doubt that the idea of having a tube as the roll bar came from the defendant's pig fender and therefore copying did take place. However, the plaintiff's pig fenders are not made exactly to the defendant's design, and I do not believe that they are made substantially to that design. Metal pig fenders must have an overall similarity due to the function they have to perform, but a person interested in their design would appreciate that the plaintiff's pig fender was of a different design to that of the defendant, although they have in common a tube as the roll bar. In that respect the two designs are substantially the same, but taken as a whole the two designs are not substantially the same. An interested man would be struck by the design features which enable the plaintiff's pig fender to be stacked. Those features not only attract the eye, but would also be seen by an interested person as being functionally significant. They contrast with the overall design features of the defendant's pig fender. The interested man looking at the plaintiff's and the defendant's pig fenders would consider the two designs to be different, but with a similar design feature - namely, the bar around the top. Therefore the defendant's claim for infringement of a design right fails.'

COMMENT

What is the difference between the test of novelty for a registered design and the test of originality for the design right? How does the test for infringement of the design right differ from that for copyright? If the judge found that copying had taken place, as he did, why did he not accept that this amounted to infringement of the design right? If the design right can apply to part of an article why should the whole article be viewed when testing for infringement rather than just the relevant parts?

Note that a designer's contribution need not necessarily be in relation to recording the design. However, the contribution must relate to the design and not to questions of manufacture and such like; see *Philip Parker* v *Stephen Tidball* [1997] FSR 680.

Ocular Sciences Ltd. v *Aspect Vision Care Ltd.* [1997] RPC 289, Patents Court

As regards the design right issues of this complex case, it suffices to say that the plaintiffs alleged that design right subsisted in the design of their soft contact lenses. The defendants, who denied copying, argued that design features of the lenses were excluded by the 'must-fit' exception or were otherwise not protected, being commonplace.

Laddie J (at 421): 'In the twenty years prior to the passing of the 1988 Act, copyright lawyers found a new area in which to enforce copyright. The copyright in production drawings was argued to be infringed by the manufacture of three dimensional articles copied, directly or indirectly, from them. The era of industrial copyright had arrived. Litigation proliferated as manufacturers of mundane industrial articles and parts used the copyright in their production drawings to prevent competitors from copying their finished products derived from those drawings. Even if the copyright work consisted of no more than a drawing of two concentric circles on a piece of paper and the alleged infringement consisted of a washer made indirectly from it, copyright could be invoked to take the competing product off the market. It is hardly surprising that not everyone was persuaded that this was the proper place for copyright or that it was of benefit to industry. The 1988 Act effectively spelt the end of industrial copyright. However in its place it put a new quasi-copyright called design right which is to be found in sections 213 to 251 of the Act. The origin of this legislation can be traced to the Semiconductor Products (Protection of Topography) Regulations 1987 SI 1987/1497. This, as its name suggests, provided for the protection of the topography, i.e. layout, of the circuits in semiconductors. This regulation was, in turn, based on a European Directive to the same effect (87/54/EEC OJ No. L24, 27/1/87). The new design right gives protection for a limited period against the copying of certain designs.

In this action the plaintiffs originally asserted that there were two groups of design rights which they owned and which had been infringed by the defendants. First design right was said to exist in certain production drawings created on or after 1 August 1989 (the commencement date of the provisions of the Act dealing with design right). The drawings were listed in two schedules annexed to the statement of claim. It was said that AVCL and Mr Geoffrey Galley infringed these rights by reproducing or authorising the reproduction of the said designs by (a) having articles made to the said designs and by (b) making design documents for the purpose of enabling such articles to be made. Secondly unregistered design right was said to subsist in the designs of the plaintiffs' lenses. All the defendants were alleged to have infringed the latter design rights by making contact lenses which reproduce them. The defendants raised extensive defences to both categories of design rights. During the plaintiffs' opening, I was told that the claims in respect of the first group of designs were not being pursued. The claim in respect of the design of the PLL lenses was maintained.

According to section 213 of the 1988 Act, design right is a property right which subsists in an "original design". Although the wording used is very similar to that employed in the Registered Designs Act, 1949, the legislative origin of these provisions is quite independent of the 1949 Act. It cannot necessarily be assumed that similar expressions have similar meanings in the two statutes. In the case of design right, "design" is defined as meaning:

" ... any aspect of the shape or configuration (whether internal or external) of the whole or any part of an article."

The proprietor can choose to assert design right in the whole or any part of his product. If the right is said to reside in the design of a teapot, this can mean that it resides in design of the whole pot, or in a part such as the spout, the handle or the lid, or, indeed, in a part of the lid. This means that the proprietor can trim his design right claim to most closely match what he believes the defendant to have taken. The defendant will not know in what the alleged monopoly resides until the letter before action or, more usually, the service of the statement of claim. This means that a plaintiff's pleading has particular importance. It not only puts forward the claim but is likely to be the only statement of what is asserted to be the design right. In this case the relevant paragraph in the statement of claim is in the following terms:

"Further, unregistered design right subsists in the designs of the lenses set out in Schedule C hereto."

Although 19 different designs are listed in that schedule, only 13 were asserted to have been copied by the defendants. However this did not mean that just 13 designs were relied upon. For example one of the designs listed in the schedule was "D 1 - Edge III Thin". This is the trade mark or name given by the plaintiffs to a family of lenses varying in power from minus to plus dioptres. Mr Waugh, who argued this part of the case on behalf of the plaintiffs, said that the pleadings meant that what was sought to be protected was each of the lenses within each of the thirteen families identified in the schedule. This was over 200 lens designs. Mr Pumfrey did not object to that and the case proceeded on the basis that the claims to design right were directed to each of those 200 odd designs. In relation to each of these, Mr Waugh said that the design comprises: (a) the front surface dimensions of the lens; (b) the rear surface dimensions; and (c) the edge characteristics. It was said that together these features, many of which are determined for each power of lens by the lens designer, make up the lens design.

At one stage during the argument, I expressed doubt as to whether the detailed dimensions on which the plaintiffs were relying could really be 'designs' within the meaning of the Act. For example the -3.00 dioptre and -3.5 dioptre lenses in the plaintiffs' DI - Edge 111 Thin range would appear to any normal observer to be identical. In fact, it would take sophisticated measuring equipment in the hands of a skilled technician to tell them apart. Surely they are a single design. They certainly look like the same design. Mr Waugh said that this was not so. He said that the use of dimension is just another way of describing or defining the shape or aspect in issue. He argued that there was nothing in the Act to indicate that a shape defined by such detailed dimensions was excluded from protection. On reconsideration, I think Mr Waugh is right. This is one of those areas in which it is necessary to bear in mind that the design right provisions are not derived from the Registered Designs Act, 1949. By section 1(1) of the latter Act, the word "design" is defined as meaning

> "features of shape, configuration, pattern or ornament applied to an article by any industrial process, being features which in the finished article appeal to and are judged by the eye."

Furthermore the 1949 Act excludes from consideration features of shape or configuration which are dictated solely by the function which the article has to perform. As that Act and numerous decisions under it demonstrate, appearance is everything where registered design law is concerned. Although the same word "design" is used in relation to design right, its meaning is different. There is no reference in the relevant provisions of the 1988 Act to features which appeal to and are judged by the eye. The Act was intended to give protection to wholly functional designs. The worth and ingenuity of a functional design over designs of similar overall appearance may be due to its detailed relative dimensions. Its detailed shape will, because of the different dimensions, be different. The eye may not be able to distinguish the shapes but that does not mean that they are not different. That being so, it seems to me that it is not possible to exclude detailed dimensional shapes on the ground that they are not designs. This does not mean that mere changes in scale produce different designs.

The defendants do not dispute that design right, if it exists, is owned by the plaintiffs. But they run three defences. First it is said that the designs have not been copied. Secondly it is said that the features relied on are not protectable as a result of the "interface" provision of section 213(3)(b)(i) of the Act. Thirdly it is said that the designs, or any parts which may have been copied, are commonplace. I will consider each of these defences.

Copying
The owner of design right in a design has the exclusive right to reproduce the design for commercial purposes, inter alia, by making articles to that design (section 226(1)). Reproduction of a design by making articles to that design is defined by section 226(2) as meaning:

> "copying the design so as to produce articles exactly or substantially to that design".

Design right is infringed by a person who does, or authorises another to do, anything which is the exclusive right of the design right owner without relevant permission (section 226(3)). To succeed in this case the plaintiffs need to show that their 200 odd individual lens designs have been copied by the defendants. It is not enough to show that the defendants have gone through an independent though very similar design exercise and have arrived at very similar designs, even if that process was undertaken to make a product which the public would accept as interchangeable. In the present case the defendants were aware, for example, that the PLL standard 55% Methafilcon design of lens had a base curve of 8.8 and an overall diameter of 14.2 mm, a nominal centre thickness of 0.12 mm at 3.00 dioptres and a power range of +5.00 to -8.00 dioptres. That is what is recorded in the schedule to the PSA. In taking some or all of those dimensions and feeding them into their spreadsheet, they were not copying the package of numerous dimensions which the plaintiffs assert constitute the total design in which their monopoly right resides. The plaintiffs have failed to prove that their individual lens designs were copied into the defendants' lens designs. The assertion of infringement fails at the first hurdle.

Furthermore to constitute an infringement the copying must be exact or substantially to the same design. Here the plaintiffs have put their case firmly on the basis that each of their lenses, differing from their neighbours' only in fine dimensional details, is to a separate design. Mr Fruth listed the relevant dimensions of the plaintiffs' lenses as: base curve, diameter, centre thickness, junction thickness, peripheral thickness, edge thickness, edge lift, optic radius, optic displacement, optic zone, peripheral radius, peripheral displacement, peripheral diameter, ramp radius, ramp displacement, ramp angle, ramp length, base curve radius, base curve diameter, base curve displacement, internal sag and external sag. A member of the public could not tell the design of one lens in a particular range from another with a different power in the same range by mere visual inspection. The fact that the defendants' lenses also can not be distinguished from the plaintiffs' on mere visual inspection does not prove that they are sufficiently close for the purposes of infringement. When a plaintiff relies on the most detailed and specific dimensions to support his claim to the existence of design right, he can only succeed on infringement if the defendants' designs are extremely close in design. Although that is the case with some of the defendants' designs it is not the case with many of them. However, in view of my finding in relation to copying, it is not necessary to go through all 220 designs to distinguish between those which are too close and those which are not.

In view of this finding, it would be possible to avoid consideration of the other defences which have been raised. However it appears to me that the nature and scope of the plaintiffs' monopoly claims are of significance not only to the defendants but to the contact lens industry in general. If the plaintiffs have enforceable design rights in their lens designs, it is likely that many other manufacturers have similar rights in their designs and anyone who wishes to copy another's product runs the risk of infringing design right. Although design right only lasts for ten years, that may well be the total effective life of most lens designs, since I was given evidence that lens designs are changed quite frequently.

The "interface" defence
Section 213(3)(b)(i) of the 1988 Act provides:

> "Design right does not subsist in ... features of shape or configuration of an article which ... enable the article to be connected to, or placed in, around or against, another article so that either article may perform its function..."

This is sometimes referred to as the interface provision. Its original purpose was to prevent the designer of a piece of equipment from using design right to prevent others from making parts which fitted his equipment. As I read it, any features of shape or configuration of an article which meet the interface criteria must be excluded from being considered as part of the design right. Furthermore a feature which meets the interface criteria must be excluded even if it performs some other purpose, for example it is attractive. There is also nothing in the provision which requires the feature to be the only one which would achieve the proper interface. If a number of designs are possible each of which enables the two articles to be fitted together in a way which allowed one or other or both to perform its function, each falls within the statutory exclusion. Mr Pumfrey argued that many of the features of the plaintiffs' lens design should be excluded from consideration by virtue of this provision.

Mr Waugh, who argued this part of the case on behalf of the plaintiffs, said that this provision could have no application to the design of contact lenses. Even if all the features of his clients' designs are there to enable the lenses to fit on the eye and under the eyelids, section 213(3)(b)(i) is irrelevant. For the latter to operate the design features of the article in suit, i.e. the contact lens, has to be there to interface with another article. But, he said, an eye is not an "article" at all. It is part of the human body. The word "article" means something inanimate which is not and has never been alive. No support for this submission is provided by any of the dictionaries I have looked at but, in the end, I do not think that this is a matter of dictionary definition. What counts is the presumed legislative intent behind the provision. It seems to me that the subsection is drafted in wide terms to exclude all interface features. The word "article" is not intended to have a restricted meaning. It could just as well have been replaced by the word "thing". I can see no reason why it should be construed so as to exclude living or formerly living things. There is no self apparent policy consideration which justifies allowing, say, the features which enable a false hip to be fitted into the hip joint of a human to fall within the ambit of design right whereas the same features on a child's doll are excluded. I reject this submission.

The question therefore is, are there any features of the plaintiffs' lenses which enable the lens to be connected to or placed in, around or against the eye or the eyeball so that either article may perform its function? To answer this it is appropriate to have in mind what are the functions of the lens and the eye. The eye's primary function is to enable us to see. It is designed to allow light to be focused on the retina. To perform this function efficiently for as long a time as possible, it needs to display an ability to focus light. It must be able to stay open for much of the time yet be washed regularly to remove debris from its front surface. It must have eyelids which can move over its surface to perform the washing function and, at night, protect it. It must have a thin living membrane on its front surface, the conjunctiva, to ensure that it is repaired when damaged and is protected from infection. The soft contact lens's function (save for those which are employed solely for cosmetic purposes) is to provide a particular correction to the light focusing ability of the eye. It must also fit in the right location on the front of the eyeball over the pupil. It should allow sufficient oxygen to pass through it to reach the conjunctiva.

With these functions in mind, it is possible to look at the various features of the plaintiffs' contact lens. I can start with the back radius. Professor Efron gave unchallenged evidence in relation to this. He said that it has been determined over many years that a soft lens with a back optic zone radius of approximately 8.8 mm will provide a good fit to an "average" eye with a central radius of curvature of 7.9 mm. Such a lens is designed to fit onto the eyeball in such a way that the lens is free to move by a small amount on each blink. Lens movement is necessary to allow debris that may build up beneath the lens (and become a source of irritation and a potential trigger for an adverse toxic or allergic reaction) to be flushed out when the patient blinks. He also explained that in the case of a large diameter soft lens (greater than 14.00 mm) made to minimal thickness, a radius of curvature of between 8.6 mm and 8.8 mm will fit virtually all eyes because such lenses are in a sense "forgiving" and will tend to drape over the eye. It is for this reason that certain lens designs are offered to practitioners in only one back optic zone radius, such as 8.8 mm. And he went on to explain how slightly different back radiuses are chosen to enable a proper fit between other designs of soft contact lenses and different eyeballs. There was no evidence to suggest that the back radius of the plaintiffs' lenses were chosen without the fit requirement in mind. I am sure they were. In any event, the subsection does not require that the designer should know that the features enable the interface, it is sufficient if they do so in fact. The back radius in each of the plaintiffs' lenses enables the lens to fit against the eyeball so as to allow the lens to perform its function of correcting the focusing ability of the eye to the desired extent and to ensure that it centres over the pupil. This feature is excluded from consideration under the subsection.

Professor Efron also gave unchallenged evidence in relation to the choice of the diameter of the soft lens. He said:

"... it is universally accepted in the contact lens industry that, for in-eye stability, a soft contact lens must be of a larger diameter than the cornea, and would generally fall within the range 12.50 mm to 15.00 mm. Because soft lenses typically 'drape' over the eye irrespective of the precise diameter of the cornea, a large diameter (14.00 mm to 15.00 mm) can be adopted for a lens that is intended to fit all eyes. A lens of, say, 12.50 mm in diameter will only properly fit the eyes of a small subset of patients who have especially small corneas, and in any case a larger lens will also generally provide a satisfactory fit for such an eye. However a disadvantage of making a lens with a diameter of 14.5 mm or greater is that the edge of a lens of this size can be readily seen against the white sclera of the eye. This might be a source of annoyance to many patients who do not wish to make it obvious to others that they are wearing contact lenses; that is, the lens is deemed to be cosmetically unacceptable. An effective and common compromise is to adopt a lens diameter of 14.20 mm, which is large enough to fit virtually all eyes, but small enough for the edge of the lens to be less visible due to the fact that the edge is 'masked" by the limbus (the transition zone between the cornea and sclera)".

On this evidence, the lens diameters chosen enable the soft lens to fit onto the eyeball and under the eyelids so as to achieve in-eye stability. They are excluded under the subsection.

From the optic zone outwards the plaintiffs' lens designs have a parallel lenticulated carrier ending in what is called a "CN bevel". The CN bevel is also known as the "Conlish bevel" and is named after its inventor. The purpose or effect of the parallel carrier and CN bevel is explained both in the plaintiffs' brochures and in their advertising video. One of the former includes the following illustration of their edge design.

This is then compared with two other types of design apparently on the market. They are illustrated as follows:

[figures in law report omitted]

The copy which is attached to these illustrations says:

"EDGE III lenses are finished with an anterior CN Bevel that places the edge apex down on the sclera for less lid interaction and greater comfort."

[figure in law report omitted]

Another refers to these peripheral features and says that they provide "better centration providing better vision". In other words they help to ensure that the lens fits more accurately on the optical centre of the eyeball. The function of the CN Bevel is described as providing "close lens edge/scleral interface for minimal lid interaction ...". This also supports the view that this feature allows the lens to fit better within the eye with less likelihood of being disturbed, by movement of the eyelid. A third advertisement states that these features give "consistent fitting characteristics with all lens powers".

In the OSI video, the advantages of the CN Bevel and parallel peripheral carrier are illustrated. An animated sequence shows how this part of the lens design enables the lens to sit stably on the front of the eye while still allowing the eyelids to move across it without turning up the edges. Dr Sammons, one of the plaintiffs' witnesses, stated in his report that one of the salient points which comes out of the OSI video was that the

"Lenticulated peripheral zone consists of parallel peripheral carrier and CN bevel which give thin edge and low mass and consistent fitting."

None of this was challenged nor was any suggestion made that it was in any way inaccurate. The detailed design of the CN Bevel and parallel peripheral carrier enables the lens to be placed in the eye and against the conjunctiva and helps the lens to perform its function of remaining in position over the cornea so as to ensure that its focus correction abilities are properly employed. It also allows the lens to fit under the eyelids when the latter move. Again, this enables the lens to remain in position to perform its focusing function. These features also are excluded from consideration by the provisions of section 213(3)(b)(i) of the 1988 Act.

This only leaves in issue the centre thickness, optic zone radius and front curve of each lens.

Commonplace
Section 213(4) of the 1988 Act provides that:

"A design is not 'original' for the purposes of this Part if it is commonplace in the design field in question at the time of its creation."

Mr Pumfrey argued that all of the designs in suit are commonplace and unprotectable by design right. He said that the expression "commonplace" covered designs which were ordinary, nothing more than banal, and trivial. He said it covered an unsurprising combination of well-known features even if nobody had made that precise combination before. Of course this was challenged by Mr Waugh. He said that the combinations of dimensions for each lens design was not shown to be used before. He said it was not permissible to divide up the designs into their component parts and then, by showing that each part was known in the trade, come to the conclusion that the combination was also. The combination of features which go to make up the full design relied on must be looked at as a whole. As such, none of the designs in issue here could be called commonplace.

The expression "commonplace" can be traced back to the European Directive upon which the original 1987 Semiconductor Products (Protection of Topography) Regulations was based. There is, therefore, no domestic material which can be used as an aid to construction on the basis of *Pepper v Hart* [1993] AC 593 and it was not suggested by counsel that there was any European material which helped either. On the other hand its origin does tell us something about its intended meaning. Semiconductor topographies are the detailed, highly functional, layouts of the layers of electronic connections inside an integrated circuit, or "chip". The layouts look rather like monochrome maps of the London Underground service, save that there are millions of lines and interconnections. Every semiconductor design team produces its own topographies, in the sense that the distribution of lines and connections will be their own particular choice to meet the functional requirements of the chip. In designing their layouts they will, no doubt, use certain conventional design considerations and functionally-conventional circuits - that is to say circuits which operate in a well known way although the actual lines and connections will be distinguishable visually from many other embodiments of the same circuitry. This can be likened to the plumbing which connects the hot and cold water taps on a bath to the hot and cold water tanks in a house. The connections are entirely common-or-garden but the actual direction and lengths of the piping will depend on the precise locations of the tanks and the bath and the intervening obstacles. If any new combination of well-known features was intended to be the subject of a monopoly, all semiconductor topographies would be protected, and the commonplace exclusion would be no exclusion at all. The same conclusion can be reached another way. It is to be assumed that the draughtsman of the European Directive was familiar, as all intellectual property lawyers are, with the concept of originality in copyright law. There it means "originated with the author without slavish copying from some preceding work". The Directive eschews adopting that concept alone in relation to semiconductor topographies. Instead it uses the expression "commonplace" which clearly envisages some objective assessment. This follows from the provisions of Article 2(2) of the Directive:

"The topography of a semiconductor product shall be protected in so far as it satisfies the conditions that it is the result of its creator's own intellectual effort *and* is not commonplace in the semiconductor industry. Where the topography of a semiconductor product consists of elements that are commonplace in the semiconductor industry, it shall be protected only to the extent that the combination of such elements, taken as a whole, fulfils the above mentioned conditions." (my emphasis)

Essentially the same words are to be found in the 1987 Regulations.

It is always undesirable to replace one ambiguous expression by another, and for that reason it is not right to redefine the word "commonplace" in the 1988 Act, but it seems to me that the flavour of the word is much along the lines suggested by Mr Pumfrey. Any design which is trite, trivial, common-or-garden, hackneyed or of the type which would excite no peculiar attention in those in the relevant art is likely to be commonplace. This does not mean that a design made up of features which, individually, are commonplace is necessarily itself commonplace. A new and exciting design can be produced from the most trite of ingredients. But to secure protection, the combination must itself not be commonplace. That is what the European Directive and the 1987 Regulations say expressly and what is implicit in the 1988 Act. In many cases the run of the mill combination of well known features will produce a combination which is itself commonplace. With this in mind it is now possible to assess the 200 odd designs the plaintiffs rely on here.

OSI's advertising video bearing the title "Clinical Considerations in Edge Design" commences with the following statement made by Mr Fruth:

> "Eye care practitioners and researchers long ago settled on the basic parameters that worked best in soft contact lens designs - the range of base curves, cord diameters and centre thickness - and most manufacturers can produce the fundamental curves required in a workable contact lens. But we know from rigid lens experience that the ability to design a high quality edge and then turn it out consistently is the hallmark of an excellent laboratory."

During the course of the trial, most of the features of the plaintiffs' lenses were analysed in detail. It is clear that, individually, all of them are well known and that all competent designers in the field have in the past had no difficulty in working out the correct dimensions to make good workable soft lenses. They pick and choose from the small range of available features, those which they want to use in their products. As Mr Stem said, that is precisely what Mr Fruth did in the early 1980s. He chose from existing designs on the market the particular features which he wanted in his lenses. Professor Efron gave extensive evidence on the lack of anything out of the ordinary in the plaintiffs' designs. He said that he was unable to identify any features that distinguish the plaintiffs' lenses from numerous other lens designs available on the market. He accepted that there were unique features about the moulded edge of these lenses, but this was an issue which he considered related more to lens manufacture than to lens design. I accept that evidence. If regard is only had to the combination of three remaining features of each lens design, they are a commonplace. Furthermore, even if I am wrong in relation to the exclusion of interface features, the plaintiffs' designs as a whole are commonplace. They do not qualify for design right protection.

For all these reasons, the plaintiffs fail on their design right case.'

COMMENT

This is an important case on design right, even though most of what was said by Laddie J was clearly *obiter*. Important features of the judgment are the discussion of the origin of the design right and the potential subsistence of the right in relation to detailed dimensions not distinguishable by the unaided human eye. Laddie J's judgment is also instructive as to the must-fit exception and the meaning of 'commonplace'.

If design right can subsist in features not distinguishable by the human eye, how is infringement tested? Is it acceptable to compare designs after they have been enlarged so as to make differences (or similarities) more readily discernible? Do you think

Laddie J was correct in deciding that the human eye was an 'article' for the purposes of design right?

There follow extracts from the 'TRIPS' Agreement relating to design law.

Agreement on Trade-Related Aspects of Intellectual Property Rights

Section 4. Industrial designs

Article 25
Requirements for protection

(1) Members shall provide for the protection of independently created industrial designs that are new or original. Members may provide that designs are not new or original if they do not significantly differ from known designs or combinations of known design features. Members may provide that such protection shall not extend to designs dictated essentially by technical or functional considerations.

(2) Each Member shall ensure that requirements for securing protection for textile designs, in particular in regard to any cost, examination or publication, do not unreasonably impair the opportunity to seek and obtain such protection. Members shall be free to meet this obligation through industrial design law *or* through copyright law.

Article 26
Protection

(1) The owner of a protected industrial design shall have the right to prevent third parties not having the owner's consent from making, selling or importing articles bearing or embodying a design which is a copy, or substantially a copy, of the protected design, when such acts are undertaken for commercial purposes.

(2) Members may provide limited exceptions to the protection of industrial designs, provided that such exceptions do not unreasonably conflict with the normal exploitation of protected industrial designs and do not unreasonably prejudice the legitimate interests of the owner of the protected design, taking account of the legitimate interests of third parties.

(3) The duration of protection available shall amount to at least 10 years.

Section 6. Layout-designs (topographies) of integrated circuits

Article 35
Relation to the IPIC Treaty

Members agree to provide protection to the layout-designs (topographies) of integrated circuits (referred to in this Agreement as 'layout-designs') in accordance with Articles 2 through 7 (other than paragraph 3 of Article 6), Article 12 and paragraph 3 of Article 16 of the Treaty on Intellectual Property in Respect of Integrated Circuits and, in addition, to comply with the following provisions.

Article 36
Scope of the protection

Subject to the provisions of paragraph 1 of Article 37, Members shall consider unlawful the following acts if performed without the authorization of the right holder:[1] importing, selling, or otherwise distributing for commercial purposes a protected layout-design, an integrated circuit in which a protected layout-design is incorporated, or an article incorporating such an integrated circuit only in so far as it continues to contain an unlawfully reproduced layout-design.

Article 37
Acts not requiring the authorization of the right holder

(1) Notwithstanding Article 36, no Member shall consider unlawful the performance of any of the acts referred to in that Article in respect of an integrated circuit incorporating an unlawfully reproduced layout-design or any article incorporating such an integrated circuit where the person performing or ordering such acts did not know and had no reasonable ground to know, when acquiring the integrated circuit or article incorporating such an integrated circuit, that it incorporated an unlawfully reproduced layout-design. Members shall provide that, after the time that such person has received sufficient notice that the layout-design was unlawfully reproduced, that person may perform any of the acts with respect to the stock on hand or ordered before such time, but shall be liable to pay to the right holder a sum equivalent to a reasonable royalty such as would be payable under a freely negotiated licence in respect of such a layout-design.

(2) The conditions set out in subparagraphs (a) through (k) of Article 31 shall apply *mutatis mutandis* in the event of any non-voluntary licensing of a layout-design or of its use by or for the government without the authorization of the right holder.

Article 38
Term of protection

(1) In Members requiring registration as a condition of protection, the term of protection of layout-designs shall not end before the expiration of a period of 10 years counted from the date of filing an application for registration or from the first commercial exploitation wherever in the world it occurs.

(2) In Members not requiring registration as a condition for protection, layout-designs shall be protected for a term of no less than 10 years from the date of the first commercial exploitation wherever in the world it occurs.

(3) Notwithstanding paragraphs 1 and 2, a Member may provide that protection shall lapse 15 years after the creation of the layout-design.

Note:
[1] The term 'right holder' in this Section shall be understood as having the same meaning as the term 'holder of the right' in the IPIC Treaty.

COMMENT

How closely does the United Kingdom's registered design comply with the minimum requirement in the TRIPS Agreement? Note that the term for protection of semiconductor topographies exactly mirrors that provided for in the United Kingdom by the modified design right. Also note that, apart from semiconductor topographies, there is no equivalent of the design right. Does the fact that the United Kingdom provides for an unregistered design right in addition to a registered design conflict with the TRIPS Agreement?

Chapter 6

Trade Marks

Introduction

Trade mark law developed from an early form of passing off. Long before the establishment of a formal system of registration of trade marks, it was usual for the courts to restrain the use by one trader of another trader's mark. The following case, *Sykes* v *Sykes*, shows that the courts were treating a trade mark as a form of proprietary right which depended upon the deceptive use of a similar mark for its enforcement.

Sykes v *Sykes* (1824) 3 B & C 541

'The declaration alleged that the plaintiff, before and at the time of committing the grievances complained of, carried on the business of a shot-belt and powder-flask manufacturer, and made and sold for profit a large quantity of shot-belts, powder-flasks, &c., which he was accustomed to mark with the words "Sykes Patent," in order to denote that they were manufactured by him, the plaintiff, and to distinguish them from articles of the same description manufactured by other persons. That plaintiff enjoyed great reputation with the public, on account of the good quality of the said articles, and made great gains by the sale of them, and that defendants, knowing the premises, and contriving, &c., did wrongfully, knowing, and fraudulently, against the will and without the licence and consent of the plaintiff, make a great quantity of shot-belts and powder-flasks, and cause them to be marked with the words "Sykes Patent," in imitation of the said mark so made by the plaintiff in that behalf as aforesaid, and in order to denote that the said shot-belts and powder-flasks, &c. were of the manufacture of the plaintiff; and did knowingly, wrongfully, and deceitfully sell, for their own lucre and gain, the said articles so made and marked as aforesaid, as and for shot-belts and powder-flasks, &c. of the manufacture of the plaintiff; whereby plaintiff was prevented from selling a great quantity of shot-belts, powder-flasks, &c., and greatly injured in reputation, the articles so manufactured and sold by the defendants being greatly inferior to those manufactured by the plaintiff. Plea, not guilty. At the trial before Bayley J, at the last Yorkshire Assizes, it was proved that some years since the plaintiff's father obtained a patent for the manufacture of the articles in question. In an action afterwards brought for infringing the patent, it was held to be invalid, on account of a defect in the specification; but the patentee, and afterwards the plaintiff, continued to mark their articles with the words "Sykes Patent," in order to distinguish them as their manufacture. The defendants afterwards commenced business, and manufactured articles of the same sort, but of an inferior description, and sold them at a reduced price to the retail dealers. They marked them with a stamp, resembling as nearly as possible that used by the plaintiff, in order that the retail dealers might, and it was proved that they actually did sell them again, as and for goods manufactured by the plaintiff; but the persons who bought these articles from the defendant, for the purpose of so reselling them, knew by whom they were manufactured. It further appeared, that the plaintiff's sale had decreased since the defendants commenced this business. It was contended for the defendants, that the plaintiffs could not maintain this action, for that one of the defendants being named Sykes, he had a right to mark his goods with that name, and had also as much right to add the word "patent" as the plaintiff, the patent granted to the latter having been declared invalid. The learned Judge overruled the objection, as the defendant had no right so to mark his goods as and for goods manufactured by the plaintiff, which is the allegation in the declaration. It was then urged that the declaration was not supported by the evidence, for that it charged that the defendants sold the goods and for goods made by the plaintiff, whereas the immediate purchasers knew them to be manufactured by the defendants. The learned Judge overruled this objection also, and left it to the jury to say, whether the defendants adopted the mark in question for the purpose of inducing the public to suppose that the articles were not manufactured by them but by the plaintiff, and they found a verdict for the plaintiff. And now

Brougham moved for a rule nisi for a new trial, and renewed the second objection taken at the trial and contended, that the facts proved did not support the declaration. The allegation should have been, not that defendants sold the goods as and for goods made by the plaintiff, but that they sold them to third persons, in order that they might be resold, as and for goods manufactured by the plaintiff.

Abbott CJ at 543: "I think that the substance of the declaration was proved. It was established most clearly, that the defendants marked the goods manufactured by them with the words 'Sykes Patent,' in order to denote that they were of the genuine manufacture of the plaintiff; and although they did not themselves sell them as goods of the plaintiff's manufacture, yet they sold them to retail dealers, for the express purpose of being resold, as goods of the plaintiff's manufacture. I think that is substantially the same thing, and that we ought not to disturb the verdict."

Rule refused.'

COMMENT

The plaintiff continued to use the mark 'Sykes Patent' even though the patent concerned had been previously held to be invalid. This is now an offence by virtue of section 110 of the Patents Act 1977. In view of the plaintiff's continued use of the word 'patent' in his mark, would he have succeeded had he brought his action in Chancery? One of the defendants argued that he had as much right to use 'Sykes Patent' as his name was also Sykes. Another argument put up by the defence was that the defendants did not sell their goods direct to consumers. Why did these defences fail to impress the court?

Registrability

The registered trade mark proved to be an immediate success when it was introduced by the Trade Marks Registration Act 1875. One major reason was that infringement actions were much more satisfactory from the plaintiff's point of view compared with a passing off action. However, the trade mark legislation had to curb the worst excesses of eager traders wishing to register words or marks that were insufficiently distinctive, deceptive or that would unduly inhibit other traders honestly describing their goods.

A legislative framework of criteria for registration was devised and the register itself was divided into two parts, Part A intended for marks that were 'very distinctive' (adapted to distinguish) and Part B for marks that would become distinctive through use (capable of distinguishing); see sections 9 and 10 of the Trade Marks Act 1938. The advantages of registration in Part A were twofold. First, there was a presumption of conclusive validity after seven years and the mark could be removed from the register only under limited circumstances (for example, that the registration was obtained by fraud or the application was not *bona fide* or through non-use for five or more years). Secondly, a defendant in an infringement action in respect of a Part B mark had a defence if he could show that the buying public were not deceived.

The Trade Marks Act 1994 has swept aside this somewhat artificial classification of trade marks. The standard for all marks is that the mark must be capable of distinguishing by section 1(1). It is instructive to look at some cases under previous legislation concerning registrability, particularly in respect of Part B marks. In the first case, *Davis v Sussex Rubber*, the meaning of 'capable of distinguishing' was considered and contrasted with the standard for a Part A mark.

Davis v *The Sussex Rubber Co. Ltd.* (1927) 44 RPC 412, Court of Appeal

Davis registered the words 'Ustikon' and 'Davis Ustikon' as trade marks in Part B of the register for use with rubber soles for boots and shoes. Sussex Rubber started using the word 'Justickon', also for rubber soles, and Davis sued for trade mark infringement and passing off. Sussex Rubber, in its defence, argued that there were two types of soles, those which 'you nail on' and those which 'you stick on' and that Davis's marks were simply misspellings of the last-mentioned type and were purely descriptive of the goods and were, consequently, incapable of being distinctive.

Sargant LJ (at 425): 'The determination of these two appeals involves somewhat different considerations.

As regards the second appeal, that in the action, the Plaintiff has rights independent of his registration. The learned Judge, relying mainly on the undoubted similarity of the two marks, both as written and as spoken, and partly on the necessarily slight evidence that was before him, has come to the conclusion that there would be a probability of confusion between the Defendants' goods and the Plaintiff's goods. And though it may be urged that this would be at least partly due to the adoption by the Plaintiff of a mark to describe a quality of the goods which is common to both sets of goods, I do not think that this common element sufficiently explains or justifies the similarity in name. The Judge, after having seen the witnesses, obviously disbelieved the story told by the Defendants as to the brain-wave which was said to have produced the earlier part of the word "Justickon" and considered that this word was suggested, though perhaps unconsciously, by the knowledge of the Defendants' agents as to the Plaintiff's Mark. And such a suggestion, even if unconscious, is in itself an indication of similarity likely to lead to confusion. Apart, therefore, from any question of fraud, which was not pleaded, there was, in my judgment, material sufficient to justify an injunction against passing off. The exact form of the injunction would no doubt be slightly different if it protected a trade name, or common law trade mark, only and not a registered trade mark. But this would be of little, if any, importance, since the Defendants have expressly disclaimed any intention of using the word "Justickon" in future.

The second appeal, namely, that in the application to remove the word "Ustikon" from the Register, is of more general importance, since it involves a consideration of the modifications with regard to the registration of trade marks which have been introduced by the Trade Marks Act, 1919. This Act materially decreases the difficulties in getting marks and particularly word-marks on the Register and especially on that division of the Register thereby constituted as Part B.

In the first place, it makes a marked alteration in Section 9, paragraph 5, of the Act of 1905 in the case of all word-marks other than those within paragraphs (1), (2), (3) and (4), by abolishing the requirement that they shall not be deemed distinctive enough for registration except by order of the Board of Trade or the Court, and substituting the far less stringent requirement that a word-mark of the kind shall not be registrable under the provisions of paragraph (5) except upon evidence of its distinctiveness.

And in the next place, it demands much less stringent evidence of distinctiveness in actual use than was ordinarily requisite under the last paragraph of Section 9 of the Act of 1905. Under that Act as interpreted in practice the evidence as to distinctiveness had to prove an actual acquired distinctiveness generally throughout the country. But under the Act of 1919 this does not seem to be necessary. Some evidence of distinctiveness has to be given under the alteration to Section 9, paragraph (5), just noticed. But so far as this is concerned, the Registrar is directed to accept an application to register in part B, unless he is not satisfied that the mark is capable of distinguishing the goods of the applicant. In the result, therefore, in the case of an application for registration in Part B of a mark in actual use for two years it is not necessary for the applicant to prove that the mark has actually become distinctive. It is sufficient for him to satisfy the Registrar that it is not incapable of becoming distinctive, a much less strenuous task, and one in which the onus lies rather on the opponent than on the applicant.

Even so, as was admitted by Mr Moritz, there is a large class of word-marks which are by their very nature incapable of becoming distinctive and which ought, therefore, on *a priori* grounds, to be refused registration, even in the B. Register. Such marks are mere laudatory epithets, such as "Good," "Best," "Excellent," "Perfect," and the like, and also marks merely describing in ordinary language some common characteristic of the goods in question, such as in the present case

"Stickable," "Attachable" or, as Mr Moritz admitted, "Stickon," however spelt. And if Mr Davis had succeeded in the object at which, according to his own evidence, he aimed, namely, to frame a word-mark which, in its ordinary sense, meant to the buying public that the soles in question could be stuck on by the purchasers themselves without employing a bootmaker, then I think that his word-mark would not have been registrable even in Part B. Such a word-mark, for instance, as "Self-attachable" or "Easy-sticking" must, I think, have been rejected by the Registrar. But in fact, Mr Davis, in the course of torturing the English language for the purpose of ultimately arriving at the word "Ustikon" has, in my judgment, been fortunate enough to arrive at a combination of letters, which, as ordinarily written or pronounced, would not definitely indicate that which he intended it to indicate, though it might perhaps suggest something with regard to the soles falling within that class of rubber soles which are stuck on rather than nailed on. And I think that there is justification for the view urged by Mr Moritz that customers first learn the word "Ustikon," the initial "U" being apparently pronounceable as in the word "Us," and later on are educated to recognise the origin and implied meaning of the word in relation to Mr Davis' soles.

On the whole, therefore, though with some doubt, I cannot say that the Registrar was bound to decide on *a priori* grounds that the mark "Ustikon" was incapable of distinguishing Mr Davis' soles. And this being so, and the other conditions of registration in Part B, having been satisfied, the registration was in order and the mark cannot now be taken off. But the case seems to me very near the line. And I hope - perhaps against hope - that the result of this decision will not be to choke the B. Register with horribly misspelt words, which were originally intended to bear and still to some extent suggest a more or less obvious reference to the ordinary characteristics of the goods they denote.'

COMMENT

Had the word 'Ustikon' not been registered, would 'Justickon' be registrable? What is a laudatory epithet and why are they not registrable as trade marks? Sargant LJ alluded to the concern that the Trade Mark Registry might be deluged with applications for 'horribly misspelt words'. The following case shows that, although such applications occasionally are made, they are rarely likely to succeed.

Electrix Ltd. v *Electrolux Ltd.* [1960] AC 722, House of Lords

In the early 1950s, the appellant sought to register the word 'Electrix' as a trade mark for vacuum cleaners, floor polishing machines and spraying machines. One application was for Part A, the others being for Part B of the register. All the applications were opposed by the respondent though registration was granted. However, the respondent's appeal to the Court of Appeal was allowed.

Viscount Simonds at (727): 'My Lords, I can conveniently state the problem to be solved by the citation of a single sentence from the judgment of the Court of Appeal: "The doctrine, as we understand it, is that, if a given word is for any reason unregistrable in its proper spelling, then, inasmuch as trade marks appeal to the ear as well as to the eye, the objection (whatever it may be) to the registration of the properly spelt word applies equally to a word which is merely its phonetic equivalent." Applying that view of the law to the facts of the present case, The Court of Appeal held that, "electrix" being the phonetic equivalent of "electrics," and that word being unregistrable, "electrix" also was unregistrable.

In my opinion the proposition or doctrine of law, upon which the Court of Appeal founded, is accurately stated and supported by authority and reason, and it was correctly applied. The more important of the cases which establish it are cited in the exhaustive judgment of the Court of Appeal. At the risk of repetition I must refer to some of them. In re *Edward Ripley & Son's Application* (1898) 15 RPC 151 the question was whether the word "Pirle" should be registered for goods in Class 34, namely, cloths and stuffs of wool, worsted and hair, the word "Pirle" being formed from the name "Ripley" with the omission of the "y." The application was refused on the ground that the word was identical in sound with "Pearl" and that "Pearl" itself was not eligible for registration, being a term of commendation. Kekewich J upheld the refusal and so did the Court of Appeal in words which I quote because they are directly apposite, Lindley MR said:

"We do not see our way to accede to this application. We cannot do it, unless we are prepared to lay down a proposition that I do not think any court should. We cannot say that a man may register, in any class of goods, a word which sounds exactly like a word that could not be registered. The reason is obvious; it would be putting a monopoly upon the public, which would be utterly unjustifiable. That is the short reason."

My Lords, the reason was short and was obvious. The judgment too was short: I have cited the whole of it. There is not a word in it to suggest that it matters why the word is unregistrable which the word proposed to be registered sounds exactly like. And in the 70 years which have passed since those very learned judges gave that clear and emphatic judgment, there has never been a suggestion that it is material why the unregistrable word is unregistrable nor any attempt to qualify the generality of its language. That case was decided under the Acts of 1883 and 1888. The next cases that I cite were heard after the passing of the Trade Marks Act, 1905. That Act made no difference to the relevant principle. Thus, in the "Perfection" and "Orlwoola" cases, In re *Joseph Crosfield & Sons Ltd.; In re H N Brock & Co. Ltd.* [1910] 1 Ch 130, Lord Cozens-Hardy MR, dealing with both cases, said (at 142):

"There is one important distinction between word marks and other marks. The former appeal to the ear as well as, and indeed more than, to the eye. The latter appeal to the eye only. It seems to follow that a word, not being an invented word, ought not to be put on the register if the spelling is phonetic and resembles in sound a word which in its proper spelling could not be put on the register."

Here again the language is general. The learned Master of the Rolls goes on to deal separately with the two marks, of which one was of a laudatory character; the other had reference to the quality or nature of the goods. In regard to "Perfection" he said:

"It was admitted by counsel that 'Perfect' could not be registered, and that admission is fatal to the case of the appellants,"

and in regard to "Orlwoola" he said:

> "It is plain that 'all wool' could not be registered, and indeed these words are disclaimed on the face of the register. This word is a mark which appeals to the ear far more than to the eye, and for reasons which I stated in my general observations I think it is obviously not distinctive."

That is to say, "Orlwoola" could not be registered, because to the ear it sounded like the unregistrable "all wool." I must pass over the judgments of Fletcher Moulton and Farwell LJJ, though there is much in them to support the doctrine laid down in the judgment of the Court of Appeal in the present case and nothing from which the appellants can derive comfort. But I cannot refrain from citing a short passage from the judgment of Fletcher Moulton LJ. With regard to "Orlwoola" he said:

> "The misspelling does not affect the words when spoken, so that we have only to decide whether the words 'all wool' are proper for registration in respect of such goods."

That was for him the sole question, just as for your Lordships the sole question is whether the word, of which "Electrix" is the phonetic equivalent, is registrable - a question that in this case admits of only one answer. So also in the *Ogee* case (*In re Garrett's Application* [1916] 1 Ch 436) Lord Cozens-Hardy MR, reiterating that a trade mark appeals to the ear as well as to the eye, said:

> "If the letters 'O.G.' could not be registered, it seems to me that the word 'Ogee' ought not to be registered ... The applicant may or may not have a right to 'Ogee' as a common law mark, but it is not a registrable mark."

It would be difficult to find words more directly applicable than these to the present case ... So also the appellants have sought to ignore the unregistrability of 'Electrics' and claimed nevertheless that "Electrix" was registrable. Thus in their formal case they say:

> "The appellants do not contend that the word 'Electrics' would be registrable,"

and they did not resile from this position in argument before the House. Let it not be thought that I criticise them for making the admission. It appears to me that, whether or not distinctiveness in fact was, or could be acquired by "Electrics," of which there was, of course, no evidence, it would be a hopeless task to persuade the tribunal that it was not inherently unregistrable. From this it follows that the word "Electrix" cannot be registered.

In my opinion the appeal must be dismissed with costs.'

COMMENT

In view of prior case law, especially in connection with 'Pirle' and 'Orlwoola', do you think it was surprising that the Trade Mark Registry initially accepted 'Electrix'? Why was it agreed by all that the word 'Electrics' was not registrable?

In the following case, the registrability or otherwise of the word mark "Treat" was considered. This mark was accepted under the 1938 Act in Part B of the Register but, when the 1994 Act came into force, the mark was transferred to the new Register and had effect as if it had been registered under the 1994 Act (para 2, schedule 3 to the 1994 Act). The registrability of the mark was, accordingly, decided under the 1994 Act.

British Sugar PLC v *James Robertson & Sons Ltd.* [1996] RPC 281

The plaintiff registered 'TREAT' for 'dessert sauces and syrups; all included in Class 30'. It used the mark with a syrup to be poured over ice-cream and known as 'Silver Spoon Treat'. The defendant started selling a sweet spread under the name 'Robertson's Toffee Treat' and sold it alongside its range of jams and preserves. It was held that the plaintiff's trade mark was invalid.

Jacob J (at 300): 'Section 47(1) of the Act provides:

"The registration of a trade mark may be declared invalid on the ground that the trade mark was registered in breach of section 3 or any of the provisions referred to in that section (absolute grounds for refusal of registration).

Where the trade mark was registered in breach of subsection (1)(b), (c) or (d) of that section, it shall not be declared invalid if, in consequence of the use which has been made of it, it has after registration acquired a distinctive character in relation to the goods or services for which it is registered."

Section 3(1) provides:

"The following shall not be registered
(a) signs which do not satisfy the requirements of section 1(1),
(b) trade marks which are devoid of any distinctive character,
(c) trade marks which consist exclusively of signs or indications which may serve, in trade, to designate the kind, quality, quantity, intended purpose, value, geographical origin, the time of production of goods or of rendering of services, or other characteristics of goods or services,
(d) trade marks which consist exclusively of signs or indications which have become customary in the current language or in the *bona fide* and established practices of the trade:
Provided that, a trade mark shall not be refused registration by virtue of paragraph (b), (c) or (d) above if, before the date of application for registration, it has in fact acquired a distinctive character as a result of the use made of it."

And section 1(1) provides:

"In this Act a 'trade mark' means any sign capable of being represented graphically which is capable of distinguishing goods or services of one undertaking from those of other undertakings."

Validity is attacked on the following grounds:

(1)   That the mark is not a "trade mark" within the meaning of section 1(1), an attack said to be permitted by section 3(1)(a);
(2)   That the mark is devoid of distinctive character (section 3(1)(b));
(3)   That the mark consists exclusively of a sign or indication specified in section 3(1)(c);
(4)   That the mark consists exclusively of a sign or indication specified in section 3(1)(d).

It is worth noting the effect on onus of the proviso to section 47(1). By section 72:

> "In all legal proceedings relating to a registered trade mark (including proceedings for rectification of the register) the registration of a person as proprietor of a trade mark shall be prima facie evidence of the validity of the original registration..."

This clearly casts the onus on he who wishes to attack the validity of the *original* registration. But once the attacker can show the registration was wrongly made (particularly for non-compliance with section 3(1)(b)-(d)) and the proprietor wishes to rely on the proviso to section 47(1) it is for the proprietor to show that his mark is distinctive. So one cannot simply look at the position at the time of the attack and say the onus lies on the attacker. Once the attacker is over the hurdle of showing the original registration was bad, the onus shifts to the proprietor if he wants to say, "never mind, I can show the mark is distinctive now".

With that in mind I must deal with the evidence - for all depends upon the conclusions to be drawn from that. I begin with the original registration. As I have said I do not have to consider whether the mark was rightly registered under the 1938 Act. By virtue of section 105 of the 1994 Act and Schedule 3 paragraph 18(2) it is section 47 of the 1994 Act which sets out the grounds upon which a mark registered under the old Act can be attacked. I have already described the evidence used to support the original registration. It was really no more than evidence of use. Now it is all too easy to be beguiled by such evidence. There is an unspoken and illogical assumption that "use equals distinctiveness". The illogicality can be seen from an example: no matter how much use a manufacturer made of the word "Soap" as a purported trade mark for soap the word would not be distinctive of his goods. He could use fancy lettering as much as he liked, whatever he did would not turn the word into a trade mark. Again, a manufacturer may coin a new word for a new product and be able to show massive use by him and him alone of that word for the product. Nonetheless the word is apt to be the name of the product, not a trade mark. Examples from old well-known cases of this sort of thing abound. The *Shredded Wheat* saga is a good example: the Canadian case is *The Canadian Shredded Wheat Co. Ltd.* v *Kellogg Co. of Canada Ltd.* (1938) 55 RPC 125 in the Privy Council and the United Kingdom case *The Shredded Wheat Co. Ltd.* v *Kellogg Co. of Great Britain Ltd* (1940) 57 RPC 137 in the House of Lords. In the former case Lord Russell said (at 145),

> "A word or words to be really distinctive of a person's goods must generally speaking be incapable of application to the goods of anyone else."

It is precisely because a common laudatory word is naturally capable of application to the goods of any trader that one must be careful before concluding that merely its use, however substantial, has displaced its common meaning and has come to denote the mark of a particular trader. This is all the more so when the mark has been used in conjunction with what is obviously taken as a trade mark.

I do not consider that the evidence filed to support the registration was anywhere near enough to support the conclusion that when the mark was registered, it was distinctive. Yes it had been used for about 5 years in conjunction with Silver Spoon, but it was not proved that the public regarded it as a trade mark - a reliable badge of trade origin - on its own. Further the use was only for what was essentially an ice cream topping. It did not cover the full range of goods covered by the registration.

What then of the position now? British Sugar rely upon more extensive evidence. First there is a great deal more use of exactly the same type as went on before. Sales figures went on going up - to nearly £3m p.a. Since introduction in 1986 sales over the 10 year period total about £13m of which over half have taken place since registration in September 1992. The product has just over 50% of the ice cream topping market sector. Next British Sugar rely upon evidence from Mrs Nash MBE. She was in public relations at British Sugar. She took telephone inquiries and dealt with letters from the general public. People sometimes complained when a flavour disappeared (blackcurrant did) or wanted information on availability (for instance when the toffee flavour came out, magazines, mainly at British Sugar's instigation, published recipes for making banoffi pie, a dessert made from bananas, toffee and ice cream). She said that customers often referred simply to "your 'Treat' range". But of course all the customers concerned, whether writing or telephoning, knew they were dealing with Silver Spoon the manufacturers. I do not think Mrs Nash's evidence establishes that the general public perceive the word "Treat" to be a badge of trade origin in itself. I think her evidence does show recognition of the word amongst British Sugar customers, but recognition does not necessarily mean recognition as a trade mark.

British Sugar also rely upon a market survey. It was conducted by National Opinion Polls ("NOP"). NOP conducted what they call an omnibus survey. Trained interviewers visited the homes of people selected essentially at random. I do not need to go into detail as to how the selection was made. The interviewers asked those of the persons selected who were willing to be interviewed a series of questions, each about a different topic. On this occasion the second topic was the "Treat" survey relied upon. The interviewer (who was equipped with a personal computer) asked the following questions:

1. Do you ever buy sweet-tasting sauces and toppings, for example sauces and syrups for use in or on desserts and ice cream?

If the interviewee said "no" the questioning proceeded to a different topic.

2. What brands of sweet-tasting sauces and toppings can you think of? Which others? Any others?

If the interviewee mentioned "Treat" then the interviewer was to proceed to Q4. Otherwise he/she showed the interviewee a card on which 5 different words appeared (Askeys, Ice Magic, Smuckers, Treat and Tops) asked:

3. Which of these other brands of sweet-tasting sauces and toppings have you heard of? Which others? Any others?

If "Treat" was mentioned at either Q2 or Q3 the subject was shown a photograph of the products and asked:

4. Is this the "Treat" product you were thinking of?

The NOP witness responsible for the survey, Mr Lees, drew the conclusion that of those who buy sweet tasting sauces and toppings 24% were aware of the product sold under the name "Treat" unprompted (Q2), and a further 40% of the total were aware of the product after prompting (Q3). This made 62-3% in all. There were a few individuals, however, who apparently were thinking of some product other than the British Sugar product, for they said "no" to Q4. The upshot of all this was said to be that 61% knew the British Sugar "Treat" product.

The procedure is open to some criticism. The first question, instead of simply covering the goods of the specification, is specifically directed at a sub-class within those goods, namely desserts and ice cream. The question as phrased in effect says "ice-cream toppings (hint hint)". I was not told who was responsible for the question, and Mr Lees did not know. There will be an obvious danger in extrapolating any conclusion to the full range of goods covered by the registration.

Next, I think there is a real problem in relation to the recording of the answers to Q2. The interviewers' computers provided them with options. If the interviewee said any of the five names I have mentioned, the interviewer was to press a number corresponding to the name. If the interviewee said anything else, the interviewer was to type in what was said. Now anyone who has had much to do with opinion polls knows there are great difficulties in recording exactly what an interviewee says, however much care is taken. So if the interviewee said "Oh there's Bird's Ice Magic and a "Silver Spoon Treat product" it is quite likely that all that would happen is that the Ice Magic and Treat numbers would have been pressed. Mr Lees acknowledged that it would have been much better, if one wanted to distinguish between those who said "Silver Spoon Treat" and simply "Treat" that the preceding should have included both as options.

Q3 I think is particularly valueless from the point of view of trying to decide whether the public perceive of "Treat" as a trade mark. It presupposes it is by including the word "brand" in the question. It could hardly lead more.

Overall there is this further point, namely that recognition is not the same thing as perception as a trade mark - as not only recognising the word but as regarding it, in itself, as denoting the goods of one particular trader.

On the question of factual distinctiveness I must also have regard to how the mark is used - how it appears on the label. I think it is fairly ambiguous. What the customer sees is "Silver Spoon Treat". The suggestion is that the syrup from "Silver Spoon" will be a "treat". Other customers may accept the word as having a trade mark meaning in context. I take the latter possibility into account in my conclusion.

Both sides invited me to have regard to the state of the register. Some traders have registered marks consisting of or incorporating the word "Treat". I do not think this assists the factual inquiry one way or the other, save perhaps to confirm that this is the sort of word in which traders would like a monopoly. In particular the state of the register does not tell you what is actually happening out in the market and in any event one has no idea what the circumstances were which led the registrar to put the marks concerned on the register. It has long been held under the old Act that comparison with other marks on the register is in principle irrelevant when considering a particular mark tendered for registration, see *e.g. MADAME Trade*

Mark [1966] RPC 541 and the same must be true under the 1994 Act. I disregard the state of the register evidence.

In the end I conclude, that whilst it is probably the case that a proportion of members of the relevant public regard the word alone as having some trade mark significance, one cannot say that most do. I think the suggested 60% figure is much too high. Overall the word has achieved some minor degree of distinctiveness in fact, but falls far short of universal or near universal acceptance as a trade mark for ice cream toppings.

How stands the law on these findings? I begin by considering the "not a trade mark" point. Section 1(1) has two parts, *sign,* and *capable of distinguishing. Sign* is not in issue: a word is plainly included within the meaning of *sign* as the remainder of section 1 indicates. But what about *capable of distinguishing?* Does this add any requirement beyond that found in section 3(1)? Section 3(1)(b) bars the registration of a mark which is *devoid of distinctive character* unless it has *in fact acquired a distinctive character.* I cannot see that the closing words of the first sentence of section 1(1) add anything to this. If a mark on its face is non-distinctive (and ordinary descriptive and laudatory words fall into this class) but is shown to have a distinctive character in fact then it must be *capable of distinguishing.* Under section 10 of the old Act, for a mark to be registrable in Part B, it also had to be *capable of distinguishing.* But the Pickwickian position was that some marks, even though 100% distinctive in fact, were not regarded as *capable of distinguishing* within the meaning of that provision. I do not think the Directive and the 1994 Act take this more limited meaning over.

Thus, *capable of distinguishing* means whether the mark can in fact do the job of distinguishing. So the phrase in section 1(1) adds nothing to section 3(1) at least in relation to any sign within section 3(1)(b)-(d). The scheme is that if a man tenders for registration a sign of this sort without any evidence of distinctiveness then he cannot have it registered unless he can prove it has a distinctive character. That is all. There is no pre-set bar saying no matter how well it is proved that a mark has become a trade mark, it cannot be registered. That is not to say that there are some signs which cannot in practice be registered. But the reason is simply that the applicant will be unable to prove the mark has become a trade mark in practice - "Soap" for "soap" is an example. The bar (no pun intended) will be factual not legal.

Next, is "Treat" within section 3(1)(b)? What does *devoid of any distinctive character* mean? I think the phrase requires consideration of the mark on its own, assuming no use. Is it the sort of word (or other sign) which cannot do the job of distinguishing without first educating the public that it is a trade mark? A meaningless word or a word inappropriate for the goods concerned ("North Pole" for bananas) can clearly do. But a common laudatory word such as "Treat" is, absent use and recognition as a trade mark, in itself (I hesitate to borrow the word from the old Act but the idea is much the same) devoid of any distinctive *inherently* [*sic,* inherent] character. I also think "Treat" falls within section 3(1)(c) because it is a trade mark which consists exclusively of a sign or indication which may serve in trade to perform a number of the purposes there specified, particularly, to designate the kind, quality and intended purpose of the product. The word probably also falls within section 3(1)(d): it is a sign which has become customary in the current language. Lots of people use "Treat" in advertisements and on goods and I have some examples in evidence.

Thus, assuming I am right so far, the question is whether British Sugar have shown that the mark now has a *distinctive character.* Is my finding that to some but not most people "Treat" has some trade mark significance enough? This depends on what is meant by a *distinctive character*. Neither the Directive nor Act throw any light on this. So I have to use what I at least regard as my common sense. Take a very descriptive or laudatory word. Suppose the proprietor can educate 10% of the public into recognising the word as his trade mark. Can that really be enough to say it has a *distinctive character* and so enough to let the proprietor lay claim to the word as a trade mark altogether? The character at this stage is part distinctive but mainly not. I do not think it would be fair to regard the character of the word as *distinctive* in that state of affairs. But if the matter were the other way round, so that to 90% of people it was taken as a trade mark, then I think it would be fair so to regard it. This all suggests that the question of factual *distinctive character* is one of degree. The proviso really means "has the mark acquired a sufficiently distinctive character that the mark has really become a trade mark." In the case of common or apt descriptive or laudatory words compelling evidence is needed to establish this. And in particular mere evidence of extensive use is unlikely to be enough on its own. Of course the power of advertising may be able to turn almost anything (save a pure description) into a trade mark, but it must be shown in a case of this sort that the mark has really become accepted by a substantial majority of persons as a trade mark - is or is almost a household word.

My findings on the facts here fall a long way short of this. Indeed even the suggested 60% figure put forward for British Sugar falls short. I do not think the mark has been shown to have a *distinctive character* and accordingly I propose to declare the registration invalid pursuant to the provisions of section 47(1). Apparently, and somewhat oddly, I do not revoke the registration (revocation is dealt with under section 46) but I should like to hear counsel on what I am to do. It seems very odd to leave the mark on the Register. This is a matter on which I may need the views of the Registrar.'

COMMENT

Does the phrase 'capable of distinguishing' have the same meaning under the Trade Marks Act 1994 as it had under the 1938 Act? If, under the latter Act, a mark was capable of distinguishing in fact, did that mean that the mark would be registrable in Class B of the Register? How has this changed under the 1994 Act?

Do you think survey evidence is useful in determining questions such as distinctiveness or whether a sign was perceived as a trade mark? Why did the survey evidence in this case fail to impress Jacob J?

ELVIS PRESLEY Trade Marks [1997] RPC 543, Chancery Division

Elvis Presley Enterprises Inc. ('Enterprises') carried on the merchandising activities of Elvis Presley and continued to do so after his death. It applied to register ELVIS, ELVIS PRESLEY and ELVIS A PRESLEY (in signature form) as trade marks under the Trade Marks Act 1938. Mr Sid David Shaw, who traded under the name 'ELVISLY YOURS' since the 1970s, opposed those applications and the oppositions were dismissed in the Trade Marks Registry. Mr Shaw appealed.

Laddie J (at 548): *'The "ELVIS" application.*
As noted above, this is an application for the name "ELVIS" *simpliciter.* It is sought to be registered under section 9 of the Act. This means that Enterprises must demonstrate that it is a distinctive mark as required by section 9(1)(e). The meaning of distinctive is dealt with by section 9(2) and (3) as follows;

"(2) For the purposes of this section 'distinctive' means adapted, in relation to the goods in respect of which a trade mark is registered or proposed to be registered, to distinguish goods with which the proprietor of the trade mark is or may be connected in the course of trade from goods in the case of which no such connection subsists, either generally or, where the trade mark is registered or proposed to be registered subject to limitations, in relation to use within the extent of the registration.

(3) In determining whether a trade mark is adapted to distinguish as aforesaid the tribunal may have regard to the extent to which -
(a) the trade mark is inherently adapted to distinguish as aforesaid; and
(b) by reason of the use of the trade mark or of any other circumstances, the trade mark is in fact adapted to distinguish as aforesaid."

The distinctiveness addressed by the Act is not a quality of the mark which exists in a vacuum. It is a particular type of distinctiveness, namely the ability to distinguish the proprietor's goods from the same or similar goods marketed by someone else. The more a proposed mark alludes to the character, quality or non-origin attributes of the goods on which it is used or proposed to be used, the lower its inherent distinctiveness. At one extreme this means that common laudatory epithets will have virtually no inherent distinctiveness. They do not inherently serve the function of distinguishing the proprietor's goods from the same goods marketed by someone else. As Mr Prescott pointed out, in *Smith Kline & French Laboratories Ltd's Trade Mark Applications* [1976] RPC 511 at page 538 Lord Diplock said that the words "inherently adapted" in section 9(3) were intended to give statutory effect to the views of Lord Parker in *W & G Du Cros Ltd's Application* (1913) 30 RPC 660 that registration should;

"largely depend on whether other traders are likely, in the ordinary course of their business and without any improper motive, to desire to use the same mark, or some mark nearly resembling it, upon or in connection with their own goods."

Those words have particular impact when it is borne in mind that the other traders' own goods can be goods having the same character, quality or non-origin attributes as those of the proprietor.
In the Registry, Mr Tuck's reasons for rejecting the opposition to the application to register "ELVIS" for Class 3 goods were expressed as follows;

"From my own knowledge, I am aware that this was the Christian or first name of a very famous individual; ... Whilst I can see, therefore, that the Registrar would take objection to any application for its registration under section 11 (as deceptive if used without authority) or in his discretion under section 17(2) (for the same reason), I cannot see that there is a prima facie objection to it under section 9. The use of feminine proper names is generally regarded as non-distinctive in Class 3, but no such objection is taken to masculine proper names used on that class of goods."

In saying this, it appears that Mr Tuck was following internal Trade Mark Registry guidelines or practice. Perhaps such a practice was a useful rule of thumb in the days when toilet preparations, perfumes, eau de colognes, preparations for the hair and teeth, soaps, bath and shower preparations, deodorants, antiperspirants, cosmetics and the like were thought to be exclusively directed at female customers. Whatever the position may have been in the past, such products are now frequently sold to and targeted at men. If there was a Registry approach that *prima facie* feminine proper names should not be registered as trade marks for cosmetics and toiletries, it now should cover masculine proper names also. But in any event, even if there are such guidelines which are useful in assisting Registry officials to adopt at least a consistent starting point for the examination of registrations, in the end whether a mark is acceptable or not for registration must depend upon the particular mark in issue, the goods for which registration is sought and the nature of the trade into which they will be sold.

Mr Meade said that the Registrar came to the wrong conclusion as to the registrability of the "ELVIS" mark. He said that there was low inherent distinctiveness. "Elvis" is merely a given name. It may be that in England it is not the most common name but it is well known, no doubt in large part because of the fame of Elvis Presley. He says that the fact that the musician's name is well known does not make the mark more inherently distinctive but less so. He says that Enterprises can not get over their problems by relying on use or other special circumstances. He says that the evidence of use is virtually non-existent and there are no other special circumstances.

Mr Prescott asked me to approach this application in an entirely different way by considering what the position would be if Elvis Presley was still alive and had made this application himself. He says that there is no doubt that he would be entitled to a registered trade mark for his own name. In fact he went further back and suggested that I consider what the position would have been had these applications been made not now but before Elvis Presley had burst onto the entertainment firmament. Before he was famous, the word "Elvis" would have been virtually unknown in England. Had he applied then he would have got the mark on the register. Mr Prescott suggested that the position can be no different if Elvis Presley had applied later once he was famous or if his estate or its successors apply after he has died.

I reject that seductive argument. What is in issue is whether, at the date of application, the mark satisfies the registration requirements of the 1938 Act. It is no help, and may be positively misleading, to consider what the position would have been in other very different circumstances. The point can be illustrated by reference to *TARZAN Trade Mark* [1970] RPC 450. In that case the applicant, Edgar Rice Burroughs Inc. of Tarzana, California, had been granted certain exclusive rights by the estate of Edgar Rice Burroughs, the author of the Tarzan stories, "to produce films, records and merchandise for distribution throughout the world, including the United Kingdom, centred on the fictional character 'Tarzan'". It applied to register "TARZAN" in Part A of the register in respect of films for exhibition and magnetic tape recordings. The application was unsuccessful in the Registry, in the High Court and in the Court of Appeal. One of the applicant's arguments was that the mark was an invented word and therefore prima facie entitled to registration under the provisions of section 9(1)(c) of the Act. By November 1965, the date of the application for registration, the word "Tarzan" had passed into the language and had become a household word. There was no doubt that originally the word had been invented by Mr Burroughs. In the Court of Appeal, Salmon LJ said at page 454:

> "It is not fatal to the application that the word had been invented many years before the application was made. For example, if a word was invented, say, in 1925, and had not passed into the language, it would still remain an invented word in 1965. The trouble facing Mr Burrell is that it seems quite plain that the word TARZAN had by 1965 passed into the language. In *Holt's Trade Mark* (1896) 13 RPC 118 there was an application to register the word TRILBY as a trade mark in relation to certain goods, and the question arose as to whether it was an invented word. Lindley, LJ said at page 121: 'It may have been once an invented word within clause (d)' - section 68 of the Act of 1883 - 'but it long ago became too well-known to fall under that head'. Smith, LJ at page 124, said: 'It is not a word coined for the first time by the owner of the trade mark, it having been used by Du Maurier in his book in 1893, and it was, therefore, not an invented work in 1895, when the appellants registered their trade mark.'
>
> For my part, as I have already indicated, it was not necessary to show that the applicant had invented the word himself in order for it to be an invented word within the meaning of the statute, but I should have thought that the word TARZAN in 1965, to quote the words of Lindley, LJ 'long ago became too well-known' to fall under the head of an invented word. It certainly, in my judgment, was at least as well-known in 1965 as the word TRILBY was in 1895, which apparently was only about two years after Du Maurier had invented it."

The whole thrust of this passage is that registrability of a mark must be assessed as of the date of application. No doubt had Edgar Rice Burroughs had the foresight, or employed a lawyer with the foresight, to realise the merchandising potential of his Tarzan character at the time he created it and before it was launched before the public, he could have obtained a registration of that word for films and a wide range of other products. Whether such a registration could have been removed from the register as a result of it becoming non-distinctive at a later date is another matter. At the time of the registration the word would have been an inherently distinctive invented word (and, incidentally, not descriptive). But that was not what happened in fact. Those interested in exploiting the Tarzan character waited until it was well known by the public before they sought the benefits of registered trade mark rights. By that time it was no longer an invented word (and was descriptive). It follows that whether a mark is registrable under the 1938 Act has to be decided on the facts and in the market conditions prevailing at the date of application.

So I approach this appeal on the basis that, at the date of application, Elvis Presley had been dead for more than 10 years but that his fame continued to exist on a large scale. There were at the date of application, and still are, many people in this country who wish to acquire recordings of his songs and films and a wide variety of domestic articles bearing his likeness and/or his name. It is not in dispute that there is a large market in Elvis Presley memorabilia. It has kept Mr Shaw in business for more than 18 years. This judgment does not deal with what Elvis Presley could have obtained by way of trade mark registration if he had applied for such rights during his life. In particular it should not be assumed that I accept Mr Prescott's assertion that there is "no doubt" that Elvis Presley would be entitled to registration of his own name. That is a proposition which is beset with difficulties but which does not arise for resolution on this appeal.

It seems to me that Mr Meade was right when he said that the word ELVIS had very low inherent distinctiveness. Not only is this a well known given name, it also will be taken by many members of the public to refer back to Elvis Presley. This accords with the view expressed by Mr Tuck:

"To me, therefore, the name Elvis means Elvis Presley."

The classification of goods for which Enterprises seeks registration covers a wide range of small value products which can carry the image of Elvis Presley. In TARZAN Salmon LJ said at page 454:

"I asked Mr Burrell during the course of his argument if he could think of a more direct reference to the character or a film dealing with some exploits of Tarzan than the description that it was a 'Tarzan' film. This was a question which Mr Burrell, despite his wide experience and ingenuity, was quite unable to answer. Indeed, it seems plain that such a film could not better be described or referred to than as a 'Tarzan' film."

Then, turning to the question of whether the mark was inherently adapted to distinguish within the meaning of section 9 of the Act, he referred to the decision of the House of Lords in *Yorkshire Copper Works Limited's Application (1954)* 71 RPC 150 and continued at page 456:

"In the present case, there is nothing at all in the word TARZAN which would suggest to the public or to the trade that a film or magnetic tape recording had anything to do with the applicant or with anyone else. The word TARZAN when used in connection with a film suggests - and suggests only - that the film has something to do with the well-known fictional person, Tarzan, a man of great strength and agility.

... TARZAN has nothing standing on its own feet, upon which it would be possible to find that it is inherently apt to distinguish the applicants' films or magnetic recordings as being the applicants' or anyone else's goods."

Similarly Cross LJ said at page 460:

"Turning now to section 9(1)(e), since it is so strongly descriptive, the word TARZAN can hardly be said to be to any appreciable extent "inherently adapted to distinguish the applicants' goods from the goods of any other trader", for, as Lord Simmonds said in the *Yorkshire Copper* case, 'the more apt a word is to describe the goods of a manufacturer, the less apt it is to distinguish them from the goods of others, for a word that is apt to describe the goods of A is likely to be apt to describe the similar goods of B'."

These passages emphasise that the more a mark has come to describe the goods to which is to be applied or to indicate some quality of those goods, the less it is inherently adapted to carry out the trade mark function of distinguishing the trade origin of the proprietor's goods from the origin of similar goods from other sources.

This is consistent with Mr Meade's argument that the more famous Elvis Presley is, the less inherently distinctive are the words "Elvis" and "Presley". They are peculiarly suitable for use on the wide range of products sold as Elvis Presley memorabilia. He therefore does not contest but adopts Enterprises' assertion that "Elvis is about as famous a name as could be, made famous by the efforts of Elvis Presley. ... Why else do members of the public wish to [purchase] Elvis merchandise?" Just as members of the public will go to see a Tarzan film because it is about Tarzan, so they will purchase Elvis merchandise because it carries the name or likeness of Elvis and not because it comes from a particular source. To adopt the approach from *W & G*, there is no reason why Mr Shaw or anyone else for that matter should not sell memorabilia and momentos of Elvis Presley, including products embellished with pictures of him, and such traders are likely, in the ordinary course of their business and without any improper motive, to desire to use the name Elvis or Elvis Presley upon or in connection with their own such goods.

Mr Prescott argued that this was not the correct approach to adopt in the late 1990's. He said I should take judicial notice of the fact that markets have changed since the days of the *Tarzan* case. There is more public awareness of character merchandising now. Therefore cases such as *Tarzan* which were lost in the 1970's would succeed now. He drew my attention *to Mirage Studios* v *Counter-Feat Clothing Co. Ltd.* [1991] FSR 145. That was a judgment of Browne-Wilkinson VC on an application for interlocutory relief in a copyright infringement and passing off action. The plaintiffs exploited on a wide variety of products the name and likeness of a group of fictitious humanoid cartoon characters called the Teenage Mutant Ninja Turtles. The defendants made drawings of rather similar looking turtle figures and licensed third parties to put their drawings on T-shirts. During the course of his judgment, the Vice-Chancellor said at page 159:

> "The second point taken by Miss Vitoria was that the plaintiffs had to prove by evidence that the public in purchasing T-shirts or other clothing carrying Turtle pictures on them would rely on the misrepresentation, namely that the picture of the Turtles was once licensed by the plaintiffs. That is to say, would the public decline to buy T-shirts if they knew that what they were buying were the defendants' counterfeits as opposed to the plaintiffs' genuine Turtles? For that purpose she relied on *Politechnika Ipari Szovetkezet* v *Dallas Print Transfers Ltd.* [1982] FSR 529. In my judgment, that case does not support the proposition. That case was purely concerned with establishing that the plaintiff in a passing off case had to show a reputation which he enjoyed in the goods, which reputation was being interfered with. It does not, as I see it, come anywhere near requiring affirmative evidence that the public will rely on the misrepresentation in acquiring the goods. In my judgment, if the misrepresentation is made there is no requirement of law for further evidence to how that the misrepresentation was the cause of the public buying the goods in question. In general, the public expect to buy what they think they are getting, namely the genuine article. So, here, a teenage child wishing to buy a Mutant Turtle as part of the craze would wish to get a genuine Turtle, one which was indeed a Teenage Mutant Ninja Turtle. In the absence of evidence, the court must infer that if the child in the present case, or the customer in any case, were aware that the object he is buying is not genuine, he would not buy it but would seek the real object."

As I have said, this was a judgment on an interlocutory application. It was given *ex tempore*. It is not clear what evidence was before the Vice-Chancellor. He appears to have held that the plaintiffs had the necessary reputation to support a passing off action, the passage quoted above only going to the issue of whether the plaintiffs needed to prove that the public relied on the misrepresentation which he had already held that the defendants had made. I do not read it as laying down a finding of fact of universal application that the products of plaintiffs in similar circumstances are viewed by the public as "genuine" and that traders in competing goods are therefore making a misrepresentation. I suspect that the difficulty arises in knowing precisely what is meant by the word "genuine". However Mr Prescott suggested that the public's awareness of merchandising practices means that they will always assume that products of famous personalities or fictitious characters come from a particular "genuine" source. By "genuine source" I assume that he meant, in the case of a dead human, either his estate or someone with "rights" granted by his estate. In the case of fictitious characters perhaps "genuine" refers to the creator or his successors.

I am quite unable to accept that proposition. It may be that in some cases a plaintiff in a passing off action or an applicant for a registered trade mark will be able to show that to be the case. But I am not willing to assume that that is the public perception generally. On the contrary, my own experience suggests that such an assumption would be false. When people buy a toy of a well known character because it depicts that character, I have no reason to believe that they care one way or the other who made, sold or licensed it. When a fan buys a poster or a cup bearing an image of his star, he is buying a likeness, not a product from a particular source. Similarly the purchaser of any one of the myriad of cheap souvenirs of the royal wedding bearing pictures of Prince Charles and Diana, Princess of Wales, wants mementoes with likenesses. He is likely to be indifferent as to the source. Of course it is possible that, as a result of the peculiarities of the way goods are marketed or advertised, an inference of association with a particular trader may be possible to draw. This may be the case when the proprietor's products bear the word "Official". But that does not mean that absent that word members of the public would draw any such inference. That type of inference appears to have been drawn by the Vice-Chancellor in the *Mirage* case. But, as I have already said, there is no reason to assume that it would be drawn in all cases for all products. In particular there is nothing here which indicates that any significant section of the public seeing any of Enterprises' products would associate them with Enterprises by reason of the use of the words "Elvis" or "Elvis Presley". On the contrary, everything is consistent with those words being used and recognised as what the relevant public want not because of any trade source they may indicate but because they are a reminder of the famous musician. As Mr Prescott put it during his submissions, the motivation for buying Elvis Presley after shave must have something to do with Elvis Presley. That does not indicate distinctiveness of trade origin. This is a matter to which I will return below. I note, in passing, that although Mr Shaw has sold millions of pounds worth of memorabilia bearing the name Elvis or Elvis Presley over the last 18 or so years, it has not been suggested that anyone has ever thought they emanated from Enterprises.

It follows that I have come to the conclusion that there is very little inherent distinctiveness in the mark "ELVIS". However this initial view may be overcome in accordance with section 9(3)(b) as a result of use of the trade mark by the proprietor or other circumstances. Enterprises relies on both of these matters to bolster its application. I shall taken them separately. ... [Neither matter succeeded in changing Laddie J's view].

The "ELVIS PRESLEY" application
This is applied for under section 10 of the Act in Part B of the Register. Enterprises accepts that it is less distinctive than the word "Elvis" alone. However the hurdles to be crossed to achieve registration under section 10 are somewhat lower than those under section 9. The former provides:

"10.(1) In order for a trade mark to be registrable in Part B of the register it must be capable, in relation to the goods in respect of which it is registered or proposed to be registered, of distinguishing goods with which the proprietor of the trade mark is or may be connected in the course of trade from goods in the case of which no such connection subsists, either generally or, where the trade mark is registered or proposed to be registered subject to limitations, in relation to use within the extent of the registration.

(2) In determining whether a trade mark is capable of distinguishing as aforesaid the tribunal may have regard to the extent to which-
    (a)   the trade mark is inherently capable of distinguishing as aforesaid; and
    (b)   by reason of the use of the trade mark or of any other circumstances, the trade mark is in fact capable of distinguishing as aforesaid."

It will be seen that the requirement of "adapted to distinguish" in section 9 is replaced by "capable of distinguishing". The obscurity introduced into our law by this difference is set out with clarity in *Kerly's Law of Trade Marks and Trade Names* (12th Edition) at paragraphs 8-74 to 8-76. Little point would be served by repeating what is said there. The essence of Part B registrations was that they allowed onto the register new unused marks and little used marks which were near the borderline of registrability under section 9. However it was still necessary to show that the mark had the ability to distinguish in a trade mark sense. That is to say, to perform the function of distinguishing the proprietor's goods from similar goods from another trader. All the factors which have led me to the conclusion that "ELVIS" is incapable of distinguishing in that sense apply equally strongly to "ELVIS PRESLEY". Neither of those marks qualifies for registration under section 10 either.

The signature mark
This is applied for under section 9. The mark is as follows;

[The Elvis Presley signature mark is shown here]

Against this, Mr Shaw has raised a number of objections. He says that Enterprises has not discharged the onus on it to show that the mark is a signature of Elvis Presley, has not shown that it is distinctive and that there are sections 11 and 12 objections to it based on his own use and registration of his "Elvisly Yours" trade mark. In the alternative, he argues that registration of the mark should be subject to suitable wide disclaimers under section 14 of the Act.

Signatures are dealt with expressly under the 1938 Act. To understand this it is useful to have in mind some of the provisions of section 9(1);

"9.(1) In order for a trade mark (other than a certification trade mark) to be registrable in Part A of the register, it must contain or consist of at least one of the following essential particulars:

(a) the name of a company, individual, or firm, represented in a special or particular manner;

(b) the signature of the applicant for registration or some predecessor in his business;

(c) ...;

(d) a word or words having no direct reference to the character or quality of the goods, and not being according to its ordinary signification a geographical name or a surname;

(e) any other distinctive mark, but a name, signature, or word or words, other than such as fall within the descriptions in the foregoing paragraphs (a), (b), (c) and (d), shall not be registrable under the provisions of this paragraph except upon evidence of its distinctiveness."

The initial words "any other distinctive mark" in section 9(1)(e) have been taken to confirm that all marks which pass muster for entry in Part A of the register must be distinctive; *Fanfold Ltd's Application* (1928) 45 RPC 325. Section 9(1)(a), (b) and (d) also indicate that names, and particularly surnames, which are not rendered in a special or particular manner or in the form of a signature are, *prima facie*, not distinctive whereas those that are so rendered are, *prima facie*, distinctive.

Although the Registry and the court must start from the premise that signatures are *prima facie* distinctive, they are not inevitably so. A person may adopt any manuscript rendering of the whole or a part of his name as a signature. It is well known, and confirmed by consulting any sizeable telephone directory, that many people have surnames which are *prima facie* descriptive or non-distinctive if used for trade mark purposes. There are many adjectival surnames such as Good, Best, Perfect, Brilliant, Most, Round, Sharp and Blunt, numerous surnames such as Gold, Silver, Bacon, Shine, Sheen, Bottom, Tough to say nothing of those names derived from well known locations like London, Glasgow, York, Hampshire, England, Scotland, Ireland and French. Someone with one of these names may adopt a signature which consists of his surname spelt out in precise capitals or in a perfect script which is indistinguishable from, say, Times Roman font. Such writings, though signatures, would be indistinguishable from the printed form of the name and, it seems to me, would not be distinctive. What makes most signatures distinctive is that they consist of a substantially unique and frequently highly distorted way of writing the author's name. They are in a sense a private graphic tied to one person. If Elvis Presley had signed his name in block capitals that signature would not be any more registrable than the "ELVIS PRESLEY" mark dealt with above. To allow registration of such a mark, simply on the basis that it was how the author signed his name, would be to give the proprietor trade mark rights which could be enforced against other traders using block capitals or any other legible script. But that is just the sort of use which, according to *W & G* should not be the subject of monopoly rights. To allow such a signature to be registered would be to forget that the mark, whether falling within section 9(1)(b) or not, still has to be distinctive.

If the signature mark in issue here is registrable, its distinctiveness must be dependent on the particular graphic style used to write it. However, particularly having regard to the wide infringement provisions of the 1994 Act, an unqualified registration of the mark might well give rise to protection far beyond the graphic style used. In effect it could well give rise to protection for the words "Elvis", "Presley", "Elvis A Presley" or "Elvis Presley" but all of those, absent the special graphic style are, for reasons already given, not distinctive. It is for this reason that Mr Shaw says that any registration should be subject to a disclaimer under section 14 of the Act. That provides:

"14. If a trade mark-
(a) contains matter common to the trade or otherwise of a non-distinctive character;
(b) the Registrar or the Board of Trade or the Court, in deciding whether the trade mark shall be entered or shall remain on the register, may require, as a condition of its being on the register, -
  (i) that the proprietor shall disclaim any right to the exclusive use of any part of the trade mark, or to the exclusive use of all or any portion of any such matter as aforesaid, to the exclusive use of which the tribunal holds him not to be entitled; or
  (ii) that the proprietor shall make such other disclaimer as the tribunal may consider necessary for the purpose of defining his rights under the registration:
Provided that no disclaimer on the register shall affect any rights of the proprietor of a trade mark except such as arise out of the registration of the trade mark in respect of which the disclaimer is made."

It seems to me that, at the very least, the signature mark contains matter common to the trade or otherwise of a non-distinctive character, namely the individual words that go to make up Elvis Presley's name. As a result it seems to me that if this mark is to be registered it must be subject to a disclaimer. I did not understand Mr Prescott to dissent from that in principle. If registered, I would subject this mark to a disclaimer in the following terms;

"Nothing in this registration shall give rise to any exclusive rights in the words 'Elvis', 'A' and 'Presley' whether used separately or together save when used in substantially the script shown."

It would be easy to say that with such a disclaimer the signature mark would not be a significant impediment to others engaged in the trade of selling Elvis Presley memorabilia and should therefore be allowed on the register. For some time I thought that this was the course that I should adopt. However in the end the onus is still on Enterprises to demonstrate that the signature mark, even with the disclaimer, is adapted to distinguish its goods from the same or similar goods of other traders.

The signature mark is not a highly stylised writing of Elvis Presley's name. In fact its most notable features are the words of the name itself. There is nothing graphically or visually distinctive about the style in which the words are written. It is just a simple, if not very fluent, cursive rendition of the name. On the face of it, the signature does not appear to me to be adapted to distinguish. Nevertheless, in accordance with the provisions of section 9(3)(b), in determining whether the mark is adapted to distinguish the court is "entitled to have regard to the extent to which by reason of the use of the trade mark or of any other circumstances" the mark is in fact adapted to distinguish the proprietor's goods. As noted above, Mr Prescott argued that the words "other circumstances" is of the widest generality. I agree. It is open to the court to look at all factors which point towards and away from distinctiveness. As was the case with the other two marks, there is no evidence that Enterprises used the signature, whether as a trade mark or otherwise, on any Class 3 goods in the United Kingdom and there is no evidence that any member of the public here has learned to treat it as a mark distinguishing goods as coming from a particular source. It therefore seems to me that none of the trading history helps Enterprises. On the contrary, such evidence as does exist showing the way that Elvis Presley memorabilia is marketed world-wide points away from distinctiveness. The catalogues exhibited to Mr Soden's statutory declaration show that there have been many instances where the names "Elvis" and "Elvis Presley" have been used in more or less cursive fonts on products but in a way which gives no suggestion that they are signatures. I have in mind particularly the following to be found in Bundle C;

[List of Products]

This is reinforced by the way in which Mr Shaw has used his own mark and the name "Elvis Presley". His mark, which appears on many of his products, his headed notepaper and as the masthead of the fan magazine he produces, is;

[stylised "Elvisly Yours"]

and over the last eighteen years he has sold a variety of products bearing the name "Elvis Presley" depicted in the following way: -

[Picture of Elvis Presley here]

I have come to the conclusion that other traders are likely, in the ordinary course of their business and without any improper motive, to desire to use the name "Elvis" or "Elvis Presley" in a cursive script which is the same as or nearly resembles the script in the signature mark upon or in connection with their own goods. The mark is not adapted to distinguish in the sense used in the 1938 Act.

In addition to this, I have come to the conclusion that Mr Shaw's objections to the signature mark on the basis of sections 11 and 12 are also made out. Section 11 provides:

"It shall not be lawful to register as a trade mark or part of a trade mark any matter the use of which would, by reason of its being likely to deceive or cause confusion or otherwise, be disentitled to protection in a court of justice, or would be contrary to law or morality, or any scandalous design."

and section 12 provides;

"(1) Subject to the provisions of subsection (2) of this section, no trade mark shall be registered in respect of any goods or description of goods that is identical with or nearly resembles a mark belonging to a different proprietor and already on the register in respect of -
  (a) the same goods,
  (b) the same description of goods, or
  (c) services or a description of services which are associated with those goods or goods of that description."

Both parties agreed that the test to be applied in deciding whether the section 11 objection is made out is that prescribed by Parker J in *Pianotist Co's Application* (1906) 23 RPC 774 at page 777:

"You must take the two words. You must judge of them, both by their look and by their sound. You must consider the goods to which they are applied. You must consider the nature and kind of customer who would be likely to buy those goods. In fact, you must consider all the surrounding circumstances; and you must further consider what is likely to happen if each of those trade marks is used in a normal way as a trade mark for the goods of the respective owners of the marks. If, considering all those circumstances, you come to the conclusion that there will be a confusion - that is to say - not necessarily that one will be injured and the other will gain illicit benefit, but that there will be a confusion in the mind of the public which will lead to confusion in the goods then you may refuse registration, or rather you must refuse the registration in that case."

Mr Prescott also drew my attention to the test adopted by Evershed J in *Smith Hayden & Co's Application* (1946) 63 RPC 97. He dealt with both sections 11 and 12 at page 101.

"(a) (under sec. 11) 'Having regard to the reputation acquired by [the superior mark], is the Court satisfied that the [junior mark], if used in a normal and fair manner in connection with any goods covered by the registration proposed, will not be reasonably likely to cause deception and confusion amongst a substantial number of persons'. (b) (under sec. 12) "Assuming user by [the opponents] of their marks ... in a normal and fair manner for any of the goods covered by the registrations of those marks ... is the Court satisfied that there will be no reasonable likelihood of deception or confusion among a substantial number of persons if [the applicants] also use their [junior] mark normally and fairly in respect of any goods covered by their proposed registration?"

Those passages make it clear that unless the applicant, i.e. Enterprises, satisfies the court that there is no reasonable likelihood of deception or confusion among a substantial number of persons, registration must be refused. So far as possible the register is to be kept clean of marks which run the risk of causing confusion or deception. I have already mentioned that Mr Tuck in the registry came to the conclusion that Mr Shaw's mark both as registered and used was a strong mark involving a degree of invention. Mr Prescott did not challenge that assessment. If, contrary to my views, Enterprises' signature mark was adapted to distinguish in the trade mark sense, then the similarity between it and Mr Shaw's mark would be likely to give rise to deception and confusion.

In the light of these findings it is not necessary for me to consider Mr Shaw's additional point that there is no relevant evidence that the writing in the signature mark is in fact the signature of Elvis Presley.

I will allow the appeal in relation to all three applications.'

COMMENT

Are any of the marks applied for by 'Enterprises' registrable under the 1994 Act? A growing number of celebrities apply to register their names or aspects of their appearance or 'catchphrases' as trade marks. Is this possible under the 1994 Act? Is 'Princess Di' or a likeness of the late Diana, Princess of Wales registrable as a trade mark? What is the function of a trade mark?

Descriptive words, including words indicating geographic origin are usually not registrable. This was also the position under the 1938 Act as the following case shows.

Geographical Names

Both the old law and the Trade Marks Act of 1994 prohibit the registration of geographical names (section 3(1)(c) of the 1994 Act provides absolute grounds for refusal of registration for marks that consist exclusively of signs or indications which may serve in trade, to designate, *inter alia*, the geographic origin of goods or services). However, under the 1994 Act an indication of geographical origin could be registrable on proof that it has, in fact, acquired a distinctive character. There are some rare examples of marks that are geographical names and there is nothing to prevent registration of a mark containing such a name providing exclusive use of the name is disclaimed by the applicant. The following case concerned a trade mark that had, in fact, become entirely distinctive of the applicant's goods.

York Trade Mark [1982] FSR 111, House of Lords

In an application to register a stylised form of the word 'York' in Part A, it was objected that it was a geographical name, a surname and not distinctive. Evidence was submitted to show that the mark was in fact 100 per cent distinctive of the applicant's lorry trailers. The mark was registered in Part B with a disclaimer of the exclusive use of the word 'York'. The applicant's appeal against the disclaimer was allowed and the Registrar appealed to the House of Lords.

Lord Wilberforce at (115): '...The second distinction (between "inherently adapted [or capable]," and "adapted [or capable] in fact") though verbally new in the Acts of 1937-8, is, on the other hand, relevant and crucial. It was not new in the law. In relation to adaptability it is sufficient to quote from a recent opinion of Lord Diplock in this House. In *Smith Kline & French Laboratories Ltd.* v *Sterling Winthrop Group Ltd.* [1976] RPC 511, 538, he said:

> "Long before the reference to inherent adaptability had been incorporated in the current statutes dealing with trade marks, it had been held upon grounds of public policy that a trader ought not to be allowed to obtain by registration under the Trade Marks Act a monopoly in what other traders may legitimately desire to use. The classic statement of this doctrine is to be found in the speech of Lord Parker in the *W & G* case (1913) 30 RPC 660 at page 672 where he said that the right to registration 'should largely depend on whether other traders are likely, in

the ordinary course of their business and without any improper motive, to desire to use the same mark, or some mark nearly resembling it, upon or in connection with their own goods'."

and there can be no doubt that exactly similar reasoning must be applied to the words "inherently capable of distinguishing" in section 10(2)(a) of the Act. They mean, in effect "capable in law of distinguishing," the relevant law being the accepted principle that, in relation to certain words, of which laudatory epithets and some geographical names were established examples, traders could not obtain a monopoly in the use of such words (however distinctive) to the detriment of members of the public who, in the future, and in connection with other goods, might desire to use them. That this principle has been firmly laid down in relation, in particular, to geographical words, by a strong current of authority, I shall now demonstrate.

I refer first to an authoritative pronouncement, to the judgment of Fletcher Moulton LJ in a case concerned with both a laudatory word ("Perfection") and a geographical word ("California Syrup of Figs") [1909] RPC 837, 854. In an extended passage, the whole of which repays study, and which has been accepted as a classic statement of the law, he described the policy of the Act as substituting for an absolute exclusion, from use as trade marks, of geographical names, a judicial examination on the merits of each individual case. This was followed in *W & G du Cros Ltd.* (1913) 30 RPC 660, concerned with the use of initials in which Lord Parker said that the right to registration should

"largely depend upon whether other traders are likely, in the ordinary course of their business and without any improper motive, to desire to use the same mark, or some mark nearly resembling it, upon or in connection with their own goods."

These cases were prior to the introduction in 1919 of the Part B section of the register. However, it was not long before a case concerned with both Part A and Part B came before the courts. This was *Liverpool Electric Cable Co. Ltd.'s Application* (1929) 46 RPC 99, where what was sought was to register "Liverpool Cables" for electric cables, this mark being accepted as distinctive of the applicants' goods. The position as regards both Part A and Part B was considered. At first instance, Romer J allowed the application holding that proof of distinctiveness established that the words were "capable of distinguishing" - essentially the respondents' argument here. But this decision was reversed by the Court of Appeal. All three members of the court dealt explicitly and at length with the position regarding Part B of the Register. As regards "capability," Lord Hanworth used these words:

"... when you come to regard the rights of the public at large, the traders at Liverpool and the like, it appears to me that the Registrar would be quite right in holding that a word of that importance and significance ought not to be used or allowed to be treated as a word capable of distinguishing, because it has not merely to be capable in fact, but it must be capable in law." *(loc. cit.* p.118)

Similar passages are to be found in the judgments of Lawrence and Russell LJJ This decision, if accepted, must conclude this appeal against the respondents and one would think would have so concluded it at first instance. What has been its subsequent history?

In 1938 it was referred to, without any sign of disapprobation, in this House, in *A Bailey & Co. Ltd.* v *Clark, Son & Morland Ltd.* (1938) 55 RPC 253, concerned with the geographical mark "Glastonburys." Lord Russell of Killowen said this:

> "It appears to me to be, from one aspect, a stronger case for refusing registration than the case of Liverpool Cables. That decision laid down no new law. It was based upon the view, well established by previous authority, that distinctiveness in fact is not conclusive upon the questions whether a Mark is 'distinctive' as defined in section 9, and whether it ought to be registered." (*loc. cit.* p.262).

This case was concerned with Part A but the reasoning is equally applicable to Part B: distinctiveness in fact is not conclusive.

In 1954 (*i.e.* after the passing of the Act of 1938) the correctness of the *Liverpool* case came directly in issue in *Yorkshire Copper Works Ltd.'s Application*, 71 RPC 150, where again, 100 per cent. distinctiveness in fact was shown. Registration was refused in both Part A and Part B. The *Liverpool* case was expressly approved by this House. It is sought to escape from the authority of this case on the basis that, as reported, counsel for the applicants conceded that registration under Part B could not be granted if the application under Part A were to fail. But this is desperate advocacy. Quite apart from the question whether the learned counsel concerned, whose determination is well-known, would have conceded the point unless he had thought it unarguable, it cannot be supposed that the members of this House, with the two adjacent sections (9 and 10) before them, would have let it pass, and given unqualified approval to the *Liverpool* case, unless they had been of the clear opinion that the argument applied to both parts of the Register. And the reasoning of Lord Simonds shows that he must have thought so. I quote two passages:

> "Just as a manufacturer is not entitled to a monopoly of a laudatory or descriptive epithet, so he is not to claim for his own a territory, whether country, county or town, which may be in the future, if it is not now, the seat of manufacture of goods similar to his own.

> There will probably be border-line cases, but there is, in my opinion, no doubt on which side of the border lies Yorkshire, a county not only of broad acres but of great manufacturing cities. If the *Liverpool Cables* case was rightly decided, as I think it clearly was, *a fortiori* the Registrar was right in refusing registration to 'Yorkshire.' And if it were a border-line case, which it is not, I think that a court, to which an appeal is brought from the Registrar, though, no doubt, it must exercise its own discretion in the matter, should be slow to differ from the experienced official whose constant duty it is to protect the interests of the public not only of today but of tomorrow and the day after." (loc. cit. p. 154).'

COMMENT

The leapfrog procedure under section 12(1) of the Administration of Justice Act 1969 was used. The parent company of the applicant was based in York, Ontario. What is the difference between 'capable in fact of distinguishing' and 'capable in law of distinguishing'? Although a Part B mark could be attacked even after seven years, under the 1938 Act there was no specific provision for removal of a mark that, through a change in circumstances, no longer qualifies for registration. The mark could not, therefore, be expunged from the register as a result of this action.

Section 11(2) of the 1994 Act provides a defence in the case of use of a mark to indicate geographical origin. Thus, a different trailer manufacturer who happened to be based in York, England could describe his trailers as made in York. Why then, is there a prohibition against registering geographical names as trade marks, in the absence of proof of distinctiveness?

Invented Words

It is often said that the best trade mark of all is an invented word, a word that is meaningless when freshly coined. The 1938 Act mentioned invented words as one of the categories of Part A marks; an invented word is, after all, *prima facie*, distinctive where first coined. The Trade Marks Act 1994 makes no specific reference to invented words but plainly such marks would be most likely to comply with the requirement of being capable of distinguishing. However, some invented words may connote some object or characteristic and then the registrability is less clear cut as the case below shows.

The Eastman Photographic Materials Co. Ltd. v *The Comptroller-General of Patents, Designs, and Trade Marks* [1898] AC 571, House of Lords

The appellants applied to register the word 'Solio' as a trade mark for photographic paper. It was turned down because it suggested 'Sol', the sun, and therefore had reference to the character or quality of goods and the Court of Appeal affirmed the decision. The appeal to the House of Lords was successful.

Earl of Halsbury LC (at 576): 'My Lords, I think ["Solio"] is an invented word within the meaning of this statute. I know of no such word as "Solio" in any sense which would make it intelligible here, although it is an Italian word meaning a throne, and although it is a Latin word in the ablative case with the same meaning.

Not much reliance, however, is placed upon the word having some meaning in a foreign tongue; but what is put is that it may have extracted from it some meaning in relation to the character or quality of the goods, because the letters, S, O, L may be understood to mean the sun, and that Shakespeare in *Troilus and Cressida* speaks of our planet "Sol" (Act 1, Sc. 3), and that inasmuch as the goods in question are photographic papers and sunlight is operative in producing impressions on photographic paper, Solio comes within the prohibition against using words which are distinctive of the character and quality of the goods in respect of which the word is sought to be registered.

My Lords, my answer is that "Solio" is not "Sol," and "Sol" is not "Solio." It certainly is a very strange thing that you should take three letters out of a word, and, by the somewhat circuitous process that has been adopted here, arrive at the conclusion that it is not an invented word and that it does describe the character and quality of the goods.

My Lords, I desire to give my opinion with reference to the particular word, and not to go behind it. I can quite understand suggesting other words - compound words, or foreign words, as to which it would be impossible to say that they were invented words, although perhaps never seen before, or that they did not indicate the character or quality of the goods, although as words of the English tongue they had never been seen before. Suppose a person were to attempt to register as a single English word "Cheapandgood," or even without taking so gross an example, using a word so slightly differing from an ordinary and recognised word as to be neither an invented word nor, avoiding the prohibited choice of a word, indicating character or quality. The line must be sometimes difficult to draw; but to my mind the substance of the enactment is intelligible enough, and the comptroller has to make up his mind whether in substance there has been an infringement of the rule. Of course also words which are merely misspelt, but which are nevertheless, in sound, ordinary English words, and the use of which may tend to deceive, ought not to be permitted.

I am satisfied in this case to say that the word "Solio" is an invented word; that it does not indicate the character or quality of the goods, and that the decision of the Court of Appeal ought to be reversed.'

COMMENT

'Solio', in Italian, means throne and 'Solium' in Latin has the same meaning. The Earl of Halsbury LC remarked that neither of those words had any reference to either photographic paper or the sun. Should the fact that an invented word, or a word closely resembling it, has a meaning in a foreign language colour the decision as to registration of the mark? Would the word mark 'soixante-dix-sept' (French for 77) be registrable in the United Kingdom?

Containers and Packaging

The Trade Marks Act 1994 allows the registration of a far wider variety of marks than was previously the case. The standard now is that the mark must be a sign capable of being represented graphically which is capable of distinguishing goods or services of one undertaking from those of other undertakings. Specifically mentioned are words, designs, letters, numerals or the shape of goods or their packaging. It would appear that sound marks and even smell marks are registrable, theoretically. In the past, registration was refused to the Coca-Cola bottle on the basis, *inter alia*, that that would lead to an undesirable monopoly in containers. Extracts from the Coca-Cola bottle case follow.

Re Coca-Cola Co's Applications [1986] 2 All ER 274, House of Lords

The Coca-Cola Co. applied to register its well-known and distinctively shaped bottle as a trade mark. The bottle had previously been registered as a design but that registration had expired some time ago. Note that the application was in respect of the bottle itself rather than a drawing or other representation of the bottle.

Lord Templeman (at 275): 'The shape of the Coca-Cola bottle was accepted as a design and was registered under the 1907 Act. The effect of this registration expired in 1940 since when any rival manufacturer has been free to use the design of the Coca-Cola bottle.

The Coca-Cola Co. now claims that during and since the period of protection for the Coca-Cola bottle under the 1907 Act the Coca-Cola Co. has been entitled to a monopoly in the Coca-Cola bottle as a trade mark. The application of the Coca-Cola Co. to register the Coca-Cola bottle as a trade mark has been rejected by the hearing officer, by Falconer J, and by the Court of Appeal (Lawton, Browne-Wilkinson LJJ and Sir Denis Buckley) [1985] FSR 315). The Coca-Cola Co., undeterred by this formidable display of judicial unanimity, now appeals with the leave of the House.

The 1938 Act confers on the proprietor of a registered trade mark the exclusive right in perpetuity, subject to payment of fees and the observance of certain conditions not here relevant, to the use of a trade mark which is distinctive ...

... It is not sufficient for the Coca-Cola bottle to be distinctive. The Coca-Cola Co. must succeed in the startling proposition that the bottle is a trade mark. If so, then any other container or any article of a distinctive shape is capable of being a trade mark. This raised the spectre of a total and perpetual monopoly in containers and articles achieved by means of the 1938 Act. Once the container or article has become associated with the manufacturer and distinctiveness has been established, with or without the help of the monopolies created by the Patents Act, the Registered Designs Act or the Copyright Act, the perpetual trade mark monopoly in the container or article can be achieved. In my opinion the 1938 Act was not intended to confer on the manufacturer of a container or on the manufacturer of an article a statutory monopoly on the ground that the manufacturer has in the eyes of the public established a connection between the shape of the container or article and the manufacturer. A rival manufacturer must be free to sell any container or article of similar shape provided the container or article is labelled or packaged in a manner which avoids confusion as to the origin of the goods in the container or the origin of the article. The Registrar of Trade Marks has always taken the view that the function of trade mark legislation is to protect the mark but not the article which is marked. I agree. By s.68(1) of the Act of 1938:

> "'mark' includes a device, brand, heading, label, ticket, name, signature, word, letter, numeral, or any combination thereof ... 'trade mark' means ... a mark used or proposed to be used in relation to goods for the purpose of indicating, or so as to indicate, a connection in the course of trade between the goods and some person having the right either as proprietor or as registered user to use the mark, whether with or without any indication of the identity of that person ..."

The word "mark" both in its normal meaning and in its statutory definition is apt only to describe something which distinguishes goods rather than the goods themselves.

A bottle is a container not a mark. The distinction between a mark and the thing which is marked is supported by authority. In *Re James's Trade Mark, James v Soulby* (1886) 33 Ch D 392, the plaintiffs sold black lead in the form of a dome and in other shapes. Their products were impressed with the representation of a dome and their labels carried a picture of a black dome. The plaintiffs were allowed to register the representation or picture of a black dome as their trade mark. Similarly, the Coca-Cola Co. has been allowed to register a line drawing of a Coca-Cola bottle as a trade mark. But, dealing with the article itself, in *Re James's Trade Mark* Lindley LJ said (at 395):

"A mark must be something distinct from the thing being marked. The thing itself cannot be a mark of itself, but here we have got the thing and we have got a mark on the thing, and the question is, whether that mark on the thing is or is not a distinctive mark within the meaning of the Act. Of course, the plaintiffs in this case have no monopoly in black lead of this shape. Anybody may make black lead of this shape provided he does not mark it as the plaintiffs mark theirs, and provided he does not pass it off as the plaintiffs' black lead. There is no monopoly in the shape, and I cannot help thinking that that has not been sufficiently kept in mind. What the plaintiffs have registered is a brand, a mark like a dome intended to represent a dome."

In the course of argument counsel for the Coca-Cola Co. relied on the decision of this House in *Smith Kline and French Laboratories Ltd.* v *Sterling-Winthrop Group Ltd.* [1975] 2 All ER 578, [1975] 1 WLR 914. In that case the plaintiffs were allowed to register 10 distinctive colour combinations as trade marks for drugs sold in pellet form within capsules. One typical example was ([1975] 2 All ER 578 at 581, [1975] 1 WLR 914 at 916):

"The trade mark consists of a maroon colour applied to one half of the capsule at one end, and the other half being colourless and transparent, and yellow, blue and white colours being each applied to a substantial number of pellets so that each pellet is of one colour only."

Lord Diplock rejected the argument that a mark could not cover the whole of the visible surface of the goods to which it was applied (see [1975] 2 All ER 578 at 584, [1975] 1 WLR 914 at 920). The *Smith Kline* case only related to the colour of goods and has no application to the goods themselves or to a container for goods. A colour combination may tend to an undesirable monopoly in colours but does not create an undesirable monopoly in goods or containers. I do not consider that the *Smith Kline* case is of assistance to the Coca-Cola Co. I would accordingly dismiss this appeal.'

COMMENT

Was Lord Templeman right to conclude that, after the design registration expired, 'any rival manufacturer has been free to use the design of the Coca-Cola bottle'? Is the Coca-Cola bottle registrable under the 1994 Act? Why were three-dimensional marks seldom registered before the 1994 Act came into force? Are colours registrable?

Disclaimers

Sometimes registration will be accepted subject to a disclaimer. For example, if the mark contains a descriptive or laudatory word registration may still be allowed providing the applicant disclaims any exclusive rights in the word. However, the non-distinctive material must not overwhelm the remainder of the mark such as where the most prominent element is, indeed, the non-distinctive word, as in the case below.

Merit Trade Marks [1989] RPC 687, Chancery Division

This was an application to register two marks for cigarettes comprising coloured stripes with a coat of arms and the word 'MERIT' which was the most prominent feature. The registrar refused the application and the applicant appealed to the Chancery Division.

Whitford J (at 692): "I was referred to a number of authorities, starting with *Ford-Werke AG's Application* [1955] 72 RPC 191. Here the mark sought to be registered was a mark consisting of two letters enclosed in a border. Lloyd-Jacob J pointed out that effectively, although it was a case in which the applicants were prepared to disclaim the use of the letters as such, if that was taken away there was really nothing left which could be said to have any distinctiveness at all.

That case was contrasted by Mr Morcom with *Mackenzie's Application* [1967] RPC 628, where on appeal - and it was an appeal which went to the Board of Trade, not to the court, and was heard by Mr Geoffrey Tookey, QC - overriding the Office, Mr Tookey allowed to go to registration a label mark which, apart from matter on the bottom half of the label, which was plainly of a wholly non-distinctive character, consisted of the word "Mackenzie" coupled with a sort of border or band of tartan with, in the centre, what is described as a seal with two deer portrayed within it. It cannot be seen very clearly in the reproduction on page 629 of the report, but effectively what was decided by Mr Tookey in that case - and it was, of course, a case in which Mr Tookey's attention was drawn to a number of relevant authorities including the *Ford-Werke* case - was that the label as a whole was *prima facie* distinctive; it was not a label which could be said to consist only of the word "Mackenzie", unlike the *Ford-Werke* case where the letters "MK" were really the only feature which stood out at all and what one had got was this word "Mackenzie" but coupled with it the distinctive tartan band and this device of a seal with deer in it, and Mr Tookey was of the view that the fact that the label might well be regarded as a "Mackenzie" label was not in itself sufficient to justify refusal.

A case which is perhaps even more strongly in Mr Morcom's favour and to which he understandably referred me is the case of another application for registration of a trade mark by the present applicants, *Philip Morris' Application* [1980] RPC 527, where one can see, albeit in black and white, the application on page 528. Again, it is effectively either a label or a panel which is going to be the front panel of a packet of cigarettes. There is the word "Mild", perhaps even more descriptive and objectionable in the context of cigarettes as being matter that could not conceivably have any distinctive character than "Merit", with, underneath the words "Philip

Morris", the words "Filter cigarettes" at the bottom of the pack, and once again, so far as I can see, the coat of arms, with possibly the letters "PM" on a shield. But the trade mark was limited to the colours gold, white and blue, though exactly how they appeared on the label in question I do not know, because one cannot see. They must have been fairly striking, I should imagine, for this application ever to have been accepted for otherwise, having regard to the *Ford-Werke* decision, it does not seem to me that even the eloquence of Mr Morcom would have been sufficient to secure registration of a label of this character. So I am left in some doubt as to exactly what the nature of this mark was - whether the colouring of gold, white and blue in whatever form it appeared was of so distinctive a character that it in itself would be considered to be such as must necessarily make the label recognisable as a trade mark. I suppose that the public in question would have asked for cigarettes thus branded as "Philip Morris Mild", and nobody would suppose that they would have been asking for "The gold, white and blue label cigarettes".

Mr Laddie, who has appeared on behalf of the Registrar felt some doubt as to the correctness of the decision that was given on this case, but then he was, as far as I am aware, in exactly the same position as I am, that is, he did not have the advantage of knowing exactly what this label looked like in its coloured form. In this case, Mr Harkness acting for the Registrar has considered the decision in the *Ford-Werke* case and the *Mackenzie case*. It does not appear that this other *Philip Morris* case was cited to him. He accepts, as I think one must, that the stripes possess an element of distinctiveness and there is no doubt that it was this element of distinctiveness and the stripes as such that secured the registration for the device alone.

Mr Harkness [of the Trade Marks Registry] takes the view that the word "Merit" is the most prominent element in this mark and I agree with that. Mr Laddie suggested that one has to consider the ways in which a mark of this kind is going to be used in practice and he drew my attention to the actual packs which have subsequently come on sale where, in addition to a front panel carrying the emblem and the words "Merit" and "Menthol", one has the word "Merit" at both ends on both sides, either alone or on no more than a sort of coloured bar, and this is effectively going to be a "Merit" mark. The whole of the emphasis is on "Merit" and Mr Laddie asked me to consider what was the object of an application for registration of this kind in view of the existing registration of the device.

Mr Harkness refers to the decision of Mr Tookey in the *Mackenzie* case. I do not go through the decision of Mr Tookey in full detail, but the effect, I think, of what Mr Tookey was saying was that where one has a mark which consists of a combination of features and a mark in which one finds a certain amount of non-distinctive matter, even though that forms quite a prominent feature of the mark in question, nonetheless, the mark may be allowed to proceed to registration if there is sufficient distinctiveness in the mark as a whole, and no doubt this is the basis upon which Mr Douglas Myall, who was acting for the Registrar in the other *Philip Morris* case, the *Philip Morris* "Mild", proceeded, although he added, as I understand it, the rider that an adverse conclusion might be reached if the view was formed that by making applications of this character what in truth was being sought to be protected was not the distinctive feature of the label as such but non-distinctive matter.

Of course, it is always alleged before any tribunal hearing a case of this kind involving a disclaimer that the interests of third parties are adequately protected by reason of the disclaimer. Mr Harkness considered this point and he was, I think, very much concerned with the fact that, as he put it, "Merit" is *a priori* unregistrable and with the point that, if it was to form a prominent feature of a mark admitted for registration, albeit with a disclaimer, that might adversely affect the rights of other traders in this field to use a word which they ought to be perfectly entitled to use. Mr Laddie in arguing the case dwelt upon this aspect of the matter and dwelt in particular upon the question of the possible effect of a disclaimer in connection with infringement proceedings. He invited me to consider a situation of another trader who wanted to use a device consisting of, let us say, diagonal stripes and he suggested the case where that trader was going to use not three diagonal stripes with what he described as ears, such as we see in the existing Philip Morris registration, but two diagonal stripes in colours other than such colours as might be particularly associated with Philip Morris. At any rate, what he suggested was that two diagonal stripes without ears could not conceivably be an infringement of Philip Morris rights under their registration number 1061882. He asked me to consider the use of two diagonal stripes without ears in association with the word "Merit" and suggested that such a use by some competing trader irrespective of the fact that there is a disclaimer to the exclusive use of the word "Merit" might nonetheless be held to be an infringement of either of the marks the subjects of the present applications if they were permitted to proceed to registration. I think, depending possibly on the exact form and content of such a mark, that one might well get a situation where, although there would be no infringement of the device mark *per se*, there might be an infringement of the device mark plus the word "Merit", irrespective of the fact that there was a disclaimer of the word "Merit".

At the end of the day, I think that cases of this kind have got to be considered, as were the *Ford-Werke* case and the *Mackenzie* case, upon a view of the mark and a balancing of the respective importance of those parts which properly can be considered as being distinctive and those parts which are plainly not distinctive but are descriptive or might otherwise be matter which ought properly to be open for use by other persons.

In my view Mr Harkness has properly considered all the matters relevant to be considered upon an application of this kind. I think that in a sense the *Mackenzie* case, where the disclaimed matter was a surname rather than a laudatory word, can be distinguished upon that basis. I think upon the application for what I have described as the "Mild" mark, these present applicants may have been fortunate, although my view in that respect might be tempered by a view of the actual mark in colour. But I am of the opinion that the conclusion which has been reached by Mr Harkness on both the present applications is correct and in the result the appeal fails.'

COMMENT

If registration is allowed subject to a disclaimer, what is the effect of the disclaimer on any infringement actions? In a previous application Philip Morris & Co. Ltd. had registered the word mark 'NERIT'. This was ordered to be expunged from the register in *Imperial Group Ltd.* v *Philip Morris & Co. Ltd.* [1982] FSR 72 where it was held that the application was not *bona fide*. Of course, the word 'MERIT' alone is inherently incapable of registrability. Why?

Infringement of a Registered Trade Mark

Infringement of a trade mark occurs, *inter alia,* when a person uses an identical or similar mark for identical or similar goods or services. However, unless both the mark and goods (or services) are identical, the plaintiff must prove that because of the use of the identical or similar mark by the defendant there exists a likelihood of confusion on the part of the public; section 10(2) of the Trade Marks Act 1994. The likelihood of deception or confusion was also relevant in infringement proceedings under the 1938 Act and cases decided under that Act should still be relevant in determining whether a likelihood of confusion exists. The following case looks at two similar marks.

The Coca-Cola Co. of Canada Ltd. v Pepsi-Cola Co. of Canada Ltd. (1942) 59 RPC 127, Privy Council

The plaintiff owned the registered trade mark 'Coca-Cola' written in stylised form and claimed that the defendant had, by its use of 'Pepsi-Cola' for similar drinks, infringed the plaintiff's mark. The case came to the Judicial Committee of the Privy Council for final determination.

Lord Russell (at 132): 'The actual question for decision in the present case may, therefore, in the light of the above definition be stated thus: Does the mark used by the Defendant so resemble the Plaintiff's registered mark, or so clearly suggest the idea conveyed by it, that its use is likely to cause dealers in or users of non-alcoholic beverages to infer that the Plaintiff assumed responsibility for the character or quality or place of origin of "Pepsi-Cola"? ...

In these circumstances the question for determination must be answered by the Court, unaided by outside evidence, after a comparison of the Defendant's mark as used with the Plaintiff's registered mark, not placing them side by side, but by asking itself whether, having due regard to relevant surrounding circumstances, the Defendant's mark as used is similar (as defined by the Act) to the Plaintiff's registered mark as it would be remembered by persons possessed of an average memory with its usual imperfections.

In the present case two circumstances exist which are of importance in this connection. The first is the information which is afforded by dictionaries in relation to the word "Cola". While questions may sometimes arise as to the extent to which a Court may inform itself by reference to dictionaries, there can, their Lordships think, be no doubt that dictionaries may properly be referred to in order to ascertain not only the meaning of a word, but also the use to which the thing (if it be a thing) denoted by the word is commonly put. A reference to dictionaries shows that "Cola" or "Kola" is a tree whose seed or nut is "largely used for chewing as a condiment and digestive" *(Murray)*, a nut of which "the extract is used as a tonic drink" *(Webster)*, and which is "imported into the United States for use in medical preparations and summer drinks" *(Encyclopædia Americana)*. "Cola" would, therefore, appear to be a word which might appropriately be used in association with beverages and in particular with that class of non-alcoholic beverages colloquially known by the description "soft drinks". That in fact the word "Cola" or "Kola" has been so used in Canada is established by the second of the two circumstances before referred to.

The Defendant put in evidence a series of twenty-two trade marks registered in Canada from time to time during a period of twenty-nine years, namely, from 1902 to 1930, in connection with beverages. They include the mark of the Plaintiff and the registered mark of the Defendant. The other twenty marks consist of two or more words or a compound word, but also containing the word "Cola" or "Kola". The following are a few samples of the bulk: "Kola Tonic Wine", "La-Kola", "Cola-Claret", "Rose-Cola", "Orange-Kola", "O'Keefe's Cola", "Royal Cola". Their Lordships agree with the Supreme Court in attributing weight to these registrations as showing that the word "Cola" (appropriate for the purpose as appears above) had been adopted in Canada as an item in the naming of different beverages.

The proper comparison must be made with that fact in mind.

Numerous cases were cited in the Courts of Canada and before the Board in which the question of infringement of various marks has been considered and decided; but, except when some general principle is laid down, little assistance is derived from authorities in which the question of infringement is discussed in relation to other marks and other circumstances.

The Plaintiff claimed that by virtue of section 23(5)(b) of the Unfair Competition Act, 1932, its registered mark was both a word mark and a design mark; and their Lordships treat it accordingly.

If it be viewed simply as a word mark consisting of "Coca" and "Cola" joined by a hyphen, and the fact be borne in mind that Cola is a word in common use in Canada in naming beverages, it is plain that the distinctive feature in this hyphenated word is the first word "Coca" and not "Cola". "Coca" rather than "Cola" is what would remain in the average memory. It is difficult, indeed impossible, to image that the mark "Pepsi-Cola" as used by the Defendant, in which the distinctive feature is, for the same reason, the first word "Pepsi" and not "Cola", would lead anyone to confuse it with the registered mark of the Plaintiff.

If it is viewed as a design mark, the same result follows. The only resemblance lies in the fact that both contain the word "Cola" and neither is written in block letters, but in script with flourishes; but the letters and flourishes in fact differ very considerably, notwithstanding the tendency of words written in script with flourishes to bear a general resemblance to each other. There is no need to specify the differences in detail; it is sufficient to say that, in their Lordships' opinion, the mark used by the Defendant, viewed as a pattern or picture, would not lead a person with an average recollection of the Plaintiff's registered mark to confuse it with the pattern or picture represented by that mark.

In the result their Lordships are of opinion that the trade mark used by the Defendant and the registered mark of the Plaintiff are not trade marks so nearly resembling each other, or so clearly suggesting the idea conveyed by each other, that the contemporaneous use of both in the same area in association with wares of the same kind would be likely to cause dealers in or users of such wares to infer that the same person assumed responsibility for their character or quality, or for the conditions under which or the class of persons by whom they were produced or for their place of origin.'

COMMENT

The plaintiff presented no evidence of confusion on the part of the public. Is a likelihood of confusion a question of law or a question of fact? Should 'Coca-Cola' only be registered subject to a disclaimer?

In the following case, the sound of the word marks as spoken was relevant to infringement.

Fisons Plc v Norton Healthcare Ltd. [1994] FSR 745, Chancery Division

The plaintiff had a number of trade mark registrations for words ending in '-CROM' including 'VICROM'. It was used for eye-drops. The defendant sold a similar product under the name 'EYE-CROM'. The plaintiff sought an interlocutory injunction restraining the defendant's use of 'EYE-CROM'. The defendant claimed that the plaintiff's mark would be pronounced 'VIC-ROM' and thus, would not be confusingly similar.

Aldous J (at 751): 'When considering infringement of a registered trade mark, it is important to bear in mind the difference between the test for infringement and that in a passing off action. In a passing off action, the court looks to see whether there is a misrepresentation; whereas the Trade Marks Act gives to the proprietor an exclusive right to the use of the mark which will be infringed in the case of identical marks and can be in the case of similar marks even though no misrepresentation actually takes place.

As Sir Wilfred Greene, MR pointed out in *Saville Perfumery Ltd.* v *June Perfect Ltd. and F W Woolworth & Co. Ltd.* (1941) 58 RPC 147 at 161, line 24:

"The statute law relating to infringement of trade marks is based on the same fundamental idea as the law relating to passing off, but it differs from the law in two particulars, namely: (1), it is concerned only with one method of passing off, namely, the use of a trade mark, and (2), the statutory protection is absolute in the sense that once a mark is shown to offend, the user of it cannot escape by showing that by something outside the actual mark itself he has distinguished his goods from those of the registered proprietor. Accordingly, in considering the question of infringement the courts have held, and it is now expressly provided by the Trade Marks Act 1938, s.4, that infringement takes place not merely by exact imitation but by the use of a mark so nearly resembling the registered mark as to be likely to deceive. Two questions therefore arise: first, is there a resemblance, and second, is the resemblance so close as to be likely to cause deception?"

In this case it is not disputed that there is a resemblance between VICROM and EYE-CROM, particularly when spoken. Thus I must go on and consider whether there is a serious issue as to whether the resemblance is such as to be likely to lead to deception or confusion.

The test is the same under section 12 as under section 4. Therefore the words of Luxmoore LJ cited with approval by Viscount Maugham in *Aristoc Ltd.* v *Rysta Ltd.* (1945) 62 RPC 65 at 72, line 46, are applicable:

"The answer to the question whether the sound of one word resembles too nearly the sound of another so as to bring the former within the limits of section 12 of the Trade Marks Act 1938, must nearly always depend on first impression, for obviously a person who is familiar with both words will neither be deceived nor confused. It is the person who only knows the one word and has perhaps an imperfect recollection of it who is likely to be deceived or confused. Little assistance, therefore, is to be obtained from a meticulous comparison of the two words, letter by letter and syllable by syllable, pronounced with the clarity to be expected from a teacher of elocution. The court must be careful to make allowance for imperfect recollection and the effect of careless pronunciation and speech on the part not only of the person seeking to buy under the trade description, but also of the shop assistant ministering to that person's wants. [And then he adds a little later] The tendency to slur a word beginning with "a" is, generally speaking, very common, and the similarity between "Rysta" and "Ristoc" would, I think, be fairly obvious."

It is the judicial ear that is decisive, but the conclusion has to be based upon all the surrounding circumstances.

The defendant submitted that VICROM would be pronounced "vic-rom". There is no evidence to support that suggestion and I conclude that the submission cannot succeed. At the very least most people would pronounce it "vi-crom".

The defendant's EYE-CROM eye drops are only available on prescription. However, the evidence shows that the public ask for repeat prescriptions by name both over the telephone and when in the surgery. Such conversations take place between the public and receptionists, and the public and doctors. That being so, the two marks are confusingly similar. EYE-CROM is as close in sound to VICROM as you can get without having identical marks. Adopting the test in the *Aristoc* case, a person who only knows of VICROM and has an imperfect recollection will inevitably be deceived and confused if asked for EYE-CROM and vice versa. Similarly, patients who have an imperfect recollection of what they had before would believe that they were getting the same product, if the doctor told them that he was prescribing EYE-CROM or VICROM. I believe the contrary to be unsustainable.'

COMMENT

The defendant also argued, unsuccessfully, that the plaintiff's mark should be expunged because of non-use in the United Kingdom. However, that argument failed because the mark was used in relation to goods for export which was covered by section 31 of the 1938 Act.

How would most people, in your opinion, pronounce 'VICROM'? How does one determine the effects of imperfect recollection and careless pronunciation?

Wagamama Ltd. v *City Centre Restaurants plc* [1995] FSR 713, Chancery Division

The plaintiff had a Japanese restaurant in London called WAGAMAMA. This was a Japanese word and a registered trade mark. The defendant opened an Indian restaurant called RAJAMAMA. After commencement of proceedings brought by the plaintiff alleging trade mark infringement and passing off, the defendant changed the name of its restaurant to RAJA MAMA'S. This change failed to satisfy the plaintiff and the case came to trial.

Laddie J (at 721): 'Infringement under the 1994 Act.
There is no dispute between the parties that such classic infringement by confusion as to the source or origin of goods or services will also constitute an infringement under section 10 of the 1994 Act. The plaintiff alleges that there is such classic infringement in this case. That is a matter to which I will return later. However the plaintiff goes further. It says that section 10 of the 1994 Act, particularly section 10(2), covers confusion in a much broader sense. It is said that the registered proprietor can prevent mere association between the marks. It is argued that there will now be infringement if, on seeing the defendant's mark, the registered mark would be "called to mind" by a customer even if there is no possibility of the customer being under any misapprehension as to the origin of the goods. This is a new concept to those steeped in British trade mark law.

To illustrate his point, Mr Fysh referred to a number of witness statements. In these various members of the public said inter alia that on hearing the name RAJAMAMA their first thoughts were of WAGAMAMA because the names sound similar. Mr Fysh said that even if their evidence had stopped there that sort of association without any more indicates trade mark infringement. He said that this was so even if the customer would have no doubt when considering just the trade marks that they are similar but unconnected. This type of association in which there is no confusion as to origin but the infringing mark "brings to mind" the registered one, I shall refer to in this judgment as "non-origin association".

The arguments advanced in favour of this wide scope to infringement are based upon the existence of the words "a likelihood of confusion on the part of the public, which includes the likelihood of association with the trade mark" which are to be found at the end of section 10(2). Mr Fysh accepted that the reference to likelihood of confusion covered classic infringement as discussed above but he argued that there were only two possible constructions which could be put upon the final words "which includes the likelihood of association with the trade mark". Either these words added nothing to the requirement of confusion and merely performed the function of clarifying that association in the classic sense was included within the scope of infringement or it is a deeming provision which has the effect of extending trade mark protection so as to cover non-origin association. He says the latter is the proper construction and in support of this he deployed a number of arguments. First he says that by applying purely domestic principles of interpretation of statutes, his construction is correct. Secondly he advances a group of arguments based upon the European origins of the 1994 Act in support of the proposition that our trade mark law must be construed to be consistent with Benelux trade mark law where non-origin association has for some years been accepted as a form of trade mark infringement. I shall consider separately each of these routes.

The domestic interpretation route
In Hill v William Hill (Park Lane) Ltd [1949] AC 530 at 546 Viscount Simon said:

"... it is to be observed that though a Parliamentary enactment (like parliamentary eloquence) is capable of saying the same thing twice over without adding anything to what has already been said once, this repetition in the case of an Act of Parliament is not to be assumed. When the legislature enacts a particular phrase in a statute the presumption is that it is saying something which has not been said immediately before. The rule that a meaning should, if possible, be given to every word in the statute implies that, unless there is good reason to the contrary, the words add something which would not be there if the words were left out."

Based on this, Mr Fysh says that the words "which includes the likelihood of association with the trade mark" at the end of section 10(2) must do more than merely repeat what is already covered by the earlier words. It must cover something other than classical infringement.

I do not accept this argument. What Viscount Simon was doing was trying to work out, from the words used, what the legislative intent was. At that time it was no doubt believed, or at least hoped, that British legislation was drafted with precision and economy. It was therefore legitimate to start from the premise that each word used in a statute was necessary and there was no tautology. Even by 1949 this was recognised as an assumption which was not always to be trusted. In the *Hill* case Viscount Jowitt pointed out at 543 that the legislature sometimes indulged in tautology. A more illuminating view was expressed by Lord Greene in the same case at 552:

"I need not cite authority for the proposition that prima facie every word in an Act of Parliament must be given an effective meaning of its own. Whether or not the legislature in any given case has condescended to tautology is a question the answer to which depends upon the language used, but in the absence of an appropriate context one statutory provision which is expressed in entirely different language from another, whether in the same or a different section, is not to be interpreted as repetitive or unnecessary."

When construing the 1994 Act it is necessary to bear in mind the legislative context. The Act was intended, amongst other things, to implement Council Directive 89/104 of December 21, 1988 (the 1988 Directive). In particular, the provisions of section 10 of the Act are intended to implement the provisions of Article 5 of that Directive. The court's task is to try to discover the intent behind the words used by the legislature. It would be wrong to apply rules of construction developed during a period when one philosophy of draftmanship was prevalent to a statute drafted when an entirely different philosophy applied. In particular it is quite artificial for the court to pretend that each word of a modern statute which has been lifted more or less verbatim from an EC directive was chosen with the economy which was believed to have been applied to the drafting of British statutes of purely domestic origin. There is no basis upon which the court can assume that the original Directive was drafted so as to avoid tautology. It follows that there is no reason to conclude that the last 10 words in section 10(2) must have been included for the purpose of expanding the scope of infringement.

Indeed, viewed solely linguistically, section 10(2) appears to point away from Mr Fysh's construction. If the words "likelihood of association with the trade mark" cover non-origin association, they cover classical infringement, that is to say likelihood of confusion, also. However, if this is so there would not be any point in including the reference in section 10(2) to "likelihood of confusion" since it is comprehended within "likelihood of association". Furthermore it is unconventional use of language to provide that the smaller (i.e. likelihood of confusion) includes the larger (i.e. likelihood of association) which would appear to be what the section says if Mr Fysh is correct.

It is therefore necessary to consider Mr Fysh's other arguments on construction.

The European interpretation route

Mr Fysh pointed to the fact that the words "the likelihood of association with the trade mark" in our Act are taken from Article 5(1) of the 1988 Directive. That Article is in the following terms:

> "The registered trade mark shall confer on the proprietor exclusive rights therein. The proprietor shall be entitled to prevent all third parties not having his consent from using in the course of trade -
> (a) any sign which is identical with the trade mark in relation to goods or services which are identical with those for which the trade mark is registered,
> (b) any sign where, because of its identity with, or similarity to, the trade mark and the identity or similarity of the goods or services covered by the trade mark and the sign, there exists a likelihood of confusion on the part of the public, which includes the likelihood of association between the sign and the trade mark."

The words "which includes the likelihood of association between the sign and the trade mark" in the Directive are said to be derived from Benelux trade mark law where they cover non-origin association. Therefore Mr Fysh says that the words must be treated as having the same meaning in the 1994 Act as they do in Benelux law. There are three arguments which he deploys in support of this. First he says that a document exists which indicates that the words in the Directive were intended to have the meaning for which he contends. Secondly he says that whether or not any document exists which so indicates, it is a matter of common knowledge that the words were inserted in the Directive for this purpose. Thirdly he says that the Directive was supposed to introduce a new era of trade mark law harmony in the European Union. Since the Benelux courts have construed their equivalent trade mark law derived from the Directive to cover non-origin association, the British courts should do likewise both as a matter of comity and to help deliver the harmony which the Directive hoped to secure.

In support of the arguments based on Benelux law, the plaintiff has adduced evidence from Professor Charles Gielen. He is Professor of Intellectual Property Law at the University of Groningen, Holland. He is also a partner in the Dutch law firm, Nauta Dutilh in Amsterdam. One of his principal areas of practice is trade mark law. In his witness statement he says as follows:

> "Whether a guiding principle or not, what is certain is that in attempting to harmonise Member States' trade mark law, the Commission have imposed upon Member States a requirement to incorporate the likelihood of association concept as developed under Benelux law."

He explained the width of the Benelux concept of likelihood of association. For example he gave the following evidence:

"Q. Can you just help me on this: if Company A has a registered trademark, and Company B comes on to the market with another trademark where the marks have similarities, but no member of the public would be confused as to origin, but some members of the public say: 'Well that has a passing similarity. It brings to mind the company A's mark, but I know that they are nothing to do with each other.' Would that be an infringement?

A. That is an infringement, yes.

Q. In that case, the infringement would have the effect of protecting Company A?

A. Yes.

Q. Well beyond what is necessary to safeguard his trade, his actual trade?

A. Well I think it protects his actual trade, because if the relevant part of the public thinks of trademark A when seeing trademark B, the effect of that is, in fact, loss of exclusivity and dilution. So, I think the Benelux concept of association includes that danger.

I will now consider each of Mr Fysh's arguments and the conclusions to which Professor Gielen has come. ...

Comity

The purpose of the 1988 Directive was to ensure a measure of uniformity between the trade mark laws of Member States of the European Union. For that reason it is right that British courts should pay regard to decisions in the courts of other Member States on equivalent provisions in their law. However it is apparent from the expert evidence of Professor Gielen that the Benelux courts have simply assumed that the Directive made no alteration to their domestic law. The contents of the Fustner and Geuze article suggests that this assumption may well have been wrong. In any event, the obligation of the English court is to decide what the proper construction is. If that construction differs from that adopted in the Benelux countries, one, at least, is wrong. It would not be right for an English court to follow the route adopted by the courts of another Member State if it is firmly of a different view simply because the other court expressed a view first. The scope of European legislation is too important to be decided on a first past the post basis.

The Court's approach to construction

Since none of the arguments on construction put forward by the plaintiff is acceptable, it is necessary to approach the Directive and the 1994 Act from first principles. Monopolies are the antithesis of competition. Intellectual property rights such as patents, trade marks and copyright can create barriers to trade within a country. They can create barriers to trade between countries. Differences between the laws of Member States of the European Union may add further obstructions to inter-state trade because what is permissible under the law of one Member State may be prohibited under the law of its neighbour. However, both at the domestic level and at the international level monopolies can be tolerated or even encouraged if they assist the development of commerce in some other way. Patent monopolies are the classic example. A valid patent may prevent competitors from entering a given field of commerce for up to 20 years. But this is a price which society, through its legislators, has agreed to pay to secure the increased investment in research and development which it is hoped patent monopolies will encourage. The important factor to bear in mind is that what justifies the monopoly is not the monopoly itself but the extent to which it gives, or is hoped to give, a benefit to commerce which compensates for the temporary restraint on competition. The monopoly is an adjunct to, and is designed to promote, commerce. This is central to the western system of commerce. Monopolies are the exception, not the rule. *Marsden v Saville Street Co.* (1878) LR 3 Ex D 203. They need to be justified. As long ago as 1615 in this country it was said that the effect of an unjustified monopoly was "to take away free trade, which is the birthright of every subject" (*The Clothworkers of Ipswich* (1615) Godbolt 252).

Trade marks have historically been used to protect the trade with which they are associated. A good summary of their function is to be found in the speech of the Advocate General in *S.A. CNL-SUCAL NV v HAG GF AG* [1990] 3 CMLR 571 *(HAG II)*. He said at 583:

> "Like patents, trade marks find their justification in a harmonious dove-tailing between public and private interests. Whereas patents reward the creativity of the inventor and thus stimulate scientific progress, trade marks reward the manufacturer who consistently produces high-quality goods and they thus stimulate economic progress. Without trade mark protection there would be little incentive for manufacturers to develop new products or to maintain the quality of existing ones. Trade marks are able to achieve that effect because they act as a guarantee, to the consumer, that all goods bearing a particular mark have been produced by, or under the control of, the same manufacturer and are therefore likely to be of similar quality. The guarantee of quality offered by a trade mark is not of course absolute, for the manufacturer is at liberty to vary the quality; however, he does so at his own risk and he - not his competitors - will suffer the consequences if he allows the quality to decline. Thus, although trade marks do not provide any form of legal guarantee of quality - the absence of which may have misled some to underestimate their significance - they do in economic terms provide such a guarantee, which is acted upon daily by consumers.

> A trade mark can only fulfil that role if it is exclusive. Once the proprietor is forced to share the mark with a competitor, he loses control over the goodwill associated with the mark. The reputation of his own goods will be harmed if the competitor sells inferior goods. From the consumer's point of view, equally undesirable consequences will ensue, because the clarity of the signal transmitted by the trade mark will be impaired. The consumer will be confused and misled."

Similarly in *The Law of Intellectual Property* (1984) Ricketson stated:

> "The primary function of a trade mark, traditionally, has been to identify the commercial or trade origin of the goods (or services) to which it is applied. This, of course, is of central importance to a trader as the mark then indicates to the market that these goods are his, even if he is not personally identified, and it becomes the focus for his growing goodwill or reputation in that market (page 603)."

That the primary function of trade marks is to indicate origin of goods or services has also been accepted by the European Court of Justice. In *HAG II* the court said at 608:

"Consequently, as the Court has stated on many occasions, the specific subject-matter of a trade mark right is to grant the owner the right to use the mark for the first marketing of a product and, in this way, to protect him against competitors who would like to abuse the position and reputation of the mark by selling products to which the mark has been improperly affixed. To determine the exact effect of this exclusive right which is granted to the owner of the mark, it is necessary to take account of the essential function of the mark, which is to give the consumer or final user a guarantee of the identity of the origin of the marked product by enabling him to distinguish, without any possible confusion, that product from others of a different provenance: see Case 102/77, *Hoffman-La Roche* and Case 3/78, *Centrafarm v American Home Products.*

...

Under these circumstances the essential function of the mark would be compromised if the owner of the right could not exercise his option under national law to prevent the importation of the similar product under a name likely to be confused with his own mark because, in this situation, consumers would no longer be able to identify with certainty the origin of the marked product and the bad quality of a product for which he is in no way responsible could be attributed to the owner of the right."

Furthermore in *Deutsche Renault AG v Audi AG [1995]* 1 CMLR 461 the Court has also indicated that the essential function of a trade mark extends to protection from association *as to origin.* In that case the Court said at 483, 484:

"... it should be noted, first, that the specific subject-matter of trade mark rights consists in protecting the proprietor of the mark against a risk of confusion such as to allow third persons to take unlawful advantage of the reputation 'of the proprietor's goods (reference made to *Centrafarm v Winthrop and HAG II)* According to German law, there is a risk of confusion between two trade marks not only when the trade concerned might mistakenly assume that the goods concerned come from one and the same undertaking (direct risk of confusion) but also when the mistaken assumption relates to the existence of an organisational or economic link between the undertakings concerned, such as a licensing agreement under which one undertaking is authorised to manufacture a product with the same properties as the product of the other (risk of confusion in the broader sense).

No exception can be taken under community law to the protection granted by a national law against this last-mentioned risk of confusion since it corresponds to the specific subject-matter of the trade mark right which, as stated above, consists in protecting the proprietor against the risk of confusion."

As mentioned above, there are two possible constructions which may be placed on Article 5 of the 1988 Directive and section 10(2) of the 1994 Act. The rights of the proprietor against alleged infringers may be limited to classic infringement which includes association as to origin or, following the Benelux route, it could cover not only classic infringement but also non-origin association. In my view, the former construction is to be preferred. If the broader scope were to be adopted, the Directive and our Act would be creating a new type of monopoly not related to the proprietor's trade but in the trade mark itself. Such a monopoly could be likened to a quasi-copyright in the mark. However, unlike copyright, there would be no fixed duration for the right and it would be a true monopoly effective against copyist and non-copyist alike. I can see nothing in the terms of the Directive (or our Act), or in any secondary material which I could legitimately take into account, which would lead me to assume that this was its objective. On the contrary, the preamble to the Directive seems to point in the opposite direction since it states:

"Whereas the protection afforded by the registered trade mark, the function of which is in particular to guarantee the trade mark as an indication of origin,..."

Furthermore there appears to be little commercial justification for any such extension of trade mark rights. If it had been the intention to make the Directive identical with Benelux law on this important issue it could have said so. Indeed, in view of the fact that to have done so would have been significantly to expand trade mark rights and thereby significantly restrict the freedom of traders to compete, I would have expected any such expansion to have been stated in clear and unambiguous words so that traders throughout the European Union would be able to appreciate that their legislators had created a new broad monopoly. As it is, no such clear and unambiguous words have been used and the language of the Directive and the 1994 Act is consistent with the rights being restricted to classical infringement.

It follows that this Court cannot follow the route adopted by the Benelux courts on this issue. This is regrettable since one of the main objectives of the 1988 Directive was to avoid differences in scope of trade mark rights which could lead to barriers to inter-state trade. Nevertheless the natural inclination to come to a conclusion which would further harmony on this issue is not so strong that I am prepared to agree that a new millstone round the neck of traders has been created when that is not my view. If the plaintiff is to succeed in its case of trade mark infringement it must do so on the classic grounds.

Does the defendant infringe?
As indicated above, when this action commenced, the defendant was using the mark RAJAMAMA. After the launch of the application for interlocutory relief the defendant changed to the use of RAJA MAMA'S. The plaintiff says that both versions infringe its rights. Mr Platts-Mills on the other hand argues that neither do and that even if the version in one word does, the version in two words does not.

The approach the court should adopt to infringement under section 10 was recently set out in by Jacob J in *Origins Natural Resources Inc.* v *Origin Clothing Limited* [1995] FSR 280 in which at 284 he said:

"section 10 of the Trade Marks Act presupposes that the plaintiff's mark is in use or will come into use. It requires the court to assume the mark of the plaintiff is used in a normal and fair manner in relation to the goods for which it is registered and then to assess the likelihood of confusion in relation to the way the defendant uses its mark, discounting external added matter or circumstances. The comparison is mark for mark."

A judge brings to the assessment of marks his own, perhaps idiosyncratic, pronunciation and view or understanding of them. Although the issue of infringement is one eventually for the judge alone, in assessing the marks he must bear in mind the impact the marks make or are likely to make on the minds of those persons who are likely to be customers for goods or services under the marks. Not all customers are the same. It is therefore sometimes of assistance for the court to hear evidence from witnesses who will help him to assess the variety of ways in which members of the target market will pronounce the marks and what, to them, will be the visual or phonetic impact of the marks. When considering infringement it is also necessary to bear in mind the possible impact of imperfect recollection on the part of members of the target market.

In this case it is conceded by the defendant that the plaintiff's mark is entirely artificial and meaningless as far as substantially all of the target market is concerned. Although it contains the letters "MAMA" it does not convey to most people the concept of motherhood. The defendant did not suggest otherwise. It is just a strange word with a pronounced internal rhythm. The defendant argues that its mark, particularly in the two word form, conveys a descriptive meaning. The letters "RAJA" mean something to do with the Raj - that is to say India, and "MAMA" conveys motherhood or an American connotation. I am not quite sure why this is said to refer to America, but that was the view expressed by Mr Naylor, Group Chief Executive of the defendant. Furthermore the defendant says that because the defendant's mark is made of two recognisable parts, it will naturally be understood as being two words and, at least in relation to the RAJA MAMA'S version, this will be confirmed when the mark is seen. Because both versions of the defendant's mark convey a meaning, the "ideas" of the plaintiff's and defendant's mark are different. My attention was also drawn to the differences in the first syllable of the marks and to paragraph 17.02 in *Kerly's Law of Trade Marks and Trade Names* (12th ed.) which suggests that first syllables are particularly important when assessing the similarity of marks. Mr Platts-Mills also drew my attention to *Coca Cola of Canada* v *Pepsi Cola of Canada* (1942) 59 RPC 127 in which Coca Cola failed to prevent the use of the trade mark Pepsi Cola because the only point of similarity was in the word "COLA" which was common to the trade. So here it is argued that the only real point of similarity between the plaintiff's and defendant's marks is in the word "MAMA" which also is common to the trade.

Whether there has been trade mark infringement is more a matter of feel than science. I have borne in mind all of the arguments advanced by the defendant. However in this case, it is significant that the marks are being used in relation to comparatively inexpensive restaurant services. This is an area where imperfect recollection is likely to play an important role. Furthermore the fact that the plaintiff's mark is quite meaningless means that imperfect recollection is more likely. Although some of the target market may consider the defendant's mark to be made of two parts, each of which has some sort of meaning, I think a significant section will not bother to analyse it in that way. To them it will be just another artificial mark. Although I accept that when seen side by side the plaintiff's and defendant's marks are easily distinguishable, this is not determinative of the issue of infringement. As the Privy Council stated in *de Cordova* v *Vick Chemical Co.* (1951) 68 RPC 103 at 106:

"A trade mark is undoubtedly a visual device, but it is well-established law that the ascertainment of an essential feature is not to be by ocular test alone. Since words can form part, or indeed the whole, of a mark, it is impossible to exclude consideration of the sound or significance of those words. ... The likelihood of confusion or deception in such cases is not disproved by placing the two marks side by side and demonstrating how small is the chance of error in any customer who places his order for goods with both the marks clearly before him, for orders are not placed, or are often not placed, under such conditions. It is more useful to observe that in most persons the eye is not an accurate recorder of visual detail, and that marks are remembered rather by general impressions or by some significant detail than by any photographic recollection of the whole."

In that case one of the registered trade marks held by the Privy Council to have been infringed is illustrated at (1951) 68 RPC 270. The defendant used the mark "KARSOTE Vapour Rub" illustrated at (1951) 68 RPC 226.

I have come to the conclusion that the defendant's mark, in either form, is so similar to the plaintiff's registered mark that in use there exists a substantial likelihood of confusion on the part of the relevant public. That confusion is likely to take the form that some members of the public as a result of imperfect recollection will think the marks are the same while others will think that they are associated in the sense that one is an extension of the other (cf. the "Rus"/"Sanrus" case) or otherwise derived from the same source. It follows that the plaintiff succeeds on the issue of trade mark infringement.'

COMMENT

Laddie J also found the allegation of passing off to be made out.

Although Laddie J found classic infringement of the trade mark (confusion as to origin) his detailed consideration of the meaning of 'likelihood of association' is very instructive. His rejection of the Benelux approach of finding infringement on the basis simply of non-origin association is surely right. In *Sabel BV v Puma AG* [1998] RPC 199, the European Court of Justice agreed that mere association made by the public between the two marks was not a sufficient ground for infringement. There must be a likelihood of confusion. Advocate General Jacobs in his opinion delivered to the court expressly approved Laddie J's view that it would be 'unconventional use of language to provide that the smaller (i.e. likelihood of confusion) includes the larger (i.e. likelihood of association)!

If non-origin association could infringe a trade mark, what undesirable consequences would this inevitably have? What is the primary purpose of a trade mark? Do they have any secondary purposes?

Comparative Advertising

Infringement by comparative advertising was introduced into trade mark law following the case of *Irving's Yeastvite Ltd.* v *Housenail* (1934) 51 RPC 110, in which it was held that advertising a product by reference to another trader's mark did not infringe. Section 4(1)(b) of the Trade Marks Act 1938 which implemented the change was one of the most difficult provisions on the statute book. Under the 1938 Act, in spite of this new form of infringement, there were relatively few cases of comparative advertising. A typical example of comparative advertising is where one trader advertises his goods or services, comparing them and/or the prices with those of another trader, using that other trader's registered trade mark, as in the case below.

The Trade Marks Act 1994 allows comparative advertising but only if it accords with honest practices and does not take unfair advantage of, and is not detrimental to, the distinctive character or repute of the other mark.

Barclays Bank plc v *RBS Advanta* [1996] RPC 307, Chancery Division

The defendant issued advertising literature which included a comparative table comparing the defendant's proposed new credit card with that of the plaintiff. The table included details of annual fees and interest rates relating to a number of credit cards and included a reference to 'Barclaycard Standard Visa'. BARCLAYCARD had been registered as a trade mark by the plaintiff in respect of credit, credit card and charge card services. The plaintiff also complained of a leaflet distributed by the defendant listing various features of the defendant's card and stating why it was 'a better credit card all round'. The leaflet, when read in conjunction with the table, infringed as it took unfair advantage of the trade mark. The leaflet, in particular failed to point out some of the ancillary benefits provided by the plaintiff but not by the defendant.

Laddie J (at 315): *'Construction of Section 10(6)*
As a general proposition, it seems to me that Mr Silverleaf is right when he says that the primary objective of section 10(6) is to allow comparative advertising. As long as the use of the competitor's mark is "honest", then there is nothing wrong with telling the public of the relative merits of competing goods or services and using registered trade marks to identify them. The proviso should not be construed in a way which effectively prohibits all comparative advertising.

First, Mr Silverleaf argued that if it is to be brought into operation, the onus is on the registered proprietor to show that the factors indicated in the proviso exist. I did not understand Mr Young to dispute this and, in my view, Mr Silverleaf is right.

Secondly, there will be no infringement unless the use of the registered mark is not in accordance with honest practices. Both counsel agreed, rightly in my view that this test is objective. This part of the proviso simply means that if the use is considered honest by members of a reasonable audience, it will not infringe. The fact that the advertising pokes fun at the proprietor's goods or services and emphasises the benefits of the defendant's is a normal incidence of comparative advertising. Its aim will be to divert customers from the proprietor. No reasonable observer would expect one trader to point to all the advantages of its competitor's business and failure to do so does not *per se* take the advertising outside what reasonable people would regard as "honest". Thus mere trade puffery, even if uncomfortable to the registered proprietor, does not bring the advertising within the scope of trade mark infringement. Much advertising copy is recognised by the public as hyperbole. The Act does not impose on the courts an obligation to try to enforce, through the back door of trade mark legislation, a more puritanical standard. If, on the other hand, a reasonable reader is likely to say, on being given the full facts, that the advertisement is not honest, for example because it is significantly misleading, then the protection from trade mark infringement is removed.

Mr Young suggested, at least in relation to section 11(2)(b), that if the registered mark is used in a trade mark sense in the comparative advertising it cannot be honest. I do not agree. Whether the mark is being used in that way has nothing to do with whether that use is honest. In any event the first half of section 10(6) exempts from infringement use of registered trade marks for the purpose of identifying goods or services as those of the proprietor or a licensee. Such use will almost invariably be used in a trade mark sense. If Mr Young's submission as to the scope of the proviso in section 11(2)(b) is correct, and applicable to the section 10(6) defence, then that defence would cease to exist, since the immunity given by the first half of the sub-section would be removed by the equal but opposite effect of the proviso. This cannot be right.

Thirdly, to come within the proviso the use must be otherwise than in accordance with honest practices in "industrial and commercial matters". It was suggested during the motion that this means that the court should look to statutory or industry-agreed codes of conduct to determine whether the advertisement is honest. That approach resulted in this case in much of the evidence on this motion being directed to the issue of whether the defendant's advertising met the specific requirements of the 1974 Act and the 1989 Regulations [The Consumer Credit Act 1974 and the Consumer Credit (Advertisements) Regulations 1989]. If this approach to the proviso is correct, it would follow that in some trades where there are very detailed and restrictive codes of practice in relation to advertising, it would be easier to breach the code and therefore harder to avoid infringement of registered trade mark. I do not believe that this is the correct way to assess honesty for the purposes of section 10(6).

No doubt the nature of the products or services will affect the degree of hyperbole acceptable. What is tolerable in advertisements for second-hand cars may well not be thought honest if used to encourage the use of powerful medicines. The nature of the goods or services may therefore affect the reasonable perception of what advertising is honest. But it is quite another thing to say that statutory or industry imposed codes of advertising conduct define honesty for the purposes of section 10(6) of the 1994 Act. Although most such codes are concerned to ensure probity, they frequently cover other matters as well. Breach of such a code therefore does not necessarily mean that the advertisement is other than honest. It follows that the provisions of the 1974 Act and 1989 Regulations are of little direct relevance to the issue of trade mark infringement. Honesty has to be gauged against what is reasonably to be expected by the relevant public of advertisements for the goods or services in issue.

Fourthly, it seems to me that the final words of the proviso

"if the use without due cause takes unfair advantage of, or is detrimental to, the distinctive character or repute of the trade mark"

in most cases adds nothing of significance to the first part of the proviso. An advertisement which makes use of a registered mark in a way which is not honest will almost always take unfair advantage of it and vice versa. At the most these final words emphasise that the use of the mark must take advantage of it or be detrimental to it. In other words the use must either give some advantage to the defendant or inflict some harm on the character or repute of the registered mark which is above the level of *de minimis*.

The strength of the parties' cases on infringement

By the time the motion came on for hearing and after the defendant had made certain amendments to its literature, the plaintiff was prepared to accept that there was nothing it could complain of, in trade mark terms, in the form or content of the comparative tables in the brochure. Although they used the mark BARCLAYCARD, the plaintiff accepted that such use was in accordance with honest practices. Furthermore the plaintiff could not complain of the contents of the leaflet *per se*. They contain no reference to the registered marks at all. It was accepted that any injunction granted on this motion could not stop that leaflet or one like it being distributed widely by the defendant. However Mr Young argued that the contents of the leaflet and the tables could not be treated as separate. They were distributed together and would be read together. Indeed, as noted above, very similar wording to that found on the leaflet is to be found on the brochure. In my view Mr Young is right. Whether or not different documents, or even different parts of the same document, are to be read together will depend on all the circumstances. An illegitimate use of a registered trade mark will not necessarily be saved from a finding of infringement by the expedient of putting the registered trade mark on one document and the dishonest part on another. If they are intended to be or likely to be read together, the advertisement should be read as a whole. In this case all the documents have been sent out and should be read together. In fact Mr Lewis, the marketing director of the defendant, described the defendant's mailshot package as a "single advertisement" in his affidavit in these proceedings.

The nub of the plaintiff's complaint is that the contents of the leaflet are not honest. As Mr Young explained it, the leaflet indicated the 15 "bullet points" which were being put forward by the defendant as showing that its credit card was better than the plaintiff's. He accepted that the plaintiff could not complain if the defendant merely said that its credit card was better. However he said that in this case the defendant had descended to detail - to be precise, 15 details - and these were not accurate since they did not compare like with like. In particular he relied on paragraph 15 of the affidavit of Mr Macfarlane sworn on behalf of the plaintiff which complains that the defendant's literature makes no mention of other ancillary benefits which the plaintiff offers its cardholders and which the defendant does not have, such as a 24 hour service relating to emergencies on the road and an overseas emergency service. He also relied on paragraph 14 of Mr Lewis' affidavit which contains the following:

"[The plaintiff's] additional benefits are not free but are, in effect, paid for by at least part of the higher interest rates charged by Barclays. RBS Advanta does not currently offer the ancillary services, which is part of the reason why RBS Advanta is able to offer lower interest rates. In my experience in the field of credit card services, many customers are attracted by lower interest rates and the absence of annual fees. The ancillary benefits are of limited importance when selecting a credit card. I believe that only a small percentage of Barclaycard customers are likely to use any of the ancillary services in any year. This is backed up by my experience at American Express ..."

This, said Mr Young, amounts to an admission that the defendant is offering a lesser service than the plaintiff and therefore to refer to the defendant's lower rates without pointing out the other advantages of using the plaintiff's card is misleading and not honest. Furthermore he said that there was no dispute between the parties that of the 15 points identified in the defendant's leaflet, 6 or 7 were common to Barclaycard as well. For example the plaintiff's card is also accepted wherever you see a VISA sign (claim 6) and can be used to obtain cash from any ATM displaying the VISA sign (claim 8). It followed that it was not honest to say that the defendant's card was better all round than the plaintiff's.

In my view the plaintiff's case on this issue is very weak. It has the onus of showing that the defendant's use of the BARCLAYCARD mark in its advertising is not honest. It appears to me that it is most unlikely that any reasonable reader would take that view. On the contrary, read fairly, the advertisements convey the message that the package of 15 features, *taken as a whole,* is believed by the defendant to offer the customer a better deal. It seems most unlikely that a reasonable reader, and particularly one to whom this advertisement is being directed - that is to say one who is being tempted to change from an existing VISA card - would be misled into thinking that the 15 features in the defendant's leaflet are, individually, only available to users of the defendant's credit card. For example it is a matter of common knowledge that all VISA cards are accepted wherever a VISA sign is displayed and can be used to draw cash from VISA AIM machines. Furthermore the advertisement does not say, and I think it is unlikely that a reasonable reader would take it to mean, that there are no features of the plaintiff's service which are better than the defendant's. The advertisement merely picks out the features taken together which are being promoted as making the defendant's product a good package.

I should point out that both parties agreed before me that the strength of the parties' cases had to be taken into consideration in deciding the question of balance of convenience. For the reasons set out above, it is my view that the plaintiff is unlikely to win this action. Whether taken into account on the balance of convenience or, for the reasons set out in *Series 5 Software,* this is a major factor in deciding whether or not to grant interlocutory relief.

The balance of convenience
In addition to the weakness of the plaintiff's case, there are other reasons advanced by the defendant why the balance of convenience points away from the grant of interlocutory relief. The type of advertising of which the plaintiff complains in this action would be to a layman very similar to many other comparative advertisements put out by other credit card companies and not complained of by the plaintiff. Examples of such other advertisements are exhibited to the affidavit of Mr Lewis. Furthermore, as pointed out above, even if an injunction were granted, it would not prevent the defendant from continuing to issue the leaflet alone. That document does not refer to the plaintiff's mark yet, because the plaintiff is the largest VISA card operator in the country, most readers would realise that the defendant is saying that its product is better than, *inter alia,* the plaintiff's. The defendant says that it would be wrong to grant an interlocutory injunction which would serve little useful purpose. In addition to this, as Mr Silverleaf points out, it will be quite easy after the trial to work out which customers for the plaintiff's card have switched to the defendant. Although not accepting that all of that switching would be referable to the alleged infringement, it would make it moderately easy to calculate the upper limit of the damage suffered by the plaintiff.

Finally the defendant argues that if it is entitled to put out these advertisements in this way and if, as it hopes, advertisements in this format will best advance the penetration of the defendant's card into the market, to force it to change its advertisements now so that the new card has to be launched with advertising material which may be less effective, will cause the defendant truly unquantifiable loss. Since this is a new venture, there are no existing data which will enable the court to decide to what extent the defendant has been held back and its market penetration blunted by its forced change of advertising material. I accept that this is so. However I think that although the damage will be unquantifiable, it is also likely to be small. Furthermore against this the plaintiff points to the fact that preservation of the status quo points in favour of granting an interlocutory injunction.

Taking all these factors into consideration, and, in particular, the weakness of the plaintiff's case, the comparative triviality of the benefit it would obtain from the grant of an injunction and the small damage which, in the light of other competitors' advertising, it would suffer as a result of the defendant's proposed advertising campaign, in my view this is not a case in which it would be appropriate to grant interlocutory relief.'

COMMENT

In another case on comparative advertising *Vodafone Group plc* v *Orange Personal Communications Services Ltd.* [1997] FSR 34, it was accepted that the public would generally expect some elasticity in price and usage in relation to mobile phones. However, in *Cable & Wireless plc* v *British Telecommunications plc* [1998] FSR 383, the court held that knowingly making a false claim could not be said to be acting in accordance with honest practices.

Laddie J spoke of the use of the mark giving some advantage to the defendant or inflicting harm on the character or repute of the registered trade mark. Is it possible to take advantage of another's mark without inflicting harm on it and still falling within what are considered to be honest practices?

Note that an amount of hyperbole is permissible. How does the audience at which the advertising is aimed know that a statement is exaggerated and not meant to be taken seriously? Do you think the public could be misled in cases such as this?

Groundless Threats of Infringement Actions

The remedy of 'groundless threats' actions was first introduced into trade mark law by the 1994 Act. Previously, it was only available in respect of patents, registered designs and the design right. The remedy is contained in section 21 of the Act and the plaintiff is entitled to relief unless the defendant (the party making the threats) can show that the use of the mark complained of does indeed infringe the mark or if the plaintiff shows that the mark is invalid or liable to be revoked in any material respect. The remedy is not available in respect of some forms of infringement, for example, applying or affixing the sign to the goods in question. Nor is mere notification that a mark is registered a groundless threat.

Trebor Bassett Ltd. v *The Football Association* [1997] FSR 211, Chancery Division

Trebor Bassett made children's sweets in packets including cards with photographs of famous footballers. Where the footballer was an England player, the photograph might show him wearing the England shirt which incorporated the England team badge with three lions on it. The badge was a registered trade mark of the Football Association, which alleged that this use of the badge amounted to an infringement of its trade mark. Trebor Bassett, the plaintiff in this case, brought a groundless threats action against the Football Association.

Rattee J (at 213): 'The essential issue in both sets of proceedings is clearly whether it is even arguable that Trebor Bassett's production and sale of the cards complained of by the FA is capable of constituting an infringement of the FA's registered trade mark, and to that question I must turn. I should first refer to the relevant provisions of the Trade Marks Act 1994. They are as follows. Section 1(1) provides:

"In this Act a 'trade mark' means any sign capable of being represented graphically which is capable of distinguishing goods or services of one undertaking from those of other undertakings.

A trade mark may, in particular, consist of words (including personal names), designs, letters, numerals or the shape of goods or their packaging."

It is in my judgment clear, as Mr Speck (on behalf of Trebor Bassett) submitted, that it is of the essence of a trade mark that its purpose is to distinguish goods and services of one undertaking from those of other undertakings. Section 9 of the Act, so far as material, provides as follows:

"(1) The proprietor of a registered trade mark has exclusive rights in the trade mark which are infringed by use of the trade mark in the United Kingdom without his consent.

The acts amounting to infringement, if done without the consent of the proprietor, are specified in section 10.

(2) References in this Act to the infringement of a registered trade mark are to any such infringement of the rights of the proprietor."

Section 10 provides:

"(1) A person infringes a registered trade mark if he uses in the course of trade a sign which is identical with the trade mark in relation to goods or services which are identical with those for which it is registered.

(2) A person infringes a registered trade mark if he uses in the course of trade a sign where because -
(a) the sign is identical with the trade mark and is used in relation to goods or services similar to those for which the trade mark is registered, or (b) the

sign is similar to the trade mark and is used in relation to goods or services identical with or similar to those for which the trade mark is registered, there exists a likelihood of confusion on the part of the public, which includes the likelihood of association with the trade mark.

(3) A person infringes a registered trade mark if he uses in the course of trade a sign which -
  (a) is identical with or similar to the trade mark, and
  (b) is used in relation to goods or services which are not similar to those for which the trade mark is registered,
where the trade mark has a reputation in the United Kingdom and the use of the sign, being without due cause, takes unfair advantage of, or is detrimental to, the distinctive character or the repute of the trade mark.

(4) For the purposes of this section a person uses a sign if, in particular, he -
  (a) affixes it to goods or the packaging thereof;
  (b) offers or exposes goods for sale, puts them on the market or stocks them for those purposes under the sign, or offers or supplies services under the sign;
  (c) imports or exports goods under the sign; or
  (d) uses the sign on business papers or in advertising."

Section 11(2) provides as follows:

"(2) A registered trade mark is not infringed by -
  (a) the use by a person of his own name or address,
  (b) the use of indications concerning the kind, quality, quantity, intended purpose, value, geographical origin, the time of production of goods or of rendering of services, or other characteristics of goods or services, or
  (c) the use of the trade mark where it is necessary to indicate the intended purpose of a product or service (in particular, as accessories or spare parts), provided the use is in accordance with honest practices in industrial or commercial matters."

Certain transitional provisions are included in Schedule 3 to the Act, and the relevant provision appears in paragraph 4(2) of Schedule 3 in these terms:

"(2) It is not an infringement of -
  (a) an existing registered mark, or
  (b) a registered trade mark of which the distinctive elements are the same or substantially the same as those of an existing registered mark and which is registered for the same goods or services, to continue after commencement any use which did not amount to infringement of the existing registered mark under the old law."

The FA alleges in the statement of claim in its action infringement within section 10(1) or, alternatively, section 10(2) of the 1994 Act. However, it was common ground between counsel in the argument before me that the England logo on the shirts worn by footballers whose pictures appear on the cards complained of is identical to the FA registered mark, and that the goods concerned (that is to say, the cards) are, for the purposes of section 10, identical with those for which the trade mark is registered in Class 16. Therefore, the alleged infringement will only be such if it falls within section 10(1) of the Act.

The FA alleges that it is at least arguable that such alleged infringement is such by virtue of section 10(1). Trebor Bassett says that it is not even arguable that it is.

Trebor Bassett ran two alternative arguments, one based on section 11(2)(b) of the 1994 Act and one on the transitional provisions in Schedule 3 para. 4(2), which I have read.

The first question, then, is whether the activities of Trebor Bassett, which are complained of in the statement of claim in the FA's action, are capable of constituting an infringement of the FA's registered trade mark under section 10(1) of the 1994 Act.

Mr Speck, on behalf of Trebor Bassett Limited, submitted that the activities complained of by the Football Association plainly do not constitute an infringement within section 10(1), because, according to his submission, Trebor Bassett is not using the England logo in relation to any goods or services, any more than is the publisher of a newspaper bearing a photograph of a footballer in the England strip as part of a news report on a football match using the logo in relation to the particular newspaper.

Mr Morcom submits that it is at least arguable (and he said, rightly, that that is sufficient for present purposes) that the activities of Trebor Bassett do fall within section 10(1). Mr Morcom relied on the case of *British Sugar Plc.* v *James Robertson & Sons Limited* [1996] RPC 281, in which, at 291, Jacob J rejected an argument that to be within section 10(1) of the 1994 Act, the use of the sign complained of has to be used as a trade mark: i.e. as identifying the provenance of the relevant goods or services.

There is no doubt, in my judgment, in the present case, that the relevant sign is not being used by Trebor Bassett as a trade mark. Mr Morcom submitted that all that is necessary to bring the case within section 10(1) is to show that Trebor Bassett has used a sign identical to the FA's registered trade mark in the course of trade in respect of identical goods and services, that is to say, in respect of the cards marketed as part of packages of confectionery by Trebor Bassett. Mr Morcom submitted that in the present case the evidence discloses that Trebor Bassett is using a sign identical with the registered trade mark in the course of its trade in relation to those cards; and that those cards are (as is, as I have already indicated, accepted by the other side, for present purposes) identical to goods for which the trade mark is registered.

Mr Morcom, in support of his argument, relies on the provisions of section 10(4) of the 1994 Act, to which I should refer again. That subsection provides a definition of certain types of use of a sign for the purposes of section 10(1), although not an exhaustive definition, and provides:

"(4)   For the purposes of this section a person uses a sign if, in particular, he -
    (a) affixes it to goods or the packaging thereof,
    (b) offers or exposes goods for sale, puts them on the market or stocks them for those purposes under the sign, or offers or supplies services under the sign."

Mr Morcom submitted that it is certainly arguable that, in distributing or offering for sale as part of the packages of confectionery these cards bearing photographs of players wearing football shirts with the England logo on them, Trebor Bassett is putting the cards on the market under a sign consisting of that logo. Mr Morcom says that if, as he submits it should do, the court will allow him to take his action to trial, he will be in a position to adduce evidence to the effect that it is of fundamental importance to Trebor Bassett's business in this particular type of confectionery that photographs included on the cards in the packets should be of players wearing the England logo.

Mr Morcom rightly stressed the fact that there are applications (one for summary judgment and the other for strike-out) neither of which I could properly accede to unless satisfied that the case is actually clear that there is no defence to Trebor Bassett's action, and that the action brought by the FA does not make any allegation or make any claim that ought properly to be allowed to go on trial.

On the other hand, Mr Speck submitted that if, as he submitted is the true view, there is no disputed issue of fact which requires evidence and a trial - and it is just a question of construing section 10(1) and deciding whether, on its construction, it is capable of applying to the undisputed facts relating to the appearance of the England players in England strip on the cards marketed by Trebor Bassett - then that is a question which can, and should properly, be decided on these summary applications, rather than putting everybody to the expense and delay of a trial - which, according to Mr Speck's submission, would inevitably result in victory for his client and failure for the FA

In deciding the questions before me, I consider it unnecessary, and therefore inappropriate, for me to decide whether I should adopt the view adopted by Jacob J in the *British Sugar Plc* case on the question whether use of a sign, to be within section 10(1), has to be used as a trade mark. I express no view on the point. I say it is unnecessary for me to do so, because I accept the argument put forward by Mr Speck, on behalf of Trebor Bassett, that it cannot seriously be argued that by publishing and marketing, on the cards concerned, photographs of players wearing the England team football strip (including the three lions logo) Trebor Bassett is in any sense using the logo in respect of the cards on which the photographs appear. In my judgment it plainly is not. The logo appears on the card only because it is worn by the player whose photograph appears on the card as part of that player's England team football strip, to show that the player himself is an England team player. The reproduction of the photograph on the card inevitably reproduces the England logo on the garments which the player was wearing when the photograph was taken. By such reproduction, in my judgment, Trebor Bassett is not even arguably using the logo, as such, in any real sense of the word 'uses', and is certainly not, in my judgment, using it as a sign in respect of its cards.

It is, I consider, unreal to say, as Mr Morcom would have me decide, that, by the activities in question, Trebor Bassett is affixing the sign comprising the England logo to its cards - and therefore to goods within the meaning of section 10(4)(a) - or that it is putting the cards on the market under the sign comprising the England logo within section 10(4)(b).

In my judgment, there is no room for further evidence to be investigated at a trial relating to this question.

The evidence is before the court and is undisputed, comprising the form of card which is marketed by Trebor Bassett and it seems to me that the question of whether the marketing of cards in that form can possibly constitute infringement within section 10(1) is a matter which requires no further evidence, and a matter which ought, in both parties' interests, to be determined as soon as possible, and that means now, on this application for summary judgment and the application to strike out.

Of course, I accept that the court should accede to neither application unless clearly satisfied that no substantial defence exists to the claim for a declaration of non-infringement sought by the plaintiff; but, in my judgment, that test is satisfied in the present case for the reasons which I have endeavoured to explain.

Accordingly, I propose to make the declaration sought by paragraph 1 of the prayer and statement of claim in the action brought by Trebor Bassett and I propose to strike out the action begun by the FA, because, in the light of my decision that Trebor Bassett is entitled to its declaration in its action, quite plainly continuation of the action started by the FA in an attempt to satisfy the court to the contrary would be nothing short of an abuse of the process of the court. For there can be nothing left in the action which has not been determined against the plaintiff in that action by the summary judgment in the action begun by Trebor Bassett.'

COMMENT

Summary judgment was given to the plaintiff in respect of the threats action. As the defendant was unable to show infringement of its trade mark, it was doomed in the threats action. A declaration was given to the effect that the production and marketing of the cards did not constitute an infringement of the Football Association's registered trade mark. The other remedies available in a threats action, an injunction and damages, were not asked for.

Because groundless threats actions are relatively new to trade mark law, care has to be taken by proprietors of trade marks seeking to warn off potential infringers. For example, in *Prince plc* v *Prince Sports Group Inc.* [1998] FSR 21, the defendant, an American company, wrote to the plaintiff alleging infringement of the former's UK registered trade mark. The court granted a declaration that the threats were unjustified and an injunction against any continuance of the threats.

In the Trebor Bassett case, Rattee J did not decide whether, for infringement, the use complained of must be use as a trade mark. What is the correct view of that issue?

Rectification and Removal of Trade Marks

Subject to the presumption of conclusive validity for Part A marks, the 1938 Act contained a number of provisions for rectification and removal from register of trade marks. The 1994 Act has broadly equivalent provisions though there are some differences; for example, under section 11 of the 1938 Act it was not lawful to register a mark which would, *inter alia*, by reason of its being likely to deceive or cause confusion or otherwise, be disentitled to protection in a court of justice. This provision was considered in the following case in which the register was rectified by removal of the defendant's mark.

Berlei (UK) Ltd. v Bali Brassiere Co. Inc. [1969] 2 All ER 812, House of Lords

The plaintiff had a registered trade mark 'Berlei' used extensively for brassières and corsets. When the defendant applied to register 'Bali', the plaintiff opposed the registration and also applied for rectification of the register by removal of an earlier mark registered by the defendant which also contained the word 'Bali'.

Lord Morris of Borth-y-Gest (at 822): 'In the Act of 1883 the latter part of that section was, with minor modification, re-enacted as s.73. By the Act of 1888 the word "exclusive" was to be omitted from s.73. That section, as amended, was replaced in the 1905 Act by s.11 which was in these terms:

"It shall not be lawful to register as a trade mark or part of a trade mark any matter, the use of which would by reason of its being calculated to deceive or otherwise be disentitled to protection in a court of justice, or would be contrary to law or morality, or any scandalous design."

By amendments made by the Trade Marks (Amendment) Act 1937 (see s.6), the section assumed its present form. Although in all the statutes from 1875 to 1938 it has been provided (e.g., see s.2 of the Trade Marks Act 1938) that proceedings may not be instituted to prevent infringement of an unregistered mark (while preserving all rights of action for passing-off) that does not alter the meaning of the words in s.11 as revealed by considering the statutory history and the state of the law before 1875.

From all this I think it follows that, in 1938, if Berlei had shown that the use of the mark "Bali" was likely to deceive or cause confusion they would have shown (quite without any reference to s.12(1)) that the use of the mark 'Bali' was disentitled to protection in a court of justice. Our attention was called to the interesting judgment of Buckley, J, in *Transfermatic Trade Mark* [1966] RPC 568. As to the decision itself no question now arises. But in the course of his judgment the learned judge said [1966] RPC at p.579:

"If an opponent to registration can show that the circumstances are such that on the ground of likelihood of deceit or confusion, the applicant could be restrained in a court of justice from using the mark sought to be registered, section 11 must prohibit registration. If all that the opponent could show was that a number of persons might entertain a reasonable doubt whether goods bearing the two marks came from the same source, falling short of grounds for relief against passing off, I, for myself, would require further argument before reaching the conclusion, apart from authority, that the section would prohibit registration."

My Lords, I do not think that the words of the learned judge need be read as saying that potential success in a passing-off action is always the test in applying s.11 or that the evidence must always be such as would warrant success in a passing-off action. If his words bore that meaning they would not be in accord with what was said in various cases. In *McDowell's* case (1927), 43 RPC, 393 where there was an application to register a word there was opposition based both on s.11 and on s.19 of the Act of 1905 (generally corresponding to s.11 and s.12(1) of the present Act). The onus was therefore on the applicant. In referring to this Warrington, LJ, said (at p.336):

"It is well settled that the onus of establishing that the proposed mark is not calculated to deceive is upon the applicant, and in this respect he is in a much less favourable position than if he were a defendant in an action for infringement, or for passing off."

Sargant, LJ, said (at p.338) that the controversy had been dealt with "too much as a litigation between the parties, and as if it had been a passing-off case": he pointed out that the predominant consideration was the protection of the public. The question was whether there was a probability of deception which the applicant had not dispelled.

So also in *Re Hack's Application* (1940) 58 RPC 91 Morton, J, said at p.103 that:

"the question whether a particular mark is calculated to deceive or cause confusion is not the same as the question whether the use of the mark will lead to passing-off."

A mark would offend against s.11 if it was likely to cause confusion or deception in the minds of persons to whom it is addressed. See also *Re Jellinek's Application* (1946) 63 RPC 59 at p.78.

The *Transfermatic* case was not one where s.13 applied, and as the applicants for rectification had not registered their mark in the United Kingdom it was not a case in which s.12 applied. The learned judge held that before the registration of the mark "Transfermatic" the applicants for rectification could have restrained the registered proprietors from using the word. The applicants for rectification succeeded.

For the reasons which I have given I consider that in the rectification proceedings in the present case the learned judge was fully justified in reaching his conclusions. It is conceded that if the appeal in the rectification proceedings is allowed and the mark no.603,390 expunged from the register there are no grounds on which it could be contended that the appeal in the opposition proceedings should not also be allowed.

I would allow the appeal and restore the judgment of Ungoed-Thomas, J.'

Lord Guest (at 823): 'The confusion which is likely to be caused arises principally from the phonetic similarity of "Bali" pronounced "Barley" and "Berlei" pronounced "Burly". The visual similarity of the two marks is negligible. The matter is very much a question of first impression and to a person who is not familiar with either word, which is the proper approach, I should have thought that there was a reasonable apprehension of confusion between the two words. There was the evidence of Mrs Lamb who made "test" orders and her evidence supports to some extent this first impression. Both the registrar and the learned judge found in favour of the appellants on this question and there was, in my view, ample material on which they could find such a likelihood of confusion.

The majority of the Court of Appeal (Lord Denning, MR and Salmon, LJ) fell into error, in my view, in placing too great reliance on the "trade evidence" led for Bali relating to the year 1964. This evidence, they said, negatived confusion. I do not so read it. These witnesses were mainly buyers or heads of departments concerned with the buying of brassieres and supervising their sale. In view of the method of trading spoken to by the witnesses, it appears unlikely that if there was confusion it would come to their notice. They were all well familiar with both "Bali" and "Berlei" marks and they would accordingly not be, in any event, likely to be confused themselves. Even if a customer was confused, it is not likely that if she was satisfied with the fit of the garment she would complain. Complaint would only arise from dissatisfaction. At any rate I do not regard this evidence as sufficiently strong to rebut the prima facie inference of confusion ensuing from the phonetic similarity and the rest of the evidence.'

COMMENT

Now, under the 1994 Act by section 64(1), an application for rectification may not be made in respect of a matter affecting the validity of the registration of a trade mark. However, a registration may be declared invalid by section 47 if it was registered in breach of section 3 or any provisions referred to in section 3. This includes a provision to the effect that a mark shall not be registered if its use is prohibited by law; section 3(4).

Compare the provisions for rectification and revocation (and invalidity) of trade marks under the 1938 Act and the 1994 Act. What are the differences?

Character Merchandising

The Trade Marks Act 1938 contained a provision to the effect that a mark could not be registered if it would tend to facilitate trafficking in the mark; section 28(6). This provision dated from a time when the buying public was not particularly knowledgeable and was in need of some protection. The whole basis of a trade mark was that it showed a connection in the course of trade between a trader and his goods. If a person allowed others to use his mark whilst exercising no control over the quality of the goods concerned this could be contrary to the public interest. Use by another was allowed in the 1938 Act under the registered user provisions but the proprietor of the trade mark had to exercise some control over the permitted use.

Character merchandising, where the owner of the rights in a typically fictional character licences the right to use it, is very common nowadays and of some commercial significance. The public is now well aware that the licensing of popular characters' names and representations is carried out and the public know that, in many cases, the owner of the rights in the character has little or no control over the quality of the goods concerned.

The Trade Marks Act 1994 was long overdue and it has brought trade mark law up to date and it has also simplified it and made it more effective. The provision against trafficking in trade marks has gone and the House of Lords' view of the provision in the case below has been vindicated.

Holly Hobbie Trade Mark [1984] FSR 199, House of Lords

The appellant was an American company which owned the rights in a drawing of a little girl in an old fashioned dress known as 'Holly Hobbie'. The drawing had been registered as a trade mark in the United States and the proprietor had licensed it to others to use in relation to greetings cards and other goods. The appellant applied to register the mark in the United Kingdom with the intention of licensing it to companies in the United Kingdom. It had also applied for registered user registrations and its registered user agreements contained provisions for quality control. However, there was no real trade connection between the appellant and the licensees. The application was refused.

Lord Bridge of Harwich (at 201): 'I find myself constrained to agree that this appeal must be dismissed, but I do so with undisguised reluctance.

There came a point in the argument when the question was posed by my noble and learned friend, Lord Diplock: "If this is not trafficking in trade marks, what is?" To that question, despite Mr Jacob's valiant efforts, no satisfactory answer has been forthcoming. Likewise, I can find no ground to quarrel with the meaning ascribed by my noble and learned friend, Lord Brightman, to the expression "trafficking in a trade mark" as "dealing in a trade mark primarily as a commodity in its own right and not primarily for the purpose of identifying or promoting merchandise in which the proprietor of the mark is interested." But these considerations lead to the conclusion that the phrase "trafficking in a trade mark" in section 28(6) of the Trade Marks Act 1938 and parallel expressions found in the report of the Goschen Committee (Cmnd. 4568 of 1934) which preceded the Act are precisely apt descriptions of the commercial activity now widely known as "character merchandising."

I can well understand that this activity, which I assume was little known, at all events on this side of the Atlantic, in the 1930s never entered the consideration of the legislators in 1938 nor of the members of the Goschen Committee on whose recommendations they acted. They were concerned that the public should not be hoodwinked and to this end set their faces against allowing the reputation for quality attaching to a trade mark to be used deceptively by a mere purchaser of the right to use the mark.

But character merchandising deceives nobody. Fictional characters capture the imagination, particularly of children, and can be very successfully exploited in the marketing of a wide range of goods. No one who buys a Mickey Mouse shirt supposes that the quality of the shirt owes anything to Walt Disney Productions.

Many marks will, of course, be protected by copyright. But when a mark consists simply in a name, it will be unprotected. It would seem from examples shown to your Lordships in the course of the argument that not a few marks in the character merchandising field have already been accepted by the registrar under section 28 before the present very large group of applications thrust the trafficking issue to the forefront. I do not pause to consider whether marks already registered which ought not to have been will be open to challenge. It will be bad enough, in my view, that the whole field of character merchandising will now be wide open to piracy. The protection, if any, of the original inventor of the character will lie in the uncertain remedy of a passing off action. This situation seems likely to generate a mass of difficult and expensive litigation which cannot be in the public interest.

In short, though I can find no escape from section 28(6) of the Act of 1938, I do not hesitate to express my opinion that it has become a complete anachronism and that the sooner it is repealed the better.'

Lord Brightman (at 206): 'There is no definition of trafficking in the Act. It is a word with several shades of meaning, ranging from ordinary reputable buying and selling to unlawful or improper commerce. When one seeks to discover the sense in which the word is used in a trade mark context, the clues are sparse. The starting point is, I think, *J. Batt and Co.'s Trade Marks* (1898) 15 RPC 262, decided at the close of the last century. In that case Romer J directed that certain marks should be expunged from the register on the ground that there had been no bona fide intention to use them. The learned judge said this (p.266):

> "... one cannot help seeing the evils that may result from allowing Trade Marks to be registered broadcast, if I may use the expression, there being no real intention of using them, or only an intention possibly of using them in respect of a few articles. The inconvenience it occasions, and the costs it occasions, are very large, and beyond that, I cannot help seeing that it would lead, in some cases, to absolute oppression, and to persons using the position they have got as registered owners of Trade Marks, which are not really bona fide Trade Marks, for the purpose of trafficking in them, and using them as a weapon to obtain money from subsequent persons who may want to use bona fide Trade Marks in respect of some classes, in respect of which they find these bogus Trade Marks registered."

There was an unsuccessful appeal to the Court of Appeal, and ultimately to your Lordships' House (1899) 16 RPC 11, where the Lord Chancellor, Lord Halsbury, picked up the same notion of trafficking when he said:

> "Here is a gentleman who, for seventeen years, has been in possession of a trade mark. There are a variety of circumstances which can be suggested - that it was needed for the purpose of trading under a particular form of mark, and so protecting the trade which he had either begun or intended to begin; or that he was disposed to register any number of trade marks for the purpose of vending them to others to whom they might appear as pleasant and attractive trade marks."

adding that there were:

> "circumstances which certainly would suggest he was a dealer in trade marks ..."

The law clearly did not recognise the entitlement of the owner of a trade mark to deal with it, like a patent, as a commodity in its own right. The same point was highlighted 15 years later in your Lordships' House in *Bowden Wire Ltd.* v *Bowden Brake Co. Ltd.* (1914) 31 RPC 385, where Lord Loreburn said this (p.392):

> "The object of the law is to preserve for a trader the reputation he has made for himself, not to help him in disposing of that reputation as of itself a marketable commodity, independent of his goodwill, to some other trader. If that were allowed, the public would be misled, because they might buy something in the

belief that it was the make of a man whose reputation they knew, whereas it was the make of someone else ... In this case the appellants parcelled out the right to use their trade mark as if they had been dealing with a patent."

The committee appointed in 1933 under the chairmanship of Viscount Goschen, to report whether any and if so what changes in the existing law and practice relating to trade marks was desirable, had this point in mind. The committee, reporting in the following year, recommended a relaxation of some of the restrictions on the assignment of trade marks, and in particular, a facility for a person to register a trade mark to be used only by others under the "registered user" provisions proposed by the committee. This recommendation was, however, subject to the proviso (p.8) that trafficking in registered trade marks is not thereby facilitated.

It was against this background that Parliament enacted section 8 of the Trade Marks (Amendment) Act 1937, which (with an immaterial exception became section 28 of the consolidating Trade Marks Act 1938).

The crucial question, then, is what is meant by trafficking in a trade mark, a tendency to facilitate which is fatal to an application by the proprietor and the proposed registered user? Or, to put the question more bluntly, if a commercial activity such as that falling to be considered by your Lordships in the instant case is not trafficking in a trade mark, what is?

It is fair to say that the *Batt* case, at first instance, is the only pre-1938 reported case discovered by counsel in which the word "trafficking" has been used judicially in a trade mark context.

Counsel for the appellants has deployed formidable arguments in support of the appellants' case that subsection (6) is not fatal to them. It is said, correctly, that a number of famous trade marks are to be found on the register in relation to classes of goods which have no conceivable connection with the goods responsible for the fame of the mark; the use of the name "Coca-Cola" on T-shirts, for example. But your Lordships do not know the circumstances in which such registrations were allowed, and in particular what weight may have been given to any advantage accruing to the licensor of a free advertisement for his products.

The appellants accept that in the case of the grant of a licence by the proprietor of a mark to another trader to use that mark on the licensee's own goods, there must always be some connection in the course of trade between the proprietor of the mark and the goods to which the mark is to be applied by the licensee, if registration is to be granted, but the appellants submit, this connection is sufficiently established if the proprietor controls or is able to control the nature and quality of the goods put on the market under the mark; see paragraph 13(b) and (c) of the appellants' case. Put shortly, quality control is said to be enough. "Trafficking," it is submitted, is confined to the sort of situation described by Romer J in *Batt,* where the mark is sought to be registered merely to enable the proprietor to use it as a means of extorting money from another who, on a later occasion, wishes to make bona fide use of the mark. No doubt in a number of cases, e.g. *BOSTITCH Trade Mark* [1963] RPC 183, a provision for quality control by the licensor over the goods of the licensee has been relevant in establishing a connection in the course of trade between the licensor and such goods. Such decisions are confined to their own factual circumstances, and I can discern no general rule that the mere ability to control quality is always to be sufficient to establish the required connection. In fact, the quality exercisable in the cases before us, so far as we have seen examples of the licence agreements, is slight. In the Oneida case it is confined to a right to inspect and to approve if the appellants so wish. In the General Mills (Chad Valley) case, the licensee must submit samples for written approval prior to use or sale.

For my part, I am quite prepared to accept that character merchandising, in the sense of the exploitation of the reputation of famous marks by making them available to a wide variety of products, has become a widespread trading practice on both sides of the Atlantic. It may well be that it is perfectly harmless and in most cases probably deceives nobody. These considerations do not, however, help to decide what Parliament intended by trafficking in trade marks or justify placing a gloss on the meaning to be attributed to what expression. I do not feel able to agree with the appellants' submission that the purpose of subsection (6) was confined to the prevention of trafficking in the *Batt* sense. Trafficking as stigmatised by Romer J in that case was in effect the stockpiling of Trade Marks, without any use or intended use in relation to the goods of the proprietor, with the intention of turning them to account when other traders wished to make use of the marks on their own goods. I see no reason for thinking that subsection (6) was solely directed against trafficking in that very narrow sense.

My Lords, although as a matter of ordinary English, trafficking in trade marks might mean the buying and selling of trade marks, it seems obvious that it is to have a more specialised meaning in a trade mark context. I have no quarrel with the definitions suggested by the assistant registrar and by Sir Denys Buckley, but perhaps one further attempt on my part may not be out of place. The courts have to grope for some means of delineating the forbidden territory, and different modes of expression may help to indicate boundaries which are not and cannot be marked out with absolute precision. To my mind, trafficking in a trade mark context conveys the notion of dealing in a trade mark primarily as a commodity in its own right and not primarily for the purpose of identifying or promoting merchandise in which the proprietor of the mark is interested. If there is no real trade connection between the proprietor of the mark and the licensee or his goods, there is room for the conclusion that the grant of the licence is a trafficking in the mark. It is a question of fact and degree in every case whether a sufficient trade connection exists. In my opinion, on the facts of these particular applications, the assistant registrar and the High Court were entitled to take the view that the registration of the licensee as a registered user, pursuant to section 28, would tend to facilitate trafficking in a trade mark.

I would dismiss this appeal.'

COMMENT

Does the ability to control quality suggest a connection in the course of trade? There is now no need to show a trade connection between the proprietor and the licensee and the 1994 Act contains comprehensive provisions for licensing and sub-licensing. Do you think that the loss of the guarantee that there is a trade connection between the proprietor and the goods will be detrimental to the buying public? Do the buying public associate particular marks with characteristics such as value for money, reliability and quality?

International Standards

Trade mark law has now been harmonised throughout the European Community. The TRIPs Agreement ought to further harmonise trade mark law on a wider scale and extracts from that Agreement relating to trade marks and indications of geographical origin are given below. Readers should note the similarities and differences compared to present United Kingdom trade mark law.

Agreement on Trade-Related Aspects of Intellectual Property Rights

Section 2. Trademarks

Article 15
Protectable subject matter

1. Any sign, or any combination of signs, capable of distinguishing the goods or services of one undertaking from those of other undertakings, shall be capable of constituting a trademark. Such signs, in particular words including personal names, letters, numerals, figurative elements and combinations of colours as well as any combination of such signs, shall be eligible for registration as trademarks. Where signs are not inherently capable of distinguishing the relevant goods or services, Members may make registrability depend on distinctiveness acquired through use. Members may require, as a condition of registration, that signs be visually perceptible.
2. Paragraph 1 shall not be understood to prevent a Member from denying registration of a trademark on other grounds, provided that they do not derogate from the provisions of the Paris Convention (1967).
3. Members may make registrability depend on use. However, actual use of a trademark shall not be a condition for filing an application for registration. An application shall not be refused solely on the ground that intended use has not taken place before the expiry of a period of three years from the date of application.
4. The nature of the goods or services to which a trademark is to be applied shall in no case form an obstacle to registration of the trademark.
5. Members shall publish each trademark either before it is registered or promptly after it is registered and shall afford a reasonable opportunity for petitions to cancel the registration. In addition, Members may afford an opportunity for the registration of a trademark to be opposed.

Article 16
Rights conferred

1. The owner of a registered trademark shall have the exclusive right to prevent all third parties not having the owner's consent from using in the course of trade

identical or similar signs for goods or services which are identical or similar to those in respect of which the trademark is registered where such use would result in a likelihood of confusion. In case of the use of an identical sign for identical goods or services, a likelihood of confusion shall be presumed. The rights described above shall not prejudice any existing prior rights, nor shall they affect the possibility of Members making rights available on the basis of use.

2. Article 6bis of the Paris Convention (1967) shall apply, *mutatis mutandis,* to services. In determining whether a trademark is well-known, Members shall take account of the knowledge of the trademark in the relevant sector of the public, including knowledge in the Member concerned which has been obtained as a result of the promotion of the trademark.

3. Article 6bis of the Paris Convention (1967) shall apply, *mutatis mutandis,* to goods or services which are not similar to those in respect of which a trademark is registered, provided that use of that trademark in relation to those goods or services would indicate a connection between those goods or services and the owner of the registered trademark and provided that the interests of the owner of the registered trademark are likely to be damaged by such use.

Article 17
Exceptions

Members may provide limited exceptions to the rights conferred by a trademark, such as fair use of descriptive terms, provided that such exceptions take account of the legitimate interests of the owner of the trademark and of third parties.

Article 18
Term of protection

Initial registration, and each renewal of registration, of a trademark shall be for a term of no less than seven years. The registration of a trademark shall be renewable indefinitely.

Article 19
Requirement of use

1. If use is required to maintain a registration, the registration may be cancelled only after an uninterrupted period of at least three years of non-use, unless valid reasons based on the existence of obstacles to such use are shown by the trademark owner. Circumstances arising independently of the will of the owner of the trademark which constitute an obstacle to the use of the trademark, such as import restrictions on or other government requirements for goods or services protected by the trademark, shall be recognised as valid reasons for non-use.

2. When subject to the control of its owner, use of a trademark by another person shall be recognised as use of the trademark for the purpose of maintaining the registration.

Article 20
Other requirements

The use of a trademark in the course of trade shall not be unjustifiably encumbered by special requirements, such as use with another trademark, use in a special form or use in a manner detrimental to its capability to distinguish the goods or services of one undertaking from those of other undertakings. This will not preclude a requirement prescribing the use of the trademark identifying the undertaking producing the goods or services along with, but without linking it to, the trademark distinguishing the specific goods or services in question of that undertaking.

Article 21
Licensing and assignment

Members may determine conditions on the licensing and assignment of trademarks, it being understood that the compulsory licensing of trademarks shall not be permitted and that the owner of a registered trademark shall have the right to assign the trademark with or without the transfer of the business to which the trademark belongs.

Section 3. Geographical indications

Article 22
Protection of geographical indications

1. Geographical indications are, for the purposes of this Agreement, indications which identify a good as originating in the territory of a Member, or a region or locality in that territory, where a given quality, reputation or other characteristic of the good is essentially attributable to its geographical origin.

2. In respect of geographical indications, Members shall provide the legal means for interested parties to prevent:

   (a) the use of any means in the designation or presentation of a good that indicates or suggests that the good in question originates in a geographical area other than the true place of origin in a manner which misleads the public as to the geographical origin of the good;

   (b) any use which constitutes an act of unfair competition within the meaning of Article 10bis of the Paris Convention (1967).

3. A Member shall, *ex officio* if its legislation so permits or at the request of an interested party, refuse or invalidate the registration of a trademark which contains or consists of a geographical indication with respect to goods not originating in the territory indicated, if use of the indication in the trademark for such goods in that Member is of such a nature as to mislead the public as to the true place of origin.

4. The protection under paragraphs 1, 2 and 3 shall be applicable against a geographical indication which, although literally true as to the territory, region or locality in which the goods originate, falsely represents to the public that the goods originate in another territory.

Article 23
Additional protection for geographical indications for wines and spirits

1. Each Member shall provide the legal means for interested parties to prevent use of a geographical indication identifying wines for wines not originating in the place indicated by the geographical indication in question or identifying spirits for spirits not originating in the place indicated by the geographical indication in question, even where the true origin of the goods is indicated or the geographical indication is used in translation or accompanied by expressions such as 'kind', 'type', 'style', 'imitation' or the like.[1]

2. The registration of a trademark for wines which contains or consists of a geographical indication identifying wines or for spirits which contains or consists of a geographical indication identifying spirits shall be refused or invalidated, *ex officio* if a Member's legislation so permits or at the request of an interested party, with respect to such wines or spirits not having this origin.

3. In the case of homonymous geographical indications for wines, protection shall be accorded to each indication, subject to the provisions of paragraph 4 of Article 22.   Each Member shall determine the practical conditions under which the homonymous indications in question will be differentiated from each other, taking into account the need to ensure equitable treatment of the producers concerned and that consumers are not misled.

4. In order to facilitate the protection of geographical indications for wines, negotiations shall be undertaken in the Council for TRIPs concerning the establishment of a multilateral system of notification and registration of geographical indications for wines eligible for protection in those Members participating in the system.

Article 24
International negotiations; exceptions

1. Members agree to enter into negotiations aimed at increasing the protection of individual geographical indications under Article 23. The provisions of paragraphs 4 through 8 below shall not be used by a Member to refuse to conduct negotiations or to conclude bilateral or multilateral agreements. In the context of such negotiations, Members shall be willing to consider the continued applicability of these provisions to individual geographical indications whose use was the subject of such negotiations.

2. The Council for TRIPs shall keep under review the application of the provisions of this Section; the first such review shall take place within two years of the entry into force of the WTO Agreement.   Any matter affecting the compliance with the obligations under these provisions may be drawn to the attention of the Council, which, at the request of a Member, shall consult with any Member or Members in respect of such matter in respect of which it has not been possible to find a satisfactory solution through bilateral or plurilateral consultations between the Members concerned.   The Council shall take such action as may be agreed to facilitate the operation and further the objectives of this Section.

3. In implementing this Section, a Member shall not diminish the protection of geographical indications that existed in that Member immediately prior to the date of entry into force of the WTO Agreement.

4. Nothing in this Section shall require a Member to prevent continued and similar use of a particular geographical indication of another Member identifying wines or spirits in connection with goods or services by any of its nationals or domiciliaries who have used that geographical indication in a continuous manner with regard to the same or related goods or services in the territory of that Member either (a) for at least 10 years preceding 15 April 1994 or (b) in good faith preceding that date.

5. Where a trademark has been applied for or registered in good faith, or where rights to a trademark have been acquired through use in good faith either:

    (a) before the date of application of these provisions in that Member as defined in Part VI; or

    (b) before the geographical indication is protected in its country of origin;

measures adopted to implement this Section shall not prejudice eligibility for or the validity of the registration of a trademark, or the right to use a trademark, on the basis that such a trademark is identical with, or similar to, a geographical indication.

6. Nothing in this Section shall require a Member to apply its provisions in respect of a geographical indication of any other Member with respect to goods or services for which the relevant indication is identical with the term customary in common language as the common name for such goods or services in the territory of that Member. Nothing in this Section shall require a Member to apply its provisions in respect of a geographical indication of any other Member with respect to products of the vine for which the relevant indication is identical with the customary name of a grape variety existing in the territory of that Member as of the date of entry into force of the WTO Agreement.

7. A Member may provide that any request made under this Section in connection with the use or registration of a trademark must be presented within five years after the adverse use of the protected indication has become generally known in that Member or after the date of registration of the trademark in that Member provided that the trademark has been published by that date, if such date is earlier than the date on which the adverse use became generally known in that Member, provided that the geographical indication is not used or registered in bad faith.

8. The provisions of this Section shall in no way prejudice the right of any person to use, in the course of trade, that person's name or the name of that person's predecessor in business, except where such name is used in such a manner as to mislead the public.

9. There shall be no obligation under this Agreement to protect geographical indications which are not or cease to be protected in their country of origin, or which have fallen into disuse in that country.

Notes:
[1] Notwithstanding the first sentence of Article 42, Members may, with respect to these obligations, instead provide for enforcement by administrative action.

Chapter 7

Passing off

Introduction

The United Kingdom has no general law of unfair competition and we must look to specific common law torts such as passing off and malicious falsehood to protect business goodwill, that intangible asset which may be of immeasurable value to a business organisation. The law of passing off has developed in a somewhat haphazard manner and, although the courts have occasionally demonstrated a willingness to adapt and extend passing off, some gaps remain in the armoury of protection of a trader's goodwill. Famous actors whose names or manner of speaking have been appropriated by traders promoting their own goods have discovered that passing off does not provide a remedy and character merchandisers have found this area of law particularly weak. This is not to say that the law of passing off is ineffective and sterile. It can, and does, give effective protection in many cases and, being common law, it is still capable of further development.

The early history of passing off is sketchy but shows the important role that equity played in the formative period.

Wadlow, C., *The Law of Passing Off* (London: Sweet & Maxwell, 1990) at p.8

'The history of passing off is sometimes presented in terms of a seamless progress in which a legal cause of action based on fraud arose by analogy with the tort of deceit and was superseded in equity as early as the mid 19th century by one based on the protection of property rights. The truth is certainly more complex but not easy to unravel. The central problem is that it is only very recently that passing off has more than occasionally been recognised as a body of law worthy of attention in its own right. Throughout the nineteenth century judges of every temperament agreed that passing off actions raised no questions of law, but only ones of fact. It is quite plausible that many early passing off cases went unreported for this very reason, as the earliest known cases of passing off being dealt with at law do not give the impression that any new legal principles were in issue. Later in the nineteenth century the problem arises in a different form. There are sufficient reported cases to work on, but little conscious analysis of how the law was developing.

The simplified view has several shortcomings and it may be convenient to summarise the development of passing off in terms of the three essential elements of misrepresentation, damage and goodwill, and the obsolete element of fraud.

First, if the reported cases are representative, then passing off was being restrained in equity before any legal cause of action was known. If so, the intervention of equity would have been as part of its original, rather than ancillary, jurisdiction. On this assumption, the parallel with deceit partly breaks down, and damage may consequently be less fundamental than in that instance or negligence, where damage is the gist of the action because both originated at law as actions on the case. In Lord Eldon's time it would have been a contradiction in terms to refer to a purely equitable tort or even to an equitable cause of action.

Equitable passing off, if it may be so called, arose from Lord Eldon's policy of granting injunctions against conduct he considered fraudulent irrespective of whether the plaintiff had a cause of action at law. In equity damage seems to have been taken for granted, and in any case a *quia timet* injunction could be granted against damage which was only prospective. With isolated exceptions, damage came to be ignored as a separate requirement in passing off, probably because ordinary passing off cases fell within a very narrow compass in which it would have been perverse to deny that damage would occur if the rest of the tort was made out. The importance of damage in its own right is a recent discovery.

There can be little doubt that fraud in one sense or another was essential to the very earliest cases, whether in equity or at law. However, the fact that the same word was used by judges in both courts is perhaps misleading. At law, there is little doubt that "fraud" was used in its everyday sense of intentional and dishonest deception. In equity the likelihood is that "fraud" was used in a very much wider sense which defies any definition except the circular one that equity would characterise as fraudulent, conduct which it was prepared to restrain. From at least as early as *Keech* v *Sandford* equity had used the word "fraud" in other contexts for behaviour which involved neither misrepresentation nor conscious dishonesty. As early as 1838 equity was expressly prepared to enjoin defendants who had acted honestly. That the common law continued to require fraud for the award of damages mattered little, because defendants were often insubstantial and the injunction was by far the more important remedy. As passing off came to be understood in terms of property, the importance of fraud waned and eventually disappeared altogether.

However, equity did not initially repudiate the need to prove *mala fides* in favour of a doctrine based on property rights, but rather for one to the effect that for the defendant to continue with deceptive behaviour after being put on notice was equivalent to fraud. When Lord Westbury interpreted the law in terms of property rights, he did so by identifying trade marks as the property protected. Goodwill was not identified as the basis of the action until the present century, and that was after a hiatus of over thirty years during which hardly any judge suggested passing off defended property rights at all.'

The Development of Passing Off

Originally, passing off was most appropriate in circumstances where one trader misrepresented his goods as being those of another trader. This is the classical form of passing off and its nature was described by the Lord Langdale, the Master of the Rolls in *Perry* v *Truefitt*.

Perry v *Truefitt* (1842) 6 Beav 66, Court of Chancery

The plaintiff obtained a secret recipe for a compound intended to encourage the growth of hair which he sold as 'Perry's Medicated Mexican Balm' claiming to have acquired a character and goodwill in the term 'Medicated Mexican Balm'. The defendant, some years later, commenced selling 'Truefitt's Medicated Mexican Balm'.

Lord Langdale MR (at 73): 'I think that the principle on which both the Courts of law and of Equity proceed, in granting relief and protection in cases of this sort, is very well understood. A man is not to sell his own goods under the pretence that they are the goods of another man; he cannot be permitted to practise such a deception, nor to use the means which contribute to that end. He cannot therefore be allowed to use names, marks, letters, or other *indicia,* by which he may induce purchasers to believe, that the goods which he is selling are the manufacture of another person. I own it does not seem to me that a man can acquire a property merely in a name or mark; but whether he has or not a property in the name or the mark, I have no doubt that another person has not a right to use that name or mark for the purposes of deception, and in order to attract to himself that course of trade, or that custom, which, without that improper act, would have flowed to the person who first used, or was alone in the habit of using the particular name or mark.

The case of *Millington* v *Fox* (3 M & Cr 338) seems to have gone to this length, that the deception need not be intentional, and that a man, though not intending any injury to another, shall not be allowed to adopt the marks by which the goods of another are designated, if the effect of adopting them would be to prejudice the trade of such other person. I am not aware that any previous case carried the principal [sic] to that extent.'

COMMENT

This case shows the early development of passing off in its traditional sense. That is, that one man is not allowed to pass off his goods as being the goods of another trader. However, Lord Langdale is not prepared to go so far as to recognise a property right in the name or mark; rather it is more a case of an equity against the defendant. Neither does there seem to be any requirement for the establishment of a goodwill associated with the name or mark. Although the defendant in this case had passed off his goods as those of the plaintiff, the Court refused to grant an injunction as the plaintiff had himself made a misrepresentation in his advertising. He had claimed that the composition was made from 'an original recipe of the learned Von Blumenbach' and that it had been presented to the plaintiff by 'a very near relation of that illustrious physiologist'. This was not true.

Before the law of trade marks was established as a separate entity by the Trade Marks Registration Act 1875, trade marks could only be protected by the law of passing off and the law's response to the dual problems of protecting trade marks and business goodwill was necessarily similar. In this way solutions to trade mark issues spilled over into the protection of goodwill and it is a trade mark case in which the existence of a property right was recognised.

The Leather Cloth Company Ltd. v The American Leather Cloth Company Ltd. (1863) 4 De G J & S 137, Court of Chancery

The plaintiff purchased from an American company a business in West Ham that made leather cloth using a patented process of tanning. The English patent and the full power to use the trade marks previously used in England by the American company were assigned to the plaintiff. The defendant later made and sold leather cloth, using a trade mark which resembled that used by the plaintiff.

Lord Westbury, Lord Chancellor (at 139): 'In equity, the right to give relief to the trader whose trade has been injured by the piracy appears to have been originally assumed by reason of the inadequacy of the remedy at law, and the necessity of protecting property of this description by injunction. But although the jurisdiction is now well settled, there is still current in several recent cases language which seems to me to give an inaccurate statement of the true ground on which it rests. In *Croft* v *Day* (7 Beav 88), and *Perry* v *Truefitt* (6 Beav 73), the late Lord Langdale is reported to have used words which place the jurisdiction of this Court to grant relief in case the piracy of trade marks entirely on the ground of the fraud that is committed when one man sells his own goods as the goods of another. The words of the learned Judge are, "I own it does not seem to me that a man can acquire a property merely in a name or mark," and in like manner the learned Vice-Chancellor, whose decision I am now reviewing, is reported to have said, "All these cases of trade mark turn not upon a question of property, but upon this, whether the act of the Defendant is such as to hold out his goods as the goods of the Plaintiff" (1 H & M 287). But with great respect this is hardly an accurate statement: for, first, the goods of one man may be sold as the goods of another without giving to that other person a right to complain, unless he sustains, or is likely to sustain, from the wrongful act some pecuniary loss or damage ...

If the Defendant adopts a mark in ignorance of the Plaintiff's exclusive right to it, and without knowing that the symbols or words so adopted and used are already current as a trade mark in the market, his acts, though innocently done, will be a sufficient ground for the interference of this Court ...

It is indeed true that, unless the mark used by the Defendant be applied by him to the same kind of goods as the goods of the Plaintiff, and be in itself such, that it may be, and is, mistaken in the market for the trade mark of the Plaintiff, the Court will not interfere, because there is no invasion of the Plaintiff's right: and thus the mistake of buyers in the market under which they in fact take the Defendant's goods as the goods of the Plaintiff, that is to say, imposition on the public, becomes the test of the property in the trade mark having been invaded and injured, and not the ground on which the Court rests its jurisdiction.

The representation which the Defendant is supposed to make, that his goods are the goods of another person, is not actually made otherwise than by his appropriating and using the trade mark which such other person has an exclusive right to use in connection with the sale of some commodity; and if the Plaintiff has an exclusive right so to use any particular mark or symbol, it becomes his property for the purposes of such application, and the act of the Defendant is a violation of such right of property, corresponding with the piracy of copyright or the infringement of the patent. I cannot therefore assent to the *dictum* that there is no property in a trade mark.

It is correct to say that there is no exclusive ownership of the symbols which constitute a trade mark apart from the use or application of them; but the word "trade mark" is the designation of these marks or symbols as and when applied to a vendible commodity, and the exclusive right to make such user or application is rightly called property. The true principle therefore would seem to be, that the jurisdiction of the Court in the protection given to trade marks rests upon property, and that the Court interferes by injunction, because that is the only mode by which property of this description can be effectually protected.'

COMMENT

Whilst clarifying the proprietary nature of a trade mark, the Lord Chancellor dismissed the Plaintiff's case because it had not come to the court with clean hands. The trade mark itself contained a number of misrepresentations as to the maker of the cloth (supposedly JR & CP Crockett, the original inventors and manufacturers) and the nature of the cloth (some untanned goods were described as having been tanned). In the words of the Lord Chancellor, the Plaintiff's case 'is condemned by the principles to which they appeal'. Apart from recognising a property right in a trade mark, the requirement for fraud is firmly renounced. The importance of a misrepresentation (express or implied) made by the defendant became clear and this permitted the law of passing off to free itself from the narrow confines of its traditional nature; that is, where one trader passes his goods off as those of another trader. In the case below, the defendant did not misrepresent the origin of the goods he advertised, rather it was their quality. Prior to that case, it had also been accepted that the property resided in the goodwill rather than a trade name or mark *simpliciter*.

Spalding v *A W Gamage Ltd.* (1915) 84 LJ Ch 449, House of Lords

The Plaintiff supplied footballs to both the trade and the public. For a number of years, the Plaintiff had described its footballs as 'Orb' footballs. It brought out an improved version that was a sewn football rather than the old moulded variety and advertised it using the phrase 'Improved Sewn Orb'. A quantity of the old moulded footballs (having been considered unsatisfactory) were sold to a waste rubber merchant who resold them to the defendant. The defendant advertised these as being the 'Improved Orb' and 'Celebrated Orb' football. There were statements which would lead a reader to conclude that the defendant was offering for sale at 4s 9d. a football sold by the Plaintiff at 10s 6d. The House of Lords considered that the defendant's advertising was calculated to deceive.

Lord Parker (at 449): 'The action in which this appeal is brought is what is known as a passing off action, and having regard to the arguments which have been addressed to your Lordships I think it well to say a few words as to the principle on which such actions are founded. This principle is stated by Lord Justice Turner in *Burgess* v *Burgess* [1853] (22 LJ Ch 675; 3 De GM & G 896), and by Lord Halsbury in *Reddaway* v *Banham & Co.* [1896] (65 LJ QB 381; [1896] AC 199), in the proposition that nobody has any right to represent his goods as the goods of somebody else. It is also sometimes stated in the proposition that nobody has the right to pass off his goods as the goods of somebody else. I prefer the former statement, for, whatever doubts may be suggested in the earlier authorities, it has long been settled that actual passing off of the defendant's goods for the plaintiff's need not be proved as a condition precedent to relief in equity either by way of an injunction or an enquiry as to profits or damages - *Edelsten* v *Edelsten* [1863] (1 De G J & S 185) and *Iron-Ox Remedy Co.* v *Co-operative Wholesale Society* [1907] (24 Rep Pat Cas 425). Nor need the representation be made fraudulently. It is enough that it has in fact been made, whether fraudulently or otherwise, and that damages may probably ensue, though the complete innocence of the party making it may be a reason for limiting the account of profits to the period subsequent to the date at which he becomes aware of the true facts. The representation is in fact treated as the invasion of a right giving rise at any rate to nominal damages, the enquiry being granted at the plaintiff's risk if he might probably have suffered more than nominal damages.

The view taken by the common law courts was somewhat different. The plaintiff's remedy is said to have been in the nature of an action for deceit, but it only resembled the action for deceit in the fact that the misrepresentation relied on must have been made fraudulently. In all other respects it differed from an action for deceit. For example, the plaintiff was not the party deceived, and, even if it were necessary to prove that someone had been deceived, nominal damages could be obtained though no actual damage was proved. Thus in *Blofield* v *Payne* [1833] (2 LJ KB 68; 4 B & Ad 410) the defendants had sold their own hones in the plaintiff's wrappers as and for the plaintiff's, but there was no evidence that any purchasers had been actually deceived. Further, though special damage was alleged in the declaration, no actual damage was proved. On motion for a nonsuit it was held in the King's Bench that the plaintiff was entitled to nominal damages. The action was, in fact, treated as one founded on the invasion of a right.

The proposition that no-one has a right to represent his goods as the goods of somebody else must, I think, as has been assumed in this case, involve as a corollary the further proposition that no-one who has in his hands the goods of another of a particular class or quality has a right to represent these goods to be the goods of that other of a different quality or belonging to a different class. Further, it is doubtful whether the principle has any application except as between rival traders. Possibly, therefore, the principle ought to be re-stated as follows: "Trader A cannot, without infringing the rights of trader B, represent goods which are not B's goods or B's goods of a particular class or quality to be B's goods or B's goods of that particular class or quality." The wrong for which relief is sought in a passing off action consists in every case of a representation of this nature.

The basis of a passing off action being a false representation by the defendant, it must be proved in each case as a fact that the false representation was made. It may, of course, have been made in express words, but cases of express misrepresentation of this sort are rare. The more common case is where the representation is implied in the use or imitation of a mark, trade name, or get-up with which the goods of another are associated in the minds of the public, or of a particular class of the public. In such cases the point to be decided is whether, having regard to all the circumstances of the case, the use by the defendant in connection with the goods of the mark, name, or get-up in question impliedly represents such goods to be the goods of the plaintiff or the goods of the plaintiff of a particular class or quality, or, as it is sometimes put, whether the defendant's use of such mark, name, or get-up is calculated to deceive. It would, however, be impossible to enumerate or classify all the possible ways in which a man may make the false representation relied on.

There appears to be considerable diversity of opinion as to the nature of the right, the invasion of which is the subject of what are known as passing off actions. The more general opinion appears to be that the right is a right of property. This view naturally demands an answer to the question, Property in what? Some authorities say, property in the mark, name, or get-up improperly used by the defendant. Others say, property in the business or goodwill likely to be injured by the misrepresentation. Lord Herschell, in *Reddaway* v *Banham & Co.* (65 LJ QB 381; [1896] AC 199) expressly dissents from the former view, and if the right invaded is a right of property at all, there are, I think, strong reasons for preferring the latter view. In the first place, cases of misrepresentation by the use of a mark, name, or get-up do not exhaust all possible cases of misrepresentation. If A says falsely, "These goods which I am selling are B's Goods," there is no mark, name, or get-up infringed unless it be B's name; and if he says falsely, "These are B's goods of a particular quality," where the goods are in fact B's goods, there is no name which is infringed at all. Further, it is extremely difficult to see how a man can be said to have property in descriptive words, such as "camel hair" in the case of *Reddaway* v *Banham & Co.* (65 LJ QB 381; [1896] AC 199), where every trader is entitled to use the words, provided only he uses them in such a way as not to be calculated to deceive. Even in the case of what are sometimes referred to as common law trade marks, the property, if any, of the so-called owner is in its nature transitory, and only exists so long as the mark is distinctive of his own goods in the eyes of the public or a class of the public. Indeed, the necessity of proving this distinctiveness in each case as a step in the proof of the false representation relied on was one of the evils sought to be remedied by the Trade Marks Act, 1875, which confers a real right of property on the owner of a registered mark.'

COMMENT

It was held that the defendant had made a misrepresentation as to the quality of the footballs it was selling and that this gave rise to a strong probability of actual damage to the plaintiffs. Because the misrepresentation was calculated to deceive, this being a question of law not fact, the plaintiff had a *prima facie* right to relief. Would any other form of intellectual property law as it has now developed provide a remedy in similar cases?

In concurring with Lord Parker's judgment, Lord Parmoor said that 'no person has a right to offer for sale, or sell, goods of another trader of an inferior or different class, under conditions calculated to represent such goods as goods of the same trader of a superior and distinctive class'. This would be an actionable wrong irrespective of motive or fraud and the plaintiff would be entitled to an injunction and, if necessary, damages. Thus, the requirement that the misrepresentation must be 'calculated to deceive' used again by Lord Diplock in *Erven Warnink* (see below) is itself deceptive and a deliberate or conscious attempt to deceive on the part of the defendant is not a pre-requisite to a passing off action. However, in other parts of his judgment in that case, Lord Diplock accepts that passing off need not be deliberate.

Undoubtedly, the leading case on the law of passing off is *Erven Warnink* v *Townend* and of particular merit are the judgments of Lords Diplock and Fraser. In addition to its status, this case is noteworthy in that it recognised a widened version of passing off, known as extended passing off, first applied in the 'Spanish Champagne' case.

Erven Warnink BV v *J Townend & Sons (Hull) Ltd.* **[1979] AC 731, House of Lords**

The plaintiffs had, in common with other Dutch companies, manufactured an alcoholic drink known as 'Advocaat' which was made from brandewijn, egg yolks and sugar. It was exported from Holland to England and enjoyed a substantial reputation. The defendant produced a drink called 'Keeling's Old English Advocaat' which was made from Cyprus sherry and dried egg powder. It captured a large share of the plaintiff's market in England.

Lord Diplock (at 739): 'My Lords, this is an action for "passing off," not in its classic form of a trader representing his own goods as the goods of somebody else, but in an extended form first recognised and applied by Danckwerts J in the champagne case (*J. Bollinger* v *Costa Brava Wine Co. Ltd.* [1960] Ch 262). The *ratio decidendi* of that case was subsequently adopted as correct by Cross J in the sherry case (*Vine Products Ltd.* v *Mackenzie & Co. Ltd.* [1969] RPC 1) and by Foster J in the Scotch whisky case (*John Walker & Sons Ltd.* v *Henry Ost & Co. Ltd.* [1970] 1 WLR 917).

 The facts of the instant case as found by Goulding J after a protracted trial make it, in my view, impossible to draw a rational distinction between the instant case and the champagne case which could reconcile acceptance of the reasoning in the champagne case with dismissal of the plaintiffs' action in the instant case. This was also the view of Goulding J; but his judgment in the plaintiffs' favour was reversed by the Court of Appeal (Buckley and Goff LJJ and Sir David Cairns) who, while expressing approval of the champagne and sherry cases, though with reservations on the Scotch whisky case, nevertheless felt able to discern a relevant distinction between those cases and the instant case. Not quite the same distinction was drawn by Buckley LJ and Goff LJ but, with respect, I think that both were mistaken: and if this be so, the question of law for your Lordships is whether this House should give the seal of its approval to the extended concept of the cause of action for passing off that was applied in the champagne, sherry and Scotch whisky cases. This question is essentially one of legal policy ...

 True it is that it could not be shown that any purchaser of "Keeling's Old English Advocaat" supposed or would be likely to suppose it to be goods supplied by Warnink or to be Dutch advocaat of any make. So Warnink had no cause of action for passing off in its classic form. Nevertheless, the learned judge was satisfied: (1) that the name "advocaat" was understood by the public in England to denote a distinct and recognisable species of beverage; (2) that Warnink's product is genuinely indicated by that name and has gained reputation and goodwill under it; (3) that Keeling's product has no natural association with the word "advocaat"; it is an egg and wine drink properly described as an "egg flip," whereas advocaat is an egg and spirit drink; these are different beverages and known as different to the public; (4) that members of the public believe and have been deliberately induced by

Keeling to believe that in buying their "Old English Advocaat" they are in fact buying advocaat; (5) that Keeling's deception of the public has caused and, unless prevented, will continue to cause, damage to Warnink in the trade and the goodwill of their business both directly in the loss of sale and indirectly in the debasement of the reputation attaching to the name "advocaat" if it is permitted to be used of alcoholic egg drinks generally and not confined to those that are spirit based.

These findings, he considered, brought the case within the principle of law laid down in the champagne case by Danckwerts J and applied in the sherry and Scotch whisky cases. He granted Warnink an injunction restraining Keeling from selling or distributing under the name or description "advocaat" any product which does not basically consist of eggs and spirit without any admixture of wine.

My Lords, these findings of fact were accepted by the Court of Appeal and have not been challenged in your Lordships' House. They seem to me to disclose a case of unfair, not to say dishonest, trading of a kind for which a rational system of law ought to provide a remedy to other traders whose business or goodwill is injured by it.

Unfair trading as a wrong actionable at the suit of other traders who thereby suffer loss of business or goodwill may take a variety of forms, to some of which separate labels have become attached in English law. Conspiracy to injure a person in his trade or business is one, slander of goods another, but most protean is that which is generally and nowadays, perhaps misleadingly, described as "passing off." The forms that unfair trading takes will alter with the ways in which trade is carried on and business reputation and goodwill acquired. Emerson's maker of the better mousetrap if secluded in his house built in the woods would today be unlikely to find a path beaten to his door in the absence of a costly advertising campaign to acquaint the public with the excellence of his wares ...

My Lords, *A G Spalding & Bros.* v *A W Gamage Ltd.,* 84 LJ Ch 449 and the later cases make it possible to identify five characteristics which must be present in order to create a valid cause of action for passing off: (1) a misrepresentation (2) made by a trader in the course of trade, (3) to prospective customers of his or ultimate consumers of goods or services supplied by him, (4) which is calculated to injure the business or goodwill of another trader (in the sense that this is a reasonably foreseeable consequence) and (5) which causes actual damage to a business or goodwill of the trader by whom the action is brought or (in a *quia timet* action) will probably do so.

In seeking to formulate general propositions of English law, however, one must be particularly careful to beware of the logical fallacy of the undistributed middle. It does not follow that because all passing off actions can be shown to present these characteristics, all factual situations which present these characteristics give rise to a cause of action for passing off. True it is that their presence indicates what a moral code would censure as dishonest trading, based as it is upon deception of customers and consumers of a trader's wares but in an economic system which has relied on competition to keep down prices and to improve products there may be practical reasons why it should have been the policy of the common law not to run the risk of hampering competition by providing civil remedies to every one competing in the market who has suffered damage to his business or goodwill in consequence of inaccurate statements of whatever kind that may be made by rival traders about their own wares. The market in which the action for passing off originated was no place for the mealy mouthed; advertisements are not on affidavit; exaggerated claims by a trader about the quality of his wares, assertions that they are better than those of his rivals even though he knows this to be untrue, have been permitted by the common law as venial "puffing" which gives no cause of action to a competitor even though he can show that he has suffered actual damage in his business as a result.

Parliament, however, beginning in the 19th century has progressively intervened in the interests of consumers to impose on traders a higher standard of commercial candour than the legal maxim *caveat emptor* calls for, by prohibiting under penal sanctions misleading descriptions of the character or quality of goods; but since the class of persons for whose protection the Merchandise Marks Acts 1887 to 1953 and even more rigorous later statutes are designed, are not competing traders but those consumers who are likely to be deceived, the Acts do not themselves give rise to any civil action for breach of statutory duty on the part of a competing trader even though he sustains actual damage as a result: *Cutler* v *Wandsworth Stadium Ltd.* [1949] AC 398 and see *London Armoury Co. Ltd.* v *Ever Ready Co. (Great Britain) Ltd.* [1941] 1 KB 742. Nevertheless the increasing recognition by Parliament of the need for more rigorous standards of commercial honesty is a factor which should not be overlooked by a judge confronted by the choice whether or not to extend by analogy to circumstances in which it has not previously been applied a principle which has been applied in previous cases where the circumstances although different had some features in common with those of the case which he has to decide. Where over a period of years there can be discerned a steady trend in legislation which reflects the view of successive Parliaments as to what the public interest demands in a particular field of law, development of the common law in that part of the same field which has been left to it ought to proceed upon a parallel rather than a diverging course.

The champagne case came before Danckwerts J in two stages: the first, *J Bollinger* v *Costa Brava Wine Co. Ltd.* [1960] Ch 262 on a preliminary point of law, the second *J Bollinger* v *Costa Brava Wine Co. Ltd. (No.2)* [1961] 1 WLR 277 on the trial of the action. The assumptions of fact on which the legal argument at the first stage was based were stated by the judge to be [1960] Ch 262, 273:

"... (1) The plaintiffs carry on business in a geographical area in France known as Champagne; (2) the plaintiffs' wine is produced in Champagne and from grapes grown in Champagne; (3) the plaintiffs' wine has been known in the trade for a long time as 'champagne' with a high reputation; (4) members of the public or in the trade ordering or seeing wine advertised as 'champagne' would expect to get wine produced in Champagne from grapes grown there; and (5) the defendants are producing a wine not produced in that geographical area and are selling it under the name of 'Spanish champagne'."

These findings disclose a factual situation (assuming that damage was thereby caused to the plaintiff's business) which contains each of the five characteristics which I have suggested must be present in order to create a valid cause of action for passing off. The features that distinguished it from all previous cases were (a) that the element in the goodwill of each of the individual plaintiffs that was represented by his ability to use without deception (in addition to his individual house mark) the word "champagne" to distinguish his wines from sparkling wines not made by the champenois process from grapes produced in the Champagne district of France, was not exclusive to himself but was shared with every other shipper of sparkling wine to England whose wines could satisfy the same condition and (b) that the class of traders entitled to a proprietary right in "the attractive force that brings in custom" represented by the ability without deception to call one's wines "champagne" was capable of continuing expansion, since it might be joined by any future shipper of wine who was able to satisfy that condition.

My Lords, in the champagne case the class of traders between whom the goodwill attaching to the ability to use the word "champagne" as descriptive of their wines was a large one, 150 at least and probably considerably more whereas in the previous English cases of shared goodwill the number of traders between whom the goodwill protected by a passing off action was shared had been two, although in the United States in 1898 there had been a case, *Pillsbury-Washburn Flour Mills Co.* v *Eagle* (1898) 86 Fed R 608, in which the successful complainants to the number of seven established their several proprietary rights in the goodwill attaching to the use of a particular geographical description to distinguish their wares from those of other manufacturers.

It seems to me, however, as it seemed to Danckwerts J, that the principle must be the same whether the class of which each member is severally entitled to the goodwill which attaches to a particular term as descriptive of his goods, is large or small. The larger it is the broader must be the range and quality of products to which the descriptive term used by the members of the class has been applied, and the more difficult it must be to show that the term has acquired a public reputation and goodwill as denoting a product endowed with recognisable qualities which distinguish it from others of inferior reputation that compete with it in the same market. The larger the class the more difficult it must also be for an individual member of it to show that the goodwill of his own business has sustained more than minimal damage as a result of deceptive use by another trader of the widely-shared descriptive term. As respects subsequent additions to the class, mere entry into the market would not give any right of action for passing off; the new entrant must have himself used the descriptive term long enough on the market in connection with his own goods and have traded successfully enough to have built up a goodwill for his business.

For these reasons the familiar argument that to extend the ambit of an actionable wrong beyond that to which effect has demonstrably been given in the previous cases would open the floodgates or, more ominously, a Pandora's box of litigation leaves me unmoved when it is sought to be applied to the actionable wrong of passing off.

I would hold the champagne case [1960] Ch 262 to have been rightly decided and in doing so would adopt the words of Danckwerts J where he said, at pp. 283-284:

"There seems to be no reason why such licence [sc. to do a deliberate act which causes damage to the property of another person] should be given to a person, competing in trade, who seeks to attach to his product a name or description with which it has no natural association so as to make use of the reputation and goodwill which has been gained by a product genuinely indicated by the name or description. In my view, it ought not to matter that the persons truly entitled to describe their goods by the name and description are a class producing goods in a certain locality, and not merely one individual. The description is part of their goodwill and a right of property. I do not believe that the law of passing off, which arose to prevent unfair trading, is so limited in scope ..."

My Lords, all the five characteristics that I have earlier suggested must be present to create a valid cause of action in passing off today were present in the instant case. Prima facie as the law stands today, I think the presence of those characteristics is enough, unless there is also present in the case some exceptional feature which justifies, on grounds of public policy, withholding from a person who has suffered injury in consequence of the deception practised on prospective customers or consumers of his product a remedy in law against the deceiver. On the facts found by the judge, and I stress their importance, I can find no such exceptional feature in the instant case.

I would allow this appeal and restore the injunction granted by Goulding J.'

Lord Fraser (at 754): 'In the champagne case, as in this case, the class, membership of which gives the plaintiff the right to sue, consists of all those who sell the genuine product in England under the distinctive name by which it is known here, and who together are the owners of the goodwill or reputation attaching to the name in England. In that case, as in this, membership of the class may vary from time to time. An existing trader who discontinues sales of the genuine product in England would cease to belong to the class and the class would thereby be reduced. Conversely, a new trader who begins to sell the genuine product would become a member of the class when he had become well enough established to have acquired a substantial right of property in the goodwill attaching to the name. In either case the class is open to new members provided they qualify themselves by acquiring the necessary goodwill, which they can do by selling, in the one case under the name "Champagne" a wine made in Champagne by the correct process from grapes grown there, and in the other case under the name "advocaat" a liqueur made according to the Dutch recipe. But although membership of the class can change, it must be definite and ascertainable at any particular time if it is to carry a right to sue an action for passing off. In the present case, as in the champagne case, the class is definite and ascertainable.

In the Court of Appeal [1978] FSR 473 Buckley LJ decided against the appellants mainly on the ground that he considered the name "advocaat" to be purely descriptive and not distinctive, in contrast to champagne which he considered to be distinctive. He said (rightly in my opinion) at p. 482 that "at least some measure of distinctiveness is essential for the trade name or description to be capable of giving rise to a claim to relief against passing off." But in my opinion the learned Lord Justice did not give sufficient weight to the findings of the judge which I have already quoted, and especially to his finding ([1978] FSR 1, 21) that advocaat "was a distinct and recognisable species of beverage." Goff LJ seems to me to have made what I regard, with all respect, as the same error, when he said [1978] FSR 473, 496 that it had not been found that "there was something to entitle the [appellant] to say that 'advocaat' ... distinguishes their product or the products of some limited class from all other beverages of the like character ...". I do not think that the terms "descriptive" and "distinctive," as applied to names of products, are mutually exclusive. Names which begin by being descriptive, such as Carrara marble and Vichy water and, of course, Champagne, may in the course of time become distinctive as well as descriptive. The name "advocaat" although never descriptive, has, as Goulding J found, become distinctive ... In my opinion [the meaning of the name] in countries other than England is immaterial because what the court is concerned to do is to protect the plaintiff's property in the goodwill attaching to the name in England and it has nothing to do with the reputation or meaning of the name elsewhere.

For these reasons I do not consider that the champagne case can be distinguished from the present case. The question therefore remains whether the champagne case itself was rightly decided or not. As I have already said, I think that the case went rather further than the previous decisions in passing off cases. I would respectfully adopt the words of traditional legal theory used by Cross J in the sherry case *Vine Products Ltd.* v *Mackenzie & Co. Ltd.* [1969] RPC 1, 23, where he said that the champagne case "uncovered a piece of common law or equity which had till then escaped notice ...". But the decision is in my opinion soundly based on the principle underlying the earlier passing off actions, which I take to be that the plaintiff is entitled to protect his right of property in the goodwill attached to a name which is distinctive of a product or class of products sold by him in the course of his business. It is essential for the plaintiff in a passing off action to show at least the following facts:- (1) that his business consists of, or includes, selling in England a class of goods to which the particular trade name applies; (2) that the class of goods is clearly defined, and that in the minds of the public, or a section of the public, in England, the trade name distinguishes that class from other similar goods; (3) that because of the reputation of the goods, there is goodwill attached to the name; (4) that he, the plaintiff, as a member of the class of those who sell the goods, is the owner of goodwill in England which is of substantial value; (5) that he has suffered, or is really likely to suffer, substantial damage to his property in the goodwill by reason of the defendants selling goods which are falsely described by the trade name to which the goodwill is attached. Provided these conditions are satisfied, as they are in the present case, I consider that the Plaintiff is entitled to protect himself by a passing off action. The argument relied on by the respondents was to the effect that, unless there has been a passing off of the defendant's goods as the plaintiff's goods, there can be no direct injury to the plaintiff entitling him to raise an action for passing off. Any other kind of unfair trading may, it was said, render the trader liable to criminal or civil proceedings under Acts such as the Food and Drugs Act 1955 or the Trade Descriptions Act 1968, or to proceedings at common law by the Attorney-General in the public interest either for criminal penalties or for an injunction, but does not amount to a tort against the party whose goodwill is damaged by the unfair competition of goods which are falsely described. If that were the law it would, I think, be unfortunate. Of course, any established trader is liable to have his goodwill damaged by fair competition, and it is not every falsehood told by a competitor that will give him a right of action. But where the falsehood is a misrepresentation that the competitor's goods are goods of definite class with a valuable reputation, and where the misrepresentation is likely to cause damage to established traders who own goodwill in relation to that class of goods, business morality seems to require that they should be entitled to protect their goodwill. The name of the tort committed by the party making the misrepresentation is not important, but in my opinion the tort is the same in kind as that which has hitherto been known as passing off.'

COMMENT

Compare and contrast the essential elements of passing off as identified by Lords Diplock and Fraser. Which do you prefer? Are either or both flawed in any way?

It is no longer necessary for one trader to pass off his goods as those of another trader and it is sufficient if the goodwill of a trader or group of traders will be harmed, for example, by being debased or eroded. The consequence of this is that a plaintiff, in such a case, does not have to show a direct or immediate loss or downturn in sales as a result of the defendant's misrepresentation. This has been confirmed by the Court of Appeal in *Taittinger S.A.* v *Allbev Ltd.* [1993] FSR 641 (see later) where the defendant was selling a non-alcoholic beverage as 'Elderflower Champagne'. Sold at £2.45 a bottle, it would be highly unlikely that anyone would be deceived into thinking that it was champagne but the danger of erosion of the goodwill residing in the name champagne was utmost in the Court's mind. Another interesting aspect of *Erven Warnink*, confirming the earlier cases on champagne, Scotch whisky and sherry, is that the goodwill can be shared amongst a number of traders.

It is not necessary for the public to know the identity of the trader having the goodwill, only that it belongs to someone and, if the defendant's goods are thought to be made by that trader, that will be sufficient for a passing off action. This is so, even if the public realise the defendant's goods are not the same as those of the plaintiff, providing the public think they originated from the same source, as the case below demonstrates.

United Biscuits (UK) Ltd. v Asda Stores Ltd. [1997] RPC 513, Chancery Division

The plaintiff made the famous 'Penguin' chocolate-coated biscuits and owned a number of trade marks including drawings of penguins and the word mark 'PENGUIN'. The wrappers were predominately red with a yellow band and a picture of a penguin and the word 'PENGUIN'.

The defendant was a supermarket chain which started selling a similar biscuit called 'PUFFIN', designed to compete with 'PENGUIN' biscuits. The appearance of the 'PUFFIN' wrappers were similar, being red with a cartoon picture of a puffin and the word 'PUFFIN'. 'PUFFIN' bars were sold by the defendant alongside 'PENGUIN' bars.

The plaintiff claimed that the defendant was guilty of passing off and was infringing the plaintiff's trade marks.

Robert Walker J (at 519): 'I have mentioned that since 1976 at least one picture of a penguin has appeared on the packaging of Penguins. I must try to summarise their general appearance and relate it to other registered trade marks which I have yet to mention. But first I should perhaps briefly record my judicial notice of relevant ornithology. Penguins are seabirds of the family of spheniscidae. There are many different varieties of different sizes but they all live in the southern hemisphere, on or close to Antarctica. Relatively few people have therefore seen them in their natural habitat but most people are familiar with them from wildlife films (and television advertisements for Penguins). Their outstanding characteristics are that they cannot fly at all, their progress on land (normally ice) appears to be ungainly, and they are most at home in the sea, where they propel their streamlined bodies with both sets of flippers, while insulated against the cold by ample layers of fat. They are more or less black with white fronts, though their plumage contains some fairly vivid yellow, especially around the neck.

A puffin (and I am here anticipating the next section of this judgment) is a seabird whose scientific name is *fratercula arctia*. It is also sometimes called a sea parrot because of its large, multi-coloured beak which is its most distinctive feature. It is more or less black but with a white front and a large and distinctive white patch around its eye, a little reminiscent of a clown. It is about the size of a pigeon; certainly a good deal smaller than normal varieties of penguin. It lives on the Atlantic coast of north-west Europe, from Brittany to North Cape, and extending to Iceland. It can fly, and has to do so to get to and from its nesting-places on cliffs and rocks. (I should perhaps add that I doubt whether the average member of the general public knows much more about the puffin than that it is a seabird with a multi-coloured beak; my own knowledge has been supplemented considerably from a handbook which counsel showed me.) ...

The products compared.
I have inspected, closely and repeatedly, the outer packaging of the three main current Penguin varieties and the four Puffin varieties. I have seen examples of individually wrapped biscuits from inside the products. I have also seen examples of Take a Break packaging and the packaging on other comparable "own brand" countline products made for (among others) Safeway, Sainsbury, Somerfield and Tesco. Apart from the name and the picture of a bird (which is of course a very important exception) some other "own brand" products (especially Tesco's and Iceland's) are more similar to Penguins because of their red and yellow colouring.

In the event of an appeal the same visual inspection will be open to higher courts. I shall not therefore attempt any minute verbal description and comparison of the ordinary Penguin packaging and the packaging of its Asda milk chocolate competitor, the red-packaged Puffin. It is sufficient to say that they are of the same size and shape and appear to use comparable though not identical materials (the Puffin packaging is semi-transparent). Red is the dominant colour on both but the yellow vignette on the Penguin has no counterpart on the Puffin, and the yellow gives particular prominence to the apparently black (but actually very dark blue), shadowed in white, of PENGUIN. PUFFIN is also edged in white and makes a similar, but not to my eye such a striking impact.

There is some authority that in a case of this sort a judge should, before having regard to the evidence of trade witnesses (and apart from factual evidence of actual confusion) form his own provisional view: see for instance the approach of Rattee J in *The European* v *The Economist Newspapers* [1996] FSR 431, especially at pages 441-2 and 445. I am of the clear view that with the very important exception of the name and the bird picture, there is nothing in the Puffin get-up that is deceptively similar to Penguin. With the name and the bird picture I have no such clear conviction. The cartoon puffin (whose multicoloured beak is reproduced, but not very clearly) could, I am inclined to think, be mistaken for a cartoon penguin. The word PUFFIN is not very different from PENGUIN. Forty per cent of Penguins are eaten by children, and children often help with the shopping even though they do not pay for it.

Had the Asda product been called for example BISON (to take another name from the original list of possibilities) with a cartoon picture of a brown woolly bison on the packaging, these proceedings could not possibly succeed. Almost certainly they would never have been brought. But the name PUFFIN and the prominent picture of an upright dark-coloured bird with a white front gives me the expectation, as a matter of first impression, that a substantial part of the public who shop in supermarkets would see an association between the Asda product and McVities Penguin. Whether that association would be sufficient to amount to deception is a matter that I shall have to come back to. ...

The law: passing off
Many authorities were cited to me, the majority on passing off rather than on trade marks. Mr Bloch's bundle contained over thirty authorities and Mr Pollock added half a dozen more, these being mostly directed to the limitations and deficiencies of public opinion surveys as evidence in this sort of case (see for instance *United Biscuits UK Ltd.* v *Burton Biscuits Ltd.* [1992] FSR 14, the Jaffa Cakes case, in which Vinelott J referred to some earlier observations of Whitford J on this topic). I do not find it necessary to refer to all or even most of the authorities which counsel's industry has put before me. In the recent decision of the Court of Appeal in *Harrods Ltd.* v *Harrodian School Ltd.* [1996] RPC 697 the judgment of Millett LJ contains a very clear summary of the main principles, with references to leading cases, under the headings "subjective intention to deceive" (pages 706-9), "the elements of passing off" (pages 712-3), "the relevant connection" (pages 712-3) and "the common field of activity" (pages 714-5). I will not attempt a further summary here but these sections of the judgment merit careful study and all but the last are in point here (there is no dispute as to common field of activity, since the two products are admittedly close competitors in a particular sector of the biscuit market).

Three points call for special attention in relation to this case: the subjective intention of the defendant (here acting through its senior employees such as Mr McLeod and Mr Blundell); the quality of the suggestion (conveyed by the get-up of the defendant's goods) of association or connection with the plaintiff's goods; and the degree to which it is necessary for the plaintiff 's name to be known to the general public as the owner of the business whose goodwill and reputation are threatened by any misrepresentation (see the remarks of Millett LJ in *Harrods Ltd.* v *Harrodian School Ltd.* [1996] RPC 697 at page 711). I will take these points in turn.

In the *Harrods* case Millett LJ said at page 706,

> "Deception is the gist of the tort of passing off, but it is not necessary for a plaintiff to establish that the defendant consciously intended to deceive the public if that is the probable result of his conduct. Nevertheless, the question why the defendant chose to adopt a particular name or get up is always highly relevant. It is "a question which falls to be asked and answered": see *Sodastream Ltd.* v *Thorn Cascade Co. Ltd.* [1982] RPC 459 at page 466 per Kerr LJ. If it is shown that the defendant deliberately sought to take the benefit of the plaintiff's goodwill for himself, the court will not "be astute to say that he cannot succeed in doing that which he is straining every nerve to do": see *Slazenger & Sons* v *Feltham & Co.* (1889) 6 RPC 531 at page 538 per Lindley LJ."

Mr Pollock accepted this as a matter of principle but said that it could have no application to this case. He stressed that Mr Blundell had readily accepted that the original artwork was "too close" to the Penguin get-up and that it had been changed in order to avoid confusion, which the defendant (as well as the plaintiff) wanted to avoid). The evidence did not explore fully how the original artwork came to be so obviously "too close"; apart from Mr Branckston's design brief, there were very few extant documents (and none as to the reasons for adoption of the name Puffin). It is certainly true that changes were made in the first design so as to lessen the risk (initially more or less a certainty) of confusion. But it seems to me likely that Mr McLeod, Mr Blundell and their subordinates and independent designers were, under advice, seeking to make only such changes as were needed in order to avoid what they judged to be an unacceptable risk of being attacked for copying, while maintaining Puffin's position as an obvious competitor and parody, and (they hoped) a "brand beater". I cannot escape the conclusion that, while aiming to avoid what the law would characterise as deception, they were taking a conscious decision to live dangerously. That is not in my judgment something that the court is bound to disregard.

The next point that calls for consideration is the witnesses' general acceptance, under Mr Pollock's questioning, that their belief that Puffins were made by the same manufacturer as Penguins was supposition, or assumption, or a guess. For one trader to induce the belief, by deceptive suggestion, that his goods are made by another trader with an established reputation can amount to actionable passing off: *Ewing* v *Buttercup Margarine Co. Ltd.* (1917) 34 RPC 232; *Wagamama Ltd.* v *City Centre Restaurants Ltd.* [1995] FSR 713. In the *Harrods* case Millett LJ (at page 712), approving what was said by Farwell J in *British Legion* v *British Legion Club (Street) Ltd.* (1931) 48 RPC 555, characterised the connection rather more widely, as a suggestion that the plaintiff was in some way responsible for the defendant's goods or services. Plainly that includes the manufacturer of a supermarket's own-brand product, even if the supermarket shares that responsibility through its own-brand commendation.

Is it sufficient for a substantial part of the general public to be led to suppose, or assume, or guess at such a connection? In *Ewing* (1917) 34 RPC 232 at page 238 Warrington LJ put it in terms of what a customer "might well think" and went on to say,

> "It seems to me that the plaintiff has proved enough. He has proved that the defendants have adopted such a name as may lead people who have dealings with the plaintiff to believe that the defendants' business is a branch of or associated with the plaintiff's business."

In *Ravenhead Brick Co. Ltd.* v *Ruabon Brick & Terra Cotta Co. Ltd.* (1937) 54 RPC 341 at page 349 (the Rus/Sanrus brick case) it was put in terms of a trade customer saying to himself "This is, or may be, a name used to describe an article of the plaintiff's manufacture." In *Wagamama* witnesses had been asked by telephone to give their immediate reaction and first thought on hearing of the opening of a restaurant called Rajamama and some of their reactions and first thoughts are recorded in the judgment ([1995] FSR 713 at page 735). These replies are expressed, naturally enough, in terms of what the witness thought, assumed, or took to be suggested. Bearing in mind that those witnesses (whose occupations are recorded) were probably of above-average articulacy, their reactions are not to my mind very different from those of witnesses in the present case. In *Wagamama* Laddie J held passing off (as well as trade mark infringement) to have been established.

Mr Pollock points out that the *Ravenhead Brick Co.* and *Wagamama* cases were both concerned with artificial and meaningless names, and that is a point of distinction. Moreover in the bricks case the customers were typically knowledgeable tradesmen, and in the restaurants case the likelihood of word-of-mouth recommendation made the sound of the names particularly important. Penguin and

Puffin, by contrast, are words denoting real creatures, and they appear on packing designed for self-service shopping in a supermarket. However they are artificial or "fancy" names in the sense that an unpalatable seabird has no obvious connection with a chocolate-coated sandwich biscuit; and Puffin is, as a word, not wholly dissimilar from Penguin. It was to the seabird, and the names in black lettering, that almost all the witnesses referred in their explanations (some more articulate than others) of why they had been led to suppose, or assume, or guess at a common manufacturer.

The third point calling for special mention is as to customers' knowledge of the identity of the company which makes Penguins and owns goodwill reflecting its reputation in those goods. That company is the plaintiff, United Biscuits. McVities is, it seems, now used as the name of a division. MacDonalds (the original manufacturer and one of the original constituent parts of United Biscuits) seems to have disappeared.

There is authority that a customer need not know or care about the name of the manufacturer who owns the goodwill, provided that the customer knows that there is such a person and cares that goods which he buys are made by that person. This point was clearly expressed by a famous American judge, Learned Hand J, in a passage in *Crescent Tool Co.* v *Kilborn & Bishop Co.* (1917) 247 F. 290 at page 300 quoted by Jacob J in *Hodgkinson & Corby Ltd.* v *Wards Mobility Services Ltd* [1994] 1 WLR 1564 at page 1573,

"It is an absolute condition to any relief whatever that the plaintiff in such cases show that the appearance of his wares has in fact come to mean that some particular person - the plaintiff may not be individually known - makes them, and the public cares who does make them."

That was said in the special context of the appearance of a product, but the point is of more general application. When witnesses called on behalf of United Biscuits said that they did not know or care who made Penguins, I did not understand them to be saying or implying that they did not expect Penguins to be of consistently high quality because of their origin from a particular source. I shall touch on this point again in a later part of this judgment. ...

Conclusions: passing off
To succeed in passing off, United Biscuits must establish the "classic trinity" of reputation (or goodwill), deception and damage. Goodwill is admitted on the pleadings, and is in any case amply established by the evidence.

At the beginning of the hearing Mr Bloch (while submitting that actual confusion of goods is notoriously difficult to establish by direct evidence, especially in the case of low-value goods) put his case on deception on the three foundations of judicial first impression, the NOP survey, and evidence of actual confusion among members of the public (including those questioned by NOP's interviewers). As I have recounted, Mr Bloch then decided that he could no longer rely on the NOP survey, and so I disregard that evidence. Mr Pollock sought to gain positive assistance from the survey (as I have mentioned above under the heading Witnesses) but for the reasons given there I think that 35 (rather than 3) out of 170 interviewees might be the more significant figure, if reliance were placed in the NOP survey. I do not attach weight to the evidence of the trade witnesses in relation to the customers' likely reactions (as opposed to their evidence of the nature of the market).

Judicial first impression is of some importance, especially where the goods in question are familiar and inexpensive (as opposed to the sort of specialised designer label goods with which Sir Nicolas Browne-Wilkinson V-C was concerned in *Guccio Gucci* v *Paolo Gucci* [1991] FSR 89: see Rattee J's comments on that case in *The European Ltd.* v *The Economist Newspapers Ltd.* [1996] FSR 431 at pages 441-2). My impression of the puffin packaging (in all four colours or varieties) is that it would cause a substantial number of members of the public to suppose that there was a connection between the Puffin biscuit and the Penguin biscuit. Despite the evidence of isolated mistakes, I do not consider that a substantial number would believe that the Asda Puffin is the McVities Penguin. But many would believe that the two must be made by the same manufacturer.

That judicial first impression was largely confirmed by the oral evidence. Witnesses repeatedly referred to the dark seabird, the black lettering and the similarity of names as the features which together induced that belief. One or two came close to saying that the Puffin biscuit must be produced by the manufacturer of the Penguin, because otherwise it would not be allowed (there is here some hint of a self-fulfilling prophecy, and this point must not be given any more weight than it merits).

I conclude that the Puffin packaging and get-up was, in the material sense, deceptively similar to those of the penguin. In reaching this conclusion I do not find that it was intended to be deceptively similar; I accept the evidence of Mr McLeod and Mr Blundell that they intended to avoid deception. But plainly they had that risk in mind, and in my judgment they miscalculated the degree of "challenge" or "matching" or "parody" that was tolerable without the product being actually deceptive (in the material sense).

As to damage, I am satisfied that United Biscuits has suffered damage, although it may be difficult to quantify for reasons discussed in Dr Bishop's report. That report is (as I have said) candid about its own limitations and cannot establish (and was not relied on by Mr Pollock as establishing) the negative proposition that no damage could have resulted from any confusion between the two products at and after the Puffin launch.'

COMMENT

Although the action in passing off succeeded, the trade mark action failed and Robert Walker J ordered that four of the plaintiff's pictorial marks be revoked on the grounds that use had been suspended for an uninterrupted period of five years. The pictures of penguins used by the plaintiffs more recently were not sufficiently similar to the registered marks.

In terms of passing off what is important is not whether the public know the identity of the trader having goodwill in question but that they will believe that the plaintiff's and defendant's products come from the same manufacturer. It appeared in this case that, after realising the first design was too close, the defendant's intention was to get as close to the plaintiff's get-up as was lawfully possible. Is such an intention a factor in determining whether there is passing off? Note that in this case there was no intention to deceive; in fact, the opposite was true. But as the case shows, trying to get close to another trader's get-up can be dangerous.

Misrepresentation

The misrepresentation may be deliberate or innocent. In the majority of passing off cases, the nature of the misrepresentation will be uncontroversial such as where one trader uses another trader's name or a name used by a group of other traders. However, the scope of the misrepresentation can be surprising and even an accurate description of one's goods can be sufficient if that name has been appropriated by another trader in the sense that it has become so associated with that trader in the minds of the buying public. The following case demonstrates this state of affairs and also provides an example of the relative width of the scope of passing off compared to trade mark law under the Trade Mark Act 1938. It is also the most recent case on passing off to be heard in the House of Lords.

Reckitt & Colman Products Ltd. v Borden Inc. [1990] 1 All ER 873, House of Lords

The respondent (Reckitt & Colman) had for a number of years sold lemon juice in plastic containers that resembled natural lemons in colour and shape. The appellant started selling lemon juice in containers of a similar shape and colour although their original container was slightly larger and had a flat side to prevent it rolling away. The respondent sued in passing off and was successful at first instance. The Court of Appeal affirmed that decision and the appellant (Borden) appealed to the House of Lords.

Lord Bridge of Harwich (at 877): '... The idea of selling preserved lemon juice in a plastic container designed to look as nearly as possible as the real thing is such a simple, obvious and inherently attractive way of marketing the product that it seems to me utterly repugnant to the law's philosophy with respect to commercial monopolies to permit any trader to acquire a *de jure* monopoly in the container as such. But, as counsel for the respondents quite rightly pointed out, the order made by the trial judge in this case does not confer any such *de jure* monopoly because the injunction restrains the appellants from marketing their product -

"in any container so nearly resembling the Plaintiff's JIF lemon shaped container ... as to be likely to deceive without making it clear that it is not of the goods of the plaintiff ..." (my emphasis.)

How then are the appellants, if they wish to sell their product in plastic containers of the shape, colour and size of natural lemons, to ensure that the buyer is not deceived? The answer, one would suppose, is by attaching a suitably distinctive label to the container. Yet here is the paradox: the trial judge found that a buyer reading the labels proposed to be attached to the appellant's Mark I, II or III containers would know at once that they did not contain Jif lemon juice and would not be deceived; but he also enjoined the appellants from selling their product as in those containers because he found, to put it shortly, that housewives buying plastic lemons in supermarkets do not read the labels but assume that whatever they buy it must be Jif. The result seems to be to give the respondents a *de facto* monopoly of the container as such, which is just as effective as *de jure* monopoly. A trader selling lemon juice would never be permitted to register a lemon as his trade mark, but the respondents have achieved the result indirectly that a container designed to look like a real lemon is to be treated, *per se*, as distinctive of their goods.

If I could find any way of avoiding this result, I would. But the difficulty is that the trial judge's findings of fact, however surprising they may seem, are not open to challenge. Given those findings, I am constrained by the reasoning in the speeches of my noble and learned friends Lord Oliver and Lord Jauncey to accept that the judge's conclusion cannot be faulted in law.

With undisguised reluctance I agree with Lord Oliver and Lord Jauncey that the appeal should be dismissed.'

Lord Oliver (at 884): '... So, it is said, the distinction between the manufactured article itself, which anyone is free to copy in the absence of patent protection, and the special trade insignia used to designate its trade origin, which the courts will protect, is clearly brought out in the speech of Lord Macnaghten in *Weingarten Bros.* v *Bayer & Co.* (1905) 92 LT 511 at 512, [1904-7] All ER Rep 877 at 878-879. The article itself cannot, it is submitted, constitute the special insignia of its own origin. All the law will protect are such capricious additions or features as may be attached to the article for the purposes of indicating origin, for instance, the embossed word "Jif" on the respondent's containers in the instant case, which serves no functional purpose.

Whether in fact the particular shape or configuration of the very object sold by a trader is incapable as a matter of law of protection in a case where it has become associated exclusively with his business is a proposition which is at least open to doubt. The decision of Buckley J in *R J Elliott & Co. Ltd.* v *Hodgson* (1902) 19 RPC 518 suggests the contrary, although it has been doubted: see *Cadbury Ltd.* v *Ulmer GmbH* [1988] FSR 385. It is clear at least from the decision of this House in *William Edge & Sons Ltd.* v *William Nicholls & Sons Ltd.* [1911] AC 693 that where the article sold is conjoined with an object which, whilst serving the functional purpose of enabling the article to be more effectively employed, is of a shape or configuration which has become specifically identified with a particular manufacturer, the latter may be entitled to protection against the deceptive use in conjunction with similar articles of [sic] objects fashioned in the same or a closely similar shape.

I find it, however, unnecessary to pursue the question further for there is, to my mind, a fallacy in the argument which begins by identifying the contents with the container and is summarised in the central proposition that "you cannot claim a monopoly in selling plastic lemons". Well, of course you cannot any more than you can claim a monopoly in the sale of dimpled bottles. The deception alleged lies not in the sale of the plastic lemons or dimpled bottles, but in the sale of lemon juice or whisky, as the case may be, in containers so fashioned to suggest that the juice or the whisky emanates from the source with which the containers of those particular configurations have become associated in the public mind: see *John Haig & Co. Ltd.* v *Forth Blending Co. Ltd.* 1954 SC 35. It is, no doubt, true that the plastic lemon-shaped container serves, as indeed does a bottle of any design, a functional purpose in the sale of lemon juice. Apart from being a container simpliciter, it is a convenient size, it is capable of convenient use by squeezing, and it is so designed as conveniently to suggest the nature of its contents without the necessity for further labelling or other identification. But those purposes are capable of being and indeed are served by a variety of distinctive containers of configurations other than those of a lemon-sized lemon. Neither the appellants nor the respondents are in the business of selling plastic lemons. Both are makers and vendors of lemon juice and the only question is whether the respondents, having acquired a public reputation for Jif juice by selling it for many years in containers of a particular shape and design which, on the evidence, has become associated with their produce, can legitimately complain of the sale by the appellants of similar produce in containers of similar, though not identical, size, shape and colouring.

So I, for my part, would reject the suggestion that the plastic lemon container is an object in itself rather than part of the get-up under which the respondent's produce is sold. But it is argued that that is not the end of the matter, for the get-up which is protected is not just a plastic lemon-shaped container, but the container plus the respondent's labelling, and it is not open to the respondents to argue that, though the labels themselves could not, fairly regarded, possibly be confused, a part, albeit perhaps a dominant part, of the get-up can, as it were, be separated and made the subject matter of protection in its own right. I confess that I do not see why not, given that the respondents establish a right to the protection of their get-up as a whole. The question is whether what the appellants are doing constitutes a misrepresentation that their juice is Jif juice, and whether that results from the similarity of their get-up to the whole of the respondents' get-up or to only the most striking part of it is wholly immaterial if, and of course this is critical, it is once established as a matter of fact that what they are doing constitutes a misrepresentation which effectively deceives the public into an erroneous belief regarding the source of the product ...

Every case depends on its own peculiar facts. For instance, even a purely descriptive term consisting of perfectly ordinary English words may, by a course of dealing over many years, become so associated with a particular trader that it acquires a secondary meaning such that it may properly be said to be descriptive of that trader's goods and of his goods alone ... these principles are aptly expressed in the speech of Lord Herschell in *Reddaway* v *Banham* [1896] AC 199 at 210, [1895-9] All ER Rep 133 at 140:

> "The name of a person, or words forming part of the common stock of language, may become so far associated with the goods of a particular maker that it is capable of proof that the use of them by themselves without explanation or qualification by another manufacturer would deceive a purchaser into the belief that he was getting the goods of A, when he was really getting the goods of B. In a case of this description the mere proof by the plaintiff that the defendant was using a name, word, or device which he had adopted to distinguish his goods would not entitle him to any relief. He could only obtain it by proving further that the defendant was using it under such circumstances or in such a manner as to put [sic] off his goods as the goods of the plaintiff. If he could succeed in proving this I think he would, on well-established principles, be entitled to an injunction."

Again Lord Herschell observed ([1896] AC 199 at 214-215, [1895-9] All ER Rep 133 at 142):

> "What right, it is asked, can an individual have to restrain another from using a common English word because he has chosen to employ it as his trade mark? I

answer he has no such right; but he has a right to insist that it shall not be used without explanation or qualification if such use would be an instrument of fraud."

In the instant case the submission that the device of selling lemon juice in a natural-sized lemon-shaped squeeze pack is something that is "common to the trade" and therefore incapable of protection at the suit of a particular trader begs the essential question. If "common to the trade" means "in general use in the trade" then, so far at least as the United Kingdom is concerned, the evidence at the trial clearly established that the lemon-sized squeeze pack was not in general use. If, on the other hand, it means, as the appellants submit, "available for use by the trade" then it is so available only if it does not become so closely associated with the respondents' goods as to render its use by the appellants deceptive; and that is the very question in issue. The trial judge has found as a fact that the natural-size squeeze pack in the form of a lemon has become so associated with Jif lemon juice that the introduction of the appellants' juice in any of the proposed get-ups will be bound to result in many housewives purchasing that juice in the belief that they are obtaining Jif juice. I cannot interpret that as anything other than a finding that the plastic lemon-shaped container has acquired, as it were, a secondary significance. It indicates not merely lemon juice but specifically Jif lemon juice ...

It is pointed out that recent decisions of this House, for instance, *British Leyland Motor Corp. Ltd.* v *Armstrong Patents Co. Ltd.* [1986] 1 All ER 850; [1986] AC 577 and *Re Coca-Cola Co.'s Applications* [1986] 2 All ER 274, [1986] 1 WLR 695, have stressed the suspicion with which this House regards any attempt to extend or perpetuate a monopoly and it is suggested again that, because it is not easy in the circumstances of this market effectively to distinguish the appellants' products from the respondents' except at considerable expense, the respondents are achieving, in effect, a perpetual monopoly in the sale of lemon juice in lemon-shaped squeeze packs. I do not accept at all that this is so, but in any event the principle that no man is entitled to steal another's trade by deceit is one of at least equal importance. The facts as found here establish that, unless the injunction is continued, that is what the appellant will be doing and it is not necessary for them to do so in order to establish their own competing business for there is nothing in the nature of the product sold which inherently requires it to be sold in the particular format which the appellants have chosen to adopt. I would dismiss the appeal.'

Lord Jauncey delivered a speech dismissing the appeal. Lords Brandon and Goff concurred with the speeches of Lords Bridge and Jauncey.

COMMENT

In this way, Reckitt & Colman obtained a monopoly in lemon-shaped containers for the sale of lemon juice. In the *Coca-Cola* case, an application to register the Coca-Cola bottle as a trade mark failed, the House of Lords pointing out that otherwise an undesirable monopoly in containers would be achieved. (However, the bottle should be registrable under the 1994 Act.) It is inconceivable that another trader could use a bottle the same shape as the Coca-Cola bottle without being guilty of passing off. How could another trader use a lemon-shaped container for lemon juice so as not to constitute passing off? It is interesting to note that Lord Oliver did not once refer to the *Advocaat* case (which was and still is considered to be the leading case on passing off) and Lord Jauncey referred to it only briefly, in passing. Why is this? Should policy have been given more weight? After all, Lord Diplock spoke of policy as being an important factor in the *Advocaat* case.

Damage to Goodwill

To be actionable, the misrepresentation must be such as to cause actual damage to the plaintiff's goodwill or, in a *quia timet* action, it will probably do so. Goodwill may be damaged if the defendant's misrepresentation is such that there is a real likelihood of confusion amongst prospective customers or ultimate consumers of the plaintiff's goods or services. Although the parties are likely to call witnesses on the point of confusion, ultimately, it is a question for the court to decide.

Mothercare U.K. Ltd. v *Penguin Books Ltd.* [1988] RPC 113, Court of Appeal

The defendant published a book entitled 'Mother Care/Other Care' and the plaintiff, which had a chain of stores selling clothes and goods for babies, expectant mothers and young children, objected on the grounds of passing off and trade mark infringement. The book was a serious work examining the problems facing working mothers who have to delegate the care of their children to other persons.

Dillon LJ (at 116): 'In making out their claim in passing off, Mothercare would have to establish at the trial the five factors listed by Lord Diplock in *Erven Warnink B V* v *Townend & Sons (Hull) Ltd.* [1979] AC 731, at 742D-E as being the five characteristics which must be present in order to create a valid cause of action for passing off. These include as (1) "a misrepresentation", which in the context of the present case must mean showing that Penguin, in publishing the book under the name *Mother Care/Other Care* have represented, contrary to the facts that the book is issued, or sponsored, by or associated with Mothercare. They also include, as (4) and (5), that the misrepresentation "is calculated to injure the business or goodwill of another trader (in the sense that this is a reasonably foreseeable consequence)" and that the misrepresentation "causes actual damage to a business or goodwill of the trader by whom the action is brought or (in a *quia timet* action) will probably do so".

The question whether there is a misrepresentation, like the question whether there is a likelihood of deception, is a question for the tribunal and not a matter for a witness:- *Kerly on Trade Marks* 12th Ed., sections 17-25 and *North Cheshire and Manchester Brewery Company* v *The Manchester Brewery Company* [1899] AC 83, per Lord Halsbury. In considering whether there is a misrepresentation, the court must consider the name *Mother Care/Other Care* as a whole. So considering the name, I am - with all respect to Falconer J. who took the opposite view - wholly unable to see any basis for saying that there is a misrepresentation in the title of the book. The name, taken as a whole, does not begin to suggest that the book has been issued or sponsored by, or is in any way associated with, Mothercare. I refer later to the evidence of the survey which Mothercare commissioned and on which the judge to some extent relied.

So far as the claim in passing off is concerned, Mothercare's case is rendered the more difficult by the nature of the damage which they claim that the publication of the book under the name *Mother Care/Other Care* will cause them.

They recognise that the mere fact, even if established, that the name of the book was erroneously understood as a representation that they were in some way associated with the book does not, by itself, cause them any damage at all. They do not suggest that the book is in competition with the *Complete Mothercare Manual* or with any other book which they are likely to issue (since they eschew controversial subjects and do not approve of the thesis which the book seeks to make out). What they claim to fear is that potential customers for the sort of goods that Mothercare sells, who suppose from the name that Mothercare is associated with the book, will be so horrified when they realise the thesis that the book is concerned to develop, vis., in brief, that the mother-child relationship is not uniquely important for the welfare of the child, that they will refuse to have anything to do with Mothercare and in particular will insist on buying any goods they need from shops other than Mothercare's shops. In my judgment such hypothetical damage is altogether too far-fetched; it is not a reasonably foreseeable consequence, in Lord Diplock's words, of the supposed misrepresentation. Beyond that, however, any potential customer who looks sufficiently far into the book to find out what it is actually about, is bound to realise that the words "Mother Care" in the title are used descriptively to refer to the care of children by their mothers as opposed to the care of children by others, and do not refer to Mothercare, or any association with Mothercare, at all; thus there will have been no misrepresentation.

Accordingly the claim in passing off is, in my judgment, bound to fail; Mothercare do not get over the first hurdle of establishing that there is a serious question to be tried.'

COMMENT

Dillon LJ was unimpressed by the results of a survey carried out by the a market research company on behalf of the plaintiff. He said that the ladies questioned were asked an unnatural question ('If you wanted further information about this book who would you approach?') in an unnatural surrounding. He further said that he did not find such surveys helpful. On the trade mark issue, it was held that the use of 'Mother Care' in the title of the book was not use as a trade mark nor in a trade mark sense. It had been claimed that there was an infringement on the basis of section 4(1)(b) of the Trade Marks Act 1938 - the difficult 'importing a reference' infringement.

The Financial Times Ltd. v *Evening Standard Co. Ltd.* [1991] FSR 7, Chancery Division.

The plaintiff published the Financial Times newspaper that had, for around 100 years, been printed on pink paper. The defendant intended to publish a new business section in its newspaper also in pink paper.

Aldous J (at 10): 'The plaintiff submits that the colour pink is so associated with it that a substantial number of persons would wrongly believe that the defendant's insert was so published. The defendant submits to the contrary. I am conscious that anything I may say as to the merits of the action could prejudice one of the parties at the hearing of the motion. However, in this case it is not possible for me to avoid this, as it has a bearing upon the extent of damage that the plaintiff may suffer and therefore the balance of convenience. If the risk of persons being misled into thinking that the *Evening Standard* pink insert is being published by or with the collaboration of the plaintiff is small, then the risk of any substantial damage pending the hearing of the motion must also be small. If, however, there is a substantial risk of persons being misled, then the likelihood of damage will be greater.

The evidence of the plaintiff is contained in the affidavit of Mr Prior-Palmer. He draws attention to the reputation of the *Financial Times*, its long and well-known use of pink paper, the promotion and advertisement using pink, and the fact that it is known as "the pink" or "the pink 'un'". He concludes, in paragraph 26 of his affidavit:

"I consider that the use of pink paper for the defendant's section will, in such circumstances, give rise to the mistaken belief that it is being published by or with the collaboration of the Financial Times."

However, I cannot accept that opinion as decisive. In *Parker-Knoll Limited* v *Knoll International Limited* [1962] RPC 243 at 285, Lord Hodson said that the question whether there is a real likelihood of deception is ultimately for the court ...

He goes on to point out that the *Financial Times* is pre-eminent in the publication of financial statistics in newspapers and he is particularly concerned about any inaccuracy in closing prices which may be published by the defendant ...

He is right that the plaintiff will not be able to control the activities of the *Evening Standard,* and therefore damage is possible if there be real deception. However, I believe that such damage be remote pending the hearing of the motion. First, I have already concluded that the risk of any substantial number of persons being deceived is remote. Secondly, I do not envisage it as likely that any shortcomings that will occur during the next 28 days or so could seriously damage the plaintiff's reputation. The *Financial Times* will continue to be published. Its reputation will be maintained by its content, and the public will turn to it as they have in the past, and to the *Evening Standard* as they have in the past. I cannot see that the change in the *Evening Standard* or any shortcomings that may occur will, over the next 28 days or so, reflect upon the reputation of the *Financial Times* built up over a very long period. The two newspapers, the *Financial Times* and the *Evening Standard* do not directly compete and will not do so over the period pending the hearing of the motion. Further, I cannot see that the *Financial Times* will suffer, during the same period, any difficulty in advertising its paper or in any other promotion that it may commence.

So far as the defendant is concerned, the *Evening Standard* pink inserts has been launched. Rumours of the launch came to the plaintiff's attention as far back as 3 September. The plaintiff took no action until 13 September, despite the fact that its media director had been informed on 11 September. Thereafter, it sought and was refused a dummy copy. I do not hold it against the plaintiff that no action was taken to prevent the launch, but the fact is that the pink insert was published on Monday, 17 September with considerable publicity. An injunction pending hearing of the motion restraining use of pink paper would be likely to cause damage which would not be readily quantifiable. It might mean a loss of increased readership which is expected and loss of goodwill amongst advertisers. Further it would cause considerable disruption and it would be likely that the *Evening Standard* would feel unable to return to the use of pink paper if it won the motion.

Weighing the damage likely to the plaintiff over the next 28 days or so against that to the defendant, I conclude that the balance comes down against granting any *ex parte* relief. I therefore refuse the plaintiff's application.'

COMMENT

In many cases concerning passing off, the court has to make a judgment on the question of whether there is likely to be any serious damage to the plaintiff's goodwill. Obviously, a well-prepared plaintiff must come to the court with strong and convincing evidence on this point. In some cases, the damage will be in the form of a loss of trade. In other cases, the damage will be less direct, where the defendant's activities will, because of the association with the plaintiff's goods, harm the plaintiff's reputation and standing. That was the argument here but the judge did not accept that sufficient numbers of persons would make that association between the two newspapers; that is, that the plaintiff was somehow involved in the pink section of the defendant's newspaper.

A mere suspicion that a defendant is misleading customers will not suffice as the case below shows.

Tamworth Herald Co. Ltd. v *Thomson Free Newspapers Ltd.* [1991] FSR 337, Chancery Division

The plaintiff published a weekly newspaper called the *Tamworth Herald,* first published in 1868. At the time of the action its price was 23p. It was circulated in the Tamworth area to about 25,000 people and there was no other paper in that area with a name including the word 'Herald'. The *Tamworth Herald* had, according to the evidence, a substantial reputation and goodwill in the area and was seen as the local weekly paper. It was known locally under its full title, that is the *Tamworth Herald* and the *Herald*. In 1980, the plaintiff also started publishing a free sheet which was delivered free to households in the area. In 1985 the name of that free sheet was changed to the *Tamworth Herald Extra.*

In the early 1970s a paper called the *Tamworth Trader* started to be published. It was published weekly and delivered free to households in the Tamworth area. The defendant purchased that paper. Because the defendant had a number of local newspapers with different titles and, in order to improve promotion of its newspapers, it decided on one name for all their local newspapers for the purpose of distinguishing between its newspapers and other local newspapers. The defendant analysed the titles it now had and found that one-third included the word 'Herald' and another third included the word 'Post'. Additionally, no newspaper was called the 'Herald and Post' or the 'Post and Herald'. The defendant therefore decided to use the two words 'Herald and Post' in combination to try and promote a new image to cover the whole of its newspapers.

Aldous J (at 339): 'The plaintiffs submit that there will be a misrepresentation leading to confusion. First, they say that the recipients of the defendants' paper will, because of the similarity of the name to that of the plaintiffs, believe that the defendants' paper is another paper delivered free but coming from the plaintiffs. I have found that suggestion difficult to understand and do not believe that it is probable. The recipients of the defendants' paper will be those who received the *Tamworth Trader* prior to the change. Prior to the change, they will be apprised of the proposed change of name and will expect that change to take place, knowing of the difference between the plaintiffs' and the defendants' papers. Further, the masthead to which I have referred makes it clear to anybody who spends more than a few seconds looking at the front page that the paper that they received, namely, the *Tamworth Herald and Post,* was formerly the *Tamworth Trader.* Those persons know that the *Tamworth Trader* is not part of the plaintiffs' organisation. Further, I believe that the difference in look between the proposed front page of the defendants' paper when it has changed its name is significant. Anybody who notices the word "Herald" in the title must, I believe, notice the rest and he will realise that it is in fact the same paper as the old *Tamworth Trader,* but produced under a different name.

Secondly, the plaintiffs submit that those who receive the defendants' paper will believe that it is the plaintiffs' paper but renamed. Again I cannot envisage that any sensible person would come to that conclusion ...

Thirdly, the plaintiffs submit that recipients of the defendants' paper would believe, by reason of the new name, that the plaintiffs had become part of the Thomson Group. I have been unable to understand how any reasonable person could conclude that from looking at the proposed front page, which is in exhibit KBL.6. There is no suggestion that the plaintiffs' paper, which will be published every Friday, has become part of the Thomson Group. The front page of the defendants' paper makes it clear that the "Herald and Post" was formerly called the *Tamworth Trader.* I cannot find any representation that the plaintiffs had become part of the Thomson Group.

Fourthly, the plaintiffs submit that this change will result in them receiving communications intended for the defendants and *vice versa.* This, they say, is the result of the misrepresentation and confusion resulting therefrom. On the evidence some confusion is in fact taking place at the moment. It may well be that there will initially be further confusion when the change is made. However, that does not, to my mind, suggest that there will be a misrepresentation which could amount to passing off. That sort of confusion, as the evidence shows, is taking place because the word "Tamworth" is used by both the plaintiffs and the defendants. The mere fact that somebody is using a word which is commonly used for newspapers, such as "Herald" may mean that typists, may, by mistake, wrongly address letters. It does not mean that in any way they are under any misapprehension caused by any misrepresentation as to where the letter should go.

The plaintiffs also submit that the defendants' change of name to the form shown in exhibit KLB.6 would cause confusion amongst potential advertisers. Such advertisers appear to fall into two basic groups, namely, members of the public who place advertisements and traders. As to the public, I have already given my reasons why I do not believe it reasonable to accept that they will be under any misapprehension. Further, they will only place advertisements having ascertained an address or a telephone number and that, in practice, will be obtained from a paper or from some reference source such as *Yellow Pages.* If the address or telephone number is taken from a paper, then the advertiser will know the paper in which he is seeking to place an advertisement. He could be under no misapprehension as to what he is seeking to do. If he uses the *Yellow Pages*, then the name that he will see will be that presently used and later that which the defendants will use to trade in that area. Again the similarity will not be such as to lead to passing off.

As to trade advertisers, they are less likely to be deceived, in that they are more skilled in deciding where to place their advertisements. I have not been able to understand how, in view of what is going to happen and the particular form of the defendants' paper pending trial, they could be confused. They should be under no misapprehension that the defendants' paper was formerly the *Tamworth Trader*. They will approach the paper in which they wish to advertise. They will see the defendants' paper, they will know of the plaintiffs' paper, they will know of the *Tamworth Trader* and they cannot really be under any misapprehension, if they look at the defendants' paper, that in fact it is that paper which was previously called the *Tamworth Trader*.

A further way in which confusion is said to be likely to occur is by reason of approaches by the papers to potential advertisers. I understand that one of the ways in which advertising revenue is secured is that those employed by the plaintiffs and the defendants will ring up potential advertisers to try to persuade them to place advertisements in their paper. The plaintiffs say that employees of the defendants seeking to obtain advertising revenue may well use language which will misrepresent that the defendants' paper is the plaintiffs' or connected or associated with it. Anything is possible and anybody can misrepresent their product or service as the product or service of another. However, I am not concerned with possibilities. I have to concern myself with probabilities that will occur on more than one or two odd occasions.

In the present case, the defendants have produced instructions, which will be given to those who telephone potential advertisers, as to what they should do ... If those instructions are followed, I do not believe that any confusion will be likely and also I believe that it would be wrong for me to assume that those instructions would not be carried out. In those circumstances, particularly as there is no attack upon the good faith of the defendants, I believe it would be not right for me to come to the conclusion that passing off is likely to occur in that way.

Lastly, the plaintiffs submitted that, because of the similarity in names, there is a likelihood that the public will refer to the defendants' paper as the "Herald" and, because their paper is known as the "Herald", any adverse comments will reflect on the plaintiffs' reputation and their paper. There is no evidence to support the suggestion that there will be adverse comments. The *Tamworth Trader* has been on the market now for many years and I have to consider the position pending trial, which will probably be in about a year's time. Further, so far as the public is concerned, there will be two papers on the market both using the word 'Herald' in their name. They are likely, if not immediately then very quickly, to refer to the defendants' paper as either the "Post" or the "Herald and Post". I believe the changes of such confusion are slim and I do not believe that there is any likelihood of any damage being caused pending trial. The possibility is so remote that there is no need for me to take it into account.

The question whether the way that the defendants will use the name *Tamworth Herald and Post* will amount to passing off is one for the court, taking into account the evidence. Without evidence of actual confusion, I find it difficult to envisage that the plaintiffs' evidence at trial would be substantially different from that which I have before me. Even contemplating amplification of that evidence to include say a market survey or evidence from the public, I do not envisage that the plaintiffs could establish that there is a serious issue to be tried in this case. Therefore, on that basis the motion fails.'

COMMENT

Could the plaintiff have improved his case in any way? In the outcome, the weakness of the plaintiff's case was lack of evidence of damage, notwithstanding the judge was unable to find a misrepresentation by the defendant. The plaintiff might have considered placing some 'trap orders', for example, by asking persons to telephoning the defendant in order to place an advertisement and asking whether they were speaking to 'The Tamworth Herald'.

Damage in the form of lost sales resulting from the defendant's misrepresentation is usually looked for in a passing off action but sometimes the damage can be more subtle as hinted at in the Spanish Champagne and Advocaat cases. If a group of traders collectively use a name to describe their product and that name signifies a quality product, then unauthorised use by another trader can cause damage by eroding or diluting the marketing power of the name itself. This is so even if there is no deception as to the origin of the defendant's goods even though the defendant may have made a misrepresentation.

Taittinger SA v *Allbev Ltd.* [1993] FSR 641, Court of Appeal

The defendant produced a non-alcoholic sparkling drink called 'Elderflower Champagne'. It was sold in bottles resembling champagne bottles and retailed at only £2.45. The word 'Champagne' appeared on the labels in cursive script. The plaintiff who was a producer of champagne and a member of associations concerned with the regulation of champagne, sued on the basis of passing off and also claimed a breach of EC Regulation 823/87 which concerns the control of the use of regional names for wines. In the Chancery Division, it was held that the defendant had made a misrepresentation which was calculated to deceive but that there was no real likelihood of serious damage because, bearing in mind the price and the fact that the defendant's drink was non-alcoholic, very few persons would be confused. It was also held that the EC Regulation must be applied in accordance with English substantive law and, therefore, there was no remedy for the plaintiff.

Peter Gibson LJ (at 661): '... The suggestion that the defendants' "Elderflower Champagne" is a traditional drink with a provenance dating back to the middle ages seems to me on the evidence to be a creative interpretation of what was known to Dr Woodall. Whilst there is a seventeenth century literary reference to an infusion of elderflowers in small ale, the earliest publication containing a recipe for home-made "elderflower champagne" that was produced in evidence was dated 1949; further the fizzy drink to which the published recipes refer depended on fermentation for its fizz, was mildly alcoholic and used white wine vinegar and no carbonated water. However the judge expressed himself satisfied that the defendant's product might be regarded as a modern type of "elderflower champagne" produced commercially.

Certainly there is no evidence of any commercial sales of "elderflower champagne" until the defendants' product was marketed.

Dr Woodall is the moving spirit among the defendants. He formed Allbev Ltd. to produce the elderflower cordial that he decided to produce first on a commercial scale. When that venture prospered, other "hedgerow" products were made and in 1989 he decided to expand the range of elderflower drinks to Elderflower Champagne. His evidence was that he knew of a drink called "elderflower champagne" from his grandmother and from recipe books and he was most keen to retain the traditional name, but he positively did not want people to believe that the product was alcoholic ...

In relation to the fifth characteristic, [erosion of uniqueness] that the misrepresentation should have caused or would probably cause actual damage to the champagne houses' goodwill, the judge held that the plaintiffs did not establish a likelihood of substantial damage. He reached this conclusion in this way. He posed the question whether it was really likely that the goodwill in the name "champagne" would be substantially affected if the defendants continued to sell Elderflower Champagne and answered that in the negative, the effect on the plaintiffs' reputation being in his view nil or minimal. He gave his reason as being that those who bought Elderflower Champagne in the belief that it was champagne made up a very small section of the public and he coupled that conclusion with the fact that the defendants' activities were on a small scale as compared with those represented by the plaintiffs. He further pointed to the absence of indication of any likely large scale enlargement of the defendants' operation.

I have already adverted to the inconsistency between his finding that many members of the public would be deceived when buying Elderflower Champagne and the description of them as constituting a very small section of the public. The deception of many members of the public cannot be *de minimis*. To this I would add the confusion of those who would think that the defendants' product had some association with champagne if it was not actually champagne. Further it cannot be right that the larger the scale of the activities of a trader suing in passing off, the less protection it will receive from the court because of a comparison with the scale of the activities of a defendant who trades on a smaller scale. The question is whether the relevant activities of the defendants are on such a small scale leading to such a small injury that it can be ignored. On the evidence of the defendants' sales, I find it impossible to say that that is the case here.

But in my judgment the real injury to the champagne houses' goodwill comes under a different head and although the judge refers to Mr Sparrow putting the point in argument, he does not deal with it specifically or give a reason for its undoubted rejection by him. Mr Sparrow had argued that if the defendants continued to market their product, there would take place a blurring or erosion of the uniqueness that now attends the word "champagne", so that the exclusive reputation of the champagne houses would be debased. He put this even more forcefully before us. He submitted that if the defendants are allowed to continue to call their product Elderflower Champagne, the effect would be to demolish the distinctiveness of the word champagne, and that would inevitably damage the goodwill of the champagne houses.

In the *Advocaat* case at first instance ([1980] RPC 31 at 52) Goulding J held that one type of damage was "a more graphical damage to the plaintiffs' business through depreciation of the reputation that their goods enjoy". He continued:

"Damage of [this] type can rarely be susceptible of positive proof. In my judgment, it is likely to occur if the word 'Advocaat' is permitted to be used of alcoholic egg drinks generally or of the defendants' product in particular."

In the House of Lords in that case Lord Diplock referred to that type of damage to goodwill as relevant damage, which he described as caused "indirectly in the debasement of the reputation attaching to the name 'advocaat'" ([1979] AC 731 at 740).

In *Vine Products Ltd.* v *MacKenzie & Co. Ltd.* [1969] RPC 1 at 23 Cross J, commenting with approval on the decision of Danckwerts J in *Bollinger* v *Costa Brava Wine Co. Ltd. (No.2)* said:

"[Danckwerts J] thought, as I read in his judgment, that if people were allowed to call sparkling wine not produced in Champagne 'Champagne', even though preceded by an adjective denoting the country of origin, the distinction between genuine Champagne and 'champagne type' wines produced elsewhere would become blurred; that the word 'Champagne' would come gradually to mean no more than 'sparkling wine', and that the part of the plaintiffs' goodwill which consisted in the name would be diluted and gradually destroyed."

That passage was referred to approvingly by Gault J in *Wineworths Ltd.* v *CIVC* [1992] 2 NZLR 327 at 341. In that case the sale of Australian sparkling wine under the name champagne was held to constitute passing off. The New Zealand Court of Appeal upheld the decision of Jeffries J who had held in *CIVC* v *Wineworths* [1991] 2 NZLR 432 at 450: "By using the word champagne on the label the defendant is deceptively encroaching on the reputation and goodwill of the plaintiffs." Jeffries J had no doubt that if relief was not granted the plaintiffs would most certainly suffer damage if the word was used on all or any sparkling wine sold in New Zealand. He thought the ordinary purchaser in New Zealand without special knowledge on wines was likely to be misled. Gault J after agreeing with Jeffries J on deception said (at p. 343):

"I find the issue of damage or likely damage to the goodwill with which the name 'Champagne' is associated equally obvious in light of the finding that there is in fact an established goodwill in New Zealand. I have no doubt that erosion of the distinctiveness of a name or mark is a form of damage to the goodwill of the business with which the name is connected. There is no clearer example of this than the debasing of the name 'Champagne' in Australia as a result of its use by local wine makers."

By parity of reasoning it seems to me no less obvious that erosion of the distinctiveness of the name champagne in this country is a form of damage to the goodwill of the business of the champagne houses. There are undoubtedly factual points of distinction between the New Zealand case and the present case, as Mr Isaacs has pointed out, and he placed particular reliance on the fact that in the New Zealand case as well as in *Bollinger* v *Costa Brava Wine Co. Ltd. (No. 2)*, the court held that there was a deliberate attempt to take advantage of the name champagne, whereas in the present case the judge found no such specific intention. In general it is no doubt easier to infer damage when a fraudulent intention is established. But that fact does not appear to have played any part in the reasoning on this particular point either of Jeffries J or of Sir Robin Cooke P, who ([1992] 2 NZLR 327 at 332) thought the case exemplified the principle that a tendency to impair distinctiveness might lead to an inference of damage to goodwill, or of Gault J; nor in logic can I see why it should. It seems to me inevitable that if the defendants, with their not insignificant trade as a supplier of drinks to Sainsbury and other retail outlets, are permitted to use the name Elderflower Champagne, the goodwill in the distinctive name champagne will be eroded with serious adverse consequences for the champagne houses.

In my judgment therefore the fifth characteristic identified in the *Advocaat* case is established. I can see no exceptional feature to this case which would justify on grounds of public policy withholding from the champagne houses the ordinary remedy of an injunction to restrain passing off. I would therefore grant an injunction to restrain the defendant from selling, offering for sale, distributing and describing, whether in advertisements or on labels or in any other way, any beverages, not being wine produced in Champagne, under or by reference to the word champagne. That injunction, I would, emphasise, does not prevent the sale of the defendants' product, provided it is not called champagne.'

Sir Thomas Bingham MR and Mann LJ delivered concurring speeches.

COMMENT

Does this case represent an extension of the law of passing off? How does it differ from the Spanish Champagne case? Why did the defendant's suggestion that the plaintiff should be denied a remedy because of acquiescence fail to find sympathy? Unfortunately, leave to appeal to the House of Lords was refused. The Court of Appeal also decided that there had been a breach of the EC Regulation which was held to be directly applicable where there was a risk of confusion. Erosion of goodwill came under judicial scrutiny again in the following case:

Harrods Ltd. v *Harrodian School Ltd.* [1996] RPC 697, Court of Appeal

Over forty years ago, the plaintiff with the famous store in Knightsbridge, used the name 'Harrodian' in relation to some of its activities, including a staff club named the 'Harrodian Club'. The plaintiff had not used the name 'Harrodian' recently and the club was finally closed in 1990. Although originally restricted to employees, eventually other people could join the club. The site was sold to the defendant in 1993.

The defendant intended to open the premises as a school and to name it 'The Harrodian School'. The plaintiff brought an action in passing off to restrain the defendant from using the name. There was no evidence of actual confusion.

Millett LJ (at 715): 'In the classic case of passing off, where the defendant represents his goods or business as the goods or business of the plaintiff, there is an obvious risk of damage to the plaintiff's business by substitution. Customers and potential customers will be lost to the plaintiff if they transfer their custom to the defendant in the belief that they are dealing with the plaintiff. But this is not the only kind of damage which may be caused to the plaintiff's goodwill by the deception of the public. Where the parties are not in competition with each other, the plaintiff's reputation and goodwill may be damaged without any corresponding gain to the defendant. In the *Lego* case, for example, a customer who was dissatisfied with the defendant's plastic irrigation equipment might be dissuaded from buying one of the plaintiff's plastic toy construction kits for his children if he believed that it was made by the defendant. The danger in such a case is that the plaintiff loses control over his own reputation.

In *Taittinger SA* v *Allbev Ltd.* [1993] FSR 641 the court appears to have recognised a different head of damage. If the defendants were allowed to market their product under the name Elderflower Champagne

> "there would take place a blurring or erosion of the uniqueness that now attends the word 'champagne', so that the exclusive reputation of the champagne houses would be debased" per Peter Gibson LJ at page 669.

It is self-evident that the application of the plaintiff's brand name to inferior goods is likely to injure the plaintiff's reputation and damage his goodwill if people take the inferior goods to be those of the plaintiff. That is a classic head of damage in cases of passing off. But Peter Gibson LJ may have had more in mind than this. He referred without disapproval to the submission of counsel for the plaintiffs that if the defendants were allowed to continue to call their product Elderflower Champagne

> "the effect would be to demolish the distinctiveness of the word champagne, and that would inevitably damage the goodwill of the champagne houses."

This is a reference to the debasement of the distinctiveness of the name champagne which would occur if it gradually came to be used by the public as a generic term to describe any kind of sparkling wine. Erosion of the distinctiveness of a brand name has been recognised as a form of damage to the goodwill of the business with which the name is connected in a number of cases, particularly in Australia and New Zealand; but unless care is taken this could mark an unacceptable extension to the tort of passing off. To date the law has not sought to protect the value of the brand name as such, but the value of the goodwill which it generates; and it insists on proof of confusion to justify its intervention. But the erosion of the distinctiveness of a brand name which occurs by reason of its degeneration into common use as a generic term is not necessarily dependent on confusion at all. The danger that if the defendant's product was called champagne then all sparkling wines would eventually come to be called champagne would still exist even if no one was deceived into thinking that such wine really was champagne. I have an intellectual difficulty in accepting the concept that the law insists upon the presence of both confusion and damage and yet recognises as sufficient a head of damage which does not depend on confusion. Counsel for the plaintiffs relied strongly on the possibility of damage of this nature, but it is in my opinion not necessary to consider it further in the present case. There is no danger of "Harrods" becoming a generic term for a retail emporium in the luxury class, and if such a danger existed the use of a different name in connection with an institution of a different kind would not advance the process.' ...

Sir Michael Kerr, dissenting, (at 724): 'The standard remedy in passing off actions is an injunction; an account to assess damages is rare. In the great majority of cases the relevant damage will not be measurable in pounds and pence, but consist in the probability of damage to the plaintiff's reputation and goodwill which is ultimately liable to lead indirectly to a reduction in trade. Loss of distinctiveness causes damage to a reputation for excellence, and loss of trade will ultimately follow. The authorities show two relevant propositions in this regard. First, a debasement or dilution of the plaintiff's reputation, as the result of the action of the defendant, is a relevant head of damage. Secondly, if the act which constitutes the passing off has the effect of raising in people's minds the mistaken belief of a connection between the defendant and the plaintiff, but which is in fact non-existent, then the court will have regard to the fact that the plaintiff has, to that extent, lost control of his reputation, and that he has therefore suffered damage to his goodwill by a potentially injurious association with the defendant against which the court will protect him by injunction.

A number of passages bear out these propositions. Inevitably, the factual contexts were different, but the aspects of principle are not open to question.

As an illustration of the first proposition one can refer to the lengthy passages in the judgments of this court in the *Taittinger* case *(supra)* at pages 668-670, 674 and 678. Thus, at pages 669 and 670, Peter Gibson LJ refers repeatedly to the danger of the blurring or erosion of the distinctiveness of the name in question, in that case "Champagne", and at page 674 Mann LJ said:

"... the impairment is a gradual debasement, dilution or erosion of what is distinctive ... The consequences of debasement, dilution or erosion are not demonstrable in figures of lost sales, but that they will be incrementally damaging to goodwill is in my opinion inescapable."

And on page 678, Sir Thomas Bingham MR answered the question why he would grant injunctive relief as follows:

"Because a reference to champagne imports nuances of quality and celebration, a sense of something privileged and special. But this is the reputation which the Champagne houses have built up over the years, and in which they have a property right. It is not in my view unfair to deny the defendants the opportunity to exploit, share or (in the vernacular) cash in on that reputation, which they have done nothing to establish. It would be very unfair to allow them to do so if the consequence was, as I am satisfied it would be, to debase and cheapen that very reputation."

In fairness to the defendants, it cannot of course be said in the present case that a similar consequence would necessarily follow, and indeed it is greatly to be hoped that this would not be the case. But that is not the test. The crucial point, as stated in the second of the foregoing propositions, is the plaintiff's inevitable loss of control of his reputation and the consequent risk of damage to it.

The validity of this second proposition can be seen from a passage in the well-known judgment of Farwell J in *The British Legion* case *(supra),* where he said at page 564:

"If the use of the Defendant's name, as it is now used, is to suggest to any ordinary person that the Plaintiff association is in some way connected with the Defendant Company or is in some way, as it were, its sponsor, then if evil befalls the Defendant Company and it finds itself (I am not suggesting it will) in trouble either under the Licensing laws or in financial trouble or in some other way of discredit, the result will be, in my judgment, that many of the persons who knew of the existence of the Defendant Club may think that the Plaintiff association has been very ill-advised and very unfortunate in having any connection with such a company, and that might well tend to prevent persons who otherwise would have supported the Plaintiff association by subscriptions or otherwise from continuing to do so... If the Defendant Company were to fall on evil days that might, although not to a great number of persons but to a certain number of persons, reflect discredit on the Plaintiff association and might result in damage to that association......"

Admittedly, the apparent connection between the parties in that case was infinitely closer than in the present case and the risk of confusion inevitably much greater. But the principle is the same, and the remainder is a question of degree. Schools are often in the news, inevitably not for the purpose of proclaiming their excellence, and in the present case the plaintiffs have already been able to refer to a number of early press reports which alleged strong parental dissatisfaction with Sir Alford's unusual educational policies. In addition there is now the further evidence which we have admitted in respect of certain unfortunate events at the school since the trial, and indeed since the main hearing of this appeal, which have resulted in Sir Alford's dismissal of his wife as the headmistress in circumstances of considerable notoriety and discreditable publicity.

Moreover, the danger of damage to the plaintiff's reputation and goodwill which is liable to result from the false impression of a connection with this school may only be the first step. It seems to me that there is a further aspect of damage to the plaintiffs which should qualify for consideration by the court in deciding whether or not to grant an injunction. It does not appear to have arisen in any of the cases to which we were referred, but it adds to the reasons for granting an injunction.

The evidence shows that the name "Harrodian" continues to be used by the plaintiffs internally in many ways, and there are also a number of clubs and associations with outside members which bear this name and which have a public connection with the plaintiffs. In addition, there are plans, which pre-date the present dispute, to use the name "Harrodian" publicly for various purposes in the Harrods Hotel to be built in Trevor Square, Knightsbridge.

However, as this case stands, the extinction of the exclusive connection between the name "Harrodian" and the plaintiffs will have the consequence that their use of this name will no doubt have to be abandoned, at any rate for public purposes. The name "Harrodian" will become generally available, and its use could only be effectively restrained by the plaintiffs, if at all, to adopt an illustration given by the judge in his judgment, "if a trader opened a shop under the style 'The Harrodian Shop' selling clothes or shoes or food, perhaps especially if the shop were situated in the Brompton Road or in Beauchamp Place or even in the Fulham Road......". Thus, if the continued use of the name by the defendants is permitted in the present case, then it seems highly likely that it would proliferate. There would then be nothing to prevent Sir Alford from also giving this name to his school in Putney and thereafter perhaps to other schools as well. The free use of the name might then spawn Harrodian garages, newsagents and other businesses, and even a moneylender might emerge under this name, though the more remote designation of "R. Harrod" would no doubt still be prohibited.

I do not think that potential developments on these lines are too far-fetched to deserve consideration. The point is a double one. The use of the adjectival form of their own name will become lost to the plaintiffs; but the false impression of a connection between the plaintiffs and unconnected businesses using the name "Harrodian" will proliferate. The plaintiffs' reputation will become involved with their fortunes or misfortunes, and become a hostage to them. In my view the plaintiffs have done nothing to deserve this detriment, nor the defendants this benefit.

Finally, I must repeat myself for emphasis. If the staff club had been called "The Harrods Club", and all other facts had been the same, it seems unthinkable that an injunction precluding the defendants from calling themselves "The Harrods School" would be refused. All the arguments about the disparity between the parties' fields of activity, the paucity of evidence of confusion, and the relative unlikelihood of damage, would go out of the window. If so, can it really make any difference that the appropriated name is not "Harrods" but Harrods in its adjectival form? That is a question for the court, and in my view the answer is "no".'

COMMENT

Beldam LJ dismissed the appeal. He thought the risk to the plaintiff's goodwill and reputation was negligible. Does this case represent a significant repudiation of passing off by erosion of goodwill? What is the position under trade mark law in respect of 'non-origin association'? Are there parallels to be drawn? (see *Wagamama Ltd.* v *City Centre Restaurants plc* [1995] FSR 713 in Chapter 6.)

Common Field of Activity

As a basic rule, for damage to occur, the parties should operate in the same field of activity. Thus, the owners of the rights in the Wombles were unable to prevent the use of the company name 'Wombles Skips Ltd.' by the defendant who hired out builders' skips for rubbish. Similarly, Granada Television could not prevent Ford naming one of its cars, the Ford Granada. However, the following case shows that the strictness of the common field of activity requirement may have been compromised.

Lego System Aktieselskab v *Lego M. Lemelstrich Ltd.* [1983] FSR 155, Chancery Division

The plaintiff made children's construction sets comprising moulded coloured plastic bricks and other items which were sold in the United Kingdom under the trade mark 'LEGO'. The plaintiff had built up a substantial reputation, the name LEGO becoming a household word. The defendant was an old established company which made plastic irrigation equipment including garden sprays and sprinklers and had used the name LEGO in other countries for some time (the name was made up from the first two letters of the partners who founded the defendant company). When it appeared that the defendant was about to market their equipment in the United Kingdom under the name LEGO, the plaintiff brought a *quia timet* action for passing off.

Falconer J (at 185): 'My finding that the use by the defendants of the trade mark or name LEGO on or in relation to their products would mislead a very substantial number of persons into thinking that those products were the goods of the plaintiffs or of a company or concern associated or connected with the plaintiffs (a finding, I should, perhaps, point out is in respect of the position in this country) establishes, in my judgment, the presence in the case of characteristics (1), (2) and (3) of the five necessary characteristics of Lord Diplock's formulation. However, as I have indicated, the defendants' case is essentially that the parties are in very different fields and the respective goods of the plaintiffs (toys such as construction sets and building bricks) and those of the defendants (irrigation equipment, particularly for gardens) are so far apart that there could be no misrepresentation, *i.e.* actionable misrepresentation, or any damage or likelihood of damage by the defendants' use of Lego on their goods.

... the recent *Advocaat* case, extending further the striking development in the *Champagne* case of passing off as a cause of action, clearly demonstrates, the law as to passing off, which is concerned with unfair trading, is constantly being developed to meet changing conditions and practices in trade. Moreover, all those earlier cases now have to be seen in the light of the authoritative statement of the law as to passing off enunciated by the House of Lords in the *Advocaat* case. I do not intend, therefore, to refer to all the cases cited by Mr Morcom, but I should make some mention of the *Uncle Mac* case *McCulloch v L A. May Ltd.* (1947) 65 RPC 58. In that case in which the plaintiff, who was well known as the "Uncle Mac" of the BBC's Children's Hour, sued the defendant, who was marketing a breakfast cereal food under the name of "Uncle Mac", Wynn-Parry J, in the course of a consideration of the nature of the cause of action in passing off, made the following much-quoted statement (at p.66, line 53):

> "I have listened with care to all the cases that have been cited and, upon analysis, I am satisfied that there is discoverable in all those in which the court has intervened this factor, namely that there was a common field of activity in which, however remotely, both the plaintiff and the defendant were engaged, and it was the presence of that factor which accounted for the jurisdiction of the court."

In that statement the expression "a common field of activity" has, in a number of cases, been read as a term of art and the statement as requiring that there should be a common field of activity between the plaintiff and the defendant to found a cause of action in passing off. The decision of Wynn-Parry J and that statement were heavily criticised by the full High Court of New South Wales in *Henderson v Radio Corpn. Pty. Ltd.* [1969] RPC 218. The majority of the full High Court (Evatt CJ and Myers J) stated at p. 234, line 14:

> "We find it impossible to accept this view without some qualification. The remedy in passing off is necessarily only available where the parties are engaged in

business, using that expression in its widest sense to include professions and callings. If they are, there does not seem to be any reason why it should also be necessary that there be an area, actual or potential, in which their activities conflict."

Manning J, giving a separate judgment to the full High Court, said, referring to the *Uncle Mac* case at p. 242, line 17:

"There is implicit in the views I have expressed, the conclusion that McCulloch v Lewis A May (Produce Distributors) Ltd. (1947) 65 RPC 58, was wrongly decided. The ratio of the decision in that case was that the plaintiff failed because the parties were not business rivals, having no common trading activities. I think it would be unsafe to adopt the view there expressed that what has been called a common field of activity must be established in every case to entitle the plaintiff to succeed."

However, I respectfully agree with the observation of Oliver J in the *Abba* case: *Lyngstad & Others* v *Anabas Products Ltd.* [1977] FSR 62 at 67:

"I think, if I may say so with respect, that the Australian case to which I have referred is to some extent based on a misconception of what Wynn-Parry J was saying in McCulloch v May. The expression 'common field of activity' is not, I think, a term of art, but merely a convenient shorthand term for indicating what the High Court of New South Wales itself recognised, that is to say, the need for a real possibility of confusion, which is the basis of the action."

That observation is justified by a reference to an earlier part of the judgment of Wynn-Parry J in 65 RPC at p.64, lines 19-35.

However, it is to the law as stated in the *Advocaat case* that we now have to look and, in Lord Diplock's formulation of the characteristics that are necessary ingredients to found a cause of action in passing off, there is no limitation as to the relation of the field of activity of the defendant to that of the plaintiff. Moreover, I have already drawn attention to the passage in his speech at p.93, lines 8-14, in which Lord Diplock specifically recognises that a cause of action for passing off may lie in a case where the plaintiff and the defendant are not competing traders in the same line of business. Although Mr Morcom contended strongly that the respective fields of the plaintiffs and the defendants, toys such as construction sets and building bricks on the one hand, and irrigation equipment, particularly for gardens, on the other, are too far apart for the defendants' use of LEGO to amount to misrepresentation and, indeed, as I have indicated, went so far as to submit that a decision in this case in favour of the plaintiffs would be extending passing off further than it has hitherto been extended in the absence of fraudulent intention, nevertheless he conceded that, in the light of all the cases including the *Advocaat* case, he could not submit that *as a matter of law* (my emphasis) passing off could never be established when the respective activities of the plaintiff and the defendant were completely unrelated. In my judgment, he was right in making that concession. Of course, that is not to say that the proximity of a defendant's field of activity to that of the plaintiff will not be relevant to whether the defendant's acts complained of amount to a misrepresentation in any particular case - plainly it will, at least in most cases. But, in my judgment, there is much force in Mr Aldous's submission, based on the extent of the plaintiffs' reputation in their mark LEGO, that if, as he contended was this case, the plaintiffs' mark has become part of the English language in the sense that everybody associates LEGO with a particular company, namely, the manufacturers of the LEGO toy construction sets and building bricks, then the misrepresentation by the defendants' use of the mark is easier to assume and to prove; on the other hand, if the mark or name concerned has only a limited field of recognition it is obviously more difficult to establish its understanding as denoting the plaintiff's goods in a field which is not directly comparable with the field of that plaintiff's goods.

Whether or not the acts of a defendant complained of in a passing off action amount to a misrepresentation must be a question of fact and, in the end, that was common ground between Mr Aldous and Mr Morcom. I think Mr Morcom expressed it correctly when, at the conclusion of that part of his argument dealing with misrepresentation, he submitted that what has to be established by a plaintiff is that there is a real risk that a substantial number of persons among the relevant section of the public will in fact believe that there is a business connection between the plaintiff and the defendant. That, as I have found, has been established by the plaintiffs in this case.

... the plaintiffs' mark LEGO with its reputation is a very valuable asset - the plaintiffs' evidence, not challenged in cross-examination, was that it is the most valuable single asset of the Lego Group. The plaintiffs' goodwill is, of course, attached to that mark with its reputation (cf. essential numbered (3) in Lord Fraser's formulation in the *Advocaat* case), indeed the reputation in the mark is such that it is probably the most important element in the plaintiffs' goodwill. Mr Aldous submitted that this is a case where the reputation of the plaintiffs' mark is so wide - the mark is, as he submitted and as I have held, a household word - that the reputation, and hence the plaintiffs' goodwill to which it is attached, extends beyond the field of toys and construction kits. That that reputation extends beyond that field and that it is wide enough to extend, in particular, to goods such as garden irrigation sprinklers made of coloured plastics materials, is, it seems to me, demonstrated by the fact, as I have found, that the defendants' use of LEGO on or in relation to such articles would mislead a very substantial number of the adult persons of the population into thinking those goods were products of the plaintiffs or of a company or concern associated or connected with the plaintiffs ...

The effect of his evidence was that, because of the reputation of Lego (meaning the plaintiffs' toy construction products), there would be an opportunity for licensing or franchising the mark LEGO in other fields, that, because of the nature of the Lego products, primarily plastic bricks, the plastics area would be a likely one to exploit and that garden implements would be an ideal market for franchising LEGO, because the purchasers of Lego toys are parents and grandparents; as he put it, the very same people who are likely to be purchasers of garden equipment. Obviously, the possibility of licensing or franchising another trader to use LEGO in the gardening equipment area would be lost if the defendants are allowed to continue using LEGO in this country in relation to their products. The effect, therefore, of the defendants continuing to use LEGO in this country in relation to their products would be to destroy that part of the plaintiffs' reputation in their mark LEGO and goodwill attached to it which extends to such goods. In view of the nature and extent of the reputation in the plaintiffs' mark LEGO, as I have held it to be, it seems to me that the defendants' use of the mark LEGO in this country in respect of their goods is calculated to injure the plaintiffs' business goodwill in that way, in the sense that it is a reasonably foreseeable consequence that it will do so, and further that such damage must result if that use is allowed to continue ...

But, as to the plaintiffs' goodwill being only in a very specific field, I do not accept that submission - their reputation in their mark LEGO, to which their goodwill is attached, is such that it extends beyond the field in which they have hitherto been engaged and, as I have held, has been demonstrated to be so extensive that its use by the defendants on goods such as their coloured plastic garden sprinklers would mislead a very substantial number of persons who would think such use denoted the plaintiffs' goods or some association or connection with the plaintiff. Mr Morcom further argued, in support of his main submission on damage, that in the absence of any common field of activity, actual or potential, *i.e.* potential, as he explained, in the sense of a natural extension of the field of the plaintiffs' existing trade, there is no basis on which any injury to the business or goodwill of the plaintiff can be foreseen, apart from exceptional cases where some dishonest activity facilitates the finding that such injury is reasonably foreseeable. It seems to me that that argument cannot be right; as I have already pointed out, in Lord Diplock's formulation of the necessary characteristics to found a cause of action in passing off, there is no limitation as to the relation of the field of activity of the defendant to that of the plaintiff and, indeed, as I have also mentioned, Mr Morcom conceded, rightly in my view, that he could *not* submit that, as a matter of law, passing off could never be established when the respective activities of the plaintiff and the defendant were completely unrelated. If passing off can be established in a case where the respective activities of plaintiff and defendant are completely unrelated, it must follow that in such a case injury to the plaintiffs' business or goodwill must be reasonably foreseeable, notwithstanding the absence of any common field of activity, actual or potential, in Mr Morcom's narrow sense.

In the result, in my judgment, the plaintiffs have established their case of passing off against the defendants and the action succeeds.'

COMMENT

From this case, it appears that the greater the goodwill, the more extensive the boundaries of the field of activity and, hence, the greater the protection afforded by the law of passing off. Was Falconer J right to take account of the possibility of licensing the use of the name LEGO or franchising when there was no evidence of any such plans for the plaintiff so to do?

In the *Wombles* case, *Wombles Ltd.* v *Wombles Skips Ltd.* [1977] RPC 99, the defendant used the name Wombles Skips Ltd. for his skip hire business. The plaintiff, who exploited the rights in the Wombles characters failed in a passing off action because the judge considered that no-one would think that the defendant's company had any business relationship with the Wombles. If there were an action today based on the same facts, would the same decision be reached? LEGO was registered as a trade mark by the plaintiff: why did the plaintiff not sue on the basis of trade mark infringement?

A Law of Unfair Competition?

As mentioned earlier, there is no general law of unfair competition in the United Kingdom as there is, for example, in Germany. In the extracts from the two articles following, the means and implications of implementing a law of unfair competition are discussed. In the first, the width and utility of an Australian statutory provision to control deceptive trade conduct is discussed. The second article questions the need for a law of unfair competition and considers whether such a law would be an unwelcome fetter on competition.

Booy, A. 'A Half-Way House for Unfair Competition in the United Kingdom - A Practitioner's Plea' [1991] 12 *EIPR* 439

'A Possible Solution
Australian jurisprudence, like that of the United Kingdom, does not recognise a general law of unfair competition. Any thought that such a cause of action existing was decisively eradicated by the decision of the High Court in *Moorgate Tobacco Company Ltd.* v *Phillip Morris Ltd. (No.2)* (1984) 156 CLR 414. This case involved a dispute between two large cigarette manufacturers. Phillip Morris Ltd. produced "Kent" cigarettes in Australia under licence, and was permitted to use the "Kent" trade mark. Subsequently, representatives of Phillip Morris Ltd. were advised of Kent plans to market "Kent Golden Lights" and there were some unsuccessful attempts to interest Phillip Morris Ltd. in the licence of this trade mark. At the time, Phillip Morris Ltd. was already marketing under the trade mark "Marlboro Lights". When it later applied for the trade mark "Golden Lights", the owner of the "Kent Golden Lights" mark sued, *inter alia,* for "unfair competition". Deane J (with whom the rest of the court agreed) firmly rejected any development of the common law in this area, stating "...'unfair competition' does not, in itself, provide a sufficient basis for relief under the law of this country".

In 1974, after an extensive review of the law in both the United States and the United Kingdom Part V, Division 1 of the federal Trade Practices Act 1974 was enacted. The "lynchpin" of this division is section 52, which provides as follows:

"A corporation shall not, in trade or commerce, engage in conduct that is misleading or deceptive or is likely to mislead or deceive."

A number of other sections deal with more specifically defined aspects of unfair trade practices such as bait advertising, referral and pyramid selling and criminal sanctions are provided for such specific offences. An injunction and civil damages may however be obtained for a breach of nearly all provisions of Part 5.

Described as a "jurisprudential freak", section 52 is a statutory prohibition against a certain form of conduct, though in itself it does not prescribe any particular sanction. The objective was to create a section "capable of flexible use to meet the imagination of defendants in avoiding the reach of more precisely drawn sections".

The simplicity of the section belies its potency and utility. Like passing off, it requires no proof of intent but unlike passing off, it is available to both consumers and competitors alike. Unlike the law of representations, it sees no difference between "existing" and "future" facts, and it is flexible enough to protect against copying of functional designs, architects' drawings, and advertising malpractice.

Although the use of section 52 has undoubtedly produced on occasion some unexpected side-effects, the legislation appears to be achieving its aim. In 1978, commentators were able to state that "the law has been instantly accepted by the community and the commercial section in particular". Indeed, the success of section 52 in the corporate sphere has led all Australian states except Tasmania to implement complementary legislation which focuses on the conduct of individuals, thus enabling the repeal of "patchwork" state legislation such as The Consumer Affairs Act, The Door to Door (Sales) Act, the Unordered Goods and Services Act and The Mock Auctions Act.

From a legal practitioner's viewpoint, section 52 has been accepted as a "valuable weapon", providing consumers and business competitors alike with formidable remedies against deceptive commercial behaviour.

Judges appear to have had little difficulty applying the concept of conduct which is "misleading or deceptive or likely to mislead or deceive", although distinctions have been drawn between "mere confusion" and "actual deception". It is now the law that to prove a breach of section 52 it is not enough to establish that the conduct complained of was "merely confusing" or "caused people to wonder" and in this respect, section 52 is narrower than passing off. In practice, however, the "mere confusion" nuance appears to serve principally as a "safety valve" in protecting corporations from over-sensitive plaintiffs.

It is true that the outer limits of section 52 are still being tested and determined by the Australian courts. Nevertheless, the section seems to have worked well in combating a wide variety of undesirable trade practices, without giving rise to the criticisms which often accompany a general law of unfair competition.'

Cornish, W.R. 'Unfair Competition under Common Law and Statute' (1985-86) 10 _Adelaide Law Review_ 32 at 35

'The West German law of unfair competition is highly developed and has come to provide the central plank of consumer protection by admitting consumers and consumer associations alongside competitors as plaintiffs in such proceedings. It is now a wide-ranging law covering not only misappropriation of marks and names and all forms of deceptive advertising and labelling but predatory practices of monopolies and cartels such as rebating, loss leading and the like. Competitors make regular use of it as a weapon in the commercial process.

Within the EEC the Germans have pressed for this model to be imposed upon the whole Common Market, the major initiative being a multi-volume study for the EC Commission of the existing laws of unfair competition, by the Max-Planck Institute for Patent, Copyright and Competition Law in Munich, led by the great Professor Eugene Ulmer. It was Ulmer's ultimate proposal that all states should adopt an unfair competition law with a general clause restraining conduct contrary to honest business practice, and that this should allow for competitors' or consumers' actions for injunctive relief and monetary compensation, including rapid interlocutory relief. The only outcome of this initiative so far has been a squib - a Directive to Member States last year, purely on the subject of misleading advertising. This in effect adopts a "lowest common denominator" approach and allows, for instance, the United Kingdom to continue with its existing consumer protection laws.

This is highly unsatisfactory to Ulmer's torch-bearers. The current director of the Max-Planck Institute, Professor Beier, in this year's Herschel Smith Lecture in London, advocated a return to the Ulmer approach. He did so in very general terms which scarcely spelled out what he found so unsatisfactory about the present position. He warned of the danger of a law that leant too strongly towards consumer interests. The future law, he said, "must give equal effect to the interests of all market participants, be they agricultural producers, industrial manufacturers, wholesalers or retailers, commercial customers or private consumers, large medium size or small business". That is all very well for a peroration but it gives little away about what is so unsatisfactory in the present position. Only one hint of this came incidentally - in the course of a reassuring demonstration that German courts do follow precedent, just like common law courts. We were invited to admire a decision of the German Supreme Court sustaining an objection to use of the Rolls-Royce grille to advertise whisky; and a consequential decision of the Munich Appeal Court enjoining the marketers of Perrier water from claiming either that it was *the* champagne of mineral waters for even *a* champagne of mineral waters: the former because consumers would be misled, Perrier being an ordinary mineral water; the latter because it involved a serious dilution of the champagne producers' name.

I have little doubt that British courts would treat claims of this nature with the same suspicion that Australian courts have been showing to some of the actions launched by competitors under s 52 [of the Australian Trade Practices Act 1974]. I would have every sympathy. This illustration from West Germany seems to show an overheated concern that none shall benefit from another's reputation without licence in any way whatsoever. It has very little to do with significant interests of consumers. To allow such claims in the name of providing them protection is a distraction from what should be the thrust of legal intervention - which should be to ensure that the buying public is not directly misinformed or led on by highly suggestive claims that play unduly upon their sensitivities and inadequacies. These are not matters which competitors can be relied upon to police systematically or satisfactorily. My hope for the Common Market is that we will develop the machinery that is directly concerned with the consumer's welfare without any distracting overlay of competitive advantage.'

COMMENT

What, if anything, would be gained by enacting a law of unfair competition and who would benefit from such a law? It should be remembered that, apart from the law of passing off, United Kingdom law has a number of ways of discouraging or tackling deceptive business practices. Of course, trade mark law may be relevant but there are a number of criminal offences such as those under the Trade Descriptions Act 1968, the Trade Marks Act 1994 (fraudulent application or use of a trade mark), the Forgery and Counterfeiting Act 1981 and the Theft Acts 1968 and 1978. However, criminal offences do not give the aggrieved trader a civil right of action and it could be argued that the basic requirements as expressed in the *Advocaat* case are too restrictive and do not fully take account of the modern advertising and trading climate. Do you agree?

Chapter 8

EC Law and Intellectual Property

Introduction

By their very nature, intellectual property rights may be used to distort the market in goods and information. Intellectual property rights place their owners in an advantageous position of power, allowing them to control imports by virtue of the fact that most intellectual property rights control importation of the subject matter by making it a form of infringement. This can operate against the free movement of goods throughout the European Community.

A further factor is that some intellectual property rights are monopolistic in nature, such as patents and trade marks. Other rights, like copyright, although not true monopoly rights in that the independent creation of a similar work will not infringe, can provide their owners with a *de facto* monopoly if the information underlying the work is not available from any other source. The existence of a monopoly will tempt the owner of the right to take maximum advantage of it. Whilst this may, in the normal run of things, be no more than sensible commercial practice, it can in some cases go further than what is generally acceptable and amount to a distortion of the relevant market. Take, for example, a case where the predominant owner of the intellectual property rights in a particular technology tries to acquire all or most of the remaining rights in that technology.

A great deal of intellectual property is exploited by means of licensing. There again the problem of abuses may be present. The owner of monopoly rights may be in a powerful position and able to force restrictive terms on a licensee severely constraining the licensee's use of the technology. Alternatively, it may work the other way round. The licensee may be the one with the stronger bargaining position.

It is difficult to reconcile the protection of intellectual property rights with the concept of a free market. United Kingdom law has attempted to do this in the past by means of domestic competition legislation and particular statutory provisions such as compulsory licensing, controls over restrictive terms and, for example, in the case of copyright, providing for permitted acts. Another example is the availability of licences of right in some cases.

European Community law has striven long and hard to reach the nirvana of a single market and most of the developments and issues dealt with in this chapter are examples of this difficult and tortuous task.

The EC Treaty

One of the main aims of the EC Treaty is to encourage trade between Member States and it achieves this in a number of ways. In terms of intellectual property, important provisions are Articles 30, 85 and 86. Article 30 prohibits quantitative restrictions and is particularly important in terms of the freedom of movement of goods. It has led to the doctrine of exhaustion of rights. That is, once particular goods are placed on the market by or with the consent of the right-owner, he can no longer use those rights to prevent further distribution and sale of those goods. To this, however, there are some qualifications as will be seen.

Article 85(1) prohibits, *inter alia*, restrictive trade agreements and is particularly important in terms of licensing agreements and other agreements for the exploitation of intellectual property. Article 86 prohibits abuses of dominant positions. Articles 30, 36 (which must be read with Article 30), 85 and 86 are reproduced below. *The numbering of the Treaty will be changed in 1999. For example, Article 85 will become Article 81 and Article 86 will become Article 82. This is a result of the Amsterdam Treaty.*

Extracts from the EC Treaty (Treaty of Rome 1957)

Article 30
Quantitative restrictions on imports and all measures having equivalent effect shall, without prejudice to the following provisions, be prohibited between Member States.

[Article 34 is expressed in similar terms for exports]

Article 36
Articles 30 to 34 shall not preclude prohibitions or restrictions on imports, exports or goods in transit justified on grounds of public morality, public policy or public security; the protection of health and life of humans, animals or plants; the protection of national treasures possessing artistic, historic or archaeological value; or the protection of industrial or commercial property. Such prohibitions or restrictions shall not, however, constitute a means of arbitrary discrimination or a disguised restriction on trade between Member States.

Article 85
1. The following shall be prohibited as incompatible with the common market: all agreements between undertakings, decisions by associations of undertakings and concerted practices which may affect trade between Member States and which have as their object or effect the prevention, restriction or distortion of competition within the common market, and in particular those which:
   - (a) directly or indirectly fix purchase or selling prices or any other trading conditions;
   - (b) limit or control production, markets, technical developments, or investment;

  (c) share markets or sources of supply;

  (d) apply dissimilar conditions to equivalent transactions with other trading parties, thereby placing them at a competitive disadvantage;

  (e) make the conclusion of contracts subject to acceptance by the other parties of supplementary obligations which, by their nature or according to commercial usage, have no connection with the subject of such contracts.

2. Any agreements or decisions prohibited pursuant to this Article shall be automatically void.

3. The provisions of paragraph 1 may, however, be declared inapplicable in the case of:
- any agreement or category of agreements between undertakings;
- any decision or category of decisions by associations of undertakings;
- any concerted practice or category of concerted practices;

which contributes to improving the production or distribution of goods or to promoting technical or economic progress, while allowing consumers a fair share of the resulting benefit, and which does not:

  (a) impose on the undertakings concerned restrictions which are not indispensable to the attainment of these objectives;

  (b) afford such undertakings the possibility of eliminating competition in respect of a substantial part of the products in question.

Article 86

Any abuse by one or more undertakings of a dominant position within the common market or in a substantial part of it shall be prohibited as incompatible with the common market in so far as it may affect trade between Member States.

Such abuse may, in particular, consist in:

  (a) directly or indirectly imposing unfair purchase or selling prices or other unfair trading conditions;

  (b) limiting production, markets or technical development to the prejudice of consumers;

  (c) applying dissimilar conditions to equivalent transactions with other trading parties, thereby placing them at a competitive disadvantage;

  (d) making the conclusion of contracts subject to acceptance by the other parties of supplementary obligations which, by their nature or according to commercial usage, have no connection with the subject of such contracts.

COMMENT

These provisions apply in a much wider context than situations where intellectual property rights are concerned but it is with the latter that this chapter is primarily concerned. A conflict immediately arises between Article 30 and Article 36. Patents, designs and trade marks are all within the definition of 'industrial property' under the Paris Convention. Is copyright 'commercial property'?

Note that Article 85(3) disapplies Article 85(1) in particular cases. This exemption allows some forms of restrictive agreements. Exemption may be by block exemption (see the 'Technology Transfer' Regulation later in this chapter) or by individual exemption. In other cases, a 'comfort letter' may be issued by the Commission indicating that either the agreement in question is thought not to be caught by Article 85(1) or to be likely to benefit from Article 85(3).

Note, in particular, the rationale for Article 85(3). What sort of agreements could take advantage of it?

Non-discrimination

It will be a relatively rare matter when Article 6 of the EC Treaty (prohibition of discrimination on the grounds of nationality) will be an issue in the context of intellectual property rights. However, as the case below shows, it can be very useful where a Member State grants better protection to its nationals than to persons from other Member States.

Collins v *Imtrat Handellgesellschaft mbH* [1994] FSR 166, European Court of Justice

Phil Collins, the British singer and composer, brought an action in the regional court in Munich against Imtrat in respect of its selling in Germany a compact disc which contained a bootleg recording of a concert by Phil Collins in the United States. At the time, German copyright law gave protection to German performers in relation to unauthorised recordings of their performances wherever those performances took place. It appeared, however, that foreign performers were not so protected if the performance was made outside Germany. As there was some doubt about the provisions, in particular, whether they offended against Article 7(1) of the EEC Treaty (now Article 6(1) of the EC Treaty), the court referred the matter to the European Court of Justice for a preliminary ruling under Article 177. It was joined with a similar case, *Patricia Im- und Export Verwaltungsgesellscahft mbH* v *EMI Electrola GmbH*, which concerned the sale of bootleg recordings of performances given by Cliff Richard in Great Britain in 1958 and 1959.

Judgment (at 170): '.. The Court ... cannot give decisions on the interpretation of national law or regulations or on their compatibility with Community law. Consequently it cannot interpret the UrhG or assess its compatibility with Community law. The Court can only give the national court guidance on interpretation under Community law which will enable it to resolve the legal problem before it: Cases 91/83 & 127/83, *Heineken Brouwerijen* [1984] ECR 3435, [1985] 1 CMLR 389.

The orders making the references mention the national rules applying to copyright and section 125 UrhG, which governs the rights of performing artists, the so-called "neighbouring rights." It is not for the Court to decide whether the main actions concern one or the other of these two types of rights. As the Commission proposes, the questions submitted should be regarded as relating to the rules applying to both.

The questions refer to Article 7(1) EEC, which lays down the general principle of non-discrimination on grounds of nationality. As the Article expressly states, such prohibition applies only within the scope of application of the Treaty.

The questions must therefore be regarded as seeking in essence to establish whether:

- copyright and related rights are within the scope of application of the Treaty within the meaning of Article 7(1) and whether the general principle of non-discrimination laid down by that Article consequently applies to those rights;
- if so, whether Article 7(1) prevents the law of a Member State from refusing authors and performing artists of other Member States and their successors in title the right, which is granted by the same law to nationals, to prohibit the marketing in national territory of a phonogram made without their consent, if the performance in question was given outside national territory;
- whether Article 7(1) EEC can be relied upon directly before a national court by an author or artist of another Member State or his successor in title in order to obtain the protection given to nationals.

Application of the Treaty to copyright and related rights

The Commission, the German and British Governments, Phil Collins and EMI Electrola contend that copyright and related rights, in so far as they are economic rights determining the conditions under which works and performances by artists can be exploited commercially, fall within the scope of application of the Treaty, as shown by the Court's judgments applying Articles 30, 36, 59, 85 and 86 EEC to those rights and by the intense legislative activity concerning them in the Communities. In the rare cases where a specific provision of the Treaty does not apply, the general principle of non-discrimination laid down by Article 7(1) EEC must in any case be applied.

Imtrat contends, on the contrary, that the conditions for according copyright and related rights affect the existence, and not the exercise, of those rights and are not within the scope of application of the Treaty, as shown by Article 222 EEC and the Court's settled case law. Patricia and Mr Kraul, repeating on this point the findings of the Federal Supreme Court, argue in particular that copyright and related rights were not, in the absence of Community rules or harmonisation measures at the time of the acts with which the main action is concerned, governed by Community law.

In the present state of Community law, and in the absence of Community measures or the harmonisation of national law, it is for the Member States to specify the conditions and rules for the protection of literary and artistic property, subject to complying with the relevant international agreements: Case 341/87, *EMI Electrola* [1989] ECR 79, [1989] 2 CMLR 413.

The specific purpose of these rights, as governed by national law, is to protect the moral and economic rights of their owners. The protection of moral rights enables authors and artists to resist any distortion, mutilation or other alteration of the work which would be prejudicial to their honour or reputation. Copyright and related rights also have economic characteristics in that they provide for the possibility of commercially exploiting the marketing of the protected work, particularly in the form of licences granted in return for the payment of royalties: Cases 55 & 57/80, *Musik-Vertrieb Membran* [1981] ECR 147, [1981] 2 CMLR 44.

As the Court observed in the last-mentioned judgment, while the commercial exploitation of copyright is a source of remuneration for the owner it also constitutes a form of control on marketing exercisable by the owner, the copyright management societies acting in his name and the grantees of licences. From this viewpoint the commercial exploitation of copyright raises the same problems as that of any other industrial or commercial property right.

Like other industrial and commercial property rights, the exclusive rights conferred by literary and artistic property are such as to affect trade in goods and services, as well as competition in the Community. For this reason, as the Court has consistently held, these rights, although governed by national law, are subject to the requirements of the Treaty and therefore fall within the scope of application.

Consequently they are subject to, for example, Articles 30 and 36 EEC on the freedom of movement of goods. As the Court has previously held, musical works are incorporated in phonograms which are goods trade in which in the Community is governed by the above mentioned provisions: Cases 55 & 57/80, cited above.

In the same way the activities of copyright management societies are subject to Articles 59 and 66 EEC, relating to the freedom to provide services. As the Court observed in Case 7/82, *GVL* v *EC Commission* [1983] ECR 483, [1983] 3 CMLR 645, these activities must not be conducted in such a way as to have the effect of impeding the free movement of services, particularly the exploitation of the rights of performers, to the extent of partitioning the Common Market.

Finally, the exclusive rights conferred by literary and artistic property are subject to the Treaty provisions concerning competition: Case 78/70, *Deutsche Grammophon* [1971] ECR 487, [1971] CMLR 631.

In addition, subsequently to the main actions, the Council adopted Directive 92/100 of 19 November 1992 on rental right and lending right and on certain rights related to copyright in the field of intellectual property [1992] OJ L346/61 on the basis of Article 57(2), 66 and 100a EEC precisely in order to avoid the risk of obstacles to trade and distortions of competition.

It follows from what has been said that copyright and related rights, which fall within the scope of application of the Treaty particularly by reason of their effects on trade in goods and services in the Community, are necessarily subject to the general principle of non-discrimination laid down by Article 7(1) EEC, and there is no requirement to attach them to the specific provisions of Articles 30, 36, 59 and 66.

Therefore the reply to the question referred must be that copyright and related rights are within the scope of application of the Treaty within the meaning of Article 7(1); the general principle of non-discrimination laid down by that Article is consequently applicable to those rights.

Discrimination within the meaning of Article 7(1) EEC
Imtrat and Patricia contend that the distinction made in the cases referred to by the national courts between German nationals and nationals of other Member States is objectively justified by the differences in national laws and by the fact that not all the Member States have yet acceded to the Rome Convention. Under these circumstances, it is said, the distinction is not contrary to Article 7(1) EEC.

The Court has consistently held that Article 7 does not apply to differences in treatment and distortions which affect persons and enterprises under the jurisdiction of the Community and which may arise from differences in the laws of the Member States if such differences affect all persons to whom they apply, according to objective criteria and without regard to nationality: Case 14/68, *Wilhelm* [1969] ECR 1, [1969] CMLR 100.

Therefore, contrary to the arguments of Imtrat and Patricia, neither the differences in national laws relating to the protection of copyright and related rights nor the fact that not all the Member States have yet acceded to the Rome Convention can justify an infringement of the principle of non-discrimination laid down by Article 7(1) EEC.

By prohibiting "any discrimination on grounds of nationality," Article 7 EEC requires that persons in a situation governed by Community law be placed on a completely equal footing with nationals of the Member State: Case 186/87, *Cowan* [1989] ECR 195, [1990] 2 CMLR 613. Where this principle applies, it precludes a Member State from making the grant of an exclusive right subject to the condition of being a national of that State.

Consequently the reply to the question must be that Article 7(1) EEC must be interpreted as meaning that it prevents the law of a Member State from refusing, under certain circumstances, authors and performing artists of other Member States and their successors in title the right, which is granted by the same law to nationals, to prohibit the marketing in national territory of a phonogram made without their consent, if the performance in question was given outside national territory.

Effects of Article 7(1)
As the Court has consistently held, the right to equal treatment laid down by Article 7(1) EEC is conferred directly by Community law: Case 186/87, cited above. The right can therefore be relied upon before the national court when asking it to set aside the discriminatory provisions of a national law which refuses nationals of other Member States the protection accorded to nationals of the State in question.

Therefore the reply to the question is that Article 7(1) EEC must be interpreted as meaning that the principle of non-discrimination which it lays down can be relied upon directly before the national court by an author or artist of a Member State or his successor in title in order to seek the protection given to national authors and artists...

On those grounds, THE COURT ... HEREBY RULES:

1. Copyright and related rights are within the scope of application of the Treaty within the meaning of Article 7(1); the general principle of non-discrimination laid down by that Article is consequently applicable to those rights.

2. Article 7(1) EEC must be interpreted as meaning that it prevents the law of a Member State from refusing authors and performing artists of other Member States and their successors in title the right, which is granted by the same law to nationals, to prohibit the marketing in national territory of a phonogram made without their consent, if the performance in question was given outside national territory.

3. Article 7(1) EEC must be interpreted as meaning that the principle of non-discrimination which it lays down can be relied upon directly before the national court by an author or artist of a Member State or his successor in title in order to seek the protection given to national authors and artists.'

COMMENT
The implications of this case are very important. Consider the changes to the term of copyright which took effect on 1 January 1996. In the United Kingdom, this resulted in the possibility of revived copyright. If the copyright in a work had expired in the United Kingdom but the work was still protected in another Member State, the United Kingdom copyright came back to life. Germany previously had a basic term of

copyright protection of 'life plus 70 years' compared with 'life plus 50 years' in the United Kingdom and some other Member States. What is the position of a work subject to United Kingdom copyright (but not German copyright) in respect of which the author died in 1940 in the light of this case?

In the 'Phil Collins case', would it have made any difference if the recordings had been made with the consent of the performer for sale in the United States only? Would your answer be the same if they had been made with the performer's consent for sale in the United Kingdom only? Note also that rights in performances have been significantly modified and improved recently.

Free Movement of Goods

A basic right in relation to a patent or trade mark is a right to prevent importation of patented products or goods to which the trade mark has been applied into the territory in which the patent or trade mark is in force. This applies to other rights also.

A typical situation where freedom of movement of goods is involved is where a proprietor of patents in two or more Member States sells the relevant patented products in different Member States at different prices. A third party might be tempted to buy the products in the Member State where they are less expensive and import them into other Member States to sell them at a lower price than the proprietor is selling them at in that other Member State. This activity is often referred to as parallel importing. The case below provides a good example.

Centrafarm BV v *Sterling Drug Inc.* [1974] 2 CMLR 480, European Court of Justice

(Note: there were two joined cases, one involving a patent, the other a trade mark. In the extracts, the trade mark judgment is omitted as similar considerations applied and the ruling was to similar effect.)

Sterling Drug Inc. was a company formed in the United States and had patents in several countries including the United Kingdom and the Netherlands for a method of preparing a drug, *acidum nalidixicum*. The trade mark for this drug, 'Negram' was owned by Sterling-Winthrop Group Ltd in the United Kingdom and by Winthrop BV in the Netherlands.

Centrafarm BV bought quantities of the drug in England and West Germany which had been properly put on the market by subsidiaries of Sterling Drug Inc. and imported them, without permission from Sterling Drug, into the Netherlands. The drugs had been made by the patented process and bore the Negram registered trade mark. Centrafarm BV made money from the price differential in the cost of the drug in the different Member States. For example, the drug was sold far more cheaply in the United Kingdom because of the buying power of the NHS.

Sterling Drug Inc. and Winthrop BV each began actions in the District Court in Rotterdam claiming interim relief and an injunction against any infringement of the patent and against direct or indirect abusive use of Winthrop's Negram trade mark. The relief was granted and Centrafarm BV and its director, Mr de Peijper (the second defendant), appealed unsuccessfully to the Dutch Court of Appeal. A further appeal was brought before the Supreme Court which referred the following questions to the European Court of Justice under Article 177 of the EC Treaty for a preliminary ruling.

The following questions were referred to the court (at 485):

'I. As regards the rules concerning the free movement of goods:
(a) Assuming that:
1. a patentee has parallel patents in several of the countries belonging to the EEC,
2. the products protected by those patents are lawfully marketed in one or more of those countries by undertakings to whom the patentee had granted licences to manufacture and/or sell,
3. those products are subsequently exported by third parties and are marketed and further dealt with in one of those other countries,
4. the patent legislation in the last-mentioned countries gives the patentee the right to take legal action to prevent products thus protected by patents from being there marketed by others, even where these products were previously lawfully marketed in another country by the patentee or by the patentee's licensee:
do the rules in the EEC Treaty concerning the free movement of the goods, notwithstanding what is stated in Article 36, prevent the patentee from using the right under 4 above?
(b) If the rules concerning the free movement of goods do not under all circumstances prevent the patentee exercising his rights under 4 above, do they however so prevent him if the exercise of that right arises exclusively, or partially, from an attempt to partition national markets from each other for products protected by the patent, or at any rate has such partitioning as an effect?
(c) Does it make any difference to the reply to the questions under (a) and (b) above that the patentee and the licensees do or do not belong to the same concern?
(d) Can the patentee, for the purpose of justifying his aforementioned right, successfully rely upon the fact that the price differences in the respective countries, which make it worthwhile for third parties in one country to market products originating in another country, and give the patentee an interest in taking action against such practices, are the consequence of governmental measures that result in the price level of these goods being lower in the exporting country than would have been the case in the absence of those measures?
(e) At any rate where the patent relates to pharmaceutical products, can the patentee for the purpose of justifying the exercise of his patent right successfully rely upon the fact that the circumstances described under (a) above prevent him from controlling the distribution of his products, such control by him being considered essential for the purpose of taking measures to protect the public where defects manifested themselves?
(f) Is it a consequence of Article 42 of the Treaty of Accession that if the rules of the EEC Treaty relating to the free movement of goods prevent the exercise of a

patent right as before mentioned, it is until 1 January 1975 not possible in Holland to rely upon these rules in relation to such goods originating in the United Kingdom?

II. As regards Article 85:

(a) Does the fact that a patentee owns parallel patents in different countries belonging to the EEC and that he has in those countries granted to different undertakings associated with the patentee licences to manufacture and sell (assuming that all of the agreements entered into with such licensees are exclusively or in part designed to regulate differently for the different countries the conditions on the market in respect of the goods protected by the patent) mean that this is a case of agreement or concerted practices of the type prohibited by Article 85 of the EEC Treaty, and must be an action for breach as referred to under I (a) above - to the extent that this must be regarded as the result of such agreements or concerted practices - for that reason be treated as unlawful?

(b) Is Article 85 also applicable if, in connection with agreements or concerted practices as there referred to, it is only undertakings belonging to the same concern that are involved?

Judgment (at 502): ' 1. By an interlocutory judgment of 1 March 1974, which reached this Court on 4 March, the Hoge Raad der Nederlanden (Supreme Court of the Netherlands) put, under Article 177 of the EEC Treaty, certain questions relating to patent rights in relation to the provisions of the Treaty and of the Act of Accession of the three new member-States.

2. The Hoge Raad, in the referring judgment, set out as follows the facts and national law it had in mind for the purpose of the reply to the questions it put:

- a patentee holds parallel patents in several States belonging to the EEC;

- the products protected by such patents are lawfully marketed in one or more of such member-States by undertakings to which the patentee has granted manufacture and sales licences or merely sales licences;

- these products are subsequently exported by third parties, put on the market in one of the other member-States and resold;

- the patent law applicable in the latter member-State gives to the patentee the right to use legal proceedings to oppose the marketing of the products protected by his patent in that country by other persons, even though the products have previously been lawfully marketed in another country by the patentee or a licensee from him.

3. It appears from the hearing that the action concerns the rights of a holder of parallel patents in several member-States who, in one of such States, grants an exclusive marketing concession for the patented product, which does not cover its manufacture, while the patentee refrains from manufacturing the patented product in that same member-State.

As to question I (a)

4. In this question the Court is asked to say whether, in the circumstances given, the rules of the Treaty on free movement of goods prevent a patentee opposing the marketing by other persons of a product protected by the patent.

5. The effect of the provisions of the Treaty on the free movement of goods, particularly Article 30, is to prohibit between member-States measures restricting imports and all measures of equivalent effect.

6. By Article 36 these provisions do not, however, prevent prohibitions or restrictions on imports justified on grounds of protection of industrial and commercial property.

7. But it appears from that same Article, particularly from its second sentence, as well as from the context, that while the Treaty does not affect the existence of the rights in industrial and commercial property recognised by the law of a member-State, the exercise of such rights may nonetheless, according to circumstances, be affected by the prohibitions in the Treaty.

8. In so far as it makes an exception to one of the fundamental principles of the Common Market, Article 36 allows derogations to the free movement of goods only to the extent that such derogations are justified for the protection of the rights which constitute the specific object of such property.

9. As regards patents, the specific object of industrial property is *inter alia* to ensure to the holder, so as to recompense the creative effort of the inventor, the exclusive right to utilise an invention with a view to the manufacture and first putting into circulation of industrial products, either directly or by the grant of licences to third parties, as well as the right to oppose any infringement.

10. The existence, in national laws on industrial and commercial property, of provisions that the right of a patentee is not exhausted by the marketing in another member-State of the patented product, so that the patentee may oppose the import into his own State of the product marketed in another State, may constitute an obstacle to the free movement of goods.

11. While such an obstacle to free movement may be justifiable for reasons of protection of industrial property when the protection is invoked against a product coming from a member-State in which it is not patentable and has been manufactured by third parties without the consent of the patentee or where the original patentees are legally and economically independent of each other, the derogation to the principle of free movement of goods is not justified when the product has been lawfully put by the patentee himself or with his consent, on the market of the member-State from which it is being imported e.g., in the case of a holder of parallel patents.

12. If a patentee could forbid the import of protected products which had been marketed in another member-State by him or with his consent he would be enabled to partition the national markets and thus to maintain a restriction on the trade between the member-States without such a restriction being necessary for him to enjoy the substance of the exclusive rights deriving from the parallel patents.

13. The plaintiff has argued along these lines that because of the variations between the national laws and practices there are no truly identical or parallel patents.

14. On that it should be noted that in spite of the variations in the national rules on industrial property resulting from lack of unification, the essential element for the judge to decide in the notion of parallel patents is the identity of the protected invention.

15. The question should therefore be answered to the effect that the exercise by a patentee of the right given him by the laws of a member-State to prohibit the marketing in that State of a product protected by the patent and put on the market in another member-State by such patentee or with his consent would be incompatible

with the rules of the EEC Treaty relating to the free movement of goods in the Common Market.

As to question I (b)

16. This question was put should the Community rules not in all circumstances oppose the patentee exercising the right conferred on him by the national law to prohibit the import of the protected product.

17. Question I(b) has become without substance following the reply given to question I(a) above.

As to question I (c)

18. By this question the Court is asked to say whether the reply to question I(a) varies according to whether the patentee and his licensees do or do not belong to the same group.

19. It follows from the reply given to question I(a) that the essential factor constituting a restriction in the trade between member-States is the territorial protection given in a member-State to a patentee against the import of the product which has been marketed in another member-State by the patentee himself or with his consent.

20. Thus the grant of a sales licence in a member-State has the result that the patentee can no longer oppose the marketing of the protected product throughout the Common Market.

21. It therefore makes no difference whether the patentee and the licensees belong to the same group or not.

As to question I (d)

22. By this question the Court is asked to say, in substance, whether the patentee may, notwithstanding the reply given to the first question, oppose the import of the protected products when there are price differences resulting from measures taken by the public authorities in the exporting country to control the prices of the goods.

23. The Community authorities have among their tasks that of eliminating factors which could be likely to distort competition between member-States, e.g., by the harmonisation of national measures for the control of prices and by the prohibition of aids incompatible with the Common Market, as well as by the exercise of their powers in competition matters.

24. The existence of such factors in a member-State, however, could not justify the maintenance or the introduction by another member-State of measures incompatible with the rules on the free movement of goods, *inter alia* relating to industrial and commercial property.

25. A negative reply should thus be given to this question.

As to question I (e)

26. By this question the Court is asked to say whether a patentee, in order to be able to control the distribution of a pharmaceutical product with a view to the protection of the public against risks from defective products, is authorised to exercise the rights conferred on him by the patent notwithstanding the Community rules on the free movement of goods.

27. The protection of the public against the risks from defective pharmaceutical products is a legitimate concern, and therefore Article 36 of the Treaty authorises

the member-States to derogate from the rules on the free movement of goods for reasons of protection of health and life of humans and animals.

28. However, the measures necessary to that end should be taken as part of the field of public health control and not by way of a misuse of the rules on industrial and commercial property.

29. Besides, the specific object of the protection of industrial and commercial property is distinct from the object of the protection of the public and any responsibilities that can imply.

30. A negative reply should therefore be given to this question.

As to question I (f)

31. By this question the Court is asked to say whether Article 42 of the Act of Accession of the three new member-States implies that the rules of the Treaty on the free movement of goods cannot be invoked in Holland before 1 January 1975 in so far as the goods in question come from the United Kingdom.

32. Article 42 of the Act of Accession provides in paragraph I that quantitative restrictions on imports and exports between the Community as originally constituted and the new member-States shall be abolished from the date of accession.

33. Under paragraph 2 of the same Article, which is more particularly in mind in the question, "measures having equivalent effect to such restrictions shall be abolished by 1 January 1975 at the latest".

34. In its context this provision can apply only to those measures of equivalent effect to quantitative restrictions which, as between the original six member-States, had to be abolished by the end of a transitional period under Articles 30 and 32 to 35 of the EEC Treaty.

35. It follows therefore that Article 42 of the Act of Accession has no effect on the import prohibitions resulting from national law on industrial and commercial property.

36. Such matters are therefore subject to the principle embedded in the Treaty and in the Act of Accession that the provisions of the Treaties instituting the European Communities regarding free movement of goods, particularly Article 30, are applicable to the new member-States as from the date of accession unless expressly provided otherwise.

37. It follows that Article 42 of the Act of Accession could not be invoked to hinder the import into Holland, even before 1 January 1975, of goods put on the United Kingdom market by the patentee or with his consent in the circumstances set out above.

As to questions I (a) and (b)

38. By these questions the Court is asked to say whether Article 85 of the Treaty is applicable to agreements and concerted practices between the holder of parallel patents in different member-States and his licensees, if the totality of the agreements and concerted practices has the aim of regulating differently according to country the market conditions for goods protected by the patents.

39. While the industrial property rights recognised by the law of a member-State are not affected in their existence by Article 85 of the Treaty, the way in which they are exercised may be covered by the prohibitions set out in that Article.

40. That may be so whenever the exercise of such a right appears as the object, means or consequence of an agreement.

41. Article 85, however, does not apply to agreements or concerted practices between undertakings belonging to the same group in the form of parent company

and subsidiary, if the undertakings form an economic unit within which the subsidiary does not have real autonomy in determining its line of conduct on the market and if the agreements or practices have the aim of establishing an internal distribution of tasks between the undertakings ...

THE COURT HEREBY RULES:

1. The exercise by a patentee of the right given him by the laws of a member-State to prohibit the marketing in that State of a product protected by the patent and put on the market in another member-State by such patentee or with his consent would be incompatible with the rules of the EEC Treaty relating to the free movement of goods in the Common Market.

2. In that connection, it makes no difference whether the patentee and the undertakings to which he has granted licences do or do not belong to the same group.

3. It also makes no difference whether there exist between the exporting member-State and the importing member-State price differences resulting from measures taken by the public authorities in the exporting State with a view to controlling the price of the product.

4. The holder of a patent for a pharmaceutical product could not evade the Community rules on the free movement of goods in order to control the distribution of the product for the protection of the public against defective products.

5. Article 42 of the Act concerning the Conditions of Accession and the Adjustments to the Treaties could not be invoked to prevent the import into Holland, even before 1 January 1975, of goods put on the market in the United Kingdom by the patentee or with his consent.

6. Article 85 of the Treaty does not apply to agreements or concerted practices between undertakings belonging to the same group in the form of parent company and subsidiary, if the undertakings form an economic unit within which the subsidiary does not have real autonomy in determining its line of conduct on the market and if the agreements or practices have the aim of establishing an internal distribution of tasks between the undertakings.'

COMMENT

In *Merck & Co. Inc.* v *Primecrown Ltd.* [1997] FSR 237 (extracts of which follow), the European Court of Justice was asked to reconsider its view on this principle in the context of a situation where a newly admitted Member State does not yet grant patents for drugs. In what way do you think it was alleged that the patent and the trade mark had been infringed? This case is interesting in that it shows how Articles 30 and 36 may be reconciled. Do you think there was any equivalent provision to the doctrine of exhaustion of rights in respect of intellectual property rights in the United Kingdom before accession to the Treaty of Rome? Could, for example, a proprietor of a patent exercise his rights to prevent further dealings with products put on the market (anywhere) by him or with his consent? If he could, was that subsequent control a result of patent law or contract law?

Merck & Co Inc. v Primecrown Ltd. [1997] FSR 237, European Court of Justice

Pharmaceutical products were imported into the United Kingdom from Spain and Portugal where they had been sold with the consent of the manufacturer. At the time of accession of Spain and Portugal to the EC Treaty, neither country afforded patents to pharmaceutical products. The manufacturer had United Kingdom patents in respect of the products. The imported drugs were sold for lower prices in Spain and Portugul. The plaintiffs sought to prevent the parallel import of the products into the United Kingdom by exercising their patent rights. In terms of the freedom of movement of goods under Article 30 of the Treaty, in *Merck v Stephar* [1981] ECR 2063 the Court of Justice held that, under Articles 30 and 36, the proprietor of a patent could not use his rights in the patent to prevent importation into one Member State from another Member State of products placed on the market in that other Member State by or with the consent of the proprietor of the patent. This was so even if the Member State in which the products had been put on the market by the proprietor did not grant patents for products of the type in question.

When Spain and Portugal joined the Community, they agreed to introduce patents for pharmaceutical products within a specified period of time and the Act of Accession provided that the rule in *Merck v Stephar* was not to apply until the end of the third year after pharmaceutical products become patentable in those States.

The plaintiffs, Merck and Beecham, brought proceedings in the High Court, Chancery Division in London, claiming infringement of their United Kingdom patents. Jacob J referred the case to the European Court of Justice for a preliminary ruling under Article 177 of the EC Treaty. The issues included whether the rule in *Merck v Stephar* should be reconsidered and when the three year period of grace from that rule would expire.

Judgment (at 244) '... *The first two questions*

17. By its first two questions, which should be examined together, the national court asks this Court to specify the dates on which the transitional periods provided for by Articles 47 and 209 of the Act of Accession expired.

18. According to both those provisions, the holder of a patent for a pharmaceutical product may, until the end of the third year after that type of product has become patentable in the Kingdom of Spain and the Portuguese Republic invoke the rights granted by that patent in order to prevent the import and marketing of pharmaceutical products put on the market in Spain and Portugal by himself or with his consent. Such products became patentable in Spain on October 7, 1992 and in Portugal on January 1, 1992.

19. As regards the different dates of expiry of the transitional arrangements envisaged in the first two questions, for the reasons given by the Advocate General in points 181 to 194 of his Opinion, only two dates may reasonably be considered in the case of each State as marking the end of the third year after pharmaceutical products became patentable, namely October 6, 1995 and December 31, 1995 in the case of the Kingdom of Spain and December 31,1994 and December 31,1995 in the case of the Portuguese Republic.

20. The choice between those two dates for each of the two Member States depends on whether the transitional period expired exactly three years after pharmaceutical products became patentable, that is to say October 6, 1995 in the case of Spain and December 31, 1994 in the case of Portugal, or whether it expired

at the end of the third calendar year after the date on which the products became patentable, that is to say December 31, 1995 in the case of both States.

21. That question cannot on any view be resolved solely on the basis of the wording of Articles 47 and 209 of the Act of Accession ... "until the end of the third year after" [the report gives the equivalent phrase in the other languages]. While the wording of most of the language versions favours the first solution, that of the other versions favours the second.

22. It is therefore appropriate to take account of other criteria of interpretation, in particular the general scheme and the purpose of the regulatory system of which the provisions in question form part.

23. In so doing, it is important to bear in mind that Articles 47 and 209 of the Act of Accession introduced a derogation from the principle of free movement of goods and that it is settled case law that such derogations are to be interpreted strictly (see, to this effect, Case C -191/90 *Generics and Harris Pharmaceuticals* [1992] 1 ECR 5335, para 41).

24. The provisions in question must therefore be interpreted in a way that the transitional periods expire on the date which ensures the earliest application, in the field concerned, of the principle of free movement of goods in Spain and Portugal.

25. Consequently, the answer to the first two questions must be that the transitional periods provided for in Articles 47 and 209 of the Act of Accession expired on October 6, 1995 in the case of the Kingdom of Spain and on December 31, 1994 in the case of the Portuguese Republic.

The third question

26. By its third question the national court asks whether Articles 30 and 36 of the Treaty preclude application of national legislation which grants the holder of a patent for a pharmaceutical product the right to oppose importation by a third party of that product from another Member State in circumstances where the holder first put the product on the market in that State after its accession to the European Community but before the product could be protected by a product patent in that State. In this regard, the national court mentions certain specific circumstances and asks what relevance they have.

27. In substance, the High Court is seeking to ascertain whether it is necessary to reconsider the rule in *Merck* v *Stephar* or whether, having regard to the specific circumstances mentioned, its scope should be limited.

28. Merck and Beecham consider that there are weighty reasons for departing from the rule in *Merck* v *Stephar*. They point out first of all that an important change in the situation has occurred since *Merck*. At the time when the Court gave that judgment, it was the exception rather than the rule for pharmaceutical products to be patentable in Europe. Nowadays, such products are patentable in all the countries of the European Economic Area, with the exception of Iceland. Similarly, the Community institutions have emphasised the importance of patents in the pharmaceutical sector, in particular by the adoption of Council Regulation (EEC) No. 1768/92 of June 18, 1992 concerning the creation of a supplementary protection certificate for medicinal products ([1992] OJ L182/1). Merck and Beecham then point to the increasingly serious financial consequences of maintaining the rule in *Merck* which, in their view, appreciably reduce the value of patents granted in the Community. Finally, they argue that the specific subject-matter of a patent can be exhausted only if the product in question is marketed with patent protection and that *Merck* is incompatible with the later case law of the Court.

29. It is first necessary to recall the Court's reasoning in *Merck*.

30. In that judgment, the Court referred to its judgment in Case 15/74 *Centrafarm v Sterling Drug* [1974] ECR 1147 in which it held, in paragraphs 8 and 9, that as an exception, on grounds of the protection of industrial and commercial property, to one of the fundamental principles of the common market, Article 36 of the Treaty admitted such derogation only in so far as it was justified for the purpose of safeguarding rights constituting the specific subject-matter of that property, which, as regards patents, is, in particular, in order to reward the creative effort of the inventor, to guarantee that the patentee has the exclusive right to use an invention with a view to manufacturing industrial products and putting them into circulation for the first time, either directly or by the grant of licences to third parties, as well as the right to oppose infringements.

31. In paragraphs 9 and 10 of *Merck,* the Court then stated that it followed from the definition of the specific purpose of a patent that the substance of a patent right lies essentially in according the inventor an exclusive right to put the product on the market for the first time, thereby allowing him a monopoly in exploiting his product and enabling him to obtain the reward for his creative effort without, however, guaranteeing such reward in all circumstances.

32. The Court held, finally, in paragraphs 11 and 13 of *Merck* that it was for the holder of the patent to decide, in the light of all the circumstances, under what conditions he would market his product, including the possibility of marketing it in a Member State where the law did not provide patent protection for the product in question. If he decides to do so, he must then accept the consequences of his choice as regards free movement of the product within the common market, this being a fundamental principle forming part of the legal and economic circumstances which the holder of the patent must take into account in determining how to exercise his exclusive right. Under those conditions, to permit an inventor to invoke a patent held by him in one Member State in order to prevent the importation of the product freely marketed by him in another Member State where that product was not patentable would cause a partitioning of national markets contrary to the aims of the Treaty.

33. For the reasons set out below, the arguments for reconsideration of the rule in *Merck* are not such as to call in question the reasoning on which the Court based that rule.

34. It is true, as Merck and Beecham point out, that it is now the norm for pharmaceutical products to be patentable. However, such a development does not mean that the reasoning underlying the rule in *Merck* is superseded.

35. The same is true in relation to the arguments based, first, on the efforts made by the Community institutions to give enhanced protection to holders of patents for pharmaceutical products and, second, on the consequences of maintaining that rule for research and development by the pharmaceutical industry.

36. There can be no doubt now, any more than at the time when the judgment in *Merck* was given, that if a patentee could prohibit the importation of protected products marketed in another Member State by him or with his consent, he would be able to partition national markets and thereby restrict trade between the Member States. By the same token, if a patentee decides, in the light of all the circumstances, to put a product on the market in a Member State where it is not patentable, he must accept the consequences of his choice as regards the possibility of parallel imports.

37. The arguments put forward in the present cases have not shown that the Court was wrong in its assessment of the balance between the principle of free movement of goods in the Community and the principle of protection of patentees' rights, albeit that, as a result of striking that balance, the right to oppose importation of a product may be exhausted by its being marketed in a Member State where it is not patentable.

38. It is important to remember in this respect that the transitional measures provided for by Articles 47 and 209 of the Act of Accession were adopted in the light of the ruling in *Merck.* Although the Member States considered it necessary to postpone the effects of that ruling for a long period, they provided that, upon expiry of the transitional arrangements, Articles 30 and 36 of the Treaty, as interpreted in *Merck,* should apply in full to trade between Spain and Portugal, on the one hand, and the existing Member States, on the other.

39. Furthermore, the situations addressed by the ruling in *Merck* are set to disappear since pharmaceutical products are now patentable in all the Member States. If, upon accession of new States to the Community, such situations were to recur, the Member States could adopt the measures considered necessary, as was the case when the Kingdom of Spain and the Portuguese Republic acceded to the Community.

40. Finally, Merck's and Beecham's argument that judgments given by the Court after *Merck,* in particular those in Case 19/84 *Pharmon* v *Hoechst* ([1985] ECR 2281) and in Case 158/86 *Warner Brothers and Metronome Video* v *Christiansen* ([1988] ECR 2605), support their point of view must be rejected.

41. Contrary to their contention, the judgment in *Pharmon* shows that the Court confirmed the principles laid down in *Merck.* In *Pharmon,* the Court emphasized the importance of the patentee's consent to the product in question being put into circulation. At paragraph 25 it held that, where the authorities of a Member State grant a third party a compulsory licence allowing him to carry out manufacturing and marketing operations which the patentee would normally have the right to prevent, the patentee cannot be deemed to have consented to those operations and he may therefore oppose importation of products made by the holder of the compulsory licence.

42. Unlike the cases now under consideration, *Warner Brothers* concerned legislation of the importing State which allowed the author of a musical or cinematographic work not only to control the initial sale but also to oppose the hiring out of videos of that work for as long as he refused specific consent for such hiring out. In that judgment, the Court held that, since there was a specific market for hiring out distinct from the market for sales, such a specific right would lose its substance if the proprietor of the work were unable to authorize hiring out, even in the case of video cassettes already put into circulation with his consent in another Member State whose legislation allowed the author to control the initial sale without giving him the right to prohibit hiring out.

43. Since none of the arguments for re-examining the rule in *Merck* which the Court has thus far considered have been accepted, the Court must next determine whether, having regard to the specific circumstances mentioned by the national court, the scope of that rule must be restricted.

44. The first question to be considered is whether the rule in *Merck* also applies where the patentee has a legal or ethical obligation to market or to continue to market his product in the exporting State. Here the national court is concerned to know what importance is to be attached to a requirement of that State's legislation or

of Community legislation that, once the product has been put on the market in that State, the patentee must supply and continue to supply sufficient quantities to satisfy the needs of domestic patients.

45. The second question is whether the rule in *Merck* applies where the legislation of the exporting State not only grants to its authorities the right, which they exercise, to fix the sale price of the product but also prohibits the sale of the product at any other price. Here the national court is concerned to know whether it is relevant that those authorities have fixed the price of the products at a level such that substantial exports of the product to the Member State of importation are foreseeable.

46. Merck and Beecham maintain in particular that, in the circumstances mentioned in the order for reference, their right to decide freely on the conditions in which they market their products is removed or considerably reduced. In their view, it follows from *Pharmon* that the rule in *Merck* does not apply in the present cases.

47. As to that, although the imposition of price controls is indeed a factor which may, in certain conditions, distort competition between Member States, that circumstance cannot justify a derogation from the principle of free movement of goods. It is well settled that distortions caused by different price legislation in a Member State must be remedied by measures taken by the Community authorities and not by the adoption by another Member State of measures incompatible with the rules on free movement of goods (see Case 16/74 *Winthrop* [1974] ECR 1183, para 17; Joined Cases 55/80 and 57/80 *Musik-Vertrieb Membran and K-tel International* v *GEMA* [1981] ECR 147, para 24; and Joined Cases C-427/93, C-429/93 and C-436193 *Bristol-Myers Squibb and Others* [1997] FSR 102, para. 46).

48. The next question which must be examined is how far the rule in *Merck* applies where patentees are legally obliged to market their products in the exporting State.

49. In answering that question it is to be remembered, first, that in *Merck* the Court emphasized the importance of the fact that the patentee had taken his decision to market his product freely and in full knowledge of all relevant circumstances and, second, that it follows from *Pharmon* that a patentee who is not in a position to decide freely how he will market his products in the exporting State may oppose importation and marketing of those products in the State where the patent is in force.

50. It follows that, where a patentee is legally bound under either national law or Community law to market his products in a Member State, he cannot be deemed, within the meaning of the ruling in *Merck,* to have given his consent to the marketing of the products concerned. He is therefore entitled to oppose importation and marketing of those products in the State where they are protected.

51. It is for the patentee to prove, before the national court from which an order prohibiting imports is sought, that there is a legal obligation to market the product concerned in the exporting State. He must in particular show, for example by reference to decisions of the competent national authorities or courts or of the competent Community authorities, that there is a genuine, existing obligation.

52. According to the information given to the Court in these proceedings and as the Advocate General observes in points 152 and 153 of his Opinion, such obligations can hardly be said to exist in the case of the imports in question.

53. Finally, as regards the argument that ethical obligations may compel patentees to provide supplies of drugs to Member States where they are needed, even if they are not patentable there, such considerations are not, in the absence of any legal obligation, such as to make it possible properly to identify the situations in which the

patentee is deprived of his power to decide freely how he will market his product. Such considerations are, at any rate in the present context, difficult to apprehend and distinguish from commercial considerations. Such ethical obligations cannot, therefore, be the basis for derogating from the rule on free movement of goods laid down in *Merck*.

54. In view of the foregoing, the answer to be given to the third question must be that Articles 30 and 36 of the Treaty preclude application of national legislation which grants the holder of a patent for a pharmaceutical product the right to oppose importation by a third party of that product from another Member State in circumstances where the holder first put the product on the market in that State after its accession to the European Community but before the product could be protected by a patent in that State, unless the holder of the patent can prove that he is under a genuine, existing legal obligation to market the product in that Member State.
...

[T]he Court ... hereby rules:

1. The transitional periods provided for in Articles 47 and 209 of the Act concerning the Conditions of Accession of the Kingdom of Spain and the Portuguese Republic and the Adjustments of the Treaties expired on October 6, 1995 in the case of the Kingdom of Spain and on December 31, 1994 in the case of the Portuguese Republic.

2. Articles 30 and 36 of the EC Treaty preclude application of national legislation which grants the holder of a patent for a pharmaceutical product the right to oppose importation by a third party of that product from another Member State in circumstances where the holder first put the product on the market in that State after its accession to the European Community but before the product could be protected by a patent in that State, unless the holder of the patent can prove that he is under a genuine, existing legal obligation to market the product in that Member State.'

COMMENT

The doctrine of exhaustion of rights is firmly entrenched and only specific and justifiable exceptions apply to it. The derogation from Article 30 and the rule in *Merck* v *Stephar* was construed as narrowly as possible in its duration (the transitional provisions relating to the accession of Spain and Portugal on this matter were ambiguous). Furthermore, only a legal obligation to place the products on the market, imposed by the proprietors of the relevant patents elsewhere, would allow the exercise of those patent rights to prevent subsequent importation into the countries where those patents existed. An ethical or moral obligation would not suffice. Do you think this decision is fair to the proprietors of the patents? The drugs were sold at a time when patents were not available in Spain or Portugal. What effect did the lack of patents for pharmaceutical products have on the sale price in those countries? Should the drug companies have refused to sell the drugs in Spain or Portugal until such time as patents were available?

Oliver, P. 'Of Split Trade Marks and Common Markets' (1991) 54 MLR 587

'The ruling of the European Court of Justice in *Van Zuylen Frères* v *Hag* [1974] ECR 731 ("Hag I") has always aroused heated controversy and its reversal in *CNL-Sucal* v *Hag* [1990] 3 CMLR 571 (*"Hag II"*) is to be warmly welcomed. One notable feature of this case is that it is thought to be the first in which the Court has expressly reversed an earlier judgment. Both cases related to Article 30 of the Treaty of Rome, which prohibits quantitative restrictions on imports between Member States and measures of equivalent effect; and to Article 36 which lays down an exception to this rule *inter alia* for measures justified for the protection of industrial and commercial property (hereafter "industrial property").

In *Hag I* the Court enunciated the doctrine of common origin, whereby a trade mark may not be relied on with a view to prohibiting the marketing in one Member State of the European Community of goods lawfully produced in another Member State under an identical trade mark having the same origin. This is to be distinguished from the principle of exhaustion of rights according to which, subject to certain exceptions, the exclusive right guaranteed by national legislation on industrial property is exhausted when a product has been lawfully distributed in one Member State by the owner of the right or with his consent; thereafter the owner of the right may not oppose the importation of the product into any other Member State. It cannot be sufficiently stressed that the principle of exhaustion is based on the *consent* of the holder of the right, whereas the doctrine of common origin was not.

The facts of *Hag I* were that from the beginning of the century Hag AG, a German company, owned the "Hag" trade mark for its coffee in a number of countries. Between the two World Wars its Belgian subsidiary acquired the trade marks for Belgium and Luxembourg. In 1944 the Belgian authorities confiscated the shares of Hag Belgium as enemy property and the trade marks for these two countries subsequently became vested in Van Zuylen. Thus the German "Hag" trade mark on the one hand and its Belgian and Luxembourg counterparts on the other, although of common origin, were now held by two totally unconnected parties. The issue which arose before the Tribunal d'Arrondissement in Luxembourg was whether Van Zuylen could prevent the German company marketing its goods in Luxembourg under the "Hag" mark. That court posed a question to the Court of Justice on this point pursuant to Article 177 of the Treaty of Rome. The following passage of the judgment of the Court deserves to be quoted in full:

"The exercise of a trade mark right tends to contribute to the partitioning off of the markets and thus to affect the free movement of goods between Member States, all the more so since - unlike other rights of industrial and commercial property - it is not subject to limitations in point of time.

Accordingly, one cannot allow the holder of a trade mark to rely upon the exclusiveness of a trade mark right - which may be the consequence of the territorial limitation of national legislations - with a view to prohibiting the marketing of goods legally produced in another Member State under an identical trade mark having the same origin.

Such a prohibition, which would legitimize the isolation of national markets, would collide with one of the essential objects of the Treaty, which is to unite national markets in a single market.

Whilst in such a market the indication of origin of a product covered by a trade mark is useful, information to consumers on this point may be insured by means other than such as would affect the free movement of goods."

This judgment has attracted considerable criticism, since it is by no means clear why the historical fact that two trade marks of a common origin should affect their exercise today, when the marks were split by an act of the public authorities, when that act occurred well before the entry into force of the Treaty and there are no continuing links between the parties.

Nevertheless, in a dictum in *Terrapin* v *Terranova* [1976] ECR 1039 the Court re-affirmed its ruling in *Hag I*, which it sought to justify on the basis that in the circumstances "the basic function of the trade mark to guarantee to consumers that the product has the same origin is already undermined by the sub-division of the original right."

It was not until *Hag II* that the Court had occasion to apply *Hag I*, since no other case involving common origin came before it in the interim. The new case arose out of the same facts as *Hag I*, except that this time it was the German company that was seeking to prevent the Belgian product from being marketed in Germany (and that CNL-Sucal had acquired the Belgian and Luxembourg marks in the meantime). The Bundesgerichsthof (The German Federal Supreme Court) posed a series of questions asking whether Articles 30 and 36 permitted this ...

Neither of the parties to the main case contested the ruling in *Hag I*: The Belgian company contended that that judgment should be applied for its benefit in these proceedings, while the German company merely wished to curtail the scope of the earlier ruling. Nor did most of the other intervenors invite the Court to reverse *Hag I* either. However, this did not deter Advocate General Jacobs from mounting a direct attack on the previous judgment ...

The Advocate General regarded it as unfortunate that *Hag I* was decided at a time when the Court's case law on intellectual property was in its infancy. It was not until some months later that it had had occasion to define the specific subject-matter of trade marks as protected by Article 36. When it had done so, it had softened its hostility to trade marks by recognising that they protected the proprietor's goodwill and saved the consumer from being misled. He also pointed to the confusion underlying the very term "common origin": "the word 'origin' in this context does not refer to the historical origin of the trade mark; it refers rather to the commercial origin of the goods. The consumer is not, I think, interested in the genealogy of trade marks; he is interested in knowing who made the goods that he purchases." Consideration was also given to the possibility of distinguishing between conflicting marks by means of additional wording, but this was dismissed as being inadequate in all but a few cases.

For the rest, the main thrust of the Advocate General's reasoning was reproduced by the Court and will therefore be considered shortly. However, the Court did not allude to his caveat in relation to "confusingly similar" trade marks. There had, he said, been instances of German courts taking an excessively broad view of this concept. In one notorious case, the Bundespatentgericht (Federal Patent Court) had gone so far as to hold that the mark "LUCKY WHIP" was liable to be confused with the mark "Schöller-Nucki" - a decision which, he remarked, 'seems to postulate a body of consumers afflicted with an acute form of dyslexia.' In his view, such an extreme approach would fall foul of Article 30 of the Treaty without being justified under Article 36; nor would it be in keeping with the First Council Directive on trade marks (1989 OJ L40/1).

The Advocate General's Opinion left the Court no honourable choice but to put Hag I out of its misery. This it proceeded to do with a few deft strokes. It began by stating that it was necessary to review this judgment in the light of its subsequent case law on industrial property. A crucial step in its reasoning was its affirmation that trade marks constitute an essential element of the system of undistorted competition which the Treaty seeks to establish and maintain; (this is a far cry indeed from its charge in Hag I that the "exercise of a trade mark tends to contribute to the partitioning of the markets"). If a trade mark was to fulfil its role in this system, it must constitute the guarantee that all the products bearing it were manufactured under the control of a single undertaking which would be responsible for maintaining their quality. The essential purpose of a trade mark would be undermined if its holder were powerless to prevent imports of goods which bore an identical or confusingly similar mark and had been produced in another Member State without his consent by another company having no legal or economic connection with him: consumers would then be confused and moreover the trade mark holder in the importing State would have no means of safeguarding his reputation, should the imported goods prove to be of inferior quality. The Court held that this position was not altered by the fact that the two marks had once been in the hands of a single owner and that one mark had been expropriated before the establishment of the Community. Accordingly, in such circumstances each of the two holders would enjoy exclusivity in his Member State, provided that the marks were identical or confusingly similar and that the products bearing them were similar.

Hag I is thus reversed and the Belgian was held to be entitled to exclude the German product bearing the mark from Belgium and Luxembourg, and vice versa. However, the terms of the judgment make it clear that no such mutual exclusivity can be enjoyed unless (a) the two marks are identical or confusingly similar and (b) the products are similar and (c) there are no legal or economic links between the parties. Unless these three cumulative conditions are met, each of the two owners may market his products in the Member State of the other.

Numerically speaking, the immediate importance of Hag II may be regarded as somewhat limited in that only a handful of trade marks are thought to have been split in similar circumstances. However, its impact will be far greater than that. By ruling that they are essential to maintaining undistorted competition within the Community, the Court has fundamentally re-assessed the role of trade marks and the repercussions of this re-assessment are likely to be felt even beyond the confines of the Treaty provisions on the free movement of goods. Moreover, as a result of Hag II other cases involving different facts might be decided differently today.

Assuming that they can show that conditions (a) to (c) above are met, where then does this ruling leave parties in the following situations:

i) two companies are manufacturing products in their respective Member States under their own marks and no links have ever existed between the parties;
ii) the two marks were once in the hands of a single owner, but he assigned his mark in one Member State, while retaining the other;

iii) an undertaking holds parallel marks in two Member States, but one of these States expropriates the mark applicable to its territory after the creation of the Community (or, in the case of a new Member State, after accession)?

Case (i) has been included only for completeness. It is not a case of common origin at all and would never have been caught by *Hag I* in the first place ...

As to case (ii), under the doctrine of common origin goods bearing the split mark could in all cases circulate freely between Member States. Henceforth this matter has to be examined in the light of the principle of the exhaustion of rights alone. The traditional formulation of the question to be asked when applying this principle is: has the party concerned consented to the marketing of the goods in the Member State in question? Yet, where the assignment occurred before the creation of the Community, both the assignor and the assignee have by definition consented to the other's marketing the goods in his respective territory; but the context in which the assignment was effected was wholly different, since at that time there was not one common market but a series of separate national markets, and it was logically impossible for the parties to divide up a common market which did not yet exist. It is therefore suggested that in these circumstances each party must be regarded as enjoying exclusive rights in his own territory, as in *Hag II*. On the other hand, any assignment of a trade mark since the Treaty of Rome came into force (or, in the case of new Member States, since accession) must be regarded as constituting consent on the part of both assignor and assignee so as to enable both their products to circulate freely. This can scarcely be a rebuttable presumption: what trade mark holder of sound mind would today split his mark unless his purpose was to divide up the market?

In case (iii) the validity of the expropriation is to some extent in issue. This delicate problem, so well known in international law, is most likely to arise when a Member State decides to nationalise all the assets of the subsidiary of a multinational company, including its trade marks. Plainly, this complex subject cannot be explored at length here. Suffice it to say then that following *Hag II* it is clear that the multinational will not have to suffer the ignominy of seeing the nationalised company marketing goods bearing the disputed mark in Member States where the multinational still owns the mark. Whether the nationalised company will be able to prevent imports into its own Member State of goods bearing the mark and produced by the multinational will presumably depend on the lawfulness of the expropriation ...

In conclusion, great credit is due to the Court for having had the courage to reverse its earlier ruling. Although few trade marks have been split in circumstances akin to those of the *Hag* cases, the importance of the new judgment should not be underestimated: not only has the Court fundamentally re-appraised the role of trade marks, but it has also laid down the principles according to which many other clashes between trade mark rights and the free movement of goods are to be solved.'

Restrictive Trade Agreements

Article 85(1) prohibits, *inter alia*, restrictive trade practices, in particular licence agreements relating to intellectual property rights. By Article 85(2) agreements that offend are declared void but this does not usually vitiate the entire agreement. Rather, it is a matter of striking out the offending terms if the agreement can reasonably operate without them.

Article 85(3) allows derogation from the rigours of Article 85(1). This may be by virtue of an individual exemption but, in many cases, parties to a licence agreement (or other agreement such as a distribution or franchising agreement) will be able to take advantage of a block exemption such as the 'Technology Transfer' Regulation, extracts from which are reproduced below.

Commission Regulation (EC) No. 240/96 of 31 January 1996 on the application of Article 85(3) of the Treaty to certain categories of technology transfer agreements, OJ L31, 9.2.1996, p.2

This regulation grants block exemption from Article 85(1) to certain types of licence agreements relating to patents, know-how or combined patent and know-how licences and particular types of terms in such agreements. It replaces the previous patent licensing regulation and the know-how licensing regulation and came into force on 1 April 1996 and continues until 31 March 2006.

The regulation declares that certain obligations in licence agreements are not caught by Article 85(1) (see Article 1 of the regulation below).

The first four Articles of the Regulation are reproduced here. Article 1 contains obligations which, because they generally are likely to contribute to the promotion of technical progress, improvement in products and the transfer of technology throughout the Community. Most are concerned with territorial restrictions on one or other party to the licence. Article 2 contains obligations commonly found in licence agreements which are not usually restrictive of competition but are also exempt from Article 85(1) in the event that, in the particular legal or economic circumstances they happen to be caught under Article 85(1). Article 3 contains a list of obligations or restrictions which must not be included in licence agreements if they are to take the benefit of the block exemption. These, therefore, comprise a 'black list' and should be avoided. Article 4 applies where an agreement contains obligations which are restrictive of competition (but not any of those in Article 3). In such a case, exemption from Article 85(1) is given if the agreement is notified to the Commission providing the Commission does not oppose the availability of the exemption within four months.

Article 1

1. Pursuant to Article 85 (3) of the Treaty and subject to the conditions set out below, it is hereby declared that Article 85 (1) of the Treaty shall not apply to pure patent licensing or know-how licensing agreements and to mixed patent and know-how licensing agreements, including those agreements containing ancillary provisions relating to intellectual property rights other than patents, to which only two undertakings are party and which include one or more of the following obligations:

(1) an obligation on the licensor not to license other undertakings to exploit the licensed technology in the licensed territory;

(2) an obligation on the licensor not to exploit the licensed technology in the licensed territory himself;

(3) an obligation on the licensee not to exploit the licensed technology in the territory of the licensor within the common market;

(4) an obligation on the licensee not to manufacture or use the licensed product, or use the licensed process, in territories within the common market which are licensed to other licensees;

(5) an obligation on the licensee not to pursue an active policy of putting the licensed product on the market in the territories within the common market which are licensed to other licensees, and in particular not to engage in advertising specifically aimed at those territories or to establish any branch or maintain an distribution depot there ;

(6) an obligation on the licensee not to put the licensed product on the market in the territories licensed to other licensees within the common market in response to unsolicited orders;

(7) an obligation on the licensee to use only the licensor's trademark or get up to distinguish the licensed product during the term of the agreement, provided that the licensee is not prevented from identifying himself as the manufacturer of the licensed products;

(8) an obligation on the licensee to limit his production of the licensed product to the quantities he requires in manufacturing his own products and to sell the licensed product only as an integral part of or a replacement part for his own products or otherwise in connection with the sale of his own products, provided that such quantities are freely determined by the licensee.

2. Where the agreement is a pure patent licensing agreement, the exemption of the obligations referred to in paragraph 1 is granted only to the extent that and for as long as the licensed product is protected by parallel patents, in the territories respectively of the licensee (points (1), (2), (7) and (8)), the licensor (point (3)) and other licensees (points (4) and (5)). The exemption of the obligation referred to in point (6) of paragraph 1 is granted for a period not exceeding five years from the date when the licensed product is first put on the market within the common market by one of the licensees, to the extent that and for as long as, in these territories, this product is protected by parallel patents.

3. Where the agreement is a pure know-how licensing agreement, the period for which the exemption of the obligations referred to in points (1) to (5) of paragraph 1 is granted may not exceed ten years from the date when the licensed product is first put on the market within the common market by one of the licensees.

The exemption of the obligation referred to in point (6) of paragraph 1 is granted for a period not exceeding five years from the date when the licensed product is first put on the market within the common market by one of the licensees.

The obligations referred to in points (7) and (8) of paragraph 1 are exempted during the lifetime of the agreement for as long as the know-how remains secret and substantial.

However, the exemption in paragraph 1 shall apply only where the parties have identified in any appropriate form the initial know-how and any subsequent improvements to it which become available to one party and are communicated to the other party pursuant to the terms of the agreement and to the purpose thereof, and only for as long as the know-how remains secret and substantial.

4. Where the agreement is a mixed patent and know-how licensing agreement, the exemption of the obligations referred to in points (1) to (5) of paragraph 1 shall apply in Member States in which the licensed technology is protected by necessary patents for as long as the licensed product is protected in those Member States by such patents if the duration of such protection exceeds the periods specified in paragraph 3.

The duration of the exemption provided in point (6) of paragraph 1 may not exceed the five-year period provided for in paragraphs 2 and 3.

However, such agreements qualify for the exemption referred to in paragraph 1 only for as long as the patents remain in force or to the extent that the know-how is identified and for as long as it remains secret and substantial whichever period is the longer.

5. The exemption provided for in paragraph 1 shall also apply where in a particular agreement the parties undertake obligations of the types referred to in that paragraph but with a more limited scope than is permitted by that paragraph.

Article 2

1. Article 1 shall apply notwithstanding the presence in particular of any of the following clauses, which are generally not restrictive of competition:

(1) an obligation on the licensee not to divulge the know-how communicated by the licensor; the licensee may be held to this obligation after the agreement has expired;

(2) an obligation on the licensee not to grant sublicences or assign the licence;

(3) an obligation on the licensee not to exploit the licensed know-how or patents after termination of the agreement in so far and as long as the know-how is still secret or the patents are still in force;

(4) an obligation on the licensee to grant to the licensor a licence in respect of his own improvements to or his new applications of the licensed technology, provided:

- that, in the case of severable improvements, such a licence is not exclusive, so that the licensee is free to use his own improvements or to license them to third parties, in so far as that does not involve disclosure of the know-how communicated by the licensor that is still secret,
- and that the licensor undertakes to grant an exclusive or non-exclusive licence of his own improvements to the licensee;

(5) an obligation on the licensee to observe minimum quality specifications, including technical specifications, for the licensed product or to procure goods or services from the licensor or from an undertaking designated by the licensor, in so far as these quality specifications, products or services are necessary for:

    (a) a technically proper exploitation of the licensed technology; or

    (b) ensuring that the product of the licensee conforms to the minimum quality specifications that are applicable to the licensor and other licensees;

and to allow the licensor to carry out related checks;

(6) obligations:

    (a) to inform the licensor of misappropriation of the know-how or of infringements of the licensed patents; or

    (b) to take or to assist the licensor in taking legal action against such misappropriation or infringements;

(7) an obligation on the licensee to continue paying the royalties:

    (a) until the end of the agreement in the amounts, for the periods and according to the methods freely determined by the parties, in the event of the know-how becoming publicly known other than by action of the licensor, without prejudice to the payment of any additional damages in the event of the know-how becoming publicly known by the action of the licensee in breach of the agreement;

    (b) over a period going beyond the duration of the licensed patents, in order to facilitate payment;

(8) an obligation on the licensee to restrict his exploitation of the licensed technology to one or more technical fields of application covered by the licensed technology or to one or more product markets;

(9) An obligation on the licensee to pay a minimum royalty or to produce a minimum quantity of the licensed product or to carry out a minimum number of operations exploiting the licensed technology;

(10) an obligation on the licensor to grant the licensee any more favourable terms that the licensor may grant to another undertaking after the agreement is entered into;

(11) an obligation on the licensee to mark the licensed product with an indication of the licensor's name or of the licensed patent;

(12) an obligation on the licensee not to use the licensor's technology to construct facilities for third parties; this is without prejudice to the right of the licensee to increase the capacity of his facilities or to set up additional

facilities for his own use on normal commercial terms, including the payment of additional royalties;

(13) an obligation on the licensee to supply only a limited quantity of the licensed product to a particular customer, where the licence was granted so that the customer might have a second source of supply inside the licensed territory; this provision shall also apply where the customer is the licensee, and the licence which was granted in order to provide a second source of supply provides that the customer is himself to manufacture the licensed products or to have them manufactured by a subcontractor;

(14) a reservation by the licensor of the right to exercise the rights conferred by a patent to oppose the exploitation of the technology by the licensee outside the licensed territory ;

(15) a reservation by the licensor of the right to terminate the agreement if the licensee contests the secret or substantial nature of the licensed know-how or challenges the validity of licensed patents within the common market belonging to the licensor or undertakings connected with him;

(16) a reservation by the licensor of the right to terminate the licence agreement of a patent if the licensee raises the claim that such a patent is not necessary;

(17) an obligation on the licensee to use his best endeavours to manufacture and market the licensed product;

(18) a reservation by the licensor of the right to terminate the exclusivity granted to the licensee and to stop licensing improvements to him when the licensee enters into competition within the common market with the licensor, with undertakings connected with the licensor or with other undertakings in respect of research and development, production, use or distribution of competing products, and to require the licensee to prove that the licensed know-how is not being used for the production of products and the provision of services other than those licensed.

2. In the event that, because of particular circumstances, the clauses referred to in paragraph 1 fall within the scope of Article 85 (1), they shall also be exempted even if they are not accompanied by any of the obligations exempted by Article 1.

3. The exemption in paragraph 2 shall also apply where an agreement contains clauses of the types referred to in paragraph 1 but with a more limited scope than is permitted by that paragraph.

Article 3

Article 1 and Article 2 (2) shall not apply where

(1)   one party is restricted in the determination of prices, components of prices or discounts for the licensed products;

(2)   one party is restricted from competing within the common market with the other party, with undertakings connected with the other party or with other undertakings in respect of research and development, production, use or distribution of competing products without prejudice to the provisions of Article 2 (1) (17) and (1 8);

(3)   one or both of the parties are required without any objectively justified reason:

   (a)   to refuse to meet orders from users or resellers in their respective territories who would market products in other territories within the common market;
   (b)   to make it difficult for users or resellers to obtain the products from other resellers within the common market, and in particular to exercise intellectual property rights or take measures so as to prevent users or rescuers from obtaining outside, or from putting on the market in the licensed territory products which have been lawfully put on the market within the common market by the licensor or with his consent;

   or do so as a result of a concerted practice between them;

(4)   the parties were already competing manufacturers before the grant of the licence and one of them is restricted, within the same technical field of use or within the same product market, as to the customers he may serve, in particular by being prohibited from supplying certain classes of user, employing certain forms of distribution or, with the aim of sharing customers, using certain types of packaging for the products, save as provided in Article 1 (1) (7) and Article 2 (1) (13);

(5)   the quantity of the licensed products one party may manufacture or sell or the number of operations exploiting the licensed technology he may carry out are subject to limitations, save as provided in Article (1) (8) and Article 2 (1) (13);

(6)   the licensee is obliged to assign in whole or in part to the licensor rights to improvements to or new applications of the licensed technology;

(7)   the licensor is required, albeit in separate agreements or through automatic prolongation of the initial duration of the agreement by the inclusion of any new improvements, for a period exceeding that referred to in Article 1 (2) and (3) not to license other undertakings to exploit the licensed technology in the licensed territory, or a party is required for a period exceeding that referred to in Article 1 (2) and (3) or Article 1 (4) not to exploit the licensed technology in the territory of the other party or of other licensees.

Article 4

1.   The exemption provided for in Articles 1 and 2 shall also apply to agreements containing obligations restrictive of competition which are not covered by those Articles and do not fall within the scope of Article 3, on condition that the agreements in question are notified to the Commission in accordance with the provisions of Articles 1, 2 and 3 of Regulation (EC) No 3385/94 and that the Commission does not oppose such exemption within a period of four months.

2.   Paragraph 1 shall apply, in particular, where:

    (a) the licensee is obliged at the time the agreement is entered into to accept quality specifications or further licences or to procure goods or services which are not necessary for a technically satisfactory exploitation of the licensed technology or for ensuring that the production of the licensee conforms to the quality standards that are respected by the licensor and other licensees;

    (b) the licensee is prohibited from contesting the secrecy or the substantiality of the licensed know-how or from challenging the validity of patents licensed within the common market belonging to the licensor or undertakings connected with him.

3.   The period of four months referred to in paragraph 1 shall run from the date on which the notification takes effect in accordance with Article 4 of Regulation (EC) No 3385/94.

4.   The benefit of paragraphs 1 and 2 may be claimed for agreements notified before the entry into force of this Regulation by submitting a communication to the Commission referring expressly to this Article and to the notification. Paragraph 3 shall apply mutatis mutandis.

5.   The Commission may oppose the exemption within a period of four months. It shall oppose exemption if it receives a request to do so from a Member State within two months of the transmission to the Member State of the notification referred to in paragraph 1 or of the communication referred to in paragraph 4. This request must be justified on the basis of considerations relating to the competition rules of the Treaty.

6.   The Commission may withdraw the opposition to the exemption at any time. However, where the opposition was raised at the request of a Member State and this request is maintained, it may be withdrawn only after consultation of the Advisory Committee on Restrictive Practices and Dominant Positions.

7.   If the opposition is withdrawn because the undertakings concerned have shown that the conditions of Article 85 (3) are satisfied, the exemption shall apply from the date of notification.

8. If the opposition is withdrawn because the undertakings concerned have amended the agreement so that the conditions of Article 85 (3) are satisfied, the exemption shall apply from the date on which the amendments take effect.

9. If the Commission opposes exemption and the opposition is not withdrawn, the effects of the notification shall be governed by the provisions of Regulation No 17.

COMMENT

'Know-how' is defined in Article 10 as 'a body of technical information that is secret, substantial and identified in any appropriate form'. The definition of 'secret' makes it clear that it does not have to be totally unknown or unobtainable outside the licensor's business but it must be not generally known or easily accessible in its precise form. Know-how is substantial if it would improve the licensee's competitive position and it is identified if it described or recorded so as to verify it is secret and substantial and so it can be set out in the licence agreement or in a separate document or recorded in another appropriate form.

The Regulation does not apply to certain types of agreement including pooling agreements, joint ventures or agreements solely for the purpose of sale (for these, individual exemption may be sought if they otherwise fall within Article 85(1)). The Regulation does, however, apply to sub-licences and to assignments of patents or know-how (or both) where the risk of exploitaiton remains with the assignor (for example where payment to the assignor is on a royalty basis) and agreements where the rights or obligations of either party are assumed by connected undertakings (for example, but not restricted to, a parent company).

The Regulation is clearly of utmost importance to those drafting patent and know-how licences (and mixed patent and know-how licences). Of particular importance are the black-listed obligations in Article 3. It is interesting to note that a licence agreement can contain some terms restrictive of competition providing the Commission does not oppose them within four months of notification. Apart from terms of the type in Articles 1 and 2 of the Regulation, what other terms would usually be found in a patent or know-how licence? Can you think of any examples of terms that could be restrictive but would be unlikely to be opposed by the Commission? In what ways do you think this Regulation will encourage technology transfer?

Abuse of a Dominant Position

Owners of monopoly rights may be, by definition, in a dominant position, especially if there is no equivalent technology and demand is high. However, being in a dominant position, *per se*, does not contravene Article 86. There must be some abuse which affects or may affect trade between Member States.

The following cases demonstrate the operation of Article 86 in the field of intellectual property. It is interesting to note:

(a) that abuses may be dealt with draconianly;

(b) controls are not limited to rights which are monpolistic, such as copyright; and

(c) lack of harmonisation inhibits the full working of Article 86.

Tetra Pak Rausing SA v EC Commission [1991] 4 CMLR 334, Court of First Instance

Tetra Pak, a Swiss company had 91.8 per cent of the market in the European Community in aseptic filling machines for UHT milk and 89.1 per cent of the market in the cartons used with the machines. Although the patents had expired, there remained considerable barriers to access to the market for aseptic filling machines. The British National Research and Development Council (NRDC), the forerunner of the British Technology Group obtained a patent for an improved sterilisation process involving the use of ultra-violet light and granted an exclusive licence to a company in the American Liquipak group of companies. Liquipak had been making machines for filling cartons for fresh milk which did not have to meet the strict aseptic conditions for UHT milk. Further patents were obtained or applied for in respect of the sterilisation process.

Elopak, a Norwegian company, was Liquipak's exclusive distributor in the European Community. The two companies collaborated in developing machines for a satisfactory aseptic filling machine. In 1986, however, Tetra Pak acquired the Liquipak group. Elopak ceased to collaborate and applied to the Commission for a finding that Tetra Pak had infringed Articles 85 and 86 of the EC Treaty. The Commission held that Tetra Pak had, by its acquisition of Liquipak, infringed Article 86.

Judgment (at 381): '... *The sole ground of action: infringement of Article 85(3) and Article 86 of the Treaty*

14. Tetra Pak challenges the Decision on the ground that it is contrary to Article 85(3) and Article 86 that the Commission should treat an agreement enjoying block exemption under Article 85(3) as prohibited under Article 86. The challenge is developed under three heads. The applicant relies, first, on a schematic analysis of the relevant rules of the Treaty and secondary sources; second, on the principle of legal certainty; and third, on the principle of the uniform application of community law.

(a) *Schematic analysis of Articles 85 and 86 of the Treaty and of secondary legislation*

15. The applicant maintains that the Commission cannot apply Article 86 to behaviour exempt under Article 85(3) because Articles 85 and 86 both pursue the same objective ...

16. In support of that argument, the applicant claims that the finding against it in the Decision relates essentially to the exclusivity granted by the licensing agreement. The applicant goes on to argue that the Commission based the application of Article 86 on a distinction, for which there is no justification in competition law, between an exclusive licence enjoying block exemption on the one hand and, on the other, acquisition of the exclusivity afforded by the licence through takeover of a competing company (in this case Liquipak) such acquisition having been held in the Decision to

constitute infringement of Article 86. Both, according to the applicant, have the same restrictive effects on competition.

17. The applicant further argued at the hearing that since, on this view, Article 86 cannot be applied to an agreement enjoying exemption under Article 85(3), the fact that an undertaking in a dominant position becomes party to an agreement enjoying such exemption cannot constitute an abuse within the meaning of Article 86 unless a supplementary element, extrinsic to the agreement and attributable to the undertaking, is present. The applicant relied in this connection on *AHMED SAEED* ([1989] ECR 803, [1990] 4 CMLR 102) where the Court of Justice said that there may be abuse of a dominant position where, in particular, an undertaking in a dominant position succeeds in imposing unfair contractual conditions on competitors or customers.

18. The applicant points out that the inapplicability of Article 86 to an exempt agreement does not jeopardise achievement of the objectives of Article 86 since it is always within the discretion of the Commission to withdraw the exemption ...

19. The applicant "accepts that there is no express exemption for the prohibition under Article 86". But, in support of its view that Article 86 is inapplicable to conduct exempt under Article 85(3), it puts forward an interpretation of the conditions for applying Article 86 based on the general scheme of Article 85. This interpretation leads in reality to accepting that there can be an implied exemption in respect of abuse of a dominant position. In determining whether conduct constitutes an abuse, one must, the applicant argues, "impliedly undertake the two-stage process which is made explicit in Article 85, namely ... ask does the conduct have the object or effect of preventing, restricting or distorting competition within the common market, and, if so, does the conduct nevertheless have overall a pro-competitive effect because it contributes to promoting technical or economic progress" ...

21. This Court notes at the outset that the problem of reconciling application of Article 86 with enjoyment of block exemption, which is the crux of the present case and arises because of the need for logical coherence in the implementation of Articles 85 and 86, has not yet been expressly determined by the Community court. However, it must be borne in mind that the relationship between Articles 85 and 86 has, to an extent, been clarified by the Court of Justice, in that the Court has expressly said that the applicability to an agreement of Article 85 does not preclude application of Article 86.

22. Resolution of the problem of reconciling application of Article 86 with exemption under Article 85(3) must therefore start from the Treaty system for the protection of competition, in particular as laid down by those two Articles of the Treaty and their implementing regulations. Articles 85 and 86 are complementary inasmuch as they pursue a common general objective, set out in Article 3(f) of the Treaty, which provides that the activities of the Community are to include "the institution of a system ensuring that competition in the common market is not distorted". But they none the less constitute, in the scheme of the Treaty, two independent legal instruments addressing different situations. This was emphasised by the Court of Justice in CONTINENTAL CAN where, having said that "Article 85 concerns agreements between undertakings, decisions of associations of undertakings and concerted practices, while Article 86 concerns unilateral activity of one or more undertakings", the Court held that "Articles 85 and 86 seek to achieve the same aim on different levels, *viz* the maintenance of effective competition within the Common Market."

23. Turning to the specific nature of the conduct whose compatibility with Article 86 is considered in the Decision, this Court holds that the mere fact that an undertaking in a dominant position acquires an exclusive licence does not *per se* constitute abuse within the meaning of Article 86. For the purpose of applying Article 86, the circumstances surrounding the acquisition, and in particular its effects on the structure of competition in the relevant market, must be taken into account. This interpretation is borne out by the case law of the Court of Justice, in which the concept of abuse is defined as "an objective concept relating to the behaviour of an undertaking in a dominant position which is such as to influence the structure of a market where, as a result of the very presence of the undertaking in question, the degree of competition is weakened and which, through recourse to methods different from those which condition normal competition in products or services on the basis of the transactions of commercial operators, has the effect of hindering the maintenance of the degree of competition still existing in the market or the growth of that competition." So, here, the Commission was right not to put in issue the exclusive licence as such, but rather to object specifically under Article 86 to the anti-competitive effect of its being acquired by the applicant. It is plain from the reasoning and conclusions of the Decision that the infringement of Article 86 found by the Commission stemmed precisely from Tetra Pak's acquisition of the exclusive licence "in the specific circumstances of this case". The specific context to which the Commission refers is expressly characterised as being the fact that acquisition of the exclusivity of the licence not only "strengthened Tetra's very considerable dominance but also had the effect of preventing, or at the very least considerably delaying, the entry of a new competitor into a market where very little if any competition is found". The decisive factor in the finding that acquisition of the exclusive licence constituted an abuse therefore lay quite specifically in the applicant's position in the relevant market and in particular, as appears from the Decision, in the fact that at the material time the right to use the process protected by the BTG licence was alone capable of giving an undertaking the means of competing effectively with the applicant in the field of the aseptic packaging of milk. The takeover of Liquipak was no more than the means - to which the Commission has attached no particular significance in applying Article 86 - by which the applicant acquired the exclusivity of the BTG licence, the effect of which was to deprive other undertakings of the means of competing with the applicant.

24. Similarly, the applicant's argument that there must be a supplementary element, external to the agreement, cannot be accepted. In this connection, it is relevant to note that in AHMED SAEED to which the applicant refers the Court of Justice held that "the application of tariffs for scheduled flights on the basis of bilateral or multilateral agreements may, in certain circumstances, constitute an abuse of a dominant position on the market in question, in particular where an undertaking in a dominant position has succeeded in imposing on other carriers the application of excessively high or excessively low tariffs or the exclusive application of only one tariff on a given route". It is true that the Court of Justice justified the concurrent application of Articles 85 and 86 to the tariff agreements there at issue by referring to the existence of a supplementary element, which in that case took the form of pressure brought to bear by the undertaking on its competitors. But the Decision in the present case does refer to the additional element that constituted an abuse within the meaning of Article 86 and justified its application. The additional element lies in the very context of the case - in the fact that Tetra Pak's acquisition of the exclusive licence had the practical effect of precluding all competition in the

relevant market. This was emphasised in the Decision and was not put in issue by the applicant.

25. In these circumstances, this Court holds that in the scheme for the protection of competition established by the Treaty the grant of exemption, whether individual or block exemption, under Article 85(3) cannot be such as to render inapplicable the prohibition set out in Article 86. This principle follows both from the wording of Article 85(3) which permits derogation, through a declaration of inapplicability, only from the prohibition of agreements, decisions and concerted practices set out in Article 85(1), and also from the general scheme of Articles 85 and 86 which, as noted above, are independent and complementary provisions designed, in general, to regulate distinct situations by different rules. Application of Article 85 involves two stages: a finding that Article 85(1) has been infringed followed, where appropriate, by exemption from that prohibition if the agreement, decision or concerted practice in question satisfies the conditions laid down in Article 85(3). Article 86, on the other hand, by reason of its very subject-matter (abuse), precludes any possible exception to the prohibition it lays down ... Moreover, in view of the principles governing the hierarchical relationship of legal rules, grant of exemption under secondary legislation could not, in the absence of any enabling provision in the Treaty, derogate from a provision of the Treaty, in this case Article 86.

26. Having established that, in principle, the grant of exemption cannot preclude application of Article 86, the question remains whether, in practice, findings made with a view to the grant of exemption under Article 85(3) preclude application of Article 86.

27. Under Article 85(3), the prohibition laid down in Article 85(1) may be declared inapplicable to agreements, decisions or concerted practices, or to categories thereof, which fulfil the conditions set out in Article 85(3). Article 85(3) provides *inter alia* that the agreement must not afford the undertakings the possibility of eliminating competition in respect of a substantial part of the products in question.

28. The way in which the question of exemption arises may in practice be different depending on whether an individual or block exemption is involved. The grant of individual exemption presupposes that the Commission has found that the agreement in question complies with the conditions set out in Article 85(3). So, where an individual exemption decision has been taken, characteristics of the agreement which would also be relevant in applying Article 86 may be taken to have been established. Consequently, in applying Article 86, the Commission must take account, unless the factual and legal circumstances have altered, of the earlier findings made when exemption was granted under Article 85(3).

29. Now it is true that regulations granting block exemption, like individual exemption decisions, apply only to agreements which, in principle, satisfy the conditions set out in Article 85(3). But unlike individual exemptions, block exemptions are, by definition, not dependent on a case-by-case examination to establish that the conditions for exemption laid down in the Treaty are in fact satisfied. In order to qualify for a block exemption, an agreement has only to satisfy the criteria laid down in the relevant block-exemption regulation. The agreement itself is not subject to any positive assessment with regard to the conditions set out in Article 85(3). So a block exemption cannot, generally speaking, be construed as having effects similar to negative clearance in relation to Article 86. The result is that, where agreements to which undertakings in a dominant position are parties fall within the scope of a block-exemption regulation (that is, where the regulation is

unlimited in scope), the effects of block exemption on the applicability of Article 86 must be assessed solely in the context of the scheme of Article 86.

30. Lastly, the possibility of applying Article 86 to an agreement covered by a block exemption is confirmed by analysis of the scheme of the block-exemption regulations. First, those regulations do not, in principle, exclude undertakings in a dominant position from qualifying the exemption and therefore do not take account of the position on the relevant markets of the parties to any given agreement. That is particularly so in the case of Regulation 2349/84 on exemptions in respect of patent licensing agreements (cited above) which is relevant in this case. Second, the possibility of applying Article 85(3) and Article 86 concurrently is expressly confirmed by certain of the block-exemption regulations where it is provided that enjoyment of block-exemption does not preclude application of Article 86 - in particular, the three block-exemption regulations in the field of air transport adopted by the Commission on 26 July 1988, each of which states expressly in the preamble that group exemption does not preclude the application of Article 86 ... Similarly, Article 8(1) of Council Regulation 4056/86, cited above, states expressly that abuse of a dominant position within the meaning of Article 86 is prohibited, no prior decision to that effect being required.

31. It follows from all the foregoing considerations that the first head of argument in support of the sole ground of action, based on a schematic analysis of Article 85(3) and Article 86, is unfounded.

(b) The principle of legal certainty

32. In support of its analysis of the relationship between Article 85(3) and Article 86 which seeks to show that application of Article 86 to an agreement exempt under Article 85(3) is inconceivable in principle, the applicant invokes the principle of legal certainty. The argument is that, interpreted in the light of the principle of legal certainty, Articles 85 and 86 require that conduct exempt under Article 85(3) cannot be prohibited under Article 86. The balance between guaranteeing legal certainty for undertakings and maintaining effective competition is secured, on this argument, by the Commission's power to withdraw the benefit of the exemption.

33. In that connection the applicant stresses that the grant of exemption, coupled with the Commission's power to withdraw the benefit of the exemption, gives undertakings a legitimate expectation that they will not be found to have infringed Articles 85 and 86 so long as the Commission has not taken a decision to withdraw the exemption.

34. The applicant considers, contrary to the Commission, that legal certainty cannot be secured by the undertaking applying for negative clearance. The need to make such an application would undermine the efficacy of the block exemption, one of whose primary functions is to enable undertakings to conclude and implement agreements without consulting the Commission. The fact that negative clearance does not afford the same degree of certainty as exemption is shown by the inclusion amongst agreements exempted under Regulation 2349/84, cited above, of certain agreements which would not normally fall within Article 85(1). The Commission justified that solution on the ground of the need for legal certainty for the undertakings concerned (paragraph [18] of the preamble and Article 2 of the regulation). More specifically the applicant points out that an application for negative clearance does not preclude the imposition of a fine in respect of conduct subsequent to the application but prior to the decision finding the infringement. Furthermore, the applicant continues, the agreement may be unenforceable in

national courts pending the Commission's investigation. Finally, negative clearance is not binding on national courts.

35. The Commission argues, to the contrary, that the block-exemption system, including the rules prompted by considerations of legal certainty for undertakings, is concerned only with application of Article 85. Article 86 establishes a prohibition which applies from the date on which the infringement is committed and, as the Court pointed out in HOFFMAN-LA ROCHE, (Case 85/76, para [134]) legal certainty can be ensured as regards the application of that provision by an application for negative clearance under Article 2 of Regulation 17, cited above.

36. The Court of Justice has consistently endorsed the principles of legal certainty and legitimate expectation, by virtue of which the effect of Community legislation must be clear and predictable for those who are subject to it ([1981] ECR 2735 at para [10]).

37. The question therefore is whether the application of Article 86 becomes unpredictable whenever an agreement fulfils the conditions for block exemption. This Court accepts that, apart from considerations of administrative simplification, one of the main purposes of block exemption is to secure legal certainty for the parties to an agreement as regards the validity of that agreement under Article 85 so long as the Commission has not withdrawn the benefit of block exemption. But that does not discharge undertakings in a dominant position from the obligation to comply with Article 86. On the contrary, the Court of Justice held in MICHELIN ([1983] ECR 3461, [1985] 1 CMLR 282) that any undertaking in a dominant position has "a special responsibility not to allow its conduct to impair genuine undistorted competition on the common market". Accordingly, an undertaking cannot rely on the alleged unpredictability of the application of Article 86 in order to escape the prohibition there laid down.

38. In any event, as far as the present case is concerned, although the requirements of legal certainty could not prevent Article 86 being applied to the applicant's acquisition of the exclusive licence, they did nonetheless prompt the Commission to mitigate the consequences of the infringement for the applicant. The Commission took into account "the fact that the contraventions ... were relatively novel" by not imposing a fine on the applicant.

39. For all of those reasons the second head of the applicant's argument is unfounded.

(c) The principle of the uniform application of Community law

40. Thirdly, the applicant bases its case on the principle of the uniform application of Community law. The applicant points out that if Article 86 were to apply to conduct enjoying block exemption then, applying the principle of the direct effect of Article 86 confirmed by the Court of Justice in Case 127/73, BRT v SABAM ([1974] ECR 51, [1974] 2 CMLR 238) national courts would have jurisdiction to prohibit under Article 86 conduct exempted by the Commission. Such a situation would, in the applicant's submission, prejudice the uniform application of Community law whose importance the Court of Justice emphasised in WALT WILHELM ([1969] ECR 1, [1969] CMLR 100). The applicant therefore argues that the only interpretation of the relationship between Article 85(3) and Article 86 which is consistent with the principle of the uniform application of Community law is to hold that application of Article 86 is incompatible with exemption.

41. The Commission observes that the argument relating to the uniform application of Community law is really based on Tetra Pak's main claim that Article 86 cannot

apply to behaviour covered by an exemption and accordingly that the applicant's premise is unsound. Further, the application of Community law by national authorities is a secondary consideration and purely hypothetical in the present case. In any event, the uniform implementation of Community law can be ensured, where there is a block exemption, by recourse to Article 177 of the Treaty.

42. On this question, the Court finds a consistent line of case law to the effect that "the prohibitions of Article 86 have a direct effect and confer on interested parties rights which the national courts must safeguard". If Community law allows Article 86 to be applied in respect of an agreement exempt under Article 85(3), there is nothing to justify limiting the power of national courts to apply Article 86 on the ground that the practice in question has been granted exemption under Article 85(3). Unlike the case of WALT WILHELM on which the applicant relies, the application of Article 86 with respect to conduct covered by an exemption under Article 85(3) does not call into question the principles of the primacy and uniformity of Community law. On the contrary, when applying Article 86, in particular to conduct exempt under Article 85(3), the national courts are acting as Community courts of general jurisdiction. They will merely be applying - as they are bound to do by virtue of the primacy and direct effect of the Community rules on competition - the principles of Community law governing the relationship between Article 85(3) and Article 86. Accordingly, where a national court applies Article 86 to conduct enjoying exemption under Article 85(3), the uniform application of Community law - in this case, Article 85(3), the provisions implementing it, and Article 86 - is fully guaranteed by the procedure for reference of questions of interpretation for a preliminary ruling under Article 177 of the Treaty.

43. Consequently, the third head of the applicant's argument is unfounded.

44. In the light of all of the foregoing considerations, the application must be dismissed.'

COMMENT

Although Articles 85 and 86 pursue the same basic objective, the two provisions are independent. Non-infringement of one does not automatically mean that the other is not infringed. Do you consider that to be a satisfactory position? Do you think Article 86 is more or less predictable in its application than Article 85? Note that the patent licensing regulation referred to in the judgment has been replaced by the Technology Transfer Regulation (extracts of which are included earlier in this chapter).

Volvo AB v Erik Veng (UK) Ltd. [1989] 4 CMLR 122, European Court of Justice

Volvo was the proprietor of a registered design in respect of front wings for Volvo 200 cars. Veng imported into the United Kingdom wings for Volvo 200s made by a third party. Most of these were made in Italy. Volvo sued Veng for infringement of its registered design. In its defence, Veng pleaded, *inter alia*, Article 86. The English Patents Courts requested the European Court of Justice for a preliminary ruling under Article 177 of the EC Treaty.

Judgment (at 134) ... '[1] By an order of 17 July 1987, which was received at the Court on 3 August 1987, the High Court of Justice of England and Wales (Chancery Division, Patents Court) referred three questions to the court under Article 177 of the EEC Treaty for a preliminary ruling on the interpretation of Article 86 of the Treaty with a view to determining whether the refusal by the proprietor of a registered design in respect of body panels for motor vehicles to grant a licence for the import and sale of such panels may, in certain circumstances, be regarded as an abuse of a dominant position within the meaning of the above mentioned Article.

[2] The questions were raised in proceedings between Volvo AB (hereinafter referred to as Volvo) and Eric Veng (UK) Ltd. (hereinafter referred to as Veng).

[3] Volvo, the proprietor in the United Kingdom of registered design no. 968 895 for the front wings of Volvo series 200 cars, instituted proceedings against Veng before the High Court of Justice for infringement of its sole and exclusive rights. Veng imports the same body panels, manufactured without authority from Volvo and markets them in the United Kingdom.

[4] In the proceedings before it, the High Court referred the following questions to the Court of Justice for a preliminary ruling:

1. If a substantial car manufacturer holds registered designs which, under the law of a member-State, confer on it the sole and exclusive right to make and import replacement body panels required to effect repair of the body of a car of its manufacture (if such body panels are not replaceable by body panels of any other design), is such a manufacturer, by reason of such sole and exclusive rights, in a dominant position within the meaning of Article 86 of the EEC Treaty with respect to such replacement parts?

2. Is it *prima facie* an abuse of such dominant position for such a manufacturer to refuse to licence others to supply such body panels, even where they are willing to pay a reasonable royalty for all articles sold under the licence (such royalty to represent an award which is just and equitable having regard to the merits of the design and all the surrounding circumstances, and to be determined by arbitration or in such other manner as the national court shall direct)?

3. Is such an abuse likely to affect trade between member-States within the meaning of Article 86 by reason of the fact that the intending licensee is thereby prevented from importing the body panels from a second member-State?

[5] It is apparent from the terms of the order for reference that the national court submitted those questions taking account of the undertaking given by the defendant in the main proceedings to abandon its contention that a comparison of the prices charged by it for the body panels in question and the higher prices charged for the same panels by the plaintiff in the main proceedings constitutes an abuse of a dominant position by the latter.

[6] Reference is made to the Report for the Hearing for a fuller account of the facts in the main proceedings, the course of the procedure and the observations submitted to the Court, which are mentioned or referred to hereinafter only in so far as is necessary for the reasoning of the Court.

The second question

[7] It must first be observed, as the Court held in its judgment of 14 September 1982 (Case 144/81, KEURKOOP v NANCY KEAN GIFTS ([1982] ECR 2853, [1983] 2 CMLR 47) with respect to the protection of designs and models, that, as

Community law stands at present and in the absence of Community standardisation or harmonisation of laws, the determination of the conditions and procedures under which protection of designs and models is granted is a matter for national rules. It is thus for the national legislatures to determine which products are to benefit from protection, even where they form part of a unit which is already protected as such.

[8] It must also be emphasised that the right of the proprietor of a protected design to prevent third parties from manufacturing and selling or importing, without its consent, products incorporating the design constitutes the very subject-matter of his exclusive right. It follows that an obligation imposed upon the proprietor of a protected design to grant to third parties, even in return for a reasonable royalty, a licence for the supply of products incorporating the design would lead to the proprietor thereof being deprived of the substance of his exclusive right, and that a refusal to grant such a licence cannot in itself constitute an abuse of a dominant position.

[9] It must however be noted that the exercise of an exclusive right by the proprietor of a registered design in respect of car body panels may be prohibited by Article 86 if it involves, on the part of an undertaking holding a dominant position, certain abusive conduct such as the arbitrary refusal to supply spare parts to independent repairers, the fixing of prices for spare parts at an unfair level or a decision no longer to produce spare parts for a particular model even though many cars of that model are still in circulation, provided that such conduct is liable to affect trade between member-States.

[10] In the present case no instance of any such conduct has been mentioned by the national court. Accordingly, and having regard to the answer given to the second question, it is unnecessary to give an answer to the first and third questions.

[11] It must therefore be stated in reply to the second question submitted by the national court that the refusal by the proprietor of a registered design in respect of body panels to grant to third parties, even in return for reasonable royalties, a licence for the supply of parts incorporating the design cannot in itself be regarded as an abuse of a dominant position within the meaning of Article 86.

On those grounds, THE COURT in reply to the questions submitted to it by the High Court of Justice of England and Wales by order of 17 July 1987 HEREBY RULES:

The refusal by the proprietor of a registered design in respect of body panels to grant to third parties even in return for reasonable royalties, a licence for the supply of parts incorporating the design cannot in itself be regarded as an abuse of a dominant position within the meaning of Article 86.'

COMMENT

Is a design such as that in this case registrable under the Registered Designs Act 1949 as it now stands? Why did the Court consider it unnecessary to decide the first and third questions? How would the Court have decided where, for example, a manufacturer of low volume cars, being a subsidiary of a very large car manufacturing company, refused to grant licences to any other company save its parent company?

This case demonstrates the extent to which a lack of harmonisation of laws throughout the Community hinders the enforcement of the competition measures of the EC Treaty.

In his submission Advocate-General Mischo said in relation to the first question:

'If a substantial car manufacturer holds registered designs which, under the law of a member-State, confer on it the sole and exclusive right to make and import replacement body panels required to effect repair of the body of a car of its manufacture (and if such body panels are not replaceable by body panels of any other design), that manufacturer is in a dominant position within the meaning of Article 86 of the EEC Treaty, by reason both of such sole and exclusive rights and of the fact that it is impossible for the consumer to obtain a substitute product'.

In relation to the third question Advocate General Mischo said:

'Since I have established that the refusal to grant a licence does not of itself constitute abuse of a dominant position, the third question is now devoid of purpose.

But what about the effect on trade between the member-States if the proprietor of the registered design abused his dominant position, for example by fixing unfair sale prices?

Like the Commission, I consider that in such cases it would be for the national court to investigate whether the undertaking abusing its dominant position imports the parts in question from one member-State into another member-State.'

Radio Telefis Eireann & Independent Television Publications Ltd v The Commission of the European Communities [1995] FSR 530, European Court of Justice

Radio Telefis Eireann ('RTE') and Independent Television Publications Ltd. ('ITP') published television guides. They allowed newspapers and others to publish details free of charge but only within 24 hours (or 48 hours in the case of a bank holiday) of the broadcast of the relevant programmes. Magill Television Guide Ltd. ('Magill') wanted to publish a weekly television guide and had been the subject of an injunction. It complained to the European Commission which held that there was a breach of Article 86 and it required RTE and ITP to grant a licence for such publication at a reasonable royalty. RTE and ITP appealed to the Court of First Instance which dismissed the appeal. At the European Court of Justice, Intellectual Property Owners Inc. ('IPO') intervened on behalf of RTE and ITP.

Judgment (at 542): ' ... *(a) Existence of a dominant position*
46. So far as dominant position is concerned, it is to be remembered at the outset that mere ownership of an intellectual property right cannot confer such a position.
47. However, the basic information as to the channel, day, time and title of programmes is the necessary result of programming by television stations, which are thus the only source of such information for an undertaking, like Magill, which wishes to publish it together with commentaries or pictures. By force of circumstance, RTE and ITP, as the agent of ITV, enjoy, along with the BBC, a *de facto* monopoly over

the information used to compile listings for the television programmes received in most households in Ireland and 30 per cent to 40 per cent of households in Northern Ireland. The appellants are thus in a position to prevent effective competition on the market in weekly television magazines. The Court of First Instance was therefore right in confirming the Commission's assessment that the appellants occupied a dominant position (see the judgment in [*Nederlandsche Banden-Industrie Michelin* v *The Commission of the European Communities* [1983] ECR 3461]) ...

(b) Existence of abuse
48. With regard to the issue of abuse, the arguments of the appellants and IPO wrongly presuppose that where the conduct of an undertaking in a dominant position consists of the exercise of a right classified by national law as "copyright", such conduct can never be reviewed in relation to Article 86 of the Treaty.

49. Admittedly, in the absence of Community standardisation or harmonisation of laws, determination of the conditions and procedures for granting protection of an intellectual property right is a matter for national rules. Further, the exclusive right of reproduction forms part of the author's rights, so that refusal to grant a licence, even if it is the act of an undertaking holding a dominant position, cannot in itself constitute abuse of a dominant position (judgment in [*AB Volvo* v *Erik Veng (UK) Ltd.* [1988] ECR 6211, [1989] 4 CMLR 122]).

50. However, it is also clear from that judgment ... that the exercise of an exclusive right by the proprietor may, in exceptional circumstances, involve abusive conduct.

51. In the present case, the conduct objected to is the appellants' reliance on copyright conferred by national legislation so as to prevent Magill - or any other undertaking having the same intention - from publishing on a weekly basis information (channel, day, time and title of programmes) together with commentaries and pictures obtained independently of the appellants.

52. Among the circumstances taken into account by the Court of First Instance in concluding that such conduct was abusive was, first, the fact that there was, according to the findings of the Court of First Instance, no actual or potential substitute for a weekly television guide offering information on the programmes for the week ahead. On this point, the Court of First Instance confirmed the Commission's finding that the complete lists of programmes for a 24-hour period - and for a 48-hour period at weekends and before public holidays - published in certain daily and Sunday newspapers, and the television sections of certain magazines covering, in addition, "highlights" of the week's programmes, were only to a limited extent substitutable for advance information to viewers on all the week's programmes. Only weekly television guides containing comprehensive listings for the week ahead would enable users to decide in advance which programmes they wished to follow and arrange their leisure activities for the week accordingly. The Court of First Instance also established that there was a specific, constant and regular potential demand on the part of consumers ...

53. Thus the appellants [were] the only sources of the basic information on programme scheduling which is the indispensable raw material for compiling a weekly television guide - gave viewers wishing to obtain information on the choice of programmes for the week ahead no choice but to buy the weekly guides for each station and draw from each of them the information they needed to make comparisons.

54. The appellants' refusal to provide basic information by relying on national copyright provisions thus prevented the appearance of a new product, a

comprehensive weekly guide to television programmes, which the appellants did not offer and for which there was a potential consumer demand. Such refusal constitutes an abuse under heading (b) of the second paragraph of Article 86 of the Treaty.

55. Second, there was no justification for such refusal either in the activity of television broadcasting or in that of publishing television magazines ...

56. Third, and finally, as the Court of First Instance also held, the appellants, by their conduct, reserved to themselves the secondary market of weekly television guides by excluding all competition on that market (see the judgment in *Commercial Solvents* v *Commission* [1974] ECR 223, para. 25) since they denied access to the basic information which is the raw material indispensable for the compilation of such a guide.

57. In the light of all those circumstances, the Court of First Instance did not err in law in holding that the appellants' conduct was an abuse of a dominant position within the meaning of Article 86 of the Treaty.

58. It follows that the plea in law alleging misapplication by the Court of First Instance of the concept of abuse of a dominant position must be dismissed as unfounded. It is therefore unnecessary to examine the reasoning of the contested judgments in so far as it is based on Article 36 of the Treaty.

Effects on trade between Member States (second plea in the appeal in Case C-241191 P)

59. With regard to the effects on trade between Member States, the Court of First Instance first reviewed the case law of the Court of Justice ... before finding ... that

> "the applicant's conduct modified the structure of competition on the market for television guides in Ireland and Northern Ireland and thus affected potential trade flows between Ireland and the United Kingdom."

60. The reasons given by the Court of First Instance for this conclusion were based on the effects of RTE's refusal to authorise third parties to publish its weekly listings on the structure of competition in the territory of Ireland and Northern Ireland. These, the Court of First Instance found, excluded all potential competition on the market in question, "thus in effect maintaining the partitioning of the markets ... [of] Ireland and Northern Ireland respectively." It found that the appreciable effect which the policy in question had on potential commercial exchanges between Ireland and the United Kingdom was evidenced by the specific demand for a general television magazine. The Court of First Instance added that

> "the relevant geographical area, within which a single market in television broadcasting services has already been achieved, likewise represents a single market for information on television programmes, particularly since trade is greatly facilitated by a common language."

61. RTE states that Community competition rules are not intended to remedy situations which are purely internal to a Member State and it disputes the finding of the Court of First Instance that RTE had "in effect maintain[ed] the partitioning of the markets represented by Ireland and Northern Ireland respectively." RTE asserts that it has observed one and the same policy in respect of the supply of weekly programme listings and licensing, irrespective of the place of establishment of the

undertakings concerned. It denies ever having stopped or hindered the export or import of television guides.

62. RTE also recalls the following facts, which are supported by the findings of the Commission and the Court of First Instance:

(i)   outside Ireland, RTE's programmes are received only in part of Northern Ireland, which represents less than 1.6 per cent of the United Kingdom television market and less than 0.3 per cent of the EEC television market;

(ii) according to the findings of the High Court of Ireland, the RTE signal is received by 30 per cent to 40 per cent of the population of Northern Ireland;

(iii) sales of RTE's television guide in the United Kingdom are less than 5 per cent of sales in Ireland.

63. RTE adds that it does not have programmes or commercials aimed at or broadcast to Northern Ireland. Its programmes can be received in Northern Ireland only because of "overspill". In Northern Ireland, approximately 100,000 households receive RTE programmes and 5,000 copies of RTE's television guide are sold.

64. According to RTE, these facts demonstrate the marginal importance of the cross-border sales of weekly guides containing RTE's programmes.

65. Moreover, following the new licensing policy applied by RTE, it appears that:

(i)   sales in Ireland of *Radio Times* and *TV Times,* originating in the United Kingdom, have decreased;

(ii) sales in Northern Ireland of the *RTE Guide,* originating in Ireland, have not increased; in general the inclusion of RTE's programme listings in a multi-channel guide does not appreciably affect sales figures of such a guide in Northern Ireland;

(iii) no other publishers have availed themselves of the new possibility of publishing comprehensive weekly television guides, including RTE's programmes, and of selling them across the border.

66. RTE concludes from this information that its licensing policy, condemned by the Commission decision, has had no effect, or no more than an insignificant effect, on commercial exchanges between Ireland and the United Kingdom. In any event, RTE states, the Commission must prove that there is an appreciable effect on trade between Member States (judgment in *United Brands* v *Commission* [1978] ECR 207), and that is something which the Court of First Instance failed to take into account. It points out that the Commission's arguments on this aspect relate only to sales in Great Britain, to ITP and to the BBC.

67. It is to be noted at the outset that the Court of Justice has consistently held that, pursuant to Article 168a of the Treaty and Article 51 of the Statute of the Court of Justice of the EEC, an appeal may rely only on grounds relating to infringement of rules of law, to the exclusion of any appraisal of the facts (judgment in *Hilti* v *Commission* [1994] ECR 1-667, para. 10). The arguments relied on by RTE must therefore be rejected in so far as they question the appraisal of the facts by the Court of First Instance.

68. Nevertheless, the condition that trade between Member States must be affected is a question of law and, as such, subject to review by the Court of Justice.

69. In order to satisfy the condition that trade between Member States must be affected, it is not necessary that the conduct in question should in fact have

substantially affected that trade. It is sufficient to establish that the conduct is capable of having such an effect (judgments in *Michelin* v *Commission,* cited above, para. 104, and in *Höfner and Elser* v *Macrotron* [1991] ECR 1-1979, para. 32).

70. In this case, the Court of First Instance found that the applicant had excluded all potential competitors on the geographical market consisting of one Member State (Ireland) and part of another Member State (Northern Ireland) and had thus modified the structure of competition on that market, thereby affecting potential commercial exchanges between Ireland and the United Kingdom. From this the Court of First Instance drew the proper conclusion that the condition that trade between Member States must be affected had been satisfied.

71. It follows that the plea in law alleging misapplication by the Court of First Instance of the concept of trade between Member States being affected must be dismissed.

The Berne Convention (third plea in the appeal in Case C-241191 P)

72. So far as the Berne Convention ("the Convention") is concerned, RTE had submitted before the Court of First Instance that Article 9(1) thereof conferred an exclusive right of reproduction and that Article 9(2) allowed a signatory State to permit reproduction only in certain special cases, provided that such reproduction did not conflict with normal exploitation of the work and did not unreasonably prejudice the legitimate interests of the author. From this RTE deduced that Article 2 of the contested decision was incompatible with the Convention inasmuch as it conflicted with the normal exploitation of RTE's copyright in the programme listings and seriously prejudiced its legitimate interests ...

73. In response to those arguments, the Court of First Instance considered whether the Convention was applicable. Its first finding was that the Community was not a party to it. After reviewing Article 234 of the EEC Treaty and the case law of the Court of Justice ... the Court of First Instance pointed out that:

"In the present case concerning Ireland and the United Kingdom, ... under Article 5 of the Act of Accession, Article 234 of the EEC Treaty applies to agreements or conventions concluded before ... 1 January 1973."

From this it deduced that:

"In intra-Comunity relations, therefore, the provisions of the Berne Convention, ratified by Ireland and the United Kingdom before 1 January 1973, cannot affect the provisions of the Treaty.... The argument that Article 2 of the decision is in conflict with Article 9(1) of the Berne Convention must therefore be dismissed, without there even being any need to inquire into its substance."

With regard to Article 9(2) of the Convention, the Court of First Instance observed that this provision:

"was introduced by the Paris revision of 1971, to which the United Kingdom has been a party since 2 January 1990 and which Ireland has not yet ratified."

The Court of First Instance then pointed out that an agreement or a convention concluded subsequent to accession without recourse to the procedure set out in Article 236 of the EEC Treaty cannot affect a provision of the Treaty ...

74. The Court of First Instance accordingly dismissed as unfounded the plea alleging infringement of the Convention ...

75. RTE claims that Article 9(2) of the Berne Convention, as revised in Paris in 1971, only allows for exceptions from authors' exclusive rights of reproduction to be made by legislation, in special cases, and provided that such reproduction does not prejudice the normal exploitation of the work or cause unreasonable prejudice to the legitimate interests of the author.

76. According to RTE, the Convention does not contain a definition of what comes under its protection but excludes only "miscellaneous news facts having the character of mere facts of press information" (Article 2(8)), an exception which must be interpreted restrictively. It is thus for the national legislature and courts to determine the scope of the Convention at national level.

77. RTE submits that the obligation imposed by the Commission's decision has not been provided for by legislation which is sufficiently clear in its terms to define the circumstances in which, and the conditions on which, reproduction is to be permitted. The decision itself cannot be regarded as "legislation". Application of competition law does not fulfil the conditions of Article 9(2). A copyright holder must be able to know on the basis of explicit legislation whether or not he may be subject to an obligation of compulsory licensing. A provision such as Article 86 of the Treaty, which merely sets out a general obligation and must be made precise and adapted from case to case, does not fulfil the conditions laid down by Article 9(2) of the Convention. Community legislation alone is capable of providing a proper legislative basis.

78. RTE submits that the Convention is part of the rules of law relating to the application of the Treaty referred to in Article 173 of the EEC Treaty. In support of that proposition, RTE refers to numerous declarations made by the Commission which show that the Convention enjoys broad international support ... According to RTE, the Commission has always regarded the Convention as establishing a minimum level of protection. It refers to the Proposal for a Council Directive on the legal protection of computer programs [1989] OJ C91/4 ... and Council Directive 91/250 of May 14, 1991 on the legal protection of computer programs [1991] OJ L122/42. The amended Commission proposal for a Council Decision concerning the accession of the Member States to the Berne Convention for the Protection of Literary and Artistic Works, as revised by the Paris Act of July 24, 1971 and the International Convention for the Protection of Performers, Producers of Phonograms and Broadcasting Organizations (Rome Convention) of October 26, 1961 [1992] OJ C57/13 states (Article la):

"In the exercise of its powers concerning copyright and neighbouring rights, the Community shall be guided by the principles and act in accordance with the provisions of the Berne Convention ..."

The Proposal for a Council Directive on the legal protection of databases, adopted on January 29, 1992, provides a legislative basis for compulsory licensing. RTE observes that, in all fields other than competition law, the Community respects the Convention.

79. RTE accordingly takes the view that, although the Community itself is not a party to the Convention, account must be taken of the rules of that Convention within the framework of Community law (judgments in *Nold* v *Commission* [1974] ECR 491, and in *Hoechst* v *Commission* [1989] ECR 2859).

80. According to RTE, the Community cannot, on the one hand, oblige the Member States to accede to and comply with the Convention and, on the other, adopt measures which do not comply with it.

81. In conclusion, it contends that examination of the scope of Articles 234 and 236 would be relevant only if a conflict between the obligations arising from the Convention and certain provisions of the EEC Treaty had been established.

82. IPO endorses this opinion and contends that harmonisation of national intellectual property law can be achieved only by legislative means, namely by a Council measure adopted in accordance with the procedure provided for in Article 100a or Article 235 of the EEC Treaty. An individual decision issued by the Commission on the basis of competition law is not the appropriate way to resolve this issue.

83. It is appropriate to observe at the outset, as the Court of First Instance did, that the Community is not a party to the Convention for the Protection of Literary and Artistic Works.

84. Next, so far as the United Kingdom and Ireland are concerned, it is true that they were already parties to the Convention when they acceded to the Community and that Article 234 of the Treaty therefore applies to that Convention, in accordance with Article 5 of the Act of Accession. It is, however, settled case law that the provisions of an agreement concluded prior to entry into force of the Treaty or prior to a Member State's accession cannot be relied on in intra-Community relations if, as in the present case, the rights of non-member countries are not involved (see, in particular, the judgment in *Ministère Public* v *Deserbais* [1988] ECR 4907, para. 18).

85. Finally, the Paris Act, which amended Article 9(1) and (2) of the Convention (the provisions relied on by RTE), was ratified by the United Kingdom only after its accession to the Community and has still not been ratified by Ireland.

86. The Court of First Instance was therefore correct to hold that Article 9 of the Convention cannot be relied on to limit the powers of the Community, as provided for in the EEC Treaty, since the Treaty can be amended only in accordance with the procedure laid down in Article 236.

87. It follows that the plea that the Court of First Instance failed to have proper regard to the Convention must be dismissed as unfounded.

The powers conferred on the Commission by Article 3 of Regulation No. 17 (second plea in the appeal in Case C-242191 P)

88. The first limb of ITP's second plea is that the Court of First Instance misconstrued Article 3 of Regulation No. 17 in holding that that provision enabled the Commission to impose compulsory licensing, on conditions approved by it, relating to intellectual property rights conferred by the laws of the Member States. Relying on the judgment in *Keurkoop* v *Nancy Kean Gifts* [1982] ECR 2853, ITP submits that only the Parliaments of Ireland and the United Kingdom may take away or replace the copyrights which they have conferred.

89. The second limb alleges infringement of the principle of proportionality in so far as the Court of First Instance held that the Commission's decision was not contrary to that principle ... ITP contends that the Court of First Instance should have taken account of a number of considerations: the decision removed not only ITP's exclusive right of reproduction, but also its right of first marketing, particularly important where, as in this case, the product has a useful life of 10 days; there is no reciprocity between ITP and the competitors (other than the BBC and RTE) to whom it is required to grant licences; many of those competitors, particularly the national

newspapers, have turnovers and profits greatly in excess of those of ITP and they also possess valuable copyrights which they protect from reproduction.

90. It is appropriate to observe that Article 3 of Regulation No. 17 is to be applied according to the nature of the infringement found and may include an order to do certain acts or things which, unlawfully, have not been done as well as an order to bring an end to certain acts, practices or situations which are contrary to the Treaty (judgment in *Commercial Solvents* [1974] 1 ECR 223, [1974] 1 CMLR 309).

91. In the present case, after finding that the refusal to provide undertakings such as Magill with the basic information contained in television programme listings was an abuse of a dominant position, the Commission was entitled under Article 3, in order to ensure that its decision was effective, to require the appellants to provide that information. As the Court of First Instance rightly found, the imposition of that obligation - with the possibility of making authorisation of publication dependent on certain conditions, including payment of royalties - was the only way of bringing the infringement to an end.

92. The Court of First Instance was also entitled to dismiss, on the basis of the same findings of fact, the allegation that the principle of proportionality had been infringed.

93. As the Court of First Instance correctly pointed out, in the context of the application of Article 3 of Regulation No. 17, the principle of proportionality means that the burdens imposed on undertakings in order to bring an infringement of competition law to an end must not exceed what is appropriate and necessary to attain the objective sought, namely re-establishment of compliance with the rules infringed ...

94. In holding, at paragraph 81 of the ITP judgment, that, in the light of the above findings, the order addressed to the applicant was an appropriate and necessary measure to bring the infringement to an end, the Court of First Instance did not commit an error of law.

The reasoning (third plea in the appeal in Case C-242191 P)

95. In its third plea ITP claims that the Court of First Instance failed to comply with Article 190 of the EEC Treaty in finding that the decision was adequately reasoned ... when the Commission did no more than state that the exercise of copyright was outside the scope of the specific subject-matter of this right and went on to conclude that an exercise of copyright consisting simply in refusing to grant a reproduction licence was an abuse of a dominant position.

96. According to ITP, the crucial question whether a mere refusal to grant a licence could constitute an abuse was dealt with by the Commission in a summary fashion. There was no analysis of the special position occupied by owners of copyright in the context of the application of Article 86. ITP maintains that such an approach fails to meet the requirements laid down in the judgment in *Hauptzollamt Munchen-Mitte* v *Technische Universitat Munchen* [1991] ECR I-5469. ITP maintains that it still does not know what the Commission meant by describing ITP's use of its copyright as falling outside the scope of the specific subject-matter of the intellectual property right.

97. ITP claims that the inadequacy of the decision's reasoning was highlighted by the numerous arguments advanced by the Commission in the course of the proceedings before the Court of First Instance. If the Commission could so act and remain within the law, Article 190 would be rendered nugatory. ITP submits that the

Court of First Instance adopted its own legal reasoning which bore no relation to the decision.

98. The Court must observe here that, according to settled case law, Commission decisions intended to find infringements of competition rules, issue directions and impose pecuniary sanctions must state the reasons on which they are based, in accordance with Article 190 of the EEC Treaty, which requires the Commission to set out the reasons which prompted it to adopt a decision, so that the Court can exercise its power of review and Member States and nationals concerned know the basis on which the Treaty has been applied (see the judgment in *Commission v BASF and Others* [1994] ECR I-2555, para. 66).

99. However, the Commission cannot be required to discuss all the matters of fact and law which may have been dealt with during the administrative proceedings (judgment in *Belasco and Others v Commission* [1989] ECR 2117, para. 55).

100. The Court of First Instance found in particular, at paragraph 64 of the ITP judgment, that:

"as regards the concept of abuse, the Commission clearly stated in the decision its reasons for finding that the applicant, by using its exclusive right to reproduce the listings as the instrument of a policy contrary to the objectives of Article 86, went beyond what was necessary to ensure the protection of the actual substance of its copyright and committed an abuse within the meaning of Article 86."

It accordingly arrived at the view that:

"Contrary to the applicant's allegations, the statement of reasons in the contested decision is ... sufficient to allow interested parties to ascertain the main legal and factual criteria on which the Commission based its findings and to enable the Court to carry out its review. It therefore fulfils the conditions relating to the respect of the right to a fair hearing as they have consistently been defined in the case-law."

101. ITP's criticisms fail to show that those assessments of the Court of First Instance are marred by an error of law.

102. It must be added that, in so far as those criticisms concern the inadequacy of the legal analysis of the situation made by the Commission in its decision, they substantially reproduce the arguments put forward to challenge the description of the appellants' conduct as an abuse of a dominant position, arguments which have already been rejected above in the examination of the first plea in law.

103. The plea of non-compliance with Article 190 of the Treaty must therefore be dismissed.

104. It follows that the appeals must be dismissed in their entirety.'

COMMENT

Why did the European Court of Justice find that there was an abuse of a dominant position when copyright law is not fully harmonised throughout the Community? Is lack of harmonisation a factor? Is the issue of whether trade between Member States is affected a question of law or fact? Does this decision conflict with the Berne Copyright Convention?

The provision for compulsory licensing in the proposal for a Directive on the legal protection of databases was omitted from the Directive as adopted (subject to the matter being reviewed by the Commission from time to time).

In the United Kingdom, section 176 of the Broadcasting Act 1990 imposes a duty to provide advance information on request about forthcoming programmes broadcast by the BBC, ITC and Welsh Authority, in return for a reasonable royalty, to be fixed by the Copyright Tribunal in the absence of agreement.

Index

A

abuse of a dominant position   *456, 466*
architect   *72*
article   *286*
assignment   *61, 66*
author   *59*

B

Berne Copyright Convention   *103*
breach of confidence
    action in   *120*
    basic requirements   *117*
    defamation   *141*
    employees   *132*
    engine   *120*
    ideas   *128*
    implied term   *136*
    innocent acquirer   *150*
    nature   *118*
    obligation of confidence   *119*
    privacy   *144*
    public interest   *141*
    restraint of trade   *137*
    risk of overhearing   *149*
    sales information   *134*
    springboard doctrine   *124, 155, 158*
    telephone conversation   *144*
    third parties   *128*
    trade secrets   *139*
breach of contract   *129*
burden of proof   *82, 205, 211, 281*

C

causation   *244*
champagne   *410*
character merchandising   *371*
Coca-Cola bottle   *341*
common field of activity   *417*
competition law   *14, 425*
compilation   *87*
computer program   *90, 217*
computer software   *87*
containers   *340, 400*

contract   *10*
contract of employment   *135*
contract of service   *62, 69*
copyright
    artistic craftsmanship   *49*
    artistic works   *15, 49, 53*
    assignment   *61, 66*
    author   *59*
    Berne Copyright Convention   *103*
    compilations   *44*
    designs, and   *272*
    dramatic format   *26*
    EC law, and   *466*
    employees   *61, 68*
    expression   *42*
    facts   *40*
    fair dealing   *100*
    false attribution   *74*
    history   *4, 37*
    ideas   *81, 89*
    infringement   *76*
    licence   *72*
    literal copyright   *94*
    literary works   *42*
    moral rights   *74*
    names   *55*
    non-literal copying   *38*
    original literary work   *55*
    originality   *42, 88*
    owner   *61, 69, 91*
    Performing Right Society   *85*
    perpetual   *5*
    piracy   *40*
    public performance   *85*
    qualification   *41*
    rationale   *8*
    subsistence   *41, 49*
    substantiality   *77, 94*
    sufficient acknowledgement   *100*
    tables   *40, 45*
    television programme listings   *466*
    test for infringement   *95*
covenant
    negative   *129*
    restrictive   *137*

D

defamation *141*
de minimis *55*
design *17, 120*
design law
    background *270*
    copyright, and *272*
    design freedom *290*
    design right *297*
    drawings, and *271*
    registrable designs *271*
design right
    commonplace *306*
    infringement *298*
    must-fit *303*
    originality *298, 306*
diaries *44*
Dickens, Charles *170*
distinctive mark *314*
drawings *53, 81, 271*

E

EC law
    abuse of a dominant position *456, 466*
    copyright *466*
    exhaustion of rights *444*
    free movement of goods *432, 439*
    non-discrimination *428*
    parallel importing *432*
    patent *432, 457*
    pharmaceuticals *439*
    registered design *463*
    restrictive trade agreements *448*
    rights in performances *428*
    split trade marks *445*
    Technology Transfer Regulation *449*
    television programme listings *466*
employees *61, 68, 132, 224*
employment contract
    implied term *136*
engine *120*
European Patent Convention *258*
examination papers *42*
exhaustion of rights *444*
expression *3, 37*

F

facts *40*
fair dealing *100*
false attribution *74*
football coupons *46*
format rights *26*
freedom of movement *432, 439*
furniture *49*

G

GATT agreement *33*
generic names *347*
genetic engineering *194*
geographical names *336*
Gillette defence *129*
goodwill *404*
groundless threats *252, 363*

I

ideas *3, 81, 89, 128, 177*
implied licence *72*
implied term *136*
implied warranty *12*
industrial application *212*
industrial revolution *171*
injunction *154*
intellectual property
    abuse of *13*
    competition law, and *14, 425*
    contract, and *10*
    international aspects *28*
    justification *7*
    models of *2*
    property theory *6*
international co-operation *28*
invented words *339*
inventive step *201, 205*

K

kit of parts *273*

L

libel *75, 141, 152*
licence *10*
    implied *72*
    patent *14, 236*

M

malicious falsehood *153*
misrepresentation *385, 400*
Monopolies and Mergers Commission *21*
monopoly *4, 8, 16*
moral rights *74*
mosaicing *204*

N

names *55, 407*
new forms of works *26*
non-derogation from grant *21*
non-discrimination *428*
novelty *173*

O

overlap of rights *1*

P

packaging *340*
Paris Convention for the Protection of
        Industrial Property *29*
parallel importing *432*
passing off
    basic requirements *388*
    champagne *410*
    colours *405*
    common field of activity *417*
    confusion *404*
    containers *400*
    damage to goodwill *404*
    development *382*
    erosion of goodwill *411*
    evidence *407*
    "extended" *388*
    goodwill *404*
    history *381*

    inferior goods *387*
    misrepresentation *385, 400*
    names *407*
    newspapers *405, 407*
    policy *404*
    privacy, and *152*
    property right *384*
    quality, and *385*
    survey evidence *405*
    traditional *383*
patent law
    anticipation *179, 180, 187, 188*
    basic requirements *173*
    claims *229*
    commercial success *203, 207*
    compensation to employees *227*
    computer program *217*
    construction of specification *230*
    damages *242*
    defences *235*
    development *163*
    EC law *432, 457*
    employees *224*
    enabling disclosure *182, 195*
    European approach *235*
    European Patent Convention *258*
    excepted matter *213*
    field trials *181*
    full disclosure *164, 175*
    genetic engineering *194*
    groundless threats *252*
    ideas *177*
    industrial application *212*
    industrial revolution *171*
    infringement *229*
    interpretation of claims *230, 233*
    invention *180*
    inventive step *201, 205*
    justification *171*
    licence agreement *236*
    made available to public *180*
    method of performing mental act *221*
    monopoly *160*
    novelty *173*
    obviousness *180, 201, 205*
    ownership *224*
    parasitic sale *242*
    pith and marrow *230*
    priority date *209*
    private Act *165*

proprietor *224*
prototype *180*
reform *170*
remedies *238*
royalties *237*
second use patents *192*
state of the art *209*
steam engine *167*
sufficiency *168, 197*
technical effect *216*
use in public *183*
Watt, James *167*
patent licences *14, 236*
Performing Right Society *85*
piracy *40*
plans *72*
priority date *209*
privacy *144*
prototype *49, 131*
public domain *39*
public interest *103, 141*
public performance *85*
public policy *139, 244*

Q

quiet enjoyment *12*

R

registered designs
article *286*
burden of proof *281*
design, meaning *272*
design freedom *290*
dictated by function *276*
EC law *463*
exceptions *275*
eye appeal *278*
infringement *295*
kit of parts *273*
method/principle of construction *279*
"must-match" *288*
novelty *284*
registrability *271*
requirements *274*
spare parts *286, 288*
remoteness of damages *246*

repair, right to *24*
restrictive covenant *137*
restrictive trade practices *448*
rights in performances *428*
royalties *237*

S

sale of goods contract *11*
source code *93*
spare parts *15, 286, 288*
springboard doctrine *124, 155, 158*
state of the art *209*
Stationers' Company *4, 37*
statutory tort *244*
subsidiary company *248*
survey evidence *405*

T

Technology Transfer Regulation *449*
telephone tap *144*
third parties *128*
trade marks
bona fide *345*
capable of distinguishing *314*
character merchandising *371*
confusion *348*
containers *340*
development *312*
disclaimers *343*
distinctiveness *320*, 324
European Community *445*
generic names *347*
geographical names *336*
groundless threats *363*
infringement *346*
invalidity *324*
invented words *339*
laudatory words *320*
mark, meaning *340*
misspelt words *316*
non-distinctive material *343*
non-origin association *350*
packaging *340*
phonetic equivalents *317, 348*
presumption *368*
property right *312*

rectification *368*
registered users *372*
registrability *314*
removal from register *368*
revocation *324*
similarity *348*
split trade marks *445*
trafficking *372*
trade secrets *139*
trespass
privacy, and *152*
TRIPs Agreement *34, 114, 158, 266, 309,
376*

U

unfair competition *389, 422*

W

work, meaning *75*
World Trade Organization *33*

Database of summaries of intellectual property cases and software copyright legislation

A computer database of summaries of important intellectual property cases is available from the author. The database usefully supplements this book and contains summaries of many of the cases referred to. The database comprises summaries of over 160 cases including some of the most recent ones. The database is provided complete with an easy-to-use computer program, having retrieval and editing facilities. Also included is a database of legislation relating to software copyright which includes extracts from the Copyright, Designs and Patents Act 1988, as amended, and from the Copyright and Rights in Databases Regulations 1997. The extracts, which are Crown copyright, are annotated by the author of this book and published by permission of the Stationery Office. The author updates the databases on a continuing basis.

The databases may be modified and added to and new databases can be created. The databases are in dBase III+ format and also may be used with most Windows database packages including MICROSOFT ACCESS, LOTUS APPROACH and DBASE for WINDOWS, allowing users to design their own forms and reports (you will need to have some familiarity with these packages to take full advantage to their powerful facilities). For users of MICROSOFT ACCESS Version 7 for WINDOWS 95, at no extra cost, a special version of the databases is available as an alternative with built in menus, forms and queries. If you want both the DOS and ACCESS versions, please make this clear and add £2.00 to your order.

The databases are available on a 3½ inch disk (1.44MB) suitable for an IBM personal computer or equivalent running DOS with a 1.44MB capacity disk drive. A hard disk is desirable. The system can be run from DOS or it can be run from Windows environment (as a DOS program) or used with the database packages mentioned above.

The databases are available for the price of £13.99 for students and academics or £19.99 for practitioners. If you want the Access Version 7 for Windows 95 version of the database, please specify ACCESS on your order. Send payment (cheque or postal order payable to David Bainbridge) to the address below, quoting reference **IP4**. Every effort will be made to deliver more quickly but allow 21 days. Prices include post and packaging for UK only.

> **Dr David Bainbridge**
> **Marketing and Law Group**
> **Aston Business School**
> **Aston University**
> **Aston Triangle**
> **BIRMINGHAM B4 7ET**

Note: if entering new materials to the database or creating new databases, please take care to avoid infringing copyright (see Chapters 6 and 7 of this book). All trade marks are acknowledged.